Fodor's 2014

ARIZONA & THE GRAND CANYON

WELCOME TO ARIZONA

From the vastness of the Grand Canyon to Sedona's red rocks and the living Sonoran Desert, Arizona's landscapes are awe-inspiring. The state's spectacular canyons, blooming deserts, raging rivers, petrified forests, and scenic mountains enthrall lovers of the outdoors in pursuit of hiking, rafting, golf, or picturesque spots to watch the sunset. But there is more to Arizona than beautiful vistas. World-renowned spas in Phoenix provide plenty of pampering, while Native American cultures thrive throughout the state.

TOP REASONS TO GO

★ **Grand Canyon:** Whether you hike, raft, or drive it, you shouldn't miss it.

★ **Native American Heritage:** There's no better place to experience these thriving cultures.

★ **Flavorful Food:** Blending Native American and Southwestern spices, Arizona's cuisine pops.

★ **Road Trips:** The wide-open spaces of Arizona dazzle anew with every curve of the road.

★ **Stunning Landscapes:** From Sedona's red rocks to Monument Valley, beauty reigns.

★ **Outdoor Experiences:** Canyons, deserts, and mountains offer adventures aplenty.

Fodor's ARIZONA & THE GRAND CANYON 2014

Publisher: Amanda D'Acierno, *Senior Vice President*

Editorial: Arabella Bowen, *Executive Editorial Director*; Linda Cabasin, *Editorial Director*

Design: Fabrizio La Rocca, *Vice President, Creative Director*; Tina Malaney, *Associate Art Director*; Chie Ushio, *Senior Designer*; Ann McBride, *Production Designer*

Photography: Melanie Marin, *Associate Director of Photography*; Jessica Parkhill and Jennifer Romains, *Researchers*

Maps: Rebecca Baer, *Senior Map Editor*; Mark Stroud (Moon Street Cartography), David Lindroth, *Cartographers*

Production: Linda Schmidt, *Managing Editor*; Evangelos Vasilakis, *Associate Managing Editor*; Angela L. McLean, *Senior Production Manager*

Sales: Jacqueline Lebow, *Sales Director*

Marketing & Publicity: Heather Dalton, *Marketing Director*; Katherine Fleming, *Senior Publicist*

Business & Operations: Susan Livingston, *Vice President, Strategic Business Planning*; Sue Daulton, *Vice President, Operations*

Fodors.com: Megan Bell, *Executive Director, Revenue & Business Development*; Yasmin Marinaro, *Senior Director, Marketing & Partnerships*

Copyright © 2014 by Fodor's Travel, a division of Random House LLC

Writers: Andrew Collins, Mara Levin, Elise Riley, Michael Weatherford

Editor: Luke Epplin

Editorial Contributor: Vanessa H. Larson

Production Editor: Carolyn Roth

ISBN 978-0-7704-3254-6

ISSN 1559–6230

SPECIAL SALES

This book is available at special discounts for bulk purchases for sales promotions or premiums. For more information, e-mail specialmarkets@randomhouse.com

PRINTED IN CHINA

10 9 8 7 6 5 4 3 2 1

CONTENTS

1 EXPERIENCE ARIZONA 9
What's Where 10
Arizona Planner 12
Arizona & the Grand Canyon
Top Attractions. 14
Quintessential Arizona &
the Grand Canyon. 16
If You Like. 18
Top Experiences 20
Arizona with Kids 21
Flavors of Arizona. 24
Great Itineraries 25

**2 PHOENIX, SCOTTSDALE,
AND TEMPE. 41**
Welcome to Phoenix,
Scottsdale, and Tempe 42
Spa Time in Arizona: Say Ahhh. . . .44
Valley of the Sun Golf:
Driving Ambition 46
Valley of the Sun Food. 48
Scottsdale Shopping 50
Phoenix, Scottsdale, and
Tempe Planner. 52
Exploring 55
Where to Eat. 69
Best Bets for Phoenix, Scottsdale,
and Tempe Dining. 71
Where to Stay 86
Best Bets for Phoenix, Scottsdale,
and Tempe Lodging. 88
Nightlife and the Arts 99
Shopping 107
Spas 112
Sports and the Outdoors 116
Side Trips Near Phoenix 124
The Apache Trail. 133

**3 GRAND CANYON
NATIONAL PARK. 141**
Welcome to Grand Canyon
National Park 142
Grand Canyon Planner. 144

Oh Starry Night:
Tips for Stargazing in Arizona. 22
Arizona Landscape Adventures 28
Exploring the Colorado River 182

Grand Canyon South Rim 150
Grand Canyon North Rim 166
The West Rim and
Havasu Canyon 172
What's Near the Grand Canyon . .177
Where to Eat. 181
Where to Stay. 193

4 NORTH-CENTRAL ARIZONA. . 199
Welcome to
North-Central Arizona 200
North-Central Arizona Planner . . .203
Flagstaff. 205
Side Trips Near Flagstaff. 218
Sedona and Oak Creek Canyon . .222
The Verde Valley, Jerome,
and Prescott 242

5 NORTHEAST ARIZONA 257
Welcome to Northeast Arizona. . .258
Native American Experience 260
Northeast Arizona Planner 265
Navajo Nation East 267
The Hopi Mesas 278
Navajo Nation West 283

Monument Valley 288
Glen Canyon Dam and
Lake Powell 296

6 EASTERN ARIZONA 311
Welcome to Eastern Arizona 312
Eastern Arizona Planner 315
The White Mountains 316
The Round Valley and
Coronado Trail 330
The Petrified Forest and Around . . 340

7 TUCSON 347
Welcome to Tucson 348
Tucson Food: North of the Border 350
Tucson and Southern
Arizona Shopping 352
Tucson Planner 354
Exploring 357
Where to Eat 374
Best Bets for Tucson Dining 375
Where to Stay 385
Best Bets for Tucson Lodging 386
Nightlife and the Arts 393
Shopping 397
Spas 401
Sports and the Outdoors 403
Saguaro National Park 409
Side Trips Near Tucson 417

8 SOUTHERN ARIZONA 423
Welcome to Southern Arizona . . . 424
Experience the Wild West 426
Southern Arizona Planner 429
Southeast Arizona 430
Southwest Arizona 460

**9 NORTHWEST ARIZONA AND
SOUTHEAST NEVADA 471**
Welcome to Northwest Arizona
and Southeast Nevada 472
Get Your Kicks on Route 66 474
Northwest Arizona and
Southeast Nevada Planner 477
Northwest Arizona 479
Southeast Nevada 492

TRAVEL SMART ARIZONA . . . 503

INDEX 515

ABOUT OUR WRITERS 532

MAPS

Downtown Phoenix 56
Greater Phoenix 60
Scottsdale 65
Tempe and Around 68
Where to Eat in Phoenix,
Scottsdale, and Tempe 72–73
Where to Stay in Phoenix,
Scottsdale, and Tempe 90–91
Side Trips Near Phoenix 126
Grand Canyon South Rim 152
Grand Canyon Village and
the Rim Trail 161
Grand Canyon North Rim 167
Flagstaff and Environs 207
Sedona and Oak Creek Canyon . . 225
The Verde Valley, Jerome,
and Prescott 243
Prescott 252
Navajo Nation East 269
Hopi Mesas 279
Navajo Nation West 286
Monument Valley 291
Glen Canyon Dam and
Lake Powell 300
The White Mountains 317
Petrified Forest National Park . . . 343
Downtown Tucson 358
The University of Arizona 363
Central Tucson and Eastside 366
Catalina Foothills 369
Westside 372
Where to Eat and Stay
in Tucson 378–379
Saguaro National Park West 411
Saguaro National Park East 413
Side Trips Near Tucson 418
Southeast Arizona 432
Southwest Arizona 461
Northwest Arizona 479
Southeast Nevada 493
Bullhead City and Laughlin 494

ABOUT
THIS GUIDE

Fodor's Recommendations
Everything in this guide is worth doing—we don't cover what isn't—but exceptional sights, hotels, and restaurants are recognized with additional accolades. **Fodor's**Choice ★ indicates our top recommendations; and **Best Bets** call attention to notable hotels and restaurants in various categories. Care to nominate a new place? Visit Fodors.com/contact-us.

Trip Costs
We list prices wherever possible to help you budget well. Hotel and restaurant price categories from $ to $$$$ are noted alongside each recommendation. For hotels, we include the lowest cost of a standard double room in high season. For restaurants, we cite the average price of a main course at dinner or, if dinner isn't served, at lunch. For attractions, we always list adult admission fees; discounts are usually available for children, students, and senior citizens.

Hotels
Our local writers vet every hotel to recommend the best overnights in each price category, from budget to expensive. Unless otherwise specified, you can expect private bath, phone, and TV in your room. For expanded hotel reviews, facilities, and deals visit Fodors.com.

Restaurants
Unless we state otherwise, restaurants are open for lunch and dinner daily. We mention dress code only when there's a specific requirement and reservations only when they're essential or not accepted. To make restaurant reservations, visit Fodors.com.

Credit Cards
The hotels and restaurants in this guide typically accept credit cards. If not, we'll say so.

Top Picks
★ **Fodor's**Choice

Listings
- ✉ Address
- ✉ Branch address
- ☎ Telephone
- 🖷 Fax
- ⊕ Website
- ✉ E-mail
- 🎟 Admission fee
- ☺ Open/closed times
- Ⓜ Subway
- ✛ Directions or Map coordinates

Hotels & Restaurants
- 🏨 Hotel
- ⟿ Number of rooms
- ⦿ Meal plans
- ✕ Restaurant
- ⚜ Reservations
- 🏛 Dress code
- ▭ No credit cards
- Ⓢ Price

Other
- ⇨ See also
- ☞ Take note
- 🏌 Golf facilities

EXPERIENCE
ARIZONA

WHAT'S WHERE

The following numbers refer to chapters.

2 Phoenix, Scottsdale, and Tempe. Rising where the Sonoran Desert meets the Superstition Mountains, the Valley of the Sun is filled with resorts and spas, shops and restaurants, and more than 200 golf courses.

3 Grand Canyon National Park. One of nature's longest-running works in progress, the canyon both exalts and humbles the human spirit. Whether you select the popular South Rim or the remote North Rim, don't just peer over the edge—take the plunge into the canyon on a mule train, on foot, or on a raft trip.

4 North-Central Arizona. Cool, laid-back towns here are as bewitching as the high-country landscape they inhabit. There are quaint escapes such as Prescott and Jerome, Sedona with its red-rock buttes, and the vibrant university town of Flagstaff.

5 Northeast Arizona. This remote area includes the stunning surroundings of Monument Valley. Alongside today's Navajo and Hopi communities, the breathtaking Canyon de Chelly and Navajo National Monument are reminders of how ancient peoples lived with the land.

6 Eastern Arizona. Summer visitors flock to the lush, green White Mountains and the warm colors of the Painted Desert. Petrified Forest National Park protects trees that stood when dinosaurs walked Earth.

7 Tucson. The modern history of Arizona begins here, where Hispanic, Anglo, and Native American cultures became intertwined in the 17th century and still are today. Farther out, city slickers enjoy horseback rides at some of the region's many guest ranches, or luxury pampering at world-class spas.

8 Southern Arizona. Splendid mountain and desert scenery evokes the romanticized spirit of the Wild West. Enduring pockets of westward expansion are the largest draw today: notorious Tombstone and the mining boomtown Bisbee.

9 Northwest Arizona and Southeast Nevada. This underexplored corner of Arizona includes Lake Havasu City and its bit of Britannia in the form of London Bridge; old-fashioned Americana around Kingman, a hub on legendary Route 66; and Hoover Dam and Laughlin's casinos, just a short jaunt away in Nevada.

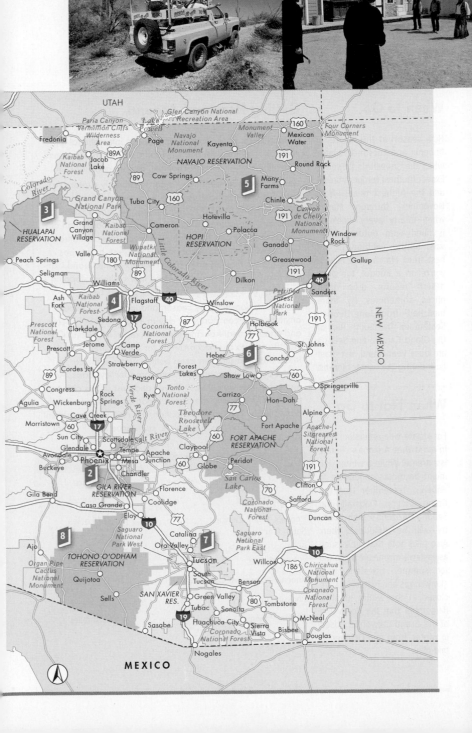

ARIZONA PLANNER

When to Go

High season at the resorts of Phoenix and Tucson is winter, when the snowbirds fly south. Expect the best temperatures—and the highest prices—from November through March, when nearly every weekend is filled with outdoor festivals. Spring wildflowers are best from March until May. If you're on a budget, the posh desert resorts drop their prices—sometimes by more than half—from June through September. The South Rim of the Grand Canyon and Sedona are busy year-round, but least busy during the winter months.

When Not to Go

For a statewide excursion, keep in mind that Arizona's climate is extreme. While a winter visit might be most comfortable in Phoenix, remember that the Grand Canyon, Flagstaff, and Sedona—Arizona's high country—will be quite cold then. Also take note that areas such as eastern Arizona are designed for summer travelers, thus many shops and restaurants are closed in the winter months. Remember that the North Rim of the Grand Canyon is closed in winter, from mid-October to mid-May.

Getting Here and Around

Getting Here: Phoenix and Tucson have international airports. Amtrak lines service Flagstaff and Tucson. Car rental is available at airports in Phoenix, Tucson, and Flagstaff.

Getting Around: You'll need a car to properly explore Arizona. Deceptively vast, Arizona is the nation's sixth-largest state at nearly 114,000 square miles. No matter where you start your journey, expect to spend a good portion of your time in the car. Fortunately, Arizona offers an attractive canvas that ranges from desert to forest. It surprises some visitors that the drive from Phoenix to the Grand Canyon takes at least a half day—and that's without stopping or taking side roads. *See more driving times below.*

Road conditions vary by season and location, so expect anything: you can start your day in 100°F heat in Phoenix and end it in near-freezing temperatures in the Grand Canyon. Be sure to plan accordingly for the weather: if driving in the desert in summer, keep bottled water in the car; in winter in the high country, be prepared for icy roads. And remember that violent flash floods and dust storms can pepper the desert during the summer monsoons. Storms usually pass quickly. For road information, the Arizona Department of Transportation has a travelers' assistance line. Just dial 511 from any phone.

TYPICAL TRAVEL TIMES

	Hours by Car	Distance
Phoenix–Flagstaff	2½	145 miles
Phoenix–Grand Canyon South Rim	4½	175 miles
Phoenix–Lake Mead/ Hoover Dam	4½	260 miles
Phoenix–Monument Valley	6	275 miles
Phoenix–Yuma	3	185 miles
Tucson–Phoenix	2	120 miles

What to Pack

Thanks to extreme climates and Western informality, you can go almost anywhere in Arizona in a pair of jeans.

■ Bring layers for trips north or east, particularly when temperatures dip after the sun sets.

■ For formal dining, call ahead for attire requirements. In most places, a shirt and dress slacks will be more than sufficient.

■ Depending on your desired level of activity, you'll need to pack different gear: golf shoes, hiking boots, or flip-flops. Most golf courses offer club and golf-cart rentals, but plan on bringing your own shoes. If the slopes are your destination, you can rent all your ski or snowboard gear before hitting the lifts.

■ No matter your plans, be prepared with water, and hats and sunscreen for sun protection. The desert heat can be intense and quite deceptive.

Tribal Lands

Arizona has 22 Native American tribes, each with its own government and culture. Most tribes have websites or phone-information lines, and it's best to contact them for information before a trip. Many require a permit for hiking or biking in scenic areas. Always be respectful of individual cultures and traditions.

How's the Weather?

Phoenix averages 325 sunny days and 7 inches of precipitation annually. The high mountains see about 25 inches of rain. The Grand Canyon is usually cool at the rim and about 20°F warmer on the floor. The North Rim is generally about 10°F cooler than the South Rim, which is open year-round. Temperatures in valley areas like Phoenix and Tucson average about 60°F to 70°F in the daytime in winter and between 100°F and 115°F in summer. Flagstaff and Sedona stay much cooler, dropping into the 30s and 40s in winter and leveling off at 80°F to 90°F in summer.

Avg. High/ Low Temps.

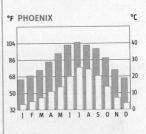

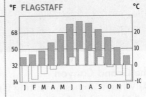

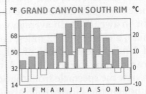

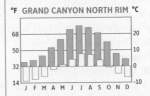

ARIZONA & THE GRAND CANYON TOP ATTRACTIONS

The Grand Canyon

(A) When it comes to visiting Grand Canyon National Park, there are statistics and there are sights, and both are sure to leave you in awe. With an average width of 10 miles, a length of 277 miles, and a depth of 1 mile, the enormity of the canyon is nearly impossible to fathom. Most choose to view the spectacle from the South Rim, although the North Rim also offers an amazing perspective. Whether exploring the area on foot, by mule, by raft, or by plane, the journey is one worth savoring.

Petrified Forest and the Painted Desert

(B) The Painted Desert takes on hues that range from blood-red to the purest pink throughout the day. View a forest of trees that stood with dinosaurs at the Petrified Forest, as well as ancient dwellings and fossils. The pieces of petrified logs look deceptively like driftwood cast upon an oceanless beach. You can enjoy the entire national park in less than a day and take in a bit of nostalgia with Route 66's vestiges in nearby Holbrook along the way.

Sedona

(C) Loved for its majestic red rocks, its spiritual energy, and its fantastic resorts and spas, Sedona is unlike any other town in America. The fracturing of the western edge of the Colorado Plateau created the red-rock buttes that loom over Sedona, and this landscape has attracted artists, entrepreneurs, and New Age followers from all over who believe the area contains some of Earth's most important vortexes of energy. Take the active route and explore Oak Creek Canyon and the surrounding area on foot or by bike or jeep, or indulge in the luxe life at a world-class spa or restaurant.

Scottsdale

(D) The West's most Western town, modern Scottsdale is equal parts kitsch and overt opulence. Resorts, spas, and golf

can easily absorb an entire vacation. Stroll through art galleries and Western boutiques in Old Town during the day, and discover chic nightlife and fine cuisine at night. The weekly Art Walk and Frank Lloyd Wright's Taliesin West are a great introduction to the local artistic scene. Scottsdale is part of the Valley of the Sun, along with Phoenix, Tempe, and some 20 other communities.

The Heard Museum

(E) One of Phoenix's cultural treasures, the Heard proudly features one of the most comprehensive collections of Native American art in the world. Interactive exhibits are alongside a staggering amount of Southwestern pottery, jewelry, kachinas, and textiles. Plus, the museum gift shop is one of the best places in town to find authentic souvenirs worth cherishing.

Monument Valley

(F) One of the most familiar sights of Arizona—thanks to dozens of Hollywood productions and the keen eye of Ansel Adams—the fantastic sculpted red-sandstone buttes, mesas, and rock formations of Monument Valley Navajo Tribal Park are yet another reminder of the abundance of nature's handiwork in the Grand Canyon state. Take a Navajo-guided tour to appreciate the nuances of the area.

Desert Botanical Garden

(G) While there are stellar museums and preserves across Arizona, none is like the Desert Botanical Garden, 150 acres just outside Downtown Phoenix dedicated to the diversity of the desert. With more than 4,000 species of cacti, succulents, trees, and flowers, visitors discover the variety and breadth of this mysterious landscape—all in the comfort of America's sixth-largest city.

QUINTESSENTIAL ARIZONA & THE GRAND CANYON

Road Trips

Arizona is *the* place to take a road trip. Get in the car, pick a destination, and go take a look at the Western landscape on historic roads like Route 66. For optimal enjoyment, avoid the interstate highways and take these smaller routes instead. It's there you'll see Arizona's most beautiful landscapes, taste its spicy cuisine, and make memories worth cherishing.

Go to Bisbee. Go to Jerome. Go to Oatman. Go to Greer. Travel AZ 260 from Payson to Show Low or historic Route 66 from Ash Fork to Topock; take AZ 60 through the Salt River Canyon, or U.S. 191 from Springerville to Clifton; and take AZ 88, the Apache Trail, from Apache Junction to Roosevelt Dam.

Wherever you go, roll down the windows, turn up the radio, and enjoy the ride. Regardless of your destination, the wide-open spaces of Arizona entice and amaze anew with every bend in the road.

Salsa and Margaritas

You're in Arizona, so join the quest to find your favorite salsa and margaritas. No two salsas are the same, and every city and town boasts its own local favorite. Spicy and chunky? Tangy and juicy? Tear-inducing? They run the gamut.

You'll find that salsa flavors change regionally, from mesquite-imbued concoctions in the east, inspired by Tex-Mex cuisine, to fresh-from-the-garden medleys in southern Arizona that are authentically Mexican. In Tucson, check out Café Poca Cosa's salsa, a deep-red blend of garlic, chiles, and tomatoes that's almost decadent. In Phoenix the brave go to Los Dos Molinos, where powerful hatch chiles punctuate every dish.

Perfectly salty-and-sour margaritas can take the sting away from a particularly robust salsa, all while washing down a delightful Mexican feast.

Arizona is known for its magnificent natural landmarks, its rich history, and its captivating cuisine. Here are some easy ways to get to know the lay of the land and start thinking like an Arizonan.

The Night Sky

Away from the metropolitan areas of the Valley of the Sun (Phoenix, Tempe, Scottsdale, and surrounds) and Tucson, where the by-products of urban life obscure the firmament, the night sky is clear and unpolluted by lights or smog. In December in the desert, the Milky Way stretches like a chiffon scarf across the celestial sphere. Lie on your back on the hood of your car at night, allow your eyes time to adjust to the darkness, and you'll see more stars than you could have possibly imagined.

For a closer look, you can visit Lowell Observatory and Northern Arizona University (both in Flagstaff), or the Kitt Peak National Observatory in southwest Arizona (outside Tucson) and look at celestial objects through large telescopes.

Rodeo

People take rodeo seriously in Arizona, whether it's a holiday extravaganza like those in Prescott or Payson (which draw top cowboys from around the country), a bull-riding competition at Camp Verde, or a bunch of working cowboys gathered for a team-roping contest in Williams.

Particularly with the emergence of bull riding as a stand-alone event—and the crowds often cheer as much for the bulls as the cowboys—rodeos these days are no longer the hayseed and cowpokey events Arizona grandpas might have enjoyed. Rock-and-roll rodeo has arrived and there's frequently live music as well as roping. And other cowboy experiences, like horseback riding and dude ranch stays, are as popular as ever. So, if you see a rodeo advertisement posted in a shop window, take a walk on the wild side and check out the fine arts of riding and roping.

IF YOU LIKE

Hiking

Arizona has a wealth of awe-inspiring natural landmarks. So you can hike in and out, up and down, or around beautiful and varied landscapes, into canyons, to a mountain summit, or just along a meandering trail through a desert or a forest.

Wherever you go, make sure you're well prepared with water, food, sunscreen, a good hat, and a camera to capture your achievement. Be sure you have a decent pair of hiking shoes, and check the weather report first. Storms can roll into the desert quickly (particularly during monsoon season), and you don't want to get caught in a flash flood or dust storm.

From the long-heralded trails such as **Bright Angel** in the Grand Canyon to iconic **Camelback Mountain** in Phoenix, there's a summit or path in every corner of the state waiting for you.

If waterfalls are your thing, check out the Grand Canyon's **Havasu Falls,** a fairly strenuous 10-mile hike that descends 3,000 feet to splashing pools of turquoise water.

The highest of the four peaks that comprise San Francisco Peaks is **Mount Humphreys,** the ultimate goal for hikers seeking the best view in the state. Timing an ascent can be tricky, though, as the snow in Flagstaff sometimes doesn't melt until mid-July, and by then the summer rains and lightning come almost daily in the afternoon. Go early in the morning and pay attention to the sky.

For some archaeology, **Walnut Canyon National Monument,** just a few minutes east of Flagstaff, has a paved and stepped trail descending 185 feet into an island of stone where you can explore prehistoric cliff dwellings. The climb out is strenuous.

Water Sports

You don't miss the water until it's not there, but Arizonans do their best to ensure that the well doesn't go completely dry. Dams and canal systems help to fill vast reservoirs, and the resulting rivers and lakes provide all manner of water-sport recreation. Of course, this is a state that considers floating in a pool or soaking in a hot tub "water-sport recreation." You can have it "easy," you can have it "rough," or you can have it "fast."

Easy is a week on a **houseboat** on a lake. Houseboats are available for rent on major lakes along the Colorado River, as well as on Lake Powell, Lake Mead, and Lake Havasu. On smaller lakes motorized boats are prohibited, but **kayaks** and **canoes** make for an enjoyable excursion along the pine-covered shorelines. You can even take a rowboat out on Tempe Town Lake, or bake in the sun while taking a lazy float down the Salt River just east of Phoenix

Rough is a **river raft trip.** There are nearly two dozen commercial rafting companies offering trips as short as three days or as long as three weeks through the Grand Canyon. Options include motorized rafts or dories rowed by Arizona's version of the California surfer—the Colorado River boatman. The Hualapai tribe, through the Hualapai River Runners, offers one-day river trips. Don't let the short duration fool you: the boatmen take you through several rapids, and thrills abound.

Fast involves a **speedboat** and water skis or Jet Skis. Both are popular on major lakes and along the Colorado River. You can go from dam to dam along the Colorado, and on lakes the size of Powell and Mead you can ski until your legs give out.

Desert

Arizona has a desert for you; actually, it has more than one. The trouble is, any desert is inhospitable to life forms unaccustomed to its harsh realities. People die in the desert here every year, from thirst, exposure, and one inexplicable trait—stupidity. Using good sense, you can explore any stretch of desert in April and May and experience a landscape festooned with flowers and blooming cacti.

To experience the desert without running the risk of leaving your bones to bleach in the sun, there are two exceptional alternatives: the **Desert Botanical Garden** in Phoenix is a showcase of the ecology of the desert with more than 4,000 different species of desert flora sustained on 150 acres. A walk through here is wonderfully soothing and extremely educational. You'll be stunned by the variety of color and texture in native desert plants. It's much more than saguaro cacti. Be sure to check out the butterfly exhibit.

There's also the **Arizona-Sonora Desert Museum** in Tucson, which isn't really a museum but a zoo and a botanical garden featuring the animals and plants of the Sonoran Desert. If you want to see a diamondback rattlesnake without jumping out of your shoes, this is the place.

And, of course, there are long drives in which you can see the wide expanses from the comfort of your car. Early spring brings the flaming-red blossoms of the ocotillo and the soft yellow-green branches of the palo verde, and the desert will be carpeted with ephemeral flowers of pink, blue, and yellow.

Along U.S. Highway 93, south of Wikieup in northwest Arizona, you can see the desert in its most abundant display, but there are countless other places, as well.

Native American Culture

John Ford Westerns and the enduring myths of the Wild West pale in comparison to the experience of seeing firsthand the Native American cultures that thrive in Arizona. You can stop at a trading post and see artisans demonstrating their crafts, visit one of Arizona's spectacular Native American museums, or explore an ancient Native American dwelling.

Hubbell Trading Post and **Cameron Trading Post** are on Navajo reservations, while **Keam's Canyon Trading Post** is on the Hopi Reservation.

The **Heard Museum**, in Phoenix, houses an impressive array of Native American cultural exhibits and has, quite possibly, the best gift shop in town if you're looking for something truly special and authentic. The **Museum of Northern Arizona,** in Flagstaff, has collections related to the natural and cultural history of the Colorado Plateau, an extensive collection of Navajo rugs, and an authentic Hopi kiva (men's ceremonial chamber). The **Colorado River Museum,** in Bullhead City, focuses on the history of the area and includes information and artifacts pertaining to the Mojave tribe. **Chiricahua Regional Museum and Research Center,** in Willcox, focuses on Apache culture.

The **Montezuma Castle National Monument** is one of the best-preserved prehistoric ruins in North America. **Tuzigoot National Monument** is not as well preserved as Montezuma Castle, but is more impressive in scope. The **Casa Grande Ruins National Monument** is a 35-foot-tall structure built by the Hohokam Indians who lived in the area.

TOP EXPERIENCES

Grand Canyon Hiking

You could spend the rest of your life hiking the Grand Canyon and never cover all the trails. There are hiking and walking trails aplenty, for all levels of fitness; we suggest you go with a guide or consult a ranger to find the best trail for you. Bright Angel Trail is the most famous, but it's tough: with an elevation change of more than 5,000 feet, don't try to hike to the Colorado River and back in one day. Less strenuous is part of the 12-mile Rim Trail, a paved, generally horizontal walk. Other outstanding choices are the South Kaibab Trail and the Hermit Trail. Many short routes lead to epic views, like the Cape Royal and Roosevelt Point trails on the North Rim.

Jeep Tours

Why drive yourself when open-air four-wheeling is available, complete with guide? Jeep tours abound in the Grand Canyon state, whether it's a rough ride on a Pink Jeep tour in the red rocks of Sedona or a Lavender Jeep tour in historic Bisbee, a weeklong excursion or an afternoon adventure. Some of these companies have special permits that provide access to national forests and an up-close view of Native American communities.

Colorado River-Rafting

Hiking too boring? Jeep tours not enough? True thrill-seekers take the plunge when they visit Arizona. There are nearly two dozen commercial river-rafting companies in Arizona that offer trips as short as a day or as long as three weeks through the Grand Canyon on the Colorado River. These rough-riding trips are popular with travelers, so be sure to make reservations very early, up to a year in advance.

Personal Pampering

If roughing it in the great outdoors isn't your vacation style, head to one of Arizona's world-class spas. Enjoy a standard mani-and-pedi afternoon, or further indulge in a specialty treatment, such as a creek-side massage at L'Auberge de Sedona, or a Native American–inspired session at the Waldorf Astoria Spa at the Boulders Resort in Carefree. Between sessions be sure to take advantage of relaxation rooms, saunas, and pools. Finish the day with a decadent meal at your resort's restaurant.

Biltmore Golfing

One of Phoenix's most historic hotels is also home to some of the Valley's most heralded golf courses. The Arizona Biltmore, Arizona's first resort, set the standard in 1929. The Biltmore has two 18-hole PGA championship courses, Adobe and Links. Arizona's climate is particularly hospitable to golfers, so greens fees are especially pricey in winter and spring. Early risers can find slightly more affordable fees in the wee hours of the morning in summer.

Native American Traditions

Westerns and the enduring myths of the Wild West don't compare to the experience of seeing firsthand the Native American cultures that thrive in Arizona. In northeast Arizona, you can visit Navajo and Hopi reservations; there are nearly two dozen tribes in the state. Stop at a trading post on a reservation to see artisans demonstrating their crafts. Visit one of Arizona's fantastic Native American museums, such as the Heard Museum in Phoenix or the Museum of Northern Arizona in Flagstaff. At spectacular national monuments, such as Montezuma Castle near Camp Verde, visitors can see 600-year-old preserved dwellings.

ARIZONA WITH KIDS

Places that are especially appealing to children are indicated throughout this guide by a family icon in the margin.

Choosing a Destination

You can make your trip one for adventure, education, or good ole American play. Stay close to the urban areas surrounding Phoenix or Tucson if you want to revel in **water parks**, swimming pools, and resort children's programs. Travel north to Sedona, where you can see **Snoopy Rock**, before exploring the wonder that is the **Grand Canyon**. If you're looking for an educational journey, don't forget to stop by Phoenix's **Heard Museum** for an introduction to Native American cultures, or spend some quality time in northeast Arizona at **Monument Valley** or **Canyon de Chelly**, two geological marvels.

Choosing a Place to Stay

This is the Old West, after all, and there's a great deal of "roughing it" that you could experience if you're staying at **campsites, dude ranches,** or **motels** near the Grand Canyon or northeast Arizona. Don't expect to always have great mobile phone reception or cable TV.

The cities of Arizona, however, have some of the most heralded **resorts** in the world. In Phoenix, check out the **Arizona Grand Resort**, which has an extensive water park. Posh resorts like the **JW Marriott Desert Ridge** and the **Westin Kierland Resort & Spa** have special kids-only programs that include evening "dive-in" movies and daytime sports and recreation instruction.

Outdoor Activities

With its majestic landscapes and sites that are right out of a Hollywood script, you're going to be spending a lot of your time in Arizona outside. Be sure to take advantage of the national parks' **Junior Ranger Programs**. Of course, there's

nothing quite as up close and personal as a mule ride down the **Grand Canyon**, an adventurous rafting trip down the **Colorado River**, or a walk back in time through **Kartchner Caverns State Park**. Let your kids make the most of their digital cameras while they document your journey. If you prefer something slightly less adventurous, be sure to check out **Oak Creek Canyon** in Sedona, and cool off at **Slide Rock State Park**. On one of your nights away from the city, take advantage of your location and search for constellations and stargaze.

Indoor Activities

On hot summer days, choose indoor activities for the afternoon, when the sun is at its most intense, and your kids are likely to be their most impatient. This might be a good time to head to Downtown Phoenix and check out the **Heard Museum**, the **Phoenix Art Museum**, and the **Arizona Science Center**, all of which are steps away from the city's light-rail system. If you're in the cooler country, take advantage of nighttime programs and events at **Lowell Observatory in Flagstaff**, where you can watch the stars in relative comfort.

Road Trip Tips

Chances are, you'll be exploring most of Arizona by car. There are kid-friendly stops along the way from Phoenix to Sedona or the Grand Canyon, including **Meteor Crater** and **Montezuma Castle**, that can help break up your hours in the car. Children and adults alike can be quite stunned by how quickly Arizona's landscape changes. Your child could start the day in the desert, and wake up from a nap driving through a ponderosa pine winter wonderland in eastern Arizona.

OH STARRY NIGHT
TIPS FOR STARGAZING IN ARIZONA

If your typical view of the night sky consists of a handful of stars dimly twinkling through a hazy, light-polluted sky, get ready for a treat. In most of Arizona, the night sky blazes with starlight—and with a little practice, you can give your family a memorable astronomical tour.

Constellations

Constellations are stories in the sky—many depict animals or figures from Greek mythology. Brush up on a few of these tales before your trip, and you'll be an instant source of nighttime entertainment.

The stars in the Northern Hemisphere appear to rotate around Polaris, the North Star, in fixed positions relative to one another. To get your celestial bearings, first find the bright stars of the Big Dipper. An imaginary line drawn through the two stars that form the outside edge of the cup (away from the handle) will point straight to Polaris (which also serves as the last star in the handle of the Little Dipper). Once you've identified Polaris, you should be able to find the other stars on our chart. Myriad astronomy books and Web sites have additional star charts; *National Geographic* has a cool interactive version with images from the Hubble Space Telescope (⊕ *www.nationalgeographic.com/stars*).

Planets

Stars twinkle, planets don't (because they're so much closer to Earth, the atmosphere doesn't distort their light as much). Planets are also bright, which makes them fairly easy to spot. Unfortunately, we can't show their positions on this star chart, because planets orbit the sun and move in relation to the stars.

The easiest planet to spot is Venus, the brightest object in the night sky besides the moon and the Earth's closest planetary neighbor. Look for it just before sunrise or just after sunset; it'll be near the point where the sun is rising or setting. (Venus and Earth orbit the sun at different speeds; when Venus is moving away from Earth, we see it in the morning, and when it's moving toward us, we see it in the evening.) Like the moon, Venus goes through phases—check it out through a pair of binoculars. You can also spot Mars, Jupiter, Saturn, and Mercury—with or without the aid of binoculars.

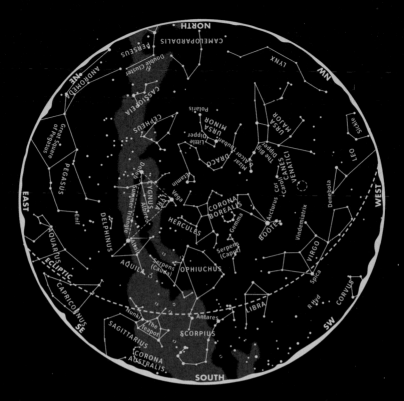

Meteors

It's hard to match the magic of a meteor shower, the natural fireworks display that occurs as Earth passes through a cloud of debris called meteoroids. These pieces of space junk—most the size of a pebble—hit our atmosphere at high speeds, and the intense friction produces brief but brilliant streaks of light. Single meteors are often called "shooting stars" or "falling stars."

Because our planet passes through the same patches of interstellar refuse each year, it's easy to roughly predict when the major meteor showers will occur. Notable ones include the Perseids (mid-August), the Orionids (late October), the Leonids (mid-November), and the Geminids (mid-December). Each shower is named after the point in the sky where meteors appear to originate. If you're not visiting during a shower, don't worry—you can spot individual meteors any time of the year.

Satellites

Right now, according to NASA, there are about 3,000 operative man-made satellites (along with 6,000 pieces of space junk) orbiting the Earth—and you can catch a glimpse of one with a little practice. Satellites look like fast-moving, non-blinking points of light; the best way to spot one is to lie on your back and scan the sky for movement. Be on the lookout for satellites an hour or two before or after sunset (though you may see them at other times as well).

You can take the guesswork out of the search with a few cool online tools (⊕ *www.nasa. gov* or *www.heavens-above.com*). Select your location, and these Web sites will help you predict—down to the minute—when certain objects will be streaking overhead. It's especially worthwhile to use these sites to look for the two brightest satellites: the International Space Station and the space shuttle.

FLAVORS OF ARIZONA

Despite the fact that it's become a culinary melting pot, Arizona has long been lumped into the spicy Southwest category of cuisine. But by pairing global influences with diverse Native American cultures, regional history, and local agriculture, creative chefs and entrepreneurs have started to earn Arizona its own star on the food walk of fame.

The Native Palate

From flash-flood farming in the south and sustained agriculture in the Verde Valley to livestock ranching in the state's northernmost reaches, Native American food customs are becoming customary off the reservations. Gourds, desert beans, mesquite pods, tree nuts, cactus fruit, agave nectar, and local game like quail and elk are buzzwords on award-winning menus. And Navajo fry bread, a tradition born from the worst of times, is one of the state's most sought-after (and caloric) treats.

Kai, Chandler. The Pima word for seed, this elegant and scenery-studded restaurant on the Gila Indian Reservation just outside Phoenix blends the local food traditions of the Tohono O'odham people with some of the finest dining in the state.

Cameron Trading Post, Cameron. If you're headed to Lake Powell, Monument Valley, or the North Rim, there's no better place to stop and try a Navajo taco made from fry bread.

Hopi Cultural Center Restaurant, Third Mesa, Hopi Reservation. This is one of the few places to find authentic *piki* (paper-thin blue-corn bread) and Hopi stew with lamb, hominy, and chiles.

Spice of Life

Arizona has long been defined by its heat. With a natural affection for everything from Mexican jalapeños to New Mexican hatch chiles, local food artists have given recipes ranging from chips and salsa to chicken mole and chilaquiles a most memorable flair.

Café Poca Cosa, Tucson. This hip family-owned eatery changes its menus daily but consistently maintains its authentic approach to Mexican cuisine.

Los Dos Molinos, Phoenix. For those who like it hot, this is the state's reigning restaurant. Signature dishes like Shrimp Veracruz are drenched in New Mexico red chiles.

The Mission, Scottsdale. Try a modern twist on old-school Mexican food like Pollo a la Brasa, chilaquiles, and avocado margaritas.

Fruits of the Desert

Arizona's local-grown wine industry is also not to be overlooked. What began as an experiment in 1973 has become a booming business in southern Arizona's Santa Cruz Valley.

Callaghan Vineyards, Elgin. Producing bold Spanish reds and a delicate white, this southeastern Arizona vineyard and winery has established itself as a favorite on area wine-tasting tours.

Keeling Schaefer Vineyards, Pearce. Featuring fruity Chardonnays, sold-out Grenaches and Syrahs, this vineyard with Mary Jane Colter–inspired architecture offers tastings and tours by appointment only.

Page Springs Cellars, Cornville. Taking a gamble on the Verde Valley's high-desert soil has paid off for winemaker Eric Glomski and his southern Rhône varietals.

1

GREAT
ITINERARIES

HIGHLIGHTS OF ARIZONA

Arizona is full of history, culture, and awe-inspiring natural landmarks. Here are some suggestions for mixing a road trip with some of the state's top attractions.

Phoenix and the Valley of the Sun: 1–2 Days

The metropolitan Phoenix area is the best place to begin your trip to Arizona, with a wealth of hotels and resorts. Reserve a day in the Valley and visit the Heard Museum and Desert Botanical Garden. Select one of the area's popular Mexican restaurants for dinner. If time permits, stroll through Old Town Scottsdale's tempting art galleries. Depending on your remaining time in the Valley, you can escape to a spa for a day of pampering, get out your clubs and hit the links, or—if the season is right—catch a Major League Baseball spring-training game.

Logistics: Sky Harbor International Airport is located at the center of the city and is 20 minutes away from most of the Valley's major resorts. Plan on driving everywhere in the greater Phoenix area, as public transportation is nearly nonexistent. The Valley of the Sun is a large area, but Phoenix itself is remarkably simple to navigate. Designed on a grid, numbered streets run north–south and named streets (Camelback Road, Glendale Avenue) run east–west. Grand Avenue, running about 20 miles from Downtown to Sun City, is the only diagonal. If you need to know which direction you're facing, you can see South Mountain, conveniently looming in the south, from nearly any point in the city.

Grand Canyon South Rim: 1–2 Days

The sight of the Grand Canyon's immense beauty has taken many a visitor's breath away. Whatever you do, though, make sure you catch a sunset or sunrise view of the canyon. A night, or even just dinner, at grand El Tovar Hotel won't disappoint, but book your reservation early (up to six months ahead). Outdoors enthusiasts will want to reserve several days to hike and explore the canyon; less-ambitious travelers can comfortably see the area in one or two days.

Logistics: Arizona is a large state; the drive north from Phoenix to the South Rim of the Grand Canyon will take several hours, so budget at least a half day to make the 225-mile trip. Take Interstate 17 north from Phoenix into Flagstaff. The best way to reach the South Rim of the canyon is via U.S. 180 northwest from Flagstaff. It's best to travel to the canyon from the city during the week—Interstate 17 fills with locals looking to escape the heat on Friday and Saturday. If you have specific plans, whether it's a mule ride and rafting trip or dining and lodging, be sure to book very early for the canyon—reservations are necessary.

Red Rocks and Spectacular Sights: 3–4 Days
Option 1: Sedona and Surrounding Area

The unusual red-rock formations in Sedona are a key destination for most visitors to Arizona, and it's no wonder. Spend at least a day exploring the town and its beauty, whether on a calm stroll or a thrilling jeep tour. The surrounding area includes Flagstaff, a college town with a love for the outdoors and the stars; Prescott, with its Whiskey Row and Victorian homes; and Jerome, a charming artists' community that thrives more with every passing year.

Logistics: If possible, visit Sedona midweek, before the city folk fill the streets on the weekend. If Sedona is too pricey for your stay, consider the nearby towns of Flagstaff or Prescott, which have ample motels and budget hotels.

Option 2: Landmarks of Indian Country

The majestic landscapes in Monument Valley and Canyon de Chelly are among the biggest draws to Arizona. Made famous by countless Western movies and famous photographs, the scenes are even more astounding firsthand. This northeast corner of the state is worth several days of exploration. The famous Four Corners, where Arizona, New Mexico, Colorado, and Utah meet, are within a short drive but there isn't much to see. For a brief trip, make Monument Valley and Canyon de Chelly the priorities. With added days, you can visit a Native American trading post, Lake Powell and Glen Canyon, and the Four Corners. On your drive, be sure to spend an hour or two at Petrified Forest National Park, where you'll see the remains of a prehistoric forest.

Logistics: Approximately 100 miles from Sedona, the fascinating sites of northeast Arizona are a destination unto themselves. Don't be fooled: this is a remote area and will take hours to reach, whether you're coming from Phoenix, Sedona, or the Grand Canyon. Most travelers view this corner of the state as a road trip heaven, as the highways offer one scenic drive after the other. Plan on making one of the main towns—Tuba City, Page, Window Rock—your base, and take day trips from there. No matter what your itinerary, plan ahead and make reservations

early: the best way to see these popular sites is via guided tour.

Scenic Drives and Historic Towns: 2–4 Days

Option 1: Tucson, the Old West, and Historic Sites

If culture and history are a bit more attractive, consider spending time in Tucson and visiting its neighboring historic communities. Spend at least a day in Tucson proper, visiting Mission San Xavier del Bac, Saguaro National Park, and the Arizona-Sonora Desert Museum. If hiking is your game, don't miss Sabino Canyon, which offers gorgeous views of the area. With Tucson as your hub, take a day trip just a bit farther south to historic Tombstone and Bisbee. On the way back to the interstate, stop by Kartchner Caverns State Park for a view of the series of spectacular wet caves. Hour-long guided tours are available by reservation; book several months in advance to guarantee entry.

Logistics: Phoenix is two hours away via Interstate 10, a relatively unscenic drive. Casa Grande is the midway point between the two cities, and is a good place to stop for a rest. History buffs might want to stop at Picacho Peak, site of the westernmost battle of the Civil War.

Option 2: The White Mountains of Eastern Arizona

If nature walks and hiking are tops on your itinerary, consider spending a few days in the White Mountains before returning to Phoenix. The breathtaking White Mountains area of eastern Arizona is a favorite for anglers and cross-country skiers. The White Mountains Trails System near Pinetop-Lakeside is considered one of the best in the nation, and can accommodate all fitness levels. Eastern Arizona is primarily a summer

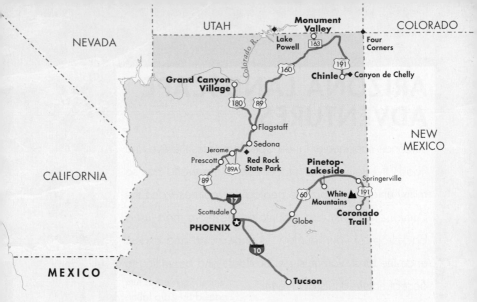

destination. Creek-side resorts with private cabins are common in the area, but many properties close from November to April, except for a few ski resorts.

Logistics: The most scenic route back to Phoenix is via the Salt River Canyon on U.S. 60 to Globe. The landscape transforms from ponderosa pine forests to high desert along the journey, marking an ideal transition from one extreme to the other. Or you can travel to Tucson from the White Mountains on one of the most scenic routes in the United States (if a bumpy and wild ride is your style). The Coronado Trail, U.S. 191 from Springerville to Clifton, is one of the world's curviest roads. The trip, which includes steep stretches and plenty of turns, will take at least four hours. Once in Clifton, you can continue south to Willcox, where Interstate 10 will take you to Tucson.

ROAD TRIP TIPS

■ If your budget permits, renting a four-wheel-drive vehicle will allow you to take advantage of side trips to remote areas.

■ Climate extremes, both heat and cold, make Arizona traveling hazardous, so heed the advice of locals. If somebody tells you it's a "little warm" to be poking around in those hills, they're probably correct.

■ Carry plenty of water, and if your vehicle should break down, put the hood up and stay with the vehicle.

■ Arizona's distances can be surprisingly vast. The drive from Phoenix to the Grand Canyon takes at least a half day.

ARIZONA LANDSCAPE ADVENTURES

Arizona's spectacular landscape dominates the eye and floods the senses. No place else in the world has so many unique and bizarre geological features—and the canyons, deserts, and mountains are more than just a backdrop for your journey. To understand and experience the land, you must get outdoors and be willing to accept nature on its own terms.

written by Melissa Kim
updated by Cara LaBrie

ARIZONA'S NATURAL FEATURES

Oak Creek Canyon, near Sedona

The diversity that these regions contain, not just in terrain but in flora and fauna, is unparalleled in the Lower 48. Resourceful plants and animals teach us so much about adapting to our surroundings and learning from nature. Some humans have also learned to survive in these harsh environments, but for most of us even a brief foray into Arizona's landscapes can be an adventure.

Canyons, mountains, and deserts are all closely related in the state's basic regions:

■ The northern section is part of the **Colorado Plateau,** a high-elevation region characterized by glowing red rocks and impossibly graceful slot canyons. It is also home to the Grand Canyon.

■ Along the state's southwestern corridor is the **Basin and Range Province,** where cactus-littered deserts and scrubby valleys rise abruptly to the San Francisco Peaks and Chiracahua Mountains.

■ In between, the **Central Highlands** contain mountain ranges where peaks drop away to canyons and desert grasslands, such as the easily accessible Saguaro National Park and the Arizona-Sonora Desert Museum.

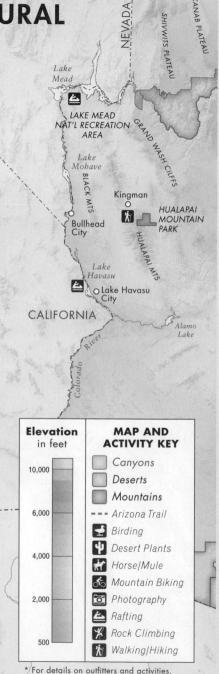

Elevation in feet	MAP AND ACTIVITY KEY
10,000	▢ Canyons
	▢ Deserts
	▢ Mountains
6,000	- - - Arizona Trail
	🦅 Birding
	🌵 Desert Plants
4,000	🐴 Horse/Mule
	🚵 Mountain Biking
2,000	📷 Photography
	🛶 Rafting
	🧗 Rock Climbing
500	🚶 Walking/Hiking

*For details on outfitters and activities, see corresponding chapters.

Lake Powell

KAIBAB PLATEAU

Page

Antelope Canyon

MARBLE CANYON

ECHO CLIFFS

MONUMENT VALLEY NAVAJO TRIBAL PARK

MONUMENT VALLEY

Four Corners Monument

BLACK MESA

CHUSKA MTS.

GRAND CANYON NATIONAL PARK

Colorado River

COCONINO PLATEAU

HAVASU CYN.

NORTH RIM

SOUTH RIM

Grand Canyon

Tusayan Museum

CANYON DE CHELLY NATIONAL MONUMENT

NEW MEXICO

PAINTED DESERT

Wupatki Nat'l Monument

SAN FRANCISCO PEAKS

Humphreys Peak 12,633ft

SUNSET CRATER VOLCANO NAT'L MONUMENT

Flagstaff

Oak Creek Canyon

Sedona

Meteor Crater

COCONINO NATIONAL FOREST

MOGOLLON PLATEAU

PETRIFIED FOREST NATIONAL PARK

VERDE VALLEY

MOGOLLON RIM

Prescott

Payson

Casa Malpais

Springerville

WHITE MOUNTAINS

SUPERSTITION MOUNTAINS

Arizona Trail

Mt. Baldy 11,404ft

APACHE-SITGREAVES NATIONAL FOREST

Scottsdale

Phoenix

Avondale

Desert Botanical Garden

Mesa

Tempe

Boyce Thompson Southwestern Arboretum

GALIURO MTS.

Casa Grande

CABEZA PRIETA NATIONAL WILDLIFE RESERVE

SANTA CATALINA MTS

Mount Lemmon

Arizona–Sonora Desert Museum

Tucson

CHIRICAHUA MOUNTAINS

CHIRICAHUA NATIONAL MONUMENT

ORGAN PIPE CACTUS NATIONAL MONUMENT

Kitt Peak

SAGUARO NATIONAL PARK

Cochise Stronghold

SULPHUR SPRINGS VALLEY

Tohono O'odham National Cultural Center

Madera Canyon

CORONADO NATIONAL FOREST

HUACHUCA MTS.

Ramsey Canyon

Douglas

SONORA

Nogales

MEXICO

CANYONS

While the Grand Canyon lives up to its impressive reputation, it is one of many such precious places in Arizona. Each canyon is a unique classroom of geology, where you can see the results of millions of years of shifts in the land.

More than 500 million years ago, a vast sea covered what is now Arizona. Sediments formed in thick layers as the sea rose and fell. Subsequent movement in the earth's crust created mountain ranges and lifted up entire sections of northern Arizona. Erosion and downcutting by rivers created deep canyons, uncovering layers of sandstone, shale, and limestone.

Forces of water and wind work to create some of Arizona's signature landscapes. High-elevation plateaus are continually eroded by rain, ice, rivers and groundwater, chipping and cracking the soft rock to form mesas and buttes, isolated hills or formations with steep sides and flat tops. What's the difference? One general rule of thumb is that a mesa is wider than it is high, while a butte is taller than it is high.

Some Grand Canyon excursions, such as mule tours (top) and rafting (opposite), are so popular they are booked up to a year in advance.

You can get your ecology credits here, too. As elevation changes from canyon floor to rim, so do the plants and animals. You can easily pass through four different biomes in a day's hike. Riparian communities on the canyon floor give way to a desert scrub, then to pinyon and Ponderosa pine forests. Where elevation exceeds 8,000 feet, spruce-fir forests make you feel as if you've somehow been transported to Canada.

ANCIENT PEOPLE AND THE LAND
Archaeologists have uncovered artifacts that show that people have lived in the Grand Canyon for at least 4,000 years. Tools, fire pits, cave paintings, and other remains indicate the presence of hunter-gatherers called the Archaic people, descendants of Paleoindians. You can see some "Archaic origami" stick figures on display at the Tusayan Museum at the South Rim.

TOP CANYON EXPERIENCES

WHITEWATER RAFTING
It's the rivers that helped create the canyons, after all, so spending time on the water is to spend time imagining the steady flow that carved out these works of natural art. About two dozen outfitters offer trips on the Colorado River through or near the Grand Canyon. Some sections are quiet and gentle, others rage and roil.

HORSE AND MULE TOURS
The best way to get a sense of the sheer scale of canyons is to be humbled by them—which means that you have to get to the bottom and look up. Hiking can be arduous, so many tour operators and parks offer horse or mule expeditions.

BIRDING
The entire state offers magnificent birding, but two extremes stand out. In the Grand Canyon, you can spot the enormous California condor's nine-foot wingspan since it was re-introduced in the 1990s. In the canyons of southeast Arizona, birders congregate in summer time to search for tiny hummingbirds.

BEYOND THE GRAND CANYON

In the northeast corner of Arizona, **Canyon de Chelly National Monument**, a National Park on Navajo Tribal Trust Land, rivals the Grand Canyon in natural splendor and can't be beat for cultural significance. People have been in residence here continuously since prehistoric times.

Antelope Canyon, called the world's most photographed slot canyon, is near Page in northern Arizona. You'll need an authorized guide to hike into this narrow sandstone canyon, which is inside the Navajo Reservation.

Just north of Sedona in north-central Arizona, you can drive through **Oak Creek Canyon**. Stop along the way to take a closer look at the red sandstone cliffs and buttes.

WORTH NOTING
- Canyon X, northeast Arizona
- Havasu Canyon, Grand Canyon
- Ramsey Canyon, southern Arizona
- Madera Canyon, southern Arizona

DESERTS

 Deserts are full of mystery, surprises, and stories of plants, animals, and people overcoming odds to survive and flourish. Track down a rare desert bloom, listen to the screech of an owl, or hear the hiss of a rattlesnake and you'll get a sense of the unique beauty and power of the landscape.

Just one of Arizona's claims to nature's hall of fame is as the only state to have all four of the major deserts in the United States within its borders. The Great Basin, the nation's largest cold desert, spills down to touch the northernmost areas of Arizona. In northwest Arizona, low shrubs such as yucca and the Joshua Tree dominate the small Mojave Desert, a hot desert, which has the nation's lowest elevation and highest temperatures. Only a few skinny fingers of the Chihuahan Desert grasslands stretch into the state's southeast corner. Arizona's largest desert, the Sonoran, is unusual with its biseasonal rainfall, mild winters, and subtropical climate that give rise to a diversity rarely seen in a desert environment.

Although deserts may look barren from a distance, a closer look reveals classic saguaros (top) and blooming prickly pear cacti (opposite).

And then there's the Painted Desert, not actually a true desert. In this high, dry region of the Colorado Plateau, colorful layers of sedimentary rocks are buckled and pitched up in grand steps, and carved into canyons and other-worldly rock formations.

ANCIENT PEOPLE AND THE LAND

Thousands of years ago, native people learned to live and thrive in the Sonoran Desert, creating canals to irrigate crops, migrating with the seasons from low valleys to cooler mountains, and harvesting desert plants. Today, the 20,000-plus members of the Tohono O'odham Nation live on more than 2.8 million acres in southwestern Arizona. To see handicrafts by tribal members and sample local food, stop by San Xavier Plaza in Tucson.

TOP DESERT EXPERIENCES

WALKING AND HIKING

Whether you're on a gentle nature stroll or a challenging scramble up a mountain, take the time for a scavenger hunt. Seek out a blooming teddy bear cholla, find a whiptail lizard sunning on a rock, or listen for the howl of a coyote at dusk.

PHOTOGRAPHY

The desert has a singular beauty that changes as the light shifts from scorching midday to shadowy dusk to evocative moonshine. With practice you can learn how to capture the best images of sweeping horizons, wildflowers, horses, cowboys, and even the wings of a hummingbird.

VIEWING DESERT PLANTS

Throughout the dry desert landscape, hardy succulents—water-retaining plants including cactus—are well-adapted to the extreme conditions. In wild parks and botanical gardens, you can observe bizzare-looking forms like the Joshua Tree as well as the more familiar saguaro, prickly pear, and barrel cactus.

TOP DESTINATIONS

Part zoo, part botanical garden, part natural history museum, the popular **Arizona-Sonora Desert Museum** allows you to sample the wildlife of the Sonoran Desert in downtown Tucson.

If you've got a little more time and energy, head for **Saguaro National Park** near Tucson. Its two districts have wonderful outdoor opportunities. For vistas of abundant cacti, try the Valley View Overlook.

For a true desert wilderness experience, head southwest to **Organ Pipe Cactus National Monument**, where organ pipe, saguaro, chollo, ocotillo, creosote, and other succulent plants flourish. Hike a trail, bike the 21-mile Ajo Mountain Drive, or camp here for pure serenity.

WORTH NOTING

- Desert Botanical Garden, Phoenix
- Boyce Thompson Arboretum, east of Phoenix
- Cabeza Prieta National Wildlife Refuge, southern Arizona
- Petrified Forest National Park, eastern Arizona

MOUNTAINS

What goes down, must come up. As Arizona's deserts and canyons were formed, so were mountain ranges. Mountain peaks reaching above 4,000 feet in elevation can be found in all parts of the state except the southwest corner.

Ancient rocky ranges with high meadows and cool alpine lakes, cratered volcanic peaks, and desert mountains that fall away to river gorges in deep canyons—Arizona has it all. The diversity of wildlife is immense and you really can travel from a cactus-covered desert to a snow-covered mountain peak in a day. The same geologic forces that created canyons—tectonic to volcanic to glacial activity—have left the state with mountains both old and young.

The rising and falling of the land created not just ranges but also isolated high-elevation areas in southern Arizona. Dubbed "sky islands," a collection of 40 forested mountain groups with lush vegetation at the top and their accompanying canyons below is surrounded by deserts or grasslands. The confluence of desert and forest communities has created habitats for rare and endemic

In warm weather, mountains can be cool escapes. Multi-use trails for bikers and hikers criss-cross the area near Sedona (top) and Flagstaff (opposite).

species, and wildlife-watching opportunities are truly unparalleled. And in eastern Arizona, the pine-covered White Mountains are a cool respite for many outdoor adventures.

ANCIENT PEOPLE AND THE LAND
As Arizona's prehistoric inhabitants evolved from hunting and gathering to agriculture, one group made its home in the forested mountain ranges and nearby valleys: the Mogollon. About 2,000 years ago, early Mogollon people hunted mountain game and gathered fruits, berries, and seeds from alpine meadows and forests to supplement what crops they could grow in the lower valleys. At Casa Malpais, in Springerville, remains of a 16-acre pueblo complex include what is thought to be a Mogollon solstice observatory, built around AD 1200.

TOP MOUNTAIN EXPERIENCES

MOUNTAIN BIKING
You can join a group ride with one of many biking clubs, take a guided tour, or venture out on your own. Recommended spots include: the Elephant Head Trail in Coronado National Forest, and trails in the Coconino National Forest, between Sedona and Flagstaff.

HIKING THE ARIZONA TRAIL
One of the eleven National Scenic Trails, this long-distance route covers about 800 miles from Mexico to Utah. People commonly take one section at a time. The trail takes you through major mountain ranges, from the Huachucas and Santa Rita in the south, through the Superstition Wilderness and over the San Francisco Peaks.

ROCK CLIMBING
Southern Arizona rock formations and towering cliffs are a great place to learn the basics of climbing. Take a course and start with basic bouldering, then learn how to rope up for multi-pitch climbs. Mount Lemmon and Cochise Stronghold, both near Tucson, are popular climbing spots.

TOP DESTINATIONS

Just north of Flagstaff, the volcanic **San Francisco Peaks** can be experienced by foot, mountain bike, horse, or even ski lift. Humphrey's Peak, the state's highest spot at 12,633 feet, is a rewarding trek for experienced hikers.

Erosion has carved out a "Wonderland of Rocks" at **Chiricahua National Monument** in the southeastern section of the state. A perfect example of a sky island, this is considered one of the most ecologically diverse regions in the entire country.

About 1,000 years ago, a series of violent erruptions formed **Sunset Crater Volcano National Monument** and destroyed plants for five miles. Now, you can hike on a lava flow, climb a cinder cone, and see signs of life regenerating.

WORTH NOTING
- Apache-Sitgreaves National Forest, eastern Arizona
- White Mountains, eastern Arizona
- Superstition Wilderness, Phoenix
- Hualapai Mountain Park, northwest Arizona
- Santa Catalina Mountains, Tucson

DISTINCTIVE ANIMALS OF ARIZONA

❶ Coatimundi

These high-energy mammals combine a long ringed tail like a monkey's, a snout like an anteater's, the lumbering walk of a bear, and the mask of a raccoon. Members of the raccoon family, they live in large social groups. Normally tree dwellers, in mountainous southeastern Arizona these nonstop foragers can make dens in caves and crevices.

❷ Desert bighorn sheep

Found primarily in the mountains of the Sonoran and Mojave Deserts, the sheep favor steep slopes and canyon walls. Unique padded hooves allow them to grab the surface of the rock. Males use their large curved horns for fighting and to break open cactus, a common food for the large grazers.

❸ Elegant trogon

This rare, distinctive bird migrates from Mexico to southeast Arizona's mountains and canyons in the summer. The foot-long birds make their nests in dead or dying sycamore trees in cavities created by woodpeckers. The colorful male has an emerald green back and throat, with a bright red breast and a white breast band.

❹ Gila woodpecker

One of the Sonoran Desert's signature species, this woodpecker works away at the saguaro cactus, creating cavities that serve as homes for itself and other animals, including owls, rats, lizards purple martins, and other birds. The very common birds don't hammer just to make holes; they also use sound to mark their territory.

❺ Western diamondback rattlesnake

Reptiles are plentiful in all of Arizona's deserts, and while most are fascinating and beautiful, the rattlesnakes can also be very dangerous. The Western Diamondback, with its triangular-shaped head and black and white ringed tail, is active late afternoon and at night, and will strike if it's disturbed. Tread carefully!

DISTINCTIVE PLANTS OF ARIZONA

❻ Ocotillo

Common in both the Sonoran and Chihuahan Deserts, this tall woody shrub has long, thin, spiny stems that rise up out of a short trunk. Reddish orange flowers bloom at the tips of these stems in spring, providing nectar—and energy—to migrating hummingbirds.

❼ Ponderosa pine

Forests of these tall stately pines cover high-elevation areas on the Colorado Plateau, and in some cases pure stands stretch for thousands of acres—such as the one from Flagstaff along the Mogollon Rim to the White Mountains. Growing more than 100 feet tall, this tree provides food and shelter to many animals and birds.

❽ Rocky Mountain iris

There's nothing quite like a mountain meadow in May, when blooming alpine wildflowers herald the season. Among the lupines, paintbrushes, lilies, and poppies, look for the Rocky Mountain iris between 6,000 and 9,000 feet elevation. Growing one or two feet high, the stems produce one to four delicate purple flowers with accents of yellow and white.

❾ Saguaro cactus

This iconic plant plays such a vital role in the Sonoran Desert, providing food and shelter to bats, bees, and birds. A giant, columnar cactus, with short stout arms that point to the sky, it can grow to be 40 feet tall or higher, with an average life span of 150 years. Its large, creamy white flowers bloom by night in late April and May, harbingers of the red juicy fruit.

❿ Yellow palo verde (foothill palo verde)

Look for this twiggy, thorny shrub on rocky hillsides. Its green bark contains chlorophyll, so it can still carry on with photosynthesis even when the shrub's leaves drop off during the dry season. The palo verde is the primary nurse plant for the saguaro cactus, providing shade for its seedlings.

A GEOLOGY PRIMER

Left: dramatic spires at the Chiracahuas. Top right: Rainbow Bridge, the world's longest natural bridge. Lower right: Monument Valley's Mittens and Merrick Butte.

ARCH This type of opening in a rock wall forms either through erosion, when wind and sand wear away the rock face, or through the freezing action of water. When water enters spaces or joints in a rock and freezes, the expansion of the ice can crack off chunks of rock.

BRIDGE If an opening through a rock is created by water flowing beneath it, it is called a bridge. You can see many natural bridges in Arizona, such as Rainbow Bridge near Lake Powell and Devil's Bridge near Sedona.

BUTTE A butte is what remains when a mesa erodes. You can see good examples of this formation in Monument Valley in northeast Arizona.

CAVES Natural underground chambers that open to the surface give you an opportunity to descend below the Earth's surface and learn about the forces of heat and water upon rocks and minerals. Kartchner Caverns, south of Tucson, is a living cave where water still flows, dissolving minerals and creating beautiful formations.

MESA A mesa, or hill with a smooth, flat, tablelike top (mesa means "table" in Spanish), is a clear example of how hard rock stands higher and protects the soft rock beneath. A single mesa may cover hundreds of square miles of land. There are many mesas in the Hopi Reservation, including the villages of First, Second, and Third Mesa.

MONUMENT This general term applies to geologic formations that are much taller than they are wide, or to formations that resemble man-made structures. These are what give Monument Valley its name.

PETRIFIED WOOD If you want to know what the desert of the Southwest used to look like, picture the Florida Everglades populated with giant dragonflies and smaller species of dinosaurs. Arizona's Petrified Forest offers a glimpse of the once lush, tropical world. Stumps and logs from the ancient woodland are now turned to rock because they were immersed in water and sealed away from the air, so normal decay did not occur. Instead, the preserved wood gradually hardened as silica, or sand, filtered into its porous spaces, almost like cement. Erosion was among the geological processes that exposed the wood.

SPIRE As a butte erodes, it may become one or more spires. You can see wonderful examples of these rock formations in southern Arizona's Chiricahua National Monument.

PHOENIX, SCOTTSDALE, AND TEMPE

WELCOME TO PHOENIX, SCOTTSDALE, AND TEMPE

TOP REASONS TO GO

★ **Resort spas:** With dozens of outstanding desert spas, Phoenix has massaged and wrapped its way to the top of the relaxation destinations list.

★ **Shops and restaurants:** Retail centers Old Town Scottsdale and Fashion Square are another way to retreat and relax in the Valley of the Sun, as are a melting pot of fine and funky dining establishments.

★ **The Heard Museum:** This small but world-renowned museum elegantly celebrates Native American people, culture, art, and history.

★ **The great outdoors:** Sure there's urban sprawl, but Phoenix also has cool and accessible places to get away from it all, like the Desert Botanical Garden, Papago Park, Tempe Town Lake, and mountain and desert preserves.

★ **Golf:** All year long, links lovers can take their pick of top-rated public and private courses—many with incredibly spectacular views.

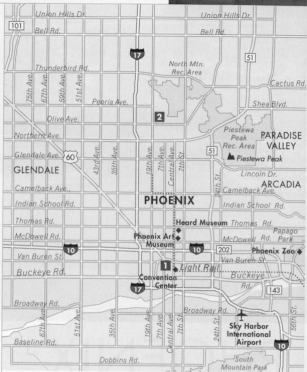

1 Downtown Phoenix. As the site of Arizona's government operations and the state's largest concentration of skyscrapers, this area used to be strictly business. Nowadays it's home to some of the Valley's major museums, performance venues, and sports arenas, plenty of high-rise homeowners, and a light-rail system that's changing the face of the city.

2 Greater Phoenix. Here's an unusual mix of attractions ranging from hip, historic neighborhoods to acres of mountain preserves, cultural and ethnic centers, and corridors of modern commercial enterprise. Hike a couple of peaks, peek at the animals in the Phoenix Zoo, zoom on over to the Phoenix Art and Heard museums, and then relax at a luxury mountainside resort—all in one day.

GETTING ORIENTED

It can be useful to think of Phoenix as a flower with petals (other communities) growing in every direction from the bud of Sky Harbor Airport. The East Valley includes Scottsdale, Paradise Valley, Ahwatukee, Tempe, Mesa, Fountain Hills, and Apache Junction. To the southeast are Chandler and Gilbert. The West Valley includes Glendale, Sun City, Peoria, and Litchfield Park. Central Avenue, which runs north and south through the heart of Downtown Phoenix, is the city's east–west dividing line. Everything east of Central is considered the East Valley and everything west of Central is the West Valley. Phoenix has grown around what was once a cluster of independent towns in Maricopa County, but the gaps between communities that were open desert space just a few short decades ago have begun to close in and blend the entire Valley into one large, sprawling community.

3 Scottsdale. Once an upscale Phoenix sibling, it now flies solo as a top American destination. A bastion of high-end and specialty shopping, historic sites, elite resorts, restaurants, spas, and golf greens next to desert views, Scottsdale can easily absorb an entire vacation.

4 Tempe and Around. The home of Arizona State University and a creative melting pot of residents, Tempe is equal parts party and performance, especially along its main artery, Mill Avenue, where commerce and culture collide.

SPA TIME IN ARIZONA: SAY AHHH

OK, so you came, you saw, you shopped, you dined, you recreated. Now it's time for some rest and relaxation at one, or even several, of the *many* area spas. Arizona's own approach to pampered repose is world-renowned and worth exploring with all of your senses.

Whether you're looking for a simple massage or an entire lifestyle change, Arizona rubs just about everyone the right way—from exclusive "immersion environments" of remote destination spas, to more accessible and affordable resort and day spas around the state. Each has its own signature style and blend of services, including purely local luxury at Sanctuary Spa on Camelback Mountain. In the midst of the Southwest's deserts and cities, you're sure to find spa menus boasting treatments and treats from around the world: Swedish and Japanese massages, French manicures and Vichy showers, Turkish-style baths, ayurvedic practices from India, California cuisine, and mood music from the Middle East and New Mexico.

Above: Royal Palms's couples massage. Upper right: A water retreat at Sanctuary on Camelback Mountain. Lower right: Moroccan-inspired treatment room in Joya Spa at Montelucia Resort

A HISTORY OF HEALING

Arizona's hot, arid climate was considered a cure-all for respiratory ailments and joint pain. The East Coast power elite (Astors, Vanderbilts, and Rockefellers, to name a few) who grew sick of brutal winters and humid summers made a second home out of local resorts and spas. The hospitality industry has been striving to meet high standards for rejuvenation and health ever since.

RULES TO RELAX BY

Observing simple spa rules can ensure ultimate spa satisfaction versus an uncomfortable experience. First, decide on a budget beforehand and research spa menus; many are available online. Plan on a 15%–20% gratuity (cash preferred) for each treatment, though some spas include gratuity in their pricing. Second, book at least a week ahead, longer for the most popular spas like Sanctuary Camelback Mountain in Paradise Valley. Third, check in at least 20 minutes prior to your first treatment. The earlier you arrive, the longer you can enjoy the spa's gratis amenities, such as pools and steam rooms.

DAY OR DESTINATION?

Day spas are just that. They keep daytime hours and offer luxury treatments, but not long-term wellness programs. Destination spas, like Mii amo at Sedona's Enchantment Resort (⇨ *See Chapter 4*) and Tucson's exclusive Canyon Ranch (⇨ *See Chapter 7*), have "immersion environments" with on-site accommodations and curricula designed for an inner- and outer-body overhaul. Most resort spas operate like day spas and don't require an overnight stay; however, hotel guests take precedence when it comes to booking.

LOCAL LURE AND LORE

A few spas are sanctioned to offer the innovative treatments and environments inspired by the traditions of local Native American tribes. Just south of Phoenix, Aji Spa at the Sheraton Wild Horse Pass Resort draws on the surrounding Pima and Maricopa communities to create unique experiences. Many of their treatments employ time-honored healing methods, approved by tribal elders.

A TOUCH OF ROMANCE

If an indulgent spa visit is your ideal romantic getaway, pick a place that truly specializes in making it special. Most spa menus include a couples' massage, but some focus on creating an entire experience for pairs. Alvadora Spa at the Royal Palms in Phoenix offers frequent romance packages (and discounted rates during the hot summer months) along with twosome-oriented treatments and amenities, while Joya at Paradise Valley's Montelucia offers a specially outfitted couples' day suite.

TASTE TREATMENT

If you're focusing on a detoxifying spa experience, the last thing you want to do is replenish with unsavory elements. Camelback Inn in Scottsdale and The Boulders in Carefree have restaurants or cafés that specialize in "spa cuisine," often surprisingly delicious, health-conscious dishes made with locally grown ingredients—good for you and the planet.

VALLEY OF THE SUN GOLF: DRIVING AMBITION

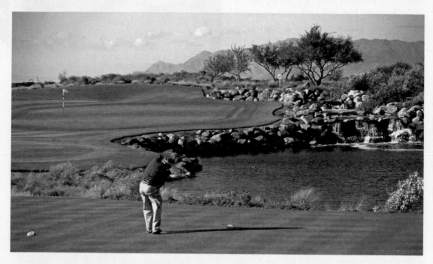

Itching to get into the swing of things? Hoping to partake in some coursework? Looking to get linked in? In other words, would you rather be golfing? You're in the right place. Despite the dry climate this place is a gold mine of lush greens and far-reaching fairways.

Above: It's easy to find greens in the Valley of the Sun. Upper right: Tournament Players Club (TPC) at the Fairmont Scottsdale Princess Resort. Lower right: The setting at The Boulders

Golf is one of Arizona's leading draws for locals and visitors from around the world. Big, professional courses mean big business in the Valley of the Sun, evidenced by the more than 200 courses that consume much of the area and surround some of its finest resorts, locally based golf companies such as Ping and Dixon, and by the Phoenix Open—an annual world-class tournament and weeklong party that takes place in North Scottsdale at the renowned Tournament Players Club (TPC). That might sound intimidating, but consider it an invitation. Whether you're an amateur or an ace, and whether you're looking out for pars, your pocketbook, or just a pretty place to play a round, there's something for all ranges here.

TEE-TIME TIP

Book online, up to weeks in advance during winter and spring. Get availability, pricing, and discounted tee-time information by visiting an individual course's website. For municipal courses, visit ⊕ *phoenix.gov/parks* or ⊕ *www.thegolfcourses. net* and search Phoenix or Scottsdale for links to all the Valley's links.

PLAN AHEAD

Call well ahead for tee times during the cooler months from January to April, especially for popular courses. In summer, it's not uncommon to schedule a round before dawn. If you're booking a room at a resort with a course, be sure to book your tee time then also. Last-minute tee times are sometimes available through online reservation services, depending on the season.

PERFECT YOUR GOLF SWING

Feel like you need to swing like a pro before you take on the Valley of the Sun's premier golf courses? Troon North has a solution: the **Callaway Golf Performance Center** (☏ *480/585–5300* ⊕ *www.troonnorthgolf.com*) is a state-of-the-art facility that analyzes your swing and fits your clubs with 3-D imagery and software designed by the experts at Callaway. Golf greats like Tiger Woods and Phil Mickelson use similar technologies to perfect their games—why shouldn't you? With only a handful of facilities like this in the country, it's definitely worth checking out.

SAVINGS TIPS

Encanto Park and Papago Golf Course are just two of the city and public courses that are a great value. Check course websites for discounts. Some golf courses offer a discounted twilight rate—and the weather is often much more amenable at this time of day.

Fees drop dramatically in summer but remember that afternoon heat can be sweltering.

"GREENER" GREENS

Short of creating sand and cactus courses, desert golf facilities are hard-pressed to answer the eco-friendly call, but some are making strides in chipping away their carbon cleat print. Most courses now use reclaimed water and are experimenting with low-water grasses.

GROUPS TO GUIDE YOU

Package deals abound at resorts as well as through booking agencies like **Scottsdale Golf Adventures** (☏ *800/398–8100* ⊕ *www.scottsdalegolfadventures.com*), who will plan and schedule a non-stop golf holiday for you. If you're looking for a little more pampering, try **Scottsdale Swing** (☏ *888/807–9464* ⊕ *www.scottsdaleswing.com*), which will arrange a complete golf holiday, including access to the area's best nightclubs. For a copy of the *Arizona Golf Guide*, contact the **Arizona Golf Association** (☏ *602/944–3035 or 800/458–8484* ⊕ *www.azgolf.org*).

VALLEY OF THE SUN FOOD

Arizona is still the state that people think of for cowboys, cactus, and "It's a dry heat," but many have thought of it as an endless possibility for creating another timeless icon: cuisine. As Old West staples get global updates, food is making lasting memories.

Above: Modern interpretations of tacos in endless varieties. Top Right: Table-side guacamole is made to taste at The Mission in Scottsdale. Lower right: Fry bread, a classic Native American dish

When the Valley's culinary innovators pull together their creations, they certainly practice safe cooking, but figuratively speaking, the gloves are off. Building on signature Sonoran Desert fruits and flavors, chefs experiment well outside the Tex-Mex box. For example, Vincent Guerithault of Vincent on Camelback combined his background in haute French cuisine with his Southwestern foreground. Matt Carter of Scottsdale's Latin-inspired The Mission had a private aptitude for roasting meats and a desire to make it public. Chandler's Kai creators wanted a sustainable restaurant reflecting the culinary lore of the surrounding Native American reservations. All good food has a history and Arizona's leading chefs are pulling from it to make their own.

FRESH-AIR FARE

Sample creations from more than 50 restaurants at the Great Arizona Picnic during the **Scottsdale Culinary Festival** (⊕ www.scottsdalefest.org) in April.

Visit the **Camelback Market** Saturdays, October to May, for fine wines, fresh produce, grilled meats, crepes, panini, pizza, and pastry.

TAKE IT SLOW

Slow-roasted pork is a Southwestern specialty that few have mastered like Valley venues have. **Barrio Cafe**'s citrus-marinated *cochinita pibil* is pork slow-roasted for 12 hours and served with spicy red pepper and sour orange seasoning. The melt-in-your-mouth red chile carne *adovada* at **Richardson's Cuisine of New Mexico** (✉ *6335 N. 16th St., Central Phoenix* ☎ *602/265–5886* ⊕ *www.richardsonsnm.com*) takes days to prepare but is usually consumed in heaven-sent minutes, while the pork shoulder at **The Mission** makes for delicious tacos.

NATIVE SUN

Native American traditions also play a strong role in the local cuisine scene. **Kai** uses locally grown, customary tribal ingredients, including native seeds, agave sap, and saguaro-blossom syrup in its organic entrées. Places like **Fry Bread House** bank on the less healthful but totally tasty traditions of fry bread and Navajo tacos.

STEAK OUT

While many restaurateurs spent years trying to break the meat-and-potatoes mold, some recognized it as an enduring dining genre and sought to reinvent the concept. For a classic spin try **Durant's**, while many of the area's resorts bid adieu to former fine dining establishments to welcome modern spins on

the American steak house. **Bourbon Steak** and **BLT Steak** offer pricey but exquisite à la carte menus featuring regional grass-fed and Kobe beef.

WINE AND DINE

Lighter, shared fare is popular among the jet set who want to see, be seen, drink, and eat a little—but not too much. Wine bars draw the happy-hour crowd and keep them through dinner with delicious tapas-style noshes. Try bruschetta at **Postino Winecafe** or a plate of international meat and cheeses at **Cheuvront Restaurant & Wine Bar,** where sharing and savoring reign supreme.

ROLLING IN DOUGH

Fresh-baked bread products have become a vital part of some of the most successful menus. It may be safe to say that **La Grande Orange** now *owns* the English muffin with their version, made on-site at LGO daily. And there are at least a bakers-dozen delicious reasons that area eateries (including LGO) clamor to serve the fresh baked and caked goods of **Tammie Coe Cakes & MJ Bread** (✉ *5210 N. Central Ave., Central Phoenix* ☎ *602/840–3644* ⊕ *www. tammiecoecakes.com*).

⇨ *Restaurants without contact details here have full listings in this chapter.*

SCOTTSDALE SHOPPING

Despite its origins as a livestock town, Scottsdale has steadily evolved from a sow's ear into a silk purse. Once a sleepy suburb of Phoenix, it's become a high-end shopping mecca—so renowned that glossy magazine ads now read: Paris, London, New York, Scottsdale.

Above: Scottsdale Fashion Square has high-end stores and great restaurants. Top Right: Art at the Wilde Meyer Galleries

When life gives you heat, become the hottest thing around. It's not Scottsdale's motto, but it should be. Not only has it built a reputation as one of the world's spending hot spots, it's made year-round vacation destinations out of trendy, temperature-controlled malls, marketplaces, and upscale plazas, exclusive department stores, and chic boutiques that are powerful magnets for old and new money, celebrities, and the diva in us all. But Scottsdale hasn't completely glossed over its rustic, cowboy beginnings and compelling heritage. In addition to finding the latest fashions, you can also find authentic Western wear; traditional Native American rugs and jewelry; Arizona novelties; fine art of every genre and medium; and historic mementos in the area's many galleries, museums, mom-and-pop shops, and specialty stores.

BEST TIME TO GO

During the summer months, your most comfortable shopping bets are the malls and centers with ample air-conditioning such as **Scottsdale Fashion Square**. The rest of the year Old Town is a great neighborhood to shop and stroll, especially during **Art Walk**, every Thursday 7–9 pm year-round in the galleries and shops of Marshall Way and Main Street arts districts.

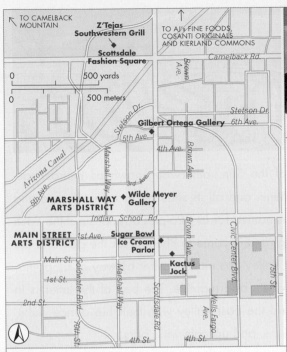

↖ TO CAMELBACK MOUNTAIN

Z'Tejas Southwestern Grill

Scottsdale Fashion Square

↑ TO AJ's FINE FOODS, COSANTI ORIGINALS AND KIERLAND COMMONS

Camelback Rd.

0 ___ 500 yards

0 ___ 500 meters

Brown Ave.

Stetson Dr.

Stetson Dr.

Gilbert Ortega Gallery 6th Ave.

5th Ave.

4th Ave.

Brown Ave.

Arizona Canal

5th Ave.

3rd Ave.

MARSHALL WAY ARTS DISTRICT

♦ **Wilde Meyer Gallery**

Marshall Way

Indian School Rd.

MAIN STREET ARTS DISTRICT

1st Ave.

Sugar Bowl Ice Cream Parlor ♦

Brown Ave.

Civic Center Blvd.

Main St.

♦ **Kactus Jock**

Goldwater Blvd.

Marshall Way

Scottsdale Rd.

Wells Fargo Ave.

75th St.

1st St.

2nd St.

79th St.

4th St.

4th St.

TOP FINDS

Local arts and crafts: For paintings and more inspired by the beauty of the Southwest, explore **Wilde Myer Galleries**. Old Town Scottsdale is a good place for Native American finds, including the many locations of **Gilbert Ortega Indian Jewelry and Gallery**. Just north of the hustle and bustle of Scottsdale Fashion Square sits the tranquil, shaded property of the **Cosanti Originals** where the signature ceramic and bronze wind-bells of renowned architect Paolo Soleri are made and sold.

Edible goods: Shopping for a foodie? Heat things up with Goldwater's salsa and Arizona Gunslinger hot sauce products. **AJ's Fine Foods** is a great place for local tastes; **Kactus Jock** has nonedible souvenirs, too.

Signature style: Bola ties are the official neckwear of Arizona. Crafted from braided leather, metal tips, and a securing ornament, these ties have long been a craft of the Hopi, Navajo, and Zuni Indian tribes and are found in shops and galleries throughout Old Town.

QUICK BITES/REFUELING

Chloe's Corner. For Kierland Commons shoppers, stop at Chloe's Corner for a light but filling bite, with gourmet sandwiches, salads, baked goods, and milk shakes. There's also a downtown Phoenix location that's a great pit stop. ✉ *15215 N. Kierland Blvd., #190, North Scottsdale, Scottsdale* ☎ *480/998–0202* ⊕ *www.chloescorneraz.com.*

Sugar Bowl Ice Cream Parlor. This iconic Scottsdale destination transports you back in time to a 1950s malt shop, complete with great burgers and lots of yummy ice-cream confections. ✉ *4005 N. Scottsdale Rd., Old Town, Scottsdale* ☎ *480/946–0051* ⊕ *www.sugarbowlscottsdale.com.*

Z'Tejas Southwestern Grill. Located in Scottsdale Fashion Square, Z'Tejas serves tasty food and ample margaritas to soothe the shopping beast. Don't miss the guacamole, which is made tableside. ✉ *7014 E. Camelback Rd., Old Town, Scottsdale* ☎ *480/946–4171* ⊕ *www.ztejas.com.*

Updated by
Elise Riley

The Valley of the Sun, otherwise known as metro Phoenix (i.e., Phoenix and all its suburbs, including Tempe and Scottsdale), is named for its 325-plus days of sunshine each year. Although many come to Phoenix for the golf and the weather, the Valley has much to offer by way of shopping, outdoor activities, and nightlife. The best of the latter is in Scottsdale and the East Valley with their hip dance clubs, old-time saloons, and upscale wine bars.

The Valley marks the northern tip of the Sonoran Desert, a prehistoric seabed that extends into northwestern Mexico with a landscape offering much more than just cacti. Palo verde and mesquite trees, creosote bushes, brittle bush, and agave dot the land, which is accustomed to being scorched by temperatures in excess of 100°F for weeks at a time. Late summer brings precious rain as monsoon storms illuminate the sky with lightning shows and the desert exudes the scent of creosote. Spring sets the Valley blooming, and the giant saguaros are crowned in white flowers for a short time in May—in the evening and cool early mornings—and masses of vibrant wildflowers fill desert crevices and span mountain landscapes.

PHOENIX, SCOTTSDALE, AND TEMPE PLANNER

WHEN TO GO

It's a common misconception that Phoenix forever hovers around 100°F. That might hold true from May to October, but the winter months have been known to push the mercury down to 35°F. The city also has experienced consecutive days of nonstop rain. Such instances are rare, but it's good to be prepared and check weather reports before you pack.

Phoenix can get pretty darn hot in summer, so plan your outdoor activities for the cooler parts of the day and save the air-conditioned stuff for when it's needed: the Heard Museum is not only a must-see, it's also inside, as are the nearby Phoenix Art Museum and many other popular attractions.

FESTIVALS AND EVENTS

JANUARY **Barrett-Jackson.** Fabulous car auctions including Barrett-Jackson attract thousands every January. ☎ *480/421-6694* ⊕ *www.barrett-jackson.com.*

PF Chang's Rock 'n' Roll Marathon. Live bands line the course and a concert follows the 26.2-mile race that attracts thousands each January. ☎ *800/311-1255* ⊕ *runrocknroll.competitor.com/arizona.*

Russo and Steele. Every January, the Russo and Steele auction features some of the most sought-after vehicles in the world. ☎ *602/252-2697* ⊕ *www.russoandsteele.com.*

Waste Management Phoenix Open. Formerly the Phoenix Open, this golf tournament is the "Greatest Show on Grass." ☎ *602/870-0163* ⊕ *www. wmphoenixopen.com.*

FEBRUARY **The Heard Museum World Championship Hoop Dance Contest.** The Heard Museum hosts the spectacular Annual World Hoop Dance Championship, with traditional music and costumes. ☎ *602/252-8840* ⊕ *www. heard.org.*

The Parada del Sol Parade and Rodeo. This annual horse-drawn parade is an Arizona tradition featuring cowboys, cowgirls, horses, and floats. ☎ *480/990-3179* ⊕ *www.paradadelsol.us.*

MARCH **Indian Fair & Market.** Every March, more than 700 Native American artists and artisans are showcased at the Heard Museum. ☎ *602/252-8840* ⊕ *www.heard.org.*

Ostrich Festival. This is a weekend of music, entertainment, and (of course) ostrich races in Chandler every March. ☎ *480/963-4571* ⊕ *www. ostrichfestival.com.*

Scottsdale Arts Festival. This weekend event in March is jam-packed with arts and crafts—and music. ☎ *480/499-8587* ⊕ *www.scottsdale artsfestival.org.*

APRIL **Scottsdale Culinary Festival.** Foodies from across the Valley mark their calendars for this week-long festival in April. Taste the creations from some of the best chefs in town at this outoor celebration of food. ☎ *480/945-7193* ⊕ *www.scottsdalefest.org.*

OCTOBER **Arizona State Fair.** Come for classic fair fun, including arm wrestling and calf roping. ☎ *602/252-6771* ⊕ *www.azstatefair.com.*

DECEMBER **Las Noches de las Luminarias.** Adjacent to the twinkling zoo, the Desert Botanical Garden lights up every night during Las Noches de las Luminarias, when thousands of luminarias (paper bags with lights inside) line the Garden's pathways. Stroll, listen to live music, and enjoy the beauty of the desert. Tickets sell out quickly, so be sure to make a reservation for this annual December event. ☎ *480/941-1225* ⊕ *www.dbg.org.*

PLANNING YOUR TIME

Three to five days is an optimal amount of time to spend in Phoenix if you want to relax, get outside to hike or golf, and see the main sites like the Heard Museum and Scottsdale. Extra time will allow you to make some interesting side trips to nearby places like Arcosanti, Wickenburg, Cave Creek, and Carefree.

Remember that the Valley of the Sun is sprawling, so planning ahead will help you save time and gas. If you're heading to the Heard Museum Downtown, for instance, you might want to visit the nearby Arizona Science Center and/or the Phoenix Art Museum, too, both of which are close to the light-rail line. If you're going to Taliesin West, do so before or after spending time in Scottsdale.

■TIP➔ If you're driving to the Grand Canyon from Phoenix, allow at least two full days, with a minimum drive time of four hours each way. You can always anticipate slow-moving traffic on Interstate 17, but in the afternoon and evening on Friday and Sunday lengthy standstills are almost guaranteed, something to remember if your plans involve getting back to Sky Harbor Airport to catch a flight out.

GETTING HERE AND AROUND
AIR TRAVEL
Phoenix Sky Harbor International Airport (PHX) is served by most major airlines. The airport is a 10-minute drive from Downtown Phoenix or Tempe, and 15 minutes to North Scottsdale. SuperShuttle vans each take up to seven passengers to different destinations. Fares are $14 to Downtown Phoenix and around $28 to Scottsdale.

Air Contacts Phoenix Sky Harbor International Airport (PHX). ☎ 602/273-3300 ⊕ www.skyharbor.com. **SuperShuttle** ☎ 602/244-9000, 800/258-3826 ⊕ www.supershuttle.com.

CAR TRAVEL
To get around Phoenix, *you will need a car.* Only the major downtown areas (Phoenix, Scottsdale, and Tempe) are pedestrian-friendly. Don't expect to nab a rental car without a reservation, especially from January to April.

Roads in Phoenix and its suburbs are laid out on an 800-square-mile grid. Grand Avenue, running 20 miles from Downtown to Sun City, is the only diagonal. Central Avenue is the main north–south grid axis: all roads parallel to and west of Central are numbered avenues; all roads parallel to and east of Central are numbered streets. The numbering begins at Central and increases in each direction.

PUBLIC TRANSPORTATION TRAVEL
The Valley's light-rail system is convenient for exploring the Downtown Phoenix museums or the area near Arizona State University. Fares are $3.50/day and multiday passes are available. Phoenix runs a free Downtown Area Shuttle (DASH), and Tempe operates the Free Local Area Shuttle (FLASH).

Public Transportation Contacts Valley Metro ☎ 602/253-5000 ⊕ www.valleymetro.org.

TAXI TRAVEL
Taxi fares are unregulated in Phoenix, except at the airport. The 800-square-mile metro area is so large that one-way fares in excess of $50 are not uncommon. Except within a compact area, travel by taxi

2

isn't recommended. Taxis charge about $3 for the first mile and $2 per mile thereafter, not including tips.

Taxi Contacts Checker/Yellow Cab ☎ *480/888-8888* ⊕ *www.aaayellowaz. com.* **Clean Air Cab** ☎ *480/777-97777* ⊕ *www.cleanaircab.com.* **Courier Cab** ☎ *602/232-2222.*

TOURS

If you'd like a break from driving, consider a tour to see the Valley's top attractions. Reservations are a must all year.

Open Road Tours. This operator offers excursions to Sedona and the Grand Canyon, Phoenix city tours, and Native American–culture trips to the Salt River Pima–Maricopa Indian Reservation. Local tours cost about $59. ☎ *602/997–6474, 855/553–8830* ⊕ *www.openroadtours. com.*

Vaughan's Southwest Tours. This 4½-hour city tour stops at the Pueblo Grande Museum, Mummy Mountain, and Old Town Scottsdale for $60. Vaughan's tours use custom vans and accommodate groups of 11 or fewer passengers. The company will also take you east to the Apache Trail. ☎ *602/971–1381, 800/513–1381* ⊕ *www.southwesttours.com.*

VISITOR INFORMATION

Most Valley cities have tourism centers where you can get maps or excursion suggestions.

Greater Phoenix Convention & Visitors Bureau ☎ *877/225-5749, 602/254–6500* ⊕ *www.visitphoenix.com* ═ *No credit cards.*

Scottsdale Convention & Visitors Bureau ☎ *800/782–1117, 480/421–1004* ⊕ *www.experiencescottsdale.com* ═ *No credit cards.*

EXPLORING

DOWNTOWN PHOENIX

Changes in the Valley over the past two decades have meant the emergence of a real Downtown in Phoenix, where people hang out: there are apartments and loft spaces; cultural and sports facilities, including Jefferson Street's Chase Field (formerly known as Bank One Ballpark and still affectionately referred to by many locals as BOB) and US Airways Center; and large areas for conventions and trade shows. It's retained a mix of past and present, too, as restored homes in Heritage Square, from the original townsite, give an idea of how far the city has come since its inception around the turn of the 20th century.

GETTING HERE AND AROUND

There are lots of parking options Downtown, and they're listed on the free map provided by Downtown Phoenix Partnership, available in many local restaurants (⊕ *www.downtownphoenix.com*). Many Downtown sites are served by the light-rail system or DASH (Downtown Area Shuttle), a free bus service.

Arizona
Science
Center **2**

Children's
Museum of
Phoenix **3**

Heritage
Square **1**

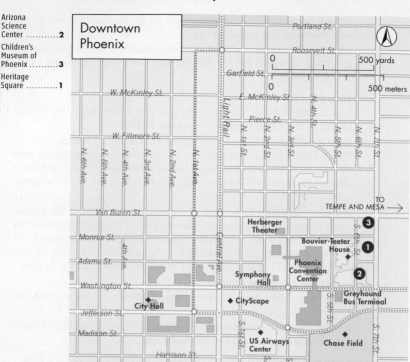

TIMING

Artlink Phoenix First Fridays. On the first Friday of every month galleries stay open late and crowds converge to view the work of emerging and established artists, listen to live music, and see impromptu street performances. It's an excellent way to check out the Phoenix arts scene. ☎ *602/256–7539* ⊕ *www.artlinkphoenix.com* ▭ *No credit cards.*

EXPLORING

FAMILY **Arizona Science Center.** With more than 300 hands-on exhibits, this is the venue for science-related exploration. You can pilot a simulated airplane flight, travel through the human body, navigate your way through the solar system in the Dorrance Planetarium, and watch a movie in a giant, five-story IMAX theater. ✉ *600 E. Washington St., Downtown Phoenix* ☎ *602/716–2000* ⊕ *www.azscience.org* 🎫 *Museum $14; combination museum, IMAX, and planetarium $30* ⊙ *Daily 10–5.*

FAMILY **Children's Museum of Phoenix.** A playground for kids of all ages, this museum features hands-on exhibits where children learn by playing. Venture through the "noodle forest," relax in the book loft, or get a crash course in economics by role-playing at the on-site market. ✉ *215 N. 7th St., Downtown Phoenix* ☎ *602/253–0501* ⊕ *www. childrensmuseumofphoenix.org* 🎫 *$11* ⊙ *Tues.–Sun. 9 am–4 pm. Closed Mon.*

2

Heritage Square. In a park-like setting from 5th to 7th streets between Monroe and Adams streets, this city-owned block contains the only remaining houses from the original Phoenix townsite. On the south side of the square, along Adams Street, stand several houses built between 1899 and 1901. The Bouvier Teeter House has a Victorian-style tearoom, and the Thomas House and Baird Machine Shop are now Pizzeria Bianco, one of the area's most popular eateries. ⊠ *Downtown Phoenix* ⊕ *phoenix.gov/parks/parks/heritagepk.html* ▭ *No credit cards.*

Arizona Doll and Toy Museum. The one-story brick Stevens House holds the Arizona Doll and Toy Museum. ⊠ *602 E. Adams St., Downtown Phoenix* ☎ *602/253–9337* ⌨ *$5* ⊙ *Tues.–Sat. 10–4, Sun. noon–4. Closed Mon. Closed Aug.*

Rosson House Museum. This 1895 Victorian in the Queen Anne style is the queen of Heritage Square. Built by a physician who served a brief term as mayor, it's the sole survivor among fewer than two dozen Victorians erected in Phoenix. It was bought and restored by the city in 1974. ⊠ *113 N 6th St., Downtown Phoenix* ☎ *602/262–5070* ⊕ *www.rossonhousemuseum.org* ⌨ *$7.50* ⊙ *Wed.–Sat. 10–3:30, Sun. noon–3:30.*

QUICK BITES

SWITCH. One of Phoenix's coolest ways to beat the summer heat, SWITCH offers a unique menu. Choose from fresh sandwiches, healthful salads, a fabulous cheese platter, gourmet burgers, steaks, seafood, baked goods, and crepes, all served in a sleek, modern setting with couch conversation pits and one of downtown's best patios, free from direct sunlight and traffic noise. ⊠ *2603 N. Central Ave., Central Phoenix* ☎ *602/264–2295* ⊕ *www. switchofarizona.com.*

GREATER PHOENIX

While suburban towns are popping up all around Phoenix, the city's core neighborhoods just outside Downtown Phoenix maintain the majority of their history and appeal. There are options aplenty to take you out hiking in the hills, or inside to some interesting cultural sites.

TOP ATTRACTIONS

FAMILY

Fodor's Choice
★

Desert Botanical Garden. Opened in 1939 to conserve and showcase the ecology of the desert, these 150 acres contain more than 4,000 different species of cacti, succulents, trees, and flowers. A stroll along the 0.5-mile-long "Plants and People of the Sonoran Desert" trail is a fascinating lesson in environmental adaptations; children enjoy playing the self-guiding game "Desert Detective." Specialized tours are available at an extra cost; check online for times and prices. ■TIP➔ The Desert Botanical Garden stays open late, to 8 pm year-round, and it's particularly lovely when lighted by the setting sun or by moonlight, so you can

CLOSE UP

Phoenix History: A City Grows in the Desert

2

As the Hohokam (the name comes from the Pima word for "people who have gone before") discovered 2,300 years ago, the miracle of water in the desert can be augmented by human hands. Having migrated from north-western Mexico, Hohokam cultivated cotton, corn, and beans in tilled, rowed, and irrigated fields for about 1,700 years, establishing more than 300 miles of canals—an engineering phenomenon when you consider the limited technology available. They constructed a great town upon whose ruins modern Phoenix is built, and then vanished. Drought, long winters, and other causes are suggested for their disappearance.

MODERN BEGINNINGS

From the time the Hohokam left until the Civil War, the once fertile Salt River valley lay forgotten, used only by occasional small bands of Pima and Maricopa Indians. Then in 1865 the U.S. Army established Fort McDowell in the mountains to the east, where the Verde River flows into the Salt River. To feed the men and the horses stationed there, a former Confederate Army officer reopened the Hohokam canals in 1867. Within a year, fields bright with barley and pumpkins earned the area the name Pumpkin-ville. By 1870 the 300 residents had decided that their new city would arise from the ancient Hohokam site, just as the mythical phoenix rose from its own ashes.

A CITY ON THE RISE

Phoenix would grow indeed. Within 20 years it had become large enough—its population was about 3,000—to wrest the title of territorial capital from Prescott. By 1912, when Arizona was admitted as the 48th state, the area, irrigated by the brand-new Roosevelt Dam and Salt River Project, had a burgeoning cotton industry. Copper was mined elsewhere but traded in Phoenix, and cattle were raised elsewhere but slaughtered and packed here in the largest stockyards outside Chicago.

Meanwhile, the climate, so long a crippling liability, became an asset. Desert air was the prescribed therapy for the respiratory ills rampant in the sooty, factory-filled East; Scottsdale began in 1901 as "30-odd tents and a half-dozen adobe houses" put up by health seekers. By 1930 travelers looking for warm winter recreation as well as rejuvenating aridity filled the elegant Wigwam Resort and Arizona Biltmore, the first of the many luxury retreats for which the area is now known worldwide. The 1950s brought residential air-conditioning, an invention that made the summers bearable for the growing workforce of the burgeoning technology industry.

PHOENIX TODAY

The Valley is very much a work still in progress, and historians are quick to point out that never in the world's history has a metropolis grown from "nothing" to attain the status of Phoenix in such a short period of time. At the heart of all the bustle, though, is a way of life that keeps its own pace: Phoenix is one of the world's largest small towns—where people dress informally and where the rugged, Old West spirit lives on in many of the Valley's nooks and crannies despite the sprawling growth. And if summer heat can be overwhelming, at least it has the restorative effect of slowing things down to an enjoyable pace.

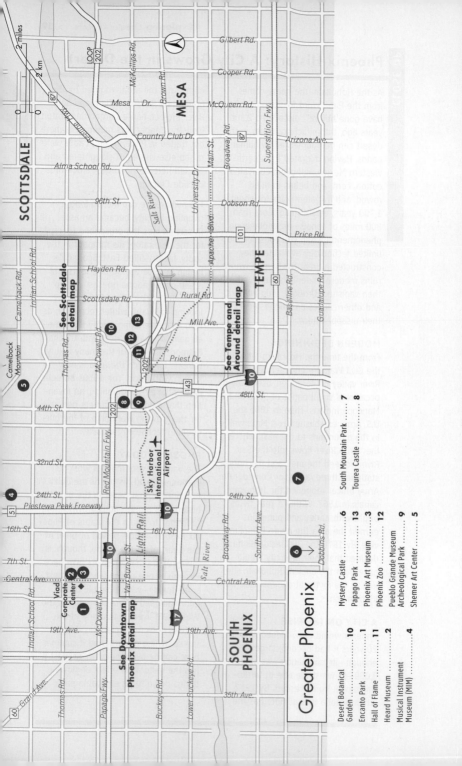

Greater Phoenix

Desert Botanical Garden	10
Encanto Park	1
Hall of Flame	11
Heard Museum	2
Musical Instrument Museum (MIM)	4
Mystery Castle	6
Papago Park	13
Phoenix Art Museum	3
Phoenix Zoo	12
Pueblo Grande Museum Archeological Park	9
Shemer Art Center	5
South Mountain Park	7
Tourea Castle	8

SCOTTSDALE

MESA

TEMPE

SOUTH PHOENIX

See Scottsdale detail map

See Tempe and Around detail map

See Downtown Phoenix detail map

Viad Corporate Center

Sky Harbor International Airport

Gilbert Rd.
Cooper Rd.
McQueen Rd.
Arizona Ave.
McKellips Rd.
Brown Rd.
Mesa Dr.
Country Club Dr.
Alma School Rd.
96th St.
Hayden Rd.
Scottsdale Rd.
Indian School Rd.
Camelback Rd.
Thomas Rd.
McDowell Rd.
44th St.
32nd St.
24th St.
16th St.
7th St.
Central Ave.
19th Ave.
Grand Ave.
Papago Fwy.
35th Ave.
Buckeye Rd.
Lower Buckeye Rd.
Van Buren St.
Light Rail
Salt River
Broadway Rd.
Southern Ave.
Central Ave.
Dobbins Rd.
Piestewa Peak Freeway
Red Mountain Fwy.
Main St.
Broadway Rd.
University Dr.
Apache Blvd.
Mill Ave.
Rural Rd.
Priest Dr.
Dobson Rd.
Price Rd.
Baseline Rd.
Guadalupe Rd.
Superstition Fwy.
48th St.
Camelback Mountain

2

plan for a cool, late visit after a full day of activities. ✉ *1201 N. Galvin Pkwy.* ☎ *480/941–1225* ⊕ *www.dbg.org* 🎟 *$18* ⊙ *Daily 8-8.*

FAMILY **Hall of Flame.** Retired firefighters lead tours through nearly 100 restored fire engines and tell harrowing tales of the "world's most dangerous profession." The museum has the world's largest collection of firefighting equipment, and children can climb on a 1916 engine, operate alarm systems, and learn fire safety lessons from the pros. Helmets, badges, and other firefighting-related articles dating from as far back as 1725 are on display. ✉ *6101 E. Van Buren St.* ☎ *602/275–3473* ⊕ *www. hallofflame.org* 🎟 *$6* ⊙ *Mon.–Sat. 9–5, Sun. noon–4.*

FAMILY
Fodor's Choice
★
Heard Museum. Pioneer settlers Dwight and Maie Heard built a Spanish colonial–style building on their property to house their collection of Southwestern art. Today the staggering collection includes such exhibits as a Navajo hogan and rooms filled with art, pottery, jewelry, kachinas, and textiles. The Heard also actively supports contemporary Indian artists and displays their work. Their fabulous signature cultural exhibition is "Home: Native People in the Southwest." Annual events include the World Championship Hoop Dance Contest in February and the Guild Indian Fair & Market in March. Children enjoy the interactive art-making exhibits. ■**TIP→ The museum also has an incredible gift shop with authentic, high-quality goods purchased directly from Native American artists.** There's a museum satellite branch in Scottsdale that has rotating exhibits. ✉ *2301 N. Central Ave., North Central Phoenix* ☎ *602/252–8848* ⊕ *www.heard.org* 🎟 *$18* ⊙ *Mon.–Sat. 9:30–5, Sun. 11–5.*

Musical Instrument Museum (MIM). A fun destination for even casual music fans, the museum offers a rare display of music and instruments going back hundreds of years—including more than 15,000 instruments and artifacts from across the globe. Special galleries highlight video demonstrations as well as audio tracks that showcase the sounds that instruments, both primitive and contemporary, create. Among the museum's dazzling array of instruments are the piano on which John Lennon composed "Imagine," and the first Steinway piano. ✉ *4725 E. Mayo Blvd.* ☎ *480/478–6000* ⊕ *www.mim.org* 🎟 *$18* ⊙ *Sun. 10–5, Mon.– Wed. 9–5, Thurs. and Fri. 9–9, Sat. 9–5.*

FAMILY **Mystery Castle.** At the foot of South Mountain lies a curious dwelling built from desert rocks by Boyce Gulley, who came to Arizona to cure his tuberculosis. Full of fascinating oddities, the castle has 18 rooms with 13 fireplaces, a downstairs grotto tavern, a roll-away bed with a mining railcar as its frame, and some original pieces of Frank Lloyd Wright–designed furniture. The pump organ belonged to Elsie, the "Widow of Tombstone," who buried six husbands under suspicious circumstances. ✉ *800 E. Mineral Rd., South Phoenix* ☎ *602/268–1581* 🎟 *$10* ⊙ *Oct.–May, Thurs.–Sun. 11–4. Call to confirm hrs.*

FAMILY **Phoenix Art Museum.** This museum is one of the most visually appealing pieces of architecture in the Southwest. Basking in natural light, the museum makes great use of its modern, open space by tastefully fitting more than 17,000 works of art from all over the world—including sculptures by Frederic Remington and paintings by Georgia O'Keeffe,

Thomas Moran, and Maxfield Parrish—within its soaring concrete walls. The museum hosts more than 20 significant exhibitions annually and has one of the most acclaimed fashion collections in the country. Complete your tour with lunch at Arcadia Farms, the in-house café that serves some of the best homemade fare in town. ⊠ *1625 N. Central Ave., Central Phoenix* ☎ *602/257–1222* ⊕ *www.phxart.org* ✉ *$12; voluntary donation Wed. 3–9 pm and during 1st Fri. evenings 6–10* ⊙ *Wed. 10–9, Thurs.–Sat. 10–5, Sun. noon–5; 1st Fri. evenings 6–10.*

FAMILY

Fodor's Choice

★

Pueblo Grande Museum Archaeological Park. Phoenix's only national landmark, this park was once the site of a 500-acre Hohokam village supporting about 1,000 people and containing homes, storage rooms, cemeteries, and ball courts. Three exhibition galleries hold displays on the Hohokam culture and archaeological methods. View the 10-minute orientation video before heading out on the 0.5-mile Ruin Trail past excavated sites that give a hint of Hohokam savvy: there's a building whose corner doorway was perfectly placed for watching the summer-solstice sunrise. Children particularly like the hands-on, interactive learning center. Guided tours by appointment only. ⊠ *4619 E. Washington St.* ☎ *602/495–0901* ⊕ *www.pueblogrande.com* ✉ *$6* ⊙ *Mon.–Sat. 9–4:45, Sun. 1–4:45. Closed Sun. and Mon. May–Sept.*

Tovrea Castle. Get a glimpse of what Phoenix was like a century ago by touring the extensive grounds and the two floors of the castle, constructed in the 1920s and early 1930s. Unfortunately, the cupola—the castle's "crown"—doesn't meet fire codes, so visitors can't get the 360-degree views that cattle baron E. A. Tovrea enjoyed. A Phoenix landmark, this 44-acre site in central Phoenix is managed jointly by the city of Phoenix and a group of loyal preservationists. ⊠ *5041 E. Van Buren St., Phoenix* ☎ *602/256–3221, 800/838–3006* ⊕ *www.tovreacastletours.com* ✉ *$15* ⊙ *Tours held Jan.–July. Call for reservations.*

WORTH NOTING

FAMILY

Encanto Park. Urban Encanto (Spanish for "enchanted") Park covers 222 acres at the heart of one of Phoenix's oldest residential neighborhoods. There are many attractions, including picnic areas, a lagoon where you can paddleboat and canoe, a municipal swimming pool, a nature trail, Enchanted Island amusement park (⊕ *www.enchantedisland.com*), fishing in the park's lake, and two public golf courses. ⊠ *1202 W. Encanto Blvd., North Central Phoenix* ☎ *602/261–8991* ⊕ *phoenix.gov/parks/encanto.html* ✉ *Park free, Enchanted Island rides $1.10 each* ⊙ *Park daily 5:30 am–11 pm; Enchanted Island hrs vary by season and weather.*

FAMILY

Papago Park. An amalgam of hilly desert terrain, streams, and lagoons, this park has picnic ramadas (shaded, open-air shelters), a golf course, a playground, hiking and biking trails, and even largemouth bass and trout fishing. (An urban fishing license is required for anglers age 15 and over. Visit ⊕ *www.azgfd.gov* for more information.) The hike up to landmark **Hole-in-the-Rock**—a natural observatory used by the native Hohokam to devise a calendar system—is steep and rocky, and a much easier climb up than down. **Governor Hunt's Tomb,** the white pyramid at the top of Ramada 16, commemorates the former Arizona leader and provides a lovely view. ✉ *625 N. Galvin Pkwy.* ☎ *602/495-5458* ⊕ *www.papagosalado.org* ✉ *Free* ⊙ *Daily 5 am–11 pm.*

FAMILY **Phoenix Zoo.** Four designated trails wind through this 125-acre zoo, replicating such habitats as an African savanna and a tropical rain forest. Meerkats, warthogs, desert bighorn sheep, and the endangered Arabian oryx are among the unusual sights. The Forest of Uco is home to the endangered spectacled bear from South America. Harmony Farm introduces youngsters to small mammals, and a stop at the Big Red Barn petting zoo provides a chance to interact with goats, cows, and more. The 30-minute narrated safari train tour costs $4 and provides a good orientation to the park. ■**TIP→** In December the zoo stays open late (6–10 pm) for the popular "ZooLights" exhibit that transforms the area into an enchanted forest of more than 225 million twinkling lights, many in the shape of the zoo's residents. Starry Safari Friday Nights in summer are fun, too. ✉ *455 N. Galvin Pkwy.* ☎ *602/273–1341* ⊕ *www.phoenixzoo.org* ✉ *$20* ⊙ *Hrs vary by month and weather. Check website for more details. Generally, Sept.–May, daily 9–4; June–Aug., daily 7–2. ZooLights extends holiday hrs until 10.*

> **PAPAGO SALADO**
>
> The word *Papago*, meaning "bean eater," was a name given by 16th-century Spanish explorers to the Hohokam, a vanished native people of the Phoenix area. Farmers of the desert, the Hohokam lived in central Arizona from about 300 BC to AD 1450, when their civilization abandoned the Salt River (Rio Salado) valley, leaving behind the remnants of their villages and also a complex system of irrigation canals.

Shemer Art Center and Museum Association. Near the Phoenician resort, the Shemer Art Center features revolving exhibits of current Arizona artists who have agreed to donate one of their pieces to the center's permanent collection. The collection is largely contemporary, and exhibits change every month or so in this former residence. ✉ *5005 E. Camelback Rd., Camelback Corridor* ☎ *602/262–4727* ⊕ *www.shemerartcenter.org* ✉ *Free* ▭ *No credit cards* ⊙ *Tues.–Sat. 10–3. Closed Sun., Mon., holidays.*

FAMILY **South Mountain Park.** This desert wonderland, the world's largest city park (almost 17,000 acres), offers a wilderness of mountain-desert trails for hikers, bikers, and horseback riders—and a great place to view sunsets. The Environmental Center has a model of the park as well as displays detailing its history, from the time of the ancient Hohokam people to gold seekers. Roads climb past picnic ramadas constructed by the Civilian Conservation Corps, winding through desert flora to the trailheads. Look for ancient petroglyphs, try to spot a desert cottontail rabbit or chuckwalla lizard, or simply stroll among the desert vegetation. Maps of all scenic drives as well as hiking, mountain biking, and horseback trails are available at the Gatehouse Entrance just inside the park boundary. ✉ *10919 S. Central Ave., South Phoenix* ☎ *602/262–7373* ⊕ *phoenix.gov/parks/trails/locations/south/index.html* ✉ *Free* ▭ *No credit cards* ⊙ *Daily 5 am–7 pm.*

SCOTTSDALE

Nationally known art galleries, souvenir shops, and a funky Old Town fill downtown Scottsdale— the third-largest artist community in the United States. Fifth Avenue is known for shopping and Native American jewelry and crafts stores, while Main Street and Marshall Way are home to the international art set with galleries and interior-design shops.

> **WORD OF MOUTH**
>
> "Don't miss Taliesin West! It's a large property, aside from the beautiful main house/studio.... Plan on a good half day so you don't have to rush." —Underhill

GETTING HERE AND AROUND

Although your tour of downtown can easily be completed on foot, there's a regular free trolley service through Scottsdale (☎ 480/421–1004 ⊕ www.scottsdaleaz.gov/trolley).

TIMING

If you have limited time in the area, spend a half day in Old Town Scottsdale and the rest of the day at Taliesin West.

Scottsdale ArtWalk. Every Thursday from 7 to 9 pm (except Thanksgiving), the galleries along Main Street and Marshall Way stay open for the Scottsdale ArtWalk, an indoor-outdoor celebration of the arts. Tour the galleries, watch street performers, and grab a bite to eat. ⊕ *www.scottsdalegalleries.com* ▭ *No credit cards.*

TOP ATTRACTIONS

5th Avenue. Whether you seek handmade Native American arts and crafts, casual clothing, or cacti, you'll find it here—at such landmark shops as Gilbert Ortega and Kactus Jock. ⊠ *5th Ave., between Civic Center Rd. and Stetson Dr., Old Town.*

Main Street Arts District. Gallery after gallery displays artwork in myriad styles—contemporary, Western realism, Native American, and traditional. Several antiques shops are also here; specialties include porcelain and china, jewelry, and Oriental rugs. ⊠ *Bounded by Main St. and 1st Ave., Scottsdale Rd. and 69th St., Old Town.*

Marshall Way Arts District. Galleries that exhibit predominantly contemporary art line the blocks of Marshall Way north of Indian School Road, and upscale gift and jewelry stores can be found here, too. Farther north on Marshall Way across 3rd Avenue are more art galleries and creative stores with a Southwestern flair. ⊠ *Marshall Way, from Indian School Rd. to 5th Ave., Old Town.*

Old Town Scottsdale. "The West's Most Western Town," this area has rustic storefronts and wooden sidewalks; it's touristy, but the closest you'll come to experiencing life here as it was 80 years ago. High-quality jewelry and Mexican imports are sold alongside kitschy souvenirs. ⊠ *Main St., from Scottsdale Rd. to Brown Ave., Old Town.*

Fodor'sChoice ★ **Taliesin West.** Ten years after visiting Arizona in 1927 to consult on designs for the Biltmore hotel, architect Frank Lloyd Wright chose 600 acres of rugged Sonoran Desert at the foothills of the McDowell Mountains as the site for his permanent winter residence. Today the site is a

5th Avenue 7

Heard Museum
North
Scottsdale 8

Main Street
Arts District 5

Marshall Way
Arts
District 6

Old Town
Scottsdale 4

Scottsdale Center
for the Performing
Arts and Scottsdale
Museum of
Contemporary
Art 2

Scottsdale
Historical
Museum 3

Taliesin
West 1

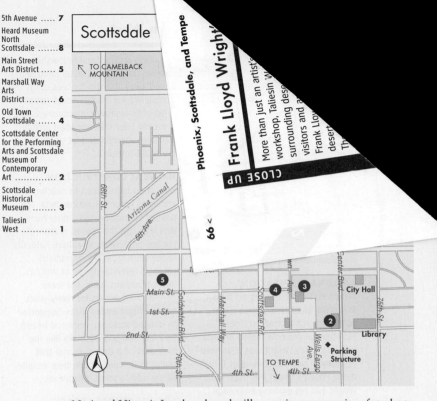

National Historic Landmark and still an active community of students and architects. Wright and apprentices constructed a desert camp here using organic architecture to integrate the buildings with their natural surroundings. In addition to the living quarters, drafting studio, and small apartments of the Apprentice Court, Taliesin West has two theaters, a music pavilion, and the Sun Trap—sleeping spaces surrounding an open patio and fireplace. Six guided tours are offered, ranging from a one-hour "panorama" tour to a three-hour behind-the-scenes tour, with other tours offered seasonally; all visitors must be accompanied by a guide. ■TIP→ Wear comfortable shoes for walking. The half-hour drive from downtown Scottsdale is very worthwhile.

Drive north on the 101 Freeway to Frank Lloyd Wright Boulevard. Follow Frank Lloyd Wright Boulevard for a few miles to the entrance at the corner of Cactus Road. ⊠ *12621 Frank Lloyd Wright Blvd., North Scottsdale* ☏ *480/860–2700* ⊕ *www.franklloydwright.org* ✉ *$24–$60* ☉ *Daily 9–4, with evening tours most days. Call to confirm.*

WORTH NOTING

Heard Museum North Scottsdale. This satellite of the big Heard in Downtown Phoenix has one gallery with its own small, permanent collection of Native American art. The gift shop is well stocked with expensive, high-quality items. ⊠ *32633 N. Scottsdale Rd., at Carefree Hwy., North*

retreat and
est and the
t still inspire both
chitects who study here.
d Wright once said, "The
abhors the straight, hard line."
ugh much of Wright's most famed
work is based on such lines, this
sprawling compound takes its environment into consideration as few desert structures do. Taliesin West mirrors the jagged shapes and earthen colors of its mountain backdrop and desert surroundings. Even Wright's interior pieces of "origami" furniture assume the mountain's unpredictable shapes.

ARIZONA INSPIRATION

Wright first came to Phoenix from Wisconsin in 1927 to act as a consultant to architect Albert Chase McArthur on the now famed Arizona Biltmore. Later Wright was also hired to design a new hotel in what is currently Phoenix South Mountain Park. Wright and his working entourage returned to the Valley and, instead of residing in apartments, they built a camp of asymmetrical cabins with canvas roofs that maximized but pleasantly diffused light, and blended into the rugged mountain backdrop.

When the hotel project failed due to the stock market crash of 1929, Wright and his crew returned to Taliesin, his Wisconsin home and site of his architectural fellowship, and the camp was disassembled and carted away. But the concept of his humble worker village would remain in Wright's creative consciousness and a decade later the renowned architect found an appropriate plot of land north of Scottsdale.

NATURAL CONSTRUCTION

Built upon foundations of caliche, known as nature's own concrete, and painted in crimson and amber hues that highlight the "desert masonry," the buildings seem to adhere naturally to the landscape. The asymmetrical roofs resemble those of Wright's South Mountain camp and were covered with canvas for many years before Wright added glass. Supported by painted-steel-and-redwood beams, they face the sun-filled sky like the hard shell of a desert animal that seems to be comfortable here despite all the odds against its survival.

ARCHITECTURAL LEGACY

The over 70-year-old property and its structures, which Wright envisioned as a "little fleet of ships," are perhaps some of the best nonnative examples of organic architecture. They also serve as desert building blocks for future generations of Wright protégés—some perhaps schooled on these very grounds—to balance man and Mother Nature.

Scottsdale ☎ *480/488–9817* ⊕ *www.heard.org* ✉ *$5* ☉ *May–Nov., Tues.–Sat. 10-5. Dec.–April, Mon.–Sat. 10–5, Sun. 11–5.*

Scottsdale Center for the Peforming Arts. Performances at this cultural and entertainment complex rotate exhibits frequently, but they typically emphasize contemporary art and artists. You might be able to catch a comical, interactive performance of the long-running "Late Night Catechism," or an installation of modern dance. The acclaimed Scottsdale Arts Festival is held annually here in March. ✉ *7380 E. 2nd St., Old*

Taliesin West was Frank Lloyd Wright's winter residence. The original Taliesin in Wisconsin was his summer home.

Town ☎ 480/499–8587 ⊕ www.scottsdaleperformingarts.org ✉ Free ⊗ *Call for performance info.*

Scottsdale Museum of Contemporary Art. SMoCA, the Scottsdale Museum of Contemporary Art, a "museum without walls," is on-site, and there's also a good museum store for unusual jewelry and stationery, posters, and art books. New installations are planned every few months, with an emphasis on contemporary art, architecture, and design. Docent-led tours are conducted on Thursday at 1:30. Kids can visit the adjacent young@art gallery for free. ⊠ *7374 E. 2nd St., Old Town* ☎ *480/874–4682* ⊕ *www.smoca.org* ✉ *$7, free Thurs.* ⊗ *Sun. 12–5. Tues.–Wed. 12–5. Thurs.–Sat. 12–9. Closed Mon.*

Scottsdale Historical Museum. Scottsdale's first schoolhouse, this redbrick building houses a reconstruction of the 1910 schoolroom, as well as photographs, original furniture from the city's founding fathers, and displays of other treasures from Scottsdale's early days. ⊠ *7333 E. Scottsdale Mall, Old Town* ☎ *480/945–4499* ⊕ *www.scottsdalemuseum. com* ✉ *Free* ⊟ *No credit cards* ⊗ *Oct.–May, Wed.–Sun. 10–5; June and Sept., Wed.–Sun. 10–2. Closed July and Aug.*

TEMPE AND AROUND

Tempe is the home of Arizona State University's main campus and a thriving student population. A 20-minute drive from Phoenix, the tree- and brick-lined Mill Avenue is the main drag, filled with student hangouts, bookstores, boutiques, eateries, and a repertory movie house. There are always things to do or see, and plenty of music venues and

Arizona
Museum of
Natural History ..**3**

Arizona Sealife
Aquarium **4**

Arizona State
University **2**

Tempe Town
Lake **1**

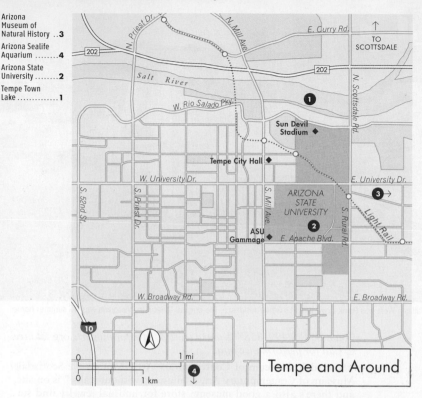

Tempe and Around

fun, casual dining spots. This is one part of town where the locals actually hang out, stroll, and sit at the outdoor cafés.

The inverted pyramid that is Tempe City Hall, on 5th Street, one block east of Mill Avenue, was constructed by local architects Rolf Osland and Michael Goodwin not just to win design awards (which they have), but also to shield city workers from the desert sun. The pyramid is built mainly of bronzed glass and stainless steel, and the point disappears in a sunken courtyard lushly landscaped with jacaranda, ivy, and flowers, out of which the pyramid widens to the sky: stand underneath and gaze up for a weird fish-eye perspective.

The banks of the Rio Salado in Tempe are the site of a new commercial and entertainment district, and Tempe Town Lake—a 2-mile-long waterway created by inflatable dams in a flood control channel—which is open for boating. There are biking and jogging paths on the perimeter.

GETTING HERE AND AROUND

Street parking is hard to find, especially amid all the construction, but you can park in the public garage at Hayden Square, just north of 5th Street and west of Mill Avenue. Get your ticket stamped by a local merchant to avoid paying parking fees. The Orbit free shuttle does a loop around Arizona State University, with stops at Mill Avenue and Sun Devil Stadium. Light-rail also stops at 3rd Street and Mill Avenue.

TIMING

Tempe Festival of the Arts. This free festival on Mill Avenue is held twice a year in early December and March–April; it has all sorts of interesting arts and crafts. ⊕ *www.tempefestivalofthearts.com* ▭ *No credit cards.*

EXPLORING

FAMILY **Arizona Museum of Natural History.** Kids young and old get a thrill out of the largest collection of dinosaur fossils in the state at this large museum where you can also pan for gold and see changing exhibits from around the world. ⊠ *53 N. Macdonald St., Mesa* ☎ *480/644–2230* ⊕ *www. azmnh.org* ⌨ *$10* ⊙ *Tues.–Fri. 10–5, Sat. 11–5, Sun. 1–5. Closed Mon.*

FAMILY **Arizona Sealife Aquarium.** For up-close views of some 5,000 creatures including sharks, sting rays, eels, and a giant octopus, head straight to this underwater menagerie in Tempe. You can walk through a 360-degree viewing tunnel in a 165,000-gallon tank that is the first of its kind. Who says there's no water in the desert? ⊠ *Arizona Mills, 5000 Arizona Mills Circle* ☎ *480/478–7600* ⊕ *www.visitsealife.com/arizona* ⌨ *$18* ⊙ *Mon.–Sat. 10–7:30, Sun. 10–6.*

Arizona State University. What began as the Tempe Normal School for Teachers—in 1886 a four-room redbrick building and 20-acre cow pasture—is now the 750-acre Tempe campus of ASU, the largest university in the Southwest. The university now has four campuses located across the Valley. As you walk around campus, you'll wind past public art and innovative architecture—including a music building that bears a strong resemblance to a wedding cake, designed by Taliesin students to echo Frank Lloyd Wright's Gammage Auditorium, and a law library shaped like an open book—and end up at the impressive 71,706-seat Sun Devil Stadium. ☎ *480/965–9011* ⊕ *www.asu.edu* ▭ *No credit cards.*

ASU Memorial Union. Stop here for maps of a self-guided walking tour of the Tempe campus. It's a long walk from Mill Avenue. ⊠ *1290 S. Normal Ave.* ☎ *480/965-5728.*

Sun Devil Stadium. Home to the school's Sun Devils, this stadium is carved out of a mountain and cradled between the Tempe buttes. ⊠ *ASU Campus, 5th St.* ☎ *480/965–9011.*

FAMILY **Tempe Town Lake.** The human-made Town Lake has turned downtown Tempe into a commercial and urban-living hot spot, and attracts college students and Valley residents of all ages. Little ones enjoy the Splash Playground, and fishermen appreciate the rainbow trout–stocked lake. You also can rent a boat and tour the lake on your own. ⊠ *550 E. Tempe Town Lake* ☎ *480/350–8625* ⊕ *www.tempe.gov/lake.*

WHERE TO EAT

Phoenix and its surroundings have metamorphosed into a melting pot for every type of cuisine imaginable, from northern to Tuscan Italian; from mom-and-pop to Mexico City Mexican; from low-key Cuban to high-end French- and Greek-inspired Southwestern; from Japanese- and Spanish-style tapas to kosher food and American classics with subtle ethnic twists.

Just as the Valley of the Sun has attracted visitors from around the world, it has also been attracting a record number of worldly residents. Fortunately for everyone, many of those people are skilled chefs and/or restaurateurs who have opted to share their gifts with the public.

Eateries like La Grande Orange grocery are revolutionizing Phoenix's "fast-food" concept with gourmet pay-and-take meals. Four-star cuisine, some concocted by celebrity chefs, also awaits all over the Valley, from Kai in Chandler to Scottsdale's Bourbon Steak, along with Binkley's and Café Bink in Carefree. Dotted with massive strip malls, Phoenix's outskirts are becoming a haven of corporate eateries, but don't worry, there's plenty of divine, independent dining for all tastes and all trends in between.

Many of the best restaurants in the Valley are in resorts, camouflaged behind courtyard walls, or tucked away in shopping malls. Newer, upscale eateries are clustered along Camelback Corridor—a veritable restaurant row, running west to east from Phoenix to Scottsdale—and in Scottsdale itself. Great Mexican food can be found throughout the Valley, but the most authentic spots are in the neighborhoods of North Central and South Phoenix.

Restaurants change hours, locations, chefs, prices, and menus frequently, so it's best to call ahead to confirm. Show up without a reservation during tourist season (October through mid-May), and you may have to head for a fast-food drive-through window to avoid a two-hour wait for a table.

Prices in the reviews are the average cost of a main course at dinner or, if dinner isn't served, at lunch. Use the coordinate (⊕ B2) at the end of each listing to locate a site on the corresponding map.

DOWNTOWN PHOENIX

$$ MODERN AMERICAN

🍴 **The Arrogant Butcher.** The attention-grabbing name is intentional, as is the in-your-face decor and cuisine of this not-quite-bar, not-quite-restaurant Downtown haunt. It's noisy, but that's part of the charm. You'll sit next to couples on their first date, bachelorette parties, families having a reunion, and concertgoers who are prepping their vocal cords for an upcoming show. Make a meal out of the charcuterie platters and to-die-for pretzel fondue. If you're craving home-cookin', order the chicken Stroganoff, and then call your mom. [$] *Average main: $22* ✉ *2 E. Jefferson St., Downtown Phoenix, Phoenix* ☎ *602/324–8502* 🌐 *www.foxrc.com/restaurants/the-arrogant-butcher* ✍ *Reservations essential* ⏲ *Closed Sun.* ⊕ *B5.*

$$ MODERN AMERICAN

🍴 **Blue Hound Kitchen.** The menu at this quirky addition to the Phoenix culinary scene features concoctions worthy of Willy Wonka's palate, from gourmet tater tots to fire-hot ancho chile caramel corn. Located inside the Palomar hotel, Blue Hound is a great place to stop for cocktails or appetizers before a show and, if you have the time, a fantastic meal. Brunch is one of the best in the Downtown area; get a reservation if you plan on dining during the weekend. [$] *Average main: $19* ✉ *2 E. Jefferson St., Downtown Phoenix, Phoenix* ☎ *602/258–0231* 🌐 *www.bluehoundkitchen.com* ⊕ *B5.*

BEST BETS FOR PHOENIX, SCOTTSDALE, AND TEMPE DINING

2

With hundreds of restaurants to choose from, how will you decide where to eat? Fodor's writers and editors have selected their favorite restaurants by price, cuisine, and experience in the Best Bets lists *below*. In the first column, Fodor's Choice properties represent the "best of the best" in every price category.

Fodor's Choice ★

Binkley's Restaurant, $$$$, p. 129

Bourbon Steak, $$$$, p. 82

Chelsea's Kitchen, $$$, p. 75

FEZ, $$, p. 79

House of Tricks, $$$, p. 86

J&G Steakhouse, $$$$, p. 75

Kai, $$$$, p. 85

La Grande Orange, $, p. 76

Matt's Big Breakfast, $, p. 74

Noca, $$$, p. 76

Pane Bianco, $$, p. 79

Pepe's Taco Villa, $, p. 79

Rancho Pinot, $$$, p. 82

T. Cook's at the Royal Palms, $$$$, p. 76

Best by Price

$

Carolina's, p. 77

Fry Bread House, p. 79

La Grande Orange, p. 76

Mrs. White's Golden Rule Café, p. 74

Pepe's Taco Villa, p. 79

$$

Pane Bianco, p. 79

Via Delosantos, p. 80

$$$–$$$$

Binkley's Restaurant, p. 129

Bourbon Steak, p. 82

Kai, p. 85

Rancho Pinot, p. 82

Best by Cuisine

BEST LOCAL EATS

La Grande Orange, $, p. 76

Mrs. White's Golden Rule Café, $, p. 74

Via Delosantos, $$, p. 80

BEST MARGARITAS

Los Dos Molinos, $$, p. 81

Pepe's Taco Villa, $, p. 79

Via Delosantos, $$, p. 80

Best by Experience

BEST BREAKFAST

La Grande Orange, $, p. 76

Matt's Big Breakfast, $, p. 74

BEST HOTEL DINING

Bourbon Steak at the Fairmont Scottsdale Princess, $$$$, p. 82

J&G Steakhouse at The Phoenician, $$$$, p. 75

Kai at Sheraton Wild Horse Pass Resort, $$$$, p. 85

T. Cook's at the Royal Palms, $$$$, p. 76

BEST PATIO WINING AND DINING

Chelsea's Kitchen, $$$, p. 75

elements, $$$$, p. 81

House of Tricks, $$$, p. 86

Olive & Ivy, $$, p. 85

BEST SPECIAL OCCASION

Binkley's Restaurant, $$$$, p. 129

Kai, $$$$, p. 85

T. Cook's at the Royal Palms, $$$$, p. 76

BEST BRUNCH

Bourbon Steak, $$$$, p. 82

Lon's at the Hermosa, $$$$, p. 81

The Mission, $$$, p. 85

GREAT VIEW

elements, $$$$, p. 81

Lon's at the Hermosa, $$$$, p. 81

T. Cook's at the Royal Palms, $$$$, p. 76

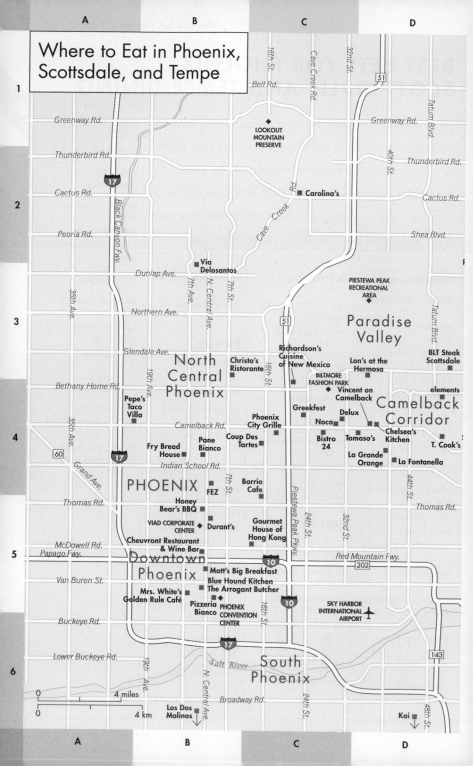

Where to Eat in Phoenix, Scottsdale, and Tempe

A B C D

1

Greenway Rd.

Bell Rd.

LOOKOUT MOUNTAIN PRESERVE

Greenway Rd.

Thunderbird Rd.

Thunderbird Rd.

Cactus Rd.

Carolina's

Cactus Rd.

2

Peoria Rd.

Shea Blvd.

Dunlap Ave.

Via Delosantos

PIESTEWA PEAK RECREATIONAL AREA

Northern Ave.

Paradise Valley

3

Glendale Ave.

Richardson's Cuisine of New Mexico

North Central Phoenix

Christo's Ristorante

Lon's at the Hermosa

BLT Steak Scottsdale

Bethany Home Rd.

BILTMORE FASHION PARK

Vincent on Camelback

elements

Pepe's Taco Villa

Greekfest

Delux

Camelback Corridor

Camelback Rd.

Phoenix City Grille

Noca

Chelsea's Kitchen

4

Fry Bread House

Pane Bianco

Coup Des Tartes

Bistro 24

Tomaso's

T. Cook's

Indian School Rd.

La Grande Orange

La Fontanella

PHOENIX

FEZ

Barrio Cafe

Thomas Rd.

Thomas Rd.

Honey Bear's BBQ

VIAD CORPORATE CENTER

Durant's

Gourmet House of Hong Kong

Cheuvront Restaurant & Wine Bar

McDowell Rd.

5

Papago Fwy.

Red Mountain Fwy.

Downtown Phoenix

Matt's Big Breakfast

Van Buren St.

Blue Hound Kitchen

The Arrogant Butcher

SKY HARBOR INTERNATIONAL AIRPORT

Mrs. White's Golden Rule Café

Pizzeria Bianco

Buckeye Rd.

PHOENIX CONVENTION CENTER

Lower Buckeye Rd.

South Phoenix

6

Salt River

0 — 4 miles
0 — 4 km

Los Dos Molinos

Broadway Rd.

Kai

A B C D

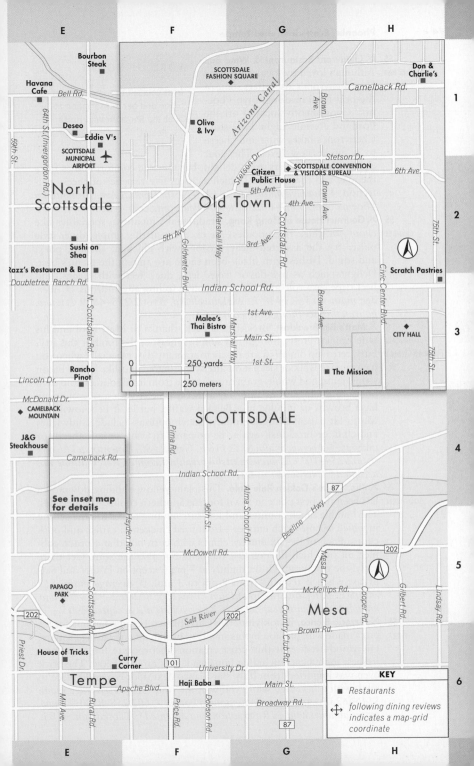

> **WORD OF MOUTH**
>
> "Treat yourself to some different cuisine and get a reservation at Kai at the Sheraton Wild Horse Pass Resort." —patandhank

$$ WINE BAR

🍴 **Cheuvront Restaurant & Wine Bar.** Although loved by locals as a wine bar, Cheuvront's also offers some of the best food in downtown Phoenix. Conveniently located off the Portland Avenue Light Rail stop, Cheuvront's takes wine and cheese to a whole new level. The goat cheese phyllo pockets are a delight, but the true comfort comes from the mac and cheese menu, which includes five varieties of cheesy perfection. [$] *Average main: $15* ✉ *1326 North Central Ave., Downtown Phoenix* ☎ *602/307–0022* 🌐 *www.cheuvronts.com* ⊕ *B5.*

$$ CHINESE

🍴 **Gourmet House of Hong Kong.** Traditional Chinatown specialties like *chow fun* (thick rice noodles) are excellent at this simple, diner-style place: try the assorted-meat version, with chicken, shrimp, pork, and squid. Dishes with black-bean sauce are among the menu's best. Delights such as five-flavor frogs' legs, duck feet with greens, and beef tripe casserole are offered, if you're feeling adventurous. [$] *Average main: $15* ✉ *1438 E. McDowell Rd.* ☎ *602/253–4859* 🌐 *www.gourmethouseofhongkong.com* ⊕ *C5.*

$ AMERICAN
Fodor's Choice ★

🍴 **Matt's Big Breakfast.** Breakfast is back, thanks to Matt Pool and his wife Erenia. Fresh, filling, and simply fantastic, the food at this itty-bitty, retro hip diner is a great way to start any day, especially when you have time to walk or sleep it off afterward. Ingredients like hearty bacon strips, jams, and whole-grain breads come from local sources, and each one is of the highest quality. Try a cheesy omelet with a side of crispy hash browns or indulge in a Belgian waffle, but let it be known that Matt's fat pancakes are legendary. Lunch options include sandwiches and chili, or breakfast, again. Be prepared to wait, or call ahead for takeout. [$] *Average main: $7* ✉ *116 E. Garfield St., Downtown Phoenix* ☎ *602/254–1074* 🌐 *www.mattsbigbreakfast.com* ✍ *Reservations not accepted* ⏲ *No dinner* ⊕ *B5.*

$ SOUTHERN

🍴 **Mrs. White's Golden Rule Café.** This plain yellow building downtown has been the best place in town for true Southern cooking for decades. The humble lunch counter and few surrounding tables are the setting in which to enjoy rich entrées—from fried chicken to catfish and pork chops. Each of the six entrées comes with corn bread and peach cobbler, all of which fill not just the belly but also the soul. Get there early: the restaurant closes nightly at 7 pm (except on Friday and Saturday, when it reopens from 9 pm to 3 am). [$] *Average main: $13* ✉ *808 E. Jefferson St., Downtown Phoenix* ☎ *602/262–9256* 🌐 *www.mrswhitesgoldenrulecafe.com* ✍ *Reservations not accepted* ⊕ *B5.*

$$ PIZZA

🍴 **Pizzeria Bianco.** Brooklyn native Chris Bianco became famous for his pizza made with passion in this small establishment on Heritage Square. His wood-fired-oven thin-crust creations incorporate the finest and freshest ingredients including homemade mozzarella cheese. The brick oven was imported from Italy. Bar Bianco next door is a good place to relax with a beverage while you wait for your table. [$] *Average main: $14* ✉ *623 E. Adams St., Downtown Phoenix* ☎ *602/258–8300* 🌐 *www.pizzeriabianco.com* ✍ *Reservations not accepted* ⏲ *Closed Sun.* ⊕ *B5.*

GREATER PHOENIX

CAMELBACK CORRIDOR

$$$ ✕**Bistro 24.** Smart and stylish, with impeccable service, the Ritz's Bistro
FRENCH 24 has one of the most attractive dining rooms in the Valley. Take a
break from shopping at the nearby Biltmore Fashion Park and enjoy
the largest Cobb salad in town. For dinner, try classic French steak *au
poivre* with *frites,* grilled fish, or sushi. Happy hour is every day from
5 to 7 in the bar. $ *Average main: $33* ✉ *Ritz-Carlton Hotel, 2401
E. Camelback Rd., Camelback Corridor* ☎ *602/468–0700* ⊕ *www.
ritzcarlton.com/en/properties/phoenix/dining/bistro24/default.htm*
◷ *No dinner Sun. and Mon.* ✛ *C4.*

$$$ ✕**Chelsea's Kitchen.** With its hip, Pacific Northwest–chic interior and a
AMERICAN patio that feels more like a secret garden, Chelsea's Kitchen can easily
Fodor's Choice make you forget you're dining in the desert. This casually sophisticated
★ establishment insists on the freshest ingredients (especially fish), used
with equally fresh and flavorful ideas that complement the restaurant's
cool but comfortable style. Specials change frequently, and are always
worth steering away from the menu, but regulars love the shrimp ceviche, burgers, and mac and cheese. $ *Average main: $20* ✉ *5040 N. 40th
St., Camelback Corridor* ☎ *602/957–2555* ⊕ *www.chelseaskitchenaz.
com* ◷ *No dinner Sun.* ✛ *D4.*

$$ ✕**Delux.** Everything exudes "cool" in this hipster burger joint. Delux
AMERICAN serves delicious salads, sandwiches, and burgers made with all-natural
Harris Ranch beef—try the Delux Burger, with Maytag blue and Gru-
yère cheeses and caramelized onions. If you can't decide what kind of
brew to wash it all down with, no worries: Order a flight of beers from
their extensive bar. Open every night until 2 am, this is a great place to
grab a late-night bite. Leave room for something cool and creamy at
the Gelato Spot across the parking lot. $ *Average main: $10* ✉ *3146
E. Camelback Rd., Camelback Corridor* ☎ *602/522–2288* ⊕ *www.
deluxburger.com* ⌦ *Reservations not accepted* ✛ *C4.*

$$ ✕**Greekfest.** This informal but elegant restaurant is lovingly decorated
GREEK with whitewashed walls, hardwood floors, and imported Greek arti-
facts. Search the menu's two pages of appetizers for *taramosalata* (cav-
iar blended with lemon and olive oil) and *saganaki* (cheese flamed with
brandy and extinguished with a squirt of lemon). The *moussaka* (lamb
casserole) is wonderful, and don't forget dessert (try *galaktoboureko,*
warm custard pie baked in phyllo). If all you seek is a sweet treat
and some genuine Greek coffee, visit the adjoining Cafestia European
dessert and coffeehouse. $ *Average main: $20* ✉ *1940 E. Camelback
Rd., Camelback Corridor* ☎ *602/265–2990* ⊕ *www.thegreekfest.com*
◷ *Closed Sun.* ✛ *C4.*

$$$$ ✕**J&G Steakhouse.** Old-school Phoenicians might balk at the thought
STEAKHOUSE that the prestigious and upper-crust French cuisine of Mary Elaine's was
Fodor's Choice shuttered for a steak house. But after one taste of Chef Jean-George
★ Vongerichten's menu, they're hooked. This is more than a steak house;
it's an experience. The menu changes seasonally, but if you're lucky
enough to be there when the sweet corn ravioli is available, stop, order,
and savor. The filet mignon is prepared to perfection, but you can spice
it up with one of a half-dozen tableside sauces if you want. $ *Average*

main: $40 ✉ The Phoenician, 6000 E. Camelback Rd., Camelback Corridor ☎ 480/214–8000 🌐 www.jgsteakhousescottsdale.com ⏲ No lunch ✥ E4.

$$$ ITALIAN 🍴 **La Fontanella.** Quality and value are a winning combination at this outstanding neighborhood restaurant. The interior is reminiscent of an Italian villa, with antiques, crisp table linens, fresh flowers, and windows dressed in lace curtains. Chef-owner Isabella Bertuccio turns out magnificent food, often using recipes from her Tuscan and Sicilian relatives. The escargots and herb-crusted rack of lamb top the list. [$] *Average main: $24 ✉ 4231 E. Indian School Rd., Camelback Corridor ☎ 602/955–1213 🌐 www.lafontanellaphx.com ⏲ No lunch ✥ D4.*

$ AMERICAN Fodor's Choice ★ 🍴 **La Grande Orange.** This San Francisco–inspired store and eatery sells artisanal nosh and novelty items, along with a formidable selection of wines. Valley residents flock to LGO, as they call it, to see and be seen, and to feast on mouthwatering sandwiches, pizzas, salads, and decadent breads and desserts. The small tables inside fill up quickly at breakfast and lunch, but there's also seating on the patio. Try the Commuter Sandwich on a homemade English muffin, the open-faced Croque Madame, or the delicious French pancakes with a sweet Spanish latte. [$] *Average main: $10 ✉ 4410 N. 40th St., Camelback Corridor ☎ 602/840–7777 🌐 www.lagrandeorangegrocery.com ✍ Reservations not accepted ✥ D4.*

$$$ AMERICAN Fodor's Choice ★ 🍴 **Noca.** This small, hidden establishment is a Valley favorite. Not only is it a fun place to see, be seen, and to sample everything, owner Eliot Wexler also wants to see everyone happy. The waitstaff are veteran fine-dining servers, and the chefs manage to turn even cotton candy into a culinary work of art. The menu changes daily—yes, daily—and features items such as Japanese Wagyu cheesesteak with Kobe beef or braised lamb ragout with rosemary bread crumbs. Every Sunday, the menu includes Noca's famous fried chicken. If you're hungry for a gourmet sandwich, stop by Nocawich, the restaurant's lunchtime conversion Tuesday through Saturday. [$] *Average main: $24 ✉ 3118 E. Camelback Rd., Camelback Corridor ☎ 602/956–6622 🌐 www.restaurantnoca.com ⏲ Closed Mon. in summer ✥ C4.*

$$$$ MEDITERRANEAN Fodor's Choice ★ 🍴 **T. Cook's at the Royal Palms.** One of the finest restaurants in the Valley, T. Cook's oozes romance, from the floor-to-ceiling windows with dramatic views of Camelback Mountain to its 1930s-style Spanish-colonial architecture and decor. The Mediterranean-influenced menu includes grilled "fireplace" fare like 21-day dry-aged rib eye, the house-specialty carbonara, and a changing selection of enticing entrées. Desserts and pastries are works of art. For special-occasion meals, call on the services of the resort's Director of Romance. [$] *Average main: $36 ✉ Royal Palms Resort & Spa, 5200 E. Camelback Rd., Camelback Corridor ☎ 602/808-0766 🌐 www.royalpalmshotel.com ✍ Reservations essential ✥ D4.*

$$ ITALIAN 🍴 **Tomaso's.** In a town where restaurants can come and go almost overnight, Tomaso's has been a favorite since 1977, and for good reason. Chef Tomaso Maggiore learned to cook at the family's restaurant in Palermo, Sicily, and honed his skills at the Culinary Institute of Rome. The result is authentic Italian cuisine that's consistently well prepared

and delicious. The house specialty, herb crusted rack of lamb, is outstanding. Other notables include risotto and osso buco. Enjoy lunch next door at Tommy V's. $ *Average main: $26* ✉ *3225 E. Camelback Rd., Camelback Corridor* ☎ *602/956–0836* ⊕ *www.tomasos.com* ⊘ *No lunch weekends* ✛ *D4.*

$$$
ECLECTIC

✗ **Vincent on Camelback.** Chef Vincent Guerithault is best known for creating French food with a Southwestern touch. The menu changes daily, but it's all delicious. You can make a meal of his famous appetizers, such as corn ravioli with white-truffle oil, or shrimp beignets with lavender dressing. The dessert menu overflows with intoxicating soufflés. The multiroom interior is intimate and elegant, but the service can be gruff. A favorite among locals is the market held in the parking lot on Saturday during cooler months. $ *Average main: $31* ✉ *3930 E. Camelback Rd., Camelback Corridor* ☎ *602/224–0225* ⊕ *www. vincentsoncamelback.com* ⊜ *Reservations essential* ⊘ *Closed Sun. No lunch* ✛ *D4.*

NORTH CENTRAL PHOENIX

$$
MEXICAN

✗ **Barrio Cafe.** Owners Wendy Gruber and Silvana Salcido Esparza have taken Mexican cuisine to a new level. Expect guacamole made to order at your table and modern Mexican specialties such as *cochinita pibil*, 12-hour slow-roasted pork with red achiote and sour orange, and *chiles en Nogada,* a delicious traditional dish from central Mexico featuring a spicy poblano pepper stuffed with fruit, chicken, and raisins. The flavor-packed food consistently draws packs of people, but you can drink in the intimate atmosphere—and a specialty margarita or *aqua fresca* (fruit water)—while you wait for a table. $ *Average main: $19* ✉ *2814 N. 16th St., North Central Phoenix* ☎ *602/636–0240* ⊕ *www.barriocafe. com* ⊜ *Reservations not accepted* ⊘ *Closed Mon.* ✛ *C4.*

$
MEXICAN

✗ **Carolina's.** This small, nondescript restaurant in north Phoenix makes the most delicious, thin-as-air flour tortillas imaginable. In-the-know locals have been lining up at Carolina's for years to partake of the homey, inexpensive Mexican food, so it makes sense that she expanded from the original downtown location to let a little more of the Valley in on the action. The tacos, tamales, burritos, flautas, and enchiladas are served on paper plates. You can buy tortillas to take away, but good luck getting home with a full bag. There is also a branch in south Phoenix at 1202 East Mohave Street (the original location) and one in Peoria. $ *Average main: $4* ✉ *2126 E. Cactus Rd.* ☎ *602/275–8231* ⊕ *www.carolinasmexicanfood.com* ⊘ *Closed Sun.* ✛ *C2.*

$$
ITALIAN

✗ **Christo's Ristorante.** Don't judge this book by its cover. Cozy and unassuming in a Phoenix strip mall, Christo's keeps its tables filled with loyal customers who enjoy fine Italian cuisine. Attentive servers ensure that your water glass never empties, and folks rave about the fresh seafood dishes, the roasted rack of lamb, the veal, and the delicious pasta dishes. Start with the delicious, panfried calamari. Dinner's main courses come with soup and salad. Before or after dinner, enjoy a cocktail in the piano bar or spend your evening snacking to the music from the bar menu. $ *Average main: $19* ✉ *6327 N. 7th St., North Central Phoenix* ☎ *602/264–1784* ⊕ *www.christos1.com* ⊘ *Closed Sun.* ✛ *B3.*

Many restaurants are tucked into strip malls, but resorts also have great restaurants, like T. Cook's at the Royal Palms.

$$$ 🍴 **Coup Des Tartes.** Tables are scattered among three small rooms and an enclosed patio of a charming old house at this country French restaurant. It's BYOB, and there's an $10 corkage fee, but all's forgiven when you taste the delicate cuisine prepared in the tiny kitchen. The menu changes seasonally, but if you're lucky it will feature the utterly unforgettable Moroccan-inspired lamb shank with harissa-spiced ragout, the pork tenderloin with a sauce made from Arizona-grown dates, or the citrus fettuccine. The banana brûlée tarte is their signature dessert, but seasonal offerings like the four-berry tarte remind mouths why they put the mind through all the guilt. [$] *Average main: $26* ✉ *4626 N. 16th St., North Central Phoenix* ☎ *602/212–1082* 🌐 *www.nicetartes.com* ✍ *Reservations essential* 🕒 *Closed Sun. and Mon.* ✣ *C4.*
FRENCH

$$$$ 🍴 **Durant's.** Durant's has endured since 1950 in the same location with the same menu and waiters who've been on staff almost as long, making it one of Phoenix's legendary eating establishments. Supreme steaks, chops, and fresh seafood, including Florida stone crab and oysters Rockefeller, dominate here; when the restaurant once tried to update its menu, regulars protested so furiously the idea was shelved. Durant's is not à la carte, like many Valley steak houses, which means their entrée prices include soup or salad and a side dish. Those in the know enter through the kitchen door and frequent the Rat Pack–style bar for jumbo martinis fit for ol' Blue Eyes himself. [$] *Average main: $34* ✉ *2611 N. Central Ave., at Virginia, North Central Phoenix* ☎ *602/264–5967* 🌐 *www.durantsfinefoods.com* ✣ *B5.*
STEAKHOUSE

2

$$
\text{ECLECTIC}
$$
Fodor's Choice
★

$$ ✕**FEZ.** From its sleek interior to its central location and diverse clientele, right down to its affordable lunch, happy hour, dinner, Sunday brunch, and late-night menus, FEZ covers everything. "American fare with a Moroccan flair" means bold culinary leaps, with choices like the half-pound grilled angus FEZ Burger, *kisras* (flat-bread pizza), and the signature crispy rosemary pomegranate chicken—but it all lands safely on the taste buds. Potables include specialty martinis and margaritas and a formidable wine list. $ *Average main: $16* ✉ *3815 N. Central Ave., North Central Phoenix* ☎ *602/287–8700* ⊕ *www.fezoncentral. com* ✛ *B4.*

$
SOUTHWESTERN

$ ✕**Fry Bread House.** Indian fry bread, a specialty of the Native American culture, is a delicious treat—pillows of deep-fried dough topped with sweet or savory toppings and folded in half. Choose from culture-crossing combinations like savory shredded chili beef with cheese, beans, green chiles, veggies, and sour cream, or try the sweeter synthesis of honey and sugar, or chocolate with butter. $ *Average main: $7* ✉ *4140 N. 7th Ave., North Central Phoenix* ☎ *602/351–2345* ⊙ *Closed Sun.* ✛ *B4.*

$$
SOUTHERN

$$ ✕**Honey Bear's BBQ.** Honey Bear's motto—"You don't need no teeth to eat our meat"—may fall short on grammar, but this place isn't packed with folks looking to improve their language skills. In 1986 childhood friends Mark Smith and Gary Clark expanded from a catering business to their first wildly successful Honey Bear's restaurant on East Van Buren Street; today they are in demand all across the Valley. This is Tennessee-style barbecue, which means smoky baby back ribs basted in a tangy sauce. The sausage-enhanced "cowbro" beans and scallion-studded potato salad are great sides, and, teeth or no teeth, finishing off with a no-frills but tasty piece of sweet-potato pie will put a smile on your face. $ *Average main: $12* ✉ *2824 N. Central., North Central Phoenix* ☎ *602/702–3060* ⊕ *www.honeybearsbbq.com* ⚭ *Reservations not accepted* ✛ *B5.*

$$
AMERICAN
Fodor's Choice
★

$$ ✕**Pane Bianco.** Chef-owner Chris Bianco spends his evenings turning out some of the Valley's best pizza at his downtown Pizzeria Bianco, and his days creating to-die-for take-out sandwiches at this minimalist shop. Order at the counter, pick up your brown-bagged meal (which always includes a piece of candy), and dine outside at a picnic table. The menu only has a few sandwich selections (the tuna with red onion, gaeta olives, and arugula is an excellent choice), but each features wood-fired-oven focaccia stuffed with farm-fresh ingredients. $ *Average main: $12* ✉ *4404 N. Central Ave., North Central Phoenix* ☎ *602/234–2100* ⊕ *www.pizzeriabianco.com* ⊙ *Closed Sun.* ✛ *B4.*

$
MEXICAN
Fodor's Choice
★

$ ✕**Pepe's Taco Villa.** The neighborhood's not fancy, and neither is this restaurant, but in a town with a lot of gringo-ized south-of-the-border fare, this is the real friendly, real deal. Tacos *rancheros*—spicy, shredded pork pungently lathered with adobo paste—are a dream, as are the green-corn tamales and authentic imported *machacado* (air-dried beef). The chiles rellenos may be the best in the state. All are perfect with a margarita from the full bar. Don't leave without trying the sensational mole, a rich sauce fashioned from chiles and chocolate. $ *Average main: $8* ✉ *2108 W. Camelback Rd., North Central Phoenix* ☎ *602/242–0379* ⊕ *www.pepestacovilla.com* ✛ *B4.*

The Phoenix-area dining scene is hot, and not just because of the many spicy Southwestern and Mexican ingredients.

$$$ AMERICAN 🍴 **Phoenix City Grille.** If you've never tasted a green chile properly prepared, head to Phoenix City Grille. From burgers to pasta, all of the quintessentially American fare served here is infused with a hint of the Southwest. For dinner, the pot roast can't be beat. If brunch is more your thing, try the griddled corn cakes with bacon—the green chiles give them just a bit of kick. [$] *Average main: $21* ✉ *5816 N. 16th St., North Central Phoenix* ☎ *602/266–3001* 🌐 *www.phoenixcitygrille.com* ✥ *C4.*

$$ SOUTHWESTERN 🍴 **Richardson's Cuisine of New Mexico.** There are two types of spicy food: dishes that you eat on a dare, and dishes that make you savor every morsel and wish for more. Richardson's has the second option mastered, and lures back locals with heat-filled dishes that test the limits of your palate—but not in a threatening way. This is fine New Mexican cuisine, which means everything (including heat and quality) is ratcheted up about three notches. The beef tenderloin chile relleno is the star of the menu, which incorporates New Mexican hatch chiles in just about every dish. If you're feeling adventurous, order a platter or a combination. You won't be disappointed. [$] *Average main: $14* ✉ *6335 N. 16th St., North Central Phoenix, Phoenix* ☎ *602/287–8900* 🌐 *richardsonsnm.com* ✍ *Reservations essential* ✥ *C4.*

$$ MEXICAN 🍴 **Via Delosantos.** The family-owned restaurant looks a little rough around the edges outside, but it's what's inside that counts—an accommodating staff, an enormous and authentic Mexican menu, and one of the best-tasting and best-priced house margaritas in town. Entrées are ample, and include more than just tired combinations of beef, beans, and cheese. Try the fajitas *calabacitas* with a yellow- and green-squash succotash; or the delicious chicken *delosantos,* a cheesy chicken breast and tortilla concoction. Expect to wait on weekends, either at the bar or outside, but the experience will be worth it. $ *Average main: $13* ✉ *9120 N. Central Ave., North Central Phoenix* 📞 *602/997–6239* 🌐 *www.viadelosantos.net* ⌨ *Reservations not accepted* ✣ *B3.*

PARADISE VALLEY

$$$$
STEAKHOUSE

✕ **BLT Steak Scottsdale.** Chef Laurent Tourondel's mini-empire includes this stylish dining room at the Camelback Inn. A knowledgeable waitstaff offer suggestions for pairing sizzling steaks with sauces (including red wine and mustard), picking sides (including stuffed mushroom caps and poached green beans), and deciding on a potato dish (a favorite: Parmesan gnocchi). Everything goes well with Gruyère popovers, which are likely to disappear from your plate within seconds (they'll bring you more if you ask). Choose from inspired desserts with deceptively modest names such as bittersweet chocolate tart. $ *Average main: $59* ✉ *Camelback Inn, 5402 E. Lincoln Dr., Paradise Valley* 📞 *480/905–7979* 🌐 *www.bltscottsdale.com* ⏱ *No lunch* ✣ *D3.*

$$$$
ECLECTIC

✕ **elements.** Perched on the side of Camelback Mountain at the Sanctuary resort, this stylish modern restaurant offers breathtaking desert-sunset and city-light views. They're the perfect complement to chef Beau MacMillan's culinary delights that fuse hearty American traditions and Asian flavors. Order such Asian-infused appetizers as the crispy sesame sweetbreads, edamame and truffle dumpling, and carrot millet pot stickers. Seasonal specials and entrées are excellent; among the best is the bacon-wrapped fillet of beef with oyster mushrooms and a merlot demi glace. $ *Average main: $35* ✉ *Sanctuary Camelback Mountain, 5700 E. McDonald Dr., Paradise Valley* 📞 *480/948–2100* 🌐 *www.elementsrestaurant.com* ⌨ *Reservations essential* ✣ *D4.*

$$$$
AMERICAN

✕ **Lon's at the Hermosa.** In an adobe hacienda hand-built by cowboy artist Lon Megargee, this romantic spot has sweeping vistas of Camelback Mountain and the perfect patio for after-dinner drinks under the stars. Megargee's art and cowboy memorabilia decorate the dining room. The menu changes seasonally and includes appetizers like Kobe beef carpaccio and foie gras. Wood-grilled Kobe New York strip, and more-exotic dishes like roasted duck breast with duck confit and black-eyed-pea cake, are main-course options. Phoenicians love the weekend brunch. $ *Average main: $35* ✉ *Hermosa Inn, 5532 N. Palo Cristi Dr., Paradise Valley* 📞 *602/955–7878* 🌐 *www.hermosainn.com/lons* ✣ *D3.*

SOUTH PHOENIX

$$
MEXICAN

✕ **Los Dos Molinos.** In a hacienda that belonged to silent-era movie star Tom Mix, this fun restaurant focuses on New Mexican–style Mexican food. That means *hot*. New Mexico chiles form the backbone and fiery breath of the dishes, and the green-chile enchilada and beef taco are potentially lethal. The red salsa and enchiladas with egg on top are excellent, as is the popular shrimp Veracruz with red chile sauce. Don't even bother asking for your dish to be prepared mild. There's no such thing at "Los Dos," and that's part of the fun. This is a must-do dining experience if you want true New Mexican–style food, but be prepared to swig lots of water. There are other locations across the Valley, but this is considered the original. $ *Average main: $12* ⊠ *8646 S. Central Ave., South Phoenix* ☎ *602/243–9113* ⊕ *www.losdosmolinosaz.com* ⚄ *Reservations not accepted* ☼ *Closed Sun. and Mon.* ✛ *B6.*

SCOTTSDALE

$$
MODERN
AMERICAN

✕ **Citizen Public House.** Everything about Citizen Public House exudes "cool," from its hip Scottsdale address to its central see-and-be-seen bar, to (most important) its menu of modern twists on traditional favorites. While the entrées here are finger-licking good—most notably the buttermilk chicken with corn-butter bean succotash—you can enjoy one of the best meals of your life by simply ordering a series of appetizers and sharing them with friends. Don't-miss items include the pork belly spaetzle and the kale Caesar. If you're looking for a taste of Phoenix culinary history, order the "original" chopped salad, and have your server explain all the elements as it's tossed table-side. $ *Average main: $21* ⊠ *711 E. 5th Ave., Old Town, Scottsdale* ☎ *480/398–4208* ⊕ *citizenpublichouse.com* ⚄ *Reservations essential* ✛ *G2.*

$$$
ECLECTIC
Fodor's Choice
★

✕ **Rancho Pinot.** The attention to quality here makes this one of the town's most lauded dining spots. The ambivalent minimalist cowboy decor and almost secret-handshake location are completely forgotten upon the first bite of food and replaced with taste-bud heaven. Chef Chrysa Robertson's inventive menu changes daily, depending on what's fresh. If you're lucky, you'll get a crack at the flatiron steak with pancetta and chimichurri sauce, the handmade pasta with fennel and chicken meatballs, or Nonni's Sunday chicken with toasted polenta. Organic and locally grown-and-raised ingredients are used whenever possible, which is just another reason why you'll want to return as many times as possible. $ *Average main: $26* ⊠ *6208 N. Scottsdale Rd., northwest of Trader Joe's in Lincoln Village Shops* ☎ *480/367–8030* ⊕ *www.ranchopinot.com* ☼ *No lunch* ✛ *E3.*

$$$
JAPANESE

✕ **Sushi on Shea.** You may be in the middle of the desert, but the sushi here will make you think you're at the ocean's edge. Fresh yellowtail, toro, shrimp, scallops, freshwater eel, and even monkfish liver pâté are among the long list of delights. The best dish? Maybe it's the *una-ju* (broiled freshwater eel with a sublime smoky scent) served over sweet rice. The fact that some people believe eel is an aphrodisiac only adds to its charm. The bento box is a good way to sample a variety of menu offerings. $ *Average main: $22* ⊠ *7000 E. Shea Blvd.* ☎ *480/483–7799* ⊕ *www.sushionshea.com* ☼ *Closed Mon.* ✛ *E2.*

NORTH SCOTTSDALE

$$$$
STEAKHOUSE
Fodor's Choice
★

✕ **Bourbon Steak.** This upscale steak restaurant run by top-rated chef Michael Mina has been living up to the royal reputation of the Fairmont Scottsdale Princess. Its severe but stunning stone-and-glass entry lets people know that they are in for something serious—seriously good.

2

WHERE TO REFUEL AROUND TOWN

Here are the most popular reliable chain restaurants, particularly for large groups (and large portions):

Elephant Bar. The predominantly Pacific Rim, elephant-size menu at this large chain offers some pleasant Cajun (catfish and jambalaya) and plain old American (New York steak, lemon herb chicken) entrées. Pacific Rim specialties include Miso Yaki fire-grilled salmon and the delicious pan-Asian vegetable-and-noodle soup with teriyaki chicken skewers. 🌐 *www.elephantbar.com.*

Garduño's. This gargantuan Mexican restaurant has several equally ample locations in the area. Try the unusually good green-chile clam chowder or the fresh guacamole made table-side for starters, and experience a grilled chimichanga or fajitas for a main course. 🌐 *www.gardunosrestaurants.com.*

Morton's of Chicago. The Windy City chain is famous for exceptional service, immense steaks, and entertaining presentations. Its business-formal atmosphere, menus, and operations are replicated at the North Scottsdale location. The monstrous 24-ounce porterhouse or 14-ounce double-cut fillet can satisfy the hungriest cowpoke. 🌐 *www.mortons.com.*

Nello's. Leave it to two brothers from Chicago to come up with the motto "In Crust We Trust," and Nello's excels in both thin-crust and deep-dish pies. Try traditional varieties heaped with homemade sausage and mushrooms, or go vegetarian with the spinach pie. Pasta entrées are very good, too, and the family-style salads are inventive and fresh. 🌐 *www.nellosscottsdale.com.*

Oregano's. Huge portions are an understatement at this nine-branch casual Chicago-theme eatery. Come hungry and feast on tasty baked sandwiches, pizza (deep-dish, thin crust, or stuffed), and pasta dishes. The young, friendly staff and kitschy 1950s decor create a fun and comfortable, family-friendly vibe. 🌐 *www.oreganos.com.*

Zoë's Kitchen. Cool, clean, fast, inexpensive, and nutritious, this national chain is great for a light but filling, Greek-inspired meal without the guilt. Each location is uniform in its bright, modern cafeteria-like setting, where first you order, then you sit. Make sure to try the Greek chicken pita or Greek salad, and the coleslaw with feta cheese. 🌐 *www.zoeskitchen.com.*

Its modern elegance is as tasty to the eyes as the food is to the palate. Select from American-grade or Japanese Kobe beef but be prepared for the prices—including one $85 steak. Even the fries are luxurious here. If you're on a budget, head to the adjacent burger bar. You won't be disappointed. [$] *Average main: $59* ✉ *Fairmont Scottsdale Princess Resort, 7575 E. Princess Dr., North Scottsdale* ☎ *480/513–6002* 🌐 *www.scottsdaleprincess.com/dining/bourbon-steak* ✍ *Reservations essential* ⏲ *Closed Sun. No lunch* ✥ *E1.*

$$$$ LATIN AMERICAN 🍴 **Deseo.** Seemingly surrounded by fine restaurants in North Scottsdale, this gem is descreetly tucked away in the Westin Kierland Resort. Designed and inspired by Douglas Rodriguez, the founder of nuevo

Latin cuisine, Deseo serves the best ceviche in town. Start with the muddle bar, where you can sip an assortment of creative mojitos that go beyond a hint of mint. The menu changes seasonally, and if fish isn't your thing, you can't go wrong with the Kobe beef carpaccio or the duck a la rioja. [$] *Average main: $32* ✉ *Westin Kierland Resort, 6902 E. Greenway Pkwy., North Scottsdale* ☎ *480/624–1202* 🌐 *www.kierlandresort.com* ⏲ *No lunch* ✣ *E1.*

$$$$ AMERICAN 🍴 **Eddie V's.** Specializing in fresh seafood done right (try the Hong Kong–style Chilean sea bass or the broiled scallops), grilled meats, and fine wines, Eddie V's is great for fine dining. But with its inviting bar and lounge area and succulent appetizers like kung pao–style calamari and a variety of fresh oysters, Eddie's is also enormously popular (and slightly more affordable) as a happy-hour spot. [$] *Average main: $33* ✉ *Scottsdale Quarter, 15323 N. Scottsdale Rd., North Scottsdale* ☎ *480/730–4800* 🌐 *www.eddiev.com* ⏲ *No lunch* ✣ *E1.*

$$$ LATIN AMERICAN 🍴 **Havana Cafe.** Tapas are marvelous at this cozy Cuban-style cantina. While sampling authentic Cuban creations like shrimp pancakes, ham and chicken croquettes, Cuban tamales, and paella heaped with a whole Maine lobster, diners can shed the stresses of an arid metropolis. New Puerto Rican menu items include stuffed green plantains and plantains with pork cracklings. There's something special for vegetarians, too: *cho cho,* a fresh chayote squash stuffed with loads of veggies and topped with a Jamaican curry sauce, and rice with pigeon peas. There's another location on Camelback Road in Phoenix. [$] *Average main: $21* ✉ *6245 E. Bell Rd., North Scottsdale* ☎ *480/991–1496* 🌐 *www.havanacafe-az.com* ⏲ *No lunch Sun.* ✣ *E1.*

$$$ ECLECTIC 🍴 **Razz's Restaurant and Bar.** There's no telling what part of the globe chef-proprietor and maestro of fusion Erasmo "Razz" Kamnitzer will use for culinary inspiration on any given day, but his creations give dormant taste buds a wake-up call: South American bouillabaisse is a fragrant fish stew stocked with veggies, and the Cuban-style green rice will turn up the heat on your palate. Count on it—Razz'll dazzle. [$] *Average main: $27* ✉ *10315 N. Scottsdale Rd., North Scottsdale* ☎ *480/905–1308* 🌐 *www.razzsrestaurant.com* ⏲ *Closed Sun. and Mon. and June–Aug. No lunch* ✣ *E2.*

OLD TOWN

$$$ STEAKHOUSE 🍴 **Don & Charlie's.** Attention sports fans! This hangout is a favorite with major-leaguers in town for spring training, college football Bowl games, or the Super Bowl. A venerable chophouse, D&C specializes in "American comforts" with prime-grade steak and sports memorabilia—the walls are covered with pictures, autographs, and uniforms. The spacious and Cheers-like interior; friendly staff; and New York sirloin, prime rib, and double-thick lamb chops are a hit. Sides include au gratin potatoes and creamed spinach. [$] *Average main: $27* ✉ *7501 E. Camelback Rd., Old Town* ☎ *480/990–0900* 🌐 *www.donandcharlies.com* ⏲ *No lunch* ✣ *H1.*

$$ THAI 🍴 **Malee's Thai Bistro.** This cozy but fashionable, casual eatery in the heart of Scottsdale's Main Street Arts District serves sophisticated, Thai-inspired fare. Try the best-selling, crispy *pla:* flash-fried whitefish fillets with fresh cilantro and sweet jalapeño garlic sauce. The vegetarian

Arizona heatwave red curry is a must, along with curries made to order with tofu, chicken, beef, pork, or seafood. You specify the spiciness—from mild to flaming—but even "mild" dishes have a bite. [$] *Average main: $15* ✉ *7131 E. Main St., Old Town* ☎ *480/947–6042* 🌐 *www.maleesthaibistro.com* ✥ *F3.*

$$$ SOUTHWESTERN 🍴 **The Mission.** Not only will the food take your taste buds to new levels, the dark and sophisticated space is also adjacent to a historic Catholic mission. Sit at the elegant bar or fireside on the patio and enjoy an avocado margarita with supreme starters or sides like table-side-crafted guacamole; Mission fries with lemon, chile, and cumin; or grits with chipotle and honey. House favorites include the pecan- and mesquite-grilled pork shoulder, and the homemade chorizo porchetta. The weekend brunch menu alone could keep this place afloat. [$] *Average main: $22* ✉ *3815 N. Brown Ave., Old Town* ☎ *480/636–5005* 🌐 *www.themissionaz.com* ✍ *Reservations essential* ✥ *G3.*

$$ MEDITERRANEAN 🍴 **Olive & Ivy.** Tucked into the south side of the high-traffic, high-priced Scottsdale waterfront complex, Olive & Ivy is a pleasant surprise. By day the light comes from the wall of windows that look out onto the ample patio with cozy couches and fire pits, as well as the man-made waterway for which the complex is named. By night the giant space becomes intimate with dim, designer lighting. A full dinner menu, featuring a mix of fish and meat creations with Italian and Mediterranean twists like veal and spinach ravioli, is available, but the delicious variety of appetizers, like bacon-wrapped Medjoul dates, beet salad with goat-cheese dressing, and flatbreads make for a good meal. Wash them down with something from their ample wine list or one of their unique, not-too-sweet peach hibiscus margaritas. [$] *Average main: $19* ✉ *7135 E. Camelback Rd., Suite 195, Old Town* ☎ *480/751–2200* 🌐 *www.foxrc.com/restaurants/olive-ivy-restaurant-marketplace* ✍ *Reservations essential* ✥ *F1.*

$$ CAFÉ 🍴 **Scratch Pastries.** Duc and Noelle Liao are a model couple, literally. The two met in Paris, where Duc worked as a fashion photographer and Noelle as a model. Now, the two are the hottest pair in pastry making. A graduate of Le Cordon Bleu, Duc Liao conjures up sublime creations, both salty and sweet, from jumbo shrimp in Japanese sauce to duck confit with pommes frites. Don't let the location in a strip mall fool you; this is a flavor trip all the way to France. [$] *Average main: $13* ✉ *7620 E. Indian School Rd., Suite 103, Old Town* ☎ *480/947–0057* 🌐 *www.scratchpastries.com* ✍ *Reservations not accepted* ⏲ *No dinner Sun.–Tues.* ✥ *H3.*

TEMPE AND AROUND

CHANDLER

$$$$ SOUTHWESTERN Fodor's Choice ★ 🍴 **Kai.** Innovative Southwestern cuisine at the prestigious and award-wining Kai ("seed" in the Pima language) uses indigenous ingredients from local tribal farms. The seasonal menu reflects the restaurant's natural setting on the Gila River Indian Community. Standout appetizers include a duo of Hudson Valley duck and citrus-and-chile-glazed sea trout. Entrées like loin of pecan-crusted Colorado lamb, and the Cheyenne River buffalo tenderloin are excellent. Try to dine at sunset:

the restaurant has huge windows that showcase gorgeous mountain and desert views. [$] *Average main: $48* ✉ *Sheraton Wild Horse Pass Resort & Spa, 5594 W. Wild Horse Pass Blvd., Chandler* ☎ *602/225–0100* 🌐 *www.wildhorsepassresort.com* ✍ *Reservations essential* ⏲ *Closed Sun. and Mon. No lunch* ✥ *D6.*

TEMPE

$ INDIAN

🍴 **Curry Corner.** In the shadow of Arizona State University, Curry Corner serves up some of the best Indian food in town. The naan is plentiful at this mom-and-pop eatery, and the chicken tikka masala is the house specialty. Don't worry if the spice gets to you—there are pitchers of water nearby to cool your palate. [$] *Average main: $11* ✉ *1212 E. Apache Blvd.* ☎ *480/894–1276* ✥ *E6.*

$ MIDDLE EASTERN

🍴 **Haji Baba.** This casual Tempe treasure is a local, hole-in-the-wall Middle Eastern favorite that gets consistent rave reviews. The reasonably priced menu includes hummus, *labni* (fresh cheese made from yogurt), fabulous falafel gyros, shawarma, and kebab plates, all served up by a friendly and efficient staff. The adjoining store stocks an ample selection of imported Middle Eastern, Mediterranean, Indian, and European foods, including everything from delicious cured olives, fava beans, and grape leaves to chocolate-covered halvah bars, rose water, and countless other hard-to-find specialties. [$] *Average main: $9* ✉ *1513 E. Apache Blvd.* ☎ *480/894–1905* ✍ *Reservations not accepted* ⏲ *No dinner Sun.* ✥ *F6.*

$$$ ECLECTIC Fodor's Choice ★

🍴 **House of Tricks.** There's nothing up the sleeves of Robert and Robin Trick, who work magic on the ever-changing eclectic menu that emphasizes the freshest available seafood, poultry, and fine meats, as well as vegetarian selections. One of the Valley's most unusual dining venues, the restaurant encompasses a completely charming 1920s home and a separate brick- and adobe-style house originally built in 1903, adjoined by an intimate wooden deck and outdoor patio shaded by a canopy of grapevines and trees. The ever-changing dinner menu serves up entrées like grilled Scottish salmon with smoked corn succotash. At lunch you can't go wrong with the quiche of the day. [$] *Average main: $30* ✉ *114 E. 7th St.* ☎ *480/968–1114* 🌐 *www.houseoftricks.com* ⏲ *Closed Sun.* ✥ *E6.*

WHERE TO STAY

The Valley of the Sun now offers locals and visitors some of the country's best choices when it comes to funky, high-fashion accommodations.

Developers and hoteliers have taken advantage of the Valley's wide-open spaces to introduce super-size, luxury resorts like the Westin Kierland and the JW Marriott Desert Ridge, offering everything from their own golf courses and water parks to four-star restaurants and shopping villages. Places like the retro-hip Hotel Valley Ho and the sleek, mountainside Sanctuary on Camelback Mountain have brought Arizona to the forefront of luxury-hotel style. Regal resorts like The Phoenician, the Four Seasons, the romantic Royal Palms Resort, and the Moroccan-inspired Montelucia keep lodging grounded in traditional, unsurpassed elegance, while plenty of boutique and business hotels keep it grounded in price.

Downtown Phoenix properties tend to be the business hotels, close to the heart of the city and the convention centers—and often closer to the average vacationer's budget. Many properties here cater to corporate travelers during the week but lower their rates on weekends to entice leisure travelers, so ask about weekend specials when making reservations. With more than 60,000 hotel rooms in the metro area, you can take your pick of anything from a luxurious resort to a guest ranch to an extended-stay hotel. For a true Western experience, guest-ranch territory is 70 miles northwest, in the town of Wickenburg.

Many people flee snow and ice to bask in the warmth of the Valley, so winter is the high season, peaking from January through March. Summer season—mid-May through the end of September—is giveaway time, when a night at a resort often goes for half of the winter price, but be forewarned: in the height of summer it can be too hot to do anything outside your air-conditioned room.

Don't be surprised if you see a "Resort Fee" on your checkout statement. Most Valley hotels charge these fees, which range from $20 to $30 and cover such amenities as parking, in-room Wi-Fi, daily newspapers, in-room coffee/tea, fitness centers, pools, and more. Ask your hotel for a complete description of what the resort fee covers.

Prices in the reviews are the lowest cost of a standard double room in high season. Use the coordinate (✣ B2) at the end of each listing to locate a site on the corresponding map. For expanded hotel reviews, visit Fodors.com.

DOWNTOWN PHOENIX

$$$$ HOTEL **Fodor's Choice** ★ 🏨 **Hotel Palomar Phoenix.** Hip and unabashedly quirky, this Downtown Phoenix boutique hotel has kicked up Phoenix's urban street cred a few notches and offers a compelling reason to stay Downtown. **Pros:** modern and luxurious furnishings; great Downtown views; attentive staff; evening wine reception; pets welcome. **Cons:** parking is costly; rowdy atmosphere could be tiresome. [$] *Rooms from: $369* ✉ *2 E. Jefferson St., Downtown Phoenix, Phoenix* ☎ *602/253–6633, 877/488–1908* 🌐 *www.hotelpalomar-phoenix.com* 🛏 *242 rooms* 🍴 *No meals* ✣ *B5.*

$$$$ HOTEL 🏨 **Hyatt Regency Phoenix.** Not just a hotel for convention-goers, the convenience of downtown Phoenix's light rail makes the Hyatt Regency an attractive destination for vacationers. **Pros:** business amenities; light rail access; views from restaurant. **Cons:** atrium blocks view on floors 8 to 10; parking gets pricey. [$] *Rooms from: $399* ✉ *122 N. 2nd St., Downtown Phoenix* ☎ *602/252–1234* 🌐 *www.phoenix.hyatt.com* 🛏 *688 rooms, 5 suites* 🍴 *No meals* ✣ *B5.*

$$$ HOTEL 🏨 **Renaissance Phoenix Downtown.** This Downtown Phoenix destination has an appealing mix of classic comfort and modern accommodations and is one of the city's architectural marvels. **Pros:** prime location for light-rail travel; great lobby bar. **Cons:** primarily oriented to business travelers, ongoing renovations are sometimes noticeable. [$] *Rooms from: $299* ✉ *50 E. Adams St., Downtown Phoenix* ☎ *602/333–0000, 800/309–8138* 🌐 *www.renaissancephoenixdowntown.com* 🛏 *447 rooms, 80 suites* 🍴 *No meals* ✣ *B6.*

BEST BETS FOR PHOENIX, SCOTTSDALE, AND TEMPE LODGING

Fodor's offers a selective listing of lodging at every price range, from the city's best budget motel to its most sophisticated luxury hotel. Here we've compiled our top picks by price and experience. The very best properties—those that provide a particularly remarkable experience in their price range—are designated with the Fodor's Choice logo.

Fodor'sChoice ★

FireSky Resort & Spa, p. 94

Four Seasons Resort Scottsdale at Troon North, p. 95

Hotel Palomar Phoenix, p. 87

Hyatt Regency Scottsdale Resort and Spa at Gainey Ranch, p. 95

JW Marriott Desert Ridge Resort & Spa, p. 93

The Phoenician, p. 92

Pointe Hilton Squaw Peak Resort, p. 93

Rancho de los Caballeros, p. 132

Royal Palms Resort and Spa, p. 92

Sanctuary on Camelback Mountain, p. 93

Westin Kierland Resort & Spa, p. 95

Best by Price

$

Best Western Plus Inn Suite, p. 92

$$

aloft Tempe, p. 98

Hampton Inn Phoenix-Biltmore, p. 89

Wingate by Wyndham Scottsdale, p. 95

$$$

Hermosa Inn, p. 93

Hotel Indigo, p. 98

Pointe Hilton Squaw Peak Resort, p. 93

$$$$

Four Seasons Resort Scottsdale at Troon North, p. 95

JW Marriott Camelback Inn Resort & Spa, p. 93

The Phoenician, p. 92

Royal Palms Resort and Spa, p. 92

Best by Experience

BEST LARGE RESORTS

Arizona Biltmore Resort & Spa, p. 89

Montelucia Resort & Spa, p. 93

JW Marriott Desert Ridge Resort & Spa, p. 93

The Phoenician, p. 92

Westin Kierland Resort & Spa, p. 95

BEST SMALL RESORTS

Hermosa Inn, p. 93

Sanctuary on Camelback Mountain, p. 93

Wigwam Resort, p. 94

BEST GOLF RESORTS

Fairmont Scottsdale Princess, p. 95

Four Seasons Resort Scottsdale at Troon North, p. 95

The Phoenician, p. 92

GREAT VIEW

JW Marriott Camelback Inn Resort & Spa, p. 93

Sanctuary on Camelback Mountain, p. 93

BEST REMOTE RETREATS

Four Seasons Resort Scottsdale at Troon North, p. 95

Rancho de los Caballeros, p. 132

BEST URBAN HOT-SPOT HOTELS

FireSky Resort & Spa, p. 94

Hotel Palomar Phoenix, p. 87

Hotel Valley Ho, p. 98

W Scottsdale, p. 98

2

$$$$ ⊡ **Sheraton Phoenix Downtown Hotel.** The grande dame of Downtown
HOTEL Phoenix hotels has positioned itself as the go-to residence of convention-
goers, but its service and the District restaurant make it desirable for
leisure travelers as well. **Pros:** restaurant has one of the best happy-hour
deals in town; great lobby for lounging or meeting people. **Cons:** hall-
ways are long and impersonal; parking is expensive. *$ Rooms from:
$579 ⊠ 340 N. 3rd St., Downtown Phoenix, Phoenix ☎ 602/262–2500,
866/837–4213 ⊕ www.sheratonphoenixdowntown.com ↩ 953 rooms,
47 suites ⦿ No meals ✢ B5.*

$$$$ ⊡ **Westin Phoenix Downtown.** This Downtown Phoenix gem offers some
HOTEL of the largest rooms in the city, which give you a feeling of seclusion in
the hustle and bustle of the city. **Pros:** large rooms with sitting areas; fantastic views; elegant furnishings and fixtures. **Cons:** tiny lobby and awkward process of getting to the hotel elevator; you have to walk through
the lobby to get to the pool. *$ Rooms from: $589 ⊠ 333 N. Central
Ave., Downtown Phoenix, Phoenix ☎ 602/429–3500, 866/961–3775
⊕ www.westinphoenixdowntown.com ↩ 214 rooms, 28 suites ⦿ No
meals ✢ B5.*

GREATER PHOENIX

CAMELBACK CORRIDOR

$$$ ⊡ **Arizona Biltmore Resort & Spa.** Designed by Frank Lloyd Wright's col-
RESORT league Albert Chase McArthur, the Biltmore has been Phoenix's pre-
mier resort since it opened in 1929. **Pros:** centrally located; stately;
historic charm. **Cons:** finding a parking spot near your room can be a
headache; hard to find lounge chairs at some pools. *$ Rooms from:
$299 ⊠ 2400 E. Missouri Ave., Camelback Corridor ☎ 602/955–6600,
800/950–0086 ⊕ www.arizonabiltmore.com ↩ 646 rooms, 90 suites
⦿ No meals ✢ C4.*

$$ ⊡ **Courtyard Phoenix Camelback.** Public areas in this four-story hotel are
HOTEL mostly glass and tile, and filled with greenery, while rooms are tastefully
done with light-colored walls and accents like plush down bedding, cher-
rywood armoires, and large, pullout desks to accommodate a business
traveler. **Pros:** great value; within walking distance of great shopping
and dining. **Cons:** few frills; business-oriented. *$ Rooms from: $219
⊠ 2101 E. Camelback Rd., Camelback Corridor ☎ 602/955–5200,
800/321–2211 ⊕ www.marriott.com/hotels/travel/phxcc-courtyard-
phoenix-camelback/ ↩ 155 rooms, 12 suites ⦿ No meals ✢ C4.*

$$ ⊡ **Hampton Inn Phoenix-Biltmore.** Conveniently located one block off
HOTEL Camelback Road, this four-story hotel is great for business travelers,
with spacious and accommodating rooms appointed with comfortable
yet modern furnishings. **Pros:** great value; central location; modern
conveniences. **Cons:** though gated, the pool area is exposed to the park-
ing lot and street. *$ Rooms from: $219 ⊠ 2310 E. Highland Ave.,
Camelback Corridor ☎ 602/956–5221 ⊕ www.phoenixbiltmorearea.
hamptoninn.com ↩ 112 rooms, 8 suites ⦿ Breakfast ✢ C4.*

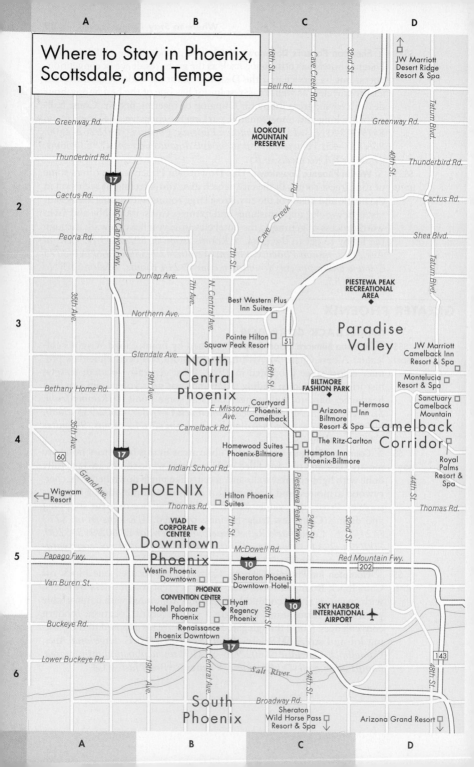

Where to Stay in Phoenix, Scottsdale, and Tempe

A   **B**   **C**   **D**

JW Marriott
Desert Ridge
Resort & Spa

Greenway Rd.

Thunderbird Rd.

Cactus Rd.

Peoria Rd.

Bell Rd.

LOOKOUT
MOUNTAIN
PRESERVE

Greenway Rd.

Thunderbird Rd.

Cactus Rd.

Shea Blvd.

16th St.

Cave Creek Rd.

32nd St.

40th St.

Tatum Blvd.

Black Canyon Fwy.

7th St.

Cave Creek Pkwy.

Dunlap Ave.

35th Ave.

Northern Ave.

Glendale Ave.

Bethany Home Rd.

19th Ave.

7th Ave.

N. Central Ave.

PIESTEWA PEAK
RECREATIONAL
AREA

Best Western Plus
Inn Suites

Pointe Hilton
Squaw Peak Resort

North
Central
Phoenix

Paradise
Valley

JW Marriott
Camelback Inn
Resort & Spa

Montelucia
Resort & Spa

Sanctuary
Camelback
Mountain

BILTMORE
FASHION PARK

E. Missouri
Ave.

Courtyard
Phoenix
Camelback

Camelback Rd.

Homewood Suites
Phoenix-Biltmore

Indian School Rd.

Arizona
Biltmore
Resort & Spa

Hermosa
Inn

Camelback
Corridor

The Ritz-Carlton

Hampton Inn
Phoenix-Biltmore

Royal
Palms
Resort &
Spa

Wigwam
Resort

PHOENIX

Thomas Rd.

VIAD
CORPORATE
CENTER

Downtown
Phoenix

Papago Fwy.

Van Buren St.

Buckeye Rd.

Lower Buckeye Rd.

Hilton Phoenix
Suites

7th St.

Thomas Rd.

McDowell Rd.

Piestewa Peak Pkwy.

24th St.

32nd St.

44th St.

Red Mountain Fwy.

Westin Phoenix
Downtown

Sheraton Phoenix
Downtown Hotel

PHOENIX
CONVENTION CENTER

Hotel Palomar
Phoenix

Hyatt
Regency
Phoenix

Renaissance
Phoenix Downtown

SKY HARBOR
INTERNATIONAL
AIRPORT

19th Ave.

N. Central Ave.

Salt River

16th St.

24th St.

48th St.

South
Phoenix

Broadway Rd.

Sheraton
Wild Horse Pass
Resort & Spa

Arizona Grand Resort

Grand Ave.

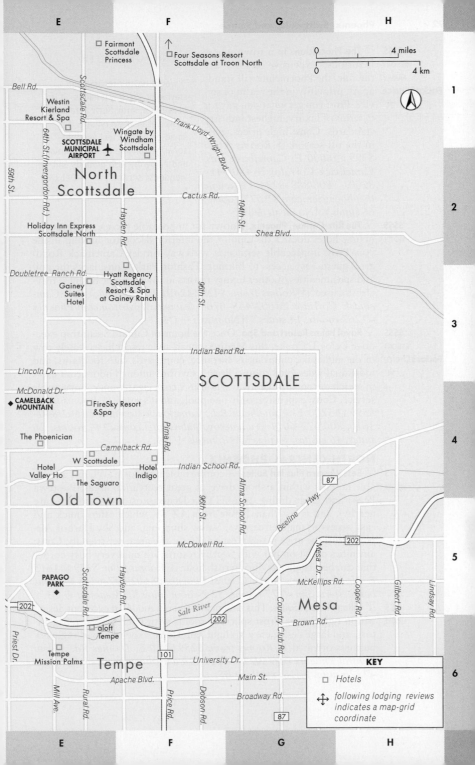

$$$$
RESORT
FAMILY
Fodor's Choice
★

The Phoenician. In a town where luxurious, expensive resorts are the rule, the Phoenician still stands apart, primarily in the realm of service. **Pros:** you get what you pay for in terms of luxury; highest industry standards. **Cons:** high prices, even in the off-season. $ *Rooms from: $799* ✉ *6000 E. Camelback Rd., Camelback Corridor* ☎ *480/941–8200,* *800/888–8234* ⊕ *www. thephoenician.com* ⤳ *577 rooms, 66 suites* ⊙ *No meals* ✛ *E4.*

$$$$
HOTEL

The Ritz-Carlton, Phoenix. Known for impeccable service, this graceful luxury hotel doesn't disappoint the interior decorator lurking inside you. **Pros:** impeccable service; a walkway (under Camelback Road) gives guests easy access to Biltmore Fashion Park. **Cons:** lacks the golf and spa amenities of other luxury resorts in town; can be business traveler–focused. $ *Rooms from: $429* ✉ *2401 E. Camelback Rd., Camelback Corridor* ☎ *602/468–0700* ⊕ *www.ritzcarlton.com/Phoenix* ⤳ *267 rooms, 14 suites* ⊙ *No meals* ✛ *C4.*

$$$$
RESORT
Fodor's Choice
★

Royal Palms Resort and Spa. Once the home of Cunard Steamship executive Delos T. Cooke, this Mediterranean-style resort has a stately row of the namesake palms at its entrance, courtyards with fountains, and individually designed rooms. **Pros:** a favorite among Fodors.com users in search of romantic getaways; houses a cozy cigar lounge; impeccable service. **Cons:** expensive; only one pool, and it's small. $ *Rooms from: $599* ✉ *5200 E. Camelback Rd., Camelback Corridor* ☎ *602/840–3610,* *800/672–6011* ⊕ *www.royalpalmshotel.com* ⤳ *44 rooms, 26 suites, 46 casitas, 3 villas* ⊙ *No meals* ✛ *D4.*

NORTH CENTRAL PHOENIX

$
HOTEL

Best Western Plus Inn Suites. A comfortable base for travel, this affordable hotel is within a short drive of great recreation areas (Piestewa Peak) and great dining options (Via Delosantos and Carolina's are nearby), and is less than 1 mile from AZ 51, which offers quick and easy access to major freeways, Valley shopping, and Sky Harbor Airport. **Pros:** the price is right, especially for the area; pet-friendly. **Cons:** amenities aren't on par with nearby resorts; it's on a very busy corner that can be a challenge during rush hour. $ *Rooms from: $129* ✉ *1615 E. Northern Ave., North Central Phoenix* ☎ *602/997–6285* ⊕ *www. bestwestern.com* ⤳ *77 rooms, 32 2-room suites* ⊙ *Breakfast* ✛ *C3.*

$$$
HOTEL

Hilton Phoenix Suites. This practical hotel is a model of excellent design within tight limits. **Pros:** spacious rooms with microwaves, refrigerators, and large desks; close to light rail. **Cons:** expensive parking; very business-oriented. $ *Rooms from: $259* ✉ *10 E. Thomas Rd., North Central Phoenix* ☎ *602/222–1111* ⊕ *www.phoenixsuites.hilton.com* ⤳ *226 suites* ⊙ *No meals* ✛ *B5.*

$$$$ | RESORT | FAMILY | Fodor's Choice ★

🏨 **JW Marriott Desert Ridge Resort & Spa.** Arizona's largest resort has an immense entryway with floor-to-ceiling windows that allow the sandstone lobby, the Sonoran Desert, and the resort's amazing water features to meld together in a single prospect. **Pros:** perfect for luxuriating with family or groups; close to north Valley restaurants, entertainmnent, and attractions. **Cons:** large size makes it a bit impersonal for the price tag; lots of walking and stairs required to get anywhere. [$] *Rooms from: $599* ✉ *5350 E. Marriott Dr.* ☎ *480/293–5000, 800/835–6206* 🌐 *www.jwdesertridgeresort.com* 🛏 *869 rooms, 81 suites* 🍴 *No meals* ✣ *D1.*

$$$ | RESORT | FAMILY | Fodor's Choice ★

🏨 **Pointe Hilton Squaw Peak Resort.** The highlight of this family-oriented Hilton is the 9-acre recreation area Hole-in-the-Wall River Ranch; it has swimming pools with waterfalls, a 130-foot waterslide, and a 1,000-foot "river" that winds past a miniature golf course, tennis courts, and artificial buttes. **Pros:** adjacent to the Phoenix Mountain Preserve, making it an ideal base for hiking and biking trips; affordable alternative to luxury resorts nearby. **Cons:** finding a parking spot can be a challenge; rooms near lobby are noisy. [$] *Rooms from: $259* ✉ *7677 N. 16th St., North Central Phoenix* ☎ *602/997–2626, 800/947–9784* 🌐 *www.pointehilton.com* 🛏 *483 suites, 80 casitas* 🍴 *No meals* ✣ *C4.*

PARADISE VALLEY

$$$ | HOTEL

🏨 **Hermosa Inn.** This boutique hotel's ranch-style lodge was the home and studio of cowboy artist Lon Megargee in the 1930s; today the adobe structure houses Lon's at the Hermosa, justly popular for its New American cuisine. **Pros:** luxurious but cozy; pet-friendly; fantastic restaurant. **Cons:** stretches the boundaries of "cozy"; lacks some luxury amenities of larger resorts nearby. [$] *Rooms from: $309* ✉ *5532 N. Palo Cristi Rd., Paradise Valley* ☎ *602/955–8614, 800/241–1210* 🌐 *www.hermosainn.com* 🛏 *13 rooms, 21 casitas* 🍴 *No meals* ✣ *D4.*

$$$$ | RESORT

🏨 **JW Marriott Camelback Inn Resort & Spa.** Built on 125 acres in the mid-1930s and gorgeously renovated to keep the cowboy character, this hacienda-style resort remains top-notch and was the first JW Marriott ever established. **Pros:** a specialty restaurant (BLT Steak); a world-class spa and golf course; stunning place to catch a sunset. **Cons:** noisy neighbors are easily heard at night; pool is small for a resort of this stature. [$] *Rooms from: $399* ✉ *5402 E. Lincoln Dr., Paradise Valley* ☎ *480/948–1700, 800/242–2635* 🌐 *www.camelbackinn.com* 🛏 *427 rooms, 26 suites* 🍴 *No meals* ✣ *D3.*

$$$$ | RESORT

🏨 **Montelucia Resort & Spa.** This luxury resort brings a touch of the Mediterranean to Paradise Valley with its exquisite dark furnishings and light stone work, its impeccable Joya Spa, its pool pavilion, and a Spanish-inspired wedding chapel. **Pros:** inner-city getaway with stellar sunset views and a new approach to luxury. **Cons:** while the grounds are beautiful, the layout is boxy, awkward, and confusing, particularly while you're trying to wheel luggage around. [$] *Rooms from: $399* ✉ *4949 E. Lincoln Dr., Paradise Valley* ☎ *480/627–3200, 888/627–3010* 🌐 *www.montelucia.com* 🛏 *251 guest rooms, 40 suites, 2 villas* 🍴 *No meals* ✣ *D3.*

$$$$ | HOTEL | Fodor's Choice ★

🏨 **Sanctuary on Camelback Mountain.** This luxurious boutique hotel is the only resort on the north slope of Camelback Mountain; secluded mountain casitas are painted in desert hues and feature breathtaking views of Paradise Valley. **Pros:** inner-city getaway with mountain seclusion; unparalleled views of Camelback's Praying Monk Rock. **Cons:** it can be hard to find your room on the sprawling property; walking between buildings can mean conquering slopes or flights of stairs; not kid-friendly. [$] *Rooms from: $569* ✉ *5700 E. McDonald Dr., Paradise Valley* ☎ *480/948–2100, 800/245–2051* 🌐 *www.sanctuaryaz.com* 🛏 *105 casitas* 🍴 *No meals* ✣ *D4.*

SOUTH PHOENIX

$$$$ RESORT FAMILY 🏨 **Arizona Grand Resort.** This beautiful all-suites resort next to South Mountain Park is home to Oasis, one of the largest water parks in the country, and one of the Valley's more challenging golf courses. **Pros:** great family or large-group location; all rooms are suites. **Cons:** huge property can overwhelm; freeway noise could be a problem in some rooms. [$] *Rooms from: $369* ✉ *8000 S. Arizona Grand Pkwy., South Phoenix* ☎ *602/438–9000, 866/267–1321* 🌐 *www.arizonagrandresort.com* 🛏 *740 suites* 🍴 *No meals* ✣ *D6.*

LITCHFIELD PARK

$$$ RESORT 🏨 **Wigwam Resort.** Built in 1918 as a retreat for executives of the Goodyear Company, the grand Wigwam Resort maintains its historical character while delivering a modern-day, first-class luxury experience. **Pros:** although only a few minutes from downtown Phoenix, this resort feels away from it all; great service. **Cons:** Odd resort layout makes it difficult to find anything; rooms can teeter on old historic charm and just plain "old." [$] *Rooms from: $299* ✉ *300 Wigwam Blvd., Litchfield Park* ☎ *623/935–3811* 🌐 *www.wigwamresort.com* 🛏 *259 rooms, 72 suites, 2 casitas* 🍴 *No meals* ✣ *A4.*

SCOTTSDALE

$$$$ HOTEL FAMILY Fodor's Choice ★ 🏨 **FireSky Resort & Spa.** This Scottsdale escape provides an elegant, intimate, eco- and family-friendly environment. **Pros:** the lavish pool and lounge area are considered among the area's nicest; pet-friendly; special rooms for tall people. **Cons:** no elevator; interior hallways can be noisy. [$] *Rooms from: $409* ✉ *4925 N. Scottsdale Rd.* ☎ *480/945–7666, 800/528–7867* 🌐 *www.fireskyresort.com* 🛏 *196 rooms, 8 suites* 🍴 *No meals* ✣ *E4.*

$$$ HOTEL FAMILY 🏨 **Gainey Suites Hotel.** This independently owned boutique hotel is a rare find for both amenities and price. **Pros:** hotel layout, price, and inclusive breakfast buffet are ideal for families and groups. **Cons:** comfortable but fairly generic decor; have to leave property to enjoy recreation amenities. [$] *Rooms from: $299* ✉ *7300 E. Gainey Suites Dr.* ☎ *480/922–6969, 800/970–4666* 🌐 *www.gaineysuiteshotel.com* 🛏 *162 suites* 🍴 *Breakfast* ✣ *E3.*

$$ HOTEL 🏨 **Holiday Inn Express Scottsdale North.** This hotel has an ideal location along the Scottsdale Road corridor, with trendy restaurants and shopping opportunities within easy walking distance, making this a comfortable, affordable, and family-friendly option. **Pros:** quiet; perfect for the price in this area. **Cons:** these affordable rooms can't meet the high-scale standards of nearby hotels and resorts. [$] *Rooms from: $171* ✉ *7350 E. Gold Dust Rd., at Scottsdale Rd.* ☎ *480/596–6559, 888/465–4329* 🌐 *www.hiexpress.com* 🛏 *121 rooms, 1 suite* 🍴 *Breakfast* ✣ *E2.*

2

$$$$
RESORT
FAMILY
Fodor's Choice
★

Hyatt Regency Scottsdale Resort and Spa at Gainey Ranch. When you stay here, it's easy to imagine that you're relaxing at an ocean-side resort instead of in the desert; shaded by towering palms and with manicured gardens and paths, the property has water everywhere—a large pool area has a beach, a three-story waterslide, waterfalls, and a lagoon. **Pros:** lots of pools for all; oasis atmosphere; best Sunday brunch in town. **Cons:** if you're early to bed, avoid a room near the lobby. $ *Rooms from: $539* ⊠ *7500 E. Doubletree Ranch Rd.* ☎ *480/444–1234* ⊕ *scottsdale.hyatt. com* ➾ *455 rooms, 7 casitas, 31 suites* �ỊỌỊ *No meals* ✛ *F2.*

$$$
HOTEL

The Saguaro. Surrounded by lush landscaping, this urban resort features two pools that are among the hottest hangouts in all of Scottsdale, and rooms that juxtapose old and new, with flat-screen TVs and retro furnishings that bring you back to the '60s. **Pros:** great location for shopping, entertainment, and Valley activities; part of the happening Scottsdale scene. **Cons:** very noisy; no elevator; furnishings are new but fixtures are very old. $ *Rooms from: $249* ⊠ *4000 N. Drinkwater Blvd., Central Scottsdale* ☎ *480/308–1100, 877/808–2440* ⊕ *www. thesaguaro.com* ➾ *194 rooms* ỊỌỊ *No meals* ✛ *E4.*

NORTH SCOTTSDALE

$$$$
RESORT
FAMILY

Fairmont Scottsdale Princess. Home of the Tournament Players Club Stadium golf course and the Phoenix Open, this resort covers 450 breathtakingly landscaped acres of desert. **Pros:** upscale favorite, especially with families; extras like in-room espresso machines; close to shopping. **Cons:** sprawling campus can be difficult to navigate; there is a parking charge. $ *Rooms from: $499* ⊠ *7575 E. Princess Dr., North Scottsdale* ☎ *480/585–4848* ⊕ *www.scottsdaleprincess.com* ➾ *505 rooms, 69 casitas, 74 suites* ỊỌỊ *No meals* ✛ *E1.*

$$$$
RESORT
Fodor's Choice
★

Four Seasons Resort Scottsdale at Troon North. A resort in every sense of the word, Four Seasons Scottsdale is tucked in the shadows of Pinnacle Peak, near the popular hiking trail, and features large, casita-style rooms with separate sitting and sleeping areas as well as fireplaces, and balconies or patios. **Pros:** amazing service; breathtaking views. **Cons:** far from everything (but maybe that's a good thing). $ *Rooms from: $449* ⊠ *10600 E. Crescent Moon Dr., North Scottsdale* ☎ *480/515–5700, 866/207-9696* ⊕ *www.fourseasons.com/scottsdale* ➾ *188 rooms, 22 suites* ỊỌỊ *No meals* ✛ *F1.*

$$$$
RESORT
FAMILY
Fodor's Choice
★

Westin Kierland Resort & Spa. Original artwork by Arizona artists is displayed throughout the Westin Kierland, and the spacious rooms all have balconies or patios with views of the mountains or the resort's water park and tubing river, where kids can enjoy programs organized by age group. **Pros:** bagpipers stroll around the courtyard at sunset; amazing beds and bedding; organic superfood menu; programs for kids' photography and scuba certification. **Cons:** bagpipers can be noisy; adults' pool very close to kids' area. $ *Rooms from: $679* ⊠ *6902 E. Greenway Pkwy.* ☎ *480/624–1000, 800/354-5892* ⊕ *www.kierlandresort. com* ➾ *732 rooms, 55 suites, 32 casitas* ỊỌỊ *No meals* ✛ *E1.*

$$
HOTEL

Wingate by Wyndham Scottsdale. Located right off the 101 freeway, this affordable hotel is an ideal base of operations; cool and modern throughout, it has clean, large, simply decorated rooms. **Pros:** clean and spacious rooms; comfortable beds; good price for location. **Cons:**

Hyatt Regency Scottsdale

FireSky Resort & Spa

Royal Palms Resort & Spa

Hotel Palomar Phoenix

Sanctuary Camelback Mountain

Pointe Hilton Squaw Peak Resort

The Phoenician

The Westin Kierland Resort & Spa

JW Marriott Desert Ridge Resort & Spa

Four Seasons Scottsdale at Troon North

more practical than perfect, primarily for business clientele. [$] *Rooms from: $189* ✉ *14255 N. 87th St., North Scottsdale* ☎ *480/922–6500, 877/570–6500* 🌐 *www.wingatehotels.com* 🛏 *82 rooms, 35 suites* 🍴 *Breakfast* ✥ *F2.*

OLD TOWN

$$$ HOTEL 🏨 **Hotel Indigo.** This Scottsdale spot is perfect for what it is: simple, modern, and, most of all, centrally located to all of Scottsdale's best bars, nightclubs, and venues where people flock to see and be seen. **Pros:** great value; ideal Scottsdale location; pet-friendly. **Cons:** noise, whether it's from music in the lobby, people in the room next door, or the bar down the street, can be annoying. [$] *Rooms from: $261* ✉ *4415 N. Civic Center Plaza, Old Town* ☎ *480/941–9400* 🌐 *www.scottsdalehiphotel.com* 🛏 *117 rooms, 9 suites* 🍴 *No meals* ✥ *F4.*

$$ HOTEL 🏨 **Hotel Valley Ho.** This Scottsdale hot-spot hotel was recently restored to its former '50s fabulousness, and the rooms don't disappoint with retro furnishings and styling. **Pros:** retro decor; great history; hip, youthful style. **Cons:** busy location; occasionally rowdy weekend crowd. [$] *Rooms from: $199* ✉ *6850 E. Main St., Old Town* ☎ *480/248–2000, 866/882–4484* 🌐 *www.hotelvalleyho.com* 🛏 *185 rooms, 6 suites* 🍴 *No meals* ✥ *E4.*

$$$$ HOTEL 🏨 **W Scottsdale.** A taste of youthful but sophisticated New York elegance, this hot-spot hotel, located in the heart of Scottsdale's shopping and social scene, caters to the wants and needs of the fashionable but fickle traveler with "Whatever/Whenever" service that provides guests with anything they want ("as long as it's legal!"). **Pros:** unpretentious elegance right across from Scottsdale Fashion Square. **Cons:** the youthful exuberance that makes the hotel so much fun during the day can get a little noisy at night. [$] *Rooms from: $699* ✉ *7277 E. Camelback Rd., Old Town* ☎ *480/970–2100* 🌐 *www.wscottsdalehotel.com* 🛏 *230 rooms, 33 suites* 🍴 *No meals* ✥ *E4.*

TEMPE AND AROUND

CHANDLER

$$$$ RESORT FAMILY 🏨 **Sheraton Wild Horse Pass Resort & Spa.** On the grounds of the Gila River Indian community, 11 miles south of Sky Harbor Airport, the culture and heritage of the Pima and Maricopa tribes are reflected in every aspect of this tranquil property. **Pros:** great views and service; peaceful; good for families and older travelers looking to escape urban chaos. **Cons:** conferences can sometimes overrun the place; beautiful hand-hewn guest room doors are very loud when they slam shut. [$] *Rooms from: $549* ✉ *5594 W. Wild Horse Pass Blvd., Chandler* ☎ *602/225–0100* 🌐 *www.wildhorsepassresort.com* 🛏 *474 rooms, 26 suites* 🍴 *No meals* ✥ *C6.*

TEMPE

$$ HOTEL 🏨 **aloft Tempe.** True to its name, this hip hotel, located right on Tempe's Rio Salado waterfront, features loft-inspired design, with modern, minimalist decor. **Pros:** flat-screen TVs; eco-friendly; highly social; adjacent to Town Lake and ASU action. **Cons:** social lodging experience not for everyone. [$] *Rooms from: $179* ✉ *951 E. Playa Del Norte Dr.*

☎ *480/621–3300, 888/867–7492* ⊕ *www.alofthotels.com/tempe* ⪢ *136 rooms* ⦿ *No meals* ✣ *E6.*

$$$
HOTEL

▦ **Tempe Mission Palms.** A handsome, casual lobby and an energetic young staff set the tone at this three-story courtyard hotel. **Pros:** nice hotel with friendly service and a rooftop pool; right at the center of ASU and Mill Avenue activity. **Cons:** all that activity can be bad for light sleepers. [$] *Rooms from: $299* ⊠ *60 E. 5th St.* ☎ *480/894–1400, 800/547–8705* ⊕ *www.missionpalms.com* ⪢ *291 rooms, 12 suites* ⦿ *No meals* ✣ *E6.*

NIGHTLIFE AND THE ARTS

Over the past decade the Valley of the Sun has gone from a "cow town" to "now town," and the nightlife and culture options are no exception. Downtown Phoenix and Scottsdale are especially packed with entertainment choices.

NIGHTLIFE

From brewpubs, sports bars, and coffeehouses to dance clubs, mega-concerts, and country venues, the Valley of the Sun offers nightlife of all types. Nightclubs, comedy clubs, upscale lounges, and wine bars abound in Downtown Phoenix, along Camelback Road in North Central Phoenix, and in Scottsdale and Tempe, as well as the other suburbs.

Among music and dancing styles, country-and-western has the longest tradition here. Jazz venues, rock clubs, and hotel lounges are also numerous and varied. Phoenix continues to get hipper and more cosmopolitan, so behind the bar you're just as likely to find a mixologist as a bartender. There are also more than 30 gay and lesbian bars, primarily on 7th Avenue, 7th Street, and the stretch of Camelback Road between the two.

You can find listings and reviews in the *New Times* free weekly newspaper, distributed Wednesday, or in the *Arizona Republic* newspaper, also online at ⊕ *www.azcentral.com,* the paper's website. The local gay scene is covered in *Echo Magazine,* which you can pick up all over town.

DOWNTOWN PHOENIX
BARS AND LOUNGES
CityScape. The best place to take part in Downtown Phoenix's thriving nightlife, CityScape offers a mix of clubs, entertainment, restaurants, and shopping, all within steps of downtown's hotels and sports arenas. ⊠ *1 E. Washington St., Downtown Phoenix* ⊕ *www.cityscapephoenix.com.*

Majerle's Sports Grill. Operated by former Suns basketball player Dan Majerle, this sports bar offers a comprehensive menu for pre- and post-game celebrations as well as some of the best people-watching potential in town. ⊠ *24 N. 2nd St., Downtown Phoenix* ☎ *602/253–0118* ⊕ *www.majerles.com.*

Rose & Crown. Next to two of the Valley's major sports complexes and inside a historic home, the Rose & Crown serves hearty, traditional, English pub grub—fish-and-chips, bangers and mash, and shepherd's pie—with equally hearty beers to wash it down. Expect a wait on game and special-event nights. ✉ *628 E. Adams St., at 7th St., Downtown Phoenix* ☎ *602/256–0223* ⊕ *www.theroseandcrownaz.com.*

Seamus McCaffrey's Irish Pub. Enjoy one of the dozen European brews on draft at this fun and friendly place. It also has the largest Scotch collection in Arizona. A small kitchen turns out traditional Irish fare. ✉ *18 W. Monroe St., Downtown Phoenix* ☎ *602/253–6081* ⊕ *www. seamusmccaffreys.com.*

COFFEEHOUSES

Lux Central. Decorated with local art and retro furniture, Lux is an eclectic gathering place where artists, architects, and downtown businesspeople enjoy excellent classic European espresso drinks. ✉ *4404 N. Central, Downtown Phoenix* ☎ *602/696–9976* ⊕ *www.luxcoffee.com.*

COMEDY

Stand Up Live. This downtown comedy club features national acts on Thursday, Friday, Saturday, and Sunday nights. ✉ *50 W. Jefferson St., Downtown Phoenix* ☎ *480/719–6100* ⊕ *standuplive.com.*

GAY AND LESBIAN BARS

Amsterdam. This bar attracts a young crowd that wants to see and be seen; it's where Phoenix's beautiful gay people hang out. ✉ *718 N. Central Ave., Downtown Phoenix* ☎ *602/258–6122.*

GREATER PHOENIX

BARS AND LOUNGES

FEZ on Central. This place is a stylish restaurant by day and a gay-friendly, hip hot spot by night. The sleek interior and fancy drinks make you feel uptown, while the happy-hour prices and location keep this place grounded. ✉ *3815 N. Central Ave., North Central Phoenix* ☎ *602/287–8700* ⊕ *www.fezoncentral.com.*

Fodor'sChoice ★ **Jade Bar.** This spot has spectacular views of Paradise Valley and Camelback Mountain; an upscale, modern bar lined with windows; and a relaxing fireplace-lighted patio. ✉ *5700 E. McDonald Dr., Sanctuary Camelback Mountain resort, Paradise Valley* ☎ *480/948–2100* ⊕ *www. sanctuaryoncamelback.com.*

Postino Wine Cafe. Postino has grown from a small neighborhood haunt into three separate destinations throughout the Valley. More than 40 wines are poured by the glass. Order a few grazing items off the menu (the bruschetta is unmatched by any in the Valley) and settle in, or carry out a bottle of wine, hunk of cheese, and loaf of bread for a twilight picnic. ✉ *3939 E. Campbell Ave., Camelback Corridor* ☎ *602/852–3939* ⊕ *www.postinowinecafe.com.*

BLUES, JAZZ, AND ROCK

Fodor'sChoice ★ **Char's Has the Blues.** This is one of the Valley's top blues clubs, with nightly bands. ✉ *4631 N. 7th Ave., North Central Phoenix* ☎ *602/230–0205* ⊕ *www.charshastheblues.com.*

Rhythm Room. Excellent local and national rock and blues artists perform here seven nights a week. ✉ *1019 E. Indian School Rd., North Central Phoenix* ☎ *602/265–4842* ⊕ *www.rhythmroom.com.*

2

CASINOS

Fort McDowell Casino. This casino is popular with the resort crowd. In addition to 150,000 square feet of slot machines, bingo, and keno games, the casino is one of the favorites in town for poker players. Take advantage of the free Valley-wide shuttle. ✉ *AZ 87 at Fort McDowell Rd., Fountain Hills* ☎ *800/843–3678* ⊕ *www.fortmcdowellcasino.com.*

GAY AND LESBIAN BARS

Cash Inn Country. This bar has an eclectic clientele of women and features music just as diverse, from Latin to country. ✉ *2140 E. McDowell Rd.* ☎ *602/244–9943* ⊕ *www.cashinncountry.net.*

Charlie's. A longtime favorite of local gay men, Charlie's has a country-western look (cowboy hats are the accessory of choice) and friendly staff. ✉ *727 W. Camelback Rd., North Central Phoenix* ☎ *602/265–0224* ⊕ *www.charliesphoenix.com.*

SCOTTSDALE

BARS AND LOUNGES

AZ88. This spot is great for feasting on huge portions of food and lavish quantities of liquor, but also for feasting your eyes on the fabulous people who flock here on weekend nights. It's a great stop before and after an Old Town event or a night of partying, Scottsdale style. ✉ *7353 Scottsdale Mall, Scottsdale Civic Center, Old Town* ☎ *480/994–5576* ⊕ *www.az88.com.*

Dos Gringos. A kitschy indoor-outdoor cantina, Dos Gringos will remind you of trips over the Mexican border, or at least spring break. Crowds (mostly college students and twentysomethings) swig margaritas and beer in a multilevel courtyard surrounded by TVs and limestone fountains. ✉ *4209 N. Craftsman Ct., Old Town* ☎ *480/423–3800* ⊕ *www. dosgringosaz.com.*

Kazimierz World Wine Bar. Enter this bar through a door marked "The Truth Is Inside," beyond which lies a dark, cavelike wine bar with comfy chairs and good music. ✉ *7137 E. Stetson Dr., Old Town* ☎ *480/946–3004* ⊕ *www.kazbar.net.*

Salty Senorita. This spot is known more for its extensive margarita selection and lively patio crowd than for its food. The restaurant-bar touts 51 different margaritas—with some recipes so secret they won't tell you what goes in them. Try the El Presidente or the Chupacabra. ✉ *3636 N. Scottsdale Rd., Old Town* ☎ *480/946–7258* ⊕ *www.saltysenorita.com.*

CASINOS

Casino Arizona at Salt River. This is the largest casino in the area, with five restaurants, four lounges, a sports bar, a 250-seat theater featuring live performances, two large blackjack rooms, and a keno parlor. There's live music and dancing most nights. ✉ *524 N. 92nd St., North Scottsdale* ☎ *480/850–7777* ⊕ *www.casinoarizona.com.*

Casino Arizona at Talking Stick Resort. Locals come here for blackjack, poker, keno, more than 200 slot machines, and a dash of Las Vegas–like nightlife. ✉ *9800 E. Indian Bend Rd.* ☎ *480/850–7777* ⊕ *www. talkingstickresort.com.*

COMEDY

The Comedy Spot. Catch local and national stand-up talent at this venue. They also offer classes for wannabe comedians on Sunday. ✉ *7117 E. 3rd Ave., Old Town* ☎ *480/945-4422* ⊕ *www.thecomedyspot.net.*

Jester'Z Improv Comedy. The improv troupe performs family-friendly comedy shows for a youngish crowd on Friday and Saturday nights. ✉ *7117 E. McDowell Rd.* ☎ *480/423-0120* ⊕ *www.jesterzimprov.com.*

> ### GAMBLING
>
> There are casinos on Native American reservations around the Valley of the Sun. Compared with Las Vegas, they offer smaller venues and a low-key atmosphere. The casinos follow Arizona gaming laws, such as no betting cash—chips only.

COUNTRY-AND-WESTERN

Fodor's Choice ★ **Greasewood Flat.** It's not fancy; in fact, it's downright ramshackle, but Greasewood Flat's burgers are delicious and the crowds friendly. There's a dance floor with live music Thursday through Sunday. In winter, wear jeans and a jacket, since everything is outside; to keep warm, folks congregate around fires burning in halved oil drums. ✉ *27375 N. Alma School Pkwy., North Scottsdale* ☎ *480/585-9430* ⊕ *www.greasewoodflat.net.*

Handlebar-J. This is a lively restaurant and bar with a Western line-dancing, 10-gallon-hat–wearing crowd. ✉ *7116 E. Becker Lane* ☎ *480/948-0110* ⊕ *www.handlebarj.com.*

DANCE CLUBS

Axis/Radius. This spot is the dress-to-impress locale where you can party at side-by-side clubs connected by a glass catwalk. ✉ *7340 E. Indian Plaza Rd.* ☎ *480/970-1112* ⊕ *www.axis-radius.com.*

GAY AND LESBIAN BARS

B.S. West. Tucked behind a shopping center on Scottsdale's main shopping drag, B.S. West draws a stylish, well-heeled gay crowd. ✉ *7125 E. 5th Ave., Old Town* ☎ *480/945-9028* ⊕ *www.bswest.com.*

MICROBREWERIES

Rock Bottom Brewery. The beer here is brewed on the premises and there's tasty pub grub—start with the giant soft pretzels served with spicy spinach dip. Watch out: the bill tends to rack up quickly. ✉ *21001 N. Tatum Blvd.* ☎ *480/513-9125* ⊕ *www.rockbottom.com.*

TEMPE AND AROUND

BARS AND LOUNGES

Casey Moore's Oyster House. A laid-back institution where students, hippies, and families come together, Casey Moore's is in a 1910 house rumored to be haunted by ghosts. Enjoy more than two-dozen beers on tap and fresh oysters at this Irish pub–style favorite. ✉ *850 S. Ash Ave.* ☎ *480/968-9935* ⊕ *www.caseymoores.com.*

The Monastery. You grill your own burgers and nosh on picnic food at this casual beer and wine pub. You can also play horseshoes, chess, or volleyball. ✉ *4810 E. McKellips, Mesa* ☎ *480/474-4477* ⊕ *www.realfunbar.com.*

2

CASINOS

Gila River Casino Wild Horse Pass. Part of the Wild Horse Pass Hotel & Casino, this casino includes 500 slots, live poker, blackjack, keno, and complimentary soft drinks. ⊠ *5040 Wild Horse Pass Blvd., Chandler* ☎ *800/946–4452* ⊕ *www.wingilariver.com.*

COMEDY

The Tempe Improv. Part of a national chain, The Tempe Improv showcases better-known headliners from Thursday to Sunday. Get there early for good seats. ⊠ *930 E. University Dr.* ☎ *480/921–9877* ⊕ *www.tempeimprov.com.*

DANCE CLUBS

School of Rock. A favorite for Arizona State University students, this is one of the most boisterous places on Mill Avenue. Wind and grind to a mix of techno and rock until the wee hours of the morning. ⊠ *411 S. Mill Ave.* ☎ *480/966–3573* ⊕ *www.schoolofrockmillave.com.*

MICROBREWERIES

Four Peaks Brewing Company. This beer spot is the former redbrick home of Bordens Creamery. Wash down an ample supply of house-made brews on tap (including some seasonal specialties) with pub grub—pizza, wings, and burgers fill the menu. There's also a location in Scottsdale. ⊠ *1340 E. 8th St.* ☎ *480/303–9967* ⊕ *www.fourpeaks.com.*

SanTan Brewing Company. Come here for good food with great beer and an energetic pub atmosphere without the tired, hole-in-the-wall or overly commercial feel. Wash down some SanTan wings and a stuffed burger with a SanTan IPA. ⊠ *8 San Marcos Pl., Chandler* ☎ *480/917–8700* ⊕ *www.santanbrewing.com.*

THE ARTS

For weekly listings of theater, arts, and music, check out Thursday's *Arizona Republic*, pick up a free issue of the independent weekly *New Times*, or check out *Where Phoenix/Scottsdale Magazine*, available free in most hotels. A good online source of information on events in the Valley is the *Arizona Republic's* website (⊕ *www.azcentral.com*).

TICKETS **Ticketmaster.** You can buy tickets for nearly every event in the Valley through Ticketmaster. ☎ *800/745–3000* ⊕ *www.ticketmaster.com.*

MAJOR PERFORMANCE VENUES

To feed its growing tourism industry Phoenix has cooked up enticing entertainment venues that attract everything from major-league sporting events to the hottest music acts and the most raved-about theater productions.

DOWNTOWN AND GREATER PHOENIX

Ashley Furniture HomeStore Pavilion. This outdoor amphitheater books major live concerts. ⊠ *2121 N. 83rd Ave.* ☎ *602/254–7200.*

Celebrity Theatre. This 2,600-seat theater-in-the-round hosts concerts and other live performances. ⊠ *440 N. 32nd St.* ☎ *602/267–1600* ⊕ *www.celebritytheatre.com.*

Frank Lloyd Wright's architectural legacy in the Valley of the Sun includes ASU Gammage Auditorium in Tempe.

Comerica Theatre. Phoenix's high-tech, state-of-the-art entertainment venue morphs from an intimate Broadway stage setup to a concert hall seating 5,000. There are great views from almost every seat. ⊠ *400 W. Washington St., Downtown Phoenix* ☎ *602/379–2800* ⊕ *www. comericatheatre.com.*

Herberger Theater Center. The permanent home of the Arizona Theatre Company and Actors Theatre of Phoenix; this theater also hosts performances of visiting dance troupes, orchestras, and Broadway shows. ⊠ *222 E. Monroe St., Downtown Phoenix* ☎ *602/254–7399* ⊕ *www. herbergertheater.org.*

Orpheum Theatre. The Spanish-colonial Orpheum Theatre, built in 1927 and renovated throughout the '90s, is a glamorous theater showcasing ballet, theater, and film festivals. The Phoenix Convention Center coordinates ticketing for the facility. ⊠ *203 W. Adams St., Downtown Phoenix* ☎ *602/262–7272* ⊕ *phoenix.gov/conventioncenter/orpheum/index.html.*

Symphony Hall. Facing the Herberger Theater is Symphony Hall, home of the Phoenix Symphony and Arizona Opera. ⊠ *75 N. 2nd St., Downtown Phoenix* ☎ *602/495–1999* ⊕ *www.phoenixsymphony.org.*

SCOTTSDALE

Kerr Cultural Center. Smaller theater, dance, and jazz performances are showcased at this center. ⊠ *6110 N. Scottsdale Rd.* ☎ *480/596–2660* ⊕ *www.asukerr.com.*

Scottsdale Center for the Performing Arts. This organization hosts cultural events on the Scottsdale Mall as well as year-round performances in two intimate theater settings. ⊠ *7380 E. 2nd St., Old Town* ☎ *480/499–8587*

⊕ *www.scottsdaleperformingarts.
org.*

TEMPE AND AROUND

ASU Gammage. Frank Lloyd Wright designed the ASU Gammage Auditorium, which presents more Broadway shows outside the Big Apple than any other venue in the nation. ⊠ *Arizona State University, Mill Ave. at Apache Blvd.* ☎ *480/965–3434* ⊕ *www.asugammage.com.*

Chandler Center for the Arts. To see some of the nation's most popular touring performances for families and children, check out the events schedule at the Chandler Center for the Arts. ⊠ *250 N. Arizona Ave., Chandler* ☎ *480/782–2680* ⊕ *www.chandlercenter.org.*

EXPERIENCE THE WILD WEST

In addition to the state and county fairs, and some seasonal shows, there are several places in and around Phoenix to get a taste of what the West was like way back when. Rawhide and the Rockin' R Ranch, closer to town, are more kid-friendly, while Pioneer Living History Village and Goldfield Ghost Town (⤳ see Apache Trail) are more sedate, with a stronger emphasis on authentic historic buildings.

Crescent Ballroom. This small music venue only accommodates 350 people, but has a loyal following for its eclectic calendar of indie acts. There is a lounge open nightly. ⊠ *308 N. 2nd Ave., Downtown Phoenix, Phoenix* ☎ *602/716–2222* ⊕ *www.crescentphx.com.*

Marquee Theatre. This venue hosts mainly headlining rock-and-roll entertainers. ⊠ *730 N. Mill Ave.* ☎ *480/829–0707* ⊕ *www.luckymanonline.com.*

Mesa Arts Center. This arts organization has risen to the demand for culture and creative art and is fast becoming one of the Valley's top destinations for exhibits, visual-art performances, and A-list concerts. ⊠ *1 E. Main St., Mesa* ☎ *480/644–6500* ⊕ *www.mesaartscenter.com.*

CLASSICAL MUSIC

Arizona Opera. This company stages an opera season in both Tucson and Phoenix. The Phoenix season runs from October to March at Symphony Hall. ⊠ *75 N. 2nd St., Downtown Phoenix, Phoenix* ☎ *602/266–7464* ⊕ *www.azopera.com.*

Phoenix Symphony Orchestra. The resident company at Symphony Hall, the Phoenix Symphony Orchestra features orchestral works from classical and contemporary composers, a chamber series, composer festivals, and outdoor pops concerts. The season runs September through May. ⊠ *75 N. 2nd St., Downtown Phoenix, Phoenix* ☎ *602/495–1999, 800/776–9080* ⊕ *www.phoenixsymphony.org.*

DANCE

Ballet Arizona. The state's professional ballet company presents a full season of classical and contemporary works (including pieces commissioned for the company) in Tucson and Phoenix. The season runs from October through May. ☎ *602/381–1096* ⊕ *www.balletaz.org.*

Rawhide Western Town, or another Wild West show with dinner, is a great recipe for family fun.

THEATER

Actors Theatre of Phoenix. The resident theater troupe at the Herberger Theater Center presents a full season of drama, comedy, and musical productions from September through May. ✉ *222 E. Monroe, Downtown Phoenix, Phoenix* ☎ *602/252–8497* ⊕ *www.atphx.org.*

Arizona Theatre Company. Based in Tuscon, the Arizona Theatre Company also performs at the Herberger Theater Center. Productions, held from September through June, range from classic dramas to musicals and new works by emerging playwrights. ✉ *222 E. Monroe, Downtown Phoenix, Phoenix* ☎ *602/256–6995* ⊕ *www.aztheatreco.org.*

The Black Theatre Troupe. This troupe presents original and contemporary dramas and musical revues, as well as adventurous adaptations, between September and May. ✉ *Downtown Phoenix, Phoenix* ☎ *602/254–2151* ⊕ *www.blacktheatretroupe.org.*

FAMILY **Childsplay.** The state's theater company for young audiences and families, Childsplay holds performances during the school year at Tempe Center for the Arts. ✉ *Tempe Center for the Arts, 700 W. Rio Salado Pkwy.* ☎ *480/921–5700* ⊕ *www.childsplayaz.org.*

FAMILY **Great Arizona Puppet Theatre.** With performances in a historic building featuring lots of theater and exhibit space, the Great Arizona Puppet Theatre mounts a yearlong cycle of inventive puppet productions that change frequently. ✉ *302 W. Latham St., Downtown Phoenix, Phoenix* ☎ *602/262–2050* ⊕ *www.azpuppets.org.*

Phoenix Theatre. Across the courtyard from the Phoenix Art Museum, Phoenix Theatre stages musical and dramatic performances. ✉ *100 E.*

McDowell Rd., Central Phoenix, Phoenix ☎ *602/254–2151* ⊕ *www.phoenixtheatre.com.*

WILD WEST SHOWS

FAMILY

Fodor's Choice

★

Rawhide Western Town and Steakhouse at Wild Horse Pass. A Valley favorite for more than four decades, Rawhide Western Town calls the 2,400-acre master-planned Wild Horse Pass Development in the Gila River Indian Community home. Featuring its legendary steak house and saloon, Main Street and all of its retail shops, and the Six Gun Theater, Rawhide is the kitschiest place in town to experience the Old West. Enjoy canal rides along the Gila River Riverwalk, train rides, and a Native American village honoring the history and culture of the Akimel O'othom and Pee Posh tribes. Immerse yourself into the Wild West, where you can watch a stunt show featuring gunslingers, have a fellow guest arrested and tossed in jail, or watch trick roping performed by the pros. ⊠ *5700 W. North Loop Rd., Gila River Indian Community, Chandler* ☎ *480/502–5600* ⊕ *www.rawhide.com.*

FAMILY

Rockin' R Ranch. This ranch includes a petting zoo, a reenactment of a Wild West shoot-out, and—the main attraction—a nightly cookout with a Western stage show. Pan for gold or take a wagon ride until the "vittles" are served, followed by music and entertainment. ⊠ *6136 E. Baseline Rd., Mesa* ☎ *480/832–1539* ⊕ *www.rockinr.net.*

SHOPPING

Since its resorts began multiplying in the 1930s and '40s, Phoenix has acquired many high-fashion clothiers and leisure-wear boutiques, but you can still find the Western clothes that in many parts of town still dominate the fashion. Jeans and boots, cotton shirts and dresses, 10-gallon hats, and bola ties (the state's official neckwear) are still the staples. On the scene as well are the arts of the Southwest's true natives—Navajo weavers, sand painters, and silversmiths; Hopi weavers and kachina-doll carvers; Pima and Tohono O'odham (Papago) basket makers and potters; and many more. Inspired by the region's rich cultural traditions, contemporary artists have flourished here, making Phoenix—particularly Scottsdale, a city with more art galleries than gas stations—one of the Southwest's largest art centers alongside Santa Fe, New Mexico.

Today's shoppers find the best of the old and the new—all presented with Southwestern style. Upscale stores, one-of-a-kind shops, and outlet malls sell the latest fashions, cowboy collectibles, handwoven rugs, traditional Mexican folk art, and contemporary turquoise jewelry.

Most of the Valley's power shopping is concentrated in central Phoenix, Old Town Scottsdale, and the Kierland area in North Scottsdale, but auctions and antiques shops cluster in odd places—and as treasure hunters know, you've always got to keep your eyes open.

GREATER PHOENIX

CAMELBACK CORRIDOR

SHOPPING CENTER

Biltmore Fashion Park. Macy's, Saks Fifth Avenue, and Ralph Lauren anchor more than 70 stores and upscale boutiques in this posh, parklike setting. It's accessible from the Camelback Esplanade and the Ritz Carlton by a pedestrian tunnel that runs beneath Camelback Road. ⊠ *2502 E Camelback Rd., Camelback Corridor* ☎ *602/955–8400* ⊕ *www.shopbiltmore.com.*

FARMERS' MARKETS

To find the fresh wares of a Valley farmers' market, visit ⊕ *www. arizonafarmersmarkets.com,* a comprehensive calendar listing started and maintained by long-time market coordinators Dee and John Logan.

MARKET

Camelback Market. On Saturdays from 9 am to 1 pm, October through May, some of the Valley's tastiest creations, from crepes to paella to panini, can be found in the parking lot of Vincent on Camelback, at the Camelback Market. The market also features a wine vendor and sellers of independent culinary curios like fresh pesto, honey, jam, and wines. ⊠ *3930 E. Camelback Rd., Camelback Corridor* ⊕ *www. vincentsoncamelback.com.*

NORTH CENTRAL PHOENIX

ARTS AND CRAFTS

Drumbeat Indian Arts. This small, interesting shop specializes in Native American music, movies, books, drums, and crafts supplies. If you're lucky, you might find authentic fry bread and Navajo tacos being cooked in the parking lot on weekends. ⊠ *4143 N. 16th St., North Central Phoenix* ☎ *602/266–4823* ⊕ *www.drumbeatindianarts.com.*

Fodor's Choice ★ **The Heard Museum Shop.** The shop at the Heard Museum is hands-down the best place in town for Southwestern Native American and other crafts, both traditional and modern. Prices tend to be high, but quality is assured, with many one-of-a-kind items among the collection of rugs, kachina dolls, pottery, and other crafts; there's also a wide selection of lower-priced gifts. The Heard Museum North Scottsdale also has a gift shop. ⊠ *2301 N. Central Ave., North Central Phoenix* ☎ *602/252–8840* ⊕ *www.heard.org.*

FOOD AND WINE

AJ's Fine Foods. The Valley's grandest upscale grocery store, AJ's is a great place to fill your basket with exclusive local creations ranging from salsas and sauces to spice mixes. It's possible to spend hours at any of the 11 identical Valley locations. It's also possible to spend far more money than you would at an average grocery store, but the vast inventory of unusual products not found together anywhere else and the first-class, one-stop shopping experience make it all worthwhile. The wine selection is among the best in town, and the sommelier-quality staff will gladly offer suggestions. Be sure to partake of the fresh, chef-prepared food offerings, like homemade soups, salad, pizza, specialty sandwiches, and gourmet take-out entrées from the bistro. ⊠ *5017 N. Central Ave., North Central Phoenix* ☎ *602/230–7015* ⊕ *www.ajsfinefoods.com.*

VINTAGE CLOTHING AND FURNITURE

Home Again. This down-home store buys and sells vintage and modern home furnishings and antiques. ✉ *4302 N. 7th Ave., North Central Phoenix* ☎ *602/424–0488.*

Melrose Vintage. The cheerful, doll-house-like yellow exterior at this store is not the only thing that makes it memorable. The no-non-sense staff knows its stuff, which includes tasteful and fun low- to high-end shabby-chic furnishings. The store is closed Sunday to Tues-day. ✉ *4238 N. 7th Ave., North Central Phoenix* ☎ *602/636–0300* ⊕ *shopmelrosevintage.com.*

PARADISE VALLEY

ARTS AND CRAFTS

Fodor'sChoice ★ **Cosanti Originals.** This is the studio where architect Paolo Soleri's famous bronze and ceramic wind chimes are made and sold. You can watch the craftspeople at work, then pick out your own—prices are surprisingly reasonable. ✉ *6433 Doubletree Ranch Rd., Paradise Valley* ☎ *800/752–3187, 480/948–6145* ⊕ *www. cosanti.com.*

FOOD AND WINE

Sportsman's Fine Wines & Spirits. This wine shop is the place to go to "lift your spirits." Sportsman's stocks fine wines and rare beverage finds from both local and international sources. They also sell cheeses and other delicious wine accompaniments including panini sandwiches, roasted garlic, hummus, bruschetta, and baked feta. ✉ *3205 E. Camel-back Rd.* ☎ *602/955–9463* ⊕ *www.sportsmans4wine.com.*

SOUTH PHOENIX

COFCO Chinese Cultural Center. Adorned with replicas of pagodas, statues, and traditional Chinese gardens, this shopping and dining facility is the place to find Asian restaurants, gift shops, and the Super L, a huge Asian grocery store. Take a stroll through the market's fish department—you'll forget you're in the desert. ✉ *668 N. 44th St.* ☎ *602/273–7268* ⊕ *www. phxchinatown.com.*

GLENDALE

A surprise to many visitors is the Old Towne district of suburban Glen-dale, with more than 80 antiques and collectibles shops nestled around historic Old Towne and Catlin Court, which are listed on the National Register of Historic Places.

Glendale Old Towne & Catlin Court. This antiques district has a plethora of shops and restaurants in colorful, century-old bungalows. Stroll the pedestrian-friendly streets and window shop, or have lunch at one of

---

VINTAGE FINDS

In certain parts of the Valley "old" is the new "new." The Melrose District, on 7th Avenue between Indian School and Camelback roads in central Phoenix, is bank-ing on its Old Phoenix charm in a slow but steady race to become the next hip historic neighbor-hood. New faces on old buildings are the perfect welcome mat for progress with forthcoming lofts, condos, eateries, and big plans for public art, but the overall charm is anchored by its variety of vintage stores. Open hours are generally 10–5, and many stores are closed Monday and Tuesday.

the neighborhood eateries to fuel up for some retail therapy. ⊠ *59th and Glendale Aves., Glendale.*

SCOTTSDALE

If you're looking for luxury, whether that's in the form of a priceless work of art or a perfectly fitting pair of jeans, head to Scottsdale. Filled with galleries, luxury boutiques, and more than enough sites to purchase a pair of cowboy boots, Scottsdale takes Western chic to a whole new level.

Scottsdale Fashion Square. This shopping complex is home to many luxury shops unique to Arizona. There are also Barney's, Nordstrom, Dillard's, Neiman Marcus, Macy's, Louis Vuitton, Tiffany, Cartier, and Gucci. A huge food court, restaurants, and a cineplex complete the picture. ⊠ *7014 East Camelback* ☎ *480/941-2140* ⊕ *www.fashionsquare.com.*

ANTIQUES AND COLLECTIBLES
NORTH SCOTTSDALE
SHOPPING CENTERS

Kierland Commons. Next to the Westin Kierland Resort is one of the city's most popular shopping areas. "Urban village" is the catchphrase for this outdoor pedestrian mall with restaurants and upscale chain retailers, among them J. Crew and Tommy Bahama. ⊠ *15205 N Kierland Blvd.* ☎ *480/348-1577* ⊕ *www.kierlandcommons.com.*

Scottsdale Quarter. Located across the street from Kierland Commons, this new outdoor mall creates a fantastic one-two punch for shoppers in search of fantastic food and dining. Stroll the largest Apple Store in the Valley, get bargain goods at H&M, and catch a luxury dine-in movie (you read that right) at iPic. ⊠ *15279 N. Scottsdale Rd., North Scottsdale, Scottsdale* ☎ *480/270-8123* ⊕ *www.scottsdalequarter.com.*

OLD TOWN
SHOPPING CENTER

Fodor's Choice ★ **Old Town Scottsdale.** This is the place to go for authentic Southwest-inspired gifts, clothing, art, and artifacts. Despite its massive modern neighbors, this area and its merchants have long respected and maintained the single-level brick storefronts that embody Scottsdale's upscale cow-town charm. More than 100 businesses meet just about any aesthetic want or need, including Gilbert Ortega, one of the premier places for fine Native American jewelry and art. Some of Scottsdale's best restaurants are also found in this pleasing maze of merchandizing. ⊠ *Between Goldwater Blvd., Brown Ave., 5th Ave. and 3rd St., Old Town.*

ARTS AND CRAFTS

Gilbert Ortega Indian Jewelry and Gallery. This retailer has many Native-American shops throughout Scottsdale. Prices are steep, but the products are authentic and the selection is among the best in town. ⊠ *7155 E. 5th Ave., Old Town* ☎ *480/941-9281.*

Fodor's Choice ★ **Wilde Meyer Galleries.** With two locations in Scottsdale and another in Tucson, this is the place to go for the true colors of the Southwest. In addition to one-of-a-kind paintings, the galleries also feature rustic, fine-art imports from around the state and the world, including furniture, sculptures, and jewelry. ⊠ *4142 N. Marshall Way, Old Town* ☎ *480/945–2323* ⊕ *www.wildemeyer.com.*

GIFTS

Kactus Jock. This somewhat kitschy Arizona souvenir store sells food, t-shirts, and some art. ⊠ *7233 E. Main St., Old Town* ☎ *480/945–3380* ⊕ *www.kactusjock.com.*

GO ANTIQUING

The central-Phoenix corridor, between 7th Street and 7th Avenue, has many antiques stores. Most shops sit north of Thomas and south of Camelback. Prices, though reasonable, are firm at most shops.

TEMPE AND AROUND

The East Valley cities of Tempe and Chandler are Phoenix's version of suburbia, offering large shopping malls that cater to families and teens. But don't knock 'em until you've tried 'em. Chandler's primary mall rivals the one in Scottsdale, and Tempe's outlet mall offers some of the best bargains in town—and the city's only aquarium.

CHANDLER

SHOPPING CENTERS

Chandler Fashion Center. This mall features anchor stores Nordstrom, Dillard's, Macy's, and Sears, along with more than 180 other national retail chains such as Coach, Pottery Barn, and the Cheesecake Factory. ⊠ *3111 W. Chandler Blvd., Chandler* ☎ *480/812–8488* ⊕ *www.shopchandlerfashioncenter.com.*

TEMPE

SHOPPING CENTERS

Arizona Mills. This mammoth retail outlet and entertainment destination features more than 175 outlet stores and sideshows, including Off 5th–Saks Fifth Avenue, and Last Call from Neiman Marcus. When you tire of bargain hunting, relax in the food court, cinemas, aquarium, or faux rainforest. ⊠ *5000 S. Arizona Mills Circle, I–10 and Baseline Rd.* ☎ *480/491–7300* ⊕ *www.arizonamills.com.*

Mill Avenue Shops. Named for the landmark Hayden Flour Mill, this is one of the Valley's favorite walk-and-shop experiences. Directly west of the Arizona State University campus and just steps from a Light Rail stop, Mill Avenue is an active melting pot of students, artists, residents, and tourists. Shops include some locally owned stores, mid-range chains, and countless bars and restaurants. The Valley Art Theater is a Mill Avenue institution and Tempe's home of indie cinema. Twice a year (in early December and March/April), the Mill Avenue area is the place to find indie arts and crafts when it hosts the Tempe Festival of the Arts. ⊠ *Mill Ave., between Rio Salado Pkwy. and University Dr.* ☎ *480/355–6060* ⊕ *www.millavenue.com.*

BOOKS

Fodor's Choice
★ **Changing Hands Bookstore.** This bookstore has a large selection of new and used books and often features special book-signings and other events with authors. ⊠ *6428 S. McClintock Dr.* ☎ *480/730–0205* ⊕ *www.changinghands.com.*

The Southwest continues to inspire contemporary artists. You can see some pieces yourself at the Wilde Meyer Galleries.

SPAS

There's no better place for relaxation than at one of Phoenix's rejuvenating resort spas. Many feature Native American–inspired treatments and use indigenous ingredients such as agave and desert clay.

If you're already preparing for a luxurious treatment at one of the Valley's renowned spas, make sure you get the most bang for the buck. Most resort spas offer complete access to spa facilities when you book a treatment. Indulge in such treats as private, rooftop pools, Swiss showers, eucalyptus-scented steam rooms, plunge pools, and more. Most also offer fitness classes and state-of-the-art workout facilities. Why book just a treatment when you could instead enjoy a whole day of pampering?

■TIP→ Be sure to ask about gratuity when you book your spa treatment. Many resorts automatically add 20% gratuity to the bill. To save a little money, consider booking a multi-treatment package. Often, these packages include built-in discounts and include gratuity. You could save up to 20% on your total bill.

Aji Spa at the Sheraton Wild Horse Pass Resort & Spa. A gem on the grounds of the Gila River Indian community, Aji incorporates its Native American surroundings into every aspect of the spa, from the name ("Aji" is Pima for sanctuary) to its Sonoran design and treatments. A complete spa experience awaits you, from the plunge pool to the steam room and exercise facilities. Therapists take extra care to explain the indigenous practices and philosophies behind your treatment, whether it's the luxurious Four Directions scrub or a soothing facial. Enjoy lunch at the always-healthy Spa Café, and relax poolside at the coed patio that overlooks the resort and surrounding desert. You might be just minutes from the hustle and bustle of the city, but this urban retreat thankfully feels much farther away. ⊠ *Sheraton Wild Horse Pass Resort & Spa, 5594 W. Wild Horse Pass Blvd., Chandler* ☎ *602/225–0100* ⊕ *www.wildhorsepassresort.com* ☞ *$135 50-minute massage or 50-minute facial; 6-hour spa day with body treatment, massage, lunch, facial, and hand and foot treatment from $530. Hair salon, hot tub (indoor), sauna, steam room. Gym with: cardiovascular machines, weight-training equipment. Services: aromatherapy, facials, hydrotherapy, massage, salon services, scrubs, Vichy shower, wraps. Classes and programs: Pilates, personal training.*

Alvadora at the Royal Palms Resort & Spa. It comes as no surprise that the on-site spa at a resort that has its own Director of Romance offers one of the most romantic spa experiences in Arizona. The full-service Alvadora Spa oozes intimacy; its couples' treatment rooms feature private patios as well as showers and tubs. Public areas include tranquil courtyards and retreat areas that offer a repose under the warm desert sun or in air-conditioned comfort. Treatments incorporate herbs, flowers, oils, and minerals from the Mediterranean—a nod to the resort's architecture—as well as orange-infused massages and facials, which are fitting, as the property was an orange grove before the resort's construction. ⊠ *5200 E. Camelback Rd., Camelback Corridor, Phoenix* ☎ *602/977-6400* ⊕ *www.royalpalmshotel.com* ☞ *$140 50-minute massage, 50-minute facial, or 50-minute orange blossom scrub. Custom spa day packages available. Hair salon, hot tub (indoor), steam room. Gym with: cardiovascular machines, weight-training equipment. Services: aromatherapy, facials, hydrotherapy, massage, salon services, scrubs, wraps. Classes and programs: meditation, personal training, Pilates, tai chi, yoga.*

Four Seasons Troon North Spa. While most think of the Four Seasons Troon North as an escape only for golfers, its spa proves that there's relaxation to be had away from the links. There are treatments especially for golfers, including a massage that incorporates warm golf balls and stretching to relieve a sub-par day. But there's plenty of pampering for those who enjoy life away from the greens. Massages and facials are administered with delicate precision, and body wraps nourish your skin after an exhilarating hike under the desert sun. Be sure to take advantage of the facility's full amenities, including the fitness center and steam room. ⊠ *10600 E. Crescent Moon Dr., North Scottsdale, Scottsdale* ☎ *480/515–5700* ⊕ *www.fourseasons.com/scottsdale* ☞ *$165 50-minute massage or 50-minute facial, 3-hour spa day with two 50-minute spa treatments, lunch, and a 25-minute spa treatment from $475. Hair salon, sauna, steam room. Gym with: cardiovascular machines, weight-training equipment. Services: aromatherapy, facials, massage, salon services, scrubs, wraps. Classes and programs: meditation, nature walk, personal training, Pilates, tai chi, yoga.*

Joya Spa at Montelucia Resort. This two-story spa offers a stairway to the heavens. Everything here is meticulously handcrafted, handpicked, or hand-placed to summon the healing spirits. Inspired by the resort's

Spanish and Moroccan designs, the spa features plush seating areas, quiet lounges with privacy draping, and a public sun deck. Offering Arizona's only hammam bathing ritual, the spa encourages visitors to linger and absorb the tranquil surroundings—the location at the base of Camelback Mountain doesn't hurt. If you're traveling with a group or searching for a romantic couples' escape, Joya offers a series of poolside treatment rooms that offer the ultimate in luxury and privacy. ✉ *4949 E. Lincoln Dr., Paradise Valley* ☎ *480/627–3200, 888/691–5692* ⊕ *www.joyaspa.com* ☞ *$149 50-minute massage or 50-minute facial, 3-hour spa day with choice of three 50-minute treatements from $365. Hair salon, sauna, pool (outdoor). Gym with: cardiovascular machines, weight-training equipment. Services: aromatherapy, aquatherapy, facials, massage, reflexology, salon services, scrubs, wraps. Classes and programs: guided hikes, personal training, Pilates, yoga.*

Jurlique Spa at FireSky Resort and Spa. With its relaxing interior, Jurlique focuses on repairing and restoring from within by relying on plant science and a combination of Eastern and Western spa philosophies. Keeping with the boutique FireSky Resort's green efforts, spa treatments incorporate natural products that are hypoallergenic and are not animal-tested. Your wallet will get some relaxation, too: While Jurlique is one of the smallest resort spas in town, it offers some of the most affordable treatments around. ✉ *4925 N. Scottsdale Rd., Scottsdale* ☎ *480/424–6072* ⊕ *www.fireskyresort.com* ☞ *$125 60-min massage or 60-min facial, 2-hr spa day with 60-min massage and facial from $240. Pool (outdoor). Gym with: cardiovascular machines, weight-training equipment. Services: aromatherapy, aquatherapy, facials, massage, scrubs.*

Fodor's Choice
★

Sanctuary Spa at Sanctuary Camelback Mountain. Savvy spa-goers continue to select Sanctuary as their destination of choice, and with good reason. This sleek spa has 12 Asian-inspired indoor-outdoor treatment rooms nestled at the base of Camelback Mountain. For a more intimate experience, indulge in the privacy of the couple's suite or the stone-walled Sanctum hideaway (only available in the winter and spring). A meditation garden is the perfect place to reflect and relax before or after your treatment; for a longer experience consider a four-day Satori Wellness retreat. Add a little sweat equity to your spa day with a customized Pilates reformer class, or a swim session guided by an Olympic gold medalist. ✉ *5700 E. McDonald Dr., Paradise Valley* ☎ *480/607-2326, 800/245-2051* ⊕ *www.sanctuaryoncamelback.com* ☞ *$150 60-minute massage or 60-minute facial, 4-hour spa day with 60-minute massage, 60-minute facial, 60-minute body treatment, manicure, and pedicure from $605. Hair salon, hot tub (indoor), pool (outdoor), steam room. Gym with: cardiovascular machines, weight-training equipment. Services: acupuncture, aromatherapy, aquatherapy, facials, hypnotherapy, massage, reflexology, salon services, scrubs, wraps. Classes and programs: aquaerobics, guided hikes, guided walks, meditation, nutritional counseling, personal training, stretching, swim instruction, Pilates, tai chi, yoga.*

The Spa at JW Marriott's Camelback Inn. One of the Valley's most popular spas blends Mediterranean and desert themes. Trained therapists will scrub, wrap, and polish your body to perfection, and use the finest products to massage your muscles and cleanse your pores. You'll want all the pampering after a one-on-one fitness session with one of the resort's trainers who specialize in Pilates and gyrokinesis. Refuel at Bloom, the on-site café, and finish your day at the outdoor heated lap pool. ⊠ *5402 E. Lincoln Dr., Scottsdale* ☎ *480/596–7040, 800/922–2635* ⊕ *www. camelbackspa.com* ☞ *$135 60-minute massage, $155 60-minute facial, 4-hour spa day with 60-minute massage, 60-minute facial, manicure, and pedicure from $360. Hair salon, pool (outdoor), sauna, steam room. Gym with: cardiovascular machines, weight-training equipment. Services: aromatherapy, aquatherapy, facials, massage, reflexology, salon services, scrubs, Vichy shower, wraps. Classes and programs: guided walks, meditation, personal training, stretching, Pilates, yoga.*

Fodor's Choice
★ **Spa Avania at the Hyatt Regency Scottsdale at Gainey Ranch.** The spa experience here is designed to match your internal clock; every treatment, meal, beverage, and moment is timed to be in tune with your body's natural rhythm. The gorgeous stone-tiled facility seeks to cleanse the body of unnatural stimuli and give equilibrium through the senses, the way nature intended. Don't feel like that standard spa music during your treatment? No worries. Choose the soothing tunes you want on your in-treatment room iPod. Conclude your day with a dip in the mineral pool, and inhale your worries away in the eucalyptus steam room. By day's end, you will indeed feel rejuvenated and back in rhythm. ⊠ *7500 E. Doubletree Ranch Rd., Scottsdale* ☎ *480/444–1234* ⊕ *www. scottsdale.hyatt.com* ☞ *$165 60-minute massage or 60-minute facial, 3-hour spa day with 60-minute massage, 60-minute facial, and 60-minute wrap from $490. Hair salon, hot tub (outdoor), pools (outdoor), sauna, steam room. Gym with: cardiovascular machines, weight-training equipment. Services: aquatherapy, facials, massage, salon services, scrubs, Vichy shower, wraps. Classes and programs: guided walks, meditation, personal training, stretching, Pilates, yoga.*

VH Spa at the Hotel Valley Ho. At the always hip Hotel Valley Ho, guests should feel comfortable entrusting renovation of the body and soul to the mod, colored-glass VH (Vitality Health) Spa. You can boost your treatments with a "flight" of antioxidants—what other people might call a glass of wine—because, hey, this is a vacation after all. If you don't feel like venturing south to the spa, you can get in-room treatments. Or, grab a cabana at the pool and get the five-star treatment there. ⊠ *6850 E. Main St., Old Town, Scottsdale* ☎ *480/248–2000* ⊕ *www. hotelvalleyho.com* ☞ *$125 60-minute massage or 60-minute facial. Hair salon, hot tub (outdoor), pool (outdoor), steam room. Gym with: cardiovascular machines, weight-training equipment. Services: acupuncture, aromatherapy, aquatherapy, facials, massage, reflexology, salon services. Classes and programs: guided hikes, Pilates, yoga.*

Fodor's Choice
★ **Willow Stream Spa at Fairmont Scottsdale Princess.** Perhaps one of the most romantic spa settings in the Valley, Willow Stream Spa is an ideal retreat for couples. A three-story experience, the spa offers more water than seems possible in a desert. Enjoy an afternoon at the rooftop pool—which also includes private cabanas—or cuddle with your loved one under the powerful waterfall that connects the men's and women's

locker facilities. Inside, the locker rooms feature plunge pools and hot tubs, aromatherapy rooms, saunas, and steam rooms. After all that relaxation, you're sure to build up an appetite. Good thing the spa café serves fantastic (and healthy) cuisine to enjoy indoors, or in the quaint outdoor atrium. ⊠ *Fairmont Scottsdale Princess Resort, 7575 E. Princess Dr., North Scottsdale, Scottsdale* ☎ *480/585–4848* ⊕ *www. willowstream.com/scottsdale* ☞ *$159 60-minute massage or 60-minute facial, 2-hour signature spa day head-to-toe body treatment $309. Hair salon, hot tub (outdoor), sauna, pool (outdoor), steam room. Gym with: cardiovascular machines, weight-training equipment. Services: aromatherapy, aquatherapy, facials, massage, reflexology, salon services, scrubs, wraps. Classes and programs: personal training, Pilates, tennis, yoga.*

SPORTS AND THE OUTDOORS

The mountains surrounding the Valley of the Sun are among its greatest assets, and outdoors enthusiasts have plenty of options within the city limits to pursue hiking, bird-watching, or mountain-biking passions. Piestewa Peak, north of Downtown Phoenix, is popular with hikers, and Camelback Mountain and the Papago Peaks are landmarks between Phoenix and Scottsdale. South of Downtown are the much less lofty peaks of South Mountain Park, which separates the Valley from the rest of the Sonoran Desert. East of the city, beyond Tempe and Mesa, the peaks of the Superstition Mountains—named for their eerie way of seeming just a few miles away—are the first of a range that stretches all the way into New Mexico.

Central Arizona's dry desert heat imposes particular restraints on outdoor endeavors—even in winter hikers and cyclists should wear lightweight opaque clothing, a hat or visor, and high-UV-rated sunglasses, and should carry a quart of water for each hour of activity. The intensity of the sun makes strong sunscreen (SPF 30 or higher) a must, and don't forget to apply it to your hands and feet. △ **From May 1 to October 1 you shouldn't jog or hike from one hour after sunrise until a half hour before sunset.** During these times the air is so hot and dry that your body will lose moisture at a dangerous, potentially lethal rate. And keep your eyes peeled in natural desert areas; rattlesnakes and scorpions could be on the prowl.

MULTISPORT OUTFITTERS

Adventures Out West and Unicorn Balloon Company. This operator has horseback riding, jeep tours, and hot-air-balloon flights that conclude with complimentary champagne, a flight certificate, and video. ☎ *480/991–3666, 800/755–0935* ⊕ *www.adventuresoutwest.com.*

Arizona Outback Adventures. The knowledgeable and personable staff at AOA leads half-day, full-day, and multiple-day adventures for hikers, bikers, rafters, and kayakers. The guides are extremely knowledgeable about local flora and fauna. Or, you can rent a road bike or a mountain bike to explore the area's mountain regions, parks, and canal

BASEBALL'S SPRING TRAINING

For dyed-in-the-wool baseball fans there's no better place than the Valley of the Sun. Baseball has become nearly a year-round activity in the Phoenix area, beginning with spring training in late February and continuing through the Arizona Fall League championships in mid-November.

SPRING

Today the Cactus League consists of 15 Major League teams that play at stadiums across the Valley. Ticket prices are reasonable, around $7 to $8 for bleacher seats and $15 to $30 for reserved seats. Many stadiums have lawn-seating areas in the outfield, where you can spread a blanket and bring a picnic. Cactus League stadiums are more intimate than big-league parks, and players often come right up to the stands to say hello and to sign autographs.

Tickets for some teams go on sale as early as December. Brochures listing game schedules and ticket information are available from the **Cactus League**'s website (⊕ www.cactusleague.com).

SUMMER

During the regular Major League season the hometown Arizona Diamondbacks (⊕ www.azdiamondbacks.com) play on natural grass at Chase Field in the heart of Downtown Phoenix. The stadium is a technological wonder; if the weather's a little too warm outside, they close the roof, turn on the gigantic air-conditioners, and keep you cool while you enjoy the game. You can tour the stadium except on afternoon-game days and holidays.

FALL

At the conclusion of the regular season the Arizona Fall League runs until the week before Thanksgiving. Each major-league team sends six of its most talented young prospects to compete with other young promising players—180 players in all. There are six teams in the league, broken down into two divisions. It's a great way to see future Hall of Famers in their early years. Tickets for Fall League games are $6.

Call **Scottsdale Stadium** (☏ 480/312–2586), one of the league's host sites, for ticket information.

paths. ✉ 16447 N. 91st St., Scottsdale ☏ 480/945–2881, 866/455–1601 ⊕ www.aoa-adventures.com.

BALLOONING

A sunrise or sunset hot-air-balloon ascent is a remarkable desert sightseeing experience. The average fee—there are more than three dozen Valley companies to choose from—is $200 per person, and hotel pickup is usually included. Since flight paths and landing sites vary with wind speeds and directions, a roving land crew follows each balloon in flight. Time in the air is generally between 1 and 1½ hours, but allow 3 hours for the total excursion.

Fodor's Choice ★ **Hot Air Expeditions.** This is the best ballooning in Phoenix. Flights are long, the staff is charming, and the gourmet snacks, catered by the acclaimed Vincent restaurant, are out of this world. ☎ *480/502–6999, 800/831–7610* ⊕ *www.hotairexpeditions.com.*

BICYCLING

There are plenty of gorgeous areas for biking in the Phoenix area, but riding in the streets isn't recommended, as there are few adequate bike lanes in the city. Popular parks such as South Mountain Park and the Tempe Town Lake have miles of trails. ⚠ Note that the desert climate can be tough on cyclists, so make sure you're prepared with lots of water.

Phoenix Parks and Recreation. The Parks and Recreation department has detailed maps of Valley bike paths. ☎ *602/262–6862* ⊕ *phoenix.gov/ parks* ⊟ *No credit cards.*

Pinnacle Peak. This is a popular place to take bikes for the ride north to Carefree and Cave Creek, or east and south over the mountain pass and down to the Verde River, toward Fountain Hills. ⊠ *26802 N. 102nd Way, 25 miles northeast of downtown Phoenix, North Scottsdale, Scottsdale* ☎ *480/312–0990* ⊕ *scottsdaleaz.gov/parks* ⊟ *No credit cards.*

Scottsdale's Indian Bend Wash. This multiuse park system has paths suitable for bikes winding among its golf courses and ponds. ⊠ *Along Hayden Rd., from Shea Blvd. south to Indian School Rd., Scottsdale* ☎ *480/312–7275* ⊕ *scottsdaleaz.gov/parks* ⊟ *No credit cards.*

Trail 100. This trail runs throughout the Phoenix Mountain preserve; it's just the thing for mountain bikers. ⊠ *Enter at Dreamy Draw park, just east of the intersection of Northern Ave. and 16th St., North Central Phoenix, Phoenix* ☎ *602/262–6862* ⊕ *www.phoenix.gov/parks* ⊟ *No credit cards.*

FOUR-WHEELING

Taking a jeep through the backcountry has become a popular way to experience the desert's saguaro-covered mountains and curious rock formations. Prices start at around $100 per person.

Desert Dog Hummer Adventures. This operator heads out on half- and full-day Humvee tours to the Four Peaks Wilderness Area in Tonto National Forest and the Sonoran Desert. U-Drive desert cars and ATV tours are also available. ⊠ *17212 E. Shea Blvd., Fountain Hills* ☎ *480/837–3966* ⊕ *www.azadventures.com.*

Desert Storm Hummer Tours. These four-hour nature tours climb 4,000 feet up the rugged trails of Tonto National Forest via Hummer. ⊠ *15525 N. 83rd Way, No. 8, North Scottsdale, Scottsdale* ☎ *480/922–0020* ⊕ *www.dshummer.com.*

Wayward Wind Tours. This operator ventures down to the Verde River on its own trail and offers wilderness cookouts for large groups. ⊠ *2418 E. Danbury St., Phoenix* ☎ *602/867–7825, 800/804–0480* ⊕ *www. waywardwindtours.com.*

Wild West Jeep Tours. Special permits allow Wild West Jeep Tours to conduct four-wheeler excursions in the Tonto National Forest, which, in addition to a wild ride, lets you also visit visit thousand-year-old Indian sites. ✉ *7127 E. Becker La., Suite 74, Scottsdale* ☎ *480/922–0144* ⊕ *www.wildwestjeeptours.com.*

GOLF

2

Arizona has more golf courses per capita than any other state west of the Mississippi River, making it one of the most popular golf destinations in the United States. The sport is also one of Arizona's major industries, and the greens fee can run from $35 at a public course to more than $500 at some of Arizona's premier golfing spots. New courses seem to pop up routinely: there are more than 200 in the Valley (some lighted at night), and the PGA's Southwest section has its headquarters here.

MUNICIPAL COURSES

Fodor's Choice
★ **ASU Karsten Golf Course.** NCAA champions train at this Arizona State University 18-hole golf course. ✉ *1125 E. Rio Salado Pkwy.* ☎ *480/921–8070* ⊕ *www.asukarsten.com* 🏌 *18 holes. 4765–7002 yds. Par 70. Slope 115–131. Greens Fee: $36–$130* ☞ *Facilities: Driving range, putting green, golf carts, rental clubs, pro shop, lessons, restaurant, bar.*

Encanto Park. There are attractive, affordable public 9- and 18-hole courses at Encanto Park. ✉ *2775 N. 15th Ave., Phoenix* ☎ *602/253–3963* ⊕ *phoenix.gov/parks* 🏌 *18 holes. 6052–6361 yds. Par 70. Slope 113–114. Green Fee: $25–$43* ☞ *Facilities: Driving range, putting green, golf carts, rental clubs, pro shop, restaurant, bar.*

Papago Golf Course. Phoenix's best municipal course, Papago Golf Course is low-priced and has 18 holes. ✉ *5595 E. Moreland St., Phoenix* ☎ *602/275–8428* ⊕ *papagogolfcourse.net* 🏌 *18 holes. 5404–7333 yds. Par 72. Slope 121–130. Greens Fee: $15–$75* ☞ *Facilities: Driving range, putting green, golf carts, rental clubs, pro shop, restaurant, bar.*

PUBLIC COURSES

Fodor's Choice
★ **Gold Canyon Golf Club.** Near Apache Junction in the East Valley, Gold Canyon Golf Club offers fantastic views of the Superstition Mountains and challenging golf. ✉ *6100 S. King's Ranch Rd., Gold Canyon* ☎ *480/982–9090, 800/827–5281* ⊕ *www.gcgr.com* 🏌 *Dinosaur Mountain: 18 holes. 5368–6653 yds. Par 72. Slope 117–143. Greens Fee: $69–$199. Sidewinder: 18 holes. 4064–6533 yds. Par 72. Slope 112–132. Greens Fee: $50–$109* ☞ *Facilities: Driving range, putting green, golf carts, rental clubs, pro shop, lessons, restaurant, bar.*

Grayhawk. This 36-hole course has beautiful mountain views. In summer the greens fee is much lower. ✉ *8620 E. Thompson Peak Pkwy., North Scottsdale, Scottsdale* ☎ *480/502–1800* ⊕ *www.grayhawkgolf.com* 🏌 *Talon: 18 holes. 5143–6973 yds. Par 72. Slope 126/146. Raptor: 18 holes. 5309–7135 yds. Par 72. Slope 124/143. Green Fee: $100–$235* ☞ *Facilities: Driving range, putting green, golf carts, rental clubs, pro shop, lessons, restaurant, bar.*

Hillcrest Golf Club. With 18 holes on 179 acres of well-designed turf, Hillcrest Golf Club is the best course in the Sun Cities development. ✉ *20002 Star Ridge Dr., Sun City West* ☎ *623/584–1500* ⊕ *www.*

hillcrestgolfclub.com ⅃ *18 holes. 5512–7002 yds. Par 70. Slope 120–126. Greens Fee: $27–$55* ☞ *Facilities: Driving range, putting green, golf carts, rental clubs, pro shop, lessons, restaurant, bar.*

Raven Golf Club – Phoenix. Thousands of Aleppo pines and Lombardy poplars at this course make it a cool, shady 18-hole haven for summertime golfers. ⊠ *3636 E. Baseline Rd., South Phoenix, Phoenix* ☎ *602/243–3636* ⊕ *www.ravenphx.com* ⅃ *18 holes. 5759–7078 yds. Par 72. Slope 119–130. Greens Fee: $110–$150* ☞ *Facilities: Driving range, putting green, golf carts, rental clubs, pro shop, lessons, restaurant, bar.*

SunRidge Canyon. East of Scottsdale, SunRidge Canyon is a great 18-hole course for both the low handicapper and those who score above 100. The incredible mountain views are almost distracting. ⊠ *13100 N. SunRidge Dr., Fountain Hills* ☎ *480/837–5100* ⊕ *www.sunridgegolf. com* ⅃ *18 holes. 5944–6823 yds. Par 72. Slope 128–142. Greens Fee: $65–$170* ☞ *Facilities: Driving range, putting green, golf carts, rental clubs, pro shop, lessons, restaurant, bar.*

Fodor'sChoice **Troon North.** This course is a challenge for the length alone (7,070 yards).
★ The million-dollar views add to the experience at this perfectly maintained 36-hole course. ⊠ *10320 E. Dynamite Blvd., North Scottsdale, Scottsdale* ☎ *480/585–7700* ⊕ *www.troonnorthgolf.com* ⅃ *Monument: 18 holes. 5099–7070 yds. Par 72. Slope 118–147. Pinnacle: 18 holes. 4883–7025 yds. Par 71. Slope 116–149. Greens Fee: $99–$295* ☞ *Facilities: Driving range, putting green, golf carts, rental clubs, pro shop, lessons, restaurant, bar.*

RESORT COURSES

Arizona Biltmore Country Club. The granddaddy of Valley golf courses, Arizona Biltmore Country Club has two 18-hole PGA championship courses, lessons, and clinics. ⊠ *Arizona Biltmore Resort & Spa, 24th St. and Missouri Ave., Camelback Corridor, Phoenix* ☎ *602/955-9655* ⊕ *www.arizonabiltmore.com* ⅃ *Adobe: 18 holes. 5417–6428 yds. Par 71. Slope 119–123. Links: 18 holes. 4747–6300 yds. Par 71. Slope 110–125. Greens Fee: $49–$185* ☞ *Facilities: Driving range, putting green, golf carts, rental clubs, pro shop, lessons, restaurant, bar.*

Camelback Golf Club. Summer twilight greens fees are as low as $29 at the two 18-hole courses at the JW Marriott's Camelback Golf Club. ⊠ *JW Marriott Camelback Inn, 7847 N. Mockingbird Lane, Paradise Valley* ☎ *480/948–1700* ⊕ *www.camelbackinn.com* ⅃ *Padre: 18 holes. 6903 yds. Par 72. Slope 125. Greens Fee: $69–$159. Indian Bend: 18 holes. 7014 yds. Par 72. Slope 122. Greens Fee: $69-$159.* ☞ *Facilities: Driving range, putting green, golf carts, rental clubs, pro shop, lessons, restaurant, bar.*

Lookout Mountain Golf Club. This property at the Pointe Hilton Tapatio Cliffs has pristine greens, beautiful mountain views, and one 18-hole, par-71 course. ⊠ *Pointe Hilton at Tapatio Cliffs, 1111 N. 7th St., North Central Phoenix, Phoenix* ☎ *602/866–6356* ⊕ *www.tapatiocliffshilton. com* ⅃ *18 holes. 4557–6535 yds. Par 71. Slope 113–135. Greens Fee: $79–$149* ☞ *Facilities: Driving range, putting green, golf carts, rental clubs, pro shop, lessons, restaurant, bar.*

Ocotillo Golf Resort. There's water in play on nearly all 27 holes at Ocotillo Golf Resort, which was designed around 95 acres of man-made lakes. Summer twilight greens fee is $29. ⊠ *3751 S. Clubhouse Dr., Chandler* ☎ *480/917–6660* ⊕ *www.ocotillogolf.com* ⅃ *Blue/Gold: 18 holes. 5128–7016 yds. Par 72. Slope 124–133. White/Gold: 18 holes. 5124–6804 yds. Par 70. Slope 118–128. Blue/White: 18 holes. 5134–6782 yds. Par 71. Slope 117–133. Greens Fee: $79–$129.* ☞ *Facilities: Driving range, putting green, golf carts, rental clubs, pro shop, lessons, restaurant, bar.*

Fodor'sChoice
★ **The Phoenician Golf Club.** Set at the base of Camelback Mountain, the Phoenician offers three nine-hole courses in one of the most picturesque settings in the Valley. Summer fees after 11 am start at $39. ⊠ *The Phoenician, 6000 E. Camelback Rd., Camelback Corridor, Scottsdale* ☎ *480/941–8200* ⊕ *www.thephoenician.com* ⅃ *Canyon/Oasis: 18 holes. 4871–6258 yds. Par 70. Slope 111–131. Desert/Canyon: 18 holes. 4777–6068 yds. Par 70. Slope 107–130. Oasis/Desert: 18 holes. 5024–6310 yds. Par 70. Slope 113–130. Greens Fee: $79–$209.* ☞ *Facilities: Driving range, putting green, golf carts, rental clubs, pro shop, lessons, restaurant, bar.*

Tournament Players Club of Scottsdale. This 36-hole course by Tom Weiskopf and Jay Morrish is the site of the PGA Waste Management Phoenix Open, which takes place in January/February. ⊠ *Fairmont Scottsdale Princess Resort, 17020 N. Hayden Rd., North Scottsdale, Scottsdale* ☎ *480/585–4334, 888/400–4001* ⊕ *www.tpc.com* ⅃ *Stadium: 18 holes. 5455–7216 yds. Par 71. Slope 124–141. Greens Fee: $75–299. Champions: 18 holes. 5342–7115 yds. Par 71. Slope 120–140. Greens Fee: $63–139* ☞ *Facilities: Driving range, putting green, golf carts, rental clubs, pro shop, lessons, restaurant, bar.*

Wigwam Golf and Country Club. This country club is the home of the famous Gold Course, as well as two other 18-hole courses. ⊠ *Wigwam Resort, 300 East Wigwam Blvd., Litchfield Park* ☎ *623/935–3811* ⊕ *www.wigwamresort.com* ⅃ *Patriot: 18 holes. 4791–6001 yds. Par 70. Slope 113–123. Gold: 18 holes. 5885–7430 yds. Par 72. Slope 119–135. Heritage: 18 holes. 5806–6852 yds. Par 72. Slope 118–126. Greens Fee: $109* ☞ *Facilities: Driving range, putting green, golf carts, rental clubs, pro shop, lessons, restaurant, bar.*

HIKING

One of the best ways to see the beauty of the Valley of the Sun is from above, so hikers of all calibers seek a vantage point in the mountains surrounding the flat Valley. A short drive from Downtown, South Mountain Park *(See Exploring)* is the jewel of the city's mountain park preserves, with more than 60 miles of marked trails for hikers, horseback riders, and mountain bikers. ■TIP➔ No matter the season, be sure to bring sunscreen, a hat, plenty of water, and a camera to capture a dazzling sunset. It's always a good idea to tell someone where you'll be and when you plan to return.

Phoenix Mountain Preserve System. Much of Phoenix's famous mountains and hiking trails are part of the Phoenix Mountain Preserve, a series

The Valley of the Sun is a popular destination for golfing with more than 200 courses in the area.

of mountains that encircles the Valley. The city's park rangers can help plan your hikes. ☎ 602/262–6862 ⊕ *www.phoenix.gov/parks.*

BEST SPOTS

Camelback Mountain and Echo Canyon Recreation Area. This recreation area has intermediate to difficult hikes up the Valley's most outstanding central landmark. *Difficult.* ⊠ *Tatum Blvd. and McDonald Dr., Paradise Valley* ☎ *602/262-6862 Phoenix Parks & Recreation Dept.* ⊕ *www.phoenix.gov/parks.*

Lost Dog Wash Trail. Part of the continually expanding McDowell-Sonoran Preserve (⊕ *www.mcdowellsonoran.org*), Lost Dog Wash Trail is a mostly gentle 4.5-mile round trip that will get you away from the bustle of the city in a hurry. The trailhead has restrooms and a map that shows a series of trails for varying skill levels. *Easy.* ⊠ *23015 N. 128th St., north of Shea Blvd., North Scottsdale, Scottsdale* ☎ *480/312–7013* ⊕ *www.scottsdaleaz.gov/preserve.*

FAMILY **The Papago Peaks.** These peaks were sacred sites for the Tohono O'odham. The soft-sandstone peaks contain accessible caves, some petroglyphs, and splendid views of much of the Valley. This is a good spot for family hikes. *Easy.* ⊠ *625 N. Galvin Pkwy., Phoenix* ☎ *602/262-6862* ⊕ *www. phoenix.gov/parks.*

Piestewa Peak. Just north of Lincoln Drive, Piestewa Peak has a series of trails for all levels of hikers. It's a great place to get views of downtown. Allow about 1½ hours for each direction. *Moderate.* ⊠ *2701 E. Piestewa Peak Dr., North Central Phoenix, Phoenix* ☎ *602/262–6862* ⊕ *www.phoenix.gov/parks.*

Pinnacle Peak Trail. This is a well-maintained trail offering a moderately challenging 3.5-mile round-trip hike—or a horseback experience for those who care to round up a horse at the local stables. Interpretive programs and trail signs along the way describe the geology, flora, fauna, and cultural history of the area. *Moderate.* ✉ *26802 N. 102nd Way, 1 mile south of Dynamite and Alma School Rds., North Scottsdale, Scottsdale* ☎ *480/312–0990* ⊕ *www.scottsdaleaz.gov/parks/pinnacle.*

FAMILY **Waterfall Trail.** Part of the 25 miles of trails available at the White Tank Mountian Regional Park, this short and easy trail is kid-friendly. Strollers and wheelchairs roll along easily to Petroglyph Plaza, which boasts 1,500-year-old boulder carvings—dozens are in clear view from the trail. From there the trail takes a rockier but manageable course to a waterfall, which, depending on area rainfall, can be cascading, creeping, or completely dry. Stop at the visitor center to view desert reptiles such as the king snake and a gopher snake in the aquariums. *Easy.* ✉ *20304 W. White Tank Mountain Rd., Waddell* ☎ *623/935–2505* ⊕ *www.maricopa.gov/parks/white_tank/.*

HORSEBACK RIDING

More than two dozen stables and equestrian-tour outfitters in the Valley attest to the saddle's enduring importance in Arizona—even in this auto-dominated metropolis. Stables offer rides for an hour, a whole day, and even some overnight adventures. Some local resorts can arrange for lessons on-site or at nearby stables.

Arizona Cowboy College. The wranglers here will teach you everything you need to know about ridin', ropin', and ranchin'. ✉ *30208 N. 152nd St., North Scottsdale, Scottsdale* ☎ *480/471–3151* ⊕ *www.cowboycollege.com.*

MacDonald's Ranch. This ranch offers one- and two-hour trail rides and guided breakfast, lunch, and dinner rides through desert foothills above Scottsdale. ✉ *26540 N. Scottsdale Rd., North Scottsdale, Scottsdale* ☎ *480/585–0239* ⊕ *www.macdonaldsranch.com.*

Fodor'sChoice **OK Corrals & Stable.** One-, two-, and four-hour horseback trail rides
★ and steak cookouts are available from this company, which also runs one- to three-day horse-packing trips. They have the oldest pack station in the history of the Superstition Mountains, and all their guides are U.S. Forest Service–licensed. ✉ *2655 E. Whiteley St., Apache Junction* ☎ *480/982–4040* ⊕ *www.okcorrals.com.*

Ponderosa Stables. You can enjoy your South Mountain experience from a higher perch. Consider renting horses at this nearby stable. This private company rents its land from the city of Phoenix, and will take you on an excursion, or send you on one of your own. Trail ride rates start at $33 an hour. ✉ *10215 S. Central Ave., South Phoenix, Phoenix* ☎ *602/268–1261* ⊕ *www.arizona-horses.com.*

RAFTING

Desert Voyagers. This operator specializes in guided raft and kayak trips on the Verde and Salt rivers. ☎ *480/998–7238* ⊕ *www.desertvoyagers.com.*

SAILPLANING–SOARING

Turf Soaring School. Scenic sailplane rides from this company last from 20 to 30 minutes. Rates are from $109 per person. ⊠ *8700 W. Carefree Hwy., Peoria* ☎ *602/439–3621* ⊕ *www.turfsoaring.com.*

TENNIS

With all the blue sky and sunshine in the Valley, it's a perfect place to play tennis or watch the pros. The Surprise Tennis and Racquet Complex, a public facility in Surprise, is the place to watch big-time tournaments such as the Fed Cup. Most major resorts, such as the Phoenician, Wigwam, Fairmont Scottsdale Princess, and JW Marriott Desert Ridge (and many smaller properties), have tennis courts. Granted, tennis plays second fiddle to golf here—but many of the larger resorts offer package tennis deals. If you're not staying at a resort, there are more than 60 public facilities in the area.

Kiwanis Park Recreation Center. This center has 15 lighted premier-surface courts (all for same-day or one-day-advance reserve). ⊠ *6111 S. All America Way* ☎ *480/350-5201* ⊕ *www.tempe.gov/kiwanis.*

Scottsdale Ranch Park. Lessons are available at this city facility, which has 12 lighted courts. ⊠ *10400 E. Via Linda, North Scottsdale, Scottsdale* ☎ *480/312-7774* ⊕ *www.scottsdaleaz.gov/parks/srp.*

Surprise Tennis and Racquet Complex. This complex features 25 public courts where you can play for 90 minutes on their state-of-the-art lighted courts for only $3. ⊠ *14469 W. Paradise Lane, Surprise* ☎ *623/222-2400* ⊕ *www.surpriseaz.com/tennis.*

TUBING

The Valley may not be known for its wealth of water, but locals manage to make the most of what there is. A popular summer stop is the northeast side of the Salt River, where sun worshippers can rent an inner tube and float down the river for an afternoon. Tubing season runs from May to September. Several Valley outfitters rent tubes. Make sure you bring lots of sunscreen, a hat, water—and a rope for attaching your cooler to a tube.

Salt River Recreation. This outfitter offers shuttle-bus service to and from your starting point and rents tubes for $17 (cash only) for the day. It's open during summer months only. ⊠ *Usery Pass and Power Rd., Mesa* ☎ *480/984-3305* ⊕ *www.saltrivertubing.com.*

SIDE TRIPS NEAR PHOENIX

There are a number of interesting sights within a 1- to 1½-hour drive of Phoenix. To the north, the thriving artist communities of Carefree and Cave Creek are popular Western attractions. Arcosanti and Wickenburg are half- or full-day trips from Phoenix. Stop along the way to visit the petroglyphs of Deer Valley Rock Art Center and the reenactments of Arizona territorial life at the Pioneer Living History Village. You also might consider Arcosanti and Wickenburg as stopovers on the way to or from Flagstaff, Prescott, or Sedona.

South of Phoenix, an hour's drive takes you back to prehistoric times and the site of Arizona's first known civilization at Casa Grande Ruins National Monument, a vivid reminder of the Hohokam who began farming this area more than 1,500 years ago.

DEER VALLEY ROCK ART CENTER

15 miles north of Downtown Phoenix.

GETTING HERE AND AROUND

Take Interstate 17 north from Phoenix for 15 miles, exit at West Deer Valley Road, and drive 2 miles west.

EXPLORING

Deer Valley Rock Art Center. This is the largest concentration of ancient petroglyphs in the metropolitan Phoenix area. Some 1,500 of the cryptic symbols are here, left behind by Native American cultures that lived in the Valley (or passed through) during the last 1,000 years. After watching a video about the petroglyphs, pick up a pair of binoculars ($1) and an informative trail map and set out on the 0.25-mile path. Telescopes point to some of the most skillful petroglyphs; they range from human and animal forms to more abstract figures. ⇨ *Also see Petroglyphs CloseUp box in Chapter 6, Eastern Arizona.* ⊠ *3711 W. Deer Valley Rd., Phoenix* ☎ *623/582–8007* ⊕ *dvrac.asu.edu* ⊠ *$7* ⊙ *Oct.–Apr., Tues.–Sat. 9–5.*

PIONEER LIVING HISTORY VILLAGE

25 miles north of Downtown Phoenix.

GETTING HERE AND AROUND

Take Interstate 17 north from Downtown Phoenix for 25 miles. Just north of Carefree Highway (AZ 74), take Exit 225, and turn left on Pioneer Road to get to the entrance.

EXPLORING

FAMILY **Pioneer Living History Museum.** This museum contains 28 original and reconstructed buildings from throughout territorial Arizona. Costumed guides filter through the bank, schoolhouse, and print shop, as well as the Pioneer Opera House, where classic melodramas are performed daily. It's popular with the grade-school field-trip set, and it's your lucky day if you can tag along for their tour of the site—particularly when John the Blacksmith forges, smelts, and answers sixth-graders' questions that adults are too know-it-all to ask. ⊠ *3901 W. Pioneer Rd., Pioneer* ☎ *623/465–1052* ⊕ *www.pioneeraz.org* ⊠ *$7* ⊙ *Oct.–May, Wed.–Sun. 9–4; June–Sept., Wed.–Sun. 8–2.*

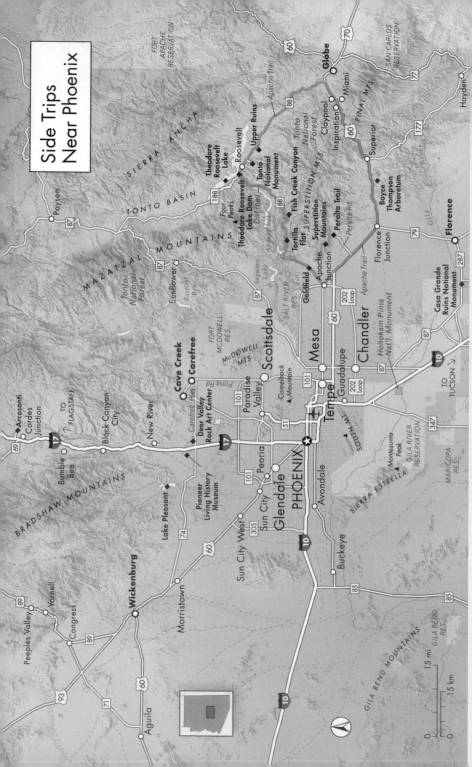

Side Trips Near Phoenix

CAVE CREEK AND CAREFREE

30 miles north of Downtown Phoenix.

Some 30 miles north of Phoenix, resting high in the Sonoran Desert at an elevation of 2,500 feet, the towns of Cave Creek and Carefree look back to a lifestyle far different from that of their more populous neighbors to the south.

Cave Creek got its start with the discovery of gold in the region. When the mines and claims "played out," the cattlemen arrived, and the sounds of horse hooves and lowing cattle replaced those of miners' picks. The area grew slowly and independently from Phoenix to the south, until a paved road connected the two in 1952. Today the mile-long main stretch of town on Cave Creek Road is a great spot to have some hot chili and cold beer, try on Western duds, or learn the two-step in a "cowboy" bar. You're likely to run into folks dressed in cowboy hats, boots, and bold belt buckles. Horseback riders and horse-drawn wagons have the right of way here, and the 25 mph speed limit is strictly enforced by county deputies. You can amble up the hill and rent a horse for a trip into the Tonto National Forest in search of some long-forgotten native petroglyphs or take a jeep tour out to the forest.

Just about the time the dirt-road era ended in Cave Creek, planners were sketching out a new community, which became neighboring Carefree. The world's largest sundial, at the town's center, is surrounded by crafts shops, galleries, artists' workshops, and cafés. Today Cave Creek and Carefree sit cheek by jowl—but the former has beans, beef, biscuits, and beer, while the latter discreetly orders up a notch or two.

GETTING HERE AND AROUND

Follow Interstate 17 north of Downtown Phoenix for 15 miles. Exit at Carefree Highway (AZ 74) and turn right, then go 12 miles. Turn left onto Cave Creek Road and go 3 miles to downtown Cave Creek, then another 4 miles on Cave Creek Road to Carefree. Pick up maps and information about the area at the Chamber of Commerce.

ESSENTIALS

Visitor Information Carefree–Cave Creek Chamber of Commerce ⊠ *748 Easy St., No. 9* ☎ *480/488–3381* ⊕ *www.carefreecavecreek.org* ⊗ *Weekdays 8–4.*

EXPLORING

Cave Creek Museum. Exhibits at the Cave Creek Museum depict pioneer living, mining, and ranching. See the last original 1920s tuberculosis cabin and a collection of Indian artifacts from the Hohokam and Yavapai tribes. ⊠ *6140 E. Skyline Dr., Cave Creek* ☎ *480/488–2764* ⊕ *www.cavecreekmuseum.org* ⊠ *$5* ⊗ *Oct.–May, Wed., Thurs., and weekends 1–4:30, Fri. 10–4:30.*

FAMILY **Frontier Town.** This pseudo-Western Frontier Town has wooden sidewalks, ramshackle buildings, and souvenir shops. ⊠ *6245 E. Cave Creek Rd., Cave Creek* ⊕ *www.frontiertownaz.com.*

QUICK BITES
Bakery Café at el Pedregal Marketplace. Adjacent to the Boulders Resort and not far from the Heard Museum North, this is a good place to pick up a breakfast or lunch of fresh-baked goods or to take a shopping break with

The Boulders Resort and Golden Door Spa

Rancho de los Caballeros

a sandwich and a cool drink. ✉ ***34505 N. Scottsdale Rd., at Carefree Hwy.*** ☎ ***480/488–4100.***

WHERE TO EAT

$$$$ MODERN AMERICAN Fodor's Choice ★

✕ **Binkley's Restaurant.** This upscale restaurant is a diamond in the Valley's last bit of rough. In a town of cowboy bars and gut bombs, chef Kevin Binkley makes a world-class impression with tasting menus featuring delicate portions of such dishes as black-truffle croque madame, red-wine-braised octopus, and duck with bok choy and ginger. The menu changes daily, so be prepared for some delicious surprises. For something a little more casual and inexpensive, try Café Bink at 36899 North Tom Darlington Drive in Carefree. Ⓢ *Average main: $45* ✉ *6920 E. Cave Creek Rd., Cave Creek* ☎ *480/437–1072* 🌐 *www.binkleysrestaurant.com* ✍ *Reservations essential.*

$$ AMERICAN

✕ **Cave Creek Smokehouse.** Some might remember this location as the Satisfied Frog, and while it keeps changing its name, locals still go here for a beer, some nachos and barbecue, and an authentic Cave Creek experience. Ⓢ *Average main: $20* ✉ *6245 E. Cave Creek Rd., Cave Creek* ☎ *480/488–3317* 🌐 *www.cavecreeksmokehouse.net.*

$$ AMERICAN

✕ **Horny Toad Restaurant.** Cave Creek's oldest restaurant is a rustic spot for barbecued pork ribs and steak, but the real star is the fried chicken. The quirky menu features a range of fare from soup "de joor" to Icelandic cod and carne asada. Ⓢ *Average main: $17* ✉ *6738 E. Cave Creek Rd., Cave Creek* ☎ *480/488–9542* 🌐 *www.thehornytoad.com.*

$$$ AMERICAN

✕ **Tonto Bar & Grill at Rancho Manana.** Old West ambience oozes from every corner of the Tonto Bar & Grill, from the hand-carved ceiling beams to the *latilla* (stick)-covered patios with views of the pristine Sonoran Desert. Try the cowboy Cobb salad or the Tonto burger piled with fried onions and cheddar for lunch; root beer–braised short ribs or onion-crusted walleye are good choices at dinner. Ⓢ *Average main: $25* ✉ *5736 E. Rancho Manana Blvd., Cave Creek* ☎ *480/488–0698* 🌐 *www.tontobarandgrill.com.*

WHERE TO STAY

For expanded hotel reviews, visit Fodors.com.

$$$$ RESORT Fodor's Choice ★

🏨 **The Boulders Resort and Golden Door Spa.** One of the country's top resorts—and one of the few with an all-organic approach—hides amid hill-size, 12-million-year-old granite boulders and the lush Sonoran Desert. **Pros:** remote desert getaway; also in the center of Cave Creek and Carefree shopping, events, and activities. **Cons:** on-site dining is priced above average; minimum 45-minute drive to Phoenix attractions. Ⓢ *Rooms from: $349* ✉ *34631 N. Tom Darlington Dr.* ☎ *480/488–9009, 888/579–2631* 🌐 *www.theboulders.com* 🛏 *160 casitas, 61 villas and haciendas* 🍽 *No meals.*

$$ HOTEL

🏨 **Cave Creek Tumbleweed Hotel.** The 1950s flavor of this Western hotel fits perfectly with Cave Creek's style. **Pros:** a true Old West experience; quite affordable compared to the very pricey area competition. **Cons:** sparse accommodations; no frills; far drive from Phoenix and Scottsdale activities. Ⓢ *Rooms from: $169* ✉ *6333 E. Cave Creek Rd., Cave Creek* ☎ *480/488–3668* 🌐 *www.tumbleweedhotel.com* 🛏 *32 rooms, 8 casitas* 🍽 *No meals.*

NIGHTLIFE

Buffalo Chip Saloon. Watch real cowboys and cowgirls two-step to live music at this saloon, where you can also gorge on mesquite-grilled chicken and buffalo chips—hot, homemade potato chips. Reservations are suggested for the all-you-can-eat Friday-night fish fry that draws crowds. There's live music and dancing just about every night. ⊠ 6811 E. Cave Creek Rd., Cave Creek ☎ 480/488–9118 ⊕ www. buffalochipsaloon.com.

Harold's Cave Creek Corral. Just across the dirt parking lot from the Buffalo Chip Saloon, Harold's has two full bars, a huge dance floor with live bands on weekends, a game room, 15 TVs, and a restaurant—serving some of the best ribs in the Valley. It's also the go-to place to watch Pittsburgh Steelers games during the NFL season. ⊠ 6895 E. Cave Creek Rd., Cave Creek ☎ 480/488–1906 ⊕ www.haroldscorral.com.

SHOPPING

Cave Creek and Carefree have a thriving arts community, with hundreds of artists and dozens of galleries.

el Pedregal. Set at the foot of a 250-foot boulder formation, el Pedregal is a two-tier shopping plaza. In spring and summer there are open-air Thursday-night concerts in the courtyard amphitheater. In addition to its posh boutiques and specialty stores, el Pedregal is home to some of the finest art galleries in the area. ⊠ 34505 N. Scottsdale Rd., at Carefree Hwy. ☎ 480/488–1072 ⊕ www.elpedregal.com.

Spanish Village. This is an outdoor shopping area complete with bell tower, fountains, courtyards, and winding alleyways. You can while away an afternoon browsing 30 shops, then contemplate dinner at one of several casual restaurants. ⊠ Ho and Hum Rds.

SPAS

Waldorf Astoria Spa at The Boulders. If you're seeking the serenity of the desert, this is the place. Influenced by Asian and Native American cultures, the soothing Southwestern spa is divided into two wings—east for relaxation and west for activity, which includes a movement studio for Pilates, tai chi, and yoga. Walk through the outdoor, Hopi-inspired tranquillity labyrinth, or schedule a visit with the spa's resident astrologer. The services menu includes traditional treatments such as masssages or facials, as well as signature Waldorf Astoria experiences such as chakra balancing, hypnotherapy, and detoxification. With a range of treatments like this, it's no wonder vacationers choose The Boulders specifically for its spa. ⊠ 34631 N. Tom Darlington Dr. ☎ 480/595–3500 ⊕ www.theboulders.com/waldorf-astoria-spa ☞ $145 50-min massage, $155 50-min facial, 4-hr spa day with complete massage, facial, wrap, and lunch from $450. Hair salon, sauna, soaking bath, pool (outdoor) steam room, whirlpool (outdoor). Gym with: cardiovascular machines, weight-training equipment. Services: acupuncture, aromatherapy, aquatherapy, facials, massage, reflexology, salon services, scrubs, Vichy shower, wraps. Classes and programs: guided walks, guided hikes, meditation, mountain biking, nature walk, personal training, Pilates, rock climbing, stretching, tai chi, water fitness, yoga.

2

SPORTS AND THE OUTDOORS

GOLF

Boulders Resort Golf Club. There are two championship 18-hole courses at this club. ⊠ *The Boulders, 34631 N. Tom Darlington Dr.* ☎ *480/488–9009, 888/579–2631* ⊕ *www.theboulders.com* ⚑ *North Course: 18 holes. 6811 yds. Par 72. Slope 137. South Course: 18 holes. 6726 yds. Par 71. Slope 140. Greens Fee: $200* ⚲ *Facilities: Driving range, putting green, golf carts, rental clubs, pro shop, lessons, restaurant, bar.*

HORSEBACK RIDING

Spur Cross Stable. Well-cared-for horses will take you on one- to six-hour rides to the high Sonoran Desert of the Spur Cross Preserve and the Tonto National Forest. Some rides include visits to petroglyph sites and a saddlebag lunch. ⊠ *44029 Spur Cross Rd., Cave Creek* ☎ *480/488–9117, 800/758–9530* ⊕ *www.horsebackarizona.com.*

WICKENBURG

70 miles northwest of Downtown Phoenix.

This town, land of guest ranches and tall tales, is named for Henry Wickenburg, whose nearby Vulture Mine was the richest gold strike in the Arizona Territory. In the late 1800s Wickenburg was a booming mining town on the banks of the Hassayampa River, with a seemingly endless supply of gold, copper, and silver. Nowadays Wickenburg's Old West history attracts visitors to its sleepy downtown and Western museum. There's a group of good antiques shops, most of which are on Tegner and Frontier streets.

GETTING HERE AND AROUND

Follow Interstate 17 north from Phoenix for about 15 miles to the Carefree Highway (AZ 74) junction. About 30 miles west on AZ 74, take U.S. 89/93 north and go another 10 miles to Wickenburg.

Maps for self-guided walking tours of the town's historic buildings are available at the Wickenburg Chamber of Commerce, in the town's old Santa Fe Depot.

ESSENTIALS

Visitor Information Wickenburg Chamber of Commerce ⊠ *216 N. Frontier St.* ☎ *928/684–5479, 800/942–5242* ⊕ *www.wickenburgchamber.com.*

EXPLORING

FAMILY **Desert Caballeros Western Museum.** Boasting one of the best collections of Western art in the nation, this museum has paintings and sculpture by Remington, Bierstadt, Joe Beeler (founder of the Cowboy Artists of America), and others. Kids enjoy the re-creation of a turn-of-the-20th-century Main Street that includes a general store, period clothing, and a large collection of cowboy gear. ⊠ *21 N. Frontier St.* ☎ *928/684–2272* ⊕ *www.westernmuseum.org* ⊠ *$9* ⊙ *Mon.–Sat. 10–5, Sun. noon–4.*

Hassayampa River Preserve. Self-guided trails here wind through lush cottonwood-willow forests, mesquite trees, and around a 4-acre, spring-fed pond and marsh habitat. Waterfowl, herons, and Arizona's rarest raptors shelter here. ⊠ *3 miles southeast of Wickenburg on U.S. 60, 49614 Hwy 60* ☎ *928/684–2772* ⊕ *www.nature.org/hassayampa* ⊠ *$5*

⏲ Mid-Sept.–mid-May, Wed.–Sun. 8–5; summer hrs vary depending on fire danger and weather. Call to confirm.

Jail Tree. On the northeast corner of Wickenburg Way and Tegner Street, check out the Jail Tree, to which prisoners were chained, the desert heat sometimes finishing them off before their sentences were served.

WHERE TO EAT AND STAY

For expanded hotel reviews, visit Fodors.com.

$ MEXICAN 🍴 **Anita's Cocina.** Reliable Tex-Mex fare is served at Anita's. The fresh tamales are tasty for lunch or dinner. Try a fruit burrito for dessert. *[$] Average main: $8 ✉ 57 N. Valentine St. ☎ 928/684–5777.*

$$$$ RESORT FAMILY Fodor's Choice ★ 🏨 **Rancho de los Caballeros.** This 20,000-acre property combines the guest-ranch experience with first-class amenities. **Pros:** large rooms, casitas, and suites; abundant activity roster; a great place for family gatherings. **Cons:** remote location; long hikes to rooms. *[$] Rooms from: $485 ✉ 1551 S. Vulture Mine Rd. ☎ 928/684–5484, 800/684–5030 🌐 www.sunc.com 🛏 79 casitas ⏲ Closed mid-May–early Oct. 🍽 All meals.*

NIGHTLIFE

Rancher Bar. Real live wranglers and cowboys meet up at this modern-day saloon to shoot some pool, and the breeze, after a hard day's work. *✉ 910 W. Wickenburg Way ☎ 928/684–5957.*

ARCOSANTI

65 miles north of Downtown Phoenix.

GETTING HERE AND AROUND

From Phoenix, take Interstate 17 north 65 miles to Exit 262 (Condes Junction). Follow the partly paved road 2½ miles northeast to the community.

EXPLORING

Arcosanti. The evolving complex and community of Arcosanti was masterminded by Italian architect Paolo Soleri to be a self-sustaining habitat in which architecture and ecology function in symbiosis. Building began in 1970, but Arcosanti hasn't quite achieved Soleri's original vision. It's still worth a stop to take a tour, have a bite at the café, and purchase one of the hand-cast bronze wind-bells made at the site. *✉ 2 miles off I-17 and Exit 262 ☎ 928/632–7135 🌐 www.arcosanti.org 🎟 Tour $10 ⏲ Daily 9–5; tours hourly 10–4.*

CASA GRANDE RUINS NATIONAL MONUMENT

36 miles southeast of Downtown Phoenix.

GETTING HERE AND AROUND

Take U.S. 60 east (Superstition Freeway) to Florence Junction (U.S. 60 and AZ 89), and head south 16 miles on AZ 89 to Florence. Casa Grande is 9 miles west of Florence on AZ 287 or, from Interstate 10, 16 miles east on AZ 387 and AZ 87. Note: follow signs to ruins, not to town of Casa Grande. When leaving the ruins, take AZ 87 north 35 miles back to U.S. 60.

EXPLORING

Casa Grande Ruins National Monument. This site, whose original purpose still eludes archaeologists, was unknown to European explorers until Father Kino, a Jesuit missionary, first recorded the site's existence in 1694. The area was set aside as federal land in 1892 and named a national monument in 1918. Although only a few prehistoric sites can be viewed, more than 60 are in the monument area, including the 35-foot-tall—that's four stories—Casa Grande (Big House). The tallest Hohokam building known, Casa Grande was built in the early 14th century and is believed by some to have been an ancient astronomical observatory or a center of government, religion, trade, or education. Allow an hour to explore the site, longer if park rangers are giving a talk or leading a tour. On your way out, cross the parking lot by the covered picnic grounds and climb the platform for a view of a ball court and two platform mounds, said to date from the 1100s. ⊠ *1100 W. Ruins Dr., Coolidge* ☎ *520/723–3172* ⊕ *www.nps.gov/cagr* ⊠ *$5* ☉ *Daily 9–5.*

THE APACHE TRAIL

Fodor's Choice
★

President Theodore Roosevelt called this 150-mile drive "the most awe-inspiring and most sublimely beautiful panorama nature ever created." A stretch of winding highway, the AZ 188 portion of the Apache Trail closely follows the route forged through wilderness in 1906 to move construction supplies for building the Roosevelt Dam, which lies at the northernmost part of the loop.

PLANNING YOUR TIME

Although the drive itself can easily be completed in less than a day, you could spend a night in Globe, continuing the loop back to Phoenix the following day.

GETTING HERE AND AROUND

From the town of Apache Junction you can choose to drive the trail in either direction; there are advantages to both. If you begin the loop going clockwise—heading eastward on AZ 188 to the Superstition Mountains, the Peralta Trail, Boyce Thompson Arboretum, Globe, Tonto National Monument, Theodore Roosevelt Lake Reservoir & Dam, and Tortilla Flat—your drive may be more relaxing; you'll be on the farthest side of this narrow dirt road some refer to as the "white-knuckle route," with its switchbacks and drop-offs straight down into spectacular Fish Creek Canyon. ■TIP→ **This 42-mile section of the drive isn't for anyone afraid of heights.** But if you follow the route counterclockwise—continuing on U.S. 60 past the town of Apache Junction—you'll be able to appreciate each attraction better.

SUPERSTITION MOUNTAINS

30 miles east of Downtown Phoenix.

GETTING HERE AND AROUND

From Phoenix, take Interstate 10 and then U.S. 60 (the Superstition Freeway) east through the suburbs of Tempe, Mesa, and Apache Junction.

EXPLORING

Superstition Mountains. As the Phoenix metro area gives way to cactus- and creosote-dotted desert, the massive escarpment of the Superstition Mountains heaves into view and slides by to the north. The Superstitions are supposedly where the legendary Lost Dutchman Mine is, the location—not to mention the existence—of which has been hotly debated since pioneer days. ⊠ *6109 N. Apache Trail, Apache Junction* ⊕ *www.azstateparks.com/parks/lodu.*

Superstition Mountain Museum. The best place to learn about the "Dutchman" Jacob Waltz and the Lost Dutchman Mine is at Superstition Mountain Museum. Exhibits include a collection of mining tools, historical maps, and artifacts relating to the "gold" age of the Superstition Mountains. ⊠ *4087 N. Apache Trail, AZ 188, Apache Junction* ☎ *480/983–4888* ⊕ *www.superstitionmountainmuseum.org* ▨ *$5* ◔ *Daily 9–4.*

Goldfield Ghost Town. Goldfield became an instant city of about 4,000 residents after a gold strike in 1892; the town dried up five years later when the gold mine flooded. Today the Goldfield Ghost Town is an interesting place to grab a cool drink, pan for gold, go for a mine tour, or take a desert Jeep ride or horseback tour of the area. The ghost town's shops are open daily 10–5, the saloon daily 11–9, and gunfights are held hourly noon–4 on weekends. ⊠ *4650 N. Mammoth Mine Rd., 4 miles northeast of Apache Junction on AZ 188, Goldfield* ☎ *480/983–0333* ⊕ *www.goldfieldghosttown.com.*

PERALTA TRAIL

35 miles east of Downtown Phoenix, located in the Superstition Mountains.

GETTING HERE AND AROUND

About 11½ miles southeast of Apache Junction, off U.S. 60, take Peralta Trail Road, just past King's Ranch Road, an 8-mile, rough gravel road that leads to the start of the Peralta Trail.

SPORTS AND THE OUTDOORS

HIKING

Peralta Trail. The 4-mile round-trip Peralta Trail winds 1,400 feet up a small valley for a spectacular view of **Weaver's Needle,** a monolithic rock formation that is one of Arizona's more famous sights. Allow a few hours for this rugged and challenging hike, bring plenty of water, sunscreen, a hat, and a snack or lunch, and don't hike it in the middle of the day in summer. *Moderate.* ⊠ *Goldfield.*

BOYCE THOMPSON ARBORETUM

60 miles east of Downtown Phoenix, 30 miles southeast of the Peralta Trail.

GETTING HERE AND AROUND

From Florence Junction, take U.S. 60 east for 12 miles.

EXPLORING

Boyce Thompson Arboretum. At the foot of Picketpost Mountain in Superior, the Boyce Thompson Arboretum is often called an oasis in the desert: the arid rocky expanse gives way to lush riparian glades home to 3,200 different desert plants and more than 230 bird and 72 terrestrial species. The arboretum offers a living album of the

WORD OF MOUTH

"I loved the Boyce Thompson Arboretum. It's a little bit of a drive from Phoenix, but you will see the desert in its unspoiled majesty. There are (easy) hiking trails and scenery to die for."

—wliwl

world's desert and semiarid region plants, including exotic species such as Canary Islands date palms and Australian eucalyptus. Trails offer breathtaking scenery in the gardens and the exhibits, especially during the spring wildflower season. A variety of tours are offered year-round. Benches with built-in misters offer relief from the heat. Bring along a picnic and enjoy the beauty. ⊠ *37615 U.S. 60, Milepost 223, Superior* ☎ *520/689–2811* ⊕ *www.arboretum.ag.arizona.edu* ⊠ *$9* ⊙ *May–Aug., daily 6–3; Sept.–Apr., daily 8–5.*

EN ROUTE   A few miles past the arboretum, **Superior** is the first of several modest mining towns and the launching point for a dramatic winding ascent through the Mescals to a 4,195-foot pass that affords panoramic views of this copper-rich range and its huge, dormant, open-pit mines. Collectors will want to watch for antiques shops, but be forewarned that quality varies considerably. A gradual descent will take you into **Miami** and **Claypool,** once-thriving boomtowns that have carried on quietly since major-corporation mining ground to a halt in the '70s. Working-class buildings are dwarfed by the mountainous piles of copper tailings. At a stoplight in Claypool, AZ 188 splits off northward to the Apache Trail, but continue on U.S. 60 another 3 miles to Globe.

GLOBE

90 miles east of Downtown Phoenix, 51 miles east of Apache Junction, 25 miles east of Superior, and 3 miles east of Claypool's AZ 188 turnoff, 30 miles east of Boyce Thompson.

In the southern reaches of Tonto National Forest, Globe is the most modern of the area's dilapidated mining towns. Initially, it was gold and silver that brought miners here—the city allegedly got its name from a large, circular boulder of silver, with lines like continents, found by prospectors—although the region is now known for North America's richest copper deposits. ■TIP→ If you're driving the Apache Trail loop, stop in Globe to fill up the tank; it's the last chance to gas up until looping all the way back to U.S. 60 at Apache Junction.

GETTING HERE AND AROUND

Globe is at the intersection of U.S. 60 and AZ 188. At the Globe Chamber of Commerce, you can pick up brochures detailing the self-guided Historic Downtown Walking Tour.

CLOSE UP

The Lost Dutchman Mine

2

Not much is known about Jacob "the Dutchman" Waltz, except that he was born around 1808 in Germany (he was "Deutsch," not "Dutch") and emigrated to the United States, where he spent several years at mining camps in the Southeast, in the West, and finally in Arizona. There's documentation that he did indeed have access to a large quantity of gold, though he never registered a claim for the mine that was attributed to him.

GOLDEN RUMORS

In 1868 Waltz appeared in the newly developing community of Pumpkinville, soon to become Phoenix. He kept to himself on his 160-acre homestead on the bank of the Salt River. From time to time he would disappear for a few weeks and return with enough high-quality ore to keep him in a wonderful fashion. Soon word was out that "Crazy Jake" had a vast gold mine in the Superstition Mountains, east of the city near the Apache Trail.

At the same time, stories about a wealthy gold mine discovered by the Peralta family of Mexico were circulating. Local Apaches raided the mine, which was near their sacred Thunder Mountain. In what became known as the Peralta Massacre, the Peraltas and more than 100 people working for them at the mine were killed. Rumors soon spread that Waltz had saved the life of a young Mexican who was part of Peralta's group—one of few who had escaped—and was shown the Peraltas' mine as a reward.

SEARCHING THE SUPERSTITIONS

As the legend of the Dutchman's mine grew, many opportunists attempted to follow Waltz into the Superstition Mountains. A crack marksman, Waltz quickly discouraged several who tried to track him. The flow of gold continued for several years.

In 1891 the Salt River flooded, badly damaging Waltz's home. When the floodwaters receded, neighbors found Waltz there in a weakened condition. He was taken to the nearby home and boardinghouse of Julia Thomas, who nursed the Dutchman for months. When his death was imminent, he reportedly gave Julia the directions to his mine.

Julia and another boarder searched for the mine fruitlessly. In her later years she sold maps to the treasure, based upon her recollections of Waltz's description. Thousands have searched for the lost mine, many losing their lives in the process—either to the brutality of fellow searchers or that of the rugged desert—and more than a century later gold seekers are still trying to connect the pieces of the puzzle.

THE LEGEND TODAY

There's no doubt that the Dutchman had a source of extremely rich gold ore. But was it in the Superstition Mountains, nearby Goldfields, or maybe even in the Four Peaks region? Wherever it was, it's still hidden. Perhaps the best-researched books on the subject are T.E. Glover's *The Lost Dutchman Mine of Jacob Waltz* and the companion book *The Holmes Manuscript*. Ron Feldman of OK Corral (☎ *480/982–4040* ⊕ *www.okcorrals. com*) in Apache Junction has become an expert on the subject during his 30-plus years in the region. He leads adventurers on pack trips into the mysterious mountains to relive the lore and legends.

ESSENTIALS

Visitor Information **Globe Chamber of Commerce** ✉ *1360 N. Broad St., 1.25 miles north of downtown on U.S. 60* ☎ *928/425–4495, 800/804–5623* 🌐 *www.globemiamichamber.com.*

EXPLORING

FAMILY **Besh-Ba-Gowah Archaeological Park.** For a step 800 years back in time, tour the 2 acres of the excavated Salado Indian site at the Besh-Ba-Gowah Archaeological Park on the southeastern side of town. After a trip through the small museum and a video introduction, enter the area full of remnants of more than 200 rooms occupied here by the Salado during the 13th and 14th centuries. Public areas include the central plaza (also the principal burial ground), roasting pits, and open patios. Besh-Ba-Gowah is a name given by the Apaches, who, arriving in the 17th century, found the pueblo abandoned, and moved in—loosely translated, the name means "metal camp," and remains left on the site point to it as part of an extensive commerce and trading network. ✉ *150 N. Pine St.* ☎ *928/425–0320* 🌐 *www.globeaz.gov/visitors/besh-ba-gowah* 🎟 *$5* 🕘 *Daily 9–5.*

WHERE TO EAT AND STAY

For expanded hotel reviews, visit Fodors.com.

$ MEXICAN 🍴 **Chalo's.** This roadside spot offers top-notch Mexican and Tex-Mex food for a slightly different flavor than your average Mexican plate. Chalo's specialty is using green chiles. Fortunately, you can request mild or spicy versions of green-chile enchiladas, burros, and practically anything else on the menu. Be sure to ask for water. Try the savory stuffed sopapillas, filled with pork and beef, beans, and red or green chiles. It's a favorite among locals, so plan for an early lunch or dinner to avoid a wait. [$] *Average main: $9* ✉ *902 E. Ash St.* ☎ *928/425–0515* 🌐 *www.chalosglobe.com.*

$ B&B/INN 🏨 **Noftsger Hill Inn.** Built in 1907, this B&B was originally the North Globe Schoolhouse; now classrooms serve as guest rooms, filled with mining-era antiques and affording fantastic views of the Pinal Mountains and historic Old Dominion Mine. **Pros:** giant windows offer pleasant natural light; many rooms have original classroom chalkboards devoted to guest comments. **Cons:** city slickers might miss modern bath fixtures and amenities. [$] *Rooms from: $125* ✉ *425 North St.* ☎ *928/425–2260, 877/780–2479* 🌐 *www.noftsgerhillinn.com* 🛏 *6 rooms* 🍽 *Breakfast.*

TONTO NATIONAL MONUMENT

30 miles northwest of Globe.

GETTING HERE AND AROUND

Tonto National Monument is located off AZ 188, approximately 25 miles north of U.S. 60. It's about a two-hour drive from the Phoenix area. If you feel like a real journey, take AZ 88, otherwise known as the Apache Trail, to Tonto National Monument. Almost half of the 47-mile trail is gravel, so be prepared for a very long and bumpy ride.

Hikers in the Superstition Mountains—perhaps searching for the riches of the Lost Dutchman Mine.

EXPLORING

Tonto National Monument. You can visit a well-preserved complex of 13th-century Salado cliff dwellings at this site. There's a self-guided walking tour of the Lower Cliff Dwellings, but if you can, take a ranger-led tour of the 40-room Upper Cliff Dwellings, offered on selected mornings from November to April. Tour reservations are required and should be made as far as a month in advance. ⊠ *26260 N. AZ Hwy. 188, Roosevelt* ☎ *928/467–2241* ⊕ *www.nps.gov/tont* ⊠ *$3* ⊗ *Daily 8–5.*

THEODORE ROOSEVELT LAKE RESERVOIR AND DAM

5 miles northwest of Tonto National Monument on AZ 188, 125 miles north of Phoenix.

GETTING HERE AND AROUND

Theodore Roosevelt Lake Reservoir and Dam is located off AZ 188, approximately 30 miles north of U.S. 60. It's on the same road as Tonto National Monument; the drive takes about two hours from Phoenix.

EXPLORING

Theodore Roosevelt Lake Reservoir & Dam. Flanked by the desolate Mazatzal and Sierra Anchas mountain ranges, Theodore Roosevelt Lake Reservoir & Dam is an aquatic recreational area—a favorite with bass anglers, water-skiers, and boaters. This is the largest masonry dam on the planet, and the massive bridge is the longest two-lane, single-span, steel-arch bridge in the nation. ⊠ *Tonto Basin Ranger Station, Roosevelt* ☎ *928/467–3200.*

EN ROUTE Past the reservoir, AZ 188 turns west and becomes a meandering dirt road, eventually winding its way back to Apache Junction via the magnificent, bronze-hued volcanic cliff walls of **Fish Creek Canyon**, with views of the sparkling lakes, towering saguaros, and, in the springtime, vast fields of wildflowers.

TORTILLA FLAT

18 miles southwest of Roosevelt Dam, 18 miles northeast of Apache Junction, 60 miles northeast of Phoenix.

GETTING HERE AND AROUND

Tortilla Flat is located off AZ 88, the bumpy and historic Apache Trail. It's about 60 miles from Downtown Phoenix, but leave at least two hours for the journey. Take U.S. 60 east of Phoenix through Apache Junction, then take the Idaho exit and head north toward AZ 88 and drive for approximately 18 miles. Be prepared for a bumpy and gravely ride on parts of AZ 88. It's historic for a reason.

EXPLORING

Tortilla Flat. Close to the end of the Apache Trail, this old-time restaurant and country store are what is left of an authentic stagecoach stop at Tortilla Flat. This is a fun place to stop for a well-earned rest and refreshment—miner- and cowboy-style grub, of course—before heading back the last 18 miles to civilization. Enjoy a hearty bowl of killer chili and some prickly-pear-cactus ice cream while sitting at the counter on a saddle bar stool. ☎ *480/984–1776* ⊕ *www.tortillaflataz.com.*

GRAND CANYON
NATIONAL PARK

WELCOME TO GRAND CANYON NATIONAL PARK

TOP REASONS TO GO

★ **Its status:** This is one of those places where you really want to say, "Been there, done that!"

★ **Awesome vistas:** Painted Desert, sandstone canyon walls, pine and fir forests, mesas, plateaus, volcanic features, the Colorado River, streams, and waterfalls make for some jaw-dropping moments.

★ **Year-round adventure:** Outdoor junkies can bike, boat, camp, fish, hike, ride mules, whitewater raft, watch birds and wildlife, cross-country ski, and snowshoe.

★ **Continuing education:** Adults and kids can have fun learning, thanks to free park-sponsored nature walks and interpretive programs.

★ **Sky-high and river-low experiences:** Experience the canyon via plane, train, and automobile, as well as by helicopter, row- or motorboat, bike, mule, or foot.

KANAB PLATEAU

Kanab Canyon

Tuweep The Dome

↙ TO
GRAND CANYON
WEST

3
WEST RIM   Supai

Havasu Canyon

• Toroweap Overlook

18
↓ TO PEAC

0 ———— 10 mi
0 ———— 10 km

1 South Rim. The South Rim is where the action is: Grand Canyon Village's lodging, camping, eateries, stores, and museums, plus plenty of trailheads into the canyon. Visitor services and facilities are open and available daily, including holidays. Four free shuttle routes cover more than 35 stops, and visitors who'd rather relax than rough it can treat themselves to comfy hotel rooms and elegant restaurant meals (lodging and camping reservations are essential).

2 North Rim. Of the nearly 5 million people who visit the park annually, 90% enter at the South Rim, but many consider the North Rim even more gorgeous—and worth the extra effort. Open only from mid-May to the end of October (or the first good snowfall), the North Rim has legitimate bragging rights: at more than 8,000 feet above sea level (1,000 feet higher than the South Rim), it has precious solitude and seven developed viewpoints. Rather than staring into the canyon's depths, you get a true sense of its expanse.

3 West Rim and Havasu Canyon. Though not in Grand Canyon National Park, the far-off-the-beaten-path western end of the canyon,

Beavertail cactus in bloom.

3

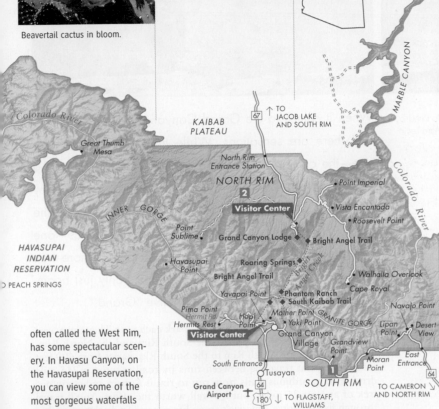

KAIBAB
PLATEAU

67 ↑ TO JACOB LAKE AND SOUTH RIM

North Rim Entrance Station

NORTH RIM

2

Visitor Center

Colorado River

MARBLE CANYON

Colorado River

• Point Imperial

• Vista Encantada

• Roosevelt Point

Point Sublime •

Grand Canyon Lodge ◆ ◆ Bright Angel Trail

Great Thumb Mesa

INNER GORGE

HAVASUPAI INDIAN RESERVATION

Havasupai Point •

Roaring Springs •

Bright Angel Trail •

Bright Angel Creek

• Walhalla Overlook

Cape Royal

○ PEACH SPRINGS

Yavapai Point ◆

◆ Phantom Ranch

South Kaibab Trail ◆

Navajo Point •

Pima Point •
Hermit Rd.
Hermits Rest •

Hopi Point •

Mather Point • GRANITE GORGE

• Yoki Point

Lipan Point •

• Desert View

Visitor Center

Grand Canyon Village

Grandview Point

Moran Point

East Entrance

South Entrance ○ Tusayan

SOUTH RIM

64

TO CAMERON AND NORTH RIM

Grand Canyon Airport ✈ 64

180 ↓ TO FLAGSTAFF, WILLIAMS

often called the West Rim, has some spectacular scenery. In Havasu Canyon, on the Havasupai Reservation, you can view some of the most gorgeous waterfalls in the United States. On the Hualapai Reservation, the Skywalk has become a major draw. This U-shape glass-floored deck juts out 3,600 feet above the Colorado River and isn't for the faint of heart.

Desert view watchtower was designed by Mary Colter in 1932.

GETTING ORIENTED

Grand Canyon National Park is a superstar—biologically, historically, and recreationally. One of the world's best examples of arid-land erosion, the canyon provides a record of three of the four eras of geological time. Almost 2 billion years' worth of Earth's history is written in the colored layers of rock stacked from the river bottom to the top of the plateau. In addition to its diverse fossil record, the park reveals long-ago traces of human adaptation to an unforgiving environment. It's also home to several major ecosystems, five of the world's seven life zones, three of North America's four desert types, and all kinds of rare, endemic, and protected plant and animal species.

Updated by
Mara Levin

When it comes to the Grand Canyon, there are statistics, and there are sensations. While the former are impressive—the canyon measures in at an average width of 10 miles, length of 277 river miles, and depth of 1 mile—they don't truly prepare you for that first impression. Seeing the canyon for the first time is an astounding experience—one that's hard to wrap your head around. In fact, it's more than an experience, it's an emotion, one that's only just beginning to be captured with the superlative "Grand."

Roughly 5 million visitors come to the park each year. They can access the canyon via two main points: the South Rim and the North Rim. The width from the North Rim to the South Rim varies from 600 feet to 18 miles, but traveling between rims by road requires a 215-mile drive. Hiking arduous trails from rim to rim is a steep and strenuous trek of at least 21 miles, but it's well worth the effort. You'll travel through five of North America's seven life zones. (To do this any other way, you'd have to journey from the Mexican desert to the Canadian woods.) In total, more than 600 miles of mostly very primitive trails traverse the canyon, with about 51 of those miles maintained. West of Grand Canyon National Park, the tribal lands of the Hualapai and the Havasupai lie along the so-called West Rim of the canyon.

GRAND CANYON PLANNER

WHEN TO GO

There's no bad time to visit the canyon, though the busiest times of year are summer and spring break. Visiting during these peak seasons, as well as holidays, requires patience and a tolerance for crowds. Note that weather changes on a whim in this exposed high-desert region. The North Rim shuts down from the end of October through mid-May due to weather conditions and related road closures.

FESTIVALS AND EVENTS

MAY **Williams Rendezvous Days.** A black-powder shooting competition, 1800s-era crafts, horse-barrel racing, and a parade fire up Memorial Day weekend in honor of Bill Williams, the town's namesake mountain man. ☎ *928/635–4061* ⊕ *www.experiencewilliams.com.*

AUGUST **Grand Canyon Music Festival.** For three weekends in late August–early September, this festival brings mostly chamber music to the Shrine of Ages amphitheater at Grand Canyon Village. In the early 1980s, music aficionados Robert Bonfiglio and Clare Hoffman hiked through the Grand Canyon and decided the stunning spectacle should be accompanied by the strains of a symphony. One of the park rangers agreed, and the wandering musicians performed an impromptu concert. Encouraged by the experience, Bonfiglio and Hoffman started the festival. ☎ *928/638–9215, 800/997–8285* ⊕ *www.grandcanyonmusicfest.org.*

DECEMBER **Mountain Village Holiday.** Williams hails the holidays with a parade of lights, ice-skating rink, and live entertainment in December–early January. ☎ *928/635–4061* ⊕ *www.experiencewilliams.com.*

PLANNING YOUR TIME

Plan ahead: mule rides require at least a six-month advance reservation, and longer for the busy season (most can be reserved up to 13 months in advance). Multiday rafting trips should be reserved at least a year in advance.

Once you arrive, pick up the free detailed map and *The Guide,* a newspaper with a schedule of free programs.

The park is most crowded on the South Rim, especially near the south entrance and in Grand Canyon Village, as well as on the scenic drives, particularly the 23-mile Desert View Drive.

GRAND CANYON IN 1 DAY

Start early, pack a picnic lunch, and drive to the South Rim's **Grand Canyon Visitor Center** just north of the south entrance, to pick up info and see your first incredible view at **Mather Point.** Continue east along **Desert View Drive** for about 2 miles to **Yaki Point**. Next, continue driving 7 miles east to **Grandview Point** for a good view of the buttes Krishna Shrine and Vishnu Temple. Go 4 miles east and catch the view at **Moran Point,** then 3 miles to the **Tusayan Ruin and Museum,** where a small display is devoted to the history of the Ancestral Puebloans. Continue another mile east to **Lipan Point** to view the Colorado River. In less than a mile, you'll arrive at **Navajo Point,** the highest elevation on the South Rim. **Desert View and Watchtower** is the final attraction along Desert View Drive.

On your return drive, stop off at any of the picnic areas for lunch. Once back at Grand Canyon Village, walk the paved **Rim Trail** to **Maricopa Point.** Along the way, pick up souvenirs in the village and stop at historic **El Tovar Hotel** for dinner (be sure to make reservations well in advance). If you have time, take the shuttle on **Hermit Road** to **Hermits Rest,** 7 miles away. Along that route, Hopi Point and Powell Point are excellent spots to watch the sunset.

GRAND CANYON IN 3 DAYS

On Day 1, follow the one-day itinerary for the morning, but spend more time exploring Desert View Drive and enjoy a leisurely picnic lunch. Later, drive 30 miles beyond Desert View to Cameron Trading Post, which has a good restaurant and is an interesting side trip. Travel Hermit Road on your second morning, and drive to Grand Canyon Airport for a late-morning small plane or helicopter tour. Have lunch in **Tusayan** and cool off at the IMAX film *Grand Canyon: The Hidden Secrets*. Back in the village, take a free ranger-led program. On your third day, hike partway down the canyon on **Bright Angel Trail**. It takes twice as long to hike back up, so plan accordingly. Get trail maps at **Grand Canyon Visitor Center,** and bring plenty of water.

Alternatively, spend days 2 and 3 exploring the remote **West Rim**, 150 miles toward Nevada or California and far away from major highways. Fill the first day with a horseback ride along the rim, a helicopter ride into the canyon, or a pontoon boat ride on the Colorado River. The next day, raft the Class V-VII rapids. Another option is to get a tribal permit and spend Days 2 and 3 in **Havasu Canyon,** a truly spiritual backcountry experience. You can opt to hike, ride horseback, or take a helicopter 8 miles down to the small village of Supai and the Havasupai Lodge.

GETTING HERE AND AROUND
SOUTH RIM

AIR TRAVEL   North Las Vegas Airport in Las Vegas is the primary air hub for charter flights to **Grand Canyon National Parks Airport** (*GCN* ☎ *928/638–2446*).

CAR TRAVEL   The best route into the park from the east or south is from Flagstaff. Take U.S. 180 northwest to the park's southern entrance and Grand Canyon Village. From the west on Interstate 40, the most direct route to the South Rim is on U.S. 180 and Highway 64.

PARK SHUTTLE TRAVEL   The South Rim is open to car traffic year-round, though access to Hermits Rest is limited to shuttle buses part of the year. There are four free shuttle routes: **The Hermits Rest Route** operates March through November, between Grand Canyon Village and Hermits Rest. **The Village Route** operates year-round in the village area near the Grand Canyon Visitor Center. **The Kaibab Rim Route** goes from the visitor center to Yaki Point, including a stop at the South Kaibab Trailhead. **The Tusayan Route** operates summer only and runs from Grand Canyon Visitor Center to the town of Tusayan. ■TIP→ In summer, South Rim roads are congested, and it's easier, and sometimes required, to park your car and take the free shuttle. Running from one hour before sunrise until one hour after sunset, shuttles arrive every 15 to 30 minutes at 30 clearly marked stops.

TAXI AND SHUTTLE TRAVEL   While there's no public transportation into the Grand Canyon, you can hire a taxi to take you from the Grand Canyon Airport or any of the Tusayan hotels. Arizona Shuttle is another option.

Shuttle and Taxi Contacts Arizona Shuttle. Arizona Shuttle has service between Phoenix, Sedona, Flagstaff, Williams, Tusayan, and Grand Canyon Village. ☎ *928/226–8060, 877/226–8060* ⊕ *www.arizonashuttle.com.* **Xanterra.** Xanterra offers 24-hour taxi service in Tusayan and the South Rim. ☎ *928/638–2822.*

TRAIN TRAVEL **Grand Canyon Railway.** There is no need to deal with all of the other drivers racing to the South Rim. Sit back and relax in the comfy train cars of the Grand Canyon Railway. Live music and storytelling enliven the trip as you journey past the landscape through prairie, ranch, and national park land to the log-cabin train station in Grand Canyon Village. You won't see the Grand Canyon from the train, but you can walk or catch the shuttle at the restored, historic Grand Canyon Railway Station. The vintage train departs from the Williams Depot every morning, and makes the 65-mile journey in 2¼ hours. You can do the round-trip in a single day; however, it's a more relaxing and enjoyable strategy to stay for a night or two at the South Rim before returning to Williams. ⇨ *See Grand Canyon Railway Hotel in Where to Stay.* ☎ 800/843-8724 ⊕ *www.thetrain.com* ☒ *$75–$190 round-trip.*

NORTH RIM

AIR TRAVEL The nearest airport to the North Rim is **St. George Municipal Airport** (☎ 435/627-4080 ⊕ *www.flysgu.com*) in Utah, 164 miles north, with regular service provided by both Delta and United Airlines.

CAR TRAVEL To reach the North Rim by car, take U.S. 89 north from Flagstaff past Cameron, turning left onto U.S. 89A at Bitter Springs. At Jacob Lake, take Highway 67 directly to the Grand Canyon North Rim. You can drive yourself to the scenic viewpoints and trailheads; the only transportation offered in the Park is a shuttle twice each morning that brings eager hikers from Grand Canyon Lodge to the North Kaibab Trailhead (a 2-mile trip). Note that the North Rim shuts down in winter following the first major snowfall (usually the end of October); Highway 67 south of Jacob Lake is closed.

SHUTTLE TRAVEL From mid-May to mid-October, the **Trans Canyon Shuttle** (☎ 928/638-2820 ⊕ *www.trans-canyonshuttle.com*) travels daily between the South and North rims—the ride takes 4½ hours each way. One-way fare is $85, round-trip $160. Reservations are required.

PARK ESSENTIALS

PARK FEES AND PERMITS

A fee of $25 per vehicle or $12 per person for pedestrians and cyclists is good for one week's access at both rims.

The $50 Grand Canyon Pass gives unlimited access to the park for 12 months. The annual America the Beautiful **National Parks and Recreational Land Pass** (☎ 888/275-8747 ⊕ *store.usgs.gov/pass* ☒ *$80*) provides unlimited access to all national parks and federal recreation areas for 12 months.

No permits are needed for day hikers; but **backcountry permits** (☎ 928/638-7875 ⊕ *www.nps.gov/grca* ☒ *$10, plus $5 per person per night*) are necessary for overnight hikers camping below the rim. Permits are limited, so make your reservation as far in advance as possible—they're taken by fax (☎ 928/638-2125) or mail only, up to four months ahead of arrival. **Camping** in the park is restricted to designated campgrounds (☎ 877/444-6777 ⊕ *www.recreation.gov*).

PARK HOURS

The South Rim is open continuously every day of the year (weather permitting), while the North Rim is open from May through the end of October. The park is in the mountain standard time zone year-round. Daylight saving time isn't observed.

CELL PHONE RECEPTION

Cell phone coverage can be spotty at both the South Rim and North Rim—though Verizon customers report better reception at the South Rim. Don't expect a strong signal anywhere in the park.

RESTAURANTS

Within the park on the South Rim, you can find everything from cafeteria food to casual café fare to creatively prepared, Western- and Southwestern-inspired American cuisine. There's even a coffeehouse with organic joe. Reservations are accepted (and recommended) only for dinner at El Tovar Dining Room; they can be made up to six months in advance with El Tovar room reservations, 30 days in advance without. You should also make dinner reservations at the Grand Canyon Lodge Dining Room on the North Rim—as the only "upscale" dining option, the restaurant fills up quickly at dinner throughout the season (the two other choices on the North Rim are a cafeteria and a chuck-wagon-style Grand Cookout experience). The dress code is casual across the board, but El Tovar is your best option if you're looking to dress up a bit and thumb through an extensive wine list. Drinking water and restrooms aren't available at most picnic spots.

Eateries outside the park generally range from mediocre to terrible— you didn't come all the way to the Grand Canyon for the food, did you? Our selections highlight your best options. Of towns near the park, Williams definitely has the leg up on culinary variety and quality, with Tusayan (near the South Rim) and Jacob Lake (to the north) offering mostly either fast food or merely adequate sit-down restaurants. Near the park, even the priciest places welcome casual dress. On the Hualapai and Havasupai reservations in Havasu Canyon and on the West Rim, dining is limited and basic.

Prices in the reviews are the average cost of a main course at dinner or, if dinner isn't served, at lunch.

HOTELS

The park's accommodations include three "historic-rustic" facilities and four motel-style lodges, all of which have undergone significant upgrades over the past decade. Of the 922 rooms, cabins, and suites, only 203, all at the Grand Canyon Lodge, are at the North Rim. Outside El Tovar Hotel, the canyon's architectural highlight, accommodations are relatively basic but comfortable, and the most sought-after rooms have canyon views. Rates vary widely, but most rooms fall in the $100 to $180 range, though the most basic units at the South Rim go for just $83.

Reservations are a must, especially during the busy summer season. ■TIP➔ **If you want to get your first choice (especially Bright Angel Lodge or El Tovar), make reservations as far in advance as possible; they're taken up to 13 months ahead.** You might find a last-minute cancellation, but you shouldn't count on it. Although lodging at the South Rim will keep you close to the action, the frenetic activity and crowded facilities are off-putting to some. With short notice, the best time to find a room on the South Rim is in winter. And though the North Rim is less crowded than the South Rim, the only lodging available is at Grand Canyon Lodge.

Just south of the South Rim park boundary, Tusayan's hotels are in a convenient location but without bargains, while Williams (about an hour's drive) can provide price breaks on food and lodging, as well as a respite from the crowds. Extra amenities (e.g., swimming pools and gyms) are also more abundant. Reservations are always a good idea. At the West Rim, lodging options are extremely limited; you can purchase a "package," which includes lodging and a visitation permit, through Hualapai Tourism.

Prices in the reviews are the lowest cost of a standard double room in high season. For expanded reviews, visit Fodors.com.

Lodging Contacts Xanterra Parks & Resorts. Xanterra Parks & Resorts operates all lodging and dining services at the South Rim as well as Phantom Ranch, deep inside the canyon. ☎ *888/297–2757* ⊕ *www.grandcanyonlodges.com.*

TOURS

Grand Canyon Field Institute. Instructors lead guided educational tours, hikes around the canyon, and weekend programs at the South Rim. With more than 200 classes a year, tour topics include everything from archaeology and backcountry medicine to photography and natural history. Contact GCFI for a schedule and price list. Private hikes can be arranged. Discounted classes are available for members; annual dues are $35. ☎ *928/638–2485, 866/471–4435* ⊕ *www.grandcanyon.org/fieldinstitute* ⊞ *$475–$850 for most classes.*

Xanterra Motorcoach Tours. Narrated by knowledgeable guides, tours include the Hermits Rest Tour, which travels along the old wagon road built by the Santa Fe Railway; the Desert View Tour, which glimpses the Colorado River's rapids and stops at Lipan Point; Sunrise and Sunset Tours; and combination tours. Children 16 and younger are free when accompanied by a paying adult. ☎ *303/297–2757, 888/297–2757* ⊕ *www.grandcanyonlodges.com* ⊞ *$21–$60.*

VISITOR INFORMATION

PARK CONTACT INFORMATION

Grand Canyon National Park. Before you go, get the complimentary *Trip Planner,* updated regularly, from the Grand Canyon National Park. ☎ *928/638–7888* ⊕ *www.nps.gov/grca.*

VISITOR CENTERS

SOUTH RIM **Desert View Information Center.** Near the watchtower, at Desert View Point, the nonprofit Grand Canyon Association store and information center has a nice selection of books, park pamphlets, gifts, and educational materials. All sales from the Association stores go to support the park programs. ⊠ *East entrance* ☎ *800/858–2808, 928/638–7888* ☉ *Daily 9–5; hrs vary in winter.*

Grand Canyon Visitor Center. The park's main orientation center, known formerly as Canyon View Information Plaza, near Mather Point, provides pamphlets and resources to help plan your sightseeing as well as engaging interpretive exhibits on the park. Rangers are on hand to answer questions and aid in planning canyon excursions. A bookstore is stocked with books covering all topics on the Grand Canyon, and a daily schedule of ranger-led hikes and evening lectures is posted on a bulletin board inside. A 20-minute film about the history, geology, and wildlife of the canyon plays every 30 minutes in the theater. There's ample parking by the information center, though it is also accessible via a short walk from Mather Point, a short ride on the shuttle bus Village Route, or a leisurely 1-mile walk on the Greenway Trail—a paved pathway that meanders through the forest. ⊠ *East side of Grand Canyon Village, 450 State Rte. 64, Grand Canyon* ☎ *928/638–7888* ⊕ *www.explorethecanyon.com* ☉ *Daily 8–5, outdoor exhibits may be viewed anytime.*

> **WORD OF MOUTH**
>
> "Take Highway 64 toward Grand Canyon Village, which will take you along the East Rim and Desert View Drive. There are over a half-dozen viewpoints on this scenic road, each with its own features and perspective on the Grand Canyon." —K_Bot

Grand Canyon Verkamp's Visitor Center. After 102 years of selling memorabilia and knickknacks on the South Rim across from El Tovar Hotel, Verkamp's Curios moved into the park's newest visitor center in 2008. The building now serves as a bookstore, ranger station, and museum with exhibits on the Verkamp family and the pioneer history of the region. ⊠ *Desert View Dr. across from El Tovar Hotel, Grand Canyon Village* ☎ *928/638–7146* ☉ *Daily 8–7; ranger station 8–5.*

Yavapai Geology Museum. Learn about the geology of the canyon at this museum and bookstore run by the Grand Canyon Association. You can also catch the park shuttle bus or pick up information for the Rim Trail here. The views of the canyon and Phantom Ranch from inside this historic building are stupendous. ⊠ *1 mile east of Market Plaza, Grand Canyon Village* ☎ *928/638–7888* ☉ *Daily 8–8; hrs vary in winter.*

NORTH RIM **North Rim Visitor Center.** View exhibits, peruse the bookstore, and pick up useful maps and brochures at this visitor center. Interpretive programs are often scheduled in summer. If you're craving coffee, it's a short walk from here to the Roughrider Saloon at the Grand Canyon Lodge. ⊠ *Near the parking lot on Bright Angel Peninsula* ☎ *928/638–7864* ⊕ *www.nps.gov/grca* ☉ *Mid-May–mid-Oct., daily 8–6; mid-Oct.–Nov., daily 9–4.*

GRAND CANYON SOUTH RIM

Visitors to the canyon converge mostly on the South Rim, and mostly in summer. Grand Canyon Village is here, with most of the park's lodging and camping, trailheads, restaurants, stores, and museums, along with a nearby airport and railroad depot. Believe it or not, the average stay in the park is a mere half day or so; this is not advised! You need to spend several days to truly appreciate this marvelous place, but at the very least, give it a full day. Hike down into the canyon, or along the rim, to get away from the crowds and experience nature at its finest.

EXPLORING

SCENIC DRIVES

Desert View Drive. This heavily traveled 23-mile stretch of road follows the rim from the East entrance to Grand Canyon Village. Starting from the less-congested entry near Desert View, road warriors can get their first glimpse of the canyon from the 70-foot-tall watchtower, the top of which provides the highest viewpoint on the South Rim. Eight overlooks, the remains of an Ancestral Puebloan dwelling at the Tusayan Ruin and Museum, and the secluded and lovely Buggeln picnic area make for great stops along the South Rim. The Kaibab Trail Route shuttle bus travels a short section of Desert View Drive and takes 50 minutes to ride round-trip without getting off at any of the stops: Grand Canyon Visitor Center, South Kaibab Trailhead, Yaki Point, and Pipe Creek Vista, Mather Point, and Yavapai Geology Museum.

Hermit Road. The Santa Fe Company built Hermit Road, formerly known as West Rim Drive, in 1912 as a scenic tour route. Nine overlooks dot this 7-mile stretch, each worth a visit. The road is filled with hairpin turns, so make sure you adhere to posted speed limits. A 1.5-mile Greenway trail offers easy access to cyclists looking to enjoy the original 1912 Hermit Rim Road. From March through November, Hermit Road is closed to private auto traffic because of congestion; during this period, a free shuttle bus carries visitors to all the overlooks. Riding the bus round-trip without getting off at any of the viewpoints takes 75 minutes; the return trip stops only at Pima, Mohave, and Powell points.

HISTORIC SITES

Kolb Studio. Built over several years beginning in 1904 by the Kolb brothers as a photographic workshop and residence, this building provides a view of Indian Garden, where, in the days before a pipeline was installed, Emery Kolb descended 3,000 feet each day to get the water he needed to develop his prints. Kolb was doing something right; he operated the studio until he died in 1976 at age 95. The gallery here has changing exhibitions of paintings, photography, and crafts. There's also a small Grand Canyon Association store here. During the winter months, a ranger-led tour of the studio illustrates the role the Kolb brothers had on the development of the Grand Canyon. Call ahead to sign up for the tour. ⊠ *Grand Canyon Village near Bright Angel Lodge* ☎ *928/638–2771* ⊕ *www.grandcanyon.org/kolb* ⊠ *Free* ⊙ *Apr.–mid-Oct., daily 8–7; mid-Oct.–Apr., daily 8–5.*

Lookout Studio. Built in 1914 to compete with the Kolbs' photographic studio, the building was designed by architect Mary Jane Colter. The combination lookout point and gift shop has a collection of fossils and geologic samples from around the world. An upstairs loft provides another excellent overlook into the gorge below. ⊠ *About 0.25 mile west of Hermit Rd. Junction on Hermit Rd.* ⊠ *Free* ⊙ *Daily 9–5.*

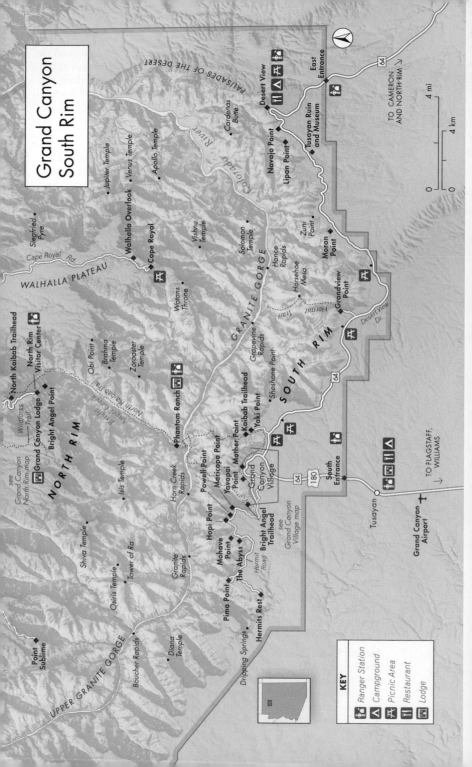

Grand Canyon South Rim

PALISADES OF THE DESERT

Colorado River

GRANITE GORGE

UPPER GRANITE GORGE

WALHALLA PLATEAU

NORTH RIM

SOUTH RIM

Cape Royal Rd.

Desert View Dr.

Hermit Trail

North Kaibab Trail

Bright Angel Trail

Wildforss Trail

Hermit Road

Points and features

Point Sublime

Siegfried Pyre

Shiva Temple

Osiris Temple

Tower of Ra

Isis Temple

Diana Temple

Boucher Rapids

Dripping Springs

Granite Rapids

Horn Creek Rapids

Hopi Point

Mohave Point

The Abyss

Pima Point

Hermits Rest

Powell Point

Maricopa Point

Yavapai Point

Mather Point

Bright Angel Trailhead

Grand Canyon Village

Kaibab Trailhead

Yaki Point

Shoshone Point

Grapevine Rapids

Horseshoe Mesa

Grandview Point

Zuni Point

Moran Point

Hance Rapids

Solomon Temple

Vishnu Temple

Wotans Throne

Obi Point

Brahma Temple

Zoroaster Temple

Phantom Ranch

North Kaibab Trailhead

North Rim Visitor Center

Grand Canyon Lodge

Bright Angel Point

Jupiter Temple

Venus Temple

Apollo Temple

Walhalla Overlook

Cape Royal

Cardenas Butte

Desert View

East Entrance

Tusayan Ruin and Museum

Navajo Point

Lipan Point

South Entrance

Tusayan

Grand Canyon Airport

see Grand Canyon North Rim map

see Grand Canyon Village map

TO CAMERON AND NORTH RIM →

TO FLAGSTAFF, WILLIAMS ←

64

180

0   4 mi

0   4 km

KEY

Ranger Station

Campground

Picnic Area

Restaurant

Lodge

BEST GRAND CANYON VIEWS

The best time of day to see the canyon is before 10 am and after 4 pm, when the angle of the sun brings out the colors of the rock, and clouds and shadows add dimension. Colors deepen dramatically among the contrasting layers of the canyon walls just before and during sunrise and sunset.

Hopi Point is the top spot on the South Rim to watch the sun set; **Yaki** and **Pima** points also offer vivid views. For a grand sunrise, try **Mather** or **Yaki** points.

■TIP➜ Arrive at least 30 minutes early for sunrise views and as much as 90 minutes for sunset views at these points. For another point of view, take a leisurely stroll along the Rim Trail and watch the color change along with the views. Timetables are listed in *The Guide* and are posted at park visitor centers.

Powell Memorial. A granite platform honors the memory of John Wesley Powell, who measured, charted, and named many of the canyons and creeks of the Colorado River. It was here that the dedication ceremony for Grand Canyon National Park took place on April 3, 1920. ⊠ *About 3 miles west of Hermit Rd. Junction on Hermit Rd.*

Tusayan Ruin and Museum. Completed in 1932, this museum offers a quick orientation to the lifestyles of the prehistoric and modern Indian populations associated with the Grand Canyon and the Colorado Plateau. Adjacent, an excavation of an 800-year-old dwelling gives a glimpse of the lives of some of the area's earliest residents. Of special interest are split-twig figurines dating back 2,000 to 4,000 years ago, a replica of a 10,000-year-old spear point, and other artifacts left behind by ancient cultures. Twice daily, a ranger leads an interpretive tour of the Ancestral Puebloan village along a 0.1-mile, paved loop trail. ⊠ *About 20 miles east of Grand Canyon Village on Desert View Dr.* ☎ *928/638–7888* ⊠ *Free* ☽ *Daily 9–5.*

SCENIC STOPS

The Abyss. At an elevation of 6,720 feet, the Abyss is one of the most awesome stops on Hermit Road, revealing a sheer drop of 3,000 feet to the Tonto Platform, a wide terrace of Tapeats sandstone about two-thirds of the way down the canyon. From the Abyss you'll also see several isolated sandstone columns, the largest of which is called the Monument. ⊠ *About 5 miles west of Hermit Rd. Junction on Hermit Rd.*

Desert View and Watchtower. From the top of the 70-foot stone-and-mortar watchtower, even the muted hues of the distant Painted Desert to the east and the Vermilion Cliffs rising from a high plateau near the Utah border are visible. In the chasm below, angling to the north toward Marble Canyon, an imposing stretch of the Colorado River reveals itself. Up several flights of stairs, the watchtower houses a glass-enclosed observatory with powerful telescopes. ⊠ *About 23 miles east of Grand Canyon Village on Desert View Dr.* ☎ *928/638–2736* ☽ *Daily 8–8; hrs vary in winter.*

DID YOU KNOW?

From the Grand Canyon's edge, the Colorado River is up to 1 mile deep. Almost 40 exposed bands of rock represent different geological periods—the oldest sections date back some 2 billion years.

Hermits Rest. This westernmost viewpoint and Hermit Trail, which descends from it, were named for "hermit" Louis Boucher, a 19th-century French-Canadian prospector who had a number of mining claims and a roughly built home down in the canyon. Views from here include Hermit Rapids and the towering cliffs of the Supai and Redwall formations. In the stone building at Hermits Rest you can buy curios and snacks. ⊠ *About 8 miles west of Hermit Rd. Junction on Hermit Rd.*

Hopi Point. From this elevation of 6,800 feet, you can see a large section of the Colorado River; although it appears as a thin line, the river is nearly 350 feet wide below this overlook. The overlook extends farther into the canyon than any other point on Hermit Road. The unobstructed views make this a popular place to watch the sunset.

Across the canyon to the north is Shiva Temple, which remained an unexplored section of the Kaibab Plateau until 1937. That year, Harold Anthony of the American Museum of Natural History led an expedition to the rock formation in the belief that it supported life that had been cut off from the rest of the canyon. Imagine the expedition members' surprise when they found an empty Kodak film box on top of the temple—it had been left behind by Emery Kolb, who felt slighted for not having been invited to partake of Anthony's tour.

Directly below Hopi Point lies Dana Butte, named for a prominent 19th-century geologist. In 1919, an entrepreneur proposed connecting Hopi Point, Dana Butte, and the Tower of Set across the river with an aerial tramway, a technically feasible plan that fortunately has not been realized. ⊠ *About 4 miles west of Hermit Rd. Junction on Hermit Rd.*

Lipan Point. Here, at the canyon's widest point, you can get an astonishing visual profile of the gorge's geologic history, with a view of every eroded layer of the canyon—you can also observe one of the longest stretches of visible Colorado River. The spacious panorama stretches to the Vermilion Cliffs on the northeastern horizon and features a multitude of imaginatively named spires, buttes, and temples—intriguing rock formations named after their resemblance to ancient pyramids. You can also see Unkar Delta, where a creek joins the Colorado to form powerful rapids and a broad beach. Ancestral Puebloan farmers worked the Unkar Delta for hundreds of years, growing corn, beans, and melons. ⊠ *About 25 miles east of Grand Canyon Village on Desert View Dr.*

Maricopa Point. This site merits a stop not only for the arresting scenery, which includes the Colorado River below, but also for its view of a defunct mine operation. On your left, as you face the canyon, are the Orphan Mine, a mine shaft, and cable lines leading up to the rim. The mine, which started operations in 1893, was worked first for copper and then for uranium until the venture came to a halt in 1969—little remains of the mine infrastructure today, but some displays along the Rim Trail discuss its history. The Battleship, the red butte directly ahead of you in the canyon, was named during the Spanish-American War, when warships were in the news. ⊠ *About 2 miles west of Hermit Rd. Junction on Hermit Rd.*

Mather Point. You'll likely get your first glimpse of the canyon from this viewpoint, one of the most impressive and accessible (and most crowded) on the South Rim. Named for the National Park Service's first director, Stephen Mather, this spot yields extraordinary views of the Grand Canyon, including deep into the inner gorge and numerous buttes: Wotans Throne, Brahma Temple, and Zoroaster Temple, among others. The Grand Canyon Lodge, on the North Rim, is almost directly north from Mather Point and only 10 miles away—yet you have to drive 215 miles to get from one spot to the other. ⊠ *Near Grand Canyon Visitor Center* ☎ *928/638–7888* ⊕ *www.nps.gov/grca.*

Mohave Point. Some of the canyon's most magnificent stone spires and buttes visible from this lesser-known overlook include the Tower of Set; the Tower of Ra; and Isis, Osiris, and Horus temples. From here you can view the 5,401-foot Cheops Pyramid, a grayish rock formation behind Dana Butte, plus some of the strongest rapids on the Colorado River. ⊠ *About 5 miles west of Hermit Rd. Junction on Hermit Rd.*

Moran Point. This point was named for American landscape artist Thomas Moran, who was especially fond of the play of light and shadows from this location. He first visited the canyon with John Wesley Powell in 1873. "Thomas Moran's name, more than any other, with the possible exception of Major Powell's, is to be associated with the Grand Canyon," wrote noted canyon photographer Ellsworth Kolb. It's fitting that Moran Point is a favorite spot of photographers and painters. ⊠ *About 17 miles east of Grand Canyon Village on Desert View Dr.*

Navajo Point. A possible site of the first Spanish view into the canyon in 1540, this overlook is also at the highest natural elevation (7,461 feet) on the South Rim. ⊠ *About 21 miles east of Grand Canyon Village on Desert View Dr.*

Pima Point. Enjoy a bird's-eye view of Tonto Platform and Tonto Trail, which winds its way through the canyon for more than 70 miles. Also to the west, two dark, cone-shape mountains—Mount Trumbull and Mount Logan—are visible on the North Rim on clear days. They rise in stark contrast to the surrounding flat-top mesas and buttes. ⊠ *About 7 miles west of Hermit Rd. Junction on Hermit Rd.*

Trailview Overlook. Look down on a dramatic view of the Bright Angel and Plateau Point trails as they zigzag down the canyon. In the deep gorge to the north flows Bright Angel Creek, one of the region's few permanent tributary streams of the Colorado River. Toward the south is an unobstructed view of the distant San Francisco Peaks, as well as Bill Williams Mountain (on the horizon) and Red Butte (about 15 miles south of the canyon rim). ⊠ *About 2 miles west of Hermit Rd. Junction on Hermit Rd.*

Yaki Point. Stop here for an exceptional view of Wotan's Throne, a flat-top butte named by François Matthes, a U.S. Geological Survey scientist who developed the first topographical map of the Grand Canyon. The overlook juts out over the canyon, providing unobstructed views of inner-canyon rock formations, South Rim cliffs, and Clear Creek canyon. About a mile south of Yaki Point, you'll come to the trailhead for the South Kaibab Trail. The point is one of the best places on the

CLOSE UP

Tips for Avoiding Grand Canyon Crowds

It's hard to commune with nature while you're searching for a parking place, dodging video cameras, and stepping away from strollers. However, this scenario is likely only during the peak summer months. One option is to bypass Grand Canyon National Park altogether and head to the West Rim of the canyon, tribal land of the Hualapai and Havasupai. If only the park itself will do, the following tips will help you to keep your distance and your cool.

TAKE ANOTHER ROUTE

Avoid road rage by choosing a different route to the South Rim, forgoing the traditional Highways 64 and U.S. 180 from Flagstaff. Take U.S. 89 north from Flagstaff instead, passing near Sunset Crater and Wupatki national monuments. When you reach the junction with Highway 64, take a break at Cameron Trading Post (1 mile north of the junction)—or stay overnight. This is a good place to shop for Native American artifacts, souvenirs, and the usual postcards, dream-catchers, recordings, and T-shirts. There are also high-quality Navajo rugs, jewelry, and other authentic handicrafts, and you can sample Navajo tacos. U.S. 64 to the west takes you directly to

the park's east entrance; the scenery along the Little Colorado River gorge en route is eye-popping. It's 23 miles from the east entrance to the visitor center at Grand Canyon Visitor Center.

SKIP THE SOUTH RIM

Although the North Rim is just 10 miles across from the South Rim, the trip to get there by car is a five-hour drive of 215 miles. At first it might not sound like the trip would be worth it, but the payoff is huge. Along the way, you'll travel through some of the prettiest parts of the state and be granted even more stunning views than those on the more easily accessible South Rim. Those who make the North Rim trip often insist it has the canyon's most beautiful views and best hiking. To get to the North Rim from Flagstaff, take U.S. 89 north past Cameron, turning left onto U.S. 89A at Bitter Springs. En route you'll pass the area known as Vermilion Cliffs. At Jacob Lake, take Highway 67 directly to the Grand Canyon North Rim. North Rim services are closed from November through mid-May because of heavy snow, but in summer months and early fall, it's a wonderful way to beat the crowds at the South Rim.

3

South Rim to watch the sunset. ⊠ *2 miles east of Grand Canyon Village on Desert View Dr.*

Fodor's Choice ★ **Yavapai Point.** This is also one of the best locations on the South Rim to watch the sunset. Dominated by the Yavapai Geology Museum and Observation Station, this point displays panoramic views of the mighty gorge through a wall of windows. Exhibits at the museum include videos of the canyon floor and the Colorado River, a scaled diorama of the canyon with national park boundaries, fossils and rock fragments used to re-create the complex layers of the canyon walls, and a display on the natural forces used to carve the chasm. Rangers dig even deeper into Grand Canyon geology with free ranger programs daily. Check ahead for special events, guided walks, and program schedules. There's

Switchbacks on the canyon's trails make the steep grade level enough for hikers (and mules).

also a bookstore. ⊠ *Adjacent to Grand Canyon Village* 🎫 *Free* ⊘ *Daily 8–8; hrs vary in winter.*

EDUCATIONAL OFFERINGS
RANGER PROGRAMS

Interpretive Ranger Programs. The National Park Service sponsors all sorts of orientation activities, such as daily guided hikes and talks, which change with the seasons. The focus may be on any aspect of the canyon—from geology and flora and fauna to history and early inhabitants. For schedules on the South Rim, go to Grand Canyon Visitor Center, pick up a free copy of *The Guide,* or check online. 🕾 *928/638–7888* ⊕ *www.nps.gov/grca* 🎫 *Free.*

FAMILY **Junior Ranger Program for Families.** The Junior Ranger Program provides a free, fun way to look at the cultural and natural history of this sublime destination. These hands-on educational programs for children ages 4 and up include guided adventure hikes, ranger-led "discovery" activities, and book readings. 🕾 *928/638–7888* ⊕ *www.nps.gov/grca/forkids/ beajuniorranger.htm* 🎫 *Free.*

SPORTS AND THE OUTDOORS

AIR TOURS

Flights by plane and helicopter over the canyon are offered by a number of companies, departing for the Grand Canyon Airport at the south end of Tusayan. Though the noise and disruption of so many aircraft buzzing the canyon is controversial, flightseeing remains a popular, if expensive, option. You'll have more visibility from a helicopter but they're louder and more expensive than the fixed-wing planes. Prices and lengths of tours vary, but you can expect to pay about $149 per adult for short plane trips and approximately $179–$250 for brief helicopter tours (and about $450 for tours leaving from Vegas). These companies often have significant discounts in winter—check the company websites to find the best deals.

TOURS

Grand Canyon Airlines. Grand Canyon Airlines flies a fixed-wing on a 50-minute tour of the eastern edge of the Grand Canyon, the North Rim, and the Kaibab Plateau. All-day combination tours combine flightseeing with 4-wheel-drive tours and float trips on the Colorado River. The company also schedules helicopter tours that leave from Las Vegas (plane flight from Las Vegas to Grand Canyon Airport, then helicopter flight into the canyon). ⊠ *Grand Canyon Airport, Tusayan* ☎ *928/638–2359, 866/235–9422* ⊕ *www.grandcanyonairlines.com.*

Maverick Helicopters. Maverick Helicopters offers 25- and 45-minute tours of the South Rim, North Rim, and Dragon Corridor of the Grand Canyon. A landing tour option for those leaving from Las Vegas sets you down in the canyon for a short snack below the rim. ⊠ *Grand Canyon Airport, 6075 South Las Vegas Blvd., Grand Canyon* ☎ *928/638–2622, 800/962–3869* ⊕ *www.flymaverick.com.*

Papillon Grand Canyon Helicopters. Papillon Grand Canyon Helicopters offers a variety of fixed-wing and helicopter tours, leaving both from Grand Canyon Airport and Vegas, of the canyon. Combination tour options include off-road jeep tours and smooth-water rafting trips. ⊠ *Grand Canyon Airport, Tusayan* ☎ *928/638–2764, 888/635–7272* ⊕ *www.papillon.com.*

BICYCLING

The South Rim's limited opportunities for off-road biking, narrow shoulders on park roads, and heavy traffic may disappoint hard-core cyclists. Bicycles are permitted on all park roads and on the multiuse Greenway System, as well as Bridle Trail (⇨ *North Rim*). Bikes are prohibited on all other trails, including the Rim Trail. Some find Hermit Road a good biking option, especially from March through November when it's closed to cars. You can ride west 8 miles and then put your bike on the free shuttle bus back into the village (or vice versa). Mountain bikers visiting the South Rim may be better off meandering through the ponderosa pine forest on the Tusayan Bike Trail. Rentals are available April to October at the South Rim only from Bright Angel Bicycles at the visitor center complex. Bicycle camping sites are available at Mather Campground for $6 per person.

HIKING

Although permits are not required for day hikes, you must have a back-country permit for longer trips (⇨ *See Park Fees and Permits at the start of this chapter*). Some of the more popular trails are listed here; more detailed information and maps can be obtained from the Backcountry Information Centers. Also, rangers can help design a trip to suit your abilities.

Remember that the canyon has significant elevation changes and, in summer, extreme temperature ranges, which can pose problems for people who aren't in good shape or who have heart or respiratory problems. ■TIP➔ **Carry plenty of water and energy foods.** The majority of each year's 400 search-and-rescue incidents result from hikers underestimating the size of the canyon, hiking beyond their abilities, or not packing sufficient food and water.

⚠ **Under no circumstances should you attempt a day hike from the rim to the river and back.** Remember that when it's 80°F on the South Rim, it's 110°F on the canyon floor. Allow two to four days if you want to hike rim to rim (it's easier to descend from the North Rim, as it's more than 1,000 feet higher than the South Rim). Hiking steep trails from rim to rim is a strenuous trek of at least 21 miles and should only be attempted by experienced canyon hikers.

EASY

Fodor's Choice
★

Rim Trail. The South Rim's most popular walking path is the 12-mile (one-way) Rim Trail, which runs along the edge of the canyon from Pipe Creek Vista (the first overlook on Desert View Drive) to Hermits Rest. This walk, which is paved to Maricopa Point and for the last 1.5 miles to Hermits Rest, visits several of the South Rim's historic landmarks. Allow anywhere from 15 minutes to a full day, depending on how much of the trail you want to cover; the Rim Trail is an ideal day hike, as it varies only a few hundred feet in elevation from Mather Point (7,120 feet) to the trailhead at Hermits Rest (6,650 feet). The trail also can be accessed from several spots in Grand Canyon Village and from the major viewpoints along Hermit Road, which are serviced by shuttle buses during the busy summer months. *Easy.* ■TIP➔ **On the Rim Trail, water is only available in the Grand Canyon Village area and at Hermits Rest.**

MODERATE

Bright Angel Trail. This well-maintained trail is one of the most scenic hiking paths from the South Rim to the bottom of the canyon (9.6 miles each way). Rest houses are equipped with water at the 1.5- and 3-mile points from May through September and at Indian Garden (4 miles) year-round. Water is also available at Bright Angel Campground, 9.25 miles below the trailhead. Plateau Point, on a spur trail about 1.5 miles below Indian Garden, is as far as you should attempt to go on a day hike; the round-trip will take six to nine hours.

Bright Angel Trail is the easiest of all the footpaths into the canyon, but because the climb out from the bottom is an ascent of 5,510 feet, the trip should be attempted only by those in good physical condition and should be avoided in midsummer due to extreme heat. The top

3

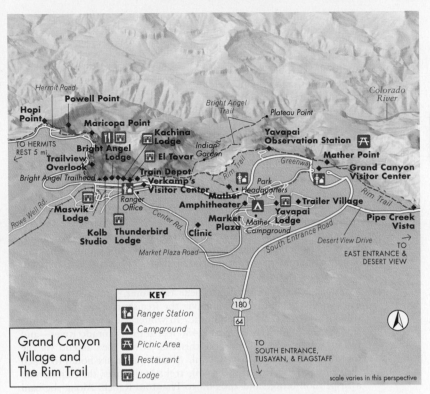

Grand Canyon Village and The Rim Trail

Hermit Road

Powell Point

Hopi Point

Maricopa Point

Bright Angel Trail

Plateau Point

Colorado River

Kachina Lodge

Yavapai Observation Station

TO HERMITS REST 5 mi.

Bright Angel Lodge

Trailview Overlook

Indian Garden

El Tovar

Mather Point

Grand Canyon Visitor Center

Bright Angel Trailhead

Train Depot

Verkamp's Visitor Center

Greenway

Rim Trail

Park Headquarters

Rim Trail

Rowe Well Rd.

Maswik Lodge

Ranger Office

Center Rd.

Mather Amphitheater

Mather Lodge

Yavapai Lodge

Trailer Village

Pipe Creek Vista

Kolb Studio

Thunderbird Lodge

Clinic

Market Plaza

Mather Campground

South Entrance Road

Desert View Drive

TO EAST ENTRANCE & DESERT VIEW

Market Plaza Road

KEY

🧑 Ranger Station
⛺ Campground
🏕 Picnic Area
🍴 Restaurant
🏨 Lodge

180
64

TO SOUTH ENTRANCE, TUSAYAN, & FLAGSTAFF

scale varies in this perspective

of the trail can be icy in winter. Originally a bighorn sheep path and later used by the Havasupai, the trail was widened late in the 19th century for prospectors and is now used for both mule and foot traffic. Also note that mule trains have the right-of-way—and sometimes leave unpleasant surprises in your path. *Moderate.* ⊠ *Trailhead: Kolb Studio, Hermits Rd.*

DIFFICULT

Grandview Trail. Accessible from the parking area at Grandview Point, the trailhead is at 7,400 feet. The path heads steeply down into the canyon for 3 miles to the junction and campsite at East Horseshoe Mesa Trail. Classified as a wilderness trail, the route is aggressive and not as heavily traveled as some of the more well-known trails, such as Bright Angel and Hermit. There is no water available along the trail, which follows a steep descent to 4,800 feet at Horseshoe Mesa, where Hopi Indians once collected mineral paints. Hike 0.7 mile farther to Page Spring, a reliable water source year-round. Parts of this trail are icy in winter, and traction crampons are mandatory. *Difficult.* ⊠ *Trailhead: Grandview Point, Desert View Dr.*

Hermit Trail. Beginning on the South Rim just west of Hermits Rest (and 7 miles west of Grand Canyon Village), this steep, unmaintained, 9.7-mile (one way) trail drops more than 5,000 feet to Hermit Creek, which usually flows year-round. It's a strenuous hike back up and is recommended for experienced long-distance hikers only; plan for six to nine hours. There's an abundance of lush growth and wildlife, including desert bighorn sheep, along this trail. The trail descends from the trailhead at 6,640 feet to the Colorado River at 2,300 feet. Day hikers should not go past Santa Maria Spring at 5,000 feet.

For much of the year, no water is available along the way; ask a park ranger about the availability of water at Santa Maria Spring and Hermit Creek before you set out. All water from these sources should be treated before drinking. The route leads down to the Colorado River and has inspiring views of Hermit Gorge and the Redwall and Supai formations. Six miles from the trailhead are the ruins of Hermit Camp, which the Santa Fe Railroad ran as a tourist camp from 1911 until 1930. *Difficult.* ⊠ *Trailhead: Hermits Rest, Hermits Rd.*

South Kaibab Trail. This trail starts near Yaki Point, 4 miles east of Grand Canyon Village and is accessible via the free shuttle bus. Because the route is so steep (and sometimes icy in winter)—descending from the trailhead at 7,260 feet down to 2,480 feet at the Colorado River—and has no water, many hikers take this trail down, then ascend via the less-demanding Bright Angel Trail. Allow four to six hours to reach the Colorado River on this 6.4-mile trek. At the river, the trail crosses a suspension bridge and runs on to Phantom Ranch. Along the trail there is no water and very little shade. There are no campgrounds, though there are portable toilets at Cedar Ridge (6,320 feet), 1.5 miles from the trailhead. Toilets and an emergency phone are also available at the Tipoff, 4.6 miles down the trail (3 miles past Cedar Ridge). The trail corkscrews down through some spectacular geology. Look for (but don't remove) fossils in the limestone when taking water breaks. ■TIP→ Even though an immense network of trails winds through the Grand Canyon, the popular corridor trails (Bright Angel and South Kaibab) are recommended for hikers new to the region. *Difficult.* ⊠ *Trailhead: Yaki Point, Desert View Dr.*

JEEP TOURS

Jeep rides can be rough; if you have had back injuries, check with your doctor before taking a 4X4 tour. It's a good idea to book a week or two ahead, and even further if you're visiting in summer or on busy weekends.

TOURS AND OUTFITTERS

Grand Canyon Jeep Tours & Safaris. If you'd like to get off the pavement and see parts of the park that are accessible only by dirt road, a jeep tour can be just the ticket. From March through November, this tour operator leads daily, 1½- to 4½-hour, off-road tours within the park, as well as in Kaibab National Forest. Combo tours adding

GRAND CANYON NATIONAL PARK: TOP PICKS HIKING TRAILS

	Grade	Miles (One Way)	Beginning Elevation	Ending Elevation	Mules	Campground	Open Info*	Water	Shuttle Access	Ranger Station	Toilet/Restroom	Emergency Telephone	Hiking Level	Trail Conditions
SOUTH RIM														
Bright Angel Trail South	Steep	9.6 mi	6,785 ft	2,480 ft (Colorado River)	Y	Y	Y/R	(Seasonal)	Y	Y	Y	Y	Moderate-Difficult	Maintained
Grandview Trail	Very Steep	3.2 mi	7,400 ft	4,900 ft (Horseshoe Mesa)		Y	Y/R	Y		Y			Difficult	Unmaintained
Hermit Trail	Steep	9.7 mi	6,640 ft	2,300 ft (Colorado River)			Y/R	(Untreated)	Y		Y ::	Y **	Difficult	Unmaintained
New Hance Trail	Steep	8 mi	6,982 ft	2,600 ft (Colorado River)			Y/R						Difficult	Unmaintained
Rim Trail	Level	9 mi	6,820 ft	7,120 ft (Mather Point)			Y/R	Y **	Y	Y	Y		Easy	Maintained
South Kaibab Trail	Steep	6.4 mi	7,200 ft	2,400 ft (Colorado River)		Y/R	Y **	Y	Y	Y	Y	Y	Difficult	Maintained
NORTH RIM														
Cape Final Trail	Level/Incline	2.0 mi	7,840 ft	7,916 ft (Cape Final)			mid-May–mid-Oct.						Easy	Maintained
Ken Patrick Trail	Level/Incline	10 mi	8,250 ft	8,803 ft (Point Imperial)			mid-May–mid-Oct.						Difficult	Unmaintained
North Kaibab Trail	Steep	7.1 mi	8,241 ft	2,400 ft (Colorado River)	Y		mid-May–mid-Oct.	Y	Y			Y	Difficult	Maintained
Transept Trail	Level	1.5 mi	8,255 ft	8,200 ft (Campground)			mid-May–mid-Oct.		Y		Y	Y	Easy	Maintained
Uncle Jim Trail	Level	2.5 mi	8,300 ft	8,244 ft (Uncle Jim Point)	Y		mid-May–mid-Oct.						Moderate	Maintained
Widforss Trail	Level/Incline	4.9 mi	8,080 ft	7,900 ft (Widforss Point)			mid-May–mid-Oct.						Moderate	Unmaintained

*South Rim trails occasionally close due to weather or trail conditions) **(Trailhead) Y/R = year-round

helicopter and airplane rides are also available. ☎ 928/638–5337 ⊕ www.grandcanyonjeeptours.com ☒ $50–$259.

Grand Canyon Store. This tour company offers off-road adventures year-round in comfortable cruisers (small luxury vans with heating and air-conditioning) rather than jeeps. There are two-hour off-road tours of the South Rim, as well as all-day trips to the inner canyon on the Hualapai Indian Reservation. Helicopter tours and smooth-water and whitewater raft tours through the canyon are available as an add-on to any trip. ✉ 24 W. Rte. 66, Flagstaff ☎ 928/638–2000, 800/716–9389 ⊕ www.discovergrandcanyon.com ☒ $39–$286.

> ### ARRANGING TOURS
>
> Transportation-services desks are maintained at Bright Angel, Maswik Lodge, and Yavapai Lodge (closed in winter) in Grand Canyon Village. The desks provide information and handle bookings for sightseeing tours, taxi and bus services, and mule rides (but don't count on last-minute availability). There's also a concierge at El Tovar that can arrange most tours, with the exception of mule rides. On the North Rim, Grand Canyon Lodge has general information about local services.

Marvelous Marv's Grand Canyon Tours. For a personalized experience, take this private tour of the Grand Canyon and surrounding sights any time of year. Tours include round-trip transportation from your hotel or campground in Williams, Tusayan, or Grand Canyon; admission to the park; scenic viewpoint stops; a short hike; and personal narration of the geology and history of the area. Note that credit cards are not accepted. ✉ Williams ☎ 928/707–0291 ⊕ www.marvelousmarv.com ☒ $100.

MULE RIDES

Fodor's Choice ★ Mule rides provide an intimate glimpse into the canyon for those who have the time, but not the stamina, to see the canyon on foot. ■ TIP→ Reservations are essential and are accepted up to 13 months in advance.

These trips have been conducted since the early 1900s. A comforting fact as you ride the narrow trail: no one's ever been killed while riding a mule that fell off a cliff. (Nevertheless, the treks are not for the faint of heart or people in questionable health.)

OUTFITTERS

Xanterra Parks & Resorts Mule Rides. These trips delve into the canyon from the South Rim to Phantom Ranch, or east along the canyon's edge (the Plateau Point rides were discontinued in 2009). Riders must be at least 55 inches tall, weigh less than 200 pounds, and understand English. Children under 15 must be accompanied by an adult. Riders must be in fairly good physical condition, and pregnant women are advised not to take these trips.

The three-hour ride along the rim costs $125 (water and snack included). An overnight with a stay at Phantom Ranch at the bottom of the canyon is $507 ($895 for two riders). Two nights at Phantom Ranch, an option available from November through March, will set you back $714 ($1,192 for two). Meals are included. Reservations (by

CLOSE UP

Freebies at the Grand Canyon

While you're here, be sure to take advantage of the many complimentary services offered at Grand Canyon National Park.

■ The most useful is undoubtedly the system of free shuttle buses at the South Rim; it caters to the road-weary, with four routes winding through or just outside the park—Hermits Rest Route, Village Route, Kaibab Rim Route, and Tusayan Route. Of the bus routes, the Hermits Rest Route runs only from March through November and the Tusayan Route only in summer; the other two run year-round, and the Kaibab Trail Route provides the only access to Yaki Point. Hikers coming or going from the Kaibab Trailhead can catch the Hikers Express, which departs three times each morning from the Bright Angel Lodge, makes a quick stop at the Backcountry Information Center, and then heads out to the South Kaibab Trailhead.

■ Ranger-led programs are always free and offered year-round, though more are scheduled during the busy spring and summer seasons. These programs might include activities such as stargazing and topics such as geology and the cultural history of prehistoric peoples. Some of the more in-depth programs may include a fossil walk or a condor talk. Check with the visitor center for seasonal programs including wildflower walks and fire ecology.

■ Kids ages 4 to 14 can get involved with the park's Junior Ranger program, with ever-changing activities including hikes and hands-on experiments.

■ Despite all of these options, rangers will tell you that the best free activity in the canyon is watching the magnificent splashes of color on the canyon walls during sunrise and sunset.

---

phone), especially during the busy summer months, are a must, but you can check at the Bright Angel Transportation Desk to see if there's last-minute availability. ☎ 888/297–2757 ⊕ *www.grandcanyonlodges. com* ⚒ *Reservations essential* ☉ *Phantom Ranch rides daily; Rim rides mid-Mar.–Oct., twice daily; Nov.–mid-Mar., once daily.*

SKIING

Tusayan Ranger District. Although you can't schuss down into the Grand Canyon, you can cross-country ski in the woods near the rim when there's enough snow, usually mid-December though early March. The ungroomed trails, suitable for beginner and intermediate skiers, begin at the Grandview Lookout and travel through the Kaibab National Forest. For details, contact the Tusayan Ranger District. ☎ *928/638–2443* ⊕ *www.fs.usda.gov/kaibab.*

SHOPPING

Nearly every lodging facility and retail store at the South Rim stocks Native American arts and crafts and Grand Canyon books and souvenirs. Prices are comparable to other souvenir outlets, though you may find some better deals in Williams. However, a portion of the proceeds from items purchased at Kolb Studio, Tusayan Museum, and all the park visitor centers go to the non-profit Grand Canyon Association.

Desert View Trading Post. A mix of traditional Southwestern souvenirs and authentic Native American arts and crafts are for sale at Desert View Trading Post. ⊠ *Desert View Dr. near the watchtower at Desert View* ☏ *928/638–3150.*

Hopi House. This shop has the widest selection of Native American handicrafts in the vicinity. ⊠ *Across from El Tovar Hotel, 4 El Tovar Rd., Grand Canyon Village* ☏ *928/638–2631.*

GRAND CANYON NORTH RIM

The North Rim stands 1,000 feet higher than the South Rim and has a more alpine climate, with twice as much annual precipitation. Here, in the deep forests of the Kaibab Plateau, the crowds are thinner, the facilities fewer, and the views even more spectacular. Due to snow, the North Rim is off-limits in winter. The buildings and concessions are closed November through mid-May. The road and entrance gate close when the snow makes them impassable—usually by the end of November.

Lodgings are limited in this more remote park, with only one historic lodge (with cabins and hotel-type rooms as well as a restaurant) and a single campground. Dining options have opened up a little with the addition of the Grand Cookout, offered nightly with live entertainment under the stars. Your best bet may be to pack your camping gear and hiking boots and take several days to explore the lush Kaibab Forest. The canyon's highest, most dramatic rim views also can be enjoyed on two wheels (via primitive dirt access roads) and on four legs (courtesy of a trusty mule).

EXPLORING

SCENIC DRIVE

Highway 67. Open mid-May to roughly mid-November (or the first big snowfall), the two-lane paved road climbs 1,400 feet in elevation as it passes through the Kaibab National Forest. Also called the "North Rim Parkway," this scenic route crosses the limestone-capped Kaibab Plateau—passing broad meadows, sun-dappled forests, and small lakes and springs—before abruptly falling away at the abyss of the Grand Canyon. Wildlife abounds in the thick ponderosa pine forests and lush mountain meadows. It's common to see deer, turkeys, and coyotes as you drive through this remote region. Point Imperial and Cape Royal branch off this scenic drive, which runs from Jacob Lake to Bright Angel Point.

HISTORIC SITE

Grand Canyon Lodge. Built in 1937 by the Union Pacific Railroad (replacing the original 1928 building, which burned in a fire), the massive stone structure is listed on the National Register of Historic Places. Its huge sunroom has hardwood floors, high-beam ceilings, and a marvelous view of the canyon through plate-glass windows. On warm days, visitors

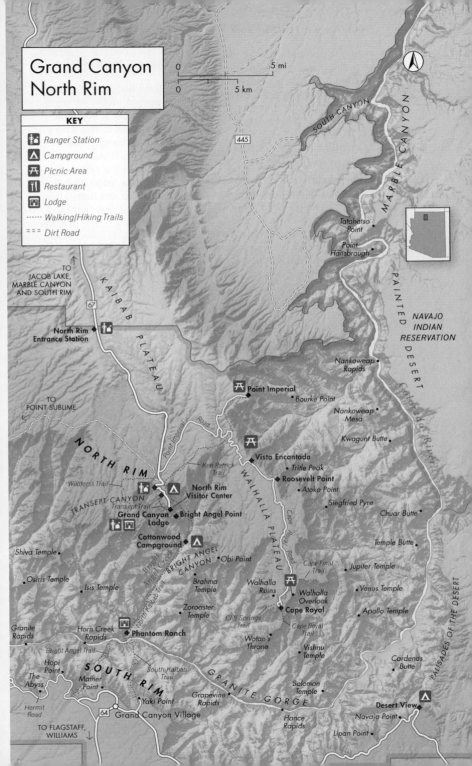

sit in the sun and drink in the surrounding beauty on an outdoor viewing deck, where National Park Service employees deliver free lectures on geology and history. ⊠ *Off Hwy. 67 near Bright Angel Point, 10 Albright St.* ☎ *928/638–2631* ⊕ *www.grandcanyonlodges.com.*

SCENIC STOPS

Bright Angel Point. This trail, which leads to one of the most awe-inspiring overlooks on either rim, starts on the grounds of the Grand Canyon Lodge and runs along the crest of a point of rocks that juts into the canyon for several hundred yards. The walk is only 0.5 mile round-trip, but it's an exciting trek accented by sheer drops on each side of the trail. In a few spots where the route is extremely narrow, metal railings ensure visitors' safety. The temptation to clamber out to precarious perches to have your picture taken could get you killed—every year several people die from falls at the Grand Canyon. ⊠ *North Rim Dr.*

Cape Royal. A popular sunset destination, Cape Royal showcases the canyon's jagged landscape; you'll also get a glimpse of the Colorado River, framed by a natural stone arch called Angels Window. In autumn, the aspens turn a beautiful gold, adding even more color to an already magnificent scene of the forested surroundings. The easy and rewarding 1-mile round-trip hike along **Cliff Springs Trail** starts here; it takes you through a forested ravine and terminates at Cliff Springs, where the forest opens to another impressive view of the canyon walls. ⊠ *Cape Royal Scenic Dr., 23 miles southeast of Grand Canyon Lodge.*

Point Imperial. At 8,803 feet, Point Imperial has the highest vista point at either rim; it offers magnificent views of both the canyon and the distant country: the Vermilion Cliffs to the north, the 10,000-foot Navajo Mountain to the northeast in Utah, the Painted Desert to the east, and the Little Colorado River canyon to the southeast. Other prominent points of interest include views of Mount Hayden, Saddle Mountain, and Marble Canyon. ⊠ *2.7 miles left off Cape Royal Rd. on Point Imperial Rd., 11 miles northeast of Grand Canyon Lodge.*

Fodor'sChoice
★

Point Sublime. You can camp within feet of the canyon's edge at this awe-inspiring site. Sunrises and sunsets are spectacular. The winding road, through gorgeous high country, is only 17 miles, but it will take you at least two hours, one way. The road is intended only for vehicles with high-road clearance (pickups and four-wheel-drive vehicles). It is also necessary to be properly equipped for wilderness road travel. Check with a park ranger or at the information desk at Grand Canyon Lodge before taking this journey. You may camp here only with a permit from the Backcountry Information Center. ⊠ *North Rim Dr., Grand Canyon; about 20 miles west of North Rim Visitor Center.*

CLOSE UP

Flora and Fauna of the Grand Canyon

Eighty-nine mammal species inhabit Grand Canyon National Park, as well as 355 species of birds, 56 kinds of reptiles and amphibians, and 17 kinds of fish. The rare Kaibab squirrel is found only on the North Rim—you can recognize them by their all-white tails and black undersides. The pink Grand Canyon rattlesnake lives at lower elevations within the canyon. Hawks and ravens are visible year-round. The endangered California condor has been reintroduced to the canyon region. Park rangers give daily talks on the magnificent birds, whose wingspan measures 9 feet. In spring, summer, and fall, mule deer, recognizable by their large ears, are abundant at the South Rim. Don't be fooled by gentle appearances; these guys can be aggressive. It's illegal to feed them, as it'll disrupt their natural habitats, and increase your risk of getting bitten or kicked.

The best times to see wildlife are early in the morning and late in the afternoon. Look for out-of-place shapes and motions, keeping in mind that animals occupy all layers in a natural habitat and not just at your eye level. Use binoculars for close-up views. While out and about try to fade into the woodwork by keeping your movements limited and noise at a minimum.

More than 1,700 species of plants color the park. The South Rim's Coconino Plateau is fairly flat, at an elevation of about 7,000 feet, and covered with stands of piñon and ponderosa pines, junipers, and Gambel's oak trees. On the Kaibab Plateau on the North Rim, Douglas fir, spruce, quaking aspen, and more ponderosas prevail. In spring you're likely to see asters, sunflowers, and lupine in bloom at both rims.

Roosevelt Point. Named after the president who gave the Grand Canyon its national monument status in 1908 (it was upgraded to national park status in 1919), Roosevelt Point is the best place to see the confluence of the Little Colorado River and the Grand Canyon. The cliffs above the Colorado River south of the junction are known as the Palisades of the Desert. A short woodland loop trail leads to this eastern viewpoint. ⊠ *Cape Royal Rd., 18 miles east of Grand Canyon Lodge.*

Vista Encantada. This point on the Walhalla Plateau offers views of the upper drainage of Nankoweap Creek, a rock pinnacle known as Brady Peak, and the Painted Desert to the east. This is an enchanting place for a picnic lunch. ⊠ *Cape Royal Rd., 16 miles southeast of Grand Canyon Lodge.*

Walhalla Overlook. One of the lowest elevations on the North Rim, this overlook has views of the Unkar Delta, a fertile region used by Ancestral Puebloans as farmland. These ancient people also gathered food and hunted game on the North Rim. A flat path leads to the remains of the Walhalla Glades Pueblo, which was inhabited from 1050 to 1150. ⊠ *Cape Royal Rd., 22.5 miles southeast of Grand Canyon Lodge.*

EDUCATIONAL OFFERINGS
RANGER PROGRAMS

FAMILY **Discovery Pack Junior Ranger Program.** In summer, children ages 6 to 14 can take part in these hands-on educational programs and earn a Junior Ranger certificate and badge. Children meet at park headquarters to attend a 1.5-hour ranger-led session first. ☎ 928/638–7967 ⊕ *www.nps.gov/grca* ✉ *Free* ☯ *Mid-June to Labor Day, meets daily at 9 am.*

Interpretive Ranger Programs. Daily guided hikes and talks during one of the programs offered may focus on any aspect of the canyon—from geology and flora and fauna to history and the canyon's early inhabitants. For schedules, go to the Grand Canyon Lodge or download a free copy of *The Guide* to the North Rim from the park website. ☎ 928/638–7967 ⊕ *www.nps.gov/grca* ✉ *Free.*

SPORTS AND THE OUTDOORS

BICYCLING

Mountain bikers can test the many dirt access roads found in this remote area. The 17-mile trek to Point Sublime is, well, sublime—though you'll share this road with high-clearance vehicles, it's rare to spot other people on most of these primitive pathways.

Bicycles and leashed pets are allowed on the well-maintained 1.2-mile (one way) **Bridle Trail,** which follows the road from Grand Canyon Lodge to the North Kaibab Trailhead. Bikes are prohibited on all other national park trails.

HIKING
EASY

Cape Final Trail. This 2-mile gravel path follows an old jeep trail through a ponderosa pine forest to the canyon overlook at Cape Final with panoramic views of the northern canyon, the Palisades of the Desert, and the impressive spectacle of Juno Temple. *Easy.* ✉ *Trailhead: dirt parking lot 5 miles south of Roosevelt Point on Cape Royal Rd.*

FAMILY **Roosevelt Point Trail.** This easy 0.2-mile round-trip trail loops through the forest to the scenic viewpoint. Allow 20 minutes for this short, secluded hike. *Easy.* ✉ *Trailhead: Cape Royal Rd.* ⊕ *www.nps.gov/grca.*

FAMILY **Transept Trail.** This 3-mile (round-trip), 1½-hour trail begins near the Grand Canyon Lodge at 8,255 feet. Well maintained and well marked, it has little elevation change, sticking near the rim before reaching a dramatic view of a large stream through Bright Angel Canyon. The route leads to a side canyon called Transept Canyon, which geologist Clarence Dutton named in 1882, declaring it "far grander than Yosemite." Check the posted schedule to find a ranger talk along this trail; it's also a great place to view fall foliage. Flash floods can occur any time of the year, especially June through September when thunderstorms develop rapidly. *Easy.* ✉ *Trailhead: near the Grand Canyon Lodge's east patio.*

MODERATE

Uncle Jim Trail. This 5-mile, three-hour loop trail starts at 8,300 feet and winds south through the forest, past Roaring Springs and Bright Angel canyons. The highlight of this rim hike is Uncle Jim Point, which, at

8,244 feet, overlooks the upper sections of the North Kaibab Trail. *Moderate.* ⊠ *Trailhead: North Kaibab Trail parking lot.*

Widforss Trail. Round-trip, Widforss Trail is 9.8 miles, with an elevation change of only 200 feet. Allow five to six hours for the hike, which starts at 8,080 feet and passes through shady forests of pine, spruce, fir, and aspen on its way to Widforss Point, at 7,900 feet. Here you'll have good views of five temples: Zoroaster, Brahma, and Deva to the southeast and Buddha and Manu to the southwest. You are likely to see wildflowers in summer, and this is a good trail for viewing fall foliage. It's named in honor of artist Gunnar M. Widforss, renowned for his paintings of national park landscapes. *Moderate.* ⊠ *Trailhead: Point Sublime Rd.*

DIFFICULT

Ken Patrick Trail. This primitive trail travels 10 miles one way (allow six hours each way) from the trailhead at 8,250 feet to Point Imperial at 8,803 feet. It crosses drainages and occasionally detours around fallen trees. The end of the road, at Point Imperial, brings the highest views from either rim. Note that there is no water along this trail. *Difficult.* ⊠ *Trailhead: east side of North Kaibab trailhead parking lot.*

North Kaibab Trail. At 8,241 feet, this trail, like the roads leading to the North Rim, is open only from May through late October or early November (depending on the weather). It is recommended for experienced hikers only, who should allow four days for the full hike. The long, steep path drops 5,840 feet over a distance of 14.5 miles to Phantom Ranch and the Colorado River, so the National Park Service suggests that day hikers not go farther than Roaring Springs (5,020 feet) before turning to hike back up out of the canyon. After about 7 miles, Cottonwood Campground (4,080 feet) has drinking water in summer, restrooms, shade trees, and a ranger. *Difficult.* ■TIP➔ A free shuttle takes hikers to the North Kaibab trailhead twice daily from Grand Canyon Lodge; reserve a spot the day before. ⊠ *Trailhead: 2 miles north of the Grand Canyon Lodge.*

MULE RIDES

FAMILY **Canyon Trail Rides.** This company leads mule rides on the easier trails of the North Rim. A one-hour ride (minimum age seven) runs $40. Half-day trips on the rim or into the canyon (minimum age 10) cost $80. Weight limits are 200 pounds for canyon rides and 220 pounds for the rim rides. Available daily from May 15 to October 15, these excursions are popular, so make reservations in advance. ☎ 435/679–8665 ⊕ *www.canyonrides.com.*

THE WEST RIM AND HAVASU CANYON

Known as "The People" of the Grand Canyon, the Pai Indians—the Hualapai and Havasupai—have lived along the Colorado River and the vast Colorado Plateau for more than 1,000 years. Both tribes traditionally moved seasonally between the plateau and the canyon, alternately hunting game and planting crops. Today, they rely on their tourism offerings outside the national park as an economic base.

GRAND CANYON WEST

186 miles northwest of Williams, 70 miles north of Kingman.

The plateau-dwelling Hualapai ("people of the tall pines") acquired a larger chunk of traditional Pai lands with the creation of their reservation in 1883. Hualapai tribal lands include diverse habitats ranging from rolling grasslands to rugged canyons, and travel from elevations of 1,500 feet at the Colorado River to more than 7,300 feet at Aubrey Cliffs. In recent years, the Hualapai have been attempting to foster tourism on the West Rim—most notably with the spectacular Skywalk, a glass walkway suspended 70 feet over the edge of the canyon rim. Not hampered by the regulations in place at Grand Canyon National Park, Grand Canyon West offers helicopter flights down into the bottom of the canyon, horseback rides to rim viewpoints, and boat trips on the Colorado River.

The Hualapai Reservation encompasses a million acres in the Grand Canyon, along 108 miles of the Colorado River. Peach Springs, a two-hour drive from the West Rim on historic Route 66, is the tribal capital and the launch site for raft trips on this stretch of the river. Lodging is available both on the rim, at Hualapai Ranch, and in Peach Springs, at the Hualapai Lodge. Although increasingly popular, the West Rim is still relatively remote and visited by far fewer people than the South Rim—keep in mind that it's more than 120 miles away from the nearest interstate highways.

GETTING HERE AND AROUND

The West Rim is a 5-hour drive from the South Rim of Grand Canyon National Park or a 2½-hour drive from Las Vegas. From Kingman, drive north 30 miles on U.S. 93, and then turn right onto Pierce Ferry Road and follow it for 28 miles. (A more scenic alternative is to drive 42 miles north on Stockton Hill Road, turning right onto Pierce Ferry Road for 7 miles, but this takes a bit longer because Stockton Hill Road has a lower speed limit than the wide, divided U.S. 93 highway.) Turn right (east) on to Diamond Bar Road and follow for 21 miles to Grand Canyon West entrance.

The dusty, bumpy 9-mile stretch of unpaved road leading to Grand Canyon West isn't recommended for RVs and low-clearance vehicles; however, this road is scheduled to be paved by early 2014. For a gentler approach to the West Rim, visitors can park at the Grand Canyon West Park & Ride Station on Pierce Ferry Road and take a shuttle to the West Rim ($16 per person); reservations are recommended.

Visitors aren't allowed to travel in their own vehicles to the viewpoints once they reach the West Rim, and must purchase a tour package—which can range from day use to horseback or helicopter rides to lodging and meals—from Hualapai Tourism.

TOURS

In addition to the exploring options provided by the Hualapai tribe, more than 30 tour and transportation companies service Grand Canyon West from Las Vegas, Phoenix, and Sedona by airplane, helicopter, coach, SUV, and Hummer. Perhaps the easiest way to visit the West Rim from Vegas is with a tour. Bighorn Wild West Tours will pick you up in a Hummer at your Vegas hotel for an all-day trip that includes the shuttle-bus package and lunch, for $249.

ESSENTIALS

Tour Operators Bighorn Wild West Tours ☎ *702/385–4676* ⊕ *www. bighorntours.com.*

Transportation Contacts Park and Ride Shuttle ✉ *Grand Canyon West, Pierce Ferry Road, Grand Canyon* ☎ *702/260–6506, 888/868–9378* ⊕ *www.hualapaitourism.com.*

Visitor Information Grand Canyon West ☎ *888/868–9378, 928/769–2636* ⊕ *www.hualapaitourism.com.*

EXPLORING INDIAN COUNTRY

When visiting Native American reservations, respect tribal laws and customs. Remember you're a guest in a sovereign nation. Don't wander into residential areas or take photographs of residents without first asking permission. Possessing or consuming alcohol is illegal on tribal lands. In general, the Hualapai and Havasupai are quiet, private people. Offer respect and don't pursue conversations or personal interactions unless invited to do so.

EXPLORING

Hualapai Tourism. At the Welcome Center, Hualapai Tourism, run by the Hualapai tribe, offers the basic Hualapai Legacy tour package ($44 per person, including taxes and fees), which includes a Hualapai visitation permit and "hop-on, hop-off" shuttle transportation to three sites. The shuttle will take you to Eagle Point, where the Indian Village walking tour visits authentic dwellings. Educational displays there uncover the culture of five different Native American tribes (Havasupai, Plains, Hopi, Hualapai, and Navajo), and intertribal, powwow-style dance performances entertain visitors at the nearby amphitheater. The shuttle also goes to Hualapai Ranch, site of Western performances, cookouts, horseback and wagon rides, and the only lodging on the West Rim; and Guano Point, where the "High Point Hike" offers panoramic views of the Colorado River. At all three areas, local Hualapai guides and roaming "ambassadors" add a Native American perspective to a canyon trip that you won't find on North and South Rim tours.

For extra fees, you can add meals (there are cafés at each of the three stops), overnight lodging at Hualapai Ranch, a helicopter trip into the canyon, a pontoon boat trip on the Colorado, a horseback ride along the canyon rim, or a walk on the Skywalk.

At this writing, a three-level, 6,000-square-foot visitor center is planned. The date of completion is currently uncertain, but eventually this complex is expected to include a museum, movie theater, gift shop, and at least two restaurants. ✉ *Grand Canyon West* ☎ *928/769–2636, 888/868–9378* ⊕ *www.hualapaitourism.com* ✉ *$44 entrance fee and taxes* ⊙ *Daily.*

Grand Canyon Skywalk. The Skywalk, which opened in 2007, is a cantilevered glass terrace suspended nearly 4,000 feet above the Colorado River and extends 70 feet from the edge of the Grand Canyon. Approximately 10 feet wide, the bridge's deck, made of tempered glass several inches thick, has 5-foot glass railings on each side creating an unobstructed open-air platform. Admission to the skywalk is a separate add-on to the basic Grand Canyon West admission. Visitors must store personal items, including cameras, cell phones, and video cameras, in lockers before entering. A professional photographer takes photographs of visitors, which can be purchased from the gift shop. ⊕ *www. hualapaitourism.com* ☞ *$29.95.*

SPORTS AND THE OUTDOORS
ADVENTURE TOURS

Hualapai River Runners. One-day combination river trips are offered by the Hualapai Tribe through the Hualapai River Runners from mid-March through October. The trips, which cost $381, leave from Peach Springs (a 2-hour drive from the West Rim) and include rafting, a hike, helicopter ride, and transport. Lunch, snacks, and beverages are provided. Children must be eight or older to take the trip, which runs several rapids with the most difficult rated as Class VII, depending on the river flow. ⊠ *5001 Buck N Doe Rd., Peach Springs* ☎ *928/769–2636, 888/868–9378* ⊕ *www.hualapaitourism.com.*

HAVASU CANYON

141 miles northwest from Williams to the head of Hualapai Hilltop.

With the establishment of Grand Canyon National Park in 1919, the Havasupai ("people of the blue green water") were confined to their summer village of Supai and the surrounding 518 acres in the 5-mile-wide and 12-mile-long Havasu Canyon. In 1975, the reservation was substantially enlarged, but is still completely surrounded by national park lands on all but its southern border. Each year, about 25,000 tourists fly, hike, or ride into Havasu Canyon to visit the Havasupai. Despite their economic reliance on tourism, the Havasupai take their guardianship of the Grand Canyon seriously, and severely limit visitation in order to protect the fragile canyon habitats. Dubbed the "Shangri-la of the Grand Canyon," the waterfalls have drawn visitors to this remote Native American reservation.

Major flooding in 2008 altered Havasu Canyon's famous landscape and it was closed to visitors for almost 10 months. Supai reopened in June 2009 but water and mud damage have changed some of the beautiful waterfalls, their streams and pools, and the amount of blue-green travertine. ■TIP→ Be sure to call the Havasupai Tourist Enterprise (☎ 928/448–2121) to make reservations before visiting.

GETTING HERE AND AROUND

Hualapai Hilltop is reached via Indian Route 18, which you follow about 65 miles north from historic Route 66 (34 miles west of Seligman and 50 miles east of Kingman). The total driving distance from the South Rim of the Grand Canyon is about 200 miles.

The Havasupai restrict the number of visitors to the canyon; you must have reservations. They ask that hikers call ahead before taking the trek into the canyon. The 8-mile Hualapai Trail begins at Hualapai Hilltop. From an elevation of 5,200 feet, the trail travels down a moderate grade to Supai village at 3,200 feet. Bring plenty of water and avoid hiking during the middle of the day, when canyon temperatures can reach into the 100s. If you'd rather ride, you can rent a horse for the trip down for $187 round-trip, or $94 one-way. Riders must be able to mount and dismount by themselves; be at least 4 feet, 7 inches; and weigh less than 250 pounds. Reservations must be made at least six weeks in advance with Havasupai Tourist Enterprise, which requires a 50% deposit. You'll need to spend the night if you're hiking or riding—you can camp at the campground 2 miles farther in ($17 per person) or stay at the Havasupai Lodge in the village.

MAIL BY MULE

Arguably the most remote mail route in the United States follows a steep 8-mile trail to the tiny town of Supai in Havasu Canyon. Havasupai tribal members living deep within the confines of the Grand Canyon rely on this route for the delivery of everything from food to furniture. During a typical week, more than a ton of mail is sent into the canyon by mule, with each animal carrying a cargo of about 130 pounds.

Another option is a helicopter ride into the canyon with Air West Helicopters. Flights leave from Hualapai Hilltop and cost $85 per person each way. Reservations aren't accepted and visitors are transported on a first-come, first-served basis. Tribal members are boarded prior to tourists.

ESSENTIALS

Transportation Contacts Air West Helicopters ☎ 623/516–2790 ⊙ Mid-Mar.–mid-Oct., Thurs., Fri., Sun., and Mon. 10–1; mid-Oct.–mid-Mar., Fri. and Sun. 10–1.

Visitor Information Havasupai Tourist Enterprise ☎ 928/448–2121 ⊕ www.havasupaitribe.com.

EXPLORING

Havasu Canyon. Havasu Canyon, south of the middle part of Grand Canyon National Park's South Rim and away from the crowds, is the home of the Havasupai, a tribe that has lived in this isolated area for centuries. You'll discover why they are known as the "people of the blue green waters" when you see the canyon's waterfalls. Accumulated travertine formations in some of the most popular pools were washed out in massive flooding decades ago and again in 2008 and 2010, but it's still a magical place.

The village of Supai, which currently has about 600 tribal members living there, is accessed by the 8-mile-long **Hualapai Trail**, which drops 2,000 feet from the canyon rim to the tiny town.

To reach Havasu's waterfalls, you must hike downstream from the village of Supai. Both **Havasu Falls** and **Mooney Falls** are still flowing and as beautiful as ever, but the flooding in 2008 washed out well-known Navajo Falls completely. Pack adequate food and supplies. Prices for food and sundries in Supai are more than double what they would be outside the reservation. The tribe does not allow alcohol, drugs, pets, or weapons. Reservations are necessary for camping or staying at the Havasupai Lodge. ⊠ *Havasupai Tourist Enterprise, Supai* ☎ *928/448–2121 general information, 928/448–2201 lodging reservations* ⊕ *www.havasupaitribe.com* ✉ *$35 entrance fee, $5 impact fee.*

WHAT'S NEAR THE GRAND CANYON

The northwest section of Arizona is geographically fascinating. In addition to the Grand Canyon, it's home to national forests, national monuments, and national recreation areas. Towns, however, are small and scattered. Many of them cater to visiting adventurers, and Native American reservations dot the map.

3

NEARBY TOWNS

Towns near the canyon's South Rim include the tiny town of Tusayan, just 1 mile south of the entrance station, and Williams, the "Gateway to the Grand Canyon," 58 miles south.

Tusayan has basic amenities and an airport that serves as a starting point for airplane and helicopter tours of the canyon. The cozy mountain town of **Williams,** founded in 1882 when the railroad passed through, was once a rough-and-tumble joint, replete with saloons and bordellos. Today it reflects a much milder side of the Wild West, with 3,300 residents and more than 25 motels and hotels. Wander along the main street—part of historic Route 66, but locally named, like the town, after trapper Bill Williams—and indulge in Route 66 nostalgia inside antiques shops or souvenir and T-shirt stores.

The communities closest to the North Rim—all of them tiny and with limited services—include Fredonia, 76 miles north; Marble Canyon, 80 miles northeast; Lees Ferry, 85 miles east; and Jacob Lake, 45 miles north.

Fredonia, a small community of about 1,050, approximately an hour's drive north of the Grand Canyon, is often referred to as the gateway to the North Rim; it's also relatively close to Zion and Bryce Canyon national parks in Utah. **Marble Canyon** marks the geographical beginning of the Grand Canyon at its northeastern tip. It's a good stopping point if you're driving U.S. 89 to the North Rim. En route from the South Rim to the North Rim is **Lees Ferry,** where most of the area's river rafts start their journey. The tiny town of **Jacob Lake,** nestled high in pine country at an elevation of 7,925 feet, was named after Mormon explorer Jacob Hamblin, also known as the "Buckskin Missionary." It has a hotel, café, campground, and lush mountain countryside.

VISITOR INFORMATION
Kaibab National Forest, North District ⊠ *430 S. Main St., Fredonia* ☎ *928/643-7395* ⊕ *www.fs.usda.gov/kaibab.* **Kaibab National Forest, Tusayan Ranger District** ⊠ *176 Lincoln Log Loop, Grand Canyon* ☎ *928/638-2443* ⊕ *www.fs.usda.gov/kaibab.* **Kaibab Plateau Visitor Center** ⊠ *Hwy. 89A/AZ 67, HC 64, Jacob Lake* ☎ *928/643-7298* ⊕ *www.fs.usda.gov/kaibab* ⊘ *Closed Dec.–mid-May.* **Williams Visitor Center** ⊠ *200 W. Railroad Ave., at Grand Canyon*

Blvd., Williams ☎ *928/635–1418, 800/863–0546* ⊕ *www.experiencewilliams.com* ⊙ *Daily 8–5.*

NEARBY ATTRACTIONS

National Geographic Visitor Center Grand Canyon. Here you can schedule and purchase tickets for air tours, buy a national park pass, and access the park by special entry lanes. However, the biggest draw at the visitor center is the six-story IMAX screen that features the 34-minute movie, *Grand Canyon: The Hidden Secrets.* You can learn about the geologic and natural history of the canyon, soar above stunning rock formations, and ride the rapids through the rocky gorge. The film is shown every hour on the half-hour. ⊠ *Hwy. 64/U.S. 180, 2 miles south of the Grand Canyon's south entrance, 450 State Rte. 64, Tusayan* ☎ *928/638–2203, 928/638–2468* ⊕ *www.explorethecanyon.com* 🎟 *$13.72 for IMAX movies* ⊙ *Mar.–Oct., daily 8 am–10 pm; Nov.–Feb., daily 10:30–6:30.*

FAMILY **Planes of Fame Air Museum.** A good stop 30 miles north of Williams, at the junction of U.S. 180 and State Route 64 in Valle, is this satellite of the Air Museum Planes of Fame in Chino, California. The museum chronicles the history of aviation with an array of historic and modern aircraft. One of the featured pieces is a C-121A Constellation "Bataan," the personal aircraft General MacArthur used during the Korean War. Guided tours of this historic plane are offered for $3. Visitors are not allowed inside the cockpits. ⊠ *755 Mustang Way, Valle* ☎ *928/635–1000* ⊕ *www.planesoffame.org* 🎟 *$6.95* ⊙ *Daily 9–5; extended summer hrs.*

Vermilion Cliffs National Monument. West from the town of Marble Canyon are these spectacular cliffs, more than 3,000 feet high in many places. Keep an eye out for condors; the giant endangered birds were reintroduced into the area in 1996. Reports suggest that the birds, once in captivity, are surviving well in the wilderness. ☎ *435/688–3200* ⊕ *www.blm.gov/az.*

SCENIC DRIVES

U.S. 89. The route north from Cameron Trading Post (Cameron, Arizona) on U.S. 89 offers a stunning view of the **Painted Desert** to the right. The desert, which covers thousands of square miles stretching to the south and east, is a vision of subtle, almost harsh beauty, with windswept plains and mesas, isolated buttes, and barren valleys in pastel patterns. About 30 miles north of Cameron Trading Post, the Painted Desert country gives way to sandstone cliffs that run for miles. Brilliantly hued and ranging in color from light pink to deep orange, the **Echo Cliffs** rise to more than 1,000 feet in many places. They are essentially devoid of vegetation, but in a few high places, thick patches of tall cottonwood and poplar trees, nurtured by springs and water seepage from the rock escarpment, manage to thrive. ⊠ *Grand Canyon.*

U.S. 89A. At Bitter Springs, 60 miles north of Cameron, U.S. 89A branches off from U.S. 89, running north and providing views of **Marble Canyon,** the geographical beginning of the Grand Canyon. Like the

Grand Canyon, Marble Canyon was formed by the Colorado River. Traversing a gorge nearly 500 feet deep is **Navajo Bridge,** a narrow steel span built in 1929 and listed on the National Register of Historic Places. Formerly used for car traffic, it now functions only as a pedestrian overpass. ⊠ *Grand Canyon.*

AREA ACTIVITIES

SPORTS AND THE OUTDOORS
BICYCLING
Arizona Bike Trail. Pedal the depths of the Kaibab National Forest on the Arizona Bike Trail-Tusayan Bike Trails System. Following linked loop trails at an elevation of 6,750 feet, you can bike as few as 3 miles or as many as 38 miles round-trip along old logging roads (parts of it paved) through ponderosa pine forest. Keep an eye out for elk, mule deer, hawks, eagles, pronghorn antelope, turkeys, coyote, and porcupines. Open for biking year-round (but most feasible March through October), the trail is accessed on the west side of Highway 64, a half mile north of Tusayan. ⊠ *Tusayan Ranger District, Hwy. 64, Box 3088, Tusayan* ☎ *928/638–2443* ⊕ *www.fs.usda.gov/kaibab.*

Historic Route 66 Mountain Bike Tour. Cyclists can enjoy the scenery along abandoned sections of Route 66 on the Historic Route 66 Mountain Bike Tour. Maps of the tour, which include the 6-mile **Ash Fork Hill Trail** and the 5-mile **Devil Dog Trail,** are available at the Williams Visitor Center.

FISHING
The stretch of ice-cold, crystal clear water at Lees Ferry off the North Rim provides arguably the best trout fishing in the Southwest. Many rafters and anglers stay the night in a campground near the river or in nearby Marble Canyon before hitting the river at dawn.

Arizona Game and Fish Department. Fish for trout, crappie, catfish, and smallmouth bass at a number of lakes surrounding Williams. To fish on public land, anglers ages 14 and older are required to obtain a fishing license from the Arizona Game and Fish Department. ☎ *928/774–5045* ⊕ *www.azgfd.gov.*

Lees Ferry Anglers. There are guides, state fishing licenses, and gear for sale at Lees Ferry Anglers. ⊠ *Milepost 547, N. U.S. 89A, HC 67, Marble Canyon* ☎ *928/355–2261, 800/962–9755* ⊕ *www.leesferry.com.*

Marble Canyon Outfitters. Marble Canyon Outfitters sells Arizona fishing licenses and offers guided fishing trips. ⊠ *0.25 mile west of Navajo Bridge on U.S. 89A, Marble Canyon* ☎ *928/645–2781, 800/533–7339* ⊕ *www.leesferryflyfishing.com.*

HORSEBACK RIDING
Apache Stables. There's nothing like a horseback ride to immerse you in the Western experience. From stables near Tusayan, these folks offer gentle horses and a ride that will meet most budgets. Choose from one- and two-hour trail rides or the popular campfire rides and horse-drawn wagon excursions. ⊠ *Forest Service Rd. 328, 1 mile north*

Lava Falls is the largest and best known of the rapids in the Grand Canyon.

of Tusayan, Tusayan 🕿 *928/638–2891* ⊕ *www.apachestables.com* ✉ *$25.50–$88.50* ⊘ *Mar.–Nov. (weather permitting), daily.*

RAFTING

Fodor's Choice
★

The National Park Service authorizes 16 concessionaires to run rafting trips through the canyon—you can view a full list at the park's website (⊕ *www.nps.gov/grca/planyourvisit/river-concessioners.htm*). Trips run from 3 to 16 days, depending on whether you opt for the upper canyon, lower canyon, or full canyon. You can also experience a one-day rafting trip, either running a few rapids in Grand Canyon West with the Hualapai tribe or floating through Glen Canyon near Page *(See Chapter 5, Northeast Arizona)*. Here are a few of the best operators for multiday trips:

Arizona Raft Adventures. Arizona Raft Adventures organizes 6- to 16-day paddle and/or motor trips through the upper, lower, or "full" canyon, for all skill levels. Trips, which run $1,985 to $4,040 (all fees and taxes included), depart April through October. ✉ *4050 East Huntington Dr., Flagstaff* 🕿 *928/526–8200, 800/786–7238* ⊕ *www.azraft.com.*

Canyoneers. With a reputation for high quality and a roster of 3- to 14-day trips, Canyoneers is popular with those who want to do some hiking as well. The five-day "Best of the Grand" trip includes a hike down to Phantom Ranch. The motorized and oar trips, available April through September, cost between $1,056 and $3,650. ✉ *Flagstaff* 🕿 *928/526–0924, 800/525–0924* ⊕ *www.canyoneers.com.*

Grand Canyon Expeditions. You can count on Grand Canyon Expeditions to take you down the Colorado River safely and in style: it limits the number of people on each boat to 14, and evening meals might include filet mignon, pork chops, or shrimp. The mid-April through mid-September trips cost $2,650 to $4,199 for 8 to 16 days. ☎ *435/644–2691, 800/544–2691* 🌐 *www.gcex.com.*

Wilderness River Adventures. One of the canyon's larger rafting outfitters, Wilderness River Adventures runs a wide variety of trips from 3 to 16 days, oar or motorized, from April to October. Their most popular trip is the seven-day motor trip. ✉ *Page* ☎ *928/645–3296, 800/992–8022* 🌐 *www.riveradventures.com.*

SKIING

FAMILY **Elk Ridge Ski and Outdoor Recreation.** Elk Ridge Ski and Outdoor Recreation is usually open from mid-December through much of March, weather permitting. There are four groomed runs (including one for beginners), areas suitable for cross-country skiing, and a hill set aside for tubing. The lodge rents skis, snowboards, and inner tubes. From Williams, take South 4th Street/Perkinsville Road for 2.5 miles, and then turn right at Ski Run Road/Forest Road 106 and go another 1.5 miles. During heavy snows, four-wheel drive or chains may be necessary. ✉ *6160 Donald Nelson Ave., Williams* ☎ *928/814–5038* 🌐 *www.elkridgeski.com.*

WHERE TO EAT

Prices in the reviews are the average cost of a main course at dinner or, if dinner isn't served, at lunch.

IN THE PARK

SOUTH RIM

$$$ STEAKHOUSE 🍴 **Arizona Room.** The canyon views from this casual Southwestern-style steak house are the best of any restaurant at the South Rim. The menu includes such delicacies as chile-crusted pan-seared wild salmon, chipotle barbecue baby back ribs, and half-pound buffalo burgers with Gorgonzola aioli. For dessert, try the cheesecake with prickly-pear syrup paired with one of the house's specialty coffee drinks. Seating is first-come, first served, so arrive early to avoid the crowds. [$] *Average main: $22* ✉ *Bright Angel Lodge, Desert View Dr., Grand Canyon Village* ☎ *928/638–2631* 🌐 *www.grandcanyonlodges.com* ✍ *Reservations not accepted* ⏲ *Closed Jan. and Feb. No lunch Nov. and Dec.*

$$ SOUTHWESTERN 🍴 **Bright Angel Restaurant.** The draw here is casual and affordable. No-surprises dishes will fill your belly at breakfast, lunch, or dinner. Entrées include such basics as salads, steaks, lasagna, burgers, fajitas, and fish tacos (sandwiches are options at lunch). Or you can step it up a notch and order some of the same selections straight from the Arizona Room menu including prime rib, baby back ribs, and wild salmon. For dessert try the warm apple grunt cake topped with vanilla ice cream. Be prepared to wait for a table: the dining room bustles all day long. The plain decor is broken up with large-pane windows and original artwork. [$] *Average main: $12* ✉ *Bright Angel Lodge, Desert View Dr., Grand Canyon Village* ☎ *928/638–2631* 🌐 *www.grandcanyonlodges.com* ✍ *Reservations not accepted.*

Continued on page 190

EXPLORING THE
COLORADO RIVER

By Carrie Frasure

High in Colorado's Rocky Mountains, the Colorado River begins as a catch-all for the snowmelt off the mountains west of the Continental Divide. By the time it reaches the Grand Canyon, the Colorado has been joined by multiple tributaries to become a raging river, red with silt as it sculpts spectacular landscapes. A network of dams can only partially tame this mighty river.

Snaking its way through five states, the Colorado River is an essential water source to the arid Southwest. Its natural course runs 1,450 miles from its origin in Colorado's La Poudre Pass Lake in Rocky Mountain National Park to its final destination in the Gulf of California, also called the Sea of Cortez. In northern Arizona, the Colorado River has been a powerful force in shaping the Grand Canyon, where it flows 4,000 to 6,000 feet below the rim. Beyond the canyon, the red river takes a lazy turn at the Arizona–Nevada border, where Hoover Dam creates the reservoir at Lake Mead. The Colorado continues at a relaxed pace along the Arizona–California border, providing energy and irrigation in Arizona, California, and Nevada before draining into northwestern Mexico.

A RIVER RUNS THROUGH IT

Stretching along 277 miles of the Colorado River is one of the seven natural wonders of the world, the Grand Canyon ranges in width from 4 to 18 miles, while the walls around it soar up to a mile high. Nearly 2 billion years of geologic history and majesty are revealed in exposed tiers of rock cut deep in the Colorado Plateau. What caused this incredible marvel of nature? Erosion by water coupled with driving wind are most likely the major culprits: under the sculpting power of wind and water, the shale layers eroded into slopes and the harder sandstone and limestone layers created terraced cliffs. Other forces that may have helped shape the canyon include ice, volcanic activity, continental drift, and earthquakes.

WHO LIVES HERE

Native tribes have lived in the canyon for thousands of years and continue to do so, looking to the river for subsistence. The plateau-dwelling Hualapai ("people of the tall pines") live on a million acres along 108 miles of the Colorado River in the West Rim. The Havasupai ("people of the blue green water") live deep within the walls of the 12-mile-long Havasu Canyon—a major side canyon connected to the Grand Canyon.

ENVIRONMENTAL CONCERNS

When the Grand Canyon achieved national park status in 1919, only 44,173 people made the grueling overland trip to see it—quite a contrast from today's nearly 5 million annual visitors. The tremendous increase in visitation has greatly impacted the fragile ecosystems, as has Lake Powell's Glen Canyon Dam, which was constructed in the 1950s and '60s. The dam has changed the composition of the Colorado River, replacing warm water rich in sediments (nature's way of nourishing the riverbed and banks) with mostly cool, much clearer water. This has introduced nonnative plants and animals that threaten the extinction of several native species. Air pollution has also affected visibility and the constant buzz of aerial tours has disturbed the natural solitude.

Above and right, views of Colorado River in the Grand Canyon from Toroweap.

DID YOU KNOW?

The North Rim's isolated Toroweap overlook (also called Tuweep) is perched 3,000 feet above the canyon floor: a height equal to stacking the Sears Tower and Empire State Building on top of each other.

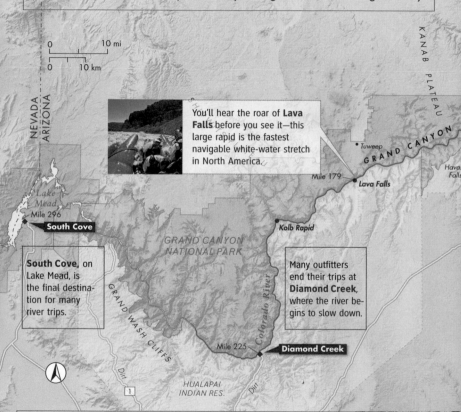

RIVER RAFTING THROUGH THE GRAND CANYON

Viewing the Colorado River from a canyon overlook is one thing, but looking up at the canyon from the middle of the river is quite another experience. If you're ready to tackle the churning white water of the Colorado River as it rumbles and hisses its way through the Grand Canyon, take a look at this map of what you might encounter along the way.

You'll hear the roar of **Lava Falls** before you see it—this large rapid is the fastest navigable white-water stretch in North America.

South Cove, on Lake Mead, is the final destination for many river trips.

Many outfitters end their trips at **Diamond Creek**, where the river begins to slow down.

KANAB PLATEAU

NEVADA
ARIZONA

Tuweep

GRAND CANYON

Hava. Falls

Mile 179

Lava Falls

Lake Mead
Mile 296

South Cove

Kolb Rapid

GRAND CANYON NATIONAL PARK

Colorado River

GRAND WASH CLIFFS

Mile 225

Diamond Creek

Dirt

1

Dirt

HUALAPAI INDIAN RES.

Peach Springs

COLORADO RIVER TRIPS		
Time and Length	Entry and Exit points	Cost/person
1 day Float trip	Glen Canyon Dam to Lees Ferry (no rapids)	$75–$89
1 day Combo trip	Diamond Creek, then helicopter to West Rim	$381
3–4 days	Lees Ferry to Phantom Ranch	*$700–$1,300
6 days, 89 mi	Phantom Ranch to Diamond Creek	$1,850–$2,300
9–10 days, 136 mi	Lees Ferry to Diamond Creek	$2,300–$3,100
14–16 days, 225 mi	Lees Ferry to South Cove	$3,300–$4,000

*Trips either begin or end at Phantom Ranch/Bright Angel Beach at the bottom of the Grand Canyon, at river mile 87

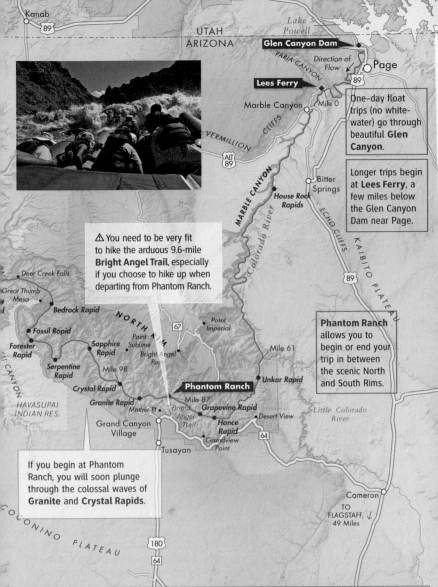

Kanab
89

UTAH
ARIZONA

Lake Powell

Glen Canyon Dam

Direction of Flow

Page
89

PARIA CANYON

Lees Ferry

Marble Canyon

Mile 0

One–day float trips (no white-water) go through beautiful **Glen Canyon**.

Longer trips begin at **Lees Ferry**, a few miles below the Glen Canyon Dam near Page.

VERMILLION

CLIFFS

ALT
89

Bitter Springs

ECHO CLIFFS

House Rock Rapids

MARBLE CANYON

Colorado River

KAIBITO PLATEAU

89

⚠ You need to be very fit to hike the arduous 9.6-mile **Bright Angel Trail**, especially if you choose to hike up when departing from Phantom Ranch.

Deer Creek Falls

Great Thumb Mesa

Bedrock Rapid

NORTH RIM

Point Imperial

67

Fossil Rapid

Forester Rapid

Sapphire Rapid

Point Sublime

Bright Angel Point

Mile 61

Serpentine Rapid

Mile 98

Phantom Ranch allows you to begin or end your trip in between the scenic North and South Rims.

Crystal Rapid

Unkar Rapid

CANYON

HAVASUPAI INDIAN RES.

Granite Rapid

Mather Pt

Phantom Ranch

Mile 87

Bright Angel Trail

Grapevine Rapid

Desert View

Little Colorado River

Grand Canyon Village

Hance Rapid

Grandview Point

64

Tusayan

If you begin at Phantom Ranch, you will soon plunge through the colossal waves of **Granite** and **Crystal Rapids**.

Cameron

TO FLAGSTAFF, ↙ 49 Miles

COCONINO PLATEAU

180

64

NOT JUST RAPIDS

Don't think that your experience will be nonstop white-water adrenaline. Most of the Colorado River features long, relaxing stretches of water, where you drift amid grandiose rock formations. You might even spot a mountain goat or two. Multiday trips include camping on the shore.

PLANNING YOUR RIVER RAFTING TRIP

OAR, MOTOR, OR HYBRID?

Base the type of trip you choose on the amount of effort you want to put in. Motor rafts, which are the roomiest of the choices, cover the most miles in less time and are the most comfortable. Guides do the rowing on oar boats and these smaller rafts offer a wilder ride. All-paddle trips are the most active and require the most involvement from guests. Hybrid trips are popular because they offer both the opportunity to paddle and to relax.

THE GEAR

Life jackets, beverages, tents, sheets, tarps, sleeping bags, dry bags, first aid, and food are provided—but you'll still need to plan ahead by packing clothing, hats, sunscreen, toiletries, and other sundries. Commercial outfitters allow each river runner two waterproof bags to store items during the day—just keep in mind that one of these will be filled up with the provided sleeping bag and tarp. ■TIP➜ Bring a rain suit: summer thunderstorms are frequent and chilly.

WHEN TO GO

Lots of people book trips for summer's peak period: June through August. If you're flexible, take advantage of the Arizona weather and go from May to early June or in September. ■TIP➜ Seats fill up quickly; make reservations for multiday trips a year or two in advance.

TOUR OPERATORS

Arizona Raft Adventures ☎ 928/526–8200 or 800/786–7238 ⊕ www.azraft.com

Canyoneers ☎ 928/526–0924 or 800/525–0924 ⊕ www.canyoneers.com

Grand Canyon Expeditions ☎ 435/644–2691 or 800/544–2691 ⊕ www.gcex.com

Hualapai River Runners
☎ 928/769–2636 or 888/868–9378 ⊕ www.hualapaitourism.com

Wilderness River Adventures ☎ 928/645–3296 or 800/992–8022 ⊕ www.riveradventures.com

⇨ See "Rafting" in the Sports and the Outdoors section of What's Nearby the Grand Canyon? for more information.

Above, Getting wet—and loving it—on an oar boat.

DID YOU KNOW?

As you're hanging on for dear life, consider this: Civil War veteran John Wesley Powell chartered these treacherous rapids in 1869—not only were conditions more dangerous then, but he had only one arm.

TOP PICNIC SPOTS

Bring your picnic basket and enjoy dining alfresco surrounded by some of the most beautiful backdrops in the country. Be sure to bring water, as it's unavailable at many of these spots, as are restrooms.

■ **Buggeln,** 15 miles east of Grand Canyon Village on Desert View Drive, has some secluded, shady spots.

■ **Cape Royal,** 23 miles south of the North Rim Visitor Center, is the most popular designated picnic area on the North Rim due to its panoramic views.

■ **Grandview Point** has, as the name implies, grand vistas; it's 12 miles east of the village on Desert View Drive.

■ **Point Imperial,** 11 miles northeast of the North Rim Visitor Center, has shade and some privacy.

$ AMERICAN

🍴 **Canyon Café at Yavapai Lodge.** Open for breakfast, lunch, and dinner, this cafeteria in the Market Plaza also serves specials such as chicken potpie, fried catfish, and fried chicken. Fast-food favorites here include pastries, burgers, and pizza. There isn't a fancy bar here, but you can order beer and wine with your meal. Resembling an old-fashioned diner, this cafeteria seats 345 guests and has easy-to-read signs that point the way to your favorite foods. Hours are limited in winter—it's best to call ahead then. [$] *Average main: $6* ✉ *Yavapai Lodge, Desert View Dr., Grand Canyon Village* ☎ *928/638–2631* 🌐 *www.grandcanyonlodges.com/canyon-cafe-423.html* ✍ *Reservations not accepted.*

$$$ SOUTHWESTERN Fodor's Choice ★

🍴 **El Tovar Dining Room.** No doubt about it—this is the best restaurant for miles. Modeled after a European hunting lodge, this rustic 19th-century dining room built of hand-hewn logs is worth a visit. The cuisine is modern Southwestern with an exotic flair. Start with the smoked salmon–and–goat cheese crostini or the acclaimed black bean soup. The dinner menu includes such hearty yet creative dishes as cherry-merlot-glazed duck with roasted poblano black bean rice, grilled New York strip steak with cornmeal-battered onion rings, and a wild salmon tostada topped with organic greens and tequila vinaigrette. The dining room also has an extensive wine list. ■ **TIP→ Dinner reservations can be made up to six months in advance with room reservations and 30 days in advance for all other visitors.** If you can't get a dinner table, consider lunch or breakfast—the best in the region with dishes like polenta corncakes with prickly pear–pistachio butter, and blackened breakfast trout and eggs. [$] *Average main: $27* ✉ *El Tovar Hotel, Desert View Dr., Grand Canyon Village* ☎ *303/297–2757, 888/297–2757 reservations only, 928/638–2631* 🌐 *www.grandcanyonlodges.com/el-tovar-421.html* ✍ *Reservations essential.*

$ AMERICAN

🍴 **Maswik Cafeteria.** You can get a burger, hot sandwich, pasta, or Mexican fare at this food court, as well as pizza by the slice and wine and beer in the adjacent Maswik Pizza Pub. This casual eatery is 0.25 mile from the rim. Lines can be long during high-season lunch and dinner, but everything moves fairly quickly. [$] *Average main: $7* ✉ *Maswik Lodge, Desert View Dr., Grand Canyon Village* 🌐 *www.grandcanyonlodges.com* ✍ *Reservations not accepted.*

NORTH RIM

$ 🍴 **Deli in the Pines.** Dining choices are very limited on the North Rim,
AMERICAN but this is your best bet for a meal on a budget. Selections include pizza, salads, deli sandwiches, hot dogs, homemade breakfast pastries and burritos, and soft-serve ice cream. Best of all, there is an outdoor seating area for dining alfresco. It's open for breakfast, lunch, and dinner. [$] *Average main: $6* ✉ *Grand Canyon Lodge, Bright Angel Point, North Rim* ☎ *928/638–2611* 🌐 *www.grandcanyonforever.com* ✍ *Reservations not accepted* ⏲ *Closed mid-Oct.–mid-May.*

$$$ 🍴 **Grand Canyon Lodge Dining Room.** The historic lodge has a huge, high-
AMERICAN ceilinged dining room with spectacular views and decent food, though
Fodor's Choice ★ the draw here is definitely the setting. You might find pecan-glazed pork chop, bison flank steak, and grilled ruby trout for dinner. The filling, simply prepared food here takes a flavorful turn with Southwestern spices and organic selections. It's also open for breakfast and lunch. A full-service bar and an impressive wine list add to the relaxed atmosphere of the only full-service, sit-down restaurant on the North Rim. Dinner reservations are essential in summer and on spring and fall weekends. [$] *Average main: $24* ✉ *Grand Canyon Lodge, Bright Angel Point, North Rim* ☎ *928/638–2611* 🌐 *www.grandcanyonforever.com* ⏲ *Closed mid-Oct.–mid-May.*

$$$ 🍴 **Grand Cookout.** Dine under the stars and enjoy live entertainment at
AMERICAN this chuck-wagon-style dining experience—a popular family-friendly
FAMILY choice among the North Rim's limited dining options. Fill up on Western favorites including barbecue beef brisket, roasted chicken, baked beans, and cowboy biscuits. The food is basic and tasty, but the real draw is the nightly performance of Western music and tall tales. Transportation from the Grand Canyon Lodge to the cookout (1 mile away) is included in the price. Be sure to call before 4 pm for dinner reservations. Advance reservations are taken by phone (during winter months) or at the Grand Canyon Lodge registration desk. [$] *Average main: $30* ✉ *Grand Canyon Lodge, North Rim* ☎ *928/638–2611, 928/645–6865 (winter)* 🌐 *www.grandcanyonforever.com* ✍ *Reservations essential* ⏲ *Closed Oct.–May.*

OUTSIDE THE PARK

TUSAYAN

$$ 🍴 **Canyon Star Restaurant and Saloon.** Relax in the rustic timber-and-stone
AMERICAN dining room at the Grand Hotel for reliable if uninspired American
FAMILY food, with an emphasis at dinner on steaks and barbecue. Other popular options include barbecue chicken and ribs, and Mexican fare. Most nights there's entertainment: live guitar or banjo music year-round, and Native American dancers in summer—all great for families. There's a kids' menu, and the Canyon Star also serves breakfast and lunch daily. In summer, be sure to reserve a table at dinner. There's also a coffee bar in the hotel lobby. [$] *Average main: $18* ✉ *Hwy. 64/U.S. 180, Tusayan* ☎ *928/638–3333* 🌐 *www.grandcanyongrandhotel.com* ⏲ *No lunch during winter.*

$$$ 🍴 **The Coronado Room.** Inside the Best Western Grand Canyon Squire
AMERICAN Inn is the most sophisticated cuisine in Tusayan in an upscale dining

room with attentive service. The menu includes well-prepared, hearty American food, with an emphasis on game (elk, venison, buffalo), plus grilled seafood, escargot, and oversize desserts. There's a good-size wine list, too. Although classier than most eateries in these parts, dress is still casual and the vibe relaxed. Reservations are a good idea, particularly in the busy season. $ *Average main: $22* ✉ *Hwy 64/U.S. 180, 100 Hwy 64, Tusayan* ☎ *928/638–2681* 🌐 *www.grandcanyonsquire.com* 🕒 *No lunch.*

DUFFEL SERVICE: LIGHTEN YOUR LOAD

Hikers staying at either Phantom Ranch or Bright Angel Campground can also take advantage of the ranch's duffel service: bags or packs weighing 30 pounds or less can be transported to the ranch by mule for a fee of $64.64 each way. As is true for many desirable things at the canyon, reservations are a must.

WILLIAMS

$$ AMERICAN FAMILY

🍴 **Cruisers Café 66.** A festive spot for a nostalgic meal, this diner patterned after a classic '50s-style, high-school hangout (but with cocktail service) pleases kids and adults with a large menu of family-priced American classics—good burgers and fries, barbecue pork sandwiches, salads, and thick malts, plus a choice steak that'll set you back about $20. The Grand Canyon Brewery, accessed by a side entrance, adds to the casual fun—just saddle up to a hand-carved log bar stool and order one of five microbrews on tap. A large mural of the town's heyday along the "Mother Road" and historic cars out front make this a Route 66 favorite. Kids enjoy the relaxed atmosphere and jukebox tunes. $ *Average main: $15* ✉ *233 W. Rte. 66, Williams* ☎ *928/635–2445* 🌐 *www.cruisers66.com.*

$$ MEXICAN

🍴 **Pancho McGullicuddy's Southwestern Bar & Grill.** Established in 1893 as the Cabinet Saloon, this restaurant is on the National Register of Historic Places. Gone are the spittoons and pipes—the colorful dining area now has Mexican-inspired decor and serves such specialties as "armadillo eggs" (deep-fried jalapeños stuffed with cheese). Other favorites include fish tacos, buzzard wings—better known as hot wings—and *pollo verde* (chicken breasts smothered in a sauce of cheese, sour cream, and green chiles). The bar has TVs tuned to sporting events and pours more than 30 tequilas, and there's live country music most evenings during the summer season. $ *Average main: $14* ✉ *141 Railroad Ave., Williams* ☎ *928/635–4150* 🌐 *www.vivapanchos.com.*

$$$ ECLECTIC Fodor's Choice ★

🍴 **Red Raven Restaurant.** Chef-owned David Haines cultivates a devoted foodie following with this dapper storefront bistro in the heart of downtown Williams that features warm lighting and romantic booth seating. Creatively presented fare blends American, Italian, and Asian ingredients—specialties include a starter of crisp tempura shrimp salad with a ginger-sesame dressing, and mains like charbroiled salmon with basil butter over cranberry–pine nut couscous, and pork tenderloin with cilantro pesto, served with mashed potatoes and sautéed local vegetables. The well-selected wine and beer list is one of the most extensive in the region. $ *Average main: $21* ✉ *135 W. Rte. 66, Williams* ☎ *928/635–4980* 🌐 *www.redravenrestaurant.com.*

$ 🍴 **Twisters.** Kick up some Route 66 nostalgia at this old-fashioned soda AMERICAN FAMILY fountain, bar, and kitschy gift shop built in 1926 on the site of an old Texaco gas station. Dine on burgers and hot dogs, a famous Twisters sundae (topped with raspberry sauce, nuts, and hot fudge), Route 66 beer float, or cherry phosphate—all to the sounds of '50s tunes. The kids' menu features cartoon characters and a selection of corn dogs, hot dogs, hamburgers, chicken strips, and peanut-butter-and-jelly sandwiches. The gift shop is a blast from the past, with Route 66 tchotchkes, classic Coca-Cola memorabilia, and fanciful items celebrating the careers of Betty Boop, James Dean, Elvis, and Marilyn Monroe. If you're thirsty, the attached bar has 20 beers on tap. [$] *Average main: $7* ✉ *417 E. Rte. 66, Williams* ☎ *928/635–0266* 🌐 *www.route66place.com* 🕓 *Closed Sun.; closed Jan.–Feb.*

3

WHERE TO STAY

Prices in the reviews are the lowest cost of a standard double room in high season. For expanded reviews, facilities, and current deals, visit Fodors.com.

IN THE PARK

SOUTH RIM

$ 🏨 **Bright Angel Lodge.** Famed architect Mary Jane Colter designed this HOTEL FAMILY 1935 log-and-stone structure, which sits within a few yards of the canyon rim and blends superbly with the canyon walls. **Pros:** some rooms have canyon vistas; all are steps away from the rim; Internet kiosks and transportation desk for the mule ride check-in are in the lobby; good value for the amazing location. **Cons:** the popular lobby is always packed; parking is a bit of a hike; lack of elevators make accessibility an issue for lodge rooms. [$] *Rooms from: $83* ✉ *Desert View Dr., Grand Canyon Village* ☎ *888/297–2757 reservations only, 928/638–2631* 🌐 *www.grandcanyonlodges.com* 🛏 *37 rooms, 18 with bath; 50 cabins* 🍽 *No meals.*

$$$ 🏨 **El Tovar Hotel.** The hotel's proximity to all of the canyon's facilities, HOTEL Fodor's Choice ★ European hunting-lodge atmosphere, attractively updated rooms and tile baths, and renowned dining room make it the best place to stay on the South Rim. **Pros:** historic lodging just steps from the South Rim; fabulous lounge with outdoor seating and canyon views; best in-park dining on-site. **Cons:** books up quickly. [$] *Rooms from: $183* ✉ *Desert View Dr., Grand Canyon Village* ☎ *888/297–2757 reservations only, 928/638–2631* 🌐 *www.grandcanyonlodges.com* 🛏 *66 rooms, 12 suites* 🍽 *No meals.*

$$$ 🏨 **Kachina Lodge.** On the rim halfway between El Tovar and Bright HOTEL Angel Lodge, this motel-style lodge has many rooms with partial canyon views ($11 extra). **Pros:** partial canyon views in half the rooms; family-friendly; steps from the best restaurants in the park. **Cons:** check-in takes place at El Tovar Hotel; limited parking; pleasant but bland furnishings. [$] *Rooms from: $180* ✉ *Desert View Dr., Grand Canyon*

Perched on the North Rim's edge—1,000 feet higher than the South Rim—is the Grand Canyon Lodge.

Village ☎ *888/297–2757 reservations only, 928/638–2631* 🌐 *www.grandcanyonlodges.com* 🛏 *49 rooms* 🍴 *No meals.*

$ HOTEL FAMILY [H] **Maswik Lodge.** Accommodations are far from crowds and noise and nestled in a shady ponderosa pine forest, with options ranging from rustic cabins to more modern motel-style rooms. **Pros:** larger rooms here than in older lodgings; good for families; affordable dining options. **Cons:** rooms lack historic charm and cabins as well as rooms in the South Section are quite plain; tucked away from the rim in the forest. [$] *Rooms from: $92* ✉ *Grand Canyon Village* ☎ *888/297–2757 reservations only, 928/638–2631* 🌐 *www.grandcanyonlodges.com* 🛏 *278 rooms* 🍴 *No meals.*

$ B&B/INN [H] **Phantom Ranch.** In a grove of cottonwood trees on the canyon floor, Phantom Ranch is accessible only to hikers and mule trekkers; there are 40 dormitory beds and 14 beds in cabins, all with shared baths. **Pros:** only inner-canyon lodging option; fabulous canyon views; remote access limits crowds. **Cons:** accessible only by foot or mule; few amenities or means of outside communication. [$] *Rooms from: $46* ✉ *On canyon floor, at intersection of Bright Angel and Kaibab trails* ☎ *303/297–2757, 888/297–2757* 🌐 *www.grandcanyonlodges.com* 🛏 *4 dormitories and 9 cabins (some cabins with outside showers reserved for mule riders)* 🍴 *Some meals.*

$$$ HOTEL [H] **Thunderbird Lodge.** This motel with comfortable, simple rooms with the modern amenities you'd expect at a typical mid-price chain hotel is next to Bright Angel Lodge in Grand Canyon Village. **Pros:** partial canyon views in some rooms; family-friendly. **Cons:** rooms lack personality; check-in takes place at Bright Angel Lodge; limited parking. [$] *Rooms from: $180* ✉ *Desert View Dr., Grand Canyon Village* ☎ *888/297–2757*

reservations only, 928/638–2631 ⊕ www.grandcanyonlodges.com ⇦ 55 rooms ⫴⚬⫴ No meals.

$$ ⊞ **Yavapai Lodge.** The largest motel-style lodge in the park is tucked in
HOTEL a piñon and juniper forest at the eastern end of Grand Canyon Village,
near the RV park. **Pros:** transportation-activities desk on-site in the
lobby; near Market Plaza in Grand Canyon Village; forested grounds.
Cons: farthest in-park lodging from the rim. Ⓢ *Rooms from: $125*
⊠ *Grand Canyon Village* ☎ *888/297–2757 reservations only, 928/638–
2961* ⊕ *www.grandcanyonlodges.com* ⇦ *358 rooms* ⊙ *Closed Jan. and
Feb.* ⫴⚬⫴ *No meals.*

NORTH RIM

$$ ⊞ **Grand Canyon Lodge.** This historic property, constructed mainly in
HOTEL the 1920s and '30s, is the premier lodging facility in the North Rim
Fodor'sChoice area. **Pros:** steps away from gorgeous North Rim views; close to sev-
★ eral easy hiking trails. **Cons:** as the only in-park North Rim lodging
option, this lodge fills up fast; few amenities and very limited Internet
access. Ⓢ *Rooms from: $124* ⊠ *Grand Canyon National Park, Hwy. 67,
North Rim* ☎ *877/386–4383, 928/638–2611 May–Oct., 928/645–6865
Nov.–Apr.* ⊕ *www.grandcanyonforever.com* ⇦ *40 rooms, 178 cabins*
⊙ *Closed mid-Oct.–mid-May* ⫴⚬⫴ *No meals.*

OUTSIDE THE PARK

TUSAYAN

$$$ ⊞ **Best Western Grand Canyon Squire Inn.** About 1 mile from the park's
HOTEL south entrance, this motel lacks the historic charm of the older lodges
FAMILY at the canyon rim, but has more amenities, including a small cow-
boy museum in the lobby, an upscale gift shop, and one of the better
restaurants in the region. **Pros:** a cool pool in summer and a hot tub
for cold winter nights; children's activities at the Family Fun Center;
close to South Rim. **Cons:** hall noise can be an issue with all of the
in-hotel activities. Ⓢ *Rooms from: $229* ⊠ *100 Hwy. 64, Grand Can-
yon* ☎ *928/638–2681, 800/622–6966* ⊕ *www.grandcanyonsquire.com*
⇦ *250 rooms, 4 suites* ⫴⚬⫴ *Breakfast.*

$$$ ⊞ **The Grand Hotel.** At the south end of Tusayan, this popular hotel has
HOTEL bright, clean rooms decorated in Southwestern colors, a cozy stone-and-
timber lobby, and free Wi-Fi. **Pros:** coffee stand for a quick morning
pick-me-up; gift shop stocked with outdoor gear and regional books.
Cons: 15-minute drive to the Grand Canyon. Ⓢ *Rooms from: $209*
⊠ *Hwy. 64/U.S. 180, 149 State Hwy. 64, Grand Canyon* ☎ *928/638–
3333, 888/634–7263* ⊕ *www.grandcanyongrandhotel.com* ⇦ *121
rooms* ⫴⚬⫴ *No meals.*

$$ ⊞ **Red Feather Lodge.** This motel and adjacent hotel are a good value
HOTEL about 6 miles from the canyon. **Pros:** good price for being so close to
park; motel rooms renovated in 2010 with new showers and mattresses.
Cons: motel rooms are small, with shower only. Ⓢ *Rooms from: $140*
⊠ *Hwy. 64/U.S. 180, 300 State Rte. 64, Tusayan* ☎ *928/638–2414,
800/538–2345* ⊕ *www.redfeatherlodge.com* ⇦ *215 rooms, 1 suite*
⫴⚬⫴ *No meals.*

Best Grand Canyon Campgrounds

Within the national park, camping is permitted only in designated campsites. Some campgrounds charge nightly camping fees in addition to entrance fees, and some accept reservations up to five months in advance through ⊕ www.recreation.gov. Others are first-come, first-served.

In-park camping in a spot other than a developed rim campground requires a permit from the Backcountry Information Center, which also serves as your reservation. Permits can be requested by mail or fax only; applying well in advance is recommended. Call ☎ 928/638–7875 between 1 pm and 5 pm Monday through Friday for information.

Outside the park boundaries, there are campgrounds near the South and North rims, and in Havasu Canyon and the Kaibab National Forest. There's no camping on the West Rim, but you can pitch a tent on the beach near the Colorado River.

SOUTH RIM

Bright Angel Campground. This backcountry campground is near Phantom Ranch, at the bottom of the canyon. There are toilet facilities and running water, but no showers. ⊠ Intersection of South and North Kaibab trails, Grand Canyon ☎ 928/638–7875.

Desert View Campground. Popular for spectacular views of the canyon from the nearby watchtower, this campground doesn't take reservations; show up before noon, as it fills up fast in summer. ⊠ Desert View Dr., 23 miles east of Grand Canyon Village off Hwy. 64, Grand Canyon National Park.

Indian Garden. Halfway down the canyon is this backcountry campground, en route to Phantom Ranch on the Bright Angel Trail. Running water and toilet facilities are available, but not showers. ⊠ Bright Angel Trail, Grand Canyon ☎ 928/638–7875.

NORTH RIM

North Rim Campground. The only designated campground at the North Rim of Grand Canyon National Park sits 3 miles north of the rim, near the general store, and has 84 RV and tent sites (no hookups). ⊠ Hwy. 67, North Rim ☎ 928/638–7888 ⊕ www.recreation.gov.

OUTSIDE THE PARK

Diamond Creek. You can camp on the banks of the Colorado River, but your peace might be interrupted by the fact that this smooth beach is a launch point for river runners. The Hualapai permit camping on their tribal lands here, with an overnight camping permit of $32.10 per person per night, which can be purchased at the Hualapai Lodge. ☎ 928/769–2210, 888/255–9550 ⊕ www.hualapaitourism.com.

Havasu Canyon. You can stay in the primitive campgrounds in Havasu Canyon for $17 per person per night, in addition to the $35-per-person entry fee plus a $5 environmental-care fee. ☎ 928/448–2121, 928/448–2174, 928/448–2180, or 928/448–2141 ⊕ www.havasupaitribe.com.

Kaibab National Forest. Both developed and undeveloped campsites are available on a first-come, first-served basis May through September at this forest that surrounds Williams and extends to the Grand Canyon. ☎ 928/699–1239, 928/638–2443 ⊕ www.fs.usda.gov/kaibab.

WILLIAMS

$ HOTEL FAMILY **Canyon Motel and RV Park.** Railcars, cabooses, and cottages make up this 13-acre property on the outskirts of Williams, about a one-hour drive to the park. **Pros:** family-friendly property with hiking, horseshoes, playground, and indoor swimming pool; general store; owners are friendly and helpful. **Cons:** a few miles from Williams dining options; RV park traffic. *[$] Rooms from: $75 ✉ 1900 E. Rodeo Rd., Rte. 66, Williams ☎ 928/635–9371, 800/482–3955 🌐 www.thecanyonmotel.com 🛏 18 rooms, 5 railcar suites 🍴 No meals.*

$$ HOTEL **Grand Canyon Railway Hotel.** Designed to resemble the train depot's original Fray Marcos lodge, this hotel features attractive Southwestern-style accommodations with large bathrooms and comfy beds with upscale linens. **Pros:** railway package options; game room and outdoor playground; short walk from historic downtown restaurants and bars. **Cons:** railroad noise. *[$] Rooms from: $169 ✉ 233 North Grand Canyon Blvd., Williams ☎ 928/635–4010, 800/843–8724 🌐 www.thetrain.com 🛏 287 rooms, 11 suites 🍴 No meals.*

$$ B&B/INN **The Red Garter.** This restored saloon and bordello from 1897 now houses a small, antiques-filled B&B. **Pros:** on-site coffeehouse and bakery; decorated in antiques and period pieces; steps from several restaurants and bars. **Cons:** all rooms are only accessible by stairs; parking is across the street; over an hour drive to canyon. *[$] Rooms from: $135 ✉ 137 Railroad Ave., Williams ☎ 928/635–1484, 800/328–1484 🌐 www.redgarter.com 🛏 4 rooms 🍴 Breakfast.*

JACOB LAKE

$$ HOTEL **Jacob Lake Inn.** The bustling lodge at Jacob Lake Inn is a popular stop for those heading to the North Rim, 45 miles south. **Pros:** grocery store, coffee shop, and restaurant; quiet rooms. **Cons:** small bathroom in cabins; worn furnishings; old-fashioned key locks. *[$] Rooms from: $139 ✉ Hwy. 67/U.S. 89A, Hwy. 89A & AZ-67, Jacob Lake ☎ 928/643–7232 🌐 www.jacoblake.com 🛏 32 rooms, 26 cabins 🍴 No meals.*

$ HOTEL **Marble Canyon Lodge.** This Arizona Strip lodge popular with anglers and rafters opened in 1929 on the same day the Navajo Bridge was dedicated; a 2010 renovation updated all rooms and bathrooms. **Pros:** convenience store, restaurant, and trading post; great fishing on the Colorado River. **Cons:** no-frills rustic lodging; more than 70 miles to the Grand Canyon North Rim. *[$] Rooms from: $80 ✉ 0.25 mile west of Navajo Bridge on U.S. 89A, Marble Canyon ☎ 928/355–2225, 800/726–1789 🌐 www.marblecanyoncompany.com 🛏 46 rooms, 8 apartments 🍴 No meals.*

WEST RIM

$$ HOTEL **Havasupai Lodge.** These are fairly spartan accommodations, but you won't mind much when you see the natural beauty surrounding you. **Pros:** near the famous waterfalls; Native American perspective on the natural and cultural history of the Grand Canyon. **Cons:** accessible only by foot, horseback, or helicopter; rooms are plain and worn; no phones, Internet, or TVs. *[$] Rooms from: $145 ✉ 159 Supai, Supai Village Trail ☎ 928/448–2111, 928/448–2201 🌐 www.havasupaitribe.com 🛏 24 rooms 🍴 No meals.*

$ HOTEL 🏨 **The Hualapai Lodge.** In Peach Springs on the longest stretch of the original historic Route 66, the hotel has a comfortable lobby with a large fireplace that is welcoming on chilly nights—it's a 19-mile scenic drive to the Colorado River (and a 2-hour drive to the West Rim). **Pros:** concierge desk arranges river trips with the Hualapai River Runners; good on-site restaurant with Native American dishes; Hualapai locals add a different perspective to the canyon experience. **Cons:** basic rooms lack historic charm; location is off the beaten path. [$] *Rooms from: $110* ✉ *900 Rte. 66, Peach Springs* ☎ *928/769–2230, 888/868–9378* 🌐 *www.hualapaitourism.com* 🛏 *60 rooms* 🍴 *Breakfast.*

$$$$ B&B/INN 🏨 **Hualapai Ranch.** Accommodations at Hualapai Ranch, the only lodging on the West Rim, are available as a package through Hualapai Tourism, and hotel rates ($153 per person) include continental breakfast, either lunch or dinner, a Hualapai visitation permit, and shuttle service to the rim overlooks at Guano Point and Eagle Point. **Pros:** front porches have relaxed desert views; rustlers tell tall tales and strike up a tune at campfire programs; dining room serves meals all day long. **Cons:** no phones, Internet, or TVs. [$] *Rooms from: $306* ✉ *Grand Canyon West* ☎ *928/769–2636, 888/868–9378* 🌐 *www.hualapaitourism.com* 🛏 *26 cabins* 🍴 *Some meals.*

NORTH-CENTRAL
ARIZONA

WELCOME TO NORTH-CENTRAL ARIZONA

TOP REASONS TO GO

★ **Mother Nature:** Stunning red rocks, snow-capped mountains, and crisp country air rejuvenate the most cynical city dwellers. Nature lovers should visit either the Coconino or Prescott national forest.

★ **Father Time:** Ancient Native American sites, such as Walnut Canyon and Montezuma's Castle, show life before Columbus "discovered" America. You can learn their history in the excellent national monument visitor centers.

★ **Main Street charm:** Jerome and Prescott exude small-town hospitality with turn-of-the-20th-century architecture and charming bed-and-breakfasts.

★ **Cool escapes:** Beat the heat in the high desert; temperatures throughout north-central Arizona are typically 20°F cooler than in the Phoenix area.

★ **Free spirits:** The energy of Sedona is delightfully infectious; even skeptics might be tempted to get their aura read.

1 Flagstaff. College-town enthusiasm and high-country charm combine to make this one of Arizona's most outdoors-friendly towns. Hiking, biking, skiing, and climbing are local passions, and there are state and national parks to explore. Stop in at a local coffee-house and get sandwiches for a picnic, then head out on a scenic trail to enjoy some solitude.

2 Sedona. Surrounded by the Coconino National Forest, Sedona's residents call their home a museum without walls. The town's red rocks lure visitors from around the world. You'll enjoy breathtaking views, fantastic cuisine, and a dash of New Age whimsy.

3 The Verde Valley, Jerome, and Prescott. Remote but still accessible, the towns of the Verde Valley embrace the life of yesteryear. You can take the Verde Canyon Railroad or visit Montezuma's Castle and see nature's untouched beauty and history. Whiskey Row in Prescott still exudes turn-of-the-20th-century charm, and Jerome, less commercial than Sedona, is emerging as a new hub for artisans and antiques dealers.

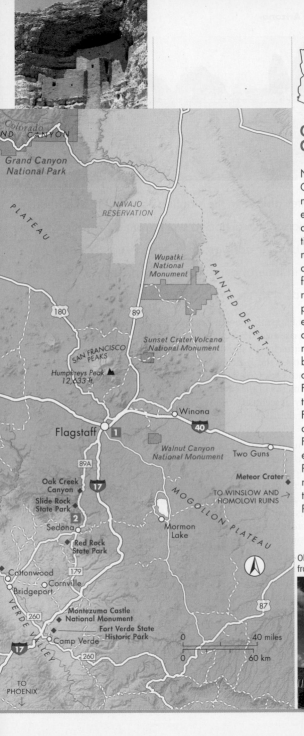

GETTING ORIENTED

Nestled between the Grand Canyon and Phoenix, north-central Arizona has enough natural beauty and sophisticated attractions to compete with its neighbors to the north and south. Most visitors flock to Sedona, world renowned for red rocks, pink jeeps, and New Age energy. The surrounding area of Verde Valley may not attract the same hordes, but this means some welcome peace and quiet. Flagstaff is surrounded by the Coconino National Forest and wrapped around the base of the San Francisco Peaks, the tallest mountains in the state. Phoenicians flee the summertime heat to cool off in the mountains and explore Prescott and Jerome.

Old Flagstaff sandstone courthouse from 1894.

Updated by
Mara Levin

Red-rock buttes ablaze in the slanting light of late afternoon, the San Francisco Peaks tipped white from a fresh snowfall, pine forests clad in dark green needles—north-central Arizona is rich in natural attractions, a landscape of vast plateaus punctuated by steep ridges and canyons.

To the north of Flagstaff the San Francisco Peaks, a string of tall volcanic mountains, rise over 12,000 feet, tapering to the 9,000-foot Mount Elden and a scattering of diminutive cinder cones. To the south, ponderosa pines cover the Colorado Plateau before the terrain plunges dramatically into Oak Creek Canyon. The canyon then opens to reveal red buttes and mesas in the high-desert areas surrounding Sedona. The desert gradually descends to the Verde Valley, crossing the Verde River before reaching the 7,000-foot Black Range, over which lies the Prescott Valley.

Flagstaff, the hub of this part of Arizona, was historically a way station en route to Southern California via the railroads and then Route 66. Many of those who were "just passing through" stayed and built a community, revitalizing downtown with cafés, an activity-filled square, eclectic shops, and festivals. The town's large network of bike paths and parks abuts hundreds of miles of trails and forest roads, an irresistible lure for outdoors enthusiasts. Not surprisingly, the typical resident of Flagstaff is outdoorsy, young, and has a large, friendly dog in tow.

Down AZ 89A in Sedona, the average age and income rises considerably. This was once a hidden hamlet used by Western filmmakers, but New Age enthusiasts flocked to the region in the 1980s, believing it was the center of spiritual powers. Well-off executives and retirees followed soon after, building clusters of McMansions. Sophisticated restaurants, upscale shops, luxe accommodations, and New Age entrepreneurs cater to both these populations, and to the thriving tourist trade. It can be difficult, though not impossible, to find a moment of serenity, even in wilderness areas.

Pioneers and miners are now part of north-central Arizona's past, but the wild and woolly days of the Old West aren't forgotten. The preserved fort at Camp Verde recalls frontier life, and the decrepit facades of the funky former mining town of Jerome have an infectious charm. The many Victorian houses in temperate Prescott attest to the attempt to bring "civilization" to Arizona's territorial capital.

North-central Arizona is also rich in artifacts from its earliest inhabitants: several national and state parks—among them Walnut Canyon, Wupatki, Montezuma Castle, and Tuzigoot national monuments—hold well-preserved evidence of the architectural accomplishments of Native American Sinagua and other Ancestral Puebloans.

■ **TIP→** It's wise, especially if you're an outdoors enthusiast, to start in the relatively lowland areas of Prescott and the Verde Valley, climbing gradually to Sedona and Flagstaff—it can take several days to grow accustomed to the high elevation in Flagstaff.

4

NORTH-CENTRAL ARIZONA PLANNER

WHEN TO GO

Autumn, when the wet season ends, the stifling desert temperatures moderate (it's 20°F cooler than Phoenix), and the mountain aspens reach their full golden splendor, is a great time to visit this part of Arizona. During the summer months many Phoenix residents travel north to escape the 100°F temperatures, meaning excessive traffic along Interstate 17 just north of Phoenix on Friday and Sunday evenings. Hotels are less expensive in winter, but mountain temperatures dip below zero, and snowstorms can occur weekly, especially near Flagstaff.

Sedona has springlike temperatures even in January, when it's snowing in Flagstaff, but summer temperatures above 90°F are common.

FESTIVALS AND EVENTS

SEPTEMBER **Festival of Science.** This 10-day series of exhibits and guest speakers—not limited to astronomy—in Flagstaff is made stellar by its observatories. ☎ *800/842-7293* ⊕ *www.scifest.org.*

Flagstaff Route 66 Days. Classic and muscle cars roar into Flagstaff the second weekend in September for this fun auto show with live music and a host of vendors. ☎ *928/451-1204* ⊕ *www.route66carclub.com.*

PLANNING YOUR TIME

Sedona will probably occupy most of your time, so plan to spend at least two days there, hiking or shopping. Oak Creek Canyon and Chapel of the Holy Cross are must-sees. Then, depending on your preferences, spend your time looking (window-shopping or stargazing) or doing (hiking, exploring). If you can, plan to be in Sedona midweek, when the weekend crowds aren't around.

Outdoors enthusiasts should head to Flagstaff for a day to enjoy the Mount Elden Trail System or hit the slopes at Arizona Snowbowl. The evening can be spent enjoying dinner at one of downtown Flagstaff's many restaurants, followed by constellation viewing at the Lowell Observatory.

Prescott and Jerome can be combined for a day or less. You can check out the pulse of downtown Prescott's art and music scene on famous Whiskey Row, then spend a night in a historic hotel; Jerome has several

HIKING HIGHLIGHTS

Ancient seas, colliding landmasses, spewing volcanoes, and other geological forces have cast and recast northern Arizona into a sprawling sculpture of contrasts. Hikes along canyon rims often look out among red-rock monoliths, and treks to the barren crests of the San Francisco Peaks overlook verdant forests stretching to the edge of the Grand Canyon to the north and the Mogollon Rim to the south. You can hike through thick woods in the Verde Valley and the Prescott National Forest (and even ascend a volcano), and amid rock formations around Sedona. Check out ⊕ *www.fs.usda.gov/coconino* for info on the Coconino, and ⊕ *www.fs.usda.gov/prescott* for more info on Prescott.

quaint B&Bs, as well as a shopping district with more affordable treasures than Sedona.

GETTING HERE AND AROUND

Don't plan on flying into Flagstaff, Sedona, or Prescott: commercial flights are limited, and besides, getting here is half the fun; the scenery is gorgeous. You'll definitely want a car, and north-central Arizona is only a two-hour drive from Phoenix.

It makes sense to rent a car in this region, since trails and monuments stretch miles past city limits and many area towns can't be reached by the major bus companies. The major rental agencies have offices in Flagstaff, Prescott, and Sedona. Avoid interstates when possible; the back ways can be more direct and have the best views of the stunning landscape. Instead of Route 17, take AZ 89A through Verde Valley and Oak Creek Canyon. Weekend traffic around Sedona can be heavy, so leave early and allow extra time.

RESTAURANTS

You'll find lots of American comfort food in this part of the country: barbecue restaurants, steak houses, and burger joints predominate. If you're looking for something different, Sedona and Flagstaff have the majority of good, multiethnic restaurants in the area, and if you're craving Mexican, you're sure to find something authentic and delicious (note that burritos are often called "burros" around here). Sedona is the best place in the area for fine dining, although Flagstaff and Prescott now boast a few upscale eateries. Some area restaurants close in January and February—the slower months in the area—so call ahead. Reservations are suggested from April through October. *Prices in the reviews are the average cost of a main course at dinner or, if dinner is not served, at lunch.*

HOTELS

Flagstaff and Prescott have the more affordable lodging options, with lots of comfortable motels and B&Bs, but no real luxury. The opposite is true in Sedona, which is filled with opulent resorts and hideaways, most offering solitude and spa services—just don't expect a bargain. Reservations are essential for Sedona and suggested for Flagstaff and

Prescott. Little Jerome has a few B&Bs, but call ahead if you think you might want to spend the night. If you're in for a thrill, many of the historic hotels have haunted rooms. *Prices in the reviews are the lowest cost of a standard double room in high season. For expanded reviews, facilities, and current deals, visit Fodors.com.*

FLAGSTAFF

146 miles northwest of Phoenix, 27 miles north of Sedona via Oak Creek Canyon.

Few travelers slow down long enough to explore Flagstaff, a town of 66,000 known locally as "Flag"; most stop only to spend the night at one of the town's many motels before making the last leg of the trip to the Grand Canyon, 80 miles north. Flag makes a good base for day trips to ancient Native American sites and the Navajo and Hopi reservations, as well as to Petrified Forest National Park and the Painted Desert, but the city is a worthwhile destination in its own right. Set against a lovely backdrop of pine forests and the snowcapped San Francisco Peaks, downtown Flagstaff retains a frontier flavor.

In summer, Phoenix residents head here seeking relief from the desert heat, since at any time of the year temperatures in Flagstaff are about 20°F cooler than in Phoenix. They also come to Flagstaff in winter to ski at the small Arizona Snowbowl, about 15 miles northeast of town among the San Francisco Peaks.

GETTING HERE AND AROUND

Flagstaff lies at the intersection of Interstate 40 (east–west) and Interstate 17 (running south from Flagstaff), 146 miles north of Phoenix via Interstate 17. If you're driving from Sedona to Flagstaff or the Grand Canyon, head north through the wooded Oak Creek Canyon: it's the most scenic route.

Flagstaff Pulliam Airport is 3 miles south of town off Interstate 17 at Exit 337. US Airways flies from Phoenix to Flagstaff. A taxi from Flagstaff Pulliam Airport to downtown should cost about $14. Cabs aren't regulated; some, but not all, have meters, so it's wise to agree on a rate before you leave for your destination.

Amtrak comes into the downtown Flagstaff station twice daily. There's no rail service into Prescott or Sedona, but Arizona Shuttle provides transportation via shuttle van or private car between Phoenix, Sedona, Flagstaff, Williams, and the Grand Canyon. Sun Taxi will take you around Flagstaff or to any place in northern Arizona.

A walking-tour map of the area is available at the visitor center in the Tudor Revival–style train depot, an excellent place to begin sightseeing.

PLANNING YOUR TIME

You can see most of Flagstaff's attractions in a day—especially if you visit the Lowell Observatory or the Northern Arizona University Observatory in the evening, which is also when the Museum Club is best experienced.

Consult the schedule of tour times if you want to visit the Riordan State Historic Park. Devote at least an hour to the excellent Museum of Northern Arizona. The Historic Downtown District is a good place for lunch or dinner. If you're a skier, spend part of a winter's day at the Arizona Snowbowl; in summer you can spend a couple of hours on the skyride and scenic trails at the top. Take your time enjoying the trails on Mount Elden, and remember to pace yourself in the higher elevations; allow a full day for hiking. The Lava River Cave is an easy—if dark—hike that can be done comfortably in an hour.

ESSENTIALS

Transportation Contacts A Friendly Cab ☎ 928/774–4444 ⊕ www. afriendlycab.com. **Arizona Shuttle** ☎ 800/888–2749 ⊕ www.arizonashuttle.com. **Sun Taxi and Tours** ☎ 928/779–1111 ⊕ www.suntaxiandtours.com/.

Visitor Information Flagstaff Visitor Center ⊠ Santa Fe Depot, 1 E. Rte. 66, Downtown ☎ 928/774–9541, 800/842–7293 ⊕ www.flagstaffarizona.org.

EXPLORING

TOP ATTRACTIONS

Arizona Snowbowl. Although the Arizona Snowball is still one of Flagstaff's biggest attractions, snowy slopes can be a luxury in times of drought. Fortunately, visitors can enjoy the beauty of the area year-round, with or without the fluffy white stuff. The Agassiz ski lift climbs to a height of 11,500 feet in 25 minutes, and doubles as a skyride through the Coconino National Forest in summer. From this vantage point you can see up to 70 miles; views may even include the North Rim of the Grand Canyon. There's a lodge at the base with a restaurant, bar, and ski school. To reach the ski area, take U.S. 180 north from Flagstaff; it's 7 miles from the Snowbowl exit to the skyride entrance. ⊠ Snowbowl Rd., North Flagstaff ☎ 928/779–1951 ⊕ www.arizonasnowbowl. com ⊠ Skyride $12 ⊙ Skyride: Memorial Day–early Sept., daily 10–4; early Sept.–mid-Oct., Fri.–Sun. 10–4, weather permitting.

Historic Downtown District. Storied Route 66 runs right through the heart of downtown Flagstaff. The late-Victorian, Tudor Revival, and early–art deco architecture in this district recalls the town's heyday as a logging and railroad center. ⊠ Downtown Historic District, Rte. 66 north to Birch Ave., and Beaver St. east to Agassiz St., Downtown.

Santa Fe Depot. The Santa Fe Depot now houses the visitor center for the Historic District. ⊠ 1 E. Rte. 66, Downtown.

Hotel Monte Vista. Highlights of the historic district include the 1927 Hotel Monte Vista, built after a community drive raised $200,000 in 60 days. The construction was promoted as a way to bolster the burgeoning tourism industry in the region. The hotel was held publicly until the early 1960s. ⊠ 100 N. San Francisco St., Downtown ☎ 928/779–6971 ⊕ www.hotelmontevista.com.

Babbitt Brothers Building. The 1888 Babbitt Brothers Building was constructed as a building-supply store and then turned into a department store by David Babbitt, the mastermind of the Babbitt empire. The Babbitts are one of Flagstaff's wealthiest founding families. Bruce

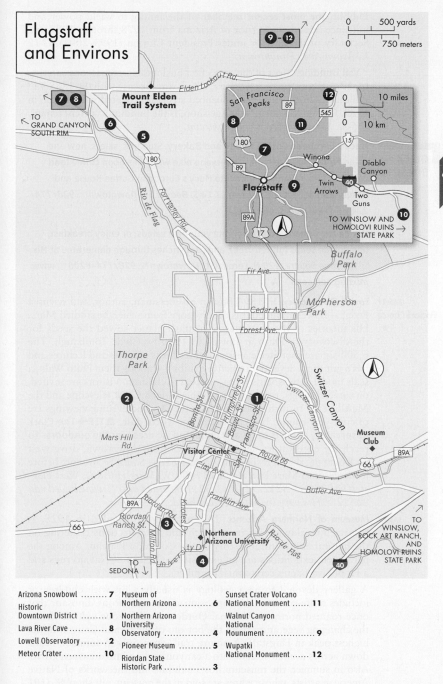

Arizona Snowbowl **7**

Historic
Downtown District **1**

Lava River Cave **8**

Lowell Observatory **2**

Meteor Crater **10**

Museum of
Northern Arizona **6**

Northern Arizona
University
Observatory **4**

Pioneer Museum **5**

Riordan State
Historic Park **3**

Sunset Crater Volcano
National Monument **11**

Walnut Canyon
National
Mounument **9**

Wupatki
National Monument **12**

Babbitt, the most recent member of the family to wield power and influence, was the governor of Arizona from 1978 through 1987 and Secretary of the Interior under President Clinton (1993–2001). ⊠ *12 E. Aspen Ave., Downtown.*

Vail Building. Most of the area's first businesses were saloons catering to railroad construction workers, which was the case with the 1888 Vail Building, a brick art deco–influenced structure covered with stucco in 1939. Crystal Magic, a New Age shop, is the building's current tenant. ⊠ *5 N. San Francisco St., Downtown.*

QUICK BITES

Macy's European Coffee House and Bakery. Students, skiers, new and aging hippies, and just about everyone else who likes good coffee (and delicious vegetarian fare) jam into Macy's European Coffee House and Bakery for the best cup in town. ⊠ *14 S. Beaver St., Downtown* ☎ *928/774–2243* ⊕ *www.macyscoffee.net.*

Mix on the Square. You can create your own salads, or enjoy breakfast, homemade soups (gluten-free), and sandwiches through dinnertime at Mix. ⊠ *Heritage Square, 120 N. Leroux St., Downtown* ☎ *928/774–8200* ⊕ *www.mixflagstaff.com.*

FAMILY
Fodor's Choice
★

Lowell Observatory. In 1894 Boston businessman, author, and scientist Percival Lowell founded this observatory from which he studied Mars. His theories of the existence of a ninth planet sowed the seeds for the discovery of Pluto at Lowell in 1930 by Clyde Tombaugh. The 6,500-square-foot Steele Visitor Center hosts exhibits and lectures and has a gift shop. Several interactive exhibits—among them Pluto Walk, a scale model of the solar system—appeal to children. Visitors are invited, on some evenings, to peer through the 24-inch Clark telescope and the McAllister, a 16-inch reflector telescope. Day and evening viewings are offered year-round, but call ahead for a schedule. ■TIP➔ The Clark observatory dome is open and unheated, so dress for the outdoors. To reach the observatory, less than 2 miles from downtown, drive west on Route 66, which resumes its former name, Santa Fe Avenue, before it merges into Mars Hill Road. ⊠ *1400 W. Mars Hill Rd., West Flagstaff* ☎ *928/233–3212, 928/233–3211 recorded info* ⊕ *www.lowell.edu* ⌑ *$12* ⊘ *Hrs vary by season; call ahead.*

FAMILY
Museum of Northern Arizona. This institution, founded in 1928, is respected worldwide for its research and its collections centering on the natural and cultural history of the Colorado Plateau. Among the permanent exhibitions are an extensive collection of Navajo rugs and a Hopi kiva (men's ceremonial chamber).

A gallery devoted to area geology is usually a hit with children: it includes a life-size model dilophosaurus, a carnivorous dinosaur that once roamed northern Arizona. Outdoors, a life-zone exhibit shows the changing vegetation from the bottom of the Grand Canyon to the highest peak in Flagstaff. A nature trail, open only in summer, heads down across a small stream into a canyon and up into an aspen grove. Also in summer, the museum hosts exhibits and the works of Native American artists, whose wares are sold in the museum gift shop. ⊠ *3101*

N. Fort Valley Rd., North Flagstaff ☎ *928/774–5213* ⊕ *www.musnaz.org* ⛄ *$10* ⊙ *Daily 9–5.*

WORTH NOTING

Lava River Cave. Subterranean lava flow formed this mile-long cave roughly 700,000 years ago. Once you descend into its boulder-strewn maw, the cave is spacious, with 40-foot ceilings, but claustrophobes take heed: about halfway through, the cave tapers to a 4-foot-high squeeze that can be a bit unnerving. A 40°F chill pervades the cave throughout the year so take warm clothing.

To reach the turnoff for the cave, go approximately 9 miles north of Flagstaff on U.S. 180, then turn west onto FR 245. Turn left at the intersection of FR 171 and look for the sign to the cave. The trip is approximately 45 minutes from Flagstaff. Although the cave is on Coconino National Forest Service property, the only thing here is an interpretive sign, so it's definitely something you tackle at your own risk. ■**TIP➜ Pack a flashlight (or two).** ⊠ *FR 171B.*

Northern Arizona University Observatory. This observatory was built in 1952 by Dr. Arthur Adel, a scientist at Lowell Observatory whose study of infrared astronomy pioneered research into molecules that absorb light passing through Earth's atmosphere. Today's studies of Earth's shrinking ozone layer rely on some of Dr. Adel's early work. Visitors to the observatory—which houses one of the largest research-grade telescopes that the public is allowed to move and manipulate—are usually hosted by friendly students and faculty members of the university's Department of Physics and Astronomy. Dr. Adel's 24-inch telescope—the first infrared scope—is also on display. ⊠ *Bldg. 47, Northern Arizona Campus Observatory, Dept. of Physics and Astronomy, S. San Francisco St., just north of Walkup Skydome, University* ☎ *928/523–7170* ⊕ *www.physics.nau.edu* ⛄ *Free* ⊙ *Viewings Fri. 7:30–10 pm, weather permitting.*

Pioneer Museum. The Arizona Historical Society operates this museum in a volcanic-rock building constructed in 1908. The structure was Coconino County's first hospital for the poor, and the current displays include one of the depressingly small nurses' rooms, an old iron lung, and a reconstructed doctor's office. Most of the exhibits, however, touch on more cheerful aspects of Flagstaff history—like road signs and pioneer children's games.

The museum holds folk-crafts festivals in the summer, with blacksmiths, weavers, spinners, quilters, and candle makers. Their crafts, and those of other local artisans, are sold in the museum's gift shop. In a wooded residential section at the northwest end of town, the museum is part of the Fort Valley Park complex. ⊠ *2340 N. Fort Valley Rd., North Flagstaff* ☎ *928/774–6272* ⊕ *www.arizonahistoricalsociety.org* ⛄ *$5* ⊙ *Mon.–Sat. 9–5.*

Riordan State Historic Park. This artifact of Flagstaff's logging heyday is near Northern Arizona University. The centerpiece is a mansion built in 1904 for Michael and Timothy Riordan, lumber-baron brothers who married two sisters. The 13,300-square-foot, 40-room log-and-stone structure—designed by Charles Whittlesley, who was also responsible for El Tovar Hotel at the Grand Canyon—contains furniture by Gustav Stickley, father of the American Arts and Crafts design movement. One room holds "Paul Bunyan's shoes," a 2-foot-long pair of boots made by Timothy in his workshop. Everything on display is original to the house. The inside of the mansion may be explored only by guided tour (hourly on the hour); reservations are suggested. ✉ *409 W. Riordan Rd., University* ☎ *928/779–4395* 🌐 *www.azstateparks.com* 🎫 *$10* 🕒 *June–Sept., daily 9:30–5; Oct.–May, Thurs.–Mon. 10:30–5.*

WHERE TO EAT

$ AMERICAN 🍴 **Beaver Street Brewery.** The Enchanted Forest (with Brie, portobello mushrooms, roasted red peppers, spinach, and artichoke pesto) is one of the most popular options among the wood-fired pizzas at this eatery. Whichever pie you order, expect serious amounts of garlic. Sandwiches, such as the Southwestern chicken with three types of cheese, come with a hefty portion of tasty fries. You won't regret ordering one of the down-home desserts, like the super-gooey chocolate bread pudding. Among the excellent microbrews usually on tap, the raspberry ale is a local favorite. [$] *Average main: $12* ✉ *11 S. Beaver St., Downtown* ☎ *928/779–0079* 🌐 *www.beaverstreetbrewery.com* ✍ *Reservations not accepted.*

$$$ AMERICAN 🍴 **Black Bart's Steakhouse Saloon.** The Wild West decor at this rollicking, brightly lit barn of a restaurant is a bit cornball, but the barbecued chicken is tender and flavorful; just don't expect to see vegetables on your plate unless they're deep-fried. Northern Arizona University music students entertain while they wait on tables, so don't be surprised if your server suddenly jumps onstage to belt out a couple of show tunes. [$] *Average main: $26* ✉ *2760 E. Butler Ave., Downtown* ☎ *928/779–3142, 800/574–4718* 🌐 *www.blackbartssteakhouse.com* 🕒 *No lunch.*

$$$ AMERICAN 🍴 **Brix Restaurant & Wine Bar.** A redbrick carriage house, built around 1910 as a garage for one the first automobiles in Flagstaff, is home to one of the city's most sophisticated restaurants. With a seasonally updated menu, the chef pairs locally raised pork and roasted duck entrées with wines from a list of almost 200 bottles (Brix refers to the sugar content of grapes at harvest). The cheese plate, served with poached natural apricots, is a great accompaniment to a glass of wine at the counter bar. The servers are friendly, the vibe is casually upscale, and the food is outstanding. [$] *Average main: $25* ✉ *413 N. San Francisco St., Downtown* ☎ *928/213–1021* 🌐 *www.brixflagstaff.com* 🕒 *No lunch.*

$$$ EUROPEAN 🍴 **Cottage Place.** Regarded by locals as one of the best special-occasion dining venues in the area, this restaurant in a cottage built in 1909 has intimate dining rooms and an extensive wine list. The menu strays slightly from Continental to include some classic American dishes, such as charbroiled lamb chops. The grilled herb salmon and the chateaubriand for two are recommended. Small plates of items such as stuffed mushrooms and grilled shrimp are less pricey and perfect for a lighter meal. [$] *Average main: $30* ✉ *126 W. Cottage Ave., Downtown* ☎ *928/774–8431* 🌐 *www.cottageplace.com* 🕒 *Closed Mon. and Tues. No lunch.*

$ 🍴 **La Bellavia.** At this favorite bohemian breakfast and lunch nook the
CAFÉ trout and eggs platter is the standard—two eggs served with Idaho trout flavored with a hint of lemon, rounded off with a buttermilk pancake. Other options include Swedish oat pancakes, seven-grain French toast, and a dozen varieties of eggs Benedict. A palette of creative sandwiches and familiar salads makes this a worthwhile lunch stop as well. The café doubles as a gallery for local artists, whose work hangs on the walls. [$] *Average main: $6* ✉ *18 S. Beaver St., Downtown* ☎ *928/774–8301* 🕒 *No dinner.*

$ 🍴 **Salsa Brava.** This cheerful Mexican restaurant, with light-wood
MEXICAN booths and colorful designs, eschews heavy Sonoran-style fare in favor of the grilled dishes found in Guadalajara. It's considered the best Mexican food in town. The fish tacos are particularly good, and you can substitute grilled vegetables for the rice and beans if you prefer a lower-carb meal. [$] *Average main: $11* ✉ *2220 E. Rte. 66, East Flagstaff* ☎ *928/779–5293* 🌐 *www.salsabravaflagstaff.com.*

$$$ 🍴 **Tinderbox Kitchen.** One of the newest entrants into Flagstaff"s fine-
MODERN AMERICAN dining scene is this trendy spot downtown. The sophisticated, modern comfort food caters to local professionals as well as foodies from out
Fodor's Choice ★ of town. Try the hot-and-sour meatballs or slow-roasted pork spareribs for starters. Signature entrées include juniper-cured venison with blue cheese grits and a grownup, Southwestern take on mac 'n' cheese, with spicy jalapeno and duck-leg confit. For cocktails and lighter fare (or if the wait for restaurant seating is lengthy), check out the sister bar next door, The Annex—it's just as hip and delicious. [$] *Average main: $25* ✉ *34 S. San Francisco St., Downtown* ☎ *928/226–8400* 🌐 *www.tinderboxkitchen.com* 🕒 *Closed Sun.*

WHERE TO STAY

Trains pass through the downtown area along Route 66 about every 15 minutes throughout the day and night. Light sleepers may prefer to stay in the south or east sections of town to avoid hearing trains rumbling through; at least the whistles are no longer blown within the downtown district.

For expanded hotel reviews, visit Fodors.com.

$$ 🏨 **Abineau Lodge.** This contemporary mountain inn with a rustic feel
B&B/INN is on 4 acres bordering the immense Coconino National Forest. **Pros:** pleasant common areas; pretty setting; sauna. **Cons:** 7 miles south of town. [$] *Rooms from: $144* ✉ *1080 Mountainaire Rd., South Flagstaff* ☎ *928/525–6212, 888/715–6386* 🌐 *www.abineaulodge.com* 🛏 *8 rooms, 1 suite* 🍴 *Breakfast.*

$ 🏨 **Hotel Weatherford.** With a columned veranda, this hotel, built in 1897,
HOTEL is a dramatic presence at the hub of town. **Pros:** historical charm mixes with a cool music scene; inexpensive. **Cons:** guests will hear noise from bars until the wee hours; dated plumbing; no elevator (all rooms require climbing one or two flights of stairs). [$] *Rooms from: $89* ✉ *23 N. Leroux St., Downtown* ☎ *928/779–1919* 🌐 *www.weatherfordhotel.com* 🛏 *11 rooms, 7 with bath* 🍴 *No meals.*

$$ 🏨 **The Inn at 410.** This downtown B&B is an inviting alternative to Flag's
B&B/INN chain motels. **Pros:** convenient downtown location; romantic; complimentary cookies and cocktails every afternoon. **Cons:** some train noise. [$] *Rooms from: $165* ✉ *410 N. Leroux St., Downtown* ☎ *928/774–0088, 800/774–2008* 🌐 *www.inn410.com* 🛏 *8 suites* 🍴 *Breakfast.*

$$ 🏨 **Little America Hotel Flagstaff.** The biggest hotel in town is deservedly
HOTEL popular. **Pros:** large, very clean rooms; many amenities including walking trails. **Cons:** large-scale property. [$] *Rooms from: $139* ✉ *2515 E. Butler Ave., Downtown* ☎ *928/779–7900, 800/865–1401* 🌐 *flagstaff.littleamerica.com* 🛏 *247 rooms* 🍴 *No meals.*

$$ 🏨 **Starlight Pines Bed and Breakfast.** If you prefer the clean lines of 1920s
B&B/INN design to Victorian froufrou, consider staying at this stylish B&B on the city's east side. **Pros:** pretty, immaculate rooms; very hospitable hosts. **Cons:** a short drive from downtown. [$] *Rooms from: $159* ✉ *3380 E. Lockett Rd., East Flagstaff* ☎ *928/527–1912, 800/752–1912* 🌐 *www.starlightpinesbb.com* 🛏 *4 rooms* 🍴 *Breakfast.*

NIGHTLIFE AND THE ARTS

NIGHTLIFE

Flagstaff's large college contingent has plenty of places to gather after dark; most are in historic downtown and charge little or no cover. It's easy to walk from one rowdy spot to the next. Use the Ale Trail Map (🌐 *www.flagstaffaletrail.com*) to guide you to six breweries within a 1-mile radius. During the summer months, catch free, family-friendly performances (music, theater, and dance) and movies Thursday to Saturday evenings outdoors at Heritage Square. For information on what's going on, pick up the free *Flagstaff Live.*

Flagstaff's Green Room. An environmentally conscious bar, typically filled with college students, Flagstaff's Green Room rolls out an eclectic mix of live music and hardy stout nightly until 2 am. ✉ *15 N. Agassiz St., Downtown* ☎ *928/226–8669* 🌐 *www.flagstaffgreenroom.com.*

Hotel Weatherford. The Hotel Weatherford has a double bill: Charly's Pub hosts late-night jazz and blues bands; the Exchange Bar tends to attract folksy ensembles. ✉ *23 N. Leroux St., Downtown* ☎ *928/779–1919* 🌐 *www.weatherfordhotel.com.*

Monte Vista Lounge. This lounge in the historic Hotel Monte Vista packs 'em in with nightly live blues, jazz, classic rock, and punk. ✉ *Hotel Monte Vista, 100 N. San Francisco St., Downtown* ☎ *928/779–6971* 🌐 *www.hotelmontevista.com.*

Museum Club Roadhouse and Danceclub. Fondly known as the Zoo, this building housed an extensive taxidermy collection in the 1930s and is now a popular country-and-Western club (a few owls still perch above the dance floor). A gigantic log cabin constructed around five trees, with a huge, wishbone-shape pine as the entryway, the venue offers a taste of Route 66 color along with live music and other events. ✉ *3404 E. Rte. 66, Downtown* ☎ *928/526–9434* 🌐 *www.themuseumclub.com.*

A visit to Meteor Crater complements Arizona's many observatories for a different look at the impact of the heavens.

San Felipe's Cantina. Head to San Felipe's Coastal Cantina for tequila, fish tacos, dancing, and a raucous spring-break atmosphere. ⊠ *103 N. Leroux, Downtown* ☏ *928/779–6000* ⊕ *www.sanfelipescantina.com.*

THE ARTS

There's no shortage of cultural entertainment in Flagstaff, including several summer festivals.

A Celebration of Native American Art. During the summer months, art festivals highlighting the Zuni (May), Hopi (July), and Navajo (August) cultures take place at the Museum of Northern Arizona. ⊠ *3101 N. Fort Valley Rd., North Flagstaff* ☏ *928/774–5213* ⊕ *www.musnaz.org.*

Flagstaff Cultural Partners/Coconino Center for the Arts. There's gallery space for exhibitions, a theater, and performance space at Flagstaff Cultural Partners/Coconino Center for the Arts. ⊠ *2300 N. Fort Valley Rd., North Flagstaff* ☏ *928/779–2300* ⊕ *www.culturalpartners.org.*

Flagstaff Symphony Orchestra. Year-round concerts, mostly held in Ardrey Auditorium on the NAU campus, are given by the Flagstaff Symphony Orchestra. ☏ *928/774–5107, 888/520–7214* ⊕ *www. flagstaffsymphony.org.*

Orpheum Theater. The 1917 Orpheum Theater features music acts, films, lectures, and plays. ⊠ *15 W. Aspen St., Downtown* ☏ *928/556–1580* ⊕ *www.orpheumpresents.com.*

Theatrikos Theatre Company. This highly regarded performance-art group produces five mainstage productions annually using a diverse base of local talent. ⊠ *11 W. Cherry Ave., Downtown* ☏ *928/774–1662* ⊕ *www.theatrikos.com.*

SHOPPING

The Artists Gallery. For fine arts and crafts—everything from ceramics and stained glass to weaving and painting—visit the Artists Gallery, a local artists' cooperative. ⊠ *17 N. San Francisco St., Downtown* ☎ *928/773–0958* ⊕ *www.flagstaffartistsgallery.com/.*

Babbitt's Backcountry Outfitters. Just about all your sporting-goods needs can be met at Babbitt's Backcountry Outfitters. ⊠ *12 E. Aspen Ave., Downtown* ☎ *928/774–4775* ⊕ *www.babbittsbackcountry.com.*

Black Hound Gallerie. This downtown gallery specializes in posters, prints, and funky kitsch of all kinds. ⊠ *120 N. Leroux St., Downtown* ☎ *928/774–2323* ⊕ *www.blackhoundgallerie.com.*

Bookmans. Packed solid with used books, music, and movies, Bookmans is also a cybercafe and a place to see live folk music. ⊠ *1520 S Riordan Ranch St., University* ☎ *928/774–0005* ⊕ *www.bookmans.com.*

Carriage House Antique & Gift Mall. Vendors sell vintage clothing and jewelry, furniture, fine china, Mexican folk art, and other collectibles at Carriage House Antique & Gift Mall. ⊠ *413 N. San Francisco St., Downtown* ☎ *928/774–1337.*

Flagstaff Soap Company. Organic bath and body products, including beautiful bar soaps, bubble baths, and lip balms, are handmade on-site at the earthy Flagstaff Soap Company. ⊠ *21 N. San Francisco St., Downtown* ☎ *928/774–9178* ⊕ *www.flagstaffsoap.com.*

Museum of Northern Arizona Gift Shop. High-quality Native American art, jewelry, and crafts can be found at the Museum of Northern Arizona Gift Shop. ⊠ *3101 N. Fort Valley Rd., North Flagstaff* ☎ *928/774–5213* ⊕ *www.musnaz.org.*

Winter Sun Trading Company. Winter Sun Trading Company sells medicinal herbs, unique fragrances, jewelry, and crafts. ⊠ *107 N. San Francisco St., Suite #1, Downtown* ☎ *928/774–2884* ⊕ *www.wintersun.com.*

Zani Cards and Gifts. Hip jewelry and gifts, handmade paper, and greeting cards are stocked at Zani. ⊠ *107 W. Phoenix Ave., Downtown* ☎ *928/774–9409* ⊕ *www.zanicardsandgifts.com.*

SPORTS AND THE OUTDOORS

HIKING

You can explore Arizona's alpine tundra in the San Francisco Peaks, part of the Coconino National Forest, where more than 80 species of plants grow on the upper elevations. The habitat is fragile, so hikers are asked to stay on established trails (there are lots of them). ■**TIP→** Flat-landers should give themselves a day or two to adjust to the altitude before lengthy or strenuous hiking. The altitude here will make even the hardiest hikers breathe a little harder, so anyone with cardiac or respiratory problems should be cautious about overexertion. Note that most of the forest trails aren't accessible during winter due to snow.

Coconino National Forest–Flagstaff Ranger District. The rangers of the Coconino National Forest maintain many of the region's trails, and can provide you with details on hiking in the area; both the forest's main office in North Flagstaff and the ranger station in East Flagstaff (5075 N. U.S 89) are open weekdays 8–4:30. ✉ *1824 S. Thompson St., North Flagstaff* ☎ *928/527–3600 main office, North Flagstaff, 928/526–0866 East Flagstaff office* ⊕ *www.fs.usda.gov/coconino.*

Mount Elden Trail System. Most trails in the Coconino National Forest's 35-mile-long Mount Elden Trail System lead to stunning views from the dormant volcanic field, across the vast ponderosa pine forest, all the way to Sedona. Keep in mind that most of the forest trails are not accessible for hiking from December through March due to snow.

Elden Lookout Trail. The most challenging trail in the Mount Elden system, which happens to be the route with the most rewarding views, is along the steep switchbacks of the Elden Lookout Trail. If you traverse the full 3 miles to the top, keep your focus on the landscape rather than the tangle of antennae and satellite dishes that greets you at the end. *Difficult.* ✉ *Off U.S. 89, 3 miles east of downtown Flagstaff.*

Sunset Trail. The 4-mile-long Sunset Trail proceeds with a gradual pitch through the pine forest, emerging onto a narrow ridge nicknamed the Catwalk. By all means take pictures of the stunning valley views, but make sure your feet are well placed. The access road to this trail is closed in winter. *Moderate.* ✉ *Off U.S. 180, 3 miles north of downtown Flagstaff, then 6 miles east on FR 420/Schultz Pass Rd.*

Humphreys Peak Trail. This trail is 9 miles round-trip, with a vertical climb of 3,843 feet to the 12,643-foot summit of Arizona's highest mountain. *Difficult.* ✉ *Trailhead: Snowbowl Rd., 7 miles north of U.S. 180.*

Kachina Trail. Those who don't want a long hike can do just the first mile of the 5-mile-long Kachina Trail; gently rolling, this route is surrounded by huge stands of aspen and offers fantastic vistas. In fall, changing leaves paint the landscape shades of yellow, russet, and amber. *Moderate.* ✉ *Trailhead: Snowbowl Rd., 7 miles north of U.S. 180.*

MOUNTAIN BIKING

With 50 miles of urban bike trails and more than 30 miles of challenging forest and mountain trails a short ride from town, it was inevitable that one of Flagstaff's best-kept secrets would leak out. The mountain biking on Mount Elden is on par with that of more celebrated trails in Colorado and Utah. While there isn't a concise loop trail such as those in Moab, Utah, experienced bikers can create one by connecting Schultz Creek Trail, Sunset Trail, and Elden Lookout Road. Beginners (as well as those looking for rewarding scenery with less of an incline) may want to start with Lower Fort Valley and Campbell Mesa. Local bike shop staff can help with advice and planning.

Coconino National Forest. Some of the best mountain biking trails in the region are in the Coconino National Forest. ☎ *928/527–3600 main office, North Flagstaff, 928/526–0866 East Flagstaff office* ⊕ *www. fs.usda.gov/coconino.*

Lower Oldham Trail. Originating on the north end of Buffalo Park in Flagstaff, the Lower Oldham Trail is steep in some sections, but

rewarding. The terrain rolls, climbing about 800 feet in 3 miles, and the trail is difficult in spots but easy enough to test your tolerance of the elevation. Many fun trails spur off this one; it's best to stop in at the local bike shop to get trail maps and discuss rides with staff who know the area. ⊠ *Trailhead: Cedar St.*

Schultz Creek Trail. The very popular Schultz Creek Trail is fun and suitable for strong beginners, although seasoned experts will be thrilled as well. Most opt to start at the top of the 600-foot-high hill and swoop down the smooth, twisting path through groves of wildflowers and stands of ponderosa pines and aspens, ending at the trailhead 4 giddy miles later. ⊠ *Trailhead: Schultz Pass Rd., near intersection with U.S. 180.*

Sunset Trail. Near the summit of Mount Elden, Sunset Trail has amazing views off the ridge rendered barren by a 1977 fire. The trail narrows into the aptly nicknamed Catwalk, with precipitous drops a few feet on either side. Fear, either from the 9,000-foot elevation or the sheer exposure, is not an option. You need to be at least a moderately experienced mountain biker to attempt this trail. When combined with Elden Lookout Road and Schultz Creek Trail, the usual loop, the trail totals 15 miles and climbs almost 2,000 feet. You can avoid the slog up Mount Elden by parking one vehicle at the top of Elden Lookout Road, at the trailhead, and a friend's vehicle at the bottom. ⊠ *Trailhead: Elden Lookout Rd., 7 miles from intersection with Schultz Pass Rd.*

Flagstaff Nordic Center. From mid-June through mid-October, the Flagstaff Nordic Center opens its cross-country trails—good for families and beginners, because they're scenic and not technically challenging. ⊠ *U.S. 180, 16 miles north of Flagstaff, North Flagstaff* ☎ *928/220–0550* ⊕ *www.flagstaffnordiccenter.com.*

Flagstaff Urban Trails System (FUTS). A map of the Urban Trails System, available at the Flagstaff Visitor Center, details low and no-traffic bike routes around town. ⊠ *Flagstaff Visitor Center, 1 E. Route 66, Downtown* ☎ *928/774–9541, 800/842–7293* ⊕ *www.flagstaffarizona.org.*

EQUIPMENT AND RENTALS **Absolute Bikes.** You can rent mountain bikes, get good advice, and purchase trail maps at Absolute Bikes. ⊠ *202 E. Route 66, Downtown* ☎ *928/779–5969* ⊕ *www.absolutebikes.net.*

ROCK CLIMBING

Flagstaff Climbing Center. The tallest indoor climbing walls in the Southwest can be found at this rock-climbing gym. Flagstaff Climbing also offers guided climbing excursions around the Flagstaff area. ⊠ *205 S. San Francisco St., Downtown* ☎ *928/556–9909* ⊕ *www.flagstaffclimbing.com.*

SKIING AND SNOWBOARDING

The ski season usually starts in mid-December and ends in mid-April.

Arizona Snowbowl. Seven miles north of Flagstaff off U.S. 180, the Arizona Snowbowl has 32 downhill runs (37% beginner, 42% intermediate, and 21% advanced), four chairlifts, and a vertical drop of 2,300 feet. There are a couple of good bump runs, but it's better for beginners or those with moderate skill; serious area skiers take a road trip to Telluride. Still, it's a fun place to ski or snowboard. The Hart Prairie Lodge has an equipment-rental shop and a SKIwee center for ages four to seven.

All-day adult lift tickets are $55. Half-day discounts are available, and group-lesson packages (including two hours of instruction, an all-day lift ticket, and equipment rental) are a good buy at $80 ($85 for snowboarding package). A children's program, which includes lunch and supervision 9:30–3, runs $89 (reservations are required). Many Flagstaff motels have ski packages that include transportation to Snowbowl. ✉ *Snowbowl Rd., North Flagstaff* ☎ *928/779–1951, 928/779–4577 snow report* ⊕ *www.arizonasnowbowl.com.*

Flagstaff Nordic Center. The Flagstaff Nordic Center is 9 miles north of Snowbowl Road. There are 25 miles of well-groomed cross-country trails here that are open 9–4 daily. Coffee, hot chocolate, and snacks are served at the lodge. A day pass for skiing costs $12 on weekdays and $18 on weekends. An instruction package costs $45, including equipment, day pass, and a 90-minute lesson. Renting equipment by itself is $16. ✉ *U.S. 180, 16 miles north of Flagstaff, North Flagstaff* ☎ *928/220–0550* ⊕ *www.flagstaffnordiccenter.com.*

SIDE TRIPS NEAR FLAGSTAFF

Travelers heading straight through town bound for the Grand Canyon often neglect the area north and east of Flagstaff, but a detour has its rewards. If you don't have time to do everything, take a quick drive to Walnut Canyon—it's only about 15 minutes out of town.

EAST OF FLAGSTAFF

GETTING HERE AND AROUND
From Flagstaff, follow Interstate 40 a few miles east to Exit 204 for Walnut Canyon National Monument. Continue east along the highway for Meteor Crater off Exit 233, a 45-minute drive. Continue east on Interstate 40, about 53 miles from Flagstaff, to see the Hopi pueblos at Homolovi Ruins State Park.

EXPLORING
Homolovi Ruins State Park. *Homolovi* is a Hopi word meaning "place of the little hills." The pueblo sites here at Homolovi Ruins State Park are thought to have been occupied between AD 1200 and 1425, and include 40 ceremonial kivas and two pueblos containing more than 1,000 rooms each. The Hopi believe their immediate ancestors inhabited this place, and they consider the site sacred. Many rooms have been excavated and recovered for protection; rangers conduct guided tours. The Homolovi Visitor Center has a small museum with Hopi pottery and Ancestral Puebloan artifacts; it also hosts workshops on native art, ethnobotany, and traditional foods. ✉ *AZ 87, 5 miles northeast of Winslow, Winslow* ☎ *928/289–4106* ⊕ *www.azstateparks.com* ✇ *$7* ☉ *Visitor center daily 8–5.*

FAMILY **Meteor Crater.** A natural phenomenon in a privately owned park 43 miles east of Flagstaff, Meteor Crater is impressive if for no other reason than its sheer size. A hole in the ground 600 feet deep, nearly 1 mile across, and more than 3 miles in circumference, Meteor Crater is large enough to accommodate the Washington Monument or 20 football fields. It was created by a meteorite crash 49,000 years ago. The area looks so much like the surface of the moon that NASA made it one of the official training sites for the Project Apollo astronauts.

You can't descend into the crater, because of the efforts of its owners to maintain its condition—scientists consider this to be the best-preserved crater on Earth—but guided rim tours, given every hour on the hour 9–2, give useful background information. There's a sandwich shop on site, and the Rock Shop sells specimens from the area and jewelry made from native stones. Take Interstate 40 east of Flagstaff to Exit 233, then drive 6 miles south on Meteor Crater Road. ☒ *Interstate 40, Exit 233, Winslow* ☎ *928/289–5898, 800/289–5898* ⊕ *www.meteorcrater.com* ☒ *$16* ☉ *June–Aug., daily 7–7; Sept.–May, daily 8–5.*

Rock Art Ranch. The Ancestral Puebloan petroglyphs of this working cattle ranch in Chevelon Canyon are startlingly vivid after more than 1,000 years. Ranch owner Brantly Baird will guide you along the 0.25-mile trail, explaining Western and archaeological history. It's mostly easy walking, except for the climb in and out of Chevelon Canyon, where there are handrails. Baird houses his Native American artifacts and pioneer farming implements in his own private museum. It's out of the way and on a dirt road, but you'll see some of the best rock art in northern Arizona. Reservations are required. ☒ *Off AZ 87, 13 miles southeast of Winslow, Winslow* ☎ *928/386–5047* ☒ *$35 per person for 1 or 2 people; less per person for larger groups* ☉ *By appointment only.*

Fodor's Choice **Walnut Canyon National Monument.** The group of cliff dwellings that make
★ up Walnut Canyon National Monument were constructed by the Sinagua people, who lived and farmed in and around the canyon starting around AD 700. The more than 300 dwellings here were built between 1080 and 1250, and abandoned, like those at so many other settlements in Arizona and New Mexico, around 1300. The Sinagua traded far and wide with other Native Americans, including people at Wupatki. Even macaw feathers, which would have come from tribes in what is now Mexico, have been excavated in the canyon. Early Flagstaff settlers looted the site for pots and "treasure"; Woodrow Wilson declared

THE SINAGUA PEOPLE

The achievements of the Sinagua people, who lived in north-central Arizona from the 8th through the 15th century, reached their height in the 12th and 13th centuries, when related groups occupied most of the San Francisco Volcanic Field and a large portion of the upper and middle Verde Valley. The Sinagua sites around modern-day Camp Verde, Clarkdale, and Flagstaff provide a window onto this remarkable culture. Some of the best examples of surviving Sinagua architecture can be found at Walnut Canyon and Wupatki National Monument, northeast of Flagstaff.

4

this a national monument in 1915, which began a 30-year process of stabilizing the site.

Part of the fascination of Walnut Canyon is the opportunity to enter the dwellings, stepping back in time to an ancient way of life. Some of the Sinagua homes are in near-perfect condition in spite of all the looting, because of the dry, hot climate and the protection of overhanging cliffs. You can reach them by descending 185 feet on the 1-mile, 240-stair, stepped **Island Trail,** which starts at the visitor center. As you follow the trail, look across the canyon for other dwellings not accessible on the path. Island Trail takes about an hour to complete at a normal pace. Those with health concerns should opt for the easier 0.5-mile **Rim Trail,** which has overlooks from which dwellings, as well as an excavated, reconstructed pit house, can be viewed. Picnic areas dot the grounds and line the roads leading to the park. Do not rely on a GPS to get here; stick to I-40. ✉ *Walnut Canyon Rd., 3 miles south of I–40, Exit 204, Winona* ☎ *928/526–3367* 🌐 *www.nps.gov/waca* 🎫 *$5* 🕒 *Nov.–Apr., daily 9–5; May–Oct., daily 8–5.*

MARY JANE COLTER

Pick a historic hotel or site of significance built in the late 19th or early 20th century in northern or eastern Arizona, and there's a good chance architect Mary Jane Colter was part of it. A student of Frank Lloyd Wright, Colter designed La Posada in Winslow, the Painted Desert Inn, and several structures at the Grand Canyon, including the Hopi House. She also decorated the canyon's El Tovar Hotel.

Winslow. Frequent flooding on the Little Colorado River frustrated the attempts of Mormon pioneers to settle here, but with the coming of the railroad the town roared into life. Later, Route 66 sustained the community until Interstate 40 passed north of town. New motels and restaurants sprouted near the interstate exits, and the downtown was all but abandoned. Still, visitors wishing to find themselves "standing on a corner in Winslow, Arizona" abound thanks to a song by The Eagles; and the historic masterpiece, La Posada, remains one of the best places to sleep and dine in the state. The town is 58 miles east of Flagstaff on Interstate 40. ✉ *Winslow.*

WHERE TO STAY

For expanded hotel reviews, visit Fodors.com.

$ HOTEL Fodor's Choice ★ 🏨 **La Posada Hotel.** One of the great railroad hotels, La Posada ("resting place") exudes the charm of an 18th-century Spanish hacienda and its restoration has been a labor of love. **Pros:** historic charm; unique architecture; impressive restaurant. **Cons:** mazes of staircases aren't very wheelchair-friendly. [$] *Rooms from: $119* ✉ *303 E. 2nd St., Winslow* ☎ *928/289–4366* 🌐 *www.laposada.org* 🛏 *53 rooms* 🍴 *No meals.*

SAN FRANCISCO VOLCANIC FIELD

The San Francisco Volcanic Field north of Flagstaff encompasses 2,000 square miles of fascinating geological phenomena, including ancient volcanoes, cinder cones, valleys carved by water and ice, and the San Francisco Peaks themselves, some of which soar to almost 13,000 feet.

There are also some of the most extensive Native American dwellings in the Southwest: don't miss Sunset Crater and Wupatki. These national monuments can be explored in relative solitude during much of the year. ■TIP→ The area is short on services, so fill up on gas and consider taking a picnic.

GETTING HERE AND AROUND

To get to both Sunset Crater and Wupatki national monuments, take U.S. 89 north out of Flagstaff. After 12 miles, turn right for Sunset Crater. Wupatki National Monument is another 19 miles north on this road.

EXPLORING

Sunset Crater Volcano National Monument. Sunset Crater, a cinder cone that rises 1,000 feet, was an active volcano 900 years ago. Its final eruption contained iron and sulfur, which give the rim of the crater its glow and thus its name. You can walk around the base, but you can't descend into the huge, fragile cone. The **Lava Flow Trail,** a half-hour, mile-long, self-guided walk, provides a good view of the evidence of the volcano's fiery power: lava formations and holes in the rock where volcanic gases vented to the surface.

If you're interested in hiking a volcano, head to **Lenox Crater,** about 1 mile east of the visitor center, and climb the 280 feet to the top of the cinder cone. The cinder is soft and crumbly, so wear closed, sturdy shoes. From **O'Leary Peak,** a 5-mile hike from the visitor center on Forest Route 545A, enjoy great views of the San Francisco Peaks, the Painted Desert, and beyond. The trail is an unpaved, rutted road (closed during winter), with a steep 2.5-mile hike to the top. Bonito Campground, just outside the monument, is open from May–October ($18) and has toilets but no hook-ups. To get to the area from Flagstaff, take Santa Fe Avenue east to U.S. 89, and head north for 12 miles; turn right onto the road marked Sunset Crater and go another 2 miles to the visitor center. ⊠ *14 miles northeast of Flagstaff, 6082 Sunset Crater Rd., Flagstaff* ☎ *928/526–0502* ⊕ *www.nps.gov/sucr* ✉ *$5, including Wupatki National Monument and Doney Mountain* ☉ *Nov.–Apr., daily 9–5; May–Oct., daily 8–5.*

Wupatki National Monument. Families from the Sinagua and other Ancestral Puebloans are believed to have lived together in harmony on the site that is now Wupatki National Monument, farming and trading with one another and with those who passed through. The eruption of Sunset Crater may have influenced migration to this area a century after the event, as freshly laid volcanic cinders held in moisture needed for crops. Although there's evidence of earlier habitation, most of the settlers moved here around 1100 and left the pueblo by about 1250. The 2,700 identified sites contain archaeological evidence of a Native American settlement.

The national monument was named for the Wupatki (meaning "tall house" in Hopi) site, which was originally three stories high, built above an unexplored system of underground fissures. The structure had almost 100 rooms and an open ball court—evidence of Southwestern trade with Mesoamerican tribes for whom ball games were a central ritual. Next to the ball court is a blowhole, a geologic phenomenon in which air is forced upward by underground pressure.

Other sites to visit are Wukoki, Lomaki, and the Citadel, a pueblo on a knoll above a limestone sink. Although the largest remnants of Native American settlements at Wupatki National Monument are open to the public, other sites are off-limits. If you're interested in an in-depth tour, consider a ranger-led overnight hike to the **Crack-in-Rock Ruin.** The 14-mile (round-trip) trek covers areas marked by ancient petroglyphs and dotted with well-preserved sites. The trips are only conducted in April and October; call by February or August if you'd like to take part in the lottery for one of the 100 available places on these $50 hikes. Between the Wupatki and Citadel ruins, **Doney Mountain** affords 360-degree views of the Painted Desert and the San Francisco Volcanic Field. It's a perfect spot for a sunset picnic. In summer, rangers give lectures. ✉ *Sunset Crater–Wupatki Loop Rd., 19 miles north of Sunset Crater visitor center* ☎ *928/679-2365* ⊕ *www.nps.gov/wupa* ▨ *$5, including Sunset Crater National Monument and Doney Mountain* ⊙ *Daily 9–5.*

SEDONA AND OAK CREEK CANYON

27 miles south of Flagstaff on AZ 89A; 114 miles north of Phoenix, Interstate 17 to AZ 179 to AZ 89A; 60 miles northeast of Prescott, U.S. 89 to AZ 89A.

It's easy to see what draws so many people to Sedona. Red-rock buttes—Cathedral Rock, Bear Mountain, Courthouse Rock, and Bell Rock, among others—reach up into an almost always blue sky, and both colors are intensified by dark-green pine forests. Surrealist Max Ernst, writer Zane Grey, and many filmmakers drew inspiration from these vistas—more than 80 Westerns were shot in the area in the 1940s and '50s alone.

These days, Sedona lures enterprising restaurateurs and gallery owners from the East and West coasts. New Age followers, who believe that the area contains some of Earth's more important vortexes (energy centers), also come in great numbers, seeking a "vibe" here that confers a sense of balance and well-being, and enhances creativity.

Expansion since the early 1980s has been rapid, and lack of planning has taken its toll in the form of unattractive developments and increased traffic.

The city of Sedona is young, and there are few historic sites; as many visitors conclude, you don't come to Sedona to tour the town itself. The main downtown activity is shopping, mostly for Southwestern-style paintings, clothing, rugs, jewelry, and Native American artifacts. Just beyond the shops and restaurants, however, canyons, creeks, ancient dwellings, and the red rocks beckon. The area is easy to hike or bike, or you can take a jeep tour.

CLOSE UP

Sedona Vortex Tour

What is a vortex? The word "vortex" comes from the Latin *vertere*, which means "to turn or whirl." In Sedona, a vortex is a funnel created by the motion of spiraling energy. Sedona has long been believed to be a center for spiritual power because of the vortexes of subtle energy in the area. This energy isn't described as electricity or magnetism, though it's said to leave a slight residual magnetism in the places where it's strongest.

New Agers believe there are four major vortexes in Sedona: Airport, Cathedral Rock, Boynton Canyon, and Bell Rock. Each manifests a different kind of energy, and this energy interacts with the individual in its presence. People come from all over the world to experience these energy forms, hoping for guidance in spiritual matters, health, and relationships.

Juniper trees, which are all over the Sedona area, are said to respond to vortex energy in a way that reveals where this energy is strongest. The stronger the energy, the more axial twist the junipers bear in their branches.

Airport Vortex is said to strengthen one's "masculine" side, aiding in self-confidence and focus. **Cathedral Rock Vortex** nurtures one's "feminine" aspects, such as patience and kindness. You'll be directed to **Boynton Canyon Vortex** if you're seeking balance between the masculine and feminine. And finally **Bell Rock Vortex**, the most powerful of all, strengthens all three aspects: masculine, feminine, and balance.

These energy centers are easily accessed, and vortex maps are available at crystal shops all over Sedona.

GETTING HERE AND AROUND

Sedona stretches along AZ 89A, its main thoroughfare, which runs roughly east–west through town. Uptown, the section with most of the shops and restaurants, is at the east end. Free parking is plentiful throughout Sedona, but especially in Uptown: the visitor center, a half block off 89A on Forest Road, has an adjacent parking lot; parking spaces along the streets are free for three hours; or park all day in the large municipal lot a few blocks farther east, off Jordan Road.

The most scenic route into town from Phoenix is taking Interstate 17 to AZ 260 toward Cottonwood, then going northeast on AZ 89A. To reach Sedona more directly from Phoenix, take Interstate 17 north for 107 miles until you come to AZ 179; it's another winding 7½ miles on that road, past the Village of Oak Creek, into town. The trip should take about 2½ hours. The 27-mile drive north from Sedona to Flagstaff on AZ 89A, which winds its way through Oak Creek Canyon, is breathtaking.

Sedona Airport, in West Sedona, is a base for several air tours but has no regularly scheduled flights.

The Sedona–Phoenix Shuttle makes eight trips daily between those cities; the fare is $50 one-way, $90 round-trip. You can also get on or off at Camp Verde, Cottonwood, or the Village of Oak Creek (7 miles outside Sedona on AZ 179). Reservations are required.

Weekend traffic near Sedona, especially during the high season, can approach gridlock on the narrow highways. Leave for your destination at first light to bypass the day-trippers, late risers, and midday heat.

Sedona is roughly divided into three neighborhoods: Uptown, which is a walkable shopping district that encompasses the areas just north and south of the "Y" (where AZ 179 and AZ 89A intersect); West Sedona, which is a 4-mile-long commercial strip; and The Village of Oak Creek, which lies a few miles south of the "Y" along AZ 179. The Verde Lynx provides bus transportation (and has wheelchair lifts) east and west along AZ 89A for $2 each way.

> ## FLAGSTAFF AND SEDONA
>
> There might only be 27 miles separating Flagstaff and Sedona, but they're very different places. Flagstaff's natural terrain and earthiness lend a "granola-y" feel to the city, and the Northern Arizona University students here enhance it. Meanwhile, Sedona's beauty is no secret, and residents (full- and part-time) pay a premium to enjoy it.

Sedona Trolley offers two types of daily orientation tours, both departing from the main bus stop in Uptown and lasting less than an hour. One goes along AZ 179 to the Chapel of the Holy Cross; the other passes through West Sedona to Boynton Canyon (Enchantment Resort). Rates are $15 for one or $25 for both.

If you want to explore the red rocks of Sedona on your own, you can rent a four-wheel-drive vehicle from one of the local agencies such as Barlow Jeep Rentals.

PLANNING YOUR TIME

In warmer months visit air-conditioned shops at midday and do hiking and jeep tours in the early morning or late afternoon, when the light is softer and the heat less oppressive. Many of the most memorable spots in Sedona are considered energy centers; vortex maps of the area are available at the visitor center.

The vistas of Sedona from Airport Mesa at sunset can't be beat. The Upper Red Rock Loop has great photo opportunities.

ESSENTIALS

Transportation Contacts Barlow Jeep Rentals ☎ *928/282–8700* ⊕ *www.barlowjeeprentals.com.* **Verde Lynx** ☎ *928/282–0938* ⊕ *www.verdelynx.az.gov.* **Sedona Airport** ☎ *928/282–4487* ⊕ *www.sedonaairport.org.* **Sedona - Phoenix Shuttle** ☎ *800/448–7988 in Arizona* ⊕ *www.sedona-phoenix-shuttle.com.* **Sedona Taxi** ☎ *928/204–9111.* **Sedona Trolley** ☎ *928/282–4211* ⊕ *www.sedonatrolley.com.*

Visitor Information Sedona Visitor Center ✉ *331 Forest Rd., just off AZ 89A* ☎ *928/282–7722, 800/288–7336* ⊕ *www.visitsedona.com.*

Sedona and
Oak Creek Canyon

EXPLORING

TOP ATTRACTIONS

Bell Rock. With its distinctive shape right out of your favorite Western film and its proximity to the main drag, this popular butte ensures a steady flow of admirers, so you may want to arrive early in the day. The parking lot next to the Bell Rock Pathway often fills by mid-morning, even midweek. The views from here are good, but an easy and fairly accessible path follows mostly gentle terrain for 1 mile to the base of the butte. Mountain bikers, parents with all-terrain baby strollers, and not-so-avid hikers should have little problem getting there. No official paths climb the rock itself, but many forge their own routes (at their own risk). ⊠ *AZ 179, several hundred yards north of Bell Rock Blvd., Village of Oak Creek.*

Cathedral Rock. It's almost impossible not to be drawn to this butte's towering, variegated spires. The approximately 1,200-foot-high Cathedral Rock looms dramatically over town. When you emerge from the narrow gorge of Oak Creek Canyon, this is the first recognizable formation you'll spot. ■TIP→ The butte is best seen toward dusk from a distance. Hikers may want to drive to the Airport Mesa and then hike the rugged but generally flat path that loops around the airfield. The trail is

0.5 mile up Airport Road off AZ 89A in West Sedona; the reward is a panoramic view of Cathedral Rock without the crowds. Those not hiking should drive through the Village of Oak Creek and 5 miles west on Verde Valley School Road to its end, where you can view the butte from a beautiful streamside vantage point and take a dip in Oak Creek

if you wish. ⊠ *5 miles to end of Verde Valley School Rd., west off AZ 179, Village of Oak Creek.*

Cathedral Rock Trail. A vigorous but nontechnical 1.5-mile scramble up the slickrock (smooth, rather than slippery, sandstone), this path leads to a nearly 360-degree view of red-rock country. Follow the cairns (rock piles marking the trail) and look for the footholds in the rock. Carry plenty of water: though short, the trail offers little shade and the pitch is steep. You can see the Verde Valley and Mingus Mountain in the distance. Look for the barely discernible "J" etched on the hillside marking the former ghost town of Jerome 30 miles away. ⊠ *Trailhead: About 0.5 mile down Back O' Beyond Rd. off AZ 179, 3 miles south of Sedona.*

Chapel of the Holy Cross. You needn't be religious to be inspired by the setting and the architecture here. Built in 1956 by Marguerite Brunwige Staude, a student of Frank Lloyd Wright, this modern landmark, with a huge cross on the facade, rises between two red-rock peaks. Vistas of the town and the surrounding area are spectacular. Though there is only one regular service—a beautiful Taizé service of prayer and song on Monday at 5 pm—all are welcome for quiet meditation.

A small gift shop sells religious artifacts and books. A trail east of the chapel leads you—after a 20-minute walk over occasional loose-rock surfaces—to a seat surrounded by voluptuous red-limestone walls, worlds away from the bustle and commerce around the chapel. ⊠ *Chapel Rd. off AZ 179, Village of Oak Creek* ☎ *928/282–4069* ⊕ *www. chapeloftheholycross.com* ⊠ *Free* ☉ *Daily 9–5.*

Oak Creek Canyon. Whether you want to swim, hike, picnic, or enjoy beautiful scenery framed through a car window, head north through the wooded Oak Creek Canyon. It's the most scenic route to Flagstaff and the Grand Canyon, and worth a drive-through even if you're not heading north. The road winds through a steep-walled canyon, where you crane your neck for views of the dramatic rock formations above. Although the forest is primarily evergreen, the fall foliage is glorious. Oak Creek, which runs along the bottom, is lined with tent campgrounds, fishing camps, cabins, motels, and restaurants. ⊠ *AZ 89A, beginning 1 mile north of Sedona, Oak Creek Canyon.*

FAMILY **Slide Rock State Park.** A good place for a picnic, Slide Rock is 7 miles north of Sedona. On a hot day you can plunge down a natural rock slide into a swimming hole (bring an extra pair of jeans or a sturdy bathing suit and river shoes to wear on the slide). The site started as an early-20th-century apple orchard, and the natural beauty attracted

Red-Rock Geology

It's hard to imagine that the land-locked desert surrounding Sedona was, for much of prehistoric time, an area of dunes and swamps on the shore of an ancient sea. The ebb and flow of this sea shaped the land. When the sea rose, it planed the dunes before dropping more sediment on top. The process continued for a few hundred million years. Eventually the sediment hardened into gray layers of limestone on top of the red sandstone. When North America collided with another continental plate, the land buckled and lifted, forming the Rocky Mountains and raising northern Arizona thousands of feet. Volcanoes erupted in the area, capping some of the rock with erosion-resistant basalt.

Oak Creek started flowing at this time, eroding through the layers of sandstone and limestone. Along with other forces of erosion, the creek carved out the canyons and shaped the buttes. Sedona's buttes stayed intact because a resilient layer of lava had hardened on top and slowed the erosion process considerably. As iron minerals in the sandstone were gradually exposed to the elements, they turned red in a process similar to rusting. The iron minerals, in turn, stained the surrounding colorless quartz and grains of sand—it only takes 2% red-iron material to give the sandstone its red color.

Like the rings of a tree, the striations in the rock document the passage of time and the events: limestone marking the rise of the sea, sandstone indicating when the region was coastline.

Hollywood—a number of John Wayne and Jimmy Stewart movies were filmed here.

A few easy hikes run along the rim of the gorge. One downside is the traffic, particularly on summer weekends; you might have to wait to get into the park after mid-morning. Unfortunately, the popularity of the stream has led to the occasional midsummer closing due to E. coli–bacteria infestations; the water is tested daily and there is a water-quality hotline at ☎ 602/542–0202. ✉ 6871 N. Hwy. 89A, Oak Creek Canyon ☎ 928/282–3034 ⊕ www.azstateparks.com ☞ $10 per vehicle for up to 4 persons; $20 per vehicle in summer ⊙ Oct–Apr, daily 8–5; May-Sept, daily 8–6 (last admission is one hour before closing).

FAMILY **Snoopy Rock.** Kids love this: when you look almost directly to the east, this butte really does look like the famed Peanuts beagle lying atop red rock instead of his doghouse. You can distinguish the formation from several places around town, including the mall in Uptown Sedona, but to get a clear view, venture up Schnebly Hill Road. Park by the trailhead on the left immediately before the paved road deteriorates to dirt. Marg's Draw, one of several trails originating here, is worthwhile, gently meandering 100 feet down-canyon, through the tortured desert flora to Morgan Road. Backtrack to the parking lot for close to a 3-mile hike. ✉ Schnebly Hill Rd. off AZ 179, Central.

WORTH NOTING

FAMILY **Blazin' M Ranch.** Western-style entertainment and activities abound at Blazin' M Ranch. After a tractor ride around the ranch, you can pitch horseshoes, hone your roping and shooting skills, and stay for a chuck-wagon dinner and Western stage show. ✉ *1875 Mabery Ranch Rd., Cottonwood* ☎ *928/634–0334, 800/937–8643* 🌐 *www.blazinm.com.*

Courthouse Butte. The red sandstone seems to catch on fire toward sunset, when this monolith is free of shadow. From the highway, Courthouse Butte sits in back of Bell Rock and can be viewed without any additional hiking or driving. ✉ *AZ 179, Village of Oak Creek.*

Rainbow Trout Farm. North-central Arizona may not be the most obvious fishing destination, but this stocked farm is a fun way to spend a few hours if you're so inclined. Anglers young and old almost always enjoy a sure catch, and you can rent a cane pole here with a hook and bait for $1. There's no charge if your catch is under 8 inches; above that it's $8 to $12, depending on the length. The real bargain is that the staff will clean and pack your fish for 50¢ each. ✉ *3500 N. AZ 89A, 3 mi north of Sedona, Oak Creek Canyon* ☎ *928/282–5799* 🌐 *www.sedonarainbowtroutfarm.com* 🎟 *$1* 🕒 *Daily 9–5.*

Red Rock State Park. Two miles west of Sedona via AZ 89A is the turnoff for this 286-acre state park, a less crowded alternative to Slide Rock State Park, though without the possibility of swimming. The 5 miles of interconnected trails are well marked, and provide beautiful vistas. There are daily naturalist-led nature walks at 10 am, a featured program at 2 pm, and bird-watching excursions on Wednesday and Saturday at 9 am. ✉ *4050 Red Rock Loop Rd., West* ☎ *928/282–6907* 🌐 *www.azstateparks.com* 🎟 *$10 per car for up to 4 persons* 🕒 *Daily 8–5.*

WHERE TO EAT

Some Sedona restaurants close in January and February, so call before you go; if you're planning a visit in high season (April to October), make reservations.

$ AMERICAN 🍴 **Coffee Pot Restaurant.** Locals and tourists alike swarm to this spacious diner for scrumptious breakfast and brunch food served by a friendly waitstaff. One hundred and one omelet options are the stars of the show, and include such concoctions as the quirky peanut butter and jelly or the basic ham and cheese. Warm homemade biscuits always hit the spot. An extensive lunch menu that includes everything from Mexican dishes to a Greek salad rounds out the offerings. [$] *Average main: $9* ✉ *2050 W Hwy. 89A, West* ☎ *928/282–6626* 🌐 *www.coffeepotsedona.com* 🕒 *No dinner.*

$$$ STEAKHOUSE 🍴 **Cowboy Club.** At this restaurant catering to carnivores, you can hang out in the casual Cowboy Club or dine in the more formal Silver Saddle Room, where suede booths are surrounded by cowboy art and a pair of large cattle horns. High-quality cuts of beef are the specialty, but the burgers and the fried chicken served with cumin mashed potatoes are delicious, too. [$] *Average main: $25* ✉ *241 N Hwy 89A, Uptown* ☎ *928/282–4200* 🌐 *www.cowboyclub.com.*

Jeep tours get you close to Sedona's red rocks while someone else does the driving.

$$$ ITALIAN 🍴 **Dahl & Di Luca Ristorante Italiano.** Lisa Dahl has created one of the most popular Italian restaurants in town, greeting diners when she's not making delicious homemade soups like white bean with ham and hearty minestrone. Specialties here include tortellini with a portobello mushroom sauce and *pollo piccata* (chicken in a lemon, capers, and chardonnay sauce). Renaissance reproductions and café seating give the impression of a Roman piazza. Make reservations or you may be seated at the bar—good food but far less romantic. [$] *Average main: $23* ✉ *2321 W Hwy 89A, West* ☎ *928/282–5219* 🌐 *www.dahlanddiluca.com* 🕒 *No lunch.*

$$ MEXICAN Fodor's Choice ★ 🍴 **Elote Café.** Traditional Mexican recipes get a creative and tasty update at this deservedly popular restaurant. Start with the namesake *elote,* roasted corn on a stick, for an appetizer: this favorite street food in Mexico is transformed into an addictive dip of grilled corn kernels, *cojita* cheese, lime, and chiles. Small plates like chicken tacos with mole sauce are delicious and affordable, and larger dishes like braised lamb shank in ancho chile sauce or chiles rellenos are equally satisfying. Enjoy the colorful interior or sit on the open-air deck for fabulous Sedona views. Just come prepared for a wait, because the word is out and they don't take reservations. [$] *Average main: $19* ✉ *771 AZ 179, Kings Ransom Sedona Hotel, Central* ☎ *928/203–0105* 🌐 *www.elotecafe.com* ✍ *Reservations not accepted* 🕒 *Closed Sun. and Mon. No lunch.*

$$$ EUROPEAN Fodor's Choice ★ 🍴 **Heartline Café.** Fresh flowers and innovative cuisine that even the staff struggles to characterize are this attractive café's hallmarks. Local ingredients pepper the menu, giving a Sedona twist to Continental fare, and favorites include pecan-crusted, Sedona-raised trout with Dijon sauce and chicken breast with pesto cream sauce. Appealing vegetarian plates

are also available, and breakfast specialties (served until 3 pm) include lemon creme–stuffed French toast and crab Benedict. Lunch sandwiches and wraps can be ordered to go for a gourmet picnic in the red rocks. Desserts include a phenomenal crème brûlée, as well as homemade truffles at the chef's whim. $ *Average main: $25* ✉ *1610 W. Hwy. 89A, West* ☎ *928/282–0785* ⊕ *www.heartlinecafe.com.*

$$$$ ✗ **L'Auberge.** The most formal dining room in Sedona, on the L'Auberge
FRENCH de Sedona resort property, promises a quiet, civilized evening of indulgence. The menu, a fusion of American cuisine with French influences, is offered as a two-, three-, or four-course meal, and can be paired with selections from the resort's 1,200-bottle wine cellar. Among the house favorites is the filet mignon with mushroom risotto. The lavish Sunday brunch is well worth the splurge; or have cocktails and lighter fare creekside at the Veranda Bar. $ *Average main: $34* ✉ *L'Auberge de Sedona, 301 L'Auberge La., Uptown* ☎ *928/282–1661* ⊕ *www. lauberge.com.*

$ ✗ **New Frontiers Natural Marketplace.** The healthful fare at this mostly
CAFÉ organic grocery and deli runs the gamut from grab-and-go sandwiches and the well-stocked salad bar to hot items like honey-glazed salmon, cheese or chicken enchiladas, and turkey meat loaf. Get supplies for your red-rock picnic or relax at the indoor-outdoor dining area. $ *Average main: $7* ✉ *1420 W. Hwy. 89A, West* ☎ *928/282–6311* ⊕ *www. newfrontiersmarket.com/sedona.*

$$ ✗ **Oaxaca Restaurant.** Tasty standards complement some of the best
MEXICAN Uptown canyon vistas at this modern Mexican restaurant with a lovely balcony. The smoky kick of the salsa, along with the sun-kissed scenery, may transport you south of the border, but dishes are prepared under the auspices of owner Carla Butler, a dietitian who shuns the traditional use of lard and cholesterol-containing oils in favor of healthier options—with delicious results. A south-of-the-border breakfast is served on weekends. $ *Average main: $16* ✉ *321 N. Hwy 89A, Uptown* ☎ *928/282–4179* ⊕ *www.oaxacarestaurant.com.*

$$$$ ✗ **René at Tlaquepaque.** Ease into the plush banquettes at this quiet,
EUROPEAN lace-curtained restaurant for classic French and Continental dishes. Recommended starters include French onion soup and the spinach-and-wild-mushroom salad in a hazelnut vinaigrette. Rack of lamb is the house specialty, and the Dover sole is a real find, far from the white cliffs. Crêpes suzette for two, prepared table-side, is an impressive dessert. There's a well-selected wine list, too. Service is formal, but resort-casual attire is acceptable. $ *Average main: $31* ✉ *Tlaquepaque Arts & Crafts Village, Unit B–117, AZ 179, Central* ☎ *928/282–9225* ⊕ *www. rene-sedona.com.*

$ ✗ **Sally's B.B.Q.** Although it offers limited indoor seating, this Uptown
SOUTHERN hideaway behind a long row of tourist shops is worth a visit. It's super-casual, with just an ordering window where you can select pulled-pork sandwiches and homemade comfort food such as beans or coleslaw. The barbecue sauce has a bit of a kick, and the french fries (also made from scratch) are fabulous. Hours vary with the season (during winter they close at 7), so call ahead. $ *Average main: $8* ✉ *250 Jordan Rd., No. 9, Uptown* ☎ *928/282–6533* ⊕ *www.sallysbbq.com.*

$$$ AMERICAN 🍴 **Shugrues Hillside.** Almost everything is good here—including the red-rock views from every seat, which have made this one of the most popular restaurants in Sedona—but the salads and meats are particularly noteworthy. The Caesar salad is refreshingly traditional, and the inventive ginger-walnut chicken salad is large enough to share. Rack of lamb and filet mignon are prepared and presented simply, and there's a small, well-priced wine list. Full entrées include soup or salad; smaller à la carte selections are lower priced. Service is friendly rather than formal, and dining views don't get much better than the upstairs deck. [$] *Average main: $30* ✉ *671 AZ 179, Central* ☎ *928/282–5300* 🌐 *www.shugrueshillside.com.*

WHERE TO STAY

For expanded hotel reviews, visit Fodors.com.

$$$ B&B/INN 🏨 **Adobe Village Graham Inn.** All of the rooms at this inn south of Sedona have either wood-burning or gas fireplaces, and some of them also have Jacuzzi tubs and balconies that look out onto the red rocks. **Pros:** way-above-average hospitality; variety of accommodations; very close to hiking and biking trails. **Cons:** drive to town. [$] *Rooms from: $179* ✉ *150 Canyon Circle Dr., Village of Oak Creek* ☎ *928/284–1425, 800/228–1425* 🌐 *www.adobevillagegrahaminn.com* 🛏 *6 rooms, 5 suites, 4 private villas* 🍽 *Breakfast.*

$$$ B&B/INN 🏨 **Alma de Sedona Bed and Breakfast Inn.** The Alma de Sedona is an enchanting bed-and-breakfast, with spectacular views and ultracomfortable beds. **Pros:** spacious and private rooms; excellent views. **Cons:** decor could use updating; some rooms require climbing stairs. [$] *Rooms from: $189* ✉ *50 Hozoni Dr., West* ☎ *928/282–2737, 800/923–2282* 🌐 *www.almadesedona.com* 🛏 *12 rooms* 🍽 *Breakfast.*

$$ RESORT 🏨 **Amara Resort Hotel & Spa.** You might not expect to find a boutique hotel in small, outdoorsy Sedona, but here at the Amara, next to gurgling Oak Creek, sleek rooms deviate from the usual Sedona look, with low-slung beds and work desks with ergonomic seating. **Pros:** good spa and restaurant; walk to Uptown. **Cons:** city-chic feels somewhat incongruous with natural setting. [$] *Rooms from: $169* ✉ *100 Amara La., Uptown* ☎ *928/282–4828, 800/815–6152* 🌐 *www.amararesort.com* 🛏 *92 rooms, 8 suites* 🍽 *No meals.*

$$$ B&B/INN 🏨 **Boots & Saddles.** Irith and Sam are the worldly and consummate hosts at this quiet inn tucked behind the main street in West Sedona. **Pros:** hosts go the extra mile to pamper and advise; private decks. **Cons:** first-floor rooms can get noise from upstairs guests. [$] *Rooms from: $250* ✉ *2900 Hopi Dr., West* ☎ *928/282–1944, 800/201–1944* 🌐 *www.oldwestbb.com* 🛏 *6 rooms* 🍽 *Breakfast.*

$$$ B&B/INN 🏨 **Briar Patch Inn.** This B&B in verdant Oak Creek canyon exudes rustic elegance in its Southwestern-themed rooms in charming wooden cabins, many with decks overlooking the creek. **Pros:** tranquil creekside setting with beautiful gardens. **Cons:** pricey; some cabins can be dark. [$] *Rooms from: $225* ✉ *3190 N. Hwy 89A, Oak Creek Canyon* ☎ *928/282–2342, 888/809–3030* 🌐 *www.briarpatchinn.com* 🛏 *19 cottages* 🍽 *Breakfast.*

Local arts and crafts often represent the Native American heritage in Arizona.

$$
B&B/INN
☷ **The Canyon Wren.** The best value in the Oak Creek canyon area, this small and serene B&B across the road from the creek has freestanding cabins with views of the canyon walls, and hosts Milena and Mike regard guests' privacy first and foremost. **Pros:** romantic yet homey; wonderful hosts and breakfast. **Cons:** some cabins are close to road; 6 miles to town. $⃞ *Rooms from: $155* ✉ *6425 N. Hwy 89A, Oak Creek Canyon* ☎ *928/282–6900, 800/437–9736* ⊕ *www.canyonwrencabins. com* ⊅ *4 cabins* ⦿❙ *Breakfast.*

$
HOTEL
☷ **Desert Quail Inn.** Close to a lion's share of the trailheads, this is a good base for outdoor adventures, and the front desk has plenty of maps and advice on offer. **Pros:** large, clean rooms. **Cons:** two-story roadside motel. $⃞ *Rooms from: $79* ✉ *6626 Hwy 179, Village of Oak Creek* ☎ *928/284–1433, 800/385–0927* ⊕ *www.desertquailinn.com* ⊅ *40 rooms* ⦿❙ *No meals.*

$$$
B&B/INN
☷ **El Portal Sedona Hotel.** This stunning hacienda is one of the most beautifully designed boutique hotels in the Southwest. **Pros:** very attractive rooms; central location next to Tlaquepaque shops and restaurants; pet-friendly rooms have private outdoor yard space. **Cons:** even breakfast is expensive. $⃞ *Rooms from: $229* ✉ *95 Portal Lane, Central* ☎ *928/203–9405, 800/313–0017* ⊕ *www.elportalsedona.com* ⊅ *12 rooms* ⦿❙ *No meals.*

$$$$
RESORT
Fodor's Choice
★
☷ **Enchantment Resort.** A few miles outside of town, serene Boynton Canyon is the setting for this luxurious resort and its world-class destination spa, Mii Amo; the rooms and suites are tucked into small, pueblo-style buildings, and accommodations come in many configurations: multiple bedrooms can be joined to create large, elaborate suites. **Pros:** gorgeous setting; state-of-the-art Mii Amo Spa; numerous on-site

activities. **Cons:** 20-minute drive into town. [$] *Rooms from: $355* ✉ *525 Boynton Canyon Rd., West* ☎ *928/282–2900, 800/826–4180* 🌐 *www.enchantmentresort.com* 🛏 *107 rooms, 115 suites* 🍴 *No meals.*

$$$ RESORT 🏨 **Junipine Resort.** These one- and two-bedroom cabins nestled in a juniper and pine forest (hence the name) are spacious and airy, with vaulted ceilings, wood-burning fireplaces, and large decks overlooking either the creek or the canyon. **Pros:** huge, well-equipped cabins (some with hot tubs); trailheads on-site. **Cons:** individually owned condo units have been individually decorated; the group appeal can mean some partying neighbors. [$] *Rooms from: $189* ✉ *8351 N. Hwy 89A, Oak Creek Canyon* ☎ *928/282–3375, 800/742–7463* 🌐 *www.junipine.com* 🛏 *50 suites* 🍴 *No meals.*

$$$ RESORT 🏨 **L'Auberge de Sedona.** This elegant resort consists of private hillside units with spectacular views and cozy cottages in the woods along Oak Creek. **Pros:** luxurious rooms and cabins; secluded setting yet close to town. **Cons:** in-house restaurant very pricey. [$] *Rooms from: $250* ✉ *301 L'Auberge Lane, Uptown* ☎ *928/282–1661, 800/905–5745* 🌐 *www.lauberge.com* 🛏 *25 lodge rooms,15 cottage suites, 4 jr. suites, 62 cottages* 🍴 *No meals.*

$$$ B&B/INN 🏨 **Lodge at Sedona.** Rooms in this rambling wood-and-stone Craftsman house have a refined rustic style; some have fireplaces, redwood decks, or hot tubs. **Pros:** tranquil setting yet short walk from West Sedona; friendly staff. **Cons:** limited views. [$] *Rooms from: $219* ✉ *125 Kallof Pl., West* ☎ *928/204–1942, 800/619–4467* 🌐 *www.lodgeatsedona.com* 🛏 *5 rooms, 9 suites* 🍴 *Breakfast.*

$ HOTEL 🏨 **Sedona Motel.** Built on a terrace removed from the highway in order to afford it the same expansive views as the pricier resorts, this motel is pretty typical in all other respects. **Pros:** good value; convenient walk to shops and restaurants; red-rock views. **Cons:** some road noise. [$] *Rooms from: $90* ✉ *218 Hwy 179, Central* ☎ *928/282–7187, 877/828–7187* 🌐 *www.thesedonamotel.com* 🛏 *16 rooms* 🍴 *No meals.*

$ HOTEL 🏨 **Sky Ranch Lodge.** There may be no better vantage point in town from which to view Sedona's red-rock canyons and sunsets than the private patios and balconies at Sky Ranch Lodge, near the top of Airport Mesa. **Pros:** good value; great views. **Cons:** older rooms are somewhat worn; driving up and down the hill into town. [$] *Rooms from: $85* ✉ *Top of Airport Rd., 1105 Airport Rd., West* ☎ *928/282–6400, 800/708–6400* 🌐 *www.skyranchlodge.com* 🛏 *92 rooms, 2 cottages* 🍴 *No meals.*

$ HOTEL 🏨 **Sugar Loaf Lodge.** Though it may be hard to believe, there are still bargains in Sedona, and this one-story, family-run motel delivers. **Pros:** it's cheap; it's clean. **Cons:** older, very basic furnishings. [$] *Rooms from: $60* ✉ *1870 W. Hwy 89A, West* ☎ *928/282–9451, 877/282–0632* 🌐 *www.sedonasugarloaf.com* 🛏 *15 rooms* 🍴 *Breakfast.*

NIGHTLIFE AND THE ARTS

Nightlife in Sedona tends to be sedate, although on high-season weekends there's usually live music at the Enchantment Resort. Shugrue's Hillside also regularly presents local musicians. Options vary from jazz to rock and pop; in all cases, call ahead.

Chamber Music Sedona. From October through May, Chamber Music Sedona hosts a concert series. They also host the "Met Live on HD" opera performances, and a bluegrass festival in early summer. ☎ *928/204–2415* ⊕ *www.chambermusicsedona.org.*

Relics Restaurant & Lounge at Rainbow's End. The closest thing to a rollicking cowboy bar in Sedona is Relics Restaurant & Lounge at Rainbow's End, a steak house with a wooden dance floor and live rock or country-and-Western music most nights. ✉ *3235 W. Hwy 89A, West* ☎ *928/282–1593* ⊕ *www.relicsrestaurant.com.*

Sedona Arts Center. The Sedona Arts Center offers classes in all mediums and hosts the Plein Air Art Festival in October. ✉ *15 Art Barn Rd., Uptown* ☎ *928/282–3809* ⊕ *www.sedonaartscenter.com.*

Sedona International Film Festival. The nine-day Sedona International Film Festival takes place in late February, and features independent films from all over the world. ✉ *2030 W. Hwy 89A, West* ☎ *928/282–1177* ⊕ *www.sedonafilm.org.*

SHOPPING

With a few exceptions, most of the stores in Uptown Sedona north of the "Y" (running along AZ 89A to the east of its intersection with AZ 179) cater to the tour-bus trade with Native American jewelry and New Age souvenirs. If this isn't your style, the largest concentration of stores and galleries is along AZ 179, just south of the "Y," with plenty of offerings for serious shoppers.

SHOPPING CENTERS

There are three main art-gallery complexes in Sedona—Hozho, Tlaquepaque, and Hillside, all located just south of the "Y." Each has smaller galleries within the larger complex.

Hillside Sedona. Half a dozen galleries and three restaurants, including Shugrues, are housed in the Hillside Sedona complex. ✉ *671 AZ 179, Uptown* ☎ *928/282–4500* ⊕ *www.hillsidesedona.net.*

Hozho Center. A minute or two north of Hillside Sedona shopping complex on AZ 179, the Hozho Center is a small, upscale complex in a beige Santa Fe–style building, with galleries and fine-art souvenirs. ✉ *431 AZ 179, Uptown.*

Tlaquepaque Arts & Crafts Village. Home to more than 100 shops and galleries and several restaurants, Tlaquepaque Arts & Crafts Village remains one of the best places for travelers to find mementos from their trip to Sedona. The complex of clay-tile-roofed buildings arranged around a series of courtyards shares its name and architectural style with a crafts village just outside Guadalajara. It's a lovely place to browse, but beware: prices tend to be high, and locals joke that it's pronounced "to-lock-your-pocket." ✉ *AZ 179 just south of "Y, Uptown* ☎ *928/282–4838* ⊕ *www.tlaq.com.*

ARTS AND CRAFTS

Esteban's. Native American crafts and ceramics are the focus at Esteban's. ⊠ *Tlaquepaque, 336 AZ 179, No. 103, Bldg. B, Uptown* ☎ *928/ 282–4686* ⊕ *www.estebanssedona.com.*

Garland's Navajo Rugs. There's a collection of new and antique rugs at Garland's Navajo Rugs, as well as Native American kachina dolls, pottery, and baskets. ⊠ *411 AZ 179, Uptown* ☎ *928/282–4070* ⊕ *www. garlandsrugs.com.*

James Ratliff Gallery. There are fun and functional pieces by not-yet-established artists at the James Ratliff Gallery. ⊠ *Hillside Sedona, 671 AZ 179, A1 and A2, Uptown* ☎ *928/282–1404* ⊕ *www.jamesratliffgallery. com.*

Kuivato Glass Gallery. There's gorgeous glass lining the shelves at the Kuivato Glass Gallery. ⊠ *Tlaquepaque, 336 Hwy 179, No. 125, Bldg. B, Uptown* ☎ *928/282–1212* ⊕ *www.kuivato.com.*

Lanning Gallery. Mostly Southwestern art and jewelry is for sale at the Lanning Gallery. ⊠ *Hozho Center, 431 Hwy 179, Uptown* ☎ *928/282– 6865* ⊕ *www.lanninggallery.com.*

Sedona Pottery. There's an eccletic mix of pieces available at Sedona Pottery, including flower-arranging bowls, egg separators, and life-size ceramic statues by shop owner Mary Margaret Sather. ⊠ *Garland Building, 411 AZ 179, Uptown* ☎ *928/282–1192* ⊕ *www.sedonapottery.net.*

CLOTHING

Isadora. There are beautiful handwoven jackets and shawls for sale at Isadora. ⊠ *Tlaquepaque, 336 Hwy 179, No. 120, Bldg. A* ☎ *928/ 282–6232.*

Looking West. The spiffiest cowgirl-style getups in town fill the racks at Looking West. ⊠ *242 N. Hwy 89A, Uptown* ☎ *928/282–4877* ⊕ *www. sedonaclothing.com.*

JEWELRY

Crystal Magic. This shop dabbles in the metaphysical, with crystals, jewelry, and books for the New Age. ⊠ *2978 W. Hwy 89A, West* ☎ *928/ 282–1622.*

SPORTS

Canyon Outfitters. This shop is good for gearing up with maps, clothing, and camping equipment before your outdoor adventures. ⊠ *2701 W. Hwy 89A, West* ☎ *928/282–5293* ⊕ *www.canyonoutfitterssedona.com.*

The Hike House. A unique shopping experience, The Hike House can not only outfit you from head to toe, they can also match you with a suitable and satisfying hiking itinerary through their interactive Trail Finder service. If you'd rather go on a guided hike, staff can arrange that as well. Grab some trail mix, scones, and strong coffee in the adjoining cafe. ⊠ *Hozho Center, 431 Hwy 179, Uptown* ☎ *928/282–5820* ⊕ *www.thehikehouse.com.*

SPAS

While some prefer to harness Sedona's rejuvenating energy at a vortex site, others seek renewal at one of the many spas in town. From all-inclusive spa retreats nestled in red-rock canyons to inexpensive body-work performed by healing arts students, Sedona has relaxing options for every budget and preference.

With its history of Native American traditions, Sedona is thought of as one of the most sacred healing spots on Earth. Spas incorporate indigenous materials, like red-rock clay, into their spa services—and choosing your treatments is part of the pleasure. Some of Sedona's spas are destinations in themselves, offering experiences tailored to individual needs and desires.

4

Fodor's Choice **Mii Amo Spa.** Guests at the Enchantment Resort can enjoy the top-
★ notch Mii Amo Spa. Set in spectacular Boynton Canyon, Mii Amo is a state-of-the-art facility with indoor and outdoor pools and treatment rooms. Meditate in the sand-floor crystal grotto before your Watsu water therapy or deep-tissue massage. Take a guided hike or try a tai chi, dance, or photography class. Afterward, dine in the spa's health-ful and tasty café (no egg yolks in these omelets), wearing only your spa robe if you like. All-inclusive spa packages are definitely the prime selection for a rejuvenating getaway—stay in one of the beautifully appointed spa casitas steps away from resort activities (three meals and two spa treatments each day are included). Otherwise, regular resort guests are welcome to partake in spa services, classes, and dining before and after their jeep tours. ⊠ *Enchantment Resort, 525 Boynton Canyon Rd., West* ☎ *928/203–8500, 888/749–2137* ⊕ *www.miiamo.com* ☞ *$150 60-min massage, $220 90-min massage; $2250–$4510 for 3-7 night all-inclusive packages. Hot tubs, pools, sauna, steam room. Gym with: Cardiovascular machines, free weights, weight-training equip-ment. Services: Bodywork, facials, massage, scrubs, nutritional coun-seling. Classes and programs: Dance, flexibility training, guided hikes, meditation, Pilates, tai chi, tennis, yoga.*

NAMTI. Students and faculty at the Northern Arizona Massage Ther-apy Institute, NAMTI, offer quality one-hour and 90-minute massage, craniosacral, reflexology, and facial treatments at much lower prices than you'll pay at resort spas in the area. A particularly invigorating treatment is the specialized Thai Massage, a two-hour combination of deep-pressure massage and stretching movements (while on the floor, clothed) that improves flexibility and relieves tension. Discounts are given for multiple treatments, such as a facial and a massage, and for adding on shorter treatments like the fine line–reducing Opal Sonic facial massage. ⊠ *2120 W. Hwy 89A, West* ☎ *928/282–7737* ⊕ *www. namti.com* ☞ *$59 60-min massage or facial; $79 90-min massage or facial; $109 for massage and facial. Services: Aromatherapy, facials massage, waxing.*

Sedona New Day Spa. The popular Sedona New Day Spa uses local ingredients for clay masks, body wraps, and crystal therapy. Their sig-nature treatment, Body and Soul Reviver—which begins with a dry-brush skin exfoliation, transitions to a scented, candle-lit bath and finishes with a hot stone massage—may just be the ultimate pampering experience. Or choose a "Soul Journey," for a psychic reading of your chakras along with a massage. For couples, they have several luxurious packages. ⊠ *1449 W. Hwy 89A, West* ☎ *928/282–7502* ⊕ *www. sedonanewdayspa.com* ☞ *$125–$165 60-min massage; $195 90-min massage; $140 60-min facial. Services: Baths, body wraps, facials, massage, nail treatment, waxing.*

The Spa at L'Auberge. As one of Sedona's upscale resorts, L'Auberge offers an array of spa amenities for both resort guests and those lodging elsewhere. Here you can indulge in an outdoor massage on the bank of gurgling Oak Creek, or restore balance to your being with an Energy Healing Therapy such as Reiki. Their signature service is the 90-minute Sedona Dreams, which incorporates a ginger-lime exfoliating scrub, aromatherapy, and a hot-stone massage. The spa is intimate, with a rustic yet elegant vibe, just like the resort. ⊠ *301 L'Auberge La, Uptown* ☎ *800/905–5745, 928/282–1661* ⊕ *www.lauberge.com* ☞ *$130 60-min; $190 90-min massage, facial, or energy work; additional $30 for creekside treatments. Outdoor hot tub, steam rooms. Gym with: Cardiovascular machines, free weights. Services: body wraps, facials, massage. Classes: yoga (for resort guests only).*

Fodor's Choice ★ **The Spa at Sedona Rouge.** The Spa at Sedona Rouge is a more understated healing environment, open to the public as well as to its boutique hotel guests. Deepak Chopra chooses this simple and tranquil setting for his weeklong "SynchroDestiny" workshop each year. Skilled spa therapists meet with clients first to discuss individual goals before embarking on treatments like the Seven Sacred Pools Massage, which brings balance to the body's seven energy centers, or chakras. Mind-body coaching services, ayurvedic treatments, and tarot readings are also popular. The gardens and interior lounges contribute to the overall nourishing experience. Yoga classes ($10) meet daily at 8 am. ⊠ *Sedona Rouge Hotel and Spa, 2250 W. Hwy 89A, West* ☎ *866/312–4111, 928/203–4111* ⊕ *www.sedonarouge.com* ☞ *$120 60-min massage; $215 90-min coaching/stress management session. Hot tub, pool, steam room. Gym with: Cardiovascular machines, free weights, weight-training equipment. Services: Massage, facials, scrubs, wraps, waxing and tinting. Classes and programs: Clairvoyant Coaching, Harmonious Healing Mind/Body/Spirit Integration, yoga.*

SPORTS AND THE OUTDOORS

The Brins Fire consumed 4,500 acres in Sedona in 2006. Although no people or structures were harmed, the human-ignited fire threatened the Oak Creek Canyon area and serves as a reminder about fire safety. Take precautions and use common sense. Extinguish all fires with water. Never toss a cigarette butt. And don't hesitate to ask questions of local park rangers.

■ **TIP→** A Red Rock Pass is required to park in the Coconino National Forest from Oak Creek Canyon through Sedona and the Village of Oak Creek. Passes cost $5 for the day, $15 for the week, or $20 for an entire year, and can be purchased online and at the **Coconino Forest Service**

Red Rock Ranger Station (⊠ *8375 AZ 179, just south of the Village of Oak Creek* ☎ *928/203–7500* ⊕ *www.redrockcountry.org*), which is open daily and has copious information on regional outdoor activities. Passes are also available from vending machines at popular trailheads—including Boynton Canyon and Bell Rock—and at the Sedona Chamber of Commerce, Circle K stores, and many Sedona hotels. Locals widely resent the pass, feeling that free access to national forests is a right. The Forest Service counters that it doesn't receive enough federal funds to maintain the land surrounding Sedona, trampled by 5 million visitors each year, and that a parking fee is the best way to raise revenue.

BALLOONING

Northern Light Balloon Expeditions. One of only two companies with permits to fly over Sedona, Northern Light Balloon Expeditions offers sunrise flights that include a post-flight breakfast picnic. ☎ *928/282–2274, 800/230–6222* ⊕ *www.northernlightballoon.com.*

Red Rock Balloon Adventures. Guests are flown over the red rocks for one to two hours with a Red Rock Balloon Adventures tour and are served a picnic upon landing. ☎ *800/258–3754* ⊕ *www.redrockballoons.com.*

GOLF

Oak Creek Country Club. The Oak Creek Country Club is a good semiprivate 18-hole, par-72 course designed by the father-son team of Robert Trent Jones Sr. and Robert Trent Jones Jr. It is a traditional, rather than desert, course with long, tree-lined fairways and slightly elevated greens amid lovely red rock views. Providing challenges for beginner through advanced golfers, this course is described as "player-friendly." Greens fee is $99 before 1 pm and $79 after 1 pm. ⊠ *690 Bell Rock Blvd., Village of Oak Creek* ☎ *928/284–1660* ⊕ *www.oakcreekcountryclub. com* ⚑ *18 holes. 6824 yds. Par 72. Greens fee: $99* ⚐ *Driving range, putting green, golf carts, rental clubs, pro shop, golf academy/lessons, restaurant, bar.*

Fodor's Choice **Sedona Golf Resort.** A gorgeous par-71 course, Sedona Golf Resort was
  ★   designed by Gary Panks to take advantage of the many changes in elevation and scenery. Golf courses are a dime a dozen in Arizona, but this one is regarded as one of the best in the state. Don't let the stunning views around every bend distract your focus from the very undulating greens and fairways. Greens fee is $95 before 1 pm and $70 after. The restaurant—with panoramic red-rock vistas—serves breakfast and lunch daily. ⊠ *35 Ridge Trail Dr., Village of Oak Creek* ☎ *928/284–9355, 877/733–6630* ⊕ *www.sedonagolfresort.com* ⚑ *18 holes. 6646 yds. Par 71. Greens fee: $95* ⚐ *Facilities: Driving range, putting green, golf carts, rental clubs, pro shop, lessons, restaurant, bar.*

HIKING AND BACKPACKING

Coconino National Forest-Red Rock Ranger District. For free detailed maps, hiking advice, and information on campgrounds, contact the rangers of the Coconino National Forest. Ask here or at your hotel for directions to trailheads for Doe's Mountain (an easy ascent, with many switchbacks), Loy Canyon, Devil's Kitchen, and Long Canyon. ✉ *8375 Hwy 179, Village of Oak Creek* ☎ *928/203–7500* ⊕ *www.redrockcountry.org* ☉ *daily 9–4:30.*

> ### BOYNTON CANYON
>
> You might want to drive out to Boynton Canyon, sacred to the Yavapai Apache, who believe it was their ancient birthplace. This is also the site of Enchantment Resort, where all are welcome to hike the canyon and stop in for lunch or a late-afternoon drink on the terrace.

West Fork Trail. Among the paths in Coconino National Forest, the popular West Fork Trail traverses Oak Creek Canyon for a 3-mile hike. A walk through the woods between sheer red-rock walls and a dip in the stream make a great summer combo. The trailhead is about 3 miles north of Slide Rock State Park. ✉ *Trailhead: AZ 89A, 9.5 miles north of Sedona.*

Any backpacking trip in the Red Rock-**Secret Mountain Wilderness** near Sedona guarantees stunning vistas, otherworldly rock formations, and Zen-like serenity, but little water, so pack a good supply. ■ **TIP→ Plan your trip for spring or fall: summer brings 100°F heat and sudden thunderstorms that flood canyons without warning.** Most individual trails in the wilderness are too short for anything longer than an overnighter, but several trails can be linked up to form a memorable multiday trip. Contact Coconino National Forest's Red Rock Ranger District in Sedona for full details.

HORSEBACK RIDING

Trail Horse Adventures. Among the tour options at Trail Horse Adventures are a midday ride with picnic and a ride along the Verde River to Native American cliff dwellings. Rides range from $64 for an hour to $125 for a 3-hour ride with lunch. ✉ *675 Dead Horse Ranch Rd., Cottonwood* ☎ *928/634–5276, 866/958–7245* ⊕ *www.trailhorseadventures.com.*

JEEP TOURS

Several jeep-tour operators headquartered along Sedona's main Uptown drag conduct excursions, some focusing on geology, some on astronomy, some on vortexes, some on all three. You can even find a combination jeep tour and horseback ride. Prices start at about $55 per person for two hours and go upward of $100 per person for four hours. Although all the excursions are safe, many aren't for those who dislike heights or bumps.

A Day in the West. With this tour operator, you can go to all the prime spots and combine a jeep tour with a horseback ride or local wine tasting. ☎ *928/282–4320, 800/973–3662* ⊕ *www.adayinthewest.com.*

Pink Jeep Tours. The ubiquitous Pink Jeep Tours are a popular choice for driving through the red rocks. ✉ *204 N. Hwy 89A, Uptown* ☎ *800/873–3662* ⊕ *www.pinkjeeptours.com.*

Red Rock Western Jeep Tours. This reliable operator spins some good cowboy tales on its jeep tours. ✉ *270 N. Hwy 89A, Uptown* ☎ *928/282–6667, 800/848–7728* ⊕ *www.redrockjeep.com.*

MOUNTAIN BIKING

Given the red-rock splendor, challenging terrain, miles of single track, and mild weather, you might think Sedona would be a mountain-biking destination on the order of Moab or Durango. Inexplicably, you won't find the Lycra-clad throngs patronizing pasta bars or throwing back microbrews on the Uptown mall, but all the better for you: the mountain-biking culture remains fervent but low-key. A few excellent, strategically located bike shops can outfit you and give advice.

As a general rule, mountain bikes are allowed on all trails and jeep paths unless designated as wilderness or private property. The rolling terrain, which switches between serpentine trails of buff red clay and mounds of slickrock, has few sustained climbs, but be careful of blind drop-offs that often step down several feet in unexpected places. The thorny trailside flora makes carrying extra inner tubes a must, and an inner-tube sealant is a good idea, too. If you plan to ride for several hours, pack a gallon of water and start early in the morning on hot days. Shade is rare, and with the exception of (nonpotable) Oak Creek, water is nonexistent.

Bell Rock Pathway. For the casual rider, Bell Rock Pathway is a scenic and easy ride traveling 3 miles through some of the most breathtaking scenery in red-rock country. Several single-track trails spur off this one, making it a good starting point for many other rides in Sedona. ✉ *Trailhead: 5 miles south of Sedona on AZ 179.*

Broken Arrow-Submarine Rock Trail. There's good reason why the Broken Arrow-Submarine Rock Trail is perhaps the most popular single-track loop in the area. The 10-mile trail is a heady mixture of prime terrain and scenery following slickrock and twisty trails up to Chicken Point, a sandstone terrace overlooking colorful buttes. The trail continues as a bumpy romp through washes, almost all downhill. Be wary of blind drop-offs in this section. It wouldn't be overly cautious to scout any parts of the trail that look sketchy. ✉ *Trailhead: 2 miles south of Sedona, off AZ 179; take Morgan Rd. to Broken Arrow Trail parking lot.*

TOURS AND
OUTFITTERS

Absolute Bikes. Close to several biking trails, Absolute Bikes is an excellent source for rentals, equipment, and advice on trails and conditions. ✉ *6101 Hwy 179, Village of Oak Creek* ☎ *877/284–1242* ⊕ *www.absolutebikes.net.*

Sedona Bike and Bean. About a block south of Bell Rock Pathway, the friendly folks at Bike and Bean offer rentals, tours, trail maps, and their own blend of coffee. ✉ *75 Bell Rock Plaza, at Hwy. 179, Village of Oak Creek* ☎ *928/284–0210* ⊕ *www.bike-bean.com.*

THE VERDE VALLEY, JEROME, AND PRESCOTT

About 90 miles north of Phoenix, as you round a curve approaching Exit 285 off Interstate 17, the valley of the Verde River suddenly unfolds in a panorama of grayish-white cliffs, tinted red in the distance and dotted with desert scrub, cottonwood, and pine. For hundreds of years many Native American communities, especially those of the southern Sinagua people, lined the Verde River. Rumors of great mineral deposits brought Europeans to the Verde Valley as early as 1583, when Hopi Indians guided Antonio de Espejo here, but it wasn't until the second half of the 19th century that this wealth was commercially exploited. The discovery of silver and gold in the Black Hills, which border the valley on the southwest, gave rise to boomtowns like Jerome—and to military installations such as Fort Verde, set up to protect the white settlers and wealth seekers from the Native American tribes they displaced. Mineral wealth was also the impetus behind the establishment of Prescott as a territorial capital by President Lincoln and other Unionists who wanted to keep the riches out of Confederate hands.

VERDE VALLEY

18 miles southwest of Sedona on U.S. 89A; 94 miles north of Phoenix on Interstate 17.

Often overlooked by travelers on trips to Sedona or Flagstaff, the Verde Valley offers several enjoyable diversions, including wine tasting in Cornville and the historical wonders at Montezuma Castle and Tuzigoot. And if you're tired of the car, the Verde Canyon Railroad in Clarkdale is a great way to get off-road without doing the driving.

GETTING HERE AND AROUND

From Phoenix, it's a leisurely and picturesque route through Verde Valley. Follow Interstate 17 north 25 miles past Cordes Junction until you see the turnoff for AZ 260, which will take you to Cottonwood in 12 miles. Here you can pick up AZ 89A, which leads southwest to Prescott (41 miles) or northeast to Sedona (19 miles).

EXPLORING
TOP ATTRACTIONS

Montezuma Castle National Monument. The five-story, 20-room cliff dwelling at Montezuma Castle National Monument was named by explorers who believed it had been erected by the Aztecs. Southern Sinagua Native Americans actually built the roughly 600-year-old structure, which is one of the best-preserved prehistoric dwellings in North America—and one of the most accessible. An easy paved trail (0.3 mile round-trip) leads to the dwelling and to the adjacent Castle A, a badly deteriorated six-story living space with about 45 rooms. No one is permitted to enter the site, but the viewing area is close by. From Interstate 17, take exit 289 and follow signs to Montezuma Castle Road. ⊠ *Montezuma Castle Rd., 7 miles northeast of Camp Verde* ☎ *928/567–3322* ⊕ *www.nps. gov/moca* ⊠ *$5 for Montezuma Castle* ⊙ *Daily 8–5.*

Montezuma Well. Somewhat less accessible than Montezuma Castle—but equally striking—is Montezuma Well, a unit of the national

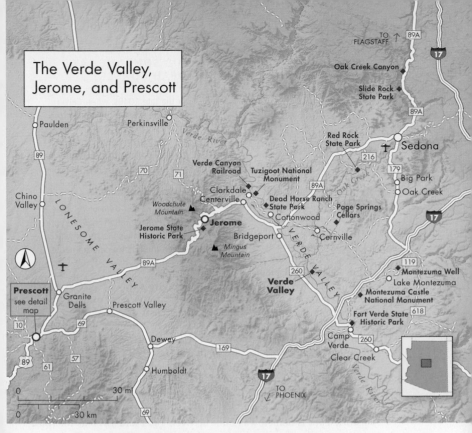

The Verde Valley, Jerome, and Prescott

park. Although there are some Sinagua and Hohokam sites here, the limestone sinkhole with a limpid blue-green pool lying in the middle of the desert is the main attraction. This cavity—55 feet deep and 365 feet across—is all that's left of an ancient subterranean cavern; the water remains at a constant 76°F year-round. It's a short hike, but the peace, quiet, and views of the Verde Valley reward the effort. To reach Montezuma Well from Montezuma Castle, return to Interstate 17 and go north to Exit 293; signs direct you to the well, which is 4 miles east of the freeway. ☎ 928/567–4521 ⊠ Free ⊙ Daily 8–5.

Verde Canyon Railroad. Train buffs come to the Verde Valley to catch the 22-mile Verde Canyon Railroad, which follows a dramatic route through the Verde Canyon, the remains of a copper smelter, and much unspoiled desert that is inaccessible by car. The destination—the city of Clarkdale—might not be that impressive, but the ride is undeniably scenic. Knowledgeable announcers regale riders with the area's colorful history and point out natural attractions along the way—in winter you're likely to see bald eagles.

This 4-hour trip is especially popular in fall-foliage season and in spring, when the desert wildflowers bloom; book well in advance. Round-trip rides cost $54.95. For $79.95 you can ride the much more comfortable living-room-like first-class cars, where hors d'oeuvres, coffee, and dessert are included in the price (a cash bar is also available). ■TIP→ **Reservations are required.** ✉ *Arizona Central Railroad, 300 N. Broadway, Clarkdale* ☎ *800/320–0718* ⊕ *www. verdecanyonrr.com* ✄ *$54.95.*

WORTH NOTING

Dead Horse Ranch State Park. The 423-acre spread of Dead Horse Ranch State Park, which combines high-desert and wetlands habitats, is a pleasant place to while away the day. You can fish in the Verde River or the well-stocked Park Lagoon, or hike on some 6 miles of trails that begin in a shaded picnic area and

> ### DID SOMEONE SAY DEAD HORSES?
>
> In the late 1940s, when Calvin "Cap" Ireys asked his family to help him choose between the ranches he was thinking about buying in the Verde Valley, his son immediately picked "the one with the dead horse on it." Ireys sold the land to the state in 1973 at one-third of its value, with the stipulation that the park into which it was to be converted retain the ranch's colorful name.

wind along the river; adjoining forest service pathways are available for those who enjoy longer treks. Birders can check off more than 100 species from the Arizona Audubon Society lists provided by the rangers. Bald eagles perch along the Verde River in winter, and the common black hawks—a misnomer for these threatened birds—nest here in summer. Campsites are also available (reserve by phone or online). The park is 1 mile north of Cottonwood, off Main Street. ✉ *675 Dead Horse Ranch Rd., Cottonwood* ☎ *928/634–5283* ⊕ *www.azstateparks. com/Parks/deho* ✄ *$7 per car for up to 4 persons* ⊙ *Daily 8–4:30.*

Fort Verde State Historic Park. The military post for which Fort Verde State Historic Park is named was built between 1871 and 1873 as the third of three fortifications in this part of the Arizona Territory. To protect the Verde Valley's farmers and miners from Tonto Apache and Yavapai raids, the fort's administrators oversaw the movement of nearly 1,500 Native Americans to the San Carlos and Fort Apache reservations. A museum details the history of the area's military installations, and three furnished officers' quarters show the day-to-day living conditions of the top brass—it's a good break from the interstate if you've been driving for too long. Signs from any of Interstate 17's three Camp Verde exits will direct you to the 10-acre park. ✉ *125 E. Hollomon St.* ☎ *928/567– 3275* ⊕ *www.azstateparks.com/Parks/fove* ✄ *$5* ⊙ *Thurs.–Mon. 9–5.*

Tuzigoot National Monument. It isn't as well preserved as Montezuma Castle, but Tuzigoot National Monument is more impressive in scope. Tuzigoot is another complex of the Sinagua people, who lived on this land overlooking the Verde Valley from about AD 1000 to 1400. The pueblo, constructed of limestone and sandstone blocks, once rose three stories and incorporated 110 rooms. Inhabitants were skilled dry farmers and traded with peoples hundreds of miles away. Implements used for food preparation, as well as jewelry, weapons, and farming tools excavated from the site, are displayed in the visitor center. Within the site, you can step into a reconstructed room. ✉ *3 miles north of Cottonwood on Broadway Rd., between Cottonwood's Old Town and*

Clarkdale, 527 S Main St., Clarkdale ☎ 928/634–5564 ⊕ *www.nps. gov/tuzi* 🎫 *$5* ⊙ *Daily 8–5.*

WINERIES

The high-desert soil of the Verde Valley seems to be working for growing grapes, and several vineyards have sprouted on the hillsides above Lower Oak Creek. Three notable vineyards are nestled together along Page Springs Road in Cornville—recently dubbed Winery Row—and offer wine tasting daily.

Javelina Leap Vineyard & Winery. Predominantly red wines with bold, dry flavors are produced by Javelina Leap Vineyard. Taste a few here and you'll be welcomed by owners Rod and Cynthia as if you were family. ✉ *1565 Page Springs Rd., Cornville* ☎ 928/649–2681 ⊕ *www. javelinaleapwinery.com* ⊙ *Daily 11–5.*

Oak Creek Vineyards & Winery. Oak Creek Vineyards, winemaker Deb Wahl offers syrah, merlot, chardonnay, and dessert wines. You can also pick up fixings for a picnic here—salami, cheeses, crackers, and chocolates. ✉ *1555 N Page Springs Rd., Cornville* ☎ 928/649–0290 ⊕ *www. oakcreekvineyards.net* ⊙ *Daily 10–6.*

Page Springs Cellars. The award-winning wines at Page Springs Cellars, produced by grape guru Eric Glomski, focus on grapes popular in the Rhône wine region of France. Sit outside on the deck overlooking Oak Creek and enjoy the wines (a tasting flight of 5 is $10), as well as antipasta plates and flatbread pizzas. ✉ *1500 N. Page Springs Rd., Cornville* ☎ 928/639–3004 ⊕ *www.pagespringscellars.com* ⊙ *Mon.-Wed. 11–7; Thurs.-Sun. 11–9.*

WHERE TO EAT

$$$ ✗**Manzanita Restaurant.** You might not expect to find sophisticated
EUROPEAN cooking in Cornville, 6 miles east of Cottonwood, but a European-born chef prepares Continental and German fare here, using organic produce and locally raised meat whenever possible. Specialties include wild game such as alligator and buffalo. Shrimp scampi and lamb shank in burgundy sauce are beautifully presented; and the sauerbraten and Weiner schnitzel don't disappoint. A lower-priced light menu is also available. 💲 *Average main: $22* ✉ *11425 E. Cornville Rd., Cornville* ☎ 928/634–8851 ⊕ *www.themanzanitarestaurant.com* ⊙ *Closed Mon.*

SPORTS AND THE OUTDOORS

Black Canyon Trail. This trail is a bit of a slog, rising more than 2,200 feet in 6 miles, but the reward is grand views from the gray cliffs of Verde Valley to the red buttes of Sedona to the blue range of the San Francisco Peaks. ✉ *AZ 260, 4 miles south of Cottonwood, west on FR 359 4.5 miles.*

Prescott National Forest. The **Verde Ranger District** office of the Prescott National Forest is a good resource for places to hike, fish, and boat along the Verde River. ✉ *300 E. AZ 260* ☎ 928/567–4121 ⊕ *www. fs.usda.gov/prescott.*

JEROME

20 miles northwest of Camp Verde, 3½ miles southwest of Clark-dale, 33 miles northeast of Prescott, 25 miles southwest of Sedona on AZ 89A.

Fodor's Choice
★

Jerome was once known as the Billion Dollar Copper Camp, but after the last mines closed in 1953 the booming population of 15,000 dwindled to 50 determined souls. Although its population has risen back to almost 500, Jerome still holds on to its "ghost town" designation, and several B&Bs and eateries regularly report spirit sightings. It's hard to imagine that this town was once the location of Arizona's largest JCPenney store and one of the state's first Safeway supermarkets. Jerome saw its first revival during the mid-1960s, when hippies arrived and turned it into an arts colony of sorts, and it has since become a tourist attraction. In addition to its shops and historic sites, Jerome is worth visiting for its scenery: it's built into the side of Cleopatra Hill, and from here you can see Sedona's red rocks, Flagstaff's San Francisco Peaks, and even eastern Arizona's Mogollon Rim country.

Jerome is about a mile above sea level, but structures within town sit at elevations that vary by as much as 1,500 feet, depending on whether they're on Cleopatra Hill or at its foot. Blasting at the United Verde (later Phelps Dodge) mine regularly shook buildings off their foundations—the town's jail slid across a road and down a hillside, where it sits today. And that's not all that was unsteady about Jerome. In 1903 a reporter from a New York newspaper called Jerome "the wickedest town in America," due to its abundance of drinking and gambling establishments; town records from 1880 list 24 saloons. Whether by divine retribution or drunken accidents, the town burned down several times.

GETTING HERE AND AROUND

You can get a map of the town's shops and its attractions at the visitor-information trailer on AZ 89A (which becomes Hull Street). The three streets in the main shopping area—Hull, Main, and Hill—run parallel to each other on the hillside. Street parking is easy to come by, but be prepared for some steep climbing up and down Cleopatra Hill when you're exploring by foot.

PLANNING YOUR TIME

The town can easily be explored in an afternoon with a stop for lunch, but the historic charm and shopping opportunities entice some visitors to stay overnight. Jerome currently has around 50 retail establishments (that's more than one for every 10 residents). Attractions and businesses don't always stay open as long as their stated hours if things are slow.

ESSENTIALS

Visitor Information Jerome Chamber of Commerce & Visitor Center ⊠ *Hwy 89A, (Hull St.)* ☎ *928/634–2900* ⊕ *www.jeromechamber.com.*

EXPLORING

Jerome State Historic Park. Of the three mining museums in town, the most inclusive is part of Jerome State Historic Park. At the edge of town, signs on AZ 89A will direct you to the turnoff for the park,

Getting there is the fun with a classic train ride on the Verde Canyon Railroad.

reached by a short, precipitous road. The museum occupies the 1917 mansion of Jerome's mining king, Dr. James "Rawhide Jimmy" Douglas Jr., who purchased Little Daisy Mine in 1912. You can see tools and heavy equipment used to grind ore, and some minerals are on display, but accounts of the town's wilder elements—such as the House of Joy brothel—are not so prominently featured. Just outside the mansion/park gates is Audrey Head Frame Park, where you can actually peer 1900 feet down into the Daisy Mineshaft. ✉ *100 Douglas Rd.* ☎ *928/634–5381* 🌐 *www.azstateparks.com* 🎟 *$5* 🕒 *Daily 8:30–5.*

Mine Museum. The Mine Museum in downtown Jerome is staffed by the Jerome Historical Society. The museum's collection of mining stock certificates alone is worth the (small) price of admission—the amount of money that changed hands in this town 100 years ago boggles the mind. ✉ *200 Main St.* ☎ *928/634–5477* 🌐 *www.jeromehistoricalsociety.com/* 🎟 *$2* 🕒 *Daily 9:30–4:30.*

WHERE TO EAT

$$$ AMERICAN 🍴 **The Asylum Restaurant.** Don't be put off by the name, a tribute to its past identity—this charming restaurant inside the Jerome Grand Hotel is the standout choice in town for fine dining, good wines, and wonderful vistas. Burgandy interior walls hung with local artists' work create a warm and romantic setting. Signature dishes include achiote-rubbed pork tenderloin and sea bass with a poblano chile–chardonnay lemon sauce. The roasted butternut squash soup, with just the right blend of sweetness and spice, is divine. [$] *Average main: $26* ✉ *200 Hill St.* ☎ *928/639–3197* 🌐 *www.asylumrestaurant.com.*

Cliff dwellings of the Sinagua people have been preserved for about 600 years at Montezuma Castle.

$ 🍴 **Flatiron Cafe.** Ask where to have lunch or a late-afternoon snack, and
AMERICAN nearly every Main Street shop owner will direct you to a tiny eatery at the fork in the road. The menu includes healthful sandwiches, such as black-bean hummus with feta cheese, and many coffee drinks. Breakfast is also served. [$] *Average main: $11* ✉ *416 Main St.* ☎ *928/634–2733* ⏲ *Closed Tues. No dinner.*

$ 🍴 **Haunted Hamburger/Jerome Palace.** After the climb up the stairs from
AMERICAN Main Street to this former boardinghouse, you'll be ready for the hearty burgers, chili, cheese steaks, and ribs that dominate the menu. Lighter fare, including such meatless selections as the guacamole quesadilla, is also available. Eat on the outside deck overlooking Verde Valley or in the upstairs dining room, where "Claire," the resident ghost, purportedly hangs out. [$] *Average main: $10* ✉ *410 Clark St.* ☎ *928/634–0554* 🌐 *www.thehauntedhamburger.com.*

WHERE TO STAY

For expanded hotel reviews, visit Fodors.com.

$ 🏨 **Ghost City Inn.** The outdoor veranda at this 1898 B&B affords sweep-
B&B/INN ing views of the Verde Valley and Sedona. **Pros:** authentic historic charm; fabulous views. **Cons:** some smaller rooms and stairs. [$] *Rooms from: $105* ✉ *541 N. Main St.* ☎ *928/634–4678, 888/634–4678* 🌐 *www.ghostcityinn.com* 🛏 *6 rooms* 🍽 *Breakfast.*

$ 🏨 **Jerome Grand Hotel.** This full-service hotel at the highest point in
HOTEL town is housed in the Jerome's former hospital, built in 1927. **Pros:** great restaurant; historic property; great ghost-hunting. **Cons:** creaky; sharing your room with ghosts. [$] *Rooms from: $120* ✉ *200 Hill St.*

☎ *928/634–8200, 888/817–6788* 🌐 *www.jeromegrandhotel.com* 🛏 *25 rooms* 🍴 *Breakfast.*

$$ B&B/INN Fodor's Choice ★ 🏨 **The Surgeon's House.** Plants, knickknacks, bright colors, and plenty of sunlight make this Mediterranean-style home a welcoming place to stay. **Pros:** friendly host; knockout vistas; unique gardens. **Cons:** rigid breakfast time; climbing some stairs is required. [$] *Rooms from: $145* ✉ *101 Hill St.* ☎ *928/639–1452, 800/639–1452* 🌐 *www.surgeonshouse.com* 🛏 *2 rooms, 2 suites* 🍴 *Breakfast.*

WORD OF MOUTH

"I just love Sedona…I made a wrong turn which took me to Jerome and it was the most delightful mistake I ever made."

—P_M

NIGHTLIFE

Jerome's a ghost town, so don't expect a hopping nightlife—although there are some places to have fun.

Paul & Jerry's Saloon. The two pool tables and old wooden bar at Paul & Jerry's Saloon attract a regular crowd (relatively speaking). ✉ *Main St.* ☎ *928/634–2603.*

Spirit Room. On weekends there's live music and a lively scene at the Spirit Room; the mural over the bar harks back to the days when it was a dining spot for the prostitutes of the red-light district. ✉ *166 Main St.* ☎ *928/634–8809* 🌐 *www.spiritroombar.com.*

SHOPPING

Jerome has its share of art galleries (some perched precariously on Cleopatra Hill), along with boutiques, and they're funkier than those in Sedona. Main Street and, just around the bend, Hull Avenue are Jerome's two primary shopping streets. Your eyes may begin to glaze over after browsing through one boutique after another, most offering tasteful Southwestern paraphernalia.

Aurum. About 30 artists are represented at Aurum, which focuses on contemporary art jewelry in silver and gold. ✉ *369 Main St., P.O. Box 847* ☎ *928/634–3330* 🌐 *www.aurumjewelry.com.*

Designs on You. This boutique carries attractively styled women's clothing and accessories. ✉ *367 Main St.* ☎ *928/634–7879* 🌐 *www.designsonyoujeromeaz.com.*

Jerome Artists Cooperative Gallery. The focus at this gallery is on jewelry, sculpture, painting, and pottery by local artists. ✉ *502 Main St.* ☎ *928/639–4276* 🌐 *www.jeromecoop.com.*

Nellie Bly Kaleidoscopes and Art Glass. This shop specializes in art glass and outstanding kaleidoscopes—in fact, they claim to have the world's largest collection of them. ✉ *136 Main St.* ☎ *928/634–0255* 🌐 *www.nbscopes.com.*

Raku Gallery. You'll find wrought-iron furniture, free-blown glass, and fountains at Raku Gallery, which stocks the work of about 300 artists. ✉ *250 Hull Ave.* ☎ *928/639–0239* 🌐 *www.rakugallery.com.*

4

Sky Fire. There are two floors of clothing and furniture at Sky Fire, from Southwestern-pattern dishes to handcrafted Mission-style hutches. ⊠ *140 Main St.* ☎ *928/634–8081* ⊕ *www.skyfirejerome.com.*

EN ROUTE

Prescott National Forest. The drive down a mountainous section of AZ 89A from Jerome to Prescott is gorgeous (if somewhat harrowing in bad weather), filled with twists and turns through Prescott National Forest. A scenic turnoff near Jerome provides one last vista and a place to apply chains during surprise snowstorms. There's camping, picnicking, and hiking at the crest of Mingus Mountain. If you're coming to Prescott from Phoenix, the route that crosses the Mogollon Rim, overlooking the Verde Valley, has nice views of rolling hills and is less precipitous. ⊕ *www.fs.usda.gov/prescott.*

PRESCOTT

33 miles southwest of Jerome on AZ 89A to U.S. 89, 100 miles northwest of Phoenix via Interstate 17 to AZ 69.

In a forested bowl 5,300 feet above sea level, Prescott is a prime summer refuge for Phoenix-area dwellers. It was proclaimed the first capital of the Arizona Territory in 1864 and settled by Yankees to ensure that gold-rich northern Arizona would remain a Union resource. (Tucson and southern Arizona were strongly pro-Confederacy.) Although early territorial settlers thought that the area's original inhabitants were of Aztec origin, today it's believed that they were ancestors of the Yavapai, whose reservation is on the outskirts of town. The Aztec theory—inspired by *The History and Conquest of Mexico,* a popular book by historian William Hickling Prescott, for whom the town was named—has left its mark on such street names as Montezuma, Cortez, and Alarcon.

Despite a devastating downtown fire in 1900, Prescott remains the "West's most Eastern town," with a rich trove of late-19th-century New England–style architecture. With two institutions of higher education, Yavapai College and Prescott College, Prescott could be called a college town, but it doesn't really feel like one, perhaps because so many retirees also reside here, drawn by the temperate climate and low cost of living.

The 1916 Yavapai County Courthouse stands in the heart of Prescott, bounded by Gurley, Goodwin, Cortez, and Montezuma streets, and guarded by an equestrian bronze of turn-of-the-20th-century journalist and lawmaker Bucky O'Neill, who died while charging San Juan Hill in Cuba with Teddy Roosevelt during the Spanish-American War. Those interested in architecture will enjoy the Victorian neighborhoods. Many Queen Annes have been beautifully restored, and a number are now B&Bs.

GETTING HERE AND AROUND

The most direct route to Prescott from Phoenix is to take Interstate 17 north for 60 miles to Cordes Junction and then drive northwest on AZ 69 for 36 miles into town. Interstate 17, a four-lane divided highway, has several steep inclines and descents (complete with a number of runaway-truck ramps), but it's generally an easy and scenic thoroughfare.

Prescott Municipal Airport is 8 miles north of town on U.S. 89. United Airlines affiliate Great Lakes Airlines (⊕ www.flygreatlakes.com) offers service to Prescott Municipal Airport from Los Angeles and Denver.

The city's main drag is Gurley Street, which AZ 69 turns into from the east. You can usually find street parking along Gurley or on the side streets as you approach town; or use the free public garage on Granite Street, between Gurley and Goodwin. Most of the town's Victorian neighborhoods, shops, and restaurants, best explored on foot, are within walking distance of the Courthouse Plaza, sitting just off Gurley Street on Montezuma. Art galleries and saloons line Cortez and Montezuma streets to the north and west of the courthouse. The Chamber of Commerce and Visitor Center is on Goodwin Street, across from the courthouse and next to the post office.

PLANNING YOUR TIME

Tourism in Prescott can be bustling on weekends but is rarely overwhelming. Any day will do to tour the Victorian homes and antiques shops, but if you enjoy museums, note that museum hours are limited on Sunday, and you won't want to rush through the extensive grounds of the Sharlot Hall Museum. Devoting a full day to tour Prescott is ample, and an overnight allows for hearing plenty of live music on Whiskey Row.

ESSENTIALS

Transportation Contact Prescott Municipal Airport ☎ *928/777–1114* ⊕ *www.cityofprescott.com/cityofprescott/airport_info.php.*

Visitor Information Prescott Chamber of Commerce & Visitor Center ✉ *117 W. Goodwin St., across from Courthouse, Prescott* ☎ *928/445–2000, 800/266–7534* ⊕ *www.prescott.org* ☉ *Mon.–Fri. 9–5; Sat.–Sun. 10–2.*

EXPLORING

Phippen Museum. The paintings and bronze sculptures of George Phippen, along with works by other artists of the West, form the permanent collection of this museum about 5 miles north of downtown. Phippen met with a group of prominent cowboy artists in 1965 to form the Cowboy Artists of America, a group dedicated to preserving the Old West as they saw it. He became the president but died the next year. A memorial foundation set up in his name opened the doors of this museum in 1984. ✉ *4701 U.S. 89N* ☎ *928/778–1385* ⊕ *www.phippenartmuseum. org* 🖼 *$7* ☉ *Tues.–Sat. 10–4, Sun. 1–4* ☉ *Closed Mon.*

FAMILY **Sharlot Hall Museum.** Local history is documented at this remarkable museum. Along with the original ponderosa pine log cabin, which housed the territorial governor, and the museum, named for historian and poet Sharlot Hall, the parklike setting contains three fully restored period homes and a transportation museum. Territorial times are the focus, but natural history and artifacts of the area's prehistoric peoples are also on display. Kids under 18 get in free. ✉ *415 W. Gurley St., 2 blocks west of Courthouse Plaza, Downtown* ☎ *928/445–3122* ⊕ *www. sharlot.org* 🖼 *$5* ☉ *Mon.–Sat. 10–4, Sun. noon–4.*

The Smoki Museum. The 1935 stone-and-log building, which resembles an Indian pueblo, is almost as interesting as the Native American artifacts

Phippen
Museum **1**

Sharlot Hall
Museum **4**

Smoki
Museum **2**

Whiskey
Row **3**

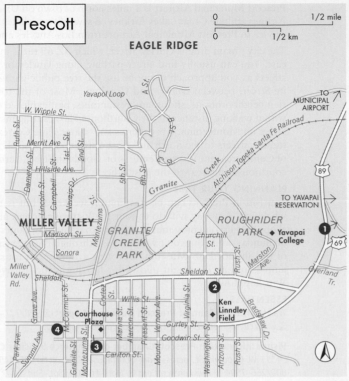

inside. Baskets, kachinas, pottery, rugs, and beadwork make up the collection, which represents Native American culture from the pre-Columbian period to the present. ☒ *147 N. Arizona Ave., Downtown* ☎ *928/445–1230* ⊕ *www.smokimuseum.org* 🎫 *$7* ⊘ *Mon.–Sat. 10–4, Sun. 1–4; Closed 1st 2 weeks in Jan.*

Whiskey Row. Twenty saloons and houses of pleasure once lined this stretch of Montezuma Street, along the west side of Courthouse Plaza. Social activity is more subdued these days, although live music pulses every evening, and the buildings have been beautifully restored. The historic bars provide an escape from the street's many boutiques. ☒ *Montezuma St., Downtown.*

WHERE TO EAT

$ × **Bistro St. Michael.** Bistro St. Michael is a great place to enjoy a coffee or bowl of black-bean chili while watching the people on Whiskey Row. The café/bar, which serves breakfast and lunch (and is open until 4 pm on weekends), has been restored to its original 1901 style. The service at the counter is brisk, and will leave you plenty of time for antiquing or museum-browsing for the remainder of the day. 🟡 *Average main: $9* ☒ *205 W. Gurley St., Downtown* ☎ *928/776–1999* ⊕ *www. stmichaelhotel.com* ⊘ *No dinner.*

AMERICAN

$$ ITALIAN 🍴 **Genovese's.** Reasonably priced, classic southern Italian fare makes this restaurant near Courthouse Plaza a local favorite. The decor is right out of 1975, but the family recipes, like chicken marsala, are fresh and flavorful and the service is extra friendly. Try the cannelloni stuffed with shrimp, crab, ricotta cheese, and spinach. Save room for spumoni ice cream or a cannoli. [$] *Average main: $14* ✉ *217 W. Gurley St., Downtown* ☎ *928/541–9089* 🌐 *www.genovesesrestaurant.com.*

$ AMERICAN 🍴 **Kendall's Famous Burgers and Ice Cream.** A classic diner, replete with booths and a 1950s-style soda fountain, Kendall's serves hamburgers cooked to order with your choice of 14 condiments. If you've seen the movie *Billy Jack*, you'll probably recognize this place from the scene where the Native Americans and the townies get into a big fight in an ice cream shop. Make sure to try the homemade french fries. [$] *Average main: $6* ✉ *113 S. Cortez St., Downtown* ☎ *928/778–3658.*

$$$ AMERICAN 🍴 **Murphy's.** Mesquite-grilled meats and beer brewed exclusively for the restaurant are the specialties at this classy bar and grill, a sort of local institution set in a restored, polished-up 1890 mercantile building. The baby back ribs, fresh steamed clams, and fresh fried catfish are standouts. Businessfolk do their moving and shaking at lunchtime here, and the spirited bar stays open until 10 pm. [$] *Average main: $22* ✉ *201 N. Cortez St., Downtown* ☎ *928/445–4044* 🌐 *www.rgtaz.com.*

$$ AMERICAN 🍴 **The Palace Restaurant and Saloon.** Legend has it that the patrons who saved the Palace's ornately carved 1880s Brunswick bar from a Whiskey Row fire in 1900 continued drinking at it while the row burned across the street. Whatever the case, the bar remains the centerpiece of the beautifully restored turn-of-the-20th-century structure, with a high, pressed-tin ceiling. Steaks and chops are the stars here, but the grilled fish and hearty corn chowder are fine, too. [$] *Average main: $20* ✉ *120 S. Montezuma St., Downtown* ☎ *928/541–1996* 🌐 *www.historicpalace.com.*

$ AMERICAN 🍴 **Prescott Brewing Company.** Good beer, good food, good service, and good prices—for a casual meal, it's hard to beat this cheerful restaurant on the town square. In addition to burgers, chili, fish-and-chips, and British-style bangers and mash, vegetarian pot-pies and salads are on the menu. Ponderosa IPA and Lodgepole Light are two popular microbrews; fresh-baked beer bread comes with many entrées. [$] *Average main: $12* ✉ *130 W. Gurley St., Downtown* ☎ *928/771–2795* 🌐 *www.prescottbrewingcompany.com.*

$$$ AMERICAN 🍴 **The Rose Restaurant.** In a well-maintained Victorian home, the Rose serves inspired dishes that straddle nouvelle and Continental fare. Choose from entrées like chateaubriand, duck breast with sweet-potato cake and orange-chipotle sauce, or almond-crusted halibut as Sinatra music plays softly in the background. Desserts, especially the apple-caramel tart, are equally stellar. [$] *Average main: $28* ✉ *234 S. Cortez St., Downtown* ☎ *928/777–8308* 🌐 *www.theroserestaurant.com* ⏰ *Closed Mon. and Tues. No lunch.*

WHERE TO STAY

For expanded hotel reviews, visit Fodors.com.

$ HOTEL 🏨 **Hassayampa Inn.** Built in 1927 for early automobile travelers, the Hassayampa Inn oozes character. **Pros:** cental location; historic charm.

Cons: thin walls; small bathrooms. [$] *Rooms from: $119* ✉ *122 E. Gurley St., Downtown* ☎ *928/778–9434, 800/322–1927* 🌐 *www.hassayampainn.com* 🛏 *58 rooms, 10 suites* 🍴 *No meals.*

$ HOTEL 🏨 **Hotel St. Michael.** Don't expect serenity on the busiest corner of Courthouse Plaza, but for low rates and historic charm it's hard to beat this hotel in operation since 1900. **Pros:** excellent breakfast; has character. **Cons:** noise from bars until the wee hours; some rooms are worn. [$] *Rooms from: $79* ✉ *205 W. Gurley St., Downtown* ☎ *928/776–1999, 800/678–3757* 🌐 *www.stmichaelhotel.com* 🛏 *71 rooms* 🍴 *Breakfast.*

$ B&B/INN 🏨 **Hotel Vendome.** This World War I–era hostelry has seen miners, health seekers, and such celebrities as cowboy star Tom Mix walk through its doors. **Pros:** central location; historical; good value. **Cons:** creaky floors raise noise factor. [$] *Rooms from: $79* ✉ *230 S. Cortez St., Downtown* ☎ *928/776–0900* 🌐 *www.vendomehotel.com* 🛏 *16 rooms, 4 suites* 🍴 *Breakfast.*

$ HOTEL 🏨 **The Motor Lodge.** Impeccably renovated to reflect its heyday as a circa-1960 motor hotel, this boutique property delivers great value as well as a fun blast to the past. **Pros:** inexpensive; comfortable beds; cheery sixties decor. **Cons:** a long-ish walk to downtown. [$] *Rooms from: $79* ✉ *503 S. Montezuma St.* ☎ *928/717–0157* 🌐 *www.themotorlodge.com* 🛏 *12 rooms* 🍴 *No meals.*

$ RESORT 🏨 **Prescott Resort Conference Center and Casino.** On a hill on the outskirts of town, this upscale property run by the Yavapai tribe has views of the mountain ranges surrounding Prescott and the valley, although many guests hardly notice, so riveted are they by the poker machines and slots in Prescott's only hotel casino. **Pros:** nicely updated; comfortable rooms. **Cons:** large-scale property may feel impersonal; drive to town center. [$] *Rooms from: $119* ✉ *1500 AZ 69* ☎ *928/776–1666, 800/967–4637* 🌐 *www.prescottresort.com* 🛏 *161 rooms* 🍴 *No meals.*

NIGHTLIFE AND THE ARTS

NIGHTLIFE

Montezuma Street's Whiskey Row, off Courthouse Plaza, is nowhere near as wild as it was in its historic heyday, but most bars have live music—with no cover charge—on weekends.

Hassayampa Inn. This upscale, art nouveau piano bar is a quieter venue for conversation than the Whiskey Row bars across the square. ✉ *122 E. Gurley St., Downtown* ☎ *928/778–9434* 🌐 *www.hassayampainn.com.*

Jersey Lilly Saloon. Located above the Palace, the Jersey Lilly Saloon is a former brothel with live entertainment, a great patio, and a large dance floor. ✉ *116 S. Montezuma St., Downtown* ☎ *928/541–7854* 🌐 *www.jerseylillysaloon.com.*

Lyzzard's Lounge. The classic Brunswick bar at Lyzzard's Lounge was shipped from England via the Colorado River. ✉ *120 N. Cortez St., Downtown* ☎ *928/778–2244* 🌐 *www.lyzzards.com.*

Matt's Saloon. For live country-Western music and two-stepping on the dance floor, mosey on over to Matt's Saloon. ✉ *112 S. Montezuma St., Downtown* ☎ *928/776–2974* 🌐 *www.mattssaloon.com.*

Raven Cafe. A contemporary and attractive coffeehouse and bar, Raven Cafe serves excellent, organically grown food and doubles as a live-music venue on weekends. ⊠ *142 N. Cortez St., Downtown* ☎ *928/717–0009* ⊕ *www.ravencafe.com* ☯ *Closed Sun. evenings.*

THE ARTS

Cowboy Poets Gathering. In August the Cowboy Poets Gathering at Yavapai Community College brings together campfire bards from around the country. ⊕ *www.azcowboypoets.org.*

Frontier Days. The town had its first organized cowboy competition in 1888, and lays claim to having the world's oldest rodeo: the annual Frontier Days roundup, held on July 4th weekend at the Prescott Rodeo Grounds. ⊕ *www.worldsoldestrodeo.com.*

Prescott Bluegrass Festival. Prescott's popular Bluegrass Festival takes place downtown at Courthouse Plaza in June. ☎ *928/445–2000* ⊕ *www.prescottbluegrassfestival.com.*

Prescott Center for the Arts. Musicals and dramas, plays for children, and a concert series are put on by the Prescott Center for the Arts. The association's gallery also presents rotating exhibits by local, regional, and national artists. ⊠ *208 N. Marina St., Downtown* ☎ *928/445–3286* ⊕ *www.pfaa.net.*

Yavapai Symphony Association. Performances by the Phoenix and Flagstaff symphonies are hosted by the Yavapai Symphony Association; call ahead for schedules and venues. ⊠ *228 N. Alarcon St., Suite B, Downtown* ☎ *928/776–4255* ⊕ *www.yavapaisymphony.org.*

SHOPPING

Shops selling antiques and collectibles line Cortez Street, just north of Courthouse Plaza. You'll find fun stuff—especially Western kitsch—as well as some good buys on valuable pieces. Courthouse Plaza, especially along Montezuma Street, is lined with artist cooperatives, specialty stores, and gift shops. Many match those in Sedona for quality.

Arts Prescott Gallery. Be sure to check out Arts Prescott, a cooperative gallery of talented local artisans. ⊠ *134 S. Montezuma St., Downtown* ☎ *928/776–7717* ⊕ *www.artsprescott.com.*

Bella Home Furnishings. Vintage home furnishings and artwork are sold at this colorful store. ⊠ *115 W. Willis St., Downtown* ☎ *928/445–0208* ⊕ *www.bellahomefurnishings.com.*

Jenny Longhorn. There's upscale Western wear for women and men at Jenny Longhorn, as well as jewelry, artwork, and home furnishings. ⊠ *152 S. Montezuma St., Downtown* ☎ *928/778–1204* ⊕ *www.jennylonghorn.com.*

The Merchandise Mart Antique Mall. At 14,000 square feet, the Merchandise Mart Antique Mall houses the largest array of antiques dealers in town. ⊠ *205 N. Cortez St., Downtown* ☎ *928/776–1728.*

Van Gogh's Ear. Exquisite work by local and national artists is beautifully displayed at Van Gogh's Ear. ⊠ *156 S. Montezuma St., Downtown* ☎ *928/776–1080* ⊕ *www.vgegallery.com.*

SPORTS AND THE OUTDOORS

HIKING AND
CAMPING

Prescott National Forest-Bradshaw Ranger District. Contact the Bradshaw Ranger District for information about hiking trails and campgrounds in the Prescott National Forest south of town down to Horse Thief Basin. Campgrounds near Prescott are generally not crowded. ⊠ *2230 E. AZ 69, Hwy. 69* ☎ *928/443–8000* ⊕ *www.fs.usda.gov/prescott.*

Thumb Butte Loop Trail. A 2-mile trek on a paved yet steep loop, the Thumb Butte Loop Trail takes you 600 feet up near the crest of its namesake. The vistas are large, but you won't be alone on this popular trail. *Easy-Moderate.* ⊠ *Trailhead: Thumb Butte Rd., 3 miles west of Prescott following Gurley St., which turns into Thumb Butte.*

HORSEBACK
RIDING

Granite Mountain Stables. This company offers guided 1-, 2-, and 4-hour trail rides, as well as Western riding lessons, starting at $35. ⊠ *2400 Shane Dr., 7 miles northeast of Prescott* ☎ *928/771–9551* ⊕ *www. granitemountainstables.com.*

NORTHEAST ARIZONA

WELCOME TO NORTHEAST ARIZONA

TOP REASONS TO GO

★ **Drive the rim roads at Canyon de Chelly:** Visit one of the most spectacular natural wonders in the Southwest—it rivals the Grand Canyon for jaw-dropping views, albeit on a much smaller scale. It's a must for photography buffs.

★ **Go boating at Glen Canyon:** Get to know this stunning, mammoth reservoir by taking a boat out amid Lake Powell's towering cliffs.

★ **Explore Hubbell Trading Post:** Take the self-guided tour to experience the relationship between early traders and the Navajo.

★ **Shop for handmade crafts on the Hopi Mesas:** Pick up crafts by some of Arizona's leading Hopi artisans, who sustain their culture through continuous occupation of the ancient villages on these mesas.

★ **Take a jeep tour through Monument Valley:** See firsthand the landscape depicted in such iconic Western films as *Stagecoach* and *The Searchers*.

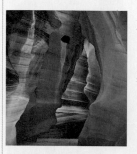

1 Navajo Nation East. Vastly underrated Canyon de Chelly National Monument offers some of the most spectacular panoramas in North America, and Window Rock is the governmental and cultural hub of the Navajo people.

2 The Hopi Mesas. An artistically rich and dramatically situated tribal land entirely surrounded by the Navajo Nation, the minimally developed Hopi Mesas rise above the high-desert floor, rife with trading posts and art studios selling fine weavings, jewelry, and crafts. Expect very few services, even relative to the rest of northeastern Arizona.

3 Navajo Nation West. Just 80 miles east of the Grand Canyon's South Rim, the bustling community of Tuba City anchors the western portions of the Navajo Nation and Hopi tribal lands—it's an excellent base for checking out the region's

painted-desert landscapes and Navajo trading posts, and for booking a tour of Hopi Mesa art studios.

4 Monument Valley. You've probably seen images of this Ancestral Puebloan stomping ground in everything from classic Western movies to Ansel Adams photos; you can explore this sweeping valley on a variety of Navajo-led

5

GETTING ORIENTED

Relatively few visitors experience the vast, sweeping northeast quadrant of Arizona, which comprises the Navajo and Hopi reservations, but efforts to spend a few days here are rewarded with stunning scenery and the chance to learn about some of the world's most vibrant indigenous communities. This is part of the West's great Four Corners Region, home to the underrated and spectacular Canyon de Chelly National Monument as well as the dramatic buttes and canyons of Monument Valley. The one portion of the area outside tribal lands is Page, the base for exploration of crystalline Lake Powell's 2,000 miles of shoreline.

tours. The region spans the Arizona and Utah borders, extending northeast from Kayenta, Arizona, nearly to Bluff, Utah.

5 Glen Canyon Dam and Lake Powell. The one section of northeastern Arizona not set on tribal lands is dominated by the nation's

second-largest man-made body of water, Lake Powell, and 710-foot-tall Glen Canyon Dam. It's a boating paradise, and the town of Page has the region's greatest number of hotels, restaurants, and bars.

NATIVE AMERICAN EXPERIENCE

With roots tracing back more than 12,000 years, Native Americans have lived in Arizona for hundreds of generations. Today, more than 250,000 people reside in sovereign nations within Arizona's state borders. Alongside ancient cliff dwellings and stunning natural monuments, the reality of the 21 tribes' cultures is best experienced on the reservations.

Above: Colorful beadwork is a popular adornment for clothing. Top right: Apache warrior Geronimo. Bottom right: Each Navajo community is known for specific rug colors and designs.

Arizona's tribes live on reservations that comprise more than a quarter of the state's lands. Though some tribes are similar to one another in certain aspects, most are culturally and spiritually distinct. Many tribes live on lands that enable them to derive income from natural resources, such as coal, but most rely upon tourism to some extent for revenue. Some tribes, such as the Navajo, open up much of their culture to visitors. Native American artisans are famed for handmade items popular with tourists, but casinos are increasingly vital to tribal economies. These often include dining, lodging, and entertainment as well.

RESERVATION REALITIES

For all the richness in culture, reservations are places where poverty is often prevalent. Some liken the tourist experience to that of visiting a developing country. Some panhandlers cluster at shopping centers and viewpoints. Visitors should respond to panhandlers with a polite but firm "no." If you wish to help, make a donation to a legitimate organization.

NAVAJO NATION AND HOPI RESERVATION RULES

Each reservation has its own government that dictates and enforces visitation rules.

Alcohol and Drugs: The possession and consumption of alcoholic beverages or illicit drugs is illegal on Hopi and Navajo land.

Camping: No open fires are allowed in reservation campgrounds; you must use grills or fireplaces. You may not gather firewood on the reservation—bring your own. Camping areas have quiet hours from 11 pm to 6 am. Pets must be kept on a leash or confined.

Hopi Shrines: Hopi spirituality is intertwined with daily life, and objects that seem ordinary to you may have deeper significance. If you see a collection of objects at or near the Hopi Mesas do not disturb them.

Permits and Permissions: No off-trail hiking, rock climbing, or other off-road travel is allowed unless you're accompanied by a local guide. A tribal permit is required for fishing. Violations of fish and game laws are punishable by heavy fines, imprisonment, or both.

Photography: Always ask permission before taking photos of locals. Even if no money is requested, consider offering a dollar or two to the person whose photo you've taken. The Navajo are very open about photographs; the Hopi don't allow photographs at all, including videos and tape recordings.

Religious Ceremonies: Should you see a ceremony in progress, look for posted signs indicating who is welcome or check with local shops or the village community. Unless you're specifically invited, stay out of kivas (ceremonial rooms) and stay on the periphery of dances or processions.

Respect for the Land: Do not wander through residential areas or disturb property. Do not disturb or remove animals, plants, rocks, petrified wood, or artifacts.

TRIBAL TIMELINE

950 The first settlements are built at Keet Seel.

1120–1210 Ancestral Puebloans occupy Wupatki Pueblo.

1150 The Hopi build the village of Old Orabi.

1250 Ancestral Puebloans are living at Keet Seel.

1276–1300 Tribes abandon northern Arizona during the "big drought."

1540–1542 Francisco Vásquez de Coronado leads an expedition in search of gold.

1863 Congress creates the Arizona Territory.

1864 Navajos forced to march 300 miles to Fort Sumner during the "Long Walk."

1868 The Navajo and the United States sign a treaty.

1886 Geronimo surrenders after evading U.S. troops for over a year.

1907 Arizona outlaws gambling.

1912 Arizona becomes 48th state.

1993 16 Arizona tribes sign gambling compacts with state.

5

SHOPPING TIPS

For big-ticket items, buy directly from the craftsmen themselves or a reputable dealer. Most products sold on the Hopi and Navajo reservations are authentic, but fakes are not unheard of.

If you're traveling in Navajoland, the Cameron Trading Post north of Flagstaff and the Hubbell Trading Post at Ganado are two spots where you can find exemplary items.

In Phoenix, the Heard Museum offers some of the finest Native American handicrafts at reasonable prices.

Trading posts are reliable, as are most roadside stands, which can offer some outstanding values, but be wary of solo vendors around parking lots.

If you're planning on shopping on the Hopi Reservation or elsewhere outside the Navajo trading posts, it's a good idea to carry cash, as not all vendors accept credit cards.

Proud craftsmen have individual logos or personal marks that are put into each piece. Authentic pieces will also indicate that the silver is sterling.

CULTURE

Heritage flavors: Native American food staples are well adapted to living in Arizona's arid lands. Corn is a universal ingredient—ground into flour to make tortillas, included in stew, or simply steamed and left on the cob. The fruits of the saguaro, prickly pear, and other cacti are commonly harvested by tribes as well as tepary beans grown from seeds handed down over generations. Fry bread—pillow-shape fried dough—is the basis of the popular Navajo taco, usually topped with beans, ground beef, and shredded cheese.

Song and dance: Ceremonies involving music and dance are central to Native American culture. Not every ceremony is accessible to visitors. Cultural centers and museums, such as the Heard in Phoenix, frequently hold powwows and other festivals that often celebrate more than one tribe.

Sacred spaces: The Hopi kivas are square- or circular-walled, mostly underground structures that are used exclusively for religious ceremonies, and often accessed by a ladder from above. Most kivas, including ruins, are off-limits to tourists. The hogan is the traditional dwelling of the Navajo and the door always faces east to welcome the rising sun. Though used as homes, hogans play an important part in Navajo spirituality and represent the universe and all things in it.

Arts and crafts: Many of the craftspeople on the reservations sell their wares, with specialties that include pottery, turquoise and sterling-silver jewelry, handwoven baskets, and Navajo wool rugs. As the Spanish ventured northward from Mexico in the late 1500s and early 1600s, they taught the Native Americans their silver-crafting skills, while tribes specializing in pottery and weaving carry on a tradition that began hundreds of years ago. Native beadwork traces its origins to trade beads from early explorers.

THE NAVAJO AND THE HOPI PEOPLE

Both the Navajo and Hopi base their cultures on the land, but they're very different from one another. The Navajo refer to themselves as the Diné (pronounced din- *eh*)—"the people"—and live on 17 million acres in Arizona, New Mexico, Utah, and Colorado, the largest Native American reservation in the country. The Hopi trace their roots to the original settlers of the area, whom they call the Hisatsinom, or "people of long ago"—they are also known as Anasazi, meaning both "ancient ones" and "ancient enemies." Hopi culture is more structured than that of the Navajo, and their religion has remained stronger and purer. For both tribes unemployment is high on the reservation, and poverty an ongoing concern.

The **Navajo** use few words and have a subtle sense of humor that can pass you by if you're not a good listener. They're taught not to talk too much, be loud, or show off. Eye contact is considered impolite; if you're conversing with Navajos, some may look down or away even though they're paying attention to you. Likewise, touching is seen differently; handshaking may be the only physical contact that you see. When shaking hands, a light touch is preferred to a firm grip, which is considered overbearing. Some of these traits are changing with younger generations, especially as technology and travel lead to less insular communities.

Although most Navajos speak English, listen closely to the language of the Diné. Stemming from the Athabascan family of languages, it's difficult for outsiders to learn because of subtle accentuation. The famous Marine Corps Navajo "code talkers" of World War II saved thousands of lives in the South Pacific by creating a code within their native Navajo language. A few code talkers still living today reside around Tuba City.

The **Hopi** Reservation is surrounded by the far larger Navajo Reservation and has begun to open up a bit more to visitors, who can now book guided tours of artists' studios. Over the years the proximity of the two tribes has been the cause of contention, often involving the assistance of the United States Government in settling land claims, yet the spirituality of the Hopi—"the peaceful ones"—is decidedly antiwar. In fact, Hopi mythology holds that a white-skinned people will save the tribe from its difficult life. Long ago, however, in the face of brutal treatment by whites, most Hopi became convinced that salvation would originate elsewhere.

ON THE GROUND

Visiting the Navajo: The Navajo are generally more relaxed than the Hopi with recording, but always ask for permission before taking someone's picture. If you aren't asked for a gratuity consider giving one anyway. Canyon De Chelly, Chaco Canyon, Monument Valley Navajo Tribal Park, and Navajo National Monument each offers a glimpse into both the past and present of Native American life and culture, including ruins of ancient dwellings and visitor centers with informative dioramas.

Visiting the Hopi: Recordings of any kind, including photographs, are prohibited in the Hopi Reservation. Central to the reservation are a handful of Hopi Mesas that contain two of the oldest continually inhabited villages in North America. Though Hopi villages offer visitors limited access, visitors can buy handicrafts directly from Hopi artisans at many shops or book a studio tour through the Moenkopi Legacy Inn in Tuba City.

(Above: A traditional Navajo hogan dwelling)

5

Updated
by Andrew
Collins

Northeast Arizona is a vast and magnificent land of lofty buttes, towering cliffs, and turquoise skies. Most of the land in the area belongs to the Navajo and Hopi, who adhere to ancient traditions based on spiritual values, kinship, and an affinity for nature. Life here has changed little during the last two centuries, and visiting this land can feel like traveling to a foreign country or going back in time.

In such towns as Tuba City and Window Rock it's not uncommon to hear the gliding vowels and soft consonants of the Navajo language, a tongue as different from Hopi as English is from Chinese. As you drive in the vicinity, tune your radio to 660 AM KTNN (⊕ *www.ktnnonline. com*), the Voice of the Navajo Nation since 1985. You'll quickly understand why the U.S. Marine Navajo "code talkers" communicating in their native tongue were able to devise a code within their language that was never broken by the Japanese.

In the Navajo Nation's approximate center sits the nearly 2,600-square-mile Hopi Reservation, a series of adobe villages built on high mesas overlooking the cultivated land. On Arizona's borders, where the Navajo Nation continues into Utah and New Mexico, the Navajo and Canyon de Chelly national monuments contain haunting cliff dwellings of ancient people who lived in the area some 1,500 years ago. Glen Canyon Dam, which abuts the northwestern corner of the reservation, holds back 185 miles of emerald waters known as Lake Powell.

Most of northeast Arizona is desert country, but it's far from boring: eerie and spectacular rock formations as colorful as desert sunsets highlight immense mesas, canyons, and cliffs; towering stands of ponderosa pine cover the Chuska Mountains to the north and east of Canyon de Chelly. Navajo Mountain to the north and west in Utah soars more than 10,000 feet, and the San Francisco Peaks climb to similar heights to the south and west by Flagstaff. According to the Navajo creation myth, these are two of the four mountainous boundaries of the sacred land where the Navajo first emerged from Earth's interior.

NORTHEAST ARIZONA PLANNER

WHEN TO GO

FESTIVALS AND EVENTS

JANUARY **Monument Valley Balloon Event.** Initiated in 2010, this well attended, mid-January, three-day weekend of hot-air ballooning at Monument Valley Navajo Tribal Park includes concerts, a family fun walk, a balloon "night glow" over the small airport at Goulding's Lodge, and a launch of more than 20 colorful balloons each morning. ☎ *435/727–5870* ⊕ *navajonationparks.org/htm/MVBallonEvent.html.*

AUGUST **Central Navajo Fair.** Several horse races, an arts-and-crafts market, the Miss Central Navajo Pageant, and several live-music performances are part of this weeklong celebration held in Chinle in late August. ☎ *928/797–7793* ⊕ *www.navajopeople.org.*

SEPTEMBER **Navajo Nation Annual Tribal Fair.** The world's largest Native American fair includes a rodeo, traditional Navajo music and dances, food booths and fry bread competitions, a Miss Navajo Nation Pageant, and an inter-tribal powwow during the first week of September after Labor Day, at Window Rock. ☎ *928/871–6478* ⊕ *www.navajonationfair.com.*

Suminangwa Harvest Festival. This celebration, which features Harvest and Butterfly social dances, is typically held the third weekend of September in the village of Sichomovi, between First Mesa and Second Mesa. ☎ *928/737–2754.*

PLANNING YOUR TIME

Northeastern Arizona encompasses an enormous area but relatively few key attractions, so it's best to use one or two primary communities (Page or Tuba City on the west side, Kayenta on the north, and Chinle or Window Rock on the east) as bases for day trips to outlying attractions.

If your time is limited, put Canyon de Chelly and Monument Valley at the top of your list—if you're ambitious, you could explore these two sites on consecutive days, spending the night in either Chinle, Kayenta, or in Monument Valley itself. Focus on the South Rim Drive at Canyon de Chelly, and in Monument Valley book a jeep tour with the highly respected Sacred Monument Tours. On travel days from one base community to another, plan a scenic drive, such as AZ 264 from Tuba City to Window Rock (don't miss the great crafts shopping at Second Mesa) or AZ 98 to U.S. 160 to U.S. 191 from Page to Chinle. Give yourself at least two days to get to know any one part of the region, and as much as a week to fully explore all of it.

■ **TIP→** Unlike the rest of Arizona (including the Hopi Reservation), the Navajo Reservation observes daylight saving time. Thus for half the year—mid-March to early November—it's an hour later on the Navajo Reservation than everywhere else in the state.

GETTING HERE AND AROUND

CAR TRAVEL

It's virtually impossible to see much of northeastern Arizona without a car—this is your best bet not only for getting here, but also for visiting attractions and communities throughout the region.

Many visitors see northeastern Arizona as part of a road-tripping adventure through the Four Corners Region, perhaps combining their visit with trips to the national parks of southern Utah and southwestern Colorado. This "en route" road-tripping strategy makes the most sense, especially given the region's stunningly scenic drives—the Navajo Nation has a terrific website (⊕ *navajoscenicroads.com*) geared toward road-tripping.

ROAD CONDI-
TIONS AND
SERVICES

Most of the 27,000 square miles of the Navajo Reservation and other areas of northeastern Arizona are off the beaten track. It's prudent to stay on the well-maintained paved thoroughfares. If you don't have the equipment for wilderness travel—including a four-wheel-drive vehicle and provisions—and lack back-country experience, stay off dirt roads unless they're signed and graded and the skies are clear. Be on the lookout for ominous rain clouds in summer or signs of snow in winter. Never drive into dips or low-lying areas during a heavy rainstorm, and be vigilant for both wildlife and livestock (the Navajo Nation is open range, meaning cattle roam freely). If you heed these simple precautions, car travel through the region is as safe as anywhere else in the Southwest. ■TIP➔ While driving around the Navajo Nation, tune in to 660 AM (KTNN) for local news and weather.

> ### HIKING IN NORTHEAST ARIZONA
>
> Some of the best hikes in this region are in Canyon de Chelly, up the streambed between the soaring vermilion, orange, and white sandstone cliffs, with the remains of the ancient Ancestral Puebloan communities frequently in view. The Navajo National Monument offers impressive hikes to Betatakin, a settlement dating back to AD 1250, and Keet Seel, which dates back as far as AD 950. Both are in alcoves at the base of gigantic overhanging cliffs. Remember, you can't hike or camp on private property or tribal land without a backcountry permit.

A tour of Navajo-Hopi country can involve driving significant distances between widely scattered communities, so a detailed, up-to-date road map is essential (relying on smartphone GPS isn't a great idea, as cell coverage is spotty). Gas stations are in all the region's major towns, but distances between them can be considerable—it's best to service your vehicle before venturing into the Navajo and Hopi reservations, and to carry emergency equipment and supplies.

RESTAURANTS

Northeastern Arizona is a vast area with small hamlets and towns scattered miles apart, and there are few stores or restaurants. With the exception of Page, which has slightly more culinary variety, the region's restaurants mostly serve basic but tasty Native American, Southwestern, and frontier-inspired American (steaks, burgers) cuisine. Navajo and Hopi favorites include mutton stew, Hopi *piki* (paper-thin, blue-corn bread), and Navajo fry bread. *Prices in the reviews are the average cost of a main course at dinner or, if dinner isn't served, at lunch.*

HOTELS

Page has the area's greatest concentration of lodgings, most of them fairly standard chain motels and hotels, but this base camp for exploring Lake Powell also has a few B&Bs as well as houseboat rentals, and the area is also home to the ultraluxurious Amangiri resort. You'll find a handful of well-maintained chains in the Navajo Nation, mostly in Kayenta, Chinle, Tuba City, and Window Rock. Additionally, Navajo's View Hotel in Monument Valley, and the Hopi's Moenkopi Legacy Inn in Tuba City are beautifully designed, contemporary hotels. This is a popular area for both tent and RV camping—you can obtain a list of campgrounds from the Page/Lake Powell Tourism Bureau and the Navajo Nation Tourism Office. *Prices in the reviews are the lowest cost of a standard double room in high season. For expanded reviews, facilities, and current deals, visit Fodors.com.*

NAVAJO NATION EAST

Land has always been central to the history of the Navajo people: it's embedded in their very name. The Tewa were the first to call them *Navahu*, which means "large area of cultivated land." But according to the Navajo creation myth, they were given the name *ni'hookaa diyan diné*—"holy earth people"—by their creators. Today tribal members call themselves the Diné (pronounced din-*eh*)—"the people." The eastern portion of the Arizona Navajo Nation (in Navajo, *diné bikéyah*) is a dry but often surprisingly green land, especially in the vicinity of the aptly named Beautiful Valley, south of Canyon de Chelly along U.S. 191. A landscape of rolling hills, wide arroyos, and small canyons, the area is dotted with traditional Navajo hogans, sheepfolds, cattle tanks, and wood racks. The region's easternmost portion is marked by tall mountains and towering sandstone cliffs cut by primitive roads that are generally accessible only on horseback or with four-wheel-drive vehicles.

ESSENTIALS

Visitor Information Navajo Nation Tourism Office ☎ *928/871–6436* ⊕ *www. discovernavajo.com.*

WINDOW ROCK

192 miles from Flagstaff; 26 miles from Gallup, New Mexico.

Named for the immense arch-shape "window" in a massive sandstone ridge above the city, Window Rock is the capital of the Navajo Nation and the center of its tribal government. With a population of around 3,050, this community serves as the business and social center for Navajo families throughout the reservation. Window Rock is a good place to stop for food, supplies, and gas.

GETTING HERE AND AROUND

From Flagstaff follow Interstate 40 east for 160 miles, then Highway 12 north. From Gallup, New Mexico follow U.S. 491 north and then NM 264 west (which becomes AZ 264). Window Rock lies on the border between the two states, with most businesses on the Arizona side.

EXPLORING

Navajo Nation Council Chambers. The murals on the walls of this handsome structure, built to resemble a large ceremonial hogan, depict scenes from the history of the tribe, and the bell beside the entrance was a gift to the tribe by the Santa Fe Railroad to commemorate the thousands of Navajos who built the railroad. Visitors can observe sessions of the council, where 88 delegates representing 110 reservation chapters meet on the third Monday of January, April, July, and October. Turn east off Indian Highway 12, about 0.5 mile north of AZ 264, to reach the Council Chambers. Nearby **Window Rock Navajo Tribal Park & Veteran's Memorial** is a memorial park honoring Navajo veterans, including the famous World War II code talkers. ⊠ *AZ 264* ☎ *928/871–6417* ⊕ *discovernavajo.com/council.html* ⊗ *Weekdays 8–5; call for weekend hrs.*

FAMILY **Navajo Nation Fair.** Many all-Indian rodeos are held near the center of downtown at the fairgrounds. The community hosts the annual multiday Fourth of July celebration with a major rodeo, ceremonial dances, and a parade. The Navajo Nation Tribal Fair, much like a traditional state fair, is held in early September. It offers standard county-fair rides, midway booths, contests, powwow competitions, and an all-Indian rodeo. ⊠ *AZ 264* ☎ *928/871–7941* ⊕ *www.navajonationfair.com* ⊠ *$5.*

FAMILY **Navajo Nation Museum.** Located on the grounds of the former Tse Bonito Park off AZ 264, this museum is devoted to the art, culture, and history of the Navajo people and has an excellent library on the Navajo Nation. Each season brings new exhibitions by Native artists call for a list of shows. There are also permanent exhibits on the Long Walk, during which the Navajo were tragically and temporarily relocated to Fort Sumner, New Mexico; and on culture and philosophies of the Navajo people. In the same building is the Navajo Nation Visitor Center, a great resource for all sorts of information on reservation activities. ⊠ *Hwy. 264 and Loop Rd., next to Quality Inn Navajo Nation* ☎ *928/871–7941* ⊕ *www.navajonationmuseum.org* ⊠ *Free* ⊗ *Mon. and Sat. 8–5, Tues.–Fri. 8–8.*

FAMILY **The Navajo Nation Zoological & Botanical Park.** Amid the sandstone monoliths on the border between Arizona and New Mexico, the Navajo Nation Zoological & Botanical Park displays about 50 species of domestic and wild animals, birds, and amphibians that figure in Navajo legends, as well as examples of plants used by traditional people. Most of the animals here were brought in as orphans or after sustaining injuries—they include black bears, mountain lions, Mexican gray wolves, bobcats, cougars, golden eagles, Gila monsters, and prairie rattlesnakes. It's the nation's only Native American–owned zoo. ⊠ *AZ 264, just east of Quality Inn; shares parking lot with Navajo Nation Museum* ☎ *928/871–6574* ⊕ *www.navajozoo.org* ⊠ *Free* ⊗ *Mon.–Sat. 10–4:30.*

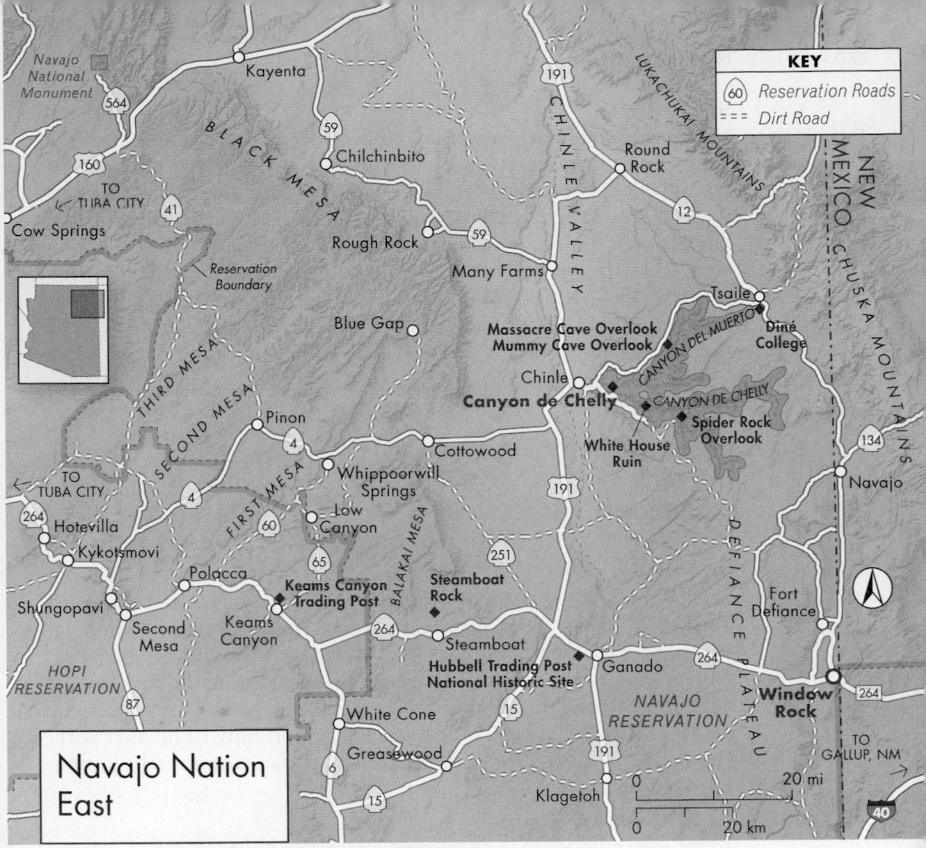

Navajo Nation East

WHERE TO EAT AND STAY

For expanded hotel reviews, visit Fodors.com.

$ AMERICAN 🍴 **Blake's Lotaburger.** The westernmost branch of a beloved New Mexico chain of old-school burger joints is technically in the Land of Enchantment (i.e. New Mexico) but just a few hundred feet over the Arizona state line, and within walking distance of the Quality Inn and Window Rock museums. Blake's began in 1952 in Albuquerque and enjoys a cult following for its Angus beef green-chile cheeseburgers, seasoned fries, breakfast burritos, and cherry milk shakes. [$] *Average main: $5* ✉ *NM 264, at Alma Dr., Gallup, New Mexico* ☎ *505/371–5400* 🌐 *www.lotaburger.com.*

$ HOTEL 🏨 **Quality Inn Navajo Nation Capital.** Rooms in this two-story beam-and-stucco hotel are decorated with an earthy Navajo-inspired palette that complements the rustic pine furniture. **Pros:** within walking distance of Navajo Museum; decent restaurant; rooms are bright and attractively furnished. **Cons:** on busy road with dull setting. [$] *Rooms from: $89* ✉ *48 W. AZ 264, at Hwy. 12* ☎ *928/871–4108* 🌐 *www.qualityinnwindowrock.com* 🛏 *56 rooms* 🍽 *Breakfast.*

SHOPPING

Fodor's Choice ★ **Navajo Arts and Crafts Enterprises.** This outlet of the Navajo Arts and Crafts Enterprises stocks tribal art purchased from craftspeople across Navajo Nation, including stunning silverwork, traditional Navajo dolls, pottery, and rugs. Local artisans are occasionally at work here. It's one of seven outlets, with four others in northeastern Arizona (Cameron, Chinle, Kayenta, Navajo National Monument), and two in northwestern New Mexico (Alamo and Shiprock). Major credit cards are accepted. ⊠ *AZ 264 at Hwy. 12, next to Quality Inn Navajo Nation Capital* ☎ *928/871–4090, 888/831–7384* ⊕ *www.gonavajo.com.*

CANYON DE CHELLY

30 miles west of Window Rock on AZ 264, then 25 miles north on U.S. 191.

GETTING HERE AND AROUND

U.S. 191 runs north–south through Chinle, the closest town to the Canyon de Chelly entrance.

Guided tours allow visits directly into the canyons, not just the park drives high above them; jeep tours even have the option of camping overnight. Each kind of tour has its pros and cons: you'll cover the most ground in a jeep; horseback trips get you close to one of the park's most notable geological formations, Spider Rock; and guided walks provide the most leisurely pace and an excellent opportunity to interact with your guide and ask questions. You can also plan custom treks lasting up to a week.

PLANNING YOUR TIME

To get even a basic sense of the park's scope and history, spend at least a full day here. If time is short, the best strategy is to visit the visitor center, where you can watch an informative 23-minute video about the canyons, and then drive the most magnificent of the two park roads, South Rim Drive. You could, if you're ambitious, drive both park roads in one day, but it's better to set aside a second day for North Rim Drive, or take the North Rim Drive as an alternative route to Kayenta, by way of Tsaile. From the different overlooks along the park roads you'll be treated to amazing photo ops of the valley floors below, and you can also access certain dwellings. For a more in-depth experience, book one of the guided hiking, jeep, or horseback tours into the canyon.

Both Canyon de Chelly and Canyon del Muerto have a paved rim drive with turnoffs and parking areas. Each drive takes a minimum of two hours—allow more if you plan to hike to White House Ruin, picnic, or spend time photographing the sites. Overlooks along the rim drives provide incredible views of the canyon; be sure to stay on trails and away from the canyon edge, and to control children and pets at all times.

The visitor center has exhibits on the history of the cliff dwellers and provides information on scheduled hikes, tours, and National Park Service programs offered throughout the summer months.

ESSENTIALS

Visitor Information Canyon de Chelly Visitor Center ✉ *Indian Hwy. 7, 3 miles east of U.S. 191, Chinle* ☎ *928/674–5500* ⊕ *www.nps.gov/cach.*

EXPLORING

Fodor'sChoice
★

Canyon de Chelly. Home to Ancestral Puebloans from AD 350 to 1300, the nearly 84,000-acre Canyon de Chelly (pronounced d'*shay*) is one of the most spectacular natural wonders in the Southwest. On a smaller scale, it rivals the Grand Canyon for beauty. Its main gorges—the 26-mile-long Canyon de Chelly ("canyon in the rock") and the adjoining 35-mile-long Canyon del Muerto ("canyon of the dead")—comprise sheer, heavily eroded sandstone walls that rise to 1,100 feet over dramatic valleys. Ancient pictographs and petroglyphs decorate some of the cliffs, and within the canyon complex there are more than 7,000 archaeological sites. Stone walls rise hundreds of feet above streams, hogans, tilled fields, and sheep-grazing lands.

You can view prehistoric sites near the base of cliffs and perched on high, sheltering ledges, some of which you can access from the park's two main drives along the canyon rims. The dwellings and cultivated fields of the present-day Navajo lie in the flatlands between the cliffs, and those who inhabit the canyon today farm much the way their ancestors did. Most residents leave the canyon in winter but return in early spring to farm.

Canyon de Chelly's South Rim Drive (36 miles round-trip with seven overlooks) starts at the visitor center and ends at **Spider Rock Overlook,** where cliffs plunge nearly 1,000 feet to the canyon floor. The view here is of two pinnacles, Speaking Rock and Spider Rock. Other highlights on the South Rim Drive are Junction Overlook, where Canyon del Muerto joins Canyon de Chelly; White House Overlook, from which a 2.5-mile round-trip trail leads to the **White House Ruin,** with remains of nearly 60 rooms and several kivas; and Sliding House Overlook, where you can see dwellings on a narrow, sloped ledge across the canyon. The carved and sometimes narrow trail down the canyon side to White House Ruin is the only access into Canyon de Chelly without a guide—but if you have a fear of heights, this may not be the hike for you.

The only slightly less breathtaking **North Rim Drive** (34 miles round-trip with four overlooks) of Canyon del Muerto also begins at the visitor center and continues northeast on Indian Highway 64 toward the town of Tsaile. Major stops include Antelope House Overlook, a large site named for the animals painted on an adjacent cliff; **Mummy Cave Overlook,** where two mummies were found inside a remarkably unspoiled pueblo dwelling; and **Massacre Cave Overlook,** which marks the spot where an estimated 115 Navajo were killed by the Spanish in 1805. (The rock walls of the cave are still pockmarked by the Spaniards' ricocheting bullets.) ✉ *Indian Hwy. 7, 3 miles east of U.S. 191, Chinle* ☎ *928/674–5500 visitor center* ⊕ *www.nps.gov/cach* ✑ *Free* ☉ *Daily 8–5.*

Chuska Mountains. To the north of Tsaile are the impressive Chuska Mountains, covered with sprawling stands of ponderosa pine. There are no established hiking trails in the Chuska Mountains, but up-to-date

CLOSE UP

Who Were the Cliff Dwellers?

The first inhabitants of the canyons arrived more than 2,000 years ago—anthropologists call them the basket makers, because baskets were the predominant artifacts they left behind. By AD 750, however, the basket makers had disappeared—their reason for leaving the region is unknown, but some speculate they were forced to leave because of encroaching cultures or climatic changes—and they were replaced by Pueblo tribes who constructed stone cliff dwellings. The departure of the Pueblo people around AD 1300 is widely believed to have resulted from changing climatic conditions, soil erosion, dwindling local resources, disease, and internal conflict. Present-day Hopi see these people as their ancestors. Beginning around AD 780, Hopi farmers settled here, followed by the Navajo around 1300. Evidence indicates that the Navajo migrated from far northern Canada, although the timing of their initial voyage south isn't clear. Despite evidence to the contrary, most Navajos hold that their people have always lived here and that the Diné passed through three previous underworlds before emerging into this, the fourth or Glittering World.

hiking information and backcountry-use permits (rarely granted if a Navajo guide does not accompany the trip) can be obtained through the Navajo Nation. ✉ *Navajo Nation Parks and Recreation Department, Bldg. 36A, E. AZ 264, Window Rock* ☎ *928/871–6647* 🌐 *www.navajonationparks.org.*

WHERE TO EAT

Chinle is the closest town to Canyon de Chelly. There are lodgings with basic restaurants, as well as a supermarket and a campground. Be aware that you may be approached by panhandlers in the grocery store parking lot.

$ AMERICAN 🍴 **Garcia's Restaurant.** The lobby restaurant at Chinle's Holiday Inn is low-key, a bit lacking in natural light, and rather ordinary; but it is one of the area's only non-fast-food dining options. It's a reliable—if unspectacular—choice for dinner. You can count on well-prepared Navajo and American fare, such as mutton stew with fry bread and honey. They also sell a box lunch. [$] *Average main: $13* ✉ *Indian Hwy. 7, Chinle* ☎ *928/674–5000* 🌐 *www.holidayinn.com* 🕒 *Limited hours mid-Nov.–Mar.; call ahead.*

$ AMERICAN 🍴 **The Junction.** Across the parking lot from the Best Western Canyon de Chelly Inn, this sun-filled, airy dining room with cream-color walls, large windows, a long granite counter, and a mix of attractive booths and tables has a cheerier feel than any other restaurant in town. The kitchen turns out pretty tasty American, Southwestern, and Chinese food, too. Specialties include posole stew, chicken-fried steak, and sheepherder's sandwiches (consisting of a tortilla or fry bread stuffed with steak, Swiss cheese, grilled onions, chiles, and tomatoes). A small kiosk by the front door sells gifts and jewelry. [$] *Average main: $10* ✉ *100 Main St., Chinle* ☎ *928/674–5875* 🌐 *www.bestwestern.com.*

WHERE TO STAY

For expanded hotel reviews, visit Fodors.com.

$ · HOTEL · **Best Western Canyon de Chelly Inn.** This two-story motel about 3 miles from Canyon de Chelly but close to the junction with U.S. 191 has cheerful rooms with modern, no-frills oak furnishings. **Pros:** usually slightly less expensive than the Holiday Inn; fun retro-motel exterior; indoor pool with hot tub and sauna is open until 9 pm. **Cons:** not within walking distance of the park; ordinary rooms. $ *Rooms from: $119 ⊠ 100 Main St., Chinle ☎ 928/674–5875, 800/780–7234 ⊕ www. bestwestern.com ⤳ 104 rooms.*

$$ · HOTEL · **Holiday Inn Canyon de Chelly.** Once Garcia's Trading Post, this hotel near Canyon de Chelly is less generic than you might expect: the exterior is territorial fort in style, although the rooms are predictably pastel and contemporary. **Pros:** attractive adobe-style building; nice pool and gym; a short drive from park entrance. **Cons:** room decor not especially memorable; dull roadside setting; priciest option in town. $ *Rooms from: $133 ⊠ Indian Hwy. 7, Chinle ☎ 928/674–5000, 888/465–4329 ⊕ www.holidayinn.com ⤳ 108 rooms* ⫶ *No meals.*

$ · HOTEL · FAMILY · **Thunderbird Lodge.** In an ideal location within the national monument's borders, this pleasant, if basic establishment has stone-and-adobe units that match the site's original 1896 trading post. **Pros:** only hotel inside the actual park borders; atmospheric architecture and decor is steeped in history; tours offered right from hotel. **Cons:** rustic decor; no high-speed Internet; cell phone service is spotty. $ *Rooms from: $127 ⊠ Indian Hwy. 7, Chinle ☎ 928/674–5841, 800/679–2473 ⊕ www.tbirdlodge.com ⤳ 73 rooms* ⫶ *No meals.*

SHOPPING

Navajo Arts and Crafts Enterprises. This branch of the respected Navajo gallery carries an excellent selection of locally made crafts and works of art. ⊠ *AZ 64 at U.S. 191, Chinle ☎ 928/328–8116 ⊕ www.gonavajo. com.*

SPORTS AND THE OUTDOORS

HIKING

From about mid-April through late September, free three-hour ranger hikes depart most mornings from the Canyon de Chelly Visitor Center—call ahead for times and to reserve a spot. Year-round, you can book a Navajo guide–led day hike or overnight camping trip through Ancient Canyon Tours. Some trails are strenuous and steep; others are easy or moderate. Those with health concerns or a fear of heights should proceed with caution.

Only one hike within Canyon de Chelly National Monument—the **White House Ruin Trail** on the South Rim Drive—can be undertaken without an authorized guide. The trail starts near White House Overlook and runs along sheer walls that drop about 550 feet. If you have concerns about heights, be aware that the path gets narrow and requires careful footing. The hike is 2½ miles round-trip, and hikers should carry their own drinking water.

Ancient Canyon Tours. This Navajo-owned tour company offers both day-hiking and overnight-camping excursions into the park's two canyons,

de Chelly and del Muerto. The moderately difficult day hikes venture into some of the park's most spectacular backcountry and can last from three to four hours, if covering the lower parts of the canyons; and to as long as nine hours for excursions into the higher terrain. The cost is $25 per hour (three-hour minimum) for up to 15 hikers; there are additional $30 per-guide and $30 per-night land-use fees for overnight trips. ⊠ *Chinle* ☎ *928/380–1563.*

HORSEBACK RIDING

Fodor'sChoice
★
Totsonii Ranch. Thirteen miles from the visitor center at the end of the paved portion of South Rim Drive (follow the signs from there), this ranch offers several types of horseback tours into different parts of Canyon de Chelly: Canyon Rim (two hours), Three Turkey Ruins (four hours), Spider Rock (four hours), White House Ruins (six hours), Canyon de Chelly overview (eight hours), and one- and two-night treks. Some of these trips are geared only toward skilled adult riders, such as the Canyon Rim trips, which encounter steep terrain and offer amazing views. Spider Rock is a great choice for virtually any skill level, and can be done in a half day—the ride leads right to the base of this 800-foot iconic pillar. Per person rates range from $63 to $250 for day trips, and $350 (one night) to $515 (two nights) for overnight adventures. ⊠ *South Rim Dr., Chinle* ☎ *928/551–0109* ⊕ *www.totsoniiranch.com.*

JEEP TOURS

Canyon de Chelly Tours. Book a private jeep tour into Canyon de Chelly or choose from group tours, overnight camping in the canyon, late-afternoon and evening tours, and bus tours along South Rim Drive. Entertainment such as storytellers, music, and Navajo legends can be arranged with advance reservation. Rates begin at $82 per person for three-hour tours, or $55 per hour per vehicle if you use your own SUV. (There's roughly a 10% discount if you pay in cash.) ⊠ *Chinle* ☎ *928/674–5433* ⊕ *www.canyondechellytours.com.*

Thunderbird Lodge Canyon Tours. Treks in six-wheel-drive vehicles are available from late spring to late fall. Half-day tours cost about $45; all-day tours, which include lunch, are around $85. ⊠ *Indian Hwy. 7, Chinle* ☎ *928/674–5841, 800/679–2473* ⊕ *www.tbirdlodge.com.*

WALKING TOURS

Footpath Journeys. Hoof it into Canyon de Chelly on a scheduled or custom four- to seven-day trek; prices start at $800 per person, not including food. ⊠ *Chinle* ☎ *928/724–3366* ⊕ *www.footpathjourneys.com.*

HUBBELL TRADING POST NATIONAL HISTORIC SITE

40 miles south of Canyon de Chelly, off AZ 264; 30 miles west of Window Rock.

GETTING HERE AND AROUND

The site is just off AZ 264, well marked from the road, and easily explored on foot once you arrive. The National Park Service Visitor Center exhibits illustrate the post's history, and you can take a self-guided tour of the grounds and Hubbell home, and visit the Hubbell Trading Post, which contains a fine display of Native American artistry.

Best Northeast Arizona Campgrounds

Cottonwood Campground. This sometimes cramped and noisy campground has RV and tent sites right in Canyon de Chelly. ⊠ *Indian Hwy. 7 near Canyon de Chelly Visitor Center, Chinle* ☎ *928/674–5500* ⊕ *www.nps. gov/cach.*

Goulding's Good Sam Campground. Views of Monument Valley are the draw at this clean, modern campground. ⊠ *Off U.S. 163, 24 miles north of Kayenta, Monument Valley Navajo Tribal Park* ☎ *435/727–3231* ⊕ *www. gouldings.com.*

Mitten View Campground. Sites are crowded together, but most offer spectacular views of Monument Valley. ⊠ *Monument Valley Navajo Tribal Park, near visitor center, off U.S. 163, 24 miles north of Kayenta* ☎ *435/727–5870* ⊕ *www. navajonationparks.org.*

Navajo National Monument Campground. Beautiful and serene with no fee, this campground has no hookups, and open fires aren't allowed (you must use camp stoves). ⊠ *AZ 564, Shonto* ☎ *928/672–2700* ⊕ *www.nps. gov/nava.*

Spider Rock Campground. Cordial Navajo owner Howard Smith makes everyone feel comfortable at this informal campground nestled in low piñons within a few hundred yards of the canyon. ⊠ *Indian Hwy. 7, 10 miles east of Canyon de Chelly Visitor Center* ☎ *928/674–8261* ⊕ *www. spiderrockcampground.com.*

Wahweap/Lake Powell RV & Campground. This campground in the Wahweap Marina complex, which is run by the National Park Service concessionaire, has views of the lake and serves both RVers and tent campers. ⊠ *U.S. 89, 5 miles north of Page near shore of Lake Powell, Wahweap* ☎ *888/896–3829* ⊕ *www.lakepowell. com.*

The visitor center has a fairly comprehensive bookstore specializing in Navajo history, art, and culture; local weavers often demonstrate their craft on-site.

EXPLORING

Fodor'sChoice
★

Hubbell Trading Post National Historic Site. John Lorenzo Hubbell, a merchant and friend of the Navajo, established this trading post in 1876. Hubbell taught, translated letters, settled family quarrels, and explained government policy to the Navajo, and during an 1886 smallpox epidemic he turned his home into a hospital and ministered to the sick and dying. He died in 1930, and is buried near the trading post.

The Hubbell Trading Post National Historic Site is famous for "Ganado red" Navajo rugs, which are sold at the store here. Rugs can cost anywhere from $100 to more than $30,000, but considering the quality and time that goes into weaving each one, the prices are quite reasonable. It's hard to resist the beautiful designs and colors, and it's a pleasure just to browse around this rustic spot, where Navajo artists frequently show their work. Documents of authenticity are provided for all works. Note: when photographing weavers, ask permission first. They expect a few dollars in return. ⊠ *AZ 264, 1 mile west of U.S. 191, Ganado*

☎ *928/755–3475* ⊕ *www.nps.gov/hutr* ✉ *Free, $2 to tour Hubbell home* ⊙ *May–Sept., daily 8–6; Oct.–Apr., daily 8–5.*

EN
ROUTE
Steamboat Rock. About 20 miles west of Hubbell Trading Post on AZ 264 is an immense, jutting peninsula of stone that resembles an early steamboat, complete with a geologically formed waterline. At Steamboat Rock you are only 5 miles from the eastern boundary of the Hopi Reservation.

THE HOPI MESAS

The Hopi occupy 12 villages in regions referred to as First Mesa, Second Mesa, and Third Mesa. Although these areas have similar languages and traditions, each has its own individual features. Generations of Hopitu, "the peaceful people," much like their Puebloan ancestors, have lived in these largely agrarian settlements of stone-and-adobe houses, which blend in with the earth so well that they appear to be natural formations. Television antennae, satellite dishes, and automobiles notwithstanding, these Hopi villages still exude the air of another time.

Descendants of the ancient Hisatsinom, the Hopi number about 12,000 people today. Their culture can be traced back more than 2,000 years, making them one of the oldest known tribes in North America. They successfully developed "dry farming," and grow many kinds of vegetables and corn (called maize) as their basic food—in fact the Hopi are often called the "corn people." They incorporate nature's cycles into most of their religious rituals. In the celebrated Snake Dance ceremony, dancers carry venomous snakes in their mouths to appease the gods and to bring rain. In addition to farming the land, the Hopi create fine pottery and basketwork and excel in wood carving of kachina dolls.

VISITOR INFORMATION

Hopi Tribe. Staff at the Hopi Tribe offices can answer basic questions and provide guidance for visiting the Hopi Mesas. ☎ *928/734–3104* ⊕ *www.hopi-nsn.gov.*

Moenkopi Legacy Inn. Although the Hopi Tribe offices can provide basic information, the staff at the Moenkopi Legacy Inn in Tuba City has become the tribe's de facto visitor information center and best overall tourism resource; they can also arrange tours led by Hopi-certified guides. ☎ *928/283–4500* ⊕ *www.experiencehopi.com.*

KEAMS CANYON TRADING POST

43 miles west of Hubbell Trading Post on AZ 264.

The trading post established by Thomas Keam in 1875 to do business with local tribes is now the area's main tourist attraction, offering a primitive campground, restaurant, service station, and shopping center, all set in a dramatic rocky canyon. An administrative center for the Bureau of Indian Affairs, Keams Canyon also has a number of government buildings. A road, accessible by passenger car, winds northeast 3 miles into the 8-mile wooded canyon. At **Inscription Rock**, about 2

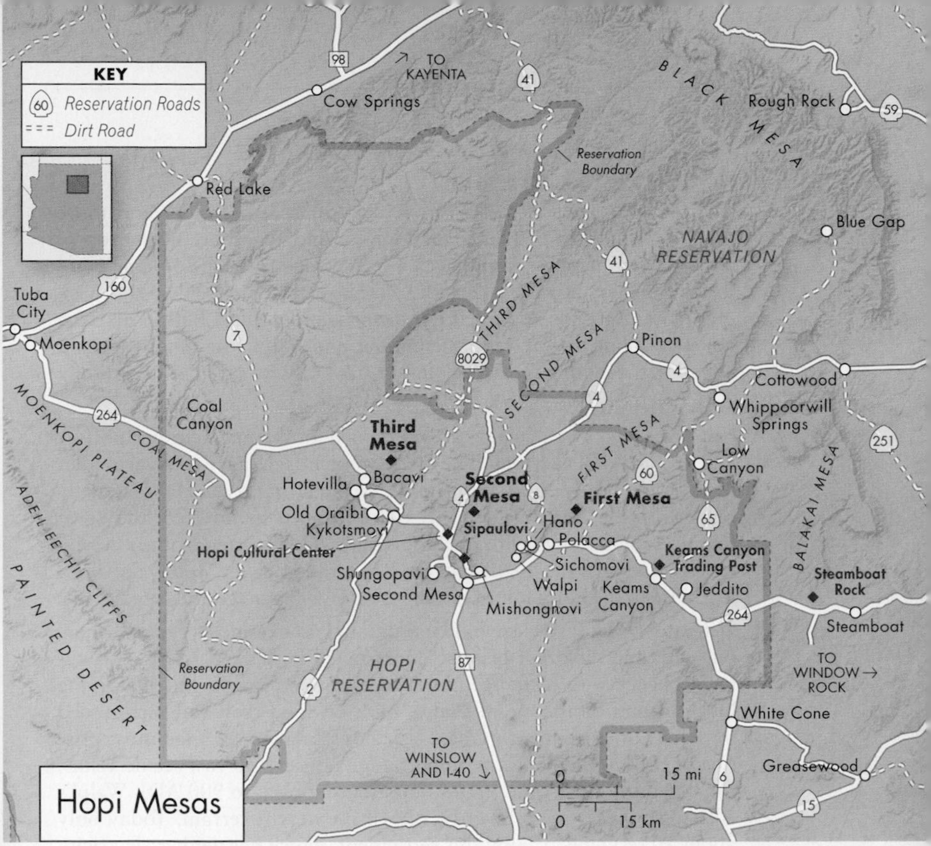
KEY
60 Reservation Roads
Dirt Road
98
TO KAYENTA
41
Cow Springs
BLACK MESA
Rough Rock
59
Reservation Boundary
Red Lake
Blue Gap
NAVAJO RESERVATION
41
THIRD MESA
Tuba City
160
7
Moenkopi
8029
SECOND MESA
Pinon
4
Cottowood
MOENKOPI PLATEAU
264
Coal Canyon
4
Whippoorwill Springs
COAL MESA
Third Mesa
FIRST MESA
Low Canyon
251
BALAKAI MESA
ADEII EECHII CLIFFS
Hotevilla
Bacavi
Second Mesa
8
60
Old Oraibi
First Mesa
Kykotsmovi
Hano
65
Sipaulovi
Polacca
Hopi Cultural Center
Keams Canyon Trading Post
Steamboat Rock
Sichomovi
Shungopavi
Walpi
Keams Canyon
Jeddito
Second Mesa
Mishongnovi
264
Steamboat
PAINTED DESERT
87
TO WINDOW ROCK
Reservation Boundary
HOPI RESERVATION
2
White Cone
TO WINSLOW AND I-40
0
15 mi
6
Greasewood
0
15 km
15
Hopi Mesas

miles down the road, frontiersman Kit Carson engraved his name in stone. There are several picnic spots in the canyon.

GETTING HERE AND AROUND

Keams Canyon is along AZ 264, the main route between Window Rock and Tuba City.

WHERE TO EAT

$ AMERICAN 🍴 **Keams Canyon Restaurant.** This typical no-frills roadside diner with Formica tabletops offers both American and Native American dishes, including Navajo tacos heaped with ground beef, chili, beans, lettuce, and grated cheese. Daily specials, offered at $1 to $2 off the regular price, may include anything from barbecued ribs to lamb chops to crab legs. There's an ice-cream stand in the same building. Come early because both the diner and ice cream counter close nightly around 8. [$] *Average main: $8* ✉ *Keams Canyon Shopping Center, AZ 264, Keams Canyon* ☎ *928/738–2296* 🕒 *Closed Sun. No dinner Sat.*

SHOPPING

McGee's Indian Art. Head upstairs from the Keams Canyon Restaurant to peruse first-rate, high-quality Hopi crafts such as handcrafted jewelry, pottery, beautiful carvings, basketry, and artwork. ✉ *AZ 264, Keams Canyon* ☎ *928/738–2295* 🌐 *www.hopiart.com.*

FIRST MESA

11 miles west of Keams Canyon, on AZ 264.

GETTING HERE AND AROUND

The first village that you approach is Polacca; the older and more impressive villages of Hano, Sichomovi, and Walpi are at the top of the sweeping mesa. From Polacca a paved road (off AZ 264) angles up to a parking lot near the village of Sichomovi, and to the Punsi Hall Visitor Center. ■TIP→ **You must get permission at Punsi Hall to take the guided walking tour of Hano, Sichomovi, and Walpi. Tour times vary; call ahead to the Moenkopi Legacy Inn in Tuba City for more information.**

EXPLORING

Fodor's Choice
★

First Mesa. First Mesa villages are renowned for their polychrome pottery and kachina-doll carvings. The older Hopi villages have structures built of rock and adobe mortar in simple architectural style. **Hano** actually belongs to the Tewa, a New Mexico Pueblo tribe. In 1696 the Tewa Indians sought refuge with the Hopi on First Mesa after an unsuccessful rebellion against the Spanish in the Rio Grande Valley. Today the Tewa live close to the Hopi but maintain their own language and ceremonies.

Sichomovi is built so close to Hano that only the residents can tell where one ends and the other begins. Constructed in the mid-1600s, this village is believed to have been built to ease overcrowding at Walpi, the highest point on the mesa. **Walpi,** built on solid rock and surrounded by steep cliffs, frequently hosts ceremonial dances. It's the most pristine of the Hopi villages, with cliff-edge houses and vast scenic vistas. Inhabited for more than 1,100 years (dating back to 900 AD), Walpi's cliff-edge houses seem to grow out of the nearby terrain. Today only about 10 residents occupy this settlement, which has neither electricity nor running water; one-hour guided tours of the village are available. Note that Walpi's steep terrain makes it a less than ideal destination for acrophobes. ⊠ *Punsi Hall Visitor Center, AZ 264, at milepost 392* ☎ *928/737–2262* ⊕ *www.experiencehopi.com/walpi.html* ☎ *Guided tours $15.*

SECOND MESA

8 miles southwest of First Mesa, on AZ 264.

GETTING HERE AND AROUND

The Second Mesa communities are reached via the main highway (AZ 264) through the Hopi Reservation.

EXPLORING

Second Mesa. The Mesas are the Hopi universe, and Second Mesa is the "Center of the Universe." **Shungopavi,** the largest and oldest village on Second Mesa, which was founded by the Bear Clan, is reached by a paved road angling south off AZ 264, between the junction of AZ 87 and the Hopi Cultural Center. The villagers here make silver overlay jewelry and coil plaques. Coil plaques are woven from galleta grass and yucca and are adorned with designs of kachinas, animals, and corn. The art of making the plaques has been passed from mother to daughter for generations, and fine coil plaques have become highly sought-after collector's items. The famous Hopi snake dances (closed to the public) are held here in August during even-numbered years.

Two smaller villages are off a paved road that runs north from AZ 264, about 2 miles east of the Hopi Cultural Center. **Mishongnovi,** the easternmost settlement, was established in the late 1600s.

Sipaulovi Hopi Information Center. Set on a high mesa with views for more than 100 miles in every direction, Sipaulovi was originally at the base of the mesa before moving to its present site in 1680. You can learn more about the community and its centuries-old traditions by watching a video at the small visitor center and taking one of the guided walking tours through the community. On these tours you have the chance to stop by local studios and talk with artists. ☎ *928/737–5426* 🌐 *www.sipaulovihopiinformationcenter.org* 🎟 *Guided tours $15* 🕒 *Tours weekdays 8–4.*

Hopi Cultural Center. You can stop for the night, learn about the people and their communities, and eat authentic Hopi cuisine. The museum here is dedicated to preserving Hopi traditions and to presenting those traditions to non-Hopi visitors. A gift shop sells works by local Hopi artisans at reasonable prices, and a modest picnic area on the west side of the building is a pleasant spot for lunch with a view of the San Francisco Peaks. ✉ *AZ 264, Second Mesa* ☎ *928/734–2401* 🌐 *www.hopiculturalcenter.com* 🎟 *Museum $3* 🕒 *Mid-Mar.–Oct., weekdays 8–5, weekends 9–3; Nov.–mid-Mar., weekdays 8–5.*

WHERE TO EAT AND STAY

For expanded hotel reviews, visit Fodors.com.

$ SOUTHWESTERN 🍴 **Hopi Cultural Center Restaurant.** The restaurant at the Hopi Cultural Center is an attractive, light-filled room where you can sample traditional tribal fare. Authentic dishes include Indian tacos, Hopi blue-corn pancakes, piki (paper-thin, blue-corn bread), fry bread (delicious with honey or salsa), and *nok qui vi* (a tasty stew made with tender bits of lamb, hominy, and mild green chiles). Breakfast is served starting at 7. [$] *Average main: $9* ✉ *5 miles west of AZ 87 on AZ 264, Second Mesa* ☎ *928/734–2401* 🌐 *www.hopiculturalcenter.com.*

$ HOTEL 🏨 **Hopi Cultural Center Inn.** This small Hopi-run motel, the only place to eat or sleep in the immediate area, occupies an attractive adobe building with a tan-and-reddish-brown exterior and clean, quiet, moderately priced rooms with coffeemakers. **Pros:** adjacent to cultural center; only place to stay for miles in either direction; peaceful setting. **Cons:** remote unless you are here to explore Hopi culture; basic, dated rooms; Wi-Fi in rooms can be slow and unreliable. [$] *Rooms from: $105* ✉ *AZ 264, 5 miles west of AZ 87, Second Mesa* ☎ *928/734–2401* 🌐 *www.hopiculturalcenter.com* 🛏 *33 rooms, 1 suite* 🍽 *No meals.*

SHOPPING

Hopi Arts and Crafts Silvercraft Cooperative Guild. The venerable guild, just west of the Hopi Cultural Center and in existence since the 1940s, hosts craftspeople selling their wares; you might even see silversmiths at work here. ✉ *383 AZ 264, Second Mesa* ☎ *928/734–2463.*

Fodor'sChoice **Hopi Arts Trail and Tours.** This Hopi-authorized tour company, run out
★ of Tuba City's Moenkopi Legacy Inn, specializes in studio tours of
the Hopi Villages, including not just Second Mesa's artists but those
in nearby villages, such as Walpi and Sipaulovi. The tours are led by
knowledgeable guides and are a great way to undertake an arts-shop-
ping adventure, especially given that many of the individual galleries
keep irregular hours and can be hard to find. At the hotel you can also
pick up a copy of the Hopi Arts Trail brochure and passport, which lists
several galleries and more than a dozen artists in the Hopi Villages with
studios open to the public—present the brochure when visiting these
establishments for discounts. Visit the Hopi Art Trails website for full
descriptions of all participating galleries and artists. ⊠ *AZ 164 at U.S.
160, Tuba City* ☎ *hopiartstrail.com.*

Hopi Cultural Center. This collection of shops carries the works of local
artists and artisans. ⊠ *AZ 264, Second Mesa* ☎ *928/734–2401* ⊕ *www.
hopiculturalcenter.com.*

Tsa-Kursh-Ovi. At this small shop, 1.5 miles east of the Hopi Cultural
Center, Hopi come to buy bundles of sweetgrass and sage, deer hooves
with which to make rattles, and ceremonial belts adorned with seashells.
Proprietors Joseph and Janice Day (she is a renowned Hopi basket
maker) are a font of information on local artwork, and the shop has
one of the largest collections of Hopi baskets in the Southwest. ⊠ *AZ
264, Second Mesa* ☎ *928/734–2478.*

THIRD MESA

12 miles northwest of Second Mesa, on AZ 264.

GETTING HERE AND AROUND

The Third Mesa communities are the closest to Tuba City, about 50
miles away along AZ 264.

EXPLORING

Third Mesa. Third Mesa villages are known for their agricultural accom-
plishments, textile weaving, wicker baskets, silver overlay, and plaques.
You'll find crafts shops and art galleries, as well as occasional roadside
vendors, along AZ 264. ■TIP→ Visit the Hopi Tribal Headquarters in
Kykotsmovi first for necessary permissions to visit the villages of Third
Mesa.

At the eastern base of Third Mesa, **Kykotsmovi,** literally "ruins on the
hills," is named for the sites on the valley floor and in the surrounding
hills. Present-day Kykotsmovi was established by Hopi people from
Oraibi—a few miles west—who either converted to Christianity or who
wished to attend school and be educated. Kykotsmovi is the seat of the
Hopi Tribal Government.

Old Oraibi, a few miles west and on top of Third Mesa at about 7,200
feet in elevation, is believed to be the oldest continuously inhabited
community in the United States, dating from around AD 1150. It was
also the site of a rare, bloodless conflict between two groups of the
Hopi people; in 1906, a dispute, settled uniquely by a "push of war" (a
pushing contest), sent the losers off to establish the town of Hotevilla.

Oraibi is a dusty spot and, as a courtesy, tourists are asked to park their cars outside and approach the village on foot.

Hotevilla and **Bacavi** are about 4 miles west of Oraibi, and their inhabitants are descended from the former residents of that village. The men of Hotevilla continue to plant crops and beautiful gardens along the mesa slopes. ✉ *Cultural Preservation Office, AZ 264* ☎ *928/734–3613* ⊕ *www.nau.edu/~hcpo-p* ☉ *Weekdays 8:30–5.*

Ancient Pathways Tours. A knowledgeable guide and member of a Hopi clan from Old Oraibi, Bertram "Tsaava" Tsavadawa leads three-hour tours of the Third Mesa area, including trips to see the Taawa Petroglyphs, which are marked with symbols of the people who have resided here for more than 1,000 years. ☎ *928/797–8145* ⊕ *www. ancientpathwaystours.com.*

EN ROUTE **Coal Canyon.** Beyond Hotevilla, AZ 264 descends from Third Mesa, exits the Hopi Reservation, and crosses into Navajo territory, past Coal Canyon, where Native Americans have long mined coal from the dark seam just below the rim. The colorful mudstone, dark lines of coal, and bleached white rock have an eerie appearance, especially by the light of the moon. Twenty miles west of the canyon, at the junction of AZ 264 and U.S. 160, is the town of Moenkopi, the last Hopi outpost. Established as a farming community, it was settled by the descendants of former Oraibi residents.

NAVAJO NATION WEST

The Hopi Reservation is like a doughnut hole surrounded by the Navajo Nation. If you approach the Grand Canyon from U.S. 89, via Flagstaff, north of the Wupatki National Monument, you'll find two significant sites in the western portions of the Navajo Reservation, the Cameron Trading Post and Tuba City (which also partly occupies Hopi land). Situated 45 miles west of the Hopi town of Hotevilla, Tuba City is a good stopover if you're traveling east to the Hopi Mesas or northeast to Page.

At Cameron, a turnoff point for the South Rim of the Grand Canyon, the Cameron Trading Post was built in 1916 and commemorates Ralph Cameron, a pre-statehood territorial-legislative delegate. The sheer walls of the Little Colorado River canyon about 10 miles west of U.S. 89 along AZ 64 are quite impressive, and also worth a stop.

TUBA CITY

52 miles northwest of Third Mesa on AZ 264.

Tuba City, believed to be named after a Hopi chief "Tsuve," has about 8,600 permanent residents and is the administrative center for the western portion of the Navajo Nation. Most of the population is Navajo, but there's also a small Hopi community—this is where you'll find the Moenkopi Legacy Inn, which acts as something of a general information center and tour desk for the Hopi tribe. In addition to two hotels and a few restaurants, this small town has a hospital, a bank, a trading

post, and a movie theater. In late October Tuba City hosts the Western Navajo Fair, a celebration combining traditional Navajo song and dance with a parade, pageant, and countless arts-and-crafts exhibits.

GETTING HERE AND AROUND

Tuba City is one of the main base communities in the Navajo and Hopi region as well as a potential base for exploring either rim of the Grand Canyon from the east. The town lies about midway between Flagstaff and Page (80 miles from each) via U.S. 89 and U.S. 160, and 60 miles from the eastern entrance to the South Rim of the Grand Canyon via AZ 64, U.S. 89, and U.S. 160.

EXPLORING

FAMILY **Dinosaur Tracks.** About 5.5 miles west of Tuba City, between mileposts 316 and 317 on U.S. 160, is a small sign for the Dinosaur Tracks. More than 200 million years ago a dilophosaurus—a carnivorous bipedal reptile over 10 feet tall—left tracks in mud that turned to sandstone. There's no charge for a look. Ask the locals about guiding you to the nearby petroglyphs and freshwater springs.

Fodor's Choice ★ **Explore Navajo Interactive Museum.** The tribe operates this enlightening 7,000-square-foot museum, which is set inside a geodesic dome-shape structure that is meant to recall a traditional Navajo hogan. Inside the dome is a vast trove of artifacts, photos, artwork, and memorabilia. One of the more poignant exhibits tells of the infamous "Long Walk" of 1864, when the U.S. military forced the Navajo to leave their native lands and march to an encampment at Fort Sumner, New Mexico, where they were confined for more than four years. Admission also includes entry to the small Navajo Code Talkers Memorial Museum in the back of the Tuba City Trading Post next door. Both facilities are adjacent to the Quality Inn Navajo Nation. ✉ *10 N. Main St., at Moenave St.* ☎ *928/640–0684* 🌐 *www.explorenavajo.com* 🎟 *$9* 🕒 *Mon.–Sat. 8–6, Sun. noon–6.*

Painted Desert. Four miles west of the dinosaur tracks on U.S. 160 is the junction with U.S. 89. This is one of the most colorful regions of the Painted Desert, with amphitheaters of maroon, orange, and red rocks facing west; it's especially glorious at sunset.

Tuba City Trading Post. The octagonal store, founded in the early 1870s, sells groceries and authentic, reasonably priced Navajo rugs, pottery, baskets, and jewelry—it's adjacent to the Quality Inn Navajo Nation and Explore Navajo Museum. ✉ *Main St., at Moenave Rd.* ☎ *928/283–5441* 🌐 *www.discovernavajo.com/tuba.*

WHERE TO EAT

$$ SOUTHWESTERN 🍴 **Hogan Restaurant.** The fare at this spot adjacent to the Quality Inn Navajo Nation is mostly Southwestern and American, but the kitchen also serves a few basic Mexican and Navajo dishes. Highlights include tasty barbecue ribs, honey-glazed ham, and herb-roasted chicken. The chicken enchiladas and beef tamales are also quite good. Breakfast is served, too. [$] *Average main: $13* ✉ *Main St.* ☎ *928/283–5260* 🌐 *www.qualityinntubacity.com.*

$ AMERICAN 🍴 **Tuuvi Café.** This casual spot inside the largest truck stop and travel center in the region serves simple but well-prepared Southwestern and

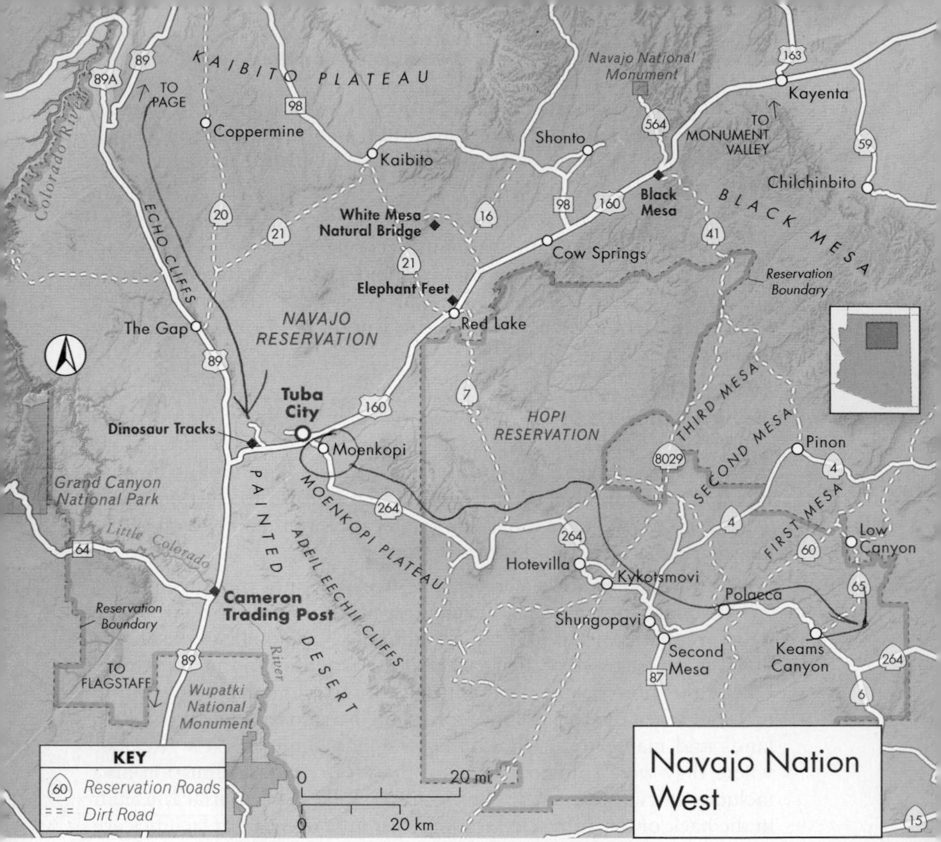

American food, from Native fry bread tacos to charbroiled burgers. There's always a stew of the day—perhaps corn-squash-and-mutton, or green-chile-and-chicken—and homemade peach pie is a dessert specialty. Noteworthy, too, are the hearty breakfasts, such as chicken-fried steak with eggs, and the Hopi Special of eggs, bacon or Spam, and homemade biscuits and gravy. [$] *Average main: $7* ✉ *U.S. 160, at AZ 264* ☎ *928/283–4374* 🌐 *www.experiencehopi.com/tuuvicafe.html.*

WHERE TO STAY

For expanded hotel reviews, visit Fodors.com.

$$ HOTEL FAMILY Fodor's Choice ★

🏨 **Moenkopi Legacy Inn & Suites.** Operated by the Hopi tribe and situated across from the Tuuvi Travel Center, this striking, contemporary hotel contains light-filled, boldly colored rooms with flat-screen TVs, work desks, and coffeemakers. **Pros:** high-quality furnishings and linens; pool is perfect spot to end a day of hiking; hotel offers guided tours to nearby Hopi villages. **Cons:** no restaurant on-site (although the Hopi run Tuuvi Café across the street and there's a Denny's next door); at a busy intersection. [$] *Rooms from: $145* ✉ *U.S. 160, at AZ 264* ☎ *928/283–4500* 🌐 *www.experiencehopi.com* 🛏 *84 rooms, 16 suites* 🍴 *Breakfast.*

$$ HOTEL

🏨 **Quality Inn Navajo Nation.** Tuba City's longest-running hotel has upgraded its rooms in an effort to better compete with the snazzy Moenkopi Legacy Inn down the street, but it's still a pretty run-of-the-mill property. **Pros:** rooms have attractive Navajo-style prints and art; Navajo museum and trading post are across parking lot; dining on-site. **Cons:** rates are a little high for what you get; an older property. $ *Rooms from: $122* ⊠ *10 N. Main St., at Moenave Rd.* ☎ *928/283–4545, 800/644–8383* ⊕ *www.qualityinn.com* ⇆ *78 rooms, 2 suites* †⊚| *Breakfast.*

SHOPPING

Native American swap meet. Bargain hunters can find great deals on jewelry, jewelry-making supplies, semiprecious stones, rugs, pottery, and other arts and crafts behind the To'Nanees'Dizi (formerly called Tuba City) Chapter House, near the town's transfer station, every Friday from 8 am on. There are also food concessions and booths selling herbs. ⊠ *Edgewater Dr. and Peshlaki Ave., beside To'Nanees'Dizi Chapter House.*

CAMERON TRADING POST

25 miles southwest of Tuba City on U.S. 89.

Cameron Trading Post and Motel, established in 1916 overlooking a spectacular gorge and vintage suspension bridge, is one of the few remaining authentic trading posts in the Southwest. A convenient stop if you're driving from the Hopi Mesas to the Grand Canyon, it has reasonably priced dining, lodging, camping, and shopping.

GETTING HERE AND AROUND

The trading post is along the main highway (U.S. 89) between Flagstaff and Page and just 30 miles from the eastern entrance to the South Rim of the Grand Canyon.

WHERE TO STAY

For expanded hotel reviews, visit Fodors.com.

$
HOTEL **Cameron Trading Post.** At the turnoff for the western entrance to the Grand Canyon's South Rim, this trading post dates back to 1916 and contains handsome Southwestern-style rooms with carved-oak furniture, tile baths, and balconies overlooking the Colorado River. **Pros:** impressive collection of Southwestern art in the trading post gallery and gift shop; restaurant serves up Native American specialties and American favorites; historic lodging with campground next door. **Cons:** high traffic volume; occasional highway noise; somewhat remote. $ *Rooms from: $99* ⊠ *466 U.S. 89* ☎ *928/679–2231, 800/338–7385* ⊕ *www.camerontradingpost.com* ⇆ *62 rooms, 4 suites* †⊚| *No meals.*

SHOPPING

Navajo Arts and Crafts Enterprises. Fine authentic Navajo products are sold at this outlet of the Navajo Arts and Crafts Enterprises, open since 1941. ⊠ *U.S. 89, at AZ 64* ☎ *928/679–2244* ⊕ *www.gonavajo.com.*

EN
ROUTE
As you proceed toward Kayenta, 22 miles northeast of Tuba City on U.S. 160, you'll come to the tiny community of Red Lake. Off to the left of the highway is a geologic phenomenon known as **Elephant Feet.** These massive eroded-sandstone buttes offer a great family photo opportunity: pose under the enormous columns. Northwest of here at the end of a

graded dirt road in Navajo backcountry is **White Mesa Natural Bridge,** a massive arch of white sandstone that extends from the edge of White Mesa. The long **Black Mesa** plateau runs for about 15 miles along U.S. 160. Above the prominent escarpments of this land formation, mining operations—a major source of revenue for the Navajo Nation—delve into the more than 20 billion tons of coal deposited there.

MONUMENT VALLEY

The magnificent Monument Valley stretches to the northeast of Kayenta into Utah. At a base altitude of about 5,500 feet, the sprawling, arid expanse was once populated by Ancestral Puebloan people (more popularly known by the Navajo word *Anasazi,* which means both "ancient ones" and "ancient enemies") and in the last few centuries has been home to generations of Navajo farmers. The soaring red buttes, eroded mesas, deep canyons, and naturally sculpted rock formations of Monument Valley are easy to enjoy on a leisurely drive.

At U.S. 163 and the Monument Valley entrance is a street of disheveled buildings called Vendor Village. Here you can purchase trinkets and souvenirs; bartering is perfectly acceptable and expected.

KAYENTA

75 miles northeast of Tuba City, on U.S. 160; 22 miles south of Monument Valley.

Kayenta, a small and rather dusty town with a couple of convenience stores, three chain hotels, and a hospital, is a good base for exploring nearby Monument Valley Navajo Tribal Park and the Navajo National Monument. The Burger King in town has an excellent "Navajo Code Talker" exhibit, with lots of memorabilia relating to this heroic World War II marine group.

GETTING HERE AND AROUND
Kayenta is the first sizable Arizona community you reach if driving to the Navajo Nation via the Four Corners on U.S. 160 or U.S. 163.

EXPLORING
FAMILY **Navajo Cultural Center of Kayenta.** Take a self-guided walking tour through the the Navajo Cultural Center of Kayenta, which includes the small Shadehouse Museum and a 2-acre outdoor cultural park. The museum is designed to resemble an authentic shade house (these wood-frame, rather crude, structures are used to shelter sheepherders in the region's often unforgiving high desert). Inside visitors will find an extensive collection of Navajo Code Talkers memorabilia and local artwork, as well as exhibits on the beliefs and traditions that have shaped North America's largest Native American tribe. As you walk through the grounds of the cultural park, note the different types of traditional hogans and sweat lodges. ⊠ *U.S. 160, between Hampton Inn and Burger King* ☎ *928/697–3170* ☒ *Free* ☉ *Daily 7am–sunset.*

WHERE TO EAT

$ SOUTHWESTERN 🍴 **Amigo Cafe.** The tables are packed with locals who frequent this small establishment, where everything is made from scratch. The delicious fry bread is the real draw. If you've never had a Navajo taco or Navajo hamburger, this is a good place to be initiated. The café also serves excellent Mexican fare and traditional American dishes. Dine on the adobe-walled patio in warm weather. [$] *Average main: $9* ✉ *U.S. 163, just north of U.S. 160* ☎ *928/697–8448* 🕒 *Closed Sun.*

$$ AMERICAN 🍴 **Reuben Heflin Restaurant.** Hampton Inn hotels aren't known for their restaurants, but this attractive spot just off the lobby serves the best food in town. Upholstered Navajo-print chairs with rustic lodgepole frames, hammered-tin sconces, a wood-beam ceiling, and a mammoth adobe fireplace set an inviting mood for the American fare with a regional bent. The Mazalon club sandwich (ham, turkey, bacon, lettuce, and tomato in a Navajo taco) is a local favorite, but also consider rosemary-citrus chicken, New York steak with grilled shrimp, fajitas, and black-bean and mesquite-chicken pizzas. [$] *Average main: $16* ✉ *Hampton Inn, U.S. 160* ☎ *928/697–3170* 🕒 *No lunch mid-Oct.–mid-Mar.*

WORD OF MOUTH

"If you can get to Monument Valley on the afternoon before spending a night in Kayenta, you could do a tour that would include sunset and then have plenty of time the next day to get to Page, perhaps with a stop at Antelope canyon on the way. Check what time sunset is when you go and be aware that Page does not do daylight savings time as it is on Arizona time, but the Navajo parks do." —emalloy

WHERE TO STAY

For expanded hotel reviews, visit Fodors.com.

$$$ HOTEL 🏨 **Hampton Inn of Kayenta.** This warm and inviting hotel is the best accommodation in Kayenta, although it's much like any other hotel in the chain except for its unusually good restaurant and Navajo-inspired design. **Pros:** clean and updated rooms; welcoming staff; excellent restaurant. **Cons:** books up many weeks in advance in summer; pricey for a Hampton Inn; on busy, unattractive stretch of road. [$] *Rooms from: $210* ✉ *U.S. 160* ☎ *928/697–3170* 🌐 *www.hamptoninn.hilton.com* 🛏 *73 rooms* 🍽 *Breakfast.*

$$ HOTEL 🏨 **Kayenta Monument Valley Inn.** This '70s-style, bland-looking cluster of buildings, formerly a Holiday Inn, overlooks a dull stretch of U.S. 160 lined with gas stations; but a welcoming staff, prosaic but clean rooms, and a decent on-site restaurant make it a worthwhile option, especially if the nearby (and typically more expensive) Hampton Inn is booked. **Pros:** friendly staff; some rooms have been recently renovated; outdoor heated pool. **Cons:** on unappealing stretch of road; high rates considering ordinary rooms and amenities. [$] *Rooms from: $149* ✉ *U.S. 160, at U.S. 163* ☎ *928/697–3221, 866/306–5458* 🌐 *www.kayentamonumentvalleyinn.com* 🛏 *156 rooms, 8 suites* 🍽 *No meals.*

$$ HOTEL 🏨 **Wetherill Inn.** This clean but very basic two-story motel with a red-tile roof has Southwestern decor and plain but new furnishings, including flat-screen TVs, hair dryers, irons, and ironing boards. **Pros:** a little

closer to Monument Valley than other properties in Kayenta; well-kept guest rooms. **Cons:** bland setting; rates a little high for such basic accommodations. [$] *Rooms from: $136* ✉ *1000 U.S. 163* ☎ *928/697-3231* 🌐 *www.wetherill-inn.com* 🛏 *54 rooms* 🍴 *Breakfast.*

MONUMENT VALLEY NAVAJO TRIBAL PARK

24 miles northeast of Kayenta, off U.S. 163.

GETTING HERE AND AROUND

It's impossible not to drive slowly on this park's bumpy roads, which are best conquered with an SUV or all-wheel-drive vehicle (especially during rainy times of year), but if you take your time and exercise caution, you can make the entire drive in a conventional car. If in doubt, inquire at the drive's entrance gate. Call ahead for road conditions in winter. The park is just off U.S. 163 north of the Arizona/Utah border and very well marked.

EXPLORING

FAMILY
Fodor's Choice ★

Monument Valley Navajo Tribal Park. For generations, the Navajo have grown crops and herded sheep in Monument Valley, considered to be one of the most scenic and mesmerizing destinations in the Navajo Nation. Within Monument Valley lies the 30,000-acre Monument Valley Navajo Tribal Park, where eons of wind and rain have carved the mammoth red-sandstone monoliths into memorable formations. The monoliths, which jut hundreds of feet above the desert floor, stand on the horizon like sentinels, frozen in time and unencumbered by electric wires, telephone poles, or fences—a scene virtually unchanged for centuries. These are the very same nostalgic images so familiar to movie buffs who recall the early Western films of John Wayne. A 17-mile self-guided driving tour on an extremely rough dirt road (there's only one road, so you can't get lost) passes the memorable **Mittens** and **Totem Pole** formations, among others. Also be sure to walk (15 minutes round-trip) from North Window around the end of Cly Butte for the views. ✉ *Monument Valley, Utah* ☎ *435/727-5874* 🌐 *www.navajonationparks.org/htm/monumentvalley.htm* 🎟 *$5* 🕒 *May–Sept., daily 6 am–8 pm; Oct.–Apr., daily 8–5.*

Monument Valley Visitor Center. The handsome Monument Valley Visitor Center contains an extensive crafts shop and exhibits devoted to ancient and modern Native American history, including a display on the World War II Navajo Code Talkers. Most of the independent guided group tours, which leave from the center, use enclosed vans and charge about $75 per person for 2½ to 3 hours; private tours are also often available, starting around $150 for up to two people. You can generally find Navajo guides—who will escort you to places that you are not allowed to visit on your own—in the center or at the booths in the parking lot. It adjoins the stunning View Hotel, which sits on a gradual rise overlooking the valley and its magnificent red-rock monoliths, with big-sky views in every direction. The park also has a campground typically open from May through September, although it was closed for construction through much of 2013; call ahead to make sure it has reopened. ✉ *Off U.S. 163, 24 miles north of Kayenta, Monument*

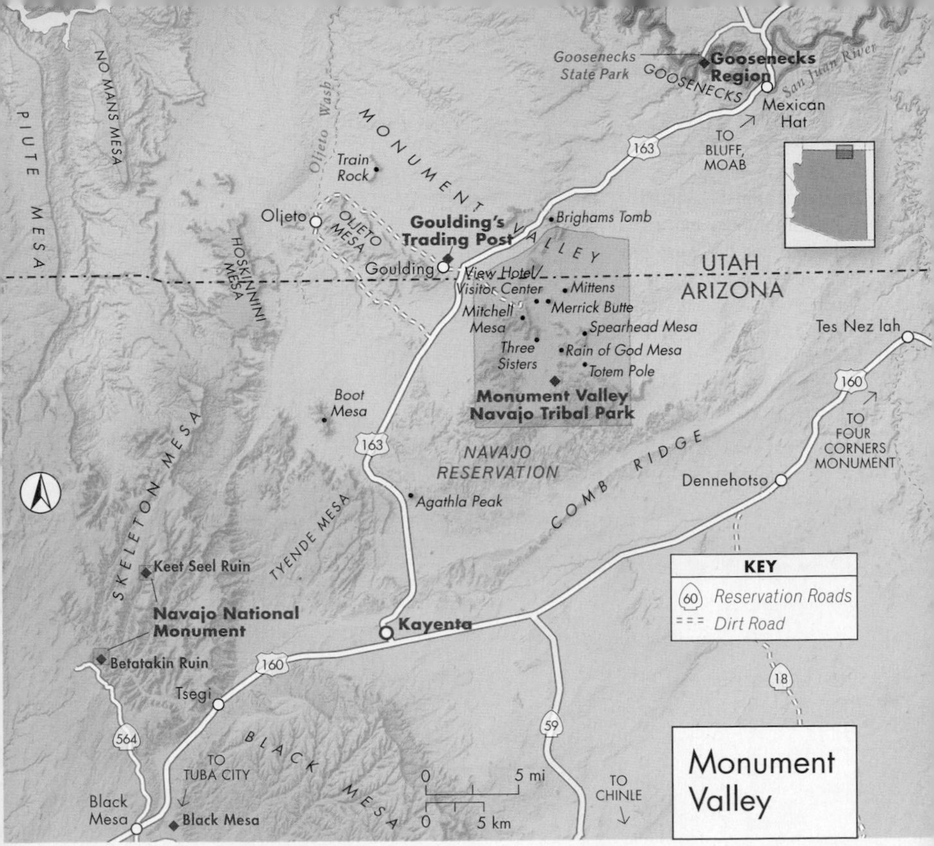

NO MANS MESA
PIUTE MESA
Goosenecks State Park
Goosenecks Region
GOOSENECKS
San Juan River
Mexican Hat
TO BLUFF, MOAB
Oljeto Wash
MONUMENT VALLEY
Train Rock
163
Oljeto
OLJETO MESA
HOSKININI MESA
Goulding's Trading Post
Goulding
Brighams Tomb
UTAH
ARIZONA
View Hotel/ Visitor Center
Mittens
Merrick Butte
Mitchell Mesa
Spearhead Mesa
Three Sisters
Rain of God Mesa
Totem Pole
Tes Nez Iah
160
TO FOUR CORNERS MONUMENT
Boot Mesa
Monument Valley Navajo Tribal Park
NAVAJO RESERVATION
COMB RIDGE
SKELETON MESA
Dennehotso
Agathla Peak
TYENDE MESA
KEY
60 Reservation Roads
Dirt Road
Keet Seel Ruin
Navajo National Monument
Kayenta
Betatakin Ruin
18
Tsegi
59
564
BLACK MESA
TO TUBA CITY
0 5 mi
0 5 km
TO CHINLE
Black Mesa
Black Mesa
Monument Valley

Valley Tribal Park, Utah ☎ 435/727–5874 🌐 www.navajonationparks.org 🎟 $5 🕒 May–Sept., daily 6 am–8 pm; Oct.–Apr., daily 8–5.

WHERE TO EAT AND STAY

For expanded hotel reviews, visit Fodors.com.

$$ SOUTHWESTERN Fodor's Choice ★ 🍴 **View Restaurant.** Connected to the View Hotel through a second-floor breezeway, this airy space comprises a few high-ceilinged rooms with massive plate-glass windows framing mesmerizing views of the valley—in warm weather you can dine outside on a terrace, awed by the same panorama. Navajo rugs and local art hang on the walls above the light-wood tables and chairs, and the tribal visitor center's extensive curio shop is attached. The food has continued to improve over the years as more-experienced chefs have come aboard, adding fresh, local ingredients, Navajo influences, and an artful flourish to typically Southwestern fare. Consider red chile–posole stew, the Navajo taco sampler plate (comprising four mini tacos), thick steaks, and the like. There's also a smaller self-serve section where you can grab sandwiches and light snacks. [$] *Average main: $18* ✉ *Off U.S. 163, 24 miles north of Kayenta* ☎ *435/727–5555* 🌐 *www.monumentvalleyview.com.*

$$$
HOTEL
Fodor's Choice
★

View Hotel. The Navajo tribe operates this sleek, three-story, red-stucco hotel, the only lodging inside Monument Valley Navajo Tribal Park. **Pros:** unbelievable panoramas from every room; eco-conscious bath products, appliances, and buildings standards; rates are similar to or less than far inferior hotels in the nearest large town, Page. **Cons:** books up weeks in advance in summer; Wi-Fi doesn't reach all rooms. $ *Rooms from: $219* ⊠ *Off U.S. 163, 24 miles north of Kayenta* ☎ *435/727–5555* ⊕ *www.monumentvalleyview.com* ⤳ *96 rooms* ○| *No meals.*

SPORTS AND THE OUTDOORS

TOURS

Black's Monument Valley Tours. A wide variety of tour options are available with this respected tour operator, from jeep and horseback adventures to hiking. You can also book an overnight stay in a Navajo hogan. ⊠ *Monument Valley, Utah* ☎ *928/429–1959* ⊕ *www.blacks monumentvalleytours.com.*

Monument Valley Tours. Some of the jeep tours on offer include entertainment and outdoor barbecues, and custom hikes into the valley are available as well. The all-day, 60-mile Monument Valley and Mystery Valley tour, which includes lunch, is especially popular. ☎ *435/727–3313* ⊕ *www.monumentvalleytours.net.*

Sacred Monument Tours. Hiking, jeep, photography, and horseback-riding tours go into Monument Valley. ⊠ *Monument Valley, Utah* ☎ *435/727–3218, 435/459–2501* ⊕ *www.monumentvalley.net.*

Simpson's Trailhandler Tours. This operator offers four-wheel-drive jeep trips, photography and hiking tours, and the chance to stay overnight in a traditional Navajo hogan. ⊠ *Monument Valley, Utah* ☎ *435/727–3362, 888/723–6236* ⊕ *www.trailhandlertours.com.*

OFF THE
BEATEN
PATH

Four Corners Monument. An inlaid brass plaque marks the only point in the United States where four states meet: Arizona, New Mexico, Colorado, and Utah. Despite the Indian wares and booths selling greasy food, there's not much else to do here but pay a fee and stay long enough to snap a photo; you'll see many a twisted tourist trying to get an arm or a leg in each state. The monument is a 75-mile drive from Kayenta and is administered by the Navajo Nation Parks and Recreation Department. ⊠ *4 Corners Rd., 7 miles northwest of the U.S. 160 and U.S. 64 junction* ☎ *928/871–6647 Navajo Parks & Recreation Dept.* ⊕ *www. navajonationparks.org/htm/fourcorners.htm* 🎟 *$3* ⊙ *Oct.–Apr., daily 8–5; May–Sept., daily 8–7.*

GOOSENECKS REGION, UTAH

Fodor's Choice
★

33 miles north of Monument Valley Navajo Tribal Park, on U.S. 163.

Monument Valley's scenic route, U.S. 163, continues from Arizona into Utah, where the land is crossed, east to west, by a stretch of the San Juan River known as the Goosenecks—named for its myriad twists and curves. This barren, erosion-blasted gorge has a stark beauty, and is a well-known take-out point for white-water runners on the San Juan, a river that vacationing sleuths will recognize as the setting of many of Tony Hillerman's Jim Chee mystery novels. The small village of Bluff (population 260), which lies at the northeastern end of the region, has an excellent hotel and restaurant, and is a good base for exploring Goosenecks and the northern reaches of Monument Valley.

GETTING HERE AND AROUND

The scenic overlook for the Goosenecks is reached by turning west from U.S. 163 onto UT 261, 4 miles north of the tiny community of **Mexican Hat,** then proceeding on UT 261 for 1 mile to a directional sign at the road's junction with UT 316. Turn left onto UT 316 and proceed 4 miles to the vista-point

parking lot. To take in spectacular scenery, drive northeast on U.S. 163 Kayenta through Monument Valley all the way past Mexican Hat to Bluff, then turn south on U.S. 191 back into Arizona, and then turn west onto U.S. 160 back to Kayenta; the 140-mile loop takes three hours without stops, but allow a full day for breaks and lunch in Bluff.

WHERE TO EAT AND STAY

For expanded hotel reviews, visit Fodors.com.

$$
ECLECTIC
Fodor's Choice
★

✕**Twin Rocks Cafe.** It's hard to miss this low-slung, timber-frame roadhouse-style restaurant in Bluffs—it's tucked beneath a sandstone ridge crowned by two rock pillars that look as though they might topple in a bad storm. Here you'll find the most varied menu and consistently delicious food in the Monument Valley region. It's well worth the 40-mile drive from Monument Valley Tribal Park for surprisingly excellent barbecue ribs and brisket for this part of the world, plus pizzas (using Navajo fry bread), country-fried steaks, and French toast breakfasts. An extensively stocked trading post lies at one end of the dining room, and there's seating on the patio during the warmer months. $ *Average main: $13* ✉ *913 E. Navajo Twins Dr., off U.S. 191, Bluff* ☎ *435/672–2341* ⊕ *www.twinrockscafe.com.*

$
HOTEL
Fodor's Choice
★

▦ **Desert Rose Inn and Cabins.** This nicely maintained motel with a handsome timber-frame facade and panoramic views of the surrounding red rocks is in Bluffs, 25 miles northeast of Mexican Hat; it's an excellent base for exploring Goosenecks State Park, the northern end of Monument Valley, and even Canyonlands National Park, to the north. **Pros:** family-owned and run by a great staff; scenic setting; good base if you're coming from points north or east. **Cons:** A (beautiful) 40-minute drive to Monument Valley Tribal Park. $ *Rooms from: $119* ✉ *701 W. U.S.191, Bluff* ☎ *435/672–2303, 888/475–7673* ⊕ *www.desertroseinn. com* ⇔ *30 rooms, 6 suites* ⎮⎮ *No meals.*

$
HOTEL

▦ **San Juan Inn & Trading Post.** This quirky motel's well-maintained, Southwestern-style, rustic rooms overlook the San Juan River in Mexican Hat, and the setting, against the red rocks, is quite inspiring, even if accommodations have few frills. **Pros:** magnificent setting; affordable rooms; parking is right outside your room. **Cons:** basic room decor—it's all about the setting. Ⓢ *Rooms from: $94* ⊠ *U.S. 163, at the San Juan River, Mexican Hat* ☎ *800/447–2022, 435/683–2220* ⊕ *www. sanjuaninn.net* ⤳ *36 rooms* ❍│*No meals.*

GOULDING'S TRADING POST

2 miles west of entrance road to Monument Valley Navajo Tribal Park, off U.S. 163 on Indian Hwy. 42.

Established in 1924 by Harry Goulding and his wife "Mike," this trading post provided a place where Navajos could exchange livestock and handmade goods for necessities. Goulding's is probably best known, though, for being used as a headquarters by director John Ford when he filmed the Western classic *Stagecoach*. Today the compound has a lodge, restaurant, museum, gift shop, grocery store, and campground. The Goulding Museum displays Native American artifacts and Goulding family memorabilia, as well as an excellent multimedia show about Monument Valley.

WHERE TO STAY
For expanded hotel reviews, visit Fodors.com.

$$$ ▨ **Goulding's Lodge.** Nestled beneath a massive red-rock monolith, this
HOTEL two-level property affords spectacular views of Monument Valley from
Fodor'sChoice each room's private balcony. **Pros:** right in heart of Monument Valley;
★ incredibly peaceful; indoor pool open all year. **Cons:** remote location; not cheap; tends to book up weeks in advance in summer. Ⓢ *Rooms from: $195* ⊠ *Off U.S. 163, 24 miles north of Kayenta, Monument Valley, Utah* ☎ *435/727–3231, 800/727–3231* ⊕ *www.gouldings.com* ⤳ *62 rooms, 8 suites* ❍│*No meals.*

NAVAJO NATIONAL MONUMENT

53 miles southwest of Goulding's Trading Post, 21 miles west of Kayenta.

GETTING HERE AND AROUND
From Kayenta, take U.S. 160 southwest to AZ 564 and follow signs 9 miles north to monument.

AZ 564 turns north off U.S. 160 at the Black Mesa gas station and convenience store, and leads to the visitor center. No food, gasoline, or hotel lodging is available at the monument, but Kayenta is about a 40-minute drive.

The visitor center houses a small museum, exhibits of prehistoric pottery, and a good crafts shop. Free campground and picnic areas are nearby, and rangers sometimes present campfire programs in summer.

EXPLORING
Fodor'sChoice **Navajo National Monument.** Two unoccupied 13th-century cliff pueblos,
★ Betatakin and Keet Seel, stand under the overhanging cliffs of Tsegi Canyon. The largest ancient dwellings in Arizona, these stone-and-mortar complexes were built by Ancestral Puebloans, obviously for permanent occupancy, but abandoned after less than half a century.

The well-preserved, 135-room **Betatakin** (Navajo for "ledge house") is a cluster of cliff dwellings from AD 1250 that seem to hang in midair before a sheer sandstone wall. When discovered in 1907 by a passing American rancher, the apartments were full of baskets, pottery, and preserved grains and ears of corn—as if the occupants had been chased away in the middle of a meal. For an impressive view of Betatakin, walk to the rim overlook about 0.5 mile from the visitor center. Ranger-led tours (a 5-mile, four-hour, strenuous round-trip hike including a 700-foot descent into the canyon) leave once or twice a day from late May to early September, and on weekends (weather-permitting) the rest of the year. No reservations are accepted; groups of no more than 25 form on a first-come, first-served basis.

Keet Seel (Navajo for "broken pottery") is also in good condition in a serene location, with 160 rooms and five kivas dating from AD 950. Explorations of Keet Seel, which lies at an elevation of 7,000 feet and is 8.5 miles from the visitor center on foot, are restricted: only 20 people are allowed to visit per day, and only between late May and early September, when a ranger is present at the site. A permit—which also allows campers to stay overnight nearby—is required. ■ TIP→ Trips to Keet Seel are very popular, so reservations are taken up to two months in advance. Anyone who suffers from vertigo might want to avoid this trip: the trail leads down a 1,100-foot, near-vertical rock face. ⊠ *AZ 564, 10 miles north of junction with U.S. 160, Shonto* ☎ *928/672–2700* ⊕ *www.nps.gov/nava* ⊠ *Free* ⊙ *Late May–mid-Sept., daily 8–5:30; mid-Sept.–late May, daily 9–5.*

SPORTS AND THE OUTDOORS
HIKING
Navajo National Monument Hiking Trails. Hiking is the best way for adventurous souls to see the Navajo National Monument. It's a fairly strenuous 5-mile hike to the Betatakin sites, permissible only with a guide from the visitor center, but if you're fit, it's well worth it to visit one of the best-preserved ancient dwellings in the Southwest. It's free, but the trail is open daily only during the summer months (May through September), and on weekends the rest of the year, when weather permits; there are two Betatakin hikes each morning. Call ahead to make a reservation; it's a good idea to reserve at least four weeks in advance. There are also three shorter self-guided hikes, open year-round, leaving from the visitor center. All are between a half-mile and a full mile round-trip. The Sandal Trail leads to a viewpoint overlooking the Betatakin/Talastima cliff dwellings, and the Canyon Trail ends at a historic ranger station and takes in expansive views of Tsegi Canyon. ⊠ *Shonto* ☎ *928/672–2700* ⊕ *www.nps.gov/nava.*

GLEN CANYON DAM AND LAKE POWELL

Lake Powell is the heart of the huge 1.25-million-acre Glen Canyon National Recreation Area. Created by the barrier of Glen Canyon Dam in the Colorado River, Lake Powell is ringed by red cliffs that twist off into 96 major canyons and countless inlets (most accessible only by boat) with huge, red-sandstone buttes randomly jutting from the sapphire waters. It extends through terrain so rugged it was the last major area of the United States to be mapped. You could spend 30 years exploring the lake and still not experience everything there is to see. In the '90s, the Sierra Club and Glen Canyon Institute started a movement to drain the lake to restore water-filled Glen Canyon, which some believe was more spectacular than the Grand Canyon, but these efforts failed to gain significant momentum, and the lake is likely to be around for years to come.

South of Lake Powell the landscape gives way to **Echo Cliffs,** orange-sandstone formations rising 1,000 feet and more above the highway in places. At **Bitter Springs** the road ascends the cliffs and provides a spectacular view of the 9,000-square-mile Arizona Strip to the west and the 3,000-foot Vermilion Cliffs to the northwest.

PAGE

90 miles west of the Navajo National Monument, 136 miles north of Flagstaff on U.S. 89.

Built in 1957 as a Glen Canyon Dam construction camp, Page is now a tourist spot and a popular base for day trips to Lake Powell; it's also become a major point of entry to the Navajo Nation. The nearby Vermilion Cliffs are where the California condor, an endangered species, has been successfully reintroduced into the wild. The town's human population of about 7,260 makes it the largest community in far-northern Arizona, and each year more than 3 million people come to play at Lake Powell.

GETTING HERE AND AROUND

Most of the motels, restaurants, and shopping centers are concentrated along **Lake Powell Boulevard,** the name given to U.S. 89 as it loops through the business district.

The only airline that offers service directly to northeastern Arizona is Great Lakes Airlines, which flies into Page Municipal Airport (PGA) from Phoenix and Prescott, as well as from Las Vegas, Denver, and Farmington, New Mexico.

ESSENTIALS

Transportation Contacts Great Lakes Airlines ☎ *800/554–5111* ⊕ *www. greatlakesav.com.* **Page Municipal Airport** ⊠ *238 10th Ave.* ☎ *928/645–4232* ⊕ *www.cityofpage.org/airport.*

Visitor Information Page/Lake Powell Tourism Bureau. There's a visitor information center inside the Powell Museum, at 6 North Lake Powell Boulevard. ☎ *888/261–7243, 928/660–3405* ⊕ *www.pagelakepowelltourism.com.*

EXPLORING

John Wesley Powell Memorial Museum. At the corner of North Navajo Drive and Lake Powell Boulevard is the John Wesley Powell Memorial Museum, whose namesake led the first known expeditions down the Green River and the rapids-choked Colorado through the Grand Canyon between 1869 and 1872. Powell mapped and kept detailed records of his trips, naming the Grand Canyon and many other geographic points of interest in northern Arizona. Artifacts from his expeditions are displayed in the museum. The museum also doubles as the town's visitor information center. A travel desk dispenses information and allows you to book boating tours, raft trips, scenic flights, accommodations in Page, or Antelope Canyon tours. When you sign up for tours here, concessionaires give a donation to the nonprofit museum with no extra charge to you. ✉ *6 N. Lake Powell Blvd.* ☎ *928/645–9496* ⊕ *www. powellmuseum.org* ✍ *$5* ⊙ *Apr.–Oct., Mon.–Sat. 9–5; Nov.–Mar., weekdays 9–5.*

WHERE TO EAT

$$
AMERICAN

✕ **Dam Bar and Grille.** The vaguely industrial-looking decor is quite urbane for this part of the world, and the kitchen turns out filling, well-prepared food. Consider the 8-ounce cowboy steak topped with sautéed mushrooms and Swiss cheese, the smoked baby back ribs, the Southwest Cobb salad, or the burger topped with bacon, cheddar, and barbecue sauce. The Dam also operates a couple of adjacent establishments: the very good Blue Buddha Sushi Lounge and the Gunsmoke Saloon. These spots are popular nightlife options as well. $ *Average main: $17* ✉ *644 N. Navajo Dr.* ☎ *928/645–2161.*

$$
MEXICAN

✕ **El Tapatio.** This small, casual cantina inside a modest-looking former fast-food restaurant is part of an affordable and consistently good chain. Take a seat in the simple but colorfully decorated dining room and peruse the astoundingly long menu, which reveals a mix of Americanized and authentic Mexican dishes, including a "cocktail" of shrimp, abalone, and octopus ceviche; charcoal-grilled *carne asada* (skirt steak); and *borrego ranchero* (grilled lamb with pico de gallo and guacamole). Mojitos, margaritas, and other colorful cocktails are served, too. $ *Average main: $12* ✉ *25 Lake Powell Blvd.* ☎ *928/645–4055* ⊕ *www. eltapatio-restaurants.com.*

WHERE TO STAY

For expanded hotel reviews, visit Fodors.com.

$$$$
HOTEL

▢ **Best Western Plus at Lake Powell.** This modern, three-story motel on a high bluff overlooking Glen Canyon Dam features dazzling views of the Vermilion Cliffs. **Pros:** excellent views; close to downtown shopping and dining; rates drop significantly late fall through late spring. **Cons:** run-of-the-mill decor and amenities don't merit the soaring summer high-season rates. $ *Rooms from: $260* ✉ *208 N. Lake Powell Blvd.* ☎ *928/645–5988, 888/794–2888* ⊕ *www.bestwestern.com* ⬗ *106 rooms, 26 suites* ¶⊙| *Breakfast.*

$$
B&B/INN

▢ **Canyon Colors Bed and Breakfast.** Run by personable New England transplants Bev and Rich Jones, this desert-country B&B occupies a simple, modern house in a quiet residential neighborhood near downtown. **Pros:** personal attention; peaceful setting; central location. **Cons:** very small; need to book well ahead in summer. $ *Rooms from: $130* ✉ *225 S. Navajo Dr.* ☎ *928/645–5979* ⊕ *www.canyoncolors.com* ⬗ *2 rooms* ¶⊙| *Breakfast.*

$$$
HOTEL

▢ **Courtyard Page at Lake Powell.** Situated just below the stunning grounds of Lake Powell National Golf Course, Page's most upscale hotel boasts airy rooms with plush bedding, large TVs, and bathrooms

Ancestral Puebloans' construction methods and their mysterious fate are worth pondering during a visit to Navajo National Monument.

with marble accents. **Pros:** lovely setting by golf course; good restaurant; the best and most modern room amenities in town. **Cons:** uphill walk to downtown restaurants and shopping; restaurant closed for dinner during slower months; steep rates in July and August. $ *Rooms from: $220 ✉ 600 Clubhouse Dr.* ☎ *928/645–5000, 877/905–4495* ⊕ *www. marriott.com* ⇔ *153 rooms* ❑ *No meals.*

$$
HOTEL
🖼 **Lake Powell Days Inn & Suites.** It may be part of an uneven budget chain, but this particular Days Inn—an attractive Southwest-style building atop a plateau with expansive views—is the best among value-oriented accommodations in the region. **Pros:** many rooms have balconies; super-friendly staff; panoramic views. **Cons:** need a car to get to downtown shopping and restaurants; on a busy road at the edge of town; better rates than competitors but can still be pricey on summer weekends. $ *Rooms from: $154 ✉ 961 N. U.S. 89* ☎ *928/645–2800, 877/525–3769* ⊕ *www.daysinn.net* ⇔ *82 rooms* ❑ *Breakfast.*

SHOPPING

There are numerous gift shops and clothing stores in the downtown area along Lake Powell Boulevard. There's lots of junk, but you can find authentic Native American arts and crafts, too.

Big Lake Trading Post. There is a gas station, convenience store, car wash, and coin laundry. ✉ *1505 Coppermine Rd., at AZ 98* ☎ *928/645–2404* ⊕ *www.biglaketradingpost.com.*

Fodor's Choice
★
Blair's Dinnebito Trading Post. Authentic Native American arts and crafts are only a small part of what this store, which has been around for more than half a century, sells. Need tack equipment, rodeo ropes, rugs, saddlery, or pottery? It's all here and reasonably priced. Wander upstairs

Glen Canyon Dam
and Lake Powell

and visit the Elijah & Claudia Blair collection and memorabilia rooms.
✉ 626 N. Navajo Dr. ☎ 928/645–3008 ⊕ www.blairstradingpost.com.

SPORTS AND THE OUTDOORS

For water sports on Lake Powell, see Wahweap.

Glen Canyon Recreation Area. Check out the park website to help plan
your Glen Canyon trip. ☎ 928/608–6200 ⊕ www.nps.gov/glca.

AIR TOURS

FAMILY **Colorado River Discovery.** Colorado River Discovery offers waterborne
Fodor'sChoice tours, including a 5½-hour guided rafting excursion down a calm por-
★ tion of the Colorado River on comfortable, motorized pontoon boats
($83). The scenery—multicolor-sandstone cliffs adorned with Native
American petroglyphs—is spectacular. The trips are offered twice daily
from May through September, and once a day in March, April, October,
and November. The company also offers full-day rowing trips along the
river, using smaller boats maneuvered by well-trained guides ($155).
These trips—offered Sunday, Monday, and Wednesday—are quieter and
more low-key, and provide a more intimate brush with this magnificent
body of water. The above prices exclude a $6 per person river-use fee.
And there's also a combination tour that includes rafting on the Colorado in the morning and kayaking on Lake Powell in the afternoon

($194), and a rafting tour through a slot canyon ($181). ⊠ *130 6th Ave.* ☎ *888/522–6644* ⊕ *www.raftthecanyon.com.*

GOLF

Lake Powell National Golf Course. Wide fairways, tiered greens with some of the steepest holes in the Southwest, and a generous lack of hazards make for a pleasant golfing experience. From the fairways you can enjoy spectacular vistas of Glen Canyon Dam and Lake Powell. ⊠ *400 Clubhouse Dr., off U.S. 89* ☎ *928/645–2023* ⊕ *www.lakepowellgolfing. com* ⅄ *18 holes. Par 72. 7064 yds. Slope 139. Greens Fee: $49* ☞ *Facilities: driving range, putting green, golf carts, rental clubs, pro shop, golf lessons, restaurant, bar.*

HIKING

Glen Canyon Hike. This hike, a short walk from the parking lot down a flight of uneven rock steps, takes you to a viewpoint on the canyon rim high above the Colorado River, and provides fantastic views of the Colorado as it flows through Glen Canyon. To reach the parking lot, turn west on Scenic View Drive, 1.5 miles south of Carl Hayden Visitor Center. ⊠ *Off U.S. 89.*

Horse Shoe Bend Trail. The views along this hike are well worth the steep up-and-down paths and the bit of deep sand to maneuver. The trail leads up to a bird's-eye view of Glen Canyon and the Colorado River downstream from Glen Canyon Dam. There are some sheer drop-offs here, so watch children. To reach the trail, drive 4 miles south of Page on U.S. 89 and turn west (right) onto a blacktop road just south of mile marker 545. It's a 0.75-mile hike from the parking area to the top of the canyon, and the entire hike can easily be done in an hour round-trip. ⊠ *Off U.S. 89* ⊕ *www.lakepowell.com/media/225945/ HorseshoeBendTrailGuide.pdf.*

ANTELOPE CANYON

4 miles east of Page on the Navajo Reservation, on AZ 98.

GETTING HERE AND AROUND

Access to Antelope Canyon is restricted by the Navajo tribe to licensed tour operators. The tribe charges a $6-per-person fee, included in the price of tours offered by the licensed concessionaires in Page. The easiest way to book a tour is in town at the John Wesley Powell Memorial Museum Visitor Center; you pay nothing extra for the museum's service. If you'd like to go directly to the tour operators, you can do that, too; visit ⊕ *www.navajonationparks.org/htm/antelopecanyon.htm* for a list of approved companies. Most companies offer 1- to 1½-hour sightseeing tours for about $35 to $45, or longer photography tours for around $80. ■TIP➔ The best time to see the canyon is between 8 am and 2 pm.

TOURS

Antelope Canyon Navajo Tours. One-hour sightseeing tours ($40) and two-hour photography tours ($80) are available. ☎ *928/698–3384* ⊕ *www. navajotours.com.*

Antelope Canyon Tours. There are several tours daily 8 am–4:30 pm for sightseers (90 min., $35–$46) and photographers. The two-and-a-half-hour photo tour ($80) gives serious and amateur photographers the opportunity to wait for the right light to photograph the canyon and get basic information on equipment setup. ☎ *928/645–9102, 435/675–9109* ⊕ *www.antelopecanyon.com.*

John Wesley Powell Memorial Museum. The visitor center in the museum offers 1½-hour tours and 2½-hour photography tours, which leave at different times throughout the morning and early afternoon. You can book online or by stopping at the museum. ☎ *928/645–9496* ⊕ *www.powellmuseum.org/tours.php.*

> ### LAKE POWELL FAST FACTS
>
> ■ Lake Powell is 185 miles long with 2,000 miles of shoreline—longer than America's Pacific Coast.
>
> ■ This is the second-largest man-made lake in the nation and it took 17 years to fill.
>
> ■ The Glen Canyon Dam is a 710-foot-tall wall of concrete.

Overland Canyon Tours. Navajo guide Harley Klemm and his company, Overland Canyon Tours, offer the only access to the isolated slot canyon known as Canyon X, which is on private property. Only one tour is given per day (departure times vary) and tours are offered by advance reservation only. Because the area is rugged, children aren't allowed, and participants should have good physical mobility to climb crevasses and some rough terrain. The company also operates popular tours to Antelope Canyon, the South Coyote Buttes, and the White Pockets rock formations. ☎ *928/608–4072* ⊕ *www.overlandcanyontours.com.*

EXPLORING

Fodor's Choice ★ **Antelope Canyon.** You've probably seen dozens of photographs of Antelope Canyon, a narrow, red-sandstone slot canyon with convoluted corkscrew formations, dramatically illuminated by light streaming down from above. And you're likely to see assorted shutterbugs waiting patiently for just the right shot of these colorful, photogenic rocks, which are actually petrified sand dunes of a prehistoric ocean that once filled this portion of North America. The best photos are taken at high noon, when light filters through the slot in the canyon surface. Be prepared to protect your camera equipment against blowing dust. ✉ *AZ 98, Page* ✛ *3 miles east of Page* ☎ *928/698–2808* ⊕ *www.navajonationparks.org/html/antelopecanyon.htm* ✉ *$6 (included in tour cost).* ☉ *Mid-Mar.–Oct., daily 8–5; Nov.–early-Mar., daily 9–3.*

WHERE TO EAT

$$
AMERICAN
✕ Ja'di' To'oh at Antelope Point Marina. The floating, sandstone restaurant and lounge at the Navajo-operated Antelope Point Marina serves reliably well-prepared American food with contemporary accents—wood-fire pizzas, fish tacos, buffalo burgers, and filet mignon with garlic-herb butter. You'll also find one of the better wine lists in the region. As good as the food is, the dramatic dining room with soaring windows overlooking a red-rock-wall section of Lake Powell is what really makes this place special. It's a long walk from the parking area to the front

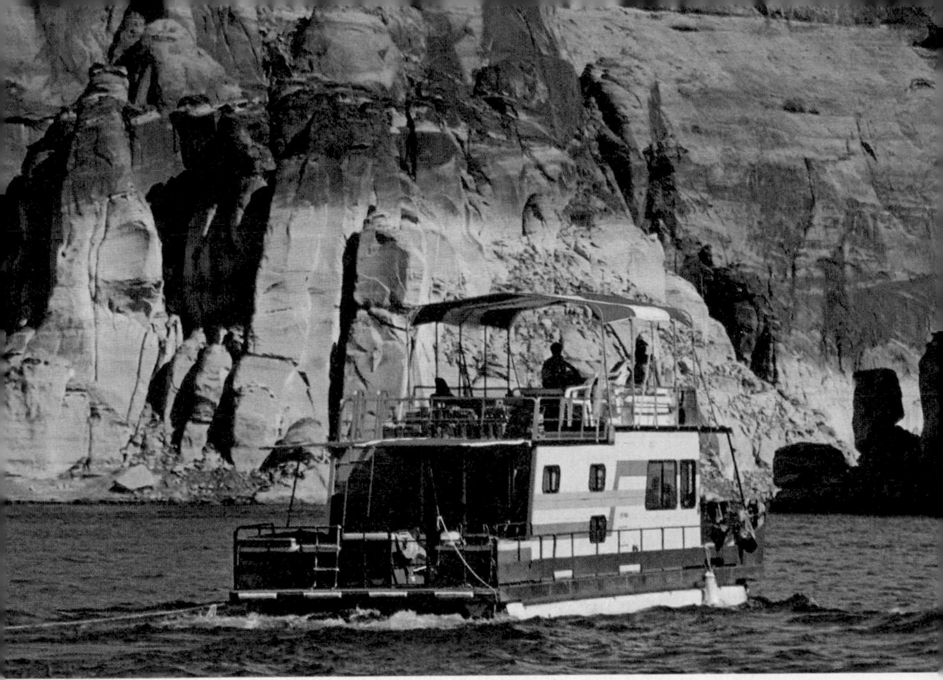

Houseboats are a unique lodging option; they're also great for exploring Lake Powell's almost 2,000 miles of shoreline.

door, but staff whisk visitors to and fro in golf carts. **■ TIP→ Hours can vary a bit in the slower winter season—call ahead to make sure it's open before driving all the way from Page.** [$] *Average main: $19* ✉ *537 Marina Pkwy., end of Indian Hwy. 22B, off of AZ 98, 9 miles northeast of Page, Page* ☎ *928/645–5900* 🌐 *www.antelopepointlakepowell.com* 🕒 *Closed Mon.–Wed. in winter.*

SPORTS AND THE OUTDOORS

BOATING

Antelope Point Marina. About 5 miles north of AZ 98, opposite the turnoff for Antelope Canyon, the Navajo Nation built Antelope Point Marina in the early 2000s on a scenic canyon of Lake Powell. This impressive 27,000-square-foot floating village has 300 wet slips for houseboats and watercraft, a variety of boat and houseboat rentals, the very good Ja'di' Tooh restaurant and lounge, a seasonal ice-cream stand, a fishing dock, and a market. From here, boaters can access the other points along the lake, including the development at Wahweap. Eventually, the Navajo plan to add luxury casitas and a Navajo Cultural Center to this dramatic compound. ✉ *End of Indian Rte. N22B, off AZ 98, 9 miles northeast of Page, Page* ☎ *928/645–5900* 🌐 *www.antelopepointlakepowell.com.*

GLEN CANYON NATIONAL RECREATION AREA

1 mile north of Page on U.S. 89.

GETTING HERE AND AROUND

Just off the highway at the north end of the bridge is the **Carl Hayden Visitor Center,** where you can learn about the controversial creation of Glen Canyon Dam and Lake Powell, enjoy panoramic views of both, and take guided tours of the dam ($5). To enter the visitor center you must go through a metal detector. Absolutely no bags or food are allowed inside, but cameras, wallets, and clear water bottles are welcome.

EXPLORING

Fodor's Choice
★

Glen Canyon Dam National Recreation Area. Once you leave the Page business district heading northwest, the Glen Canyon Dam National Recreation Area and Lake Powell behind it immediately become visible. This concrete-arch dam—all 5 million cubic feet of it—was completed in September 1963, its power plant an engineering feat that rivaled the Hoover Dam. The dam's crest is 1,560 feet across and rises 710 feet from bedrock and 583 feet above the waters of the Colorado River. When Lake Powell is full, it's 560 feet deep at the dam. The plant generates some 1.3 million kilowatts of electricity when each generator's 40-ton shaft is producing nearly 200,000 horsepower. Power from the dam serves a five-state grid consisting of Colorado, Arizona, Utah, California, and New Mexico, and provides energy for more than 1.5 million users.

With only 8 inches of annual rainfall, the Lake Powell area enjoys blue skies nearly year-round. Summer temperatures range from the 60s to the 90s. Fall and spring are usually balmy, with daytime temperatures often in the 70s and 80s, but chilly weather can set in. Nights are cool even in summer, and in winter the risk of a cold spell increases, but all-weather houseboats and tour boats make for year-round cruising.

Boaters and campers should note that regulations require the use of portable toilets on the lake and lakeshore to prevent water pollution. ✉ *U.S. 89, 2 miles northwest of town, Page* ☎ *928/608–6200* ⊕ *www. nps.gov/glca* ☑ *$15 per vehicle or $7 per person (entering on foot or by bicycle), good for up to 7 days; $16 per wk boating fee* ☉ *Visitor center: June–Aug., daily 8–6; Sept.–Oct. and Mar.–May, daily 8–5; Nov.–Feb., daily 8:30–4:30.*

WAHWEAP

5 miles north of Glen Canyon Dam on U.S. 89.

Most waterborne-recreational activity on the Arizona side of the lake is centered on this vacation village, where everything needed for a lakeside holiday is available: tour boats, fishing, boat rentals, dinner cruises, and more. The Lake Powell Resorts have excellent views of the lake area, and you can take a boat tour from the Wahweap Marina.

GETTING HERE AND AROUND

Wahweap has two well-marked entrance roads off U.S. 89, one just north of Glen Canyon Dam, and the other about 3½ miles north and more direct if arriving from Utah. Keep in mind that you must pay the Glen Canyon National Recreation Area entry fee upon entering Wahweap—this is true even if you're just passing through or having a meal at Lake Powell Resorts (although the fee collection stations are often closed in winter, meaning you can pass through freely).

SLOT CANYONS

Slot canyons are unique to the Southwest. Carved through sandstone by wind and water, they're narrow at the top—some are only a foot wide on the surface—and wider at the bottom, which can be more than 100 feet below ground level. The play of light as it filters down through the slot onto the sandstone walls makes them remarkable subjects for photographs, but they're dangerous, particularly during the summer rainy season when flash floods can rush through them and sweep away an unwary hiker. Before hiking into a slot canyon, consult with locals and pay attention to weather forecasts.

5

EXPLORING

Rainbow Bridge National Monument. A boat tour to the monument is a great way to see the enormity of the lake and its incredible, rugged beauty. This 290-foot red-sandstone arch is the world's largest natural bridge, and can be reached by boat or strenuous hike *(⇨ See Hiking)*. The lake level is down due to the prolonged drought throughout the region, so expect a 1.5-mile hike from the boat dock to the monument. The bridge can also be viewed by air. To the Navajos this is a sacred area with deep religious and spiritual significance, so outsiders are asked not to hike underneath the arch itself. *☎ 928/608–6200, 888/896–3829 for boat tour information 🌐 www.nps.gov/rabr.*

WHERE TO EAT AND STAY

For expanded hotel reviews, visit Fodors.com.

$$$ AMERICAN Fodor's Choice ★ 🍴 **Rainbow Room.** The bi-level signature restaurant at the Lake Powell Resort occupies a cavernous round room affording 270-degree views of the lake, surrounding vermilion cliffs, and massive Navajo Mountain in the distance. Serving the best food in the region, the kitchen focuses on organic, healthful ingredients in producing such toothsome dishes as a serrano-citrus–brinded pork porterhouse with apple-chipotle gastrique, pan-wilted spinach, mashed potatoes, and salsa verde; and ancho-honey–glazed salmon with spicy black-bean sauce, charred-jalapeño crema, and roasted sweet potatoes. There's a lavish breakfast buffet in the mornings. When Rainbow Room is closed in winter, you can still dine at the casual Driftwood Lounge restaurant. [$] *Average main: $22 ✉ 100 Lake Shore Dr., 7 miles north of Page off U.S. 89 ☎ 928/645–2433 🌐 www.lakepowell.com ⏲ Closed Nov.–Mar.*

$$$$ RESORT Fodor's Choice ★ 🏨 **Amangiri.** One of just two U.S. properties operated by the famously luxurious Aman resort company, this ultraplush 34-suite compound lies just a few miles north of Lake Powell on a 600-acre plot of rugged high desert, soaring red-rock cliffs, and jagged mesas. [$] *Rooms from: $1100 ✉ 1 Kayenta Rd., 15 miles northwest of Page off U.S. 89, Canyon Point,*

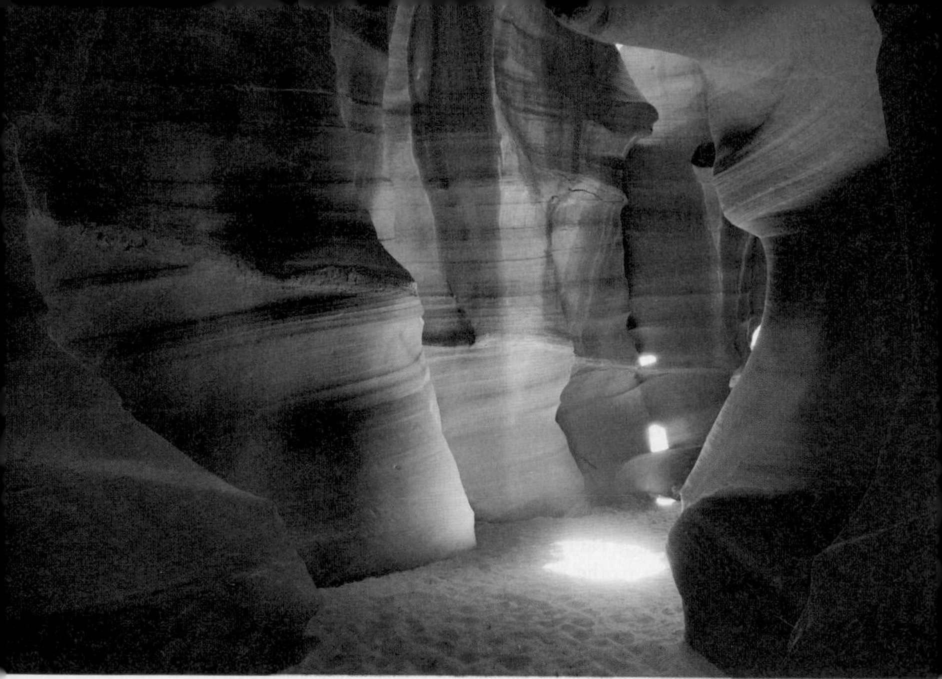

Midday light on Antelope Canyon's sandstone walls is a favorite shot for many photographers.

Utah ☎ *435/675–3999, 877/695–3999* 🌐 *www.amanresorts.com* 🛏 *34 suites* 🍴 *No meals.*

$$ **B&B/INN** 🏨 **Dreamkatchers' B&B.** This sleek, contemporary Southwestern-style home sits on a bluff a few miles northwest of Lake Powell and 15 miles from Page, its grounds affording dramatic views of the lake, mountains, and sweeping high-desert mesas. **Pros:** peaceful and secluded location that's perfect for stargazing at night; delicious breakfasts; laid-back, friendly hosts. **Cons:** often booked more than a couple of months in advance; two-night minimum stay. [$] *Rooms from: $135* ✉ *1055 S. American Way, Big Water, Utah* ☎ *435/675–5828* 🌐 *www.dreamkatcherslakepowell.com* 🛏 *3 rooms* 🕒 *Closed mid-Nov.–mid-Apr.* 🍴 *Breakfast.*

$$$ **RESORT** **FAMILY** 🏨 **Lake Powell Resorts & Marinas.** This sprawling property consisting of several one- and two-story buildings, run by Aramark, sits on a promontory above Lake Powell and serves as the center for recreational activities in the area. **Pros:** stunning lake setting; couldn't be closer to the water; all rooms have patios or balconies. **Cons:** it can be a long way from your room to the restaurant and lobby. [$] *Rooms from: $180* ✉ *100 Lake Shore Dr., 7 miles north of Page off U.S. 89* ☎ *888/896–3829* 🌐 *www.lakepowell.com* 🛏 *350 rooms* 🍴 *No meals.*

HOUSEBOATS Without a doubt, the most popular and fun way to vacation on Lake Powell is to rent a houseboat. Houseboats, ranging in size from 46 to 75 feet and sleeping 6 to 12 people, come complete with marine radios, fully equipped kitchens, and bathrooms with hot showers; you need only bring sheets and towels. The larger, luxury boats are a good choice in hot summer months, since they have air-conditioning.

Aramark's Lake Powell Resorts & Marinas (☎ 888/896–3829 ⊕ *www. lakepowell.com*) is the only concessionaire that rents boats on Lake Powell. There are many vacation packages available. A smaller, more basic houseboat that sleeps up to 12 runs from $3,300 for a week in winter to about $4,500 for a week during the summer peak. At the other end of the spectrum, 75-foot luxury houseboats, some of which can sleep up to 22, cost as much as $15,000 in high season for seven nights. You receive hands-on instruction before you leave the marina.

Lake Powell Resorts & Marinas. Houseboat rentals at this marina range widely in size, amenities, and price, depending upon season. You may want to rent a powerboat or personal watercraft along with a house-boat to explore the many narrow canyons and waterways on the lake. A 19-foot powerboat for seven passengers runs approximately $400 and up per day. Kayaks rent for $43 per day, and wakeboards, water skis, and jet skis are also available. ☎ 928/645–2433, 888/896–3829 ⊕ *www.lakepowell.com*.

SHOPPING

Lake Powell Resort. The gift shop at Lake Powell Resort carries authentic Native American rugs, pottery, jewelry, and baskets, as well as tourist T-shirts and postcards. ⊠ *100 Lake Shore Dr.* ☎ *928/645–2433* ⊕ *www. lakepowell.com*.

SPORTS AND THE OUTDOORS

BOATING

One of the most scenic lakes of the American West, Lake Powell has 185 miles of clear sapphire waters edged with vast canyons of red and orange rock. Ninety-six major side canyons intricately twist and turn into the main channel of Lake Powell, into what was once the main artery of the Colorado River through Glen Canyon. In some places the lake is 500 feet deep, and by June the lake's waters begin to warm and stay that way well into October.

Wahweap Marina. The largest and most impressive of the five full-service Lake Powell marinas run by Aramark's Lake Powell Resorts & Marinas has more than 900 slips and the most facilities, including a decent diner, public launch ramp, camping, extensive docks, fishing guide and pri-vate tour services, and marina store where you can buy fishing licenses and other necessities. It's the only full-service marina on the Arizona side of the lake (the other four—Dangling Rope, Hite, Bullfrog, and Halls Crossing—are in Utah). ⊠ *100 Lake Shore Dr.* ☎ *888/896–3829* ⊕ *www.lakepowell.com/executive-marina.aspx*.

TOURS **Lake Powell Resort.** Excursions on double-decker scenic cruisers piloted by experienced guides leave from the dock of Lake Powell Resort. The most popular tour is the full-day trip to Rainbow Bridge National Mon-ument for $115 (a box lunch is included); a half-day version is avail-able, too. There's also a two-hour sunset dinner cruise ($75) featuring a prime-rib dinner (vegetarian option available in advance). It's served on the fully enclosed decks of the sleek and modern *Canyon Princess* ship. Two-hour Antelope Canyon cruises are another favorite, costing about $42, and there's also a longer and more extensive Canyon Adventure tour that visits both Antelope Canyon and Navajo Canyon for $65.

Most tours are available year-round; the dinner cruises run May–late September. ✉ *100 Lake Shore Dr.* ☎ *928/645–2433, 888/896–3829* ⊕ *www.lakepowell.com/tours/scenic-boat-tours.aspx.*

CAMPING

Beautiful campsites are abundant on Lake Powell, from large beaches to secluded coves, with the most desirable areas accessible only by boat. You're allowed to camp anywhere along the shores of the lake unless it's restricted by the National Park Service; however, camping within ¼ mile of the shoreline requires a portable toilet or bathroom facilities on your boat. Campfires are allowed on the shoreline, but since there's little firewood available around the lake you'll need to bring your own.

FISHING

Marina Store at Wahweap Marina. Anglers delight in the world-class bass fishing on Lake Powell. You'll hear over and over how the big fish are "biting in the canyons," so you'll need a small vessel if you plan on fishing for the big one. Landing a 20-pound striper isn't unusual (the locals' secret is to use anchovies for bait). Fishing licenses for both Arizona and Utah are available at the Marina Store at Wahweap Marina. ✉ *100 Lake Shore Dr.* ☎ *888/896–3829* ⊕ *www.lakepowell.com/executive-marina.aspx.*

Stix Bait & Tackle. Come here for supplies and fishing guide recommendations. ✉ *5 S. Lake Powell Blvd., Page* ☎ *928/645–2891.*

HIKING

Bring plenty of water when hiking and drink often. It's important to remember when hiking at Lake Powell to watch the sky for storms: it may not be raining where you are, but flooding can occur in downstream canyons—particularly slot canyons—from a storm miles away.

Rainbow Bridge. Only seasoned hikers in good physical condition will want to try either of the trails leading to Rainbow Bridge; both are about 26 to 28 miles round-trip through challenging and rugged terrain. This site is considered sacred by the Navajo, and it's requested that visitors show respect by not walking under the bridge. Take Indian Highway 16 north toward the Utah state border. At the fork in the road, take either direction for about 5 miles to the trailhead leading to Rainbow Bridge. Excursion boats pull in at the dock near the arch, but no supplies are sold there.

Navajo Parks & Recreation. Get backcountry permits ($5 per person, per day), which must be obtained before hiking to Rainbow Bridge, here. Call the office, and allow about a month to process the paperwork. Alternatively, on weekdays from 8 until 5, you can stop by the Antelope Canyon Tribal Park Office in Page, on Coppermine Road (3 miles south of downtown Page), next to the LeChee Chapter House. ✉ *Window Rock* ☎ *928/871–6647 Navajo Parks Dept., 928/698–2808 Antelope Canyon Tribal Park Office* ⊕ *www.navajonationparks.org/permits.htm.*

EASTERN
ARIZONA

WELCOME TO EASTERN ARIZONA

TOP REASONS TO GO

★ **Get outside:** No place for couch potatoes, Eastern Arizona is home to some of the state's best recreation areas for skiing, fishing, camping, and exploring. If you love the outdoor life, you might fall in love with this place.

★ **Be petrified:** Marvel at huge fossilized logs and the dazzling colors of nature at Petrified Forest National Park.

★ **View nature's handiwork at Salt River Canyon:** Watch the desert cacti disappear as the country's pines delight your senses. U.S. 60 dramatically switchbacks down—and back up—2,000 feet of eroded canyon.

★ **Hit the road:** Whether you're traveling the Coronado Trail National Scenic Byway or getting your kicks on Route 66, these roads were made for travelers.

★ **Discover native traditions:** The rich culture and heritage of Native American tribes permeates this area.

1 The White Mountains. In a state known for its extreme temperatures, residents of the White Mountains are proud of their home's relatively staid climate. The comfortable conditions and panoramic mountain views draw thousands here in summer, making the region a playground for golfers, hikers, and fishermen. But there's plenty to do if you don't want to get your hands dirty.

2 The Round Valley and Coronado Trail. Considered one of the most scenic drives in the country—though not for the faint of heart—this 123-mile stretch of highway takes you through terrifying switchbacks and majestic pine forests, unveiling the beauty of Arizona. Fill up your gas tank in Springerville, head south toward Clifton, and enjoy the ride.

3 The Petrified Forest and Around. Forget about indoor natural history exhibits—the Petrified Forest actually takes you back in time. One of Arizona's most unusual sites, the park has yielded fossils dating back 225 million years. A visit to the forest is like exploring an outdoor museum. It's worth the trip to see the park's beautiful Painted Desert—especially if you catch the brilliant colors of the landscape at midday.

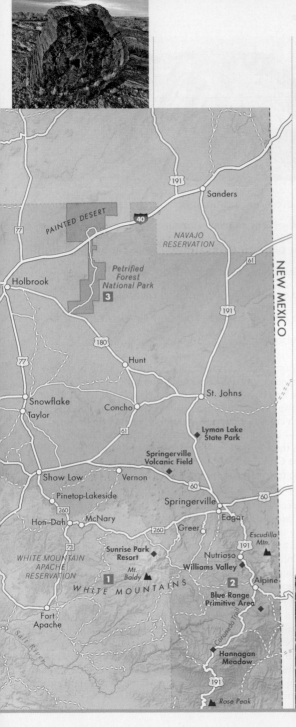

GETTING ORIENTED

Eastern Arizona is a large, somewhat loosely defined series of small towns and historic sites along the Mogollon Rim. Pronounced "*muh*-gee-on," the rim is a 200-mile-long area of volcanic and sedimentary rock that marks a distinct change in the topography of the state. Say goodbye to cacti and desert, and hello to forests of towering trees. Visitors searching for an escape from the desert heat head for the White Mountains and their majestic vistas of ponderosa pines. Others seek history and head northeast to the 221,000-acre Petrified Forest National Park and the Painted Desert. No matter the destination, don't forget to experience the area's local flavor, whether it's a museum of Native American crafts or a drive through a town whose name was derived from a winning hand of cards.

6

Updated by
Elise Riley

In a state of dramatic natural wonders, Eastern Arizona is often overlooked—this is unfortunate, as it's one of Arizona's great outdoor playgrounds. In the White Mountains, northeast of Phoenix, you can hike, fish, swim, and, at night, gaze upward at millions of twinkling stars. The region's winter sports are just as varied: you can ski downhill or cross-country, snowboard, snowshoe, and snowmobile.

The White Mountains are unspoiled high country at its best. In vast tracts of preserved primitive wilderness, the air is punctuated with piercing cries of hawks and eagles, and majestic herds of elk graze in verdant, wildflower-laden meadows. Past volcanic activity has left the land strewn with cinder cones, and the whole region is bounded by the Mogollon Rim— a 200-mile geologic upthrust that splits the state— made famous as the "Tonto Rim" in the books of the best-selling Western author Zane Grey. Much of the plant life is unique to this region; this is one of the few places in the country where such desert plants as juniper and manzanita grow intermixed with mountain pines and aspen.

The human aspects of the landscape are equally appealing. Historic Western towns are outposts of down-home hospitality, and the prehistoric sites are reminders of the native cultures that once flourished here and are still a vital presence. The Fort Apache Indian Reservation, home to the White Mountain Apache tribe, is to the north of the Salt River, and the San Carlos Apache Indian Reservation is to the south. Visitors are welcome to explore most reservation lands with a permit, which can be obtained from tribal offices.

Historic sites and natural wonders also attract visitors to Eastern Arizona. To the north, along historic Route 66, are the Painted Desert and Petrified Forest National Park. The austere mesas of the Painted Desert are famous for their multihued sedimentary layers. In Triassic times the Petrified Forest was a great, steamy swampland; some 225 million years ago, seismic activity forced the swamp's decaying plant matter deep underground, where it eventually turned to stone.

EASTERN ARIZONA PLANNER

WHEN TO GO

If you're not a winter-sports enthusiast, it's best to plan your trip to Eastern Arizona for the high season (May through October). Residents of Phoenix and Tucson flock here to escape unbearably hot temperatures, but you can still find some solitude if you rent a cabin or choose a smaller, more remote resort or bed-and-breakfast.

If you're a skier, winter is the time to tour the White Mountains. Sunrise Park Resort has 10 lifts and 65 trails, and a private snowboarders' park. ■TIP→ Eastern Arizona is enjoyable year-round, but many lodging facilities, restaurants, and tourist attractions are closed in autumn and winter. It's wise to call ahead from November through April, as the opening and closing dates of many seasonal properties are dependent on when the snow starts (and when it melts). Snowstorms can close the highways that lead into the area, so if you plan on making the trip from Phoenix or even Flagstaff, make sure you have an alternative plan.

PLANNING YOUR TIME

The Petrified Forest is the main attraction for most of Eastern Arizona's visitors; it's easy to see the fossils and petroglyphs in just a few hours. Plan to reserve a day for the park and the surrounding Painted Desert, with one or two additional days for exploring the nearby towns and areas. Depending on your preferences, you can add day trips and excursions. Fans of the great outdoors have their choice of activities in the White Mountains. Those who like a little less sweat in their vacations can hit the open road and explore historic Route 66 or the Coronado Trail.

Pinetop-Lakeside, with its wide range of lodging facilities and amenities, might be the best base for your trip. Neighboring area towns, such as Snowflake-Taylor, have memorable motels and B&Bs. If solitude is your goal, consider staying at a lodge surrounded by private forest.

GETTING HERE AND AROUND

CAR TRAVEL

There isn't much choice: you'll be driving to and around Eastern Arizona. Amtrak runs limited service, but it isn't that helpful for travelers. Part of the experience in Eastern Arizona is the drive. Rent a car in Phoenix or Tucson, or even Flagstaff, and enjoy the open road.

If you're arriving from points west via Flagstaff, Interstate 40 leads directly to Holbrook, where drivers can take AZ 77 south into Show Low or U.S. 180 southeast to Springerville-Eagar. From Phoenix, take the scenic drive northeast on U.S. 60, or the slightly faster (and less curvy) AZ 87 north to AZ 260 east, both of which lead to Show Low. From Tucson, AZ 77 north connects with U.S. 60 at Globe, and continues through Show Low up to Holbrook. For those who want to drive the Coronado Trail south-to-north, U.S. 70 and AZ 78 link up with U.S. 191 from Globe to the west and New Mexico to the east, respectively.

WINTER ROAD CONDITIONS Weather conditions change rapidly in Eastern Arizona. Before heading out on a daylong excursion—particularly in winter—be sure to

TOP OUTDOOR ACTIVITIES

Hiking: Hikers and mountain bikers of all abilities enjoy the White Mountains' 225 miles of interconnecting loop trails, open to visitors on foot or on nonmotorized wheels. Ranger stations have maps. Allow an hour for each 2 miles of trail, plus an additional hour for every 1,000 feet gained in altitude. Carry water, wear sunscreen, and watch out for poison ivy.

Fishing: Anglers flock to the more than 65 lakes, streams, and reservoirs in the White Mountains. In winter only artificial lures and flies are permitted. An Arizona fishing license is required; on tribal land you'll also need a White Mountain Apache fishing license. Want an easier catch?

Some lodges have private lakes stocked with trout.

Golfing: The high country's links draw golfers from all over, and these mountain fairways angle through lush forests and past lakes and springs.

Skiing: The 11,000-foot White Mountains have hilly, wooded landscapes that invite downhill and cross-country skiing adventurers. Greer's nearby Pole Knoll Trail System and surrounding Forest Service roads make for 33 miles of cross-country trails. No matter where you stay in the White Mountains, Sunrise Park Resort is never more than an hour's drive away.

call the Arizona Department of Transportation's Traveler Information Service (☎ *511*).

RESTAURANTS

Luxury travel this is not. Fine dining is difficult to find; home-style cooking, steak houses, and the occasional authentic Mexican joint pepper most towns. Casual is the norm. A pair of jeans will gain you entrance to just about any eatery in the area—any dressier and you might be overdone. Reservations are helpful during the busy summer months, and remember that some places are closed from November to April. *Prices in the reviews are the average cost of a main course at dinner or, if dinner isn't served, at lunch.*

HOTELS

Most places supply clean rooms without many frills. These aren't the world-class resorts and spas of Phoenix, but that isn't necessarily a bad thing. "Resort" in this area means you'll probably have a room with a kitchenette and occasional (but not daily) maid service in a picturesque, woodsy setting. Plan on bringing your own toiletries and the like; there's a reason some of these prices are so affordable. *Prices in the reviews are the lowest cost of a standard double room in high season. For expanded reviews, facilities, and current deals, visit Fodors.com.*

THE WHITE MOUNTAINS

With elevations climbing to more than 11,000 feet, the White Mountains area of east-central Arizona is a winter wonderland and a summer haven from the desert heat. In the 1870s, the U.S. soldier John Gregory

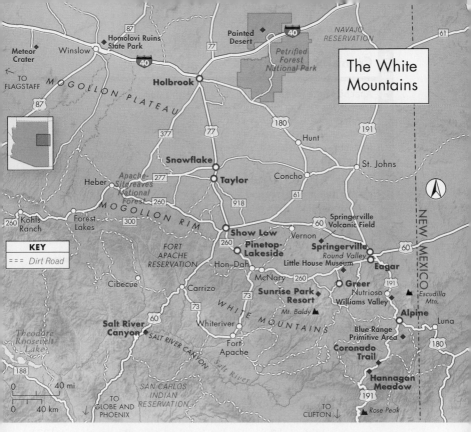

The White Mountains

NAVAJO RESERVATION

Painted Desert

Petrified Forest National Park

Meteor Crater

Winslow
Homolovi Ruins State Park

TO FLAGSTAFF

MOGOLLON PLATEAU

Holbrook

Snowflake
Taylor

Heber
Apache-Sitgreaves National Forest

Kohls Ranch
Forest Lakes

MOGOLLON RIM

Hunt

St. Johns

Concho

Springerville Volcanic Field

Show Low
Pinetop-Lakeside
Vernon
Springerville
Round Valley
Little House Museum
Eagar

FORT APACHE RESERVATION
Hon-Dah

Cibecue
Carrizo

McNary

Sunrise Park Resort

Greer
Nutrioso
Williams Valley

Escudilla Mtn.

WHITE MOUNTAINS

Mt. Baldy

Alpine
Luna

Salt River Canyon
SALT RIVER CANYON

Whiteriver

Fort Apache

Salt River

Blue Range Primitive Area

Coronado Trail

Theodore Roosevelt Lake

SAN CARLOS INDIAN RESERVATION

Hannagan Meadow

NEW MEXICO

KEY
=== Dirt Road

0   40 mi
0   40 km

TO GLOBE AND PHOENIX

TO CLIFTON ↓

Rose Peak

Bourke wrote in his diary that the White Mountains region was "a strange upheaval, a freak of nature, a mountain canted up on one side; one rides along the edge and looks down two or three thousand feet . . . into a weird scene of grandeur and rugged beauty." The area, although much less remote than in Bourke's time, is still grand and rugged, carved by deep river canyons and tall cliffs covered with ponderosa pine.

SALT RIVER CANYON

40 miles north of Globe on U.S. 60.

Exposing a time lapse of 500 million years, the multicolored spires, buttes, mesas, and walls of the Salt River Canyon have inspired its nickname, the Mini–Grand Canyon. Approaching the Salt River Canyon from Phoenix, U.S. 60 climbs through rolling hills, and the terrain changes from high desert with cactus and mesquite trees to forests of ponderosa pine. After entering the San Carlos Indian Reservation, the highway drops 2,000 feet and makes a series of hairpin turns to the Salt River. **Hieroglyphic Point** is just one of the viewpoints along the scenic drive. Stop to stretch your legs at the viewing and interpretive display area before crossing the bridge. Wander along the banks below and enjoy the rock-strewn rapids. On hot days slip your shoes off and dip your feet into the chilly water. ■TIP→ The river and canyon are open

Camping Resources

Apache-Sitgreaves National Forests has a listing of all public camping facilities in the region, most of which operate from April to November. ☎ *928/333–4301* ⊕ *www.fs.usda.gov/asnf.*

To reserve a site at a fee campground, use the **National Recreation Reservation Service**, which charges a reservation fee of $10 per transaction.

☎ *877/444–6777* ⊕ *www.recreation.gov.*

Book your campground site well in advance with the Game and Fish Department of the **White Mountain Apache Tribe**. ☎ *928/338–4385* ⊕ *www.wmatoutdoors.org.*

to hiking, fishing, and white-water rafting, but you need a permit, as this is tribal land. For information and recreational permits, contact the individual tribes.

The Apache people migrated to the Southwest around the 10th century. Divided into individual bands instead of functioning as a unified tribe, they were a hunting and gathering culture, moving with the seasons to gather food, and their crafts—baskets, beadwork, and cradleboards (traditional baby-carriers)—were compatible with their mobile lifestyle. The U.S. government didn't understand that different Apache bands might be hostile to each other, and tried to gather separate tribes on one reservation, compounding relocation problems. Eventually, the government established the San Carlos Apache Indian Reservation in 1871 and the Fort Apache Indian Reservation in 1897. Both tribes hold on fiercely to their cultures. The native language is still spoken and taught in schools, and tribal ceremonies continue to be held. Both tribes have highly acclaimed "hot-shot" crews that immediately respond to forest fires throughout the West. The Salt River forms the boundary between these two large Apache reservations in Eastern Arizona.

WHEN TO GO
As with most of Eastern Arizona, it's best to visit Salt River Canyon in the summer, when there are no worries about winter storms.

GETTING HERE AND AROUND
From the Phoenix area, take U.S. 60 east through Globe, and then continue north for 40 miles. From rim to rim, the road into the canyon itself is 9 miles, but allow extra time to slow down for the tight turns—and to enjoy the views. It's a three-hour drive from Phoenix through Globe.

ESSENTIALS
Recreational Permits and Information San Carlos Apache Tribe
☎ *928/475–2343* ⊕ *www.sancarlosapache.com.* **White Mountain Apache Tribe**
☎ *928/338–4346* ⊕ *www.wmat.nsn.us.*

EXPLORING

Apache Cultural Museum. The entrance price buys access to three great places to visit on the Fort Apache Indian Reservation. The museum explains the history, culture, and artistic traditions of the Apaches, and sells local crafts and books. The **Fort Apache Historical Park** harks back to cavalry days with horse barns, parade grounds, log cabins, and officers' homes. **Kinishba Ruins,** 5 miles west of Fort Apache (get directions and a map at the Cultural Center), is a partly restored sandstone pueblo, and the only Native American ruin on the reservation open to visitors. ⊠ *0.5 miles east of junction of AZ 73 and Indian Rte. 46, 5 miles south of Whiteriver* ☏ *928/338–4625* ☜ *$5* ☉ *Weekdays 8–5.*

Cultural Center. Exhibits on Apache history and culture are displayed at the San Carlos Apache Cultural Center, along with explanations of cultural traditions, such as the Changing Women Ceremony, a girls' puberty rite. Crafts are sold here as well. ⊠ *Hwy. 70, Milepost 272, Peridot* ☏ *928/475–2894* ☜ *$4* ☉ *Weekdays 9–5.*

Fort Apache Indian Reservation. The 2,500-square-mile Fort Apache Indian Reservation is the ancestral home of the White Mountain Apache Tribe. The elevation of the tribal lands ranges from 3,000 feet at the bottom of Salt River to 11,000 feet in the White Mountains, and the area provides some of the best outdoor recreation in the state. Most of the more than 15,000 tribal members live in nine towns, the largest, Whiteriver (population 5,200), serving as tribal headquarters. Tribal enterprises include Sunrise Ski Resort, Hon-Dah Resort Casino, cattle ranching, and lumber. ☏ *928/338–4346* ⊕ *www.wmat.nsn.us.*

San Carlos Apache Indian Reservation. Established in 1871 for various Apache tribes, the San Carlos Apache Indian Reservation covers 1.8 million acres southeast of Salt River Canyon. One-third of the reservation is covered with forest, and the rest is desert. The San Carlos Apaches number about 12,500 and are noted for their beadwork and basketry. Peridot, a beautiful yellow-green stone resembling the emerald, is mined near the town of the same name and made into jewelry. ☏ *928/475–2361 for tribal offices* ⊕ *www.sancarlosapache.com.*

EN ROUTE The road out of the Salt River Canyon climbs along the canyon's northern cliffs, providing views of this truly spectacular chasm, unfairly overlooked in a state full of world-famous gorges. The highway continues some 50 miles northward to the **Mogollon Rim**—a huge geologic ledge that bisects much of Arizona—and its cool upland pinewoods.

SHOW LOW

60 miles north of the Salt River Canyon on U.S. 60.

Show Low has little of the charm of its neighboring White Mountains communities, but it's the main commercial center for the high country. The city is also a crossing point for east–west traffic along the Mogollon Rim and traffic headed for Holbrook and points north. If you're heading up to the Painted Desert and Petrified Forest from Phoenix, you might want to spend the night here.

U.S. 60 descends 2,000 feet into the Salt River Canyon on a series of tight switchbacks with great views.

WHEN TO GO

You'll have to pass through the Salt River Canyon to reach Show Low (or take Highways 87 and 260 through Payson). Either way, it means you'll be driving through mountains; be prepared in winter for storms and cold weather.

GETTING HERE AND AROUND

Show Low is a fairly good central location from which to explore Eastern Arizona by car. You can take AZ 260 south to reach Pinetop-Lakeside, or travel north on AZ 77 to Snowflake-Taylor and, eventually, Petrified Forest National Park.

WHERE TO EAT

$$ MEXICAN 🍴 **Licano's Mexican Food and Steakhouse.** Along with what locals claim are the best enchiladas on the mountain, Licano's also serves shrimp tacos, prime rib, and lobster tail, making for a fairly broad menu. The spacious lounge, with a weekday happy hour from 4:30 to 6:30, stays open to 9 nightly. Its convenient downtown location places it within walking distance from most Show Low hotels. [$] *Average main: $11* ✉ *573 W. Deuce of Clubs* ☎ *928/537–8220* 🌐 *www.licanos.net.*

$ AMERICAN 🍴 **Native New Yorker.** With 30 TVs in the dining room and the adjacent sports bar, this regional chain restaurant is a good place to keep up with the team. As you might expect, they're famous for their wings and bar food, but their chili will warm you up, too. If you're looking for a late-night scene, this is your best bet for the area: the bar stays open on weekends until 2 am. [$] *Average main: $9* ✉ *391 W. Deuce of Clubs* ☎ *928/532–5100* 🌐 *www.nativenewyorker.com.*

WHERE TO STAY

For expanded hotel reviews, visit Fodors.com.

$ **Best Western Paint Pony Lodge.** Spacious rooms have wood accents
HOTEL and picture windows overlooking the pine-studded high country. **Pros:**
affordable, large rooms; free hot breakfast; modern conveniences. **Cons:**
no frills. $ *Rooms from: $109* ✉ *581 W. Deuce of Clubs* ☎ *928/537–
5773* ⊕ *www.bestwestern.com* ⇝ *48 rooms, 2 suites* ⦿ *Breakfast.*

$ **Holiday Inn Express.** Larger rooms and more conveniences than much
HOTEL of its competition make for a comfortable night's rest. **Pros:** the closest
thing to a "big-city" hotel in Show Low; everything you expect from a
brand-name property. **Cons:** limited sightseeing opportunities nearby
mean this is better for a pit stop than a vacation. $ *Rooms from: $118*
✉ *151 W. Deuce of Clubs* ☎ *928/537–5115* ⊕ *www.hiexpress.com*
⇝ *71 rooms* ⦿ *Breakfast.*

$ **KC Motel.** Victorian decorating and large rooms help this not-so-typi-
HOTEL cal two-story motel stand out. **Pros:** good value; Continental breakfast
included. **Cons:** as expected for a motel, there are few frills; style not
for everyone. $ *Rooms from: $72* ✉ *60 W. Deuce of Clubs* ☎ *928/537–
4433, 800/531–7152* ⊕ *www.kcmotelinshowlow.com* ⇝ *35 rooms*
⦿ *Breakfast.*

SPORTS AND THE OUTDOORS

FISHING

Fool Hollow Lake Recreational Area. In addition to fishing, this year-round
park is popular for boating, camping, and wildlife-viewing. Set amid a
piney 800 acres, the lake is stocked with rainbow trout, walleye, and
bass. There are five fishing platforms available, plus two fish-cleaning
stations at the park. ✉ *1500 N. Fool Hollow Lake Rd., 2 miles north of
U.S. 60 off AZ 260, Show Low* ☎ *928/537–3680* ⊕ *www.azstateparks.
com.*

FAMILY **Show Low Lake.** Show Low Lake, south of town and 1 mi off AZ 260,
holds the state record for the largest walleye catch. It's well stocked with
largemouth bass, bluegill, and catfish. Lucky anglers have pulled out
9-pound rainbow trout. Facilities include a bait shop, a marina with
boat rentals, and campsites with bathrooms and showers. ✉ *Show Low
Lake Rd.* ☎ *928/537–4126.*

GOLF

Bison Golf. Designed by Billy Mayfair, Bison Golf has a back nine in
the pines and a front nine in a more open meadow. The course is open
year-round, but expect to encounter course closings throughout the
winter. The club also has a fitness center. ✉ *860 N. 36th Dr., at AZ 260*
☎ *928/537–4564* ⊕ *www.bisongolf.net* 🏌 *18 holes. 5916 yds. Par 71.
Slope 114. Greens Fee: $47* ☞ *Facilities: Driving range, putting green,
golf carts, rental clubs, pro shop.*

Silver Creek Golf Club. Silver Creek Golf Club is 5 miles east of town on
U.S. 60, then 7.5 miles north on Bourdon Ranch Road. This championship course opened to rave reviews in the 1980s, and was voted
by the PGA as one of the top 10 golf courses in Arizona—no small
feat in a state that lives and breathes golf. It's also one of the more
affordable courses in the area. Given its lower elevation, this course

6

is usually a few degrees warmer than Show Low and stays open year-round. Sandbaggers Bar & Grill has breakfast and lunch (dinner on weekends). ✉ *2051 Silver Lake Blvd.* ☎ *928/537–2744, 888/537–3673* 🌐 *www.silvercreekgolfclub.com* 🏌 *18 holes. 6813 yds. Par 71. Slope 135. Greens Fee: $60* ☞ *Facilities: Driving range, putting green, golf carts, rental clubs, lessons, restaurant, bar.*

PINETOP-LAKESIDE

15 miles southeast of Show Low on AZ 260.

At 7,200 feet, the community of Pinetop-Lakeside borders the world's largest stand of ponderosa pine. Two towns, Pinetop and Lakeside, were incorporated in 1984 to form this municipality—although they still retain separate post offices. The year-round population is just 4,200, but in summer months it can jump to as high as 30,000. Once popular only with retirees and those with summerhouses, the city now lures thousands of "flatlanders" up from the Valley of the Sun with gorgeous scenery, excellent multiuse trails, premier golf courses, and temperatures that rarely exceed 85°F.

WHEN TO GO

Desert dwellers flock to Pinetop-Lakeside in summer to escape the heat. In winter, it's a wonderland of snow and mountains, but be prepared, as U.S. 60 and Interstate 40 are routinely closed and impassable during snowstorms.

GETTING HERE AND AROUND

A 15-minute drive from Show Low, Pinetop-Lakeside is ideal for exploring by car. The main drag is known as both AZ 260 and White Mountain Boulevard.

WHERE TO EAT

$$ STEAKHOUSE 🍴 **Charlie Clark's Steak House.** Attracting golfers relishing a successful day on the links as well as locals in search of good food, Charlie Clark's has been the meeting place of the White Mountains since it opened in 1938. Furnished with lots of wood, the building has been added on to in the decades since. Prime rib is the house specialty, and make sure to try a cup of the French onion soup. Minnesota walleye adds a Midwestern spin to the menu. [$] *Average main: $23* ✉ *1701 E. White Mountain Blvd., Pinetop* ☎ *928/367–4900, 888/333-0259* 🌐 *www.charlieclarks.com.*

$ MEXICAN 🍴 **Los Corrales.** Bright yellows and oranges make this a cheerful family-style eatery. Locals come for Mexican seafood dishes such as *camarones a la crema* (shrimp and mushrooms in cream sauce) and lunch specials. Dessert specialties include fried ice cream and apple *chimichanga*. [$] *Average main: $8* ✉ *845 E. White Mountain Blvd., Lakeside* ☎ *928/367–5585.*

WHERE TO STAY

For expanded hotel reviews, visit Fodors.com.

$$ HOTEL 🏨 **Hon-Dah Resort Casino and Conference Center.** Stuffed high-country animals atop a mountain of boulders welcome you to Hon-Dah, which is operated by the White Mountain Apache Tribe (the name means

"welcome to my home" in Apache). **Pros:** best destination for travelers who aren't interested in roughing it; big draw for the casino crowd. **Cons:** can get noisy in the evening, and the term "resort" can be misleading. $ *Rooms from: $124* ✉ *777 Hwy 260, Pinetop* ☎ *928/369–0299, 800/929–8744* ⊕ *www.hon-dah.com* ⤳ *126 rooms, 2 suites* ⦿ *No meals.*

$
RESORT

⌘ **Lake of the Woods Resort.** Whether you're looking for a modern cabin with all the creature comforts or something a little more cozy and rustic, this resort has what you want. **Pros:** on Lakeside's main street, with a rural, but not removed, atmosphere; stocked private lake. **Cons:** only phone for guests is a pay phone in the main building; Internet in lobby only. $ *Rooms from: $99* ✉ *2244 W. White Mountain Blvd., Lakeside* ☎ *928/368–5353* ⊕ *www.lakeofthewoodsaz.com* ⤳ *26 cabins, 7 houses* ⦿ *No meals.*

$$
RESORT
FAMILY

⌘ **Northwoods Resort.** Each of the 14 fully furnished cottages at this mountain retreat has its own covered porch and a grill. **Pros:** no highway noise; ideal for a family vacation in solitude; Wi-Fi available. **Cons:** cabins are close together, so there isn't a ton of privacy. $ *Rooms from: $119* ✉ *AZ 260, Milepost 352* ☎ *928/367–2966, 800/813–2966* ⊕ *www.northwoodsaz.com* ⤳ *14 cabins* ⦿ *No meals.*

$$
RESORT

⌘ **Whispering Pines Resort.** On 12 acres bordering the Apache-Sitgreaves National Forest, these well-maintained cabins are in walking distance of Woodland Lake and Walnut Creek. **Pros:** great accommodations for large parties; extremely private. **Cons:** older furnishings in rooms; icy roads in the resort can be difficult to navigate in winter. $ *Rooms from: $120* ✉ *AZ 260, just beyond Milepost 352, 237 E. White Mountain Blvd.* ☎ *928/367–4386, 800/840–3867* ⊕ *www.whisperingpinesaz.com* ⤳ *38 cabins* ⦿ *No meals.*

SPORTS AND THE OUTDOORS
BICYCLING AND HIKING

Listed in the American Hiking Society's "Trail Town Hall of Fame," Pinetop-Lakeside is the primary trailhead for the White Mountains Trails System, which includes roughly 200 miles of interconnecting multiuse loop trails that span the White Mountains. All these trails are open to mountain bikers, horseback riders, and hikers.

Apache-Sitgreaves National Forests. You can get trail brochures or other information from the Apache-Sitgreaves National Forests, including a $2 booklet on the White Mountains Trail System. ✉ *Lakeside Ranger Station, 2022 W. White Mountain Blvd., Lakeside* ☎ *928/368–2100* ⊕ *www.fs.usda.gov/asnf.*

Big Springs Environmental Study Area. Half a mile off AZ 260 on Woodland Road, Big Springs Environmental Study Area is a 0.5–mi loop trail that wanders by riparian meadows, two streams, and a spring-fed pond. A series of educational signs is devoted to the surrounding flora and fauna. *Easy.* ✉ *Woodland Rd. and AZ 260, Lakeside* ☎ *928/368–6700* ⊕ *ci.pinetop-lakeside.az.us/bigsprings.htm.*

Country Club Trail. The trailhead for Country Club Trail is at the junction of Forest Service roads 182 and 185; these 3.5 mi of moderately dif-

6

ficult mountain-biking and hiking trails can be spiced up by following the spur-trail to the top of Pat Mullen Mountain and back. *Moderate.*

Mogollon Rim Interpretive Trail. The well-traveled and easy Mogollon Rim Interpretive Trail follows a small part of the 19th-century **Crook Trail** along the Mogollon Rim; the 0.25-mi path, with a trailhead just west of the Pinetop-Lakeside city limits, is well marked with placards describing local wildlife and geography. *Easy.*

Panorama Trail. The 8-mile Panorama Trail, rated moderate, comes with astonishing views from the top of extinct double volcanoes known as the Twin Knolls, and passes through a designated wildlife habitat area; the trailhead is 6 miles east on Porter Mountain Road, off AZ 260. *Moderate.*

FISHING

Hawley Lake. East of Pinetop-Lakeside and 9 miles south of AZ 260, 260-acre Hawley Lake sits on Apache territory and yields mostly rainbow trout; rental boats are available in the marina. Tribal permits are required for all recreational activities: contact **White Mountain Apache Game & Fish Department** (☎ *928/338–4385* ⊕ *www.wmatoutdoors. org*) for details. ⊠ *AZ 473, Hawley Lake.*

Paradise Creek Anglers. Paradise Creek Anglers offers fishing advice, lessons, and equipment rentals. They share business space with Skiers Edge, so you can get year-round service and advice. ⊠ *560 W. White Mountain Blvd., Lakeside* ☎ *928/367–6200, 800/231–3831* ⊕ *www. paradisecreekanglers.com.*

GOLF

Pinetop Lakes Golf & Country Club. Pinetop Lakes Golf & Country Club has fewer trees than other area courses, but it includes several water hazards to compensate. The shorter course is wonderful for public play. The club also has tennis courts; it's open April to October. ⊠ *4643 Buck Springs Rd., Pinetop* ☎ *928/369–4531* ⊕ *www.pinetoplakesgolf. com* ⚑ *18 holes. 4558 yds. Par 63. Slope 94. Greens Fee: $63* ☞ *Facilities: Driving range, putting green, golf carts, rental clubs, lessons, restaurant, bar.*

SKIING AND SNOW SPORTS

The Skier's Edge. The Skier's Edge has cross-country and downhill skis as well as snowboards and boots. They share business space with Paradise Creek Anglers, so you can get year-round service and advice. ⊠ *560 W. White Mountain Blvd., Pinetop* ☎ *928/367–6200, 800/231–3831* ⊕ *www.skiersedgepinetop.com.*

Snowriders Board & Ski Rentals. From December through mid-March, Snowriders Board & Ski Rentals sells and rents skis, snowboards, and gear, weather permitting. ⊠ *857 E. White Mountain Blvd., Pinetop* ☎ *928/367-5638* ⊕ *www.azsnowriders.com.*

SNOWFLAKE-TAYLOR

30 miles north of Pinetop-Lakeside on Route 260 and AZ 77.

Snowflake-Taylor is a good jumping-off point for exploring Eastern Arizona. The towns are also a less crowded alternative for summer trips into the nearby White Mountains. Most Phoenix weekenders head for the higher towns, so Snowflake and Taylor don't get the crush of summer visitors that results in higher prices at hotels and restaurants. Sandwiched between the White Mountains and the Colorado Plateau, the communities enjoy year-round pleasant weather, with summer highs in the 90s. Yes, it snows in Snowflake, but it seldom lasts more than a day. It's also an easy day trip to the Petrified Forest.

Snowflake and Taylor were settled by Mormons in the 1870s and named for Mormon church leaders. Snowflake's unusual name is a combination of Erastus Snow, an apostle in the early Mormon church of Salt Lake City, and William Flake, one of the town founders. One of Arizona's two Mormon temples sits on Temple Hill (to the west of Snowflake), and the towns still have a large Mormon contingent in their combined population of 9,000. You can take a walking tour of Snowflake's historical district, with pioneer homes and antiques stores.

WHEN TO GO

Since Snowflake-Taylor isn't as far into the White Mountains as other communities it's somewhat easier to reach in winter. Still, most visitors explore this area in summer.

GETTING HERE AND AROUND

From Show Low off AZ 77, Snowflake-Taylor is about one-third of the way to Interstate 40.

EXPLORING

Stinson Museum. The Stinson Museum once served as a schoolhouse. James Stinson, the first rancher in the valley, was the original resident of the small adobe home. William J. Flake bought out Stinson's holdings and founded the town of Snowflake. Flake added on to the structure, which today is a museum containing pioneer memorabilia, quilts, Native American artifacts, and a small gift shop. ⊠ *102 N. 1st St. East* ☎ *928/536–4331 Snowflake-Taylor Chamber of Commerce* 🖃 *Donations accepted* ☉ *Mon.–Sat. 10–2.*

Taylor Museum. A small local museum with pioneer and Native American exhibits, the Taylor Museum celebrates July 4th by "firing the anvil" at sunrise. At 4 am revelers place an anvil on the ground, a newspaper and gunpowder on top, then another anvil. When the gunpowder is lighted, the anvil flies a few feet into the air with a deafening bang. The rest of the year, the anvil resides at the museum along with the Jennings drum, which was brought to town by early Mormon settlers. ⊠ *2 North Main St., Taylor* ☎ *928/536–4331 Snowflake-Taylor Chamber of Commerce* 🖃 *Donations accepted* ☉ *Mon.,Tues., and Thurs.–Sat. 10–2.*

WHERE TO EAT

$$
ITALIAN
✕ **Enzo's Ristorante Italiano.** At the only Italian restaurant in town, sauces and breads are made from scratch by Enzo himself, and although they may take a while, the minestrone soup, baked pastas, and shrimp Alfredo are worth the wait. Bring your own bottle of wine; Enzo provides the glasses. 💲 *Average main: $15* ⊠ *423 W. 3rd St. N* ☎ *928/243–0450* ⟁ *Reservations not accepted* 🖃 *No credit cards* ☉ *Closed Sun.–Tues. No lunch.*

$
MEXICAN

✕ **La Cocina de Eva.** Any trip to Arizona should become a tour of different styles of Mexican food, and if you like trying different interpretations of Sonoran cuisine, stop here. The green-corn tamales and enchiladas are delicious, and locals go for the bean burrito smothered in green chili sauce. Portions are large, and the service is friendly at this popular spot, which is decorated in a homey combination of South-of-the-border knickknacks and Western paintings. $ *Average main: $8* ⊠ *201 N. Main St.* ☎ *928/536–7683* ⊗ *Closed Sun.*

$
AMERICAN

✕ **Trapper's Cafe.** Opened in 1973 by "Trapper" Hatch, this family-owned diner is decorated with Hatch's old trapping equipment and animal paintings by local artists. Chicken-fried steak and homemade barbecue sauce draw a loyal crowd, as do the steaks. People drive out of their way just for a piece of pie, especially the banana cream. Have a slice at the counter with a cup of coffee. $ *Average main: $8* ⊠ *9 S. Main St., Taylor* ☎ *928/536–7758* ⊗ *Closed Sun.*

WHERE TO STAY
For expanded hotel reviews, visit Fodors.com.

$
B&B/INN
Fodor's Choice
★

▦ **Heritage Inn Bed & Breakfast.** Elegantly furnished with Victorian antiques and filled with pioneer style, this popular redbrick bed-and-breakfast has charm to spare. **Pros:** quiet B&B setting with modern conveniences, including Internet access and DVD players; exceptional service and great breakfast. **Cons:** some rooms only have a Jacuzzi tub with no shower. $ *Rooms from: $105* ⊠ *161 N. Main St.* ☎ *928/536–3322, 866/486–5947* ⊕ *www.heritage-inn.net* ⊅ *10 rooms, 1 cottage* ⍟ *Breakfast.*

$
B&B/INN

▦ **Silver Creek Rodeway Inn.** Simply furnished, clean, and handy to fast-food restaurants, Silver Creek attracts regulars who travel through the area often. **Pros:** convenient town location; inexpensive. **Cons:** intended for travelers just passing through; no on-site restaurant. $ *Rooms from: $59* ⊠ *825 N. Main St., Taylor* ☎ *928/536–2600* ⊕ *www.rodewayinn. com* ⊅ *42 rooms* ⍟ *Breakfast.*

SPORTS AND THE OUTDOORS
GOLF
Snowflake Municipal Golf Course. One of the least expensive golf courses in the White Mountains, the Snowflake Municipal Golf Course is open year-round, with fees that are lower October through April. With scenic red rocks and waterfalls, the course also includes a water hazard. The restaurant is open May through October. ⊠ *90 N. Country Club Dr.* ☎ *928/536–7233* ⅃ *18 holes. 6172 yds. Par 72. Slope 116. Greens Fee: $40* ⊂ *Facilities: Driving range, putting green, golf carts, rental clubs, restaurant.*

HIKING
Petroglyph Hike. At the junction of Silver Creek Canyon and Five-Mile Canyon, 5 miles north of Snowflake, ancient peoples left petroglyphs made by carving through dark varnish, revealing the light sandstone of the canyon walls. Petroglyph Hike, the trail from the canyon top down to the petroglyphs, is short but steep. Trail access is regulated by the city of Snowflake. To check in and get directions, contact the

Snowflake-Taylor Chamber of Commerce (☎ *928/536–4331* 🌐 *www.snowflaketaylorchamber.org*). *Moderate.* ✉ *Silver Creek Canyon.*

SUNRISE PARK RESORT

27 miles southeast of Pinetop-Lakeside on AZ 260 and AZ 273.

WHEN TO GO

Sunrise is one of Arizona's top two destinations for skiing and winter recreation. You can also visit in summer, however, for horseback riding, mountain biking, and chairlift rides—all with great views of the White Mountains.

GETTING HERE AND AROUND

The resort is 7 miles south of the intersection of AZ 260 and AZ 273.

EXPLORING

FAMILY **Sunrise Park Resort.** In winter and early spring, skiers and other snow lovers flock to Sunrise Park Resort. There's plenty more than downhill and cross-country skiing here, including snowboarding, snowmobiling, snowshoeing, ice fishing, and sleigh rides. The resort has 10 lifts and 65 trails on three mountains rising to 11,000 feet. Eighty percent of the downhill runs are for beginning or intermediate skiers, and many less-intense trails begin at the top, so skiers of varying skill levels can ride the chairlifts together. There's a "ski-wee" hill for youngsters. The Sunrise Express high-speed chairlift anchors the 10 lifts. One-day lift tickets are $51. Sunrise's Snowboard Park has jumps of all difficulty levels and its own sound system, and is exclusively for snowboarders—so there's no tension on the hill between boarders and skiers. Cross-country skiers enjoy 13.5 miles of interconnecting trails. You can rent equipment at the ski shop. In summer a marina is open for boat rentals on Sunrise Lake. ✉ *AZ 273, 7 mi south of AZ 260* ☎ *928/735–7669* 🌐 *www.sunriseskipark.com.*

WHERE TO STAY

For expanded hotel reviews, visit Fodors.com.

$$ HOTEL 🏨 **Sunrise Park Resort.** Catering to those who want to be as close as possible to the lifts, this hotel has comfortable rooms with ski racks and runs a shuttle to the slopes every half hour. **Pros:** convenient location and proximity to slopes. **Cons:** this is not a resort like many travelers are accustomed to—accommodations are no-frills; closed between seasons. [$] *Rooms from: $124* ✉ *AZ 273, 7 miles south of AZ 260* ☎ *928/735–7669* 🌐 *www.sunriseskipark.com* 🛏 *100 rooms, 1 suite* 🍴 *No meals.*

GREER

12 miles east of Sunrise Park Resort, 35 miles southeast of Pinetop-Lakeside, 15 miles southwest of Springerville-Eagar on AZ 260.

The charming community of Greer sits among pine, spruce, willow, and aspen on the banks of the Little Colorado River. At an elevation of 8,500 feet, this portion of gently sloping National Forest land is covered with meadows and reservoirs and is dominated by 11,590-foot Baldy Peak. Much of the surrounding area remains under the control of the White Mountain Apache Tribe, which has its own laws regulating camping and hiking.

WHEN TO GO

When compared to other areas of Eastern Arizona, Greer is relatively temperate. As in most towns in the area, summers are great here for getting away from the heat; winters are snowy but not frigid.

GETTING HERE AND AROUND

Take AZ 373 south from AZ 260. AZ 373 is also Greer's main street, and after it crosses the Little Colorado River it eventually comes to a dead end. It's affectionately called the Road to Nowhere.

EXPLORING

Butterfly Lodge Museum. Listed on the National Register of Historic Places, the Butterfly Lodge Museum was built as a hunting lodge in 1914 for author James Willard Schultz and his artist son, Lone Wolf, a prolific painter of Indian and Western scenes. There's a small gift shop. Take time to watch the surrounding meadow come to life with the lodge's fluttering butterflies. (The lodge was built by John Butler, the husband of "Aunt Molly," of Molly Butler Lodge fame.) ✉ *AZ 373 at CR 1126* ☎ *928/735–7514* 🌐 *www.butterflylodgemuseum.org* 🎟 *$2* 🕒 *June–Aug., Thurs.–Sun. 10–5.*

WHERE TO EAT AND STAY

For expanded hotel reviews, visit Fodors.com.

$ AMERICAN 🍴 **Greer Mountain Resort Country Cafe.** Decorated with hanging plants, this diner-café has a straightforward, unremarkable interior and exterior. Grab a seat by the fireplace and sample the homemade ranch beans, a grilled-cheese sandwich with tomato and green chiles—because every dish in Arizona tastes better with green chiles—or fresh-baked cobbler. When it's cold outside, the homemade soups will take away the chill. The cafe is open daily 7 am–3 pm. [$] *Average main: $7* ✉ *38742 AZ 373, 1.5 mi south of AZ 260* ☎ *928/735–7560* 🌐 *www.greermountainresort.com* 🕒 *No dinner.*

$ AMERICAN 🍴 **Rendezvous Diner.** This popular local diner has earned a reputation for serving up some of Greer's tastiest dishes, not to mention the area's best hot spiced cider, a perfect choice during the chilly winter months. Of particular note are the pineapple teriyaki, green-chile burgers, and generous portions of homemade cobblers; the rhubarb is a specialty. The place is open year-round for breakfast and lunch. [$] *Average main: $7* ✉ *117 Main St.* ☎ *928/735–7483* 🕒 *Closed Tues. No dinner.*

$ RENTAL 🏨 **Greer Mountain Resort.** Budget travelers and families appreciate these cabin-style accommodations. **Pros:** on-site restaurant and in-room kitchens; good value. **Cons:** small resort with few other amenities. [$] *Rooms from: $95* ✉ *AZ 373, 1.5 miles south of AZ 260* ☎ *928/735–7560* 🌐 *www.greermountainresort.com* 🛏 *9 units* 🍽 *No meals.*

$$ RENTAL 🏨 **Molly Butler Lodge & Cabins.** Colorful quilts and wood furnishings fill the history-themed rooms at Arizona's oldest lodge, which also includes dozens of cabins in the Greer area for larger parties and extended stays. **Pros:** historic charm; range of accommodations. **Cons:** minimal services; you're on your own (which could be a good thing). [$] *Rooms from:*

Eastern Arizona attracts outdoor lovers for horseback riding, hiking, fishing, golfing, and skiing.

$125 ⊠ *109 Main St.* ☎ *928/735–7617* ⊕ *www.mollybutlerlodge.com*
⊋ *3 rooms, 49 cabins* ⦿ *No meals.*

NIGHTLIFE

Molly Butler Lodge. Tiny Greer's nightlife is limited to the bar and lounge of the Molly Butler Lodge, where you can listen to vintage tunes on the jukebox, sink into a cozy seat near the fireplace, play an arcade game, or challenge a local to a game of pool or darts. The bar usually closes by 11 in winter and just past midnight during the busier summer months. ⊠ *109 Main St.* ☎ *928/735–7226* ⊕ *www.mollybutlerlodge.com.*

SPORTS AND THE OUTDOORS

Lazy Trout Trading Post. The Lazy Trout Trading Post sells sleds in winter and tackle the rest of the year. Fishing licenses, groceries, and other supplies are for sale, which is helpful considering the nearest large grocery store is more than a half-hour away. You can grab a cup of joe, buy supplies for an afternoon picnic, and feel free to use their Wi-Fi for a quick email check. ⊠ *38940 AZ 373* ☎ *928/735–7540* ⊕ *www.lazytrout.com.*

FISHING

Greer Lakes. The three Greer Lakes are actually the Bunch, River, and Tunnel reservoirs. Bait and fly-fishing options are scenic and plentiful, and there are several places to launch a boat. Winding through Greer, the Little Colorado River's West Fork is well stocked with brook and rainbow trout, and has 23 miles of fishable waters.

HIKING

Mount Baldy Trail. The difficult but accessible Mount Baldy Trail begins at **Sheeps Crossing,** southwest of Greer on AZ 273. In just under 8 miles (one way) the trail climbs the northern flank of 11,590-foot Mount Baldy, the second-highest peak in Arizona. Note that the summit of Baldy is on the White Mountain Apache Reservation. Considered sacred land, this final 0.25 mile is off-limits to non-Apaches. Please respect this boundary, no matter how much you wish to continue to the peak. *Moderate.*

SKIING

Apache-Sitgreaves National Forests. Trail maps are available from the Apache-Sitgreaves National Forests. ⊠ *Springerville Ranger District, 165 S. Mountain Ave., Springerville* ☎ *928/333–6200* ⊕ *www.fs.usda. gov/asnf.*

Pole Knoll Trail System. Cross-country skiers find Greer an ideally situated hub for some of the mountain's best trails. About 2.5 miles west of AZ 373 on AZ 260, a trailhead marks the starting point for the Pole Knoll Trail System, nearly 30 miles of well-marked, groomed cross-country trails interlacing through the Apache-Sitgreaves National Forests and color-coded by experience level. ⊠ *Springerville Ranger District* ☎ *928/333-4372* ⊕ *www.fs.usda.gov/asnf.*

THE ROUND VALLEY AND CORONADO TRAIL

Named by Basque settlers in the late 1800s, the "Valle Redondo," or Round Valley, is a circular, high-mountain basin on the back side of the massive 10,912-foot Escudilla Mountain. This area once served as a unique Old West haven for the lawless—it was a great place to conceal stolen cattle and hide out for a while. Butch Cassidy, the Clantons, and the Smith Gang all spent time here. Home to sister cities Springerville and Eagar, the Round Valley is the ideal start to any journey on the Coronado Trail, a historic 123-mile switchback highway that starts in pine forests and ends with the cacti of the Sonoran Desert in Clifton. Along the way, you'll find quaint towns, charming inns, and plenty of reasons to marvel at what Mother Nature created.

CORONADO TRAIL

The 123-mile stretch of U.S. 191 from Springerville to Clifton.

WHEN TO GO

It's best to drive in summer. The road is curvy—it was once called the Devil's Highway for a reason. Don't drive on it in snow or ice.

GETTING HERE AND AROUND

Take U.S. 191 for 123 miles from Springerville to Clifton, and be prepared for an eye-opening ride. Allow a good four hours to make the steep, winding drive, more if you plan on making stops and having a leisurely trip.

EXPLORING

Coronado Trail. Surely one of the world's curviest roads, the twisting Coronado Trail portion of U.S. 191 was referred to as the Devil's Highway in its prior incarnation as U.S. 666. The route parallels the one allegedly followed more than 450 years ago by Spanish explorer Francisco Vásquez de Coronado on his search for the legendary Seven Cities of Cibola, where he'd heard that the streets were paved with gold and jewels.

This 123-mile stretch of highway is renowned for the transitions of its spectacular scenery over a dramatic 5,000-foot elevation change—from rolling meadows to spruce- and ponderosa pine-covered mountains, down into the Sonoran Desert's piñon pine, grassland savannas, juniper stands, and cacti. A trip down the Coronado Trail crosses through the Apache-Sitgreaves National Forests, as well as the Fort Apache and San Carlos Apache Indian reservations.

Pause at **Blue Vista,** perched on the edge of the Mogollon Rim, about 30 miles outside Alpine, to take in views of the Blue Range Mountains to the east and the succession of tiered valleys dropping some 4,000 feet back down into the Sonoran Desert. Still above the rim, this is one of your last opportunities to enjoy the blue spruce, ponderosa pine, and high-country mountain meadows.

About 17 miles south of Blue Vista, the Coronado Trail continues to twist and turn, eventually crossing under 8,786-foot **Rose Peak.** Named for the wild roses growing on its mountainside, Rose Peak is also home to a fire lookout tower from which peaks more than 100 miles away can be seen on a clear day. This is a great picnic-lunch stop.

After Rose Peak, enjoy the remaining scenery some 70 more miles until you reach the less scenic towns of Clifton and Morenci, homes to a massive copper mine. U.S. 191 then swings back west, links up with U.S. 70, and provides a fairly straight shot to Globe.

SPRINGERVILLE-EAGAR

17 miles northeast of Greer, 45 miles east of Pinetop-Lakeside on AZ 260, 67 miles southeast of Petrified Forest National Park on U.S. 180.

Sister cities Springerville and Eagar are the self-proclaimed "Gateway to the White Mountains." Insulated by the unique geography of the Round Valley where they sit, Springerville and Eagar occupy a different climate belt from nearby Greer and Sunrise Park Resort, which means less severe winter temperatures and lighter snowfall than in neighboring mountain towns.

WHEN TO GO

■TIP➔ The Round Valley is the favorite of skiers in the know, who appreciate the location as they commute to the lifts at Sunrise with the sun always at their back—important when you consider the glare off those blanketed snowscapes between the resort and Pinetop-Lakeside. There's also a lot less traffic on this less-icy stretch of AZ 260.

On the other hand, although Springerville-Eagar doesn't get as much snow as other parts of the region, it remains a very remote area. It can be hard to reach—and leave—in winter.

GETTING HERE AND AROUND

It's about an hour drive from Pinetop-Lakeside to this isolated area.

EN
ROUTE

Springerville Volcanic Field. The junction of U.S. 180/191 and U.S. 60, just north of Springerville, is the perfect jumping-off spot for a driving tour of the Springerville Volcanic Field, which covers an area larger than the state of Rhode Island. On the southern edge of the Colorado Plateau, it's spread across a high-elevation plain similar to the Tibetan Plateau. Six miles north of Springerville on U.S. 180/191 are sweeping westward views of the **Twin Knolls**—double volcanoes that erupted twice here 700,000 years ago. As you travel west on U.S. 60, Green's Peak Road and various south-winding Forest Service roads make for a leisurely, hour-long drive past **St. Peter's Dome** and a stop for impressive views from **Green's Peak,** the topographic high point of the Springerville Field. A free, detailed driving-tour brochure of the Springerville Volcanic Field is available from the **Springerville-Eagar Regional Chamber of Commerce** (*318 Main St. Box 31, Springerville 85938* ☎ *928/333–2123* ⊕ *www.sechamber.com*).

EXPLORING

Casa Malpais Archaeological Park. The 14.5-acre Casa Malpais Archaeological Park pueblo complex, built in the 13th century, has a series of narrow terraces lining eroded edges of basalt (hardened lava flow) cliff, as well as an extensive system of subterranean rooms nestled within Earth's fissures underneath. Strategically designed gateways in the walls of the "House of the Badlands," as Spanish settlers called it, allow streams of sunlight to illuminate significant petroglyphs prior to the setting equinox or solstice sun. Casa Malpais's Great Kiva (any kiva over 30 feet is considered great) is square-cornered instead of round, consistent with Ancestral Puebloan practice. Some archaeologists believe the pueblo served as a regional ceremonial center for the Mogollon people. Both the Hopi and Zuni tribes trace their history to Casa Malpais. Start your visit at the Springerville Heritage Center, home of the Casa Malpais Museum. Two-hour tours leave at 9, 11, and 2. ⊠ *418 E. Main St.* ☎ *928/333–5375* ⊕ *www.casamalpais.org* ☜ *$8* ⊙ *Museum Mon.–Sat. 8–4, weather permitting; call ahead to confirm. Tours only offered March–Nov.*

Little House Museum. The Little House Museum has a collection of local pioneer and ranching memorabilia, but it's the mesmerizing tones from a rare collection of automatic musical instruments that you remember—as well as the museum's colorful curator, Wink Crigler, with her tales of this region's lively past. Tours to archaeological digs and petroglyphs are available by appointment. To reach the ranch, go 10 miles southwest of Eagar on AZ 260, turn south onto South Fork Road, and go 3 miles. ⊠ *X Diamond Ranch, S. Fork Rd., 10 mi southwest of Eagar, Greer* ☎ *928/333–2286* ⊕ *www.xdiamondranch.com/museum.html* ☜ *$12* ⊙ *By reservation only.*

The White Mountains' elevation makes the area a great place to stay cool in summer.

Renée Cushman Art Collection Museum. The Renée Cushman Art Collection Museum is one of the highlights of the Springerville Heritage Center. Renée Cushman's extensive collection of objets d'art—some acquired on her travels, some collected with the accumulated resources of three wealthy husbands, and some willed to her by her artistic father—includes a Rembrandt engraving, pen-and-inks by Tiepolo, and an impressive collection of European antiques, some dating back to the 15th century. ✉ *Springerville Heritage Center, 418 E. Main Street* ☎ *928/333-2123* 🎟 *Donation only* 🕒 *Mon.–Sat. 8–4.*

WHERE TO EAT

$ AMERICAN 🍴 **Booga Reds.** The delicious comfort food here, such as fish-and-chips and a roast-beef dinner, is worth a stop. Should your palate demand something spicier, try one of the many Mexican dishes—the enchiladas are wonderful. Save room for the daily fruit or cream pie. Booga Reds closes at 8 pm, so make your dinner an early one. [$] *Average main: $8* ✉ *521 E. Main St.* ☎ *928/333–2640.*

$ AMERICAN 🍴 **Java Blues.** With a coffeehouse vibe (overstuffed couches and stained-glass windows), this isn't your typical mountain eatery. Salads, soups, sandwiches, and a Greek Board—a variety of meats and cheeses served with toasted baguette—are on the lunch menu. A separate dinner menu and a full bar make it a favorite evening spot, too—don't miss the chicken-fried steak. The restaurant opens early and serves dinner every day but Sunday. [$] *Average main: $7* ✉ *341 E. Main St.* ☎ *928/333–5282* 🕒 *No dinner Sun.*

WHERE TO STAY

For expanded hotel reviews, visit Fodors.com.

$ **Reed's Lodge.** It's an older motel, but a town favorite. **Pros:** well
HOTEL priced; fantastic service. **Cons:** modest accommodations; few frills;
some rooms in need of updating. *$ Rooms from: $58 ⊠ 514 E. Main
St. ☎ 928/333–4323, 800/814–6451 ⊕ www.k5reeds.com ⤳ 45 rooms,
5 suites ⊙ No meals.*

$ **Rode Inn.** Two cardboard figures of John Wayne in full cowboy regalia
B&B/INN are perched on a walkway above the lobby, and his photos decorate the
walls. **Pros:** comfortable; free wi-fi. **Cons:** take away the kitschy acces-
sories and it's just an old Ramada Inn. *$ Rooms from: $80 ⊠ 242 E.
Main St. ☎ 928/333–4365 ⊕ www.rodeinnmotels.com ⤳ 60 rooms, 3
suites ⊙ Breakfast.*

$ **X Diamond Ranch.** This magnificent ranch has log cabins complete
RESORT with porches, fireplaces, and full kitchens. **Pros:** one of the best-known
and most picturesque spots in the area. **Cons:** no on-site restaurant,
so plan on making your own meals. *$ Rooms from: $110 ⊠ S. Fork
Rd., 10 mi southwest of Eagar off AZ 260 ☎ 928/333–2286 ⊕ www.
xdiamondranch.com ⤳ 7 cabins ⊙ No meals.*

NIGHTLIFE

Tequila Reds. Springerville and Eagar aren't known for their nightlife,
but Tequila Reds is the best place around to catch a televised sporting
event. It's behind Booga Reds restaurant and stays open until at least
11 most nights. *⊠ 521 E. Main St. ☎ 928/333–5036.*

SHOPPING

Reed's Lodge / K5 Adventures & Gallery. Reed's Lodge / K5 Adventures &
Gallery sells wares created by White Mountains artists and local craftspeople, including those from nearby reservations. The gallery teems
with Western-themed paintings, books on local history, wildlife, cowboy poetry, and even John Wayne paper dolls. *⊠ Reed's Lodge, 514 E.
Main St. ☎ 928/333–4323 ⊕ www.k5reeds.com.*

SPORTS AND THE OUTDOORS

Sweat Shop. For your mountain-sports needs, the Sweat Shop rents
skis, snowboards, and mountain bikes. *⊠ 42 N. Main St., Eagar
☎ 928/333–2950.*

FISHING

Becker Lake. Trout fishing is the specialty at Becker Lake; call for seasonal bait requirements. *⊠ U.S. 60, 2 miles northwest of Springerville
☎ 928/367–4281 ⊕ www.azgfd.gov.*

Big Lake. Known to many as the "queen of all trout lakes," Big Lake is
stocked each spring and fall with rainbow, brook, and cutthroat trout.
*⊠ Springerville Ranger District, AZ 273, 24 miles south of AZ 260
☎ 928/333-6200.*

Nelson Reservoir. Between Springerville-Eagar and Alpine, Nelson Reservoir is well stocked with rainbow, brown, and brook trout. *⊠ U.S.
191, Nutrioso ☎ 928/333-4301.*

TOURS AND OUTFITTERS **Western United Drug.** Open 365 days a year, Western United Drug has a well-stocked sporting-goods and outdoor-equipment section. ⊠ *105 E. Main St.* ☎ *928/333–4321.*

ALPINE

27 miles south of Springerville-Eagar on U.S. 191.

Known as the Alps of Arizona, the tiny, scenic village of Alpine promotes its winter recreation opportunities most heavily, but outdoors enthusiasts find that the town, sitting on the lush plains of the San Francisco River, is also an ideal base for hiking, fishing, and mountain-biking excursions during the warmer months. There are summer cabins tucked in the pines, campgrounds, 11 lakes, and 200 miles of trout streams within a 30-mile radius.

WHEN TO GO
This area of the Apache-Sitgreaves National Forests is as remote as it gets, and the name Alpine should indicate the climate. If you're there in winter, expect road closures or delays if there's a storm. In summer, this is a great place to transition from green forests to, eventually, brown desert and cacti.

GETTING HERE AND AROUND
Take U.S. 191 south from Springerville for 27 miles. This is a good stop along the Coronado Trail.

EXPLORING
Blue Range Primitive Area. Directly east of Hannagan Meadow, these unspoiled 170,000 acres, lovingly referred to by locals as "the Blue," are the last designated primitive area in the United States. The diverse terrain surrounds the Blue River and is crossed by the Mogollon Rim from east to west. No motorized or mechanized equipment is allowed, and that includes mountain bikes; passage is restricted to foot or horseback. Many trails interlace the Blue: prehistoric paths of the ancient native peoples, cowboy trails to move livestock between pastures and water sources, access routes to lookout towers and fire trails. Avid backpackers and campers may want to spend a few days exploring the dozens of hiking trails. Even though trail access is fairly good, hikers need to remember that this is primitive, rough country, and it's essential to carry adequate water and other supplies. ⊠ *Alpine Ranger District* ☎ *928/339-5000.*

WHERE TO STAY
For expanded hotel reviews, visit Fodors.com.

$ RENTAL **Downs' Ranch Hide-Away.** If you're looking for a vacation that is really back-of-beyond, do as the locals do and go "down on the Blue." **Pros:** a truly one-of-a-kind way to commune with Mother Nature; open year-round. **Cons:** zero amenities; no credit cards. *$ Rooms from: $75* ⊠ *On Forest Service Road 281, 35 miles south of Alpine, Blue* ☎ *928/339–4952* ⊕ *www.dcoutfitters.com/downsRanch.php* ⋄ *4 cabins* ⊟ *No credit cards* ⊗ *No meals.*

$ B&B/INN **Tal-Wi-Wi Lodge.** This lodge draws many repeat visitors—particularly driving and motorcycle enthusiasts—to its lush meadows, a favorite for bird-watchers. **Pros:** best place to stay in Alpine; in-room Wi-Fi. **Cons:** only a few rooms have king-size beds; no phones in room; only open nine months a year. [$] *Rooms from: $90* ✉ *U.S. 191* ☎ *928/339–4319* 🌐 *www.talwiwilodge.com* 🛏 *20 rooms* ⏲ *Closed Jan.–Mar.* 🍴 *No meals.*

SPORTS AND THE OUTDOORS

BICYCLING

Luna Lake Trail. The 8-mile Luna Lake Trail, 5 miles east of U.S. 191, is a good two-hour ride for beginner and intermediate cyclists. The trail-head is on the north side of the lake, before the campground entrance. ✉ *Apline Ranger District, U.S. 180* ☎ *928/339-5000.*

FISHING

Luna Lake. A divergence of the San Francisco River's headwaters, 80-acre Luna Lake, 5 miles east of U.S. 191, is well stocked with rainbow trout. ✉ *Alpine Ranger District, U.S. 180* ☎ *928/339-5000.*

Tackle Shop. At the junction of U.S. 180 and 191, Tackle Shop carries trout and fly-fishing supplies. ✉ *Junction Hwy 180E &191S* ☎ *928/339–4338* 🌐 *www.thetackleshopaz.com.*

GOLF

Alpine Country Club. At 8,500 feet above sea level, Alpine Country Club is one of the highest golf courses in the Southwest. Even if you don't play golf, stop in for New Mexican–style food—enchiladas here are stacked, not rolled—and breathtaking scenery at the club's Aspen Room Restaurant. It's 1 mile south of Alpine, off U.S. 180 on Blue River Road. The course is closed from November to April, and the restaurant is closed Monday. ✉ *58 County Rd. 2122* ☎ *928/339–4944* 🌐 *www.alpinegolfandcountryclub.com* ⛳ *18 holes. 5595 yds. Par 70. Slope 107. Greens Fee: $30* ☞ *Facilities: restaurant.*

HIKING

Escudilla National Recreation Trail. A 3-mile trail that is more idyllic than arduous, the Escudilla National Recreation Trail winds through the Escudilla Wilderness to the summit of towering, 10,912-foot **Escudilla Mountain,** Arizona's third-tallest peak. The trail climbs 1,300 feet to a fire tower 0.25 mile from the summit. From Alpine, take U.S. 191 north and follow the signs to Hulsey Lake (about 5 miles). *Moderate.* ✉ *Alpine Ranger District, U.S. 191, Hulsey Lake* ☎ *928/339–5000.*

SNOW SPORTS

Williams Valley Winter Sports Area. This winter recreation area, 2.5 miles west of town, has 12.5 miles of cross-country and snowshoe trails of varying difficulty. Toboggan Hill is a favorite with families who sled, toboggan, and tube. Shelters, picnic facilities, and toilets are available. Pick up an Apache-Sitgreaves National Forests map and "Winter Sports" brochure from the Alpine Ranger District, and call for conditions prior to heading out. ✉ *Alpine Ranger District, FSR 249* ☎ *928/339–5000.*

HANNAGAN MEADOW

23 miles south of Alpine, 50 miles south of Springerville-Eagar.

WHEN TO GO

Just like other towns in Eastern Arizona, Hannagan Meadow is warm (not hot!) in summer and cold and snowy in winter. It's a good place to stop for the night and enjoy some time away from it all.

GETTING HERE AND AROUND

The Coronado Trail stretch of U.S. 191 passes through this remote part of the state.

EXPLORING

Hannagan Meadow. Hannagan Meadow is home to elk, deer, and range cattle, as well as blue grouse, wild turkeys, and the occasional eagle. At 9,500 feet, it's a lush, isolated, and mesmerizing spot. Adjacent to the meadow is the Blue Range Primitive Area, which provides access to miles of untouched wilderness and some stunning rugged terrain. It's a designated recovery area for the endangered Mexican gray wolf. Francisco Vásquez de Coronado and his party may have come through the meadow on their famed expedition in 1540 to find the Seven Cities of Cibola. ✉ *Alpine Ranger District, Hannagan Meadow* ☎ *928/339-5000.*

WHERE TO STAY

For expanded hotel reviews, visit Fodors.com.

$ RESORT 🏨 **Hannagan Meadow Lodge.** Antiques and floral prints impart a genteel, Victorian quality to this lodge. **Pros:** gorgeous surroundings and fantastic service. **Cons:** you should not rely on daily room cleaning; much more lodge than hotel. [$] *Rooms from: $85* ✉ *U.S. 191, 22 mi south of Alpine, HC 61, P.O. Box 335, Hannagan Meadow* ☎ *928/339–4370* 🌐 *www.hannaganmeadow.com* ➪ *7 rooms, 8 cabins* 🍴 *No meals.*

SPORTS AND THE OUTDOORS

Want to get away from it all? The **Apache Ranger District** of the Apache-Sitgreaves National Forests has secluded spaces for outdoor adventures year-round. Hikers and anglers can check out the 11,000-acre **Bear Wallow Wilderness Area** (west of U.S. 191 and bordered by FSR 25 and 54), which has cool, flowing streams stocked with native Apache trout. The **Rose Spring Trail** is a pleasant 5.5-mile hike with a moderate gradient and magnificent views from the Mogollon Rim's edge; the trailhead is at the end of Forest Service Road 54. **Reno Trail** and **Gobbler Trail** both drop into the main canyon from well-marked trailheads off Forest Service Road 25. Reno Trail meanders 2 miles through conifer forest and aspen, while Gobbler Trail is 2.5 miles long, with views overlooking the Black River and Fort Apache Indian Reservation. This designated wilderness (and some of its trails) borders the San Carlos Apache Indian Reservation, where an advance permit is required for entry.

Hannagan Meadow Winter Recreation Area. In winter, try the 8.5 miles of groomed cross-country trails of the Hannagan Meadow Winter Recreation Area, which also is part of the Apache-Sitgreaves National Forest. The 4.5-mile **Clell Lee Loop** is an easy route; the more advanced, ungroomed **KP Rim Loop** traverses upper elevations of the Blue Range Primitive Area and provides some of the most varied (and tranquil)

CLOSE UP

Petroglyphs: The Writing on the Wall

The rock art of early Native Americans is carved or painted on basalt boulders, on canyon walls, and on the underside of overhangs throughout the area. No one knows the exact meaning of these signs, and interpretations vary; they've been seen as elements in shamanistic or hunting rituals, as clan signs, maps, or even indications of visits by extraterrestrials.

WHERE TO FIND IT

Susceptible to (and often already damaged by) vandalism, many rock-art sites aren't open to the public. Two good petroglyphs to check out at **Petrified Forest National Park** are Newspaper Rock, an overlook near mile marker 12, and Puerco Pueblo, near mile marker 11. Other sites in Arizona include **Hieroglyphic Point** in Salt River Canyon, and **Five-Mile Canyon** in Snowflake.

DETERMINING ITS AGE

It's just as difficult to date a "glyph" as it is to understand it. Archaeologists try to determine a general time frame by judging the style, the date of the ruins and pottery in the vicinity, the amount of patination (formation of minerals) on the design, or the superimposition of newer images on top of older ones. Most of Eastern Arizona's rock art is estimated to be at least 1,000 years old, and many of the glyphs were created even earlier.

VARIED IMAGES

Some glyphs depict animals like bighorn sheep, deer, bear, and mountain lions; others are geometric patterns. The most unusual are the anthropomorphs, strange humanlike figures with elaborate headdresses. Concentric circles are a common design. A few of these circles served as solstice signs, indicating the summer and winter solstice and other important dates. At the solstice, when the angle of the sun is just right, a shaft of light shines through a crack in a nearby rock, illuminating the center of the circle. Archaeologists believe that these solar calendars helped determine the time for ceremonies and planting.

Many solstice signs are in remote regions, but you can visit Petrified Forest National Park around June 20 to see a concentric circle illuminated during the summer solstice. The glyph, reached by a paved trail just a few hundred yards from the parking area, is visible year-round, but light shines directly in the center during the week of the solstice. The phenomenon occurs at 9 am, a reasonable hour for looking at the calendar.

■TIP➔ Do not touch petroglyphs or pictographs—the oil from your hands can damage the images.

---

remote skiing in the state. The area just northeast of U.S. 191 is a snowmobiling playground. Trailheads are at U.S. 191 and Forest Service Road 576. There are no rental shops nearby, so bring your own equipment.

Contact **Apache-Sitgreaves National Forests'** Alpine Ranger District (☎ 928/339–5000 ⊕ www.fs.usda.gov/asnf) for trail maps and information. ⊠ *Alpine Ranger District, U.S. 191, Hannagan Meadow.*

THE PETRIFIED FOREST AND AROUND

Only about 1½ hours from Show Low and the lush, verdant forests of the White Mountains, Arizona's diverse and dramatic landscape changes from pine-crested mountains to sunbaked terrain. Inside the lunar landscape of the Painted Desert is the fossil-filled Petrified Forest.

PETRIFIED FOREST NATIONAL PARK

Northern Entrance: 160 miles north of Hannagan Meadow on AZ 191 and Interstate 40, 27 miles east of Holbrook on Interstate 40; Southern Entrance: 18 miles east of Holbrook on U.S. 180.

There are few places where the span of geologic and human history is as wide or apparent as it is at Petrified Forest National Park. Fossilized trees and countless other fossils date back to the Triassic Period, while a stretch of the famed Route 66 of more modern lore is protected within park boundaries. Ancestors of the Hopi, Zuni, and Navajo left petroglyphs, pottery, and even structures built of petrified wood. Nine park sites are on the National Register of Historic Places; one, the Painted Desert Inn, is one of only 3% of such sites that are also listed as National Historic Landmarks.

The good thing is that most of Petrified Forest's treasures can easily be viewed without a great amount of athletic conditioning. Much can be seen by driving along the main road, from which historic sites are readily accessible. By combining a drive along the park road with a short hike here and there and a visit to one of the park's landmarks, you can see most of the sights in as little as half a day.

WHEN TO GO
The park is rarely crowded. Weather-wise, the best time to visit is autumn, when nights are chilly but daytime temperatures hover near 70°F. Half of all yearly rain falls between June and August, so it's a good time to spot blooming wildflowers. The park is least crowded in winter, because of cold winds and occasional snow, though daytime temperatures are in the 50s and 60s.

PLANNING YOUR TIME
PETRIFIED
FOREST IN
ONE DAY

A nonstop drive through the park (28 miles) takes only 45 minutes, but you can spend a half day or more exploring if you stop along the way. From almost any vantage point you can see the multicolored rocks and hills that were home to prehistoric humans and ancient dinosaurs.

Entering from the north, stop at **Painted Desert Visitor Center** for a 20-minute introductory film. Two miles in, the **Painted Desert Inn National Historic Landmark** provides guided ranger tours. Drive south 8 miles to reach **Puerco Pueblo,** a 100-room pueblo built before 1400. Continuing south, you'll find Puebloan petroglyphs at **Newspaper Rock** and, just beyond, **the Tepees,** cone-shape rock formations.

Blue Mesa is roughly the midpoint of the drive, and the start of a 1-mile, moderately steep loop hike that leads you around badland hills made of bentonite clay. Drive on for 5 miles until you come to **Jasper Forest,** just past **Agate Bridge,** with views of the landscape strewn with petrified logs.

Crystal Forest, about 20 miles south of the north entrance, is named for the smoky quartz, amethyst, and citrine along the 0.8-mile loop trail. **Rainbow Forest Museum,** at the park's south entrance, has restrooms, a bookstore, and exhibits. Just behind Rainbow Forest Museum is **Giant Logs,** a 0.4-mile loop that takes you to "Old Faithful," the largest log in the park, estimated to weigh 44 tons.

LOOK AND TOUCH— BUT DON'T TAKE

One of the most commonly asked questions about the Petrified Forest is, "Can I touch the wood?" Yes! Feel comfortable to touch anything, pick it up, inspect it…just make sure you put it back where you found it. It's illegal to remove even a small sliver of fossilized wood from the park.

GETTING HERE AND AROUND

Holbrook, the nearest large town with services such as gas or food, is on U.S. 40, roughly 30 miles from either of the park's two entrances.

Parking is free, and there's ample space at all trailheads, as well as at the visitor center and the museum. The main park road extends 28 miles from the Painted Desert Visitor Center (north entrance) to the Rainbow Forest Museum (south entrance). For park road conditions, call ☎ 928/524–6228.

PARK ESSENTIALS

PARK FEES AND PERMITS
Entrance fees are $10 per car for seven consecutive days or $5 per person on foot, bicycle, motorcycle, or bus. Backcountry hiking and camping permits are free (limit of 15 days) at the Painted Desert Visitor Center or the Rainbow Forest Museum before 4 pm.

PARK HOURS
It's a good idea to call ahead or check the website, since the park's hours vary so much; as a rule of thumb, the park is open daily from sunrise to sunset, and keep in mind that the area does not observe daylight saving time. Hours are approximately: 8 am–5 pm from November to February, daily 7 am–6:30 pm in March and April, daily 7 am–7:30 pm from May to August, and daily 7 am–6 pm in September and October.

VISITOR INFORMATION

Park Contact Information Petrified Forest National Park ✉ *1 Park Rd., Petrified Forest* ☎ *928/524–6228* ⊕ *www.nps.gov/pefo.*

VISITOR CENTERS
Painted Desert Inn National Historic Landmark. This third visitor center at the park isn't as large as the others, but here you can get information as well as view cultural history exhibits. ✉ *2 miles north of Painted Desert Visitor Center.*

Painted Desert Visitor Center. This is the place to go for general park information and an informative 20-minute film on the park. Proceeds from books purchased here will fund continued research and interpretive activities for the park. ✉ *North entrance, off I–40, 27 miles east of Holbrook* ☎ *928/524–6228.*

Rainbow Forest Museum and Visitor Center. The museum houses artifacts of early reptiles, dinosaurs, and petrified wood. Be sure to see Gurtie, a skeleton of a phytosaur, a crocodile-like carnivore. ✉ *South entrance, off U.S. 180, 18 miles southeast of Holbrook* ☎ *928/524–6228.*

Walking Petrified Forest's short trails can be a nice break from driving along Interstate 40, which crosses the park.

EXPLORING
SCENIC DRIVE

Painted Desert Scenic Drive. A 28-mile scenic drive takes you through the park from one entrance to the other. If you begin at the north end, the first 5 miles of the drive take you along the edge of a high mesa, with spectacular views of the Painted Desert. Beyond lies the desolate Painted Desert Wilderness Area. After the 5-mile point, the road crosses Interstate 40, then swings south toward the Puerco River across a landscape covered with sagebrush, saltbrush, sunflowers, and Apache plume. Past the river, the road climbs onto a narrow mesa leading to Newspaper Rock, a panel of Pueblo Indian rock art. Then the road bends southeast, enters a barren stretch, and passes teepee-shaped buttes in the distance. Next you come to Blue Mesa, roughly the park's midpoint and a good place to stop for views of petrified logs. The next stop on the drive is Agate Bridge, really a 100-foot log over a wide wash. The remaining overlooks are Jasper Forest and Crystal Forest, where you can get a further glimpse of the accumulated petrified wood. On your way out of the park, stop at the Rainbow Forest Museum for a rest and to shop for a memento. ⊠ *Begins at Painted Desert Visitor Center.*

HISTORIC SITES

Agate House. This eight-room pueblo is thought to have been built entirely of petrified wood 700 years ago. Researchers believe it might have been used as a temporary dwelling by seasonal farmers or traders from one of the area tribes. ⊠ *Rainbow Forest Museum parking area.*

Newspaper Rock. See huge boulders covered with petroglyphs believed to have been carved by the Pueblo Indians more than 500 years ago.

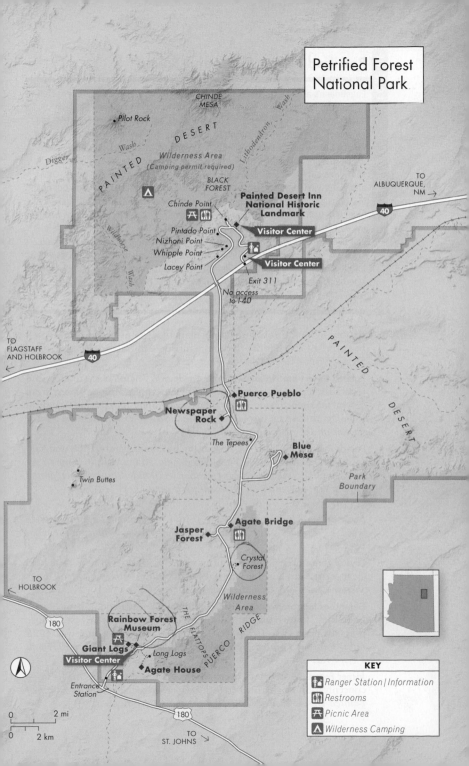

Petrified Forest National Park

CHINDE MESA

• Pilot Rock

P A I N T E D   D E S E R T

Wash

Digger

Wilderness Area
(Camping permit required)

BLACK FOREST

⛺

Chinde Point
🥧 🚻

Painted Desert Inn National Historic Landmark

◆ **Visitor Center**

Pintado Point
Nizhoni Point
Whipple Point
🏛🚻

Lacey Point

◆ **Visitor Center**

Exit 311

No access to I-40

Wildhorse

Wash

Lithodendron

Wash

TO ALBUQUERQUE, NM →

🛣 40

TO FLAGSTAFF AND HOLBROOK ←
🛣 40

P A I N T E D

◆ **Puerco Pueblo**
🚻

Newspaper Rock
◆

The Tepees

◆ **Blue Mesa**

D E S E R T

•
Twin Buttes

Park Boundary

Jasper Forest
◆

Agate Bridge
🚻

Crystal Forest
•

Wilderness Area

TO HOLBROOK ←

🛣 180

Rainbow Forest Museum
🥧

Giant Logs
🏛🚻
◆ **Visitor Center**

Long Logs

Agate House
◆

Entrance Station

T H E   F L A T T O P S

P U E R C O   R I D G E

🧭

0	2 mi
0	2 km

🛣 180

TO ST. JOHNS ↓

KEY

🏛 *Ranger Station | Information*
🚻 *Restrooms*
🥧 *Picnic Area*
⛺ *Wilderness Camping*

Petrified Forest Flora and Fauna

Engelmann's asters and sunflowers are among the blooms in the park each summer. Juniper trees, cottonwoods, and willows grow along Puerco River wash, providing shelter for all manner of wildlife. You might spot mule deer, coyotes, prairie dogs, and foxes, while other inhabitants, like porcupines and bobcats, tend to hide. Bird-watchers should keep an eye out for mockingbirds, red-tailed and Swainson's hawks, roadrunners, swallows, and hummingbirds. Look for all three kinds of lizards—collared, side-blotched, and southern prairie—in rocks.

Beware of rattlesnakes. They're common but can generally be easily avoided: Watch where you step, and don't step anywhere you can't see. If you do come across a rattler, give it plenty of space, and let it go its way before you continue on yours. Other reptiles are just as common but not as dangerous. The gopher snake looks similar to a rattlesnake, but is nonpoisonous. The collared lizard, with its yellow head, can be seen scurrying out of your way in bursts measured at up to 15 mph. They aren't poisonous, but will bite in the rare instance of being caught.

Be sure to look through the binoculars that are provided here—you'll be surprised at what the naked eye misses. ⊠ *6 miles south of Painted Desert Visitor Center on the main park road.*

Painted Desert Inn National Historic Landmark. A nice place to stop and rest in the shade, this site offers vast views of the Painted Desert from several lookouts. Inside, cultural-history exhibits, murals, and American Indian crafts are on display. ⊠ *2 miles north of Painted Desert Visitor Center on the main park road.*

Puerco Pueblo. This is a 100-room pueblo, built before 1400 and said to have housed Ancestral Puebloan people. Many visitors come to see petroglyphs, as well as a solar calendar. ⊠ *10 miles south of the Painted Desert Visitor Center on the main park road.*

SCENIC STOPS

Agate Bridge. Here you'll see a 100-foot log spanning a 40-foot-wide wash. ⊠ *19 miles south of Painted Desert Visitor Center on the main park road.*

Crystal Forest. The fragments of petrified wood strewn here once held clear quartz and amethyst crystals. ⊠ *20 miles south of Painted Desert Visitor Center on the main park road.*

Giant Logs Interpretive Loop Trail. A short walk leads you past the park's largest log, known as Old Faithful. It's considered the largest because of its diameter (9 feet, 9 inches), as well as how tall it once was. ⊠ *28 miles south of Painted Desert Visitor Center on the main park road, 1 Park Rd.*

Jasper Forest. More of an overlook than a forest, this spot has a large concentration of petrified trees in jasper or red. ⊠ *17 miles south of Painted Desert Visitor Center on the main park road.*

Different minerals in different concentrations cause the rich colors in petrified wood and in the Painted Desert.

The Tepees. Witness the effects of time on these cone-shaped rock formations colored by iron, manganese, and other minerals. ⊠ *8 miles south of Painted Desert Visitor Center on the main park road.*

WHERE TO EAT AND STAY

There's no lodging or campgrounds within the Petrified Forest. Backcountry camping is allowed if you obtain a free permit at the visitor center or museum; the only camping allowed is minimal-impact camping in a designated zone in the wilderness area. Group size is limited to eight. RVs aren't allowed. There are no fire pits, nor is any shade available. Also note that if it rains, that pretty Painted Desert rock formation turns to sticky clay.

Dining in the park is limited to a cafeteria in the Painted Desert Visitor Center and snacks in the Rainbow Forest Museum. You may want to pack a lunch and eat at one of the park's picnic areas.

SPORTS AND THE OUTDOORS

Because the park goes to great pains to maintain the integrity of the fossil- and artifact-strewn landscape, sports and outdoor options in the park are limited to on-trail hiking.

HIKING

All trails begin off the main road, with restrooms at or near the trailheads. Most maintained trails are relatively short, paved, clearly marked, and, with a few exceptions, easy to moderate in difficulty. Hikers with greater stamina can make their own trails in the wilderness area, located just north of the Painted Desert Visitor Center. Watch your step for rattlesnakes, which are common in the park—if left alone and given a wide berth, they're passed easily enough.

HOLBROOK

Downtown Holbrook is a monument to Route 66 kitsch. The famous "Mother Road" traveled through the center of Holbrook before Interstate 40 replaced it as the area's major east-west artery, and remnants of the "good ole days" can be found all over town. Navajo Boulevard, the town's main thoroughfare, is known for its cartoonish models of brightly colored dinosaurs. If you're looking for a memorable photo op, it's here. Although it's probably not worth staying overnight, the town's iconic Wigwam Motel (⊕ *www.galerie-kokopelli.com/wigwam*) is a quirky and highly iconic option if you do find yourself needing a rest.

EASY **Crystal Forest Trail.** This easy 0.75-mile loop leads you past petrified wood that once held quartz crystals and amethyst chips. *Easy.* ⊠ *Trailhead: 20 miles south of the Painted Desert Visitor Center.*

Giant Logs Trail. At 0.4 mile, Giant Logs is the park's shortest trail. The loop leads you to Old Faithful, the park's largest petrified log—9 feet, 9 inches at its base, weighing an estimated 44 tons. *Easy.* ⊠ *Trailhead: directly behind Rainbow Forest Museum, 28 miles south of Painted Desert Visitor Center.*

Long Logs Trail. Although barren, this easy 1.6-mile loop passes the largest concentration of wood in the park. *Easy.* ⊠ *Trailhead: 26 miles south of Painted Desert Visitor Center.*

FAMILY **Puerco Pueblo Trail.** A relatively flat and interesting 0.3-mile trail takes you past remains of a home of the Ancestral Puebloan people, built before 1400. The trail is paved and wheelchair accessible. *Easy.* ⊠ *Trailhead: 10 miles south of Painted Desert Visitor Center.*

Fodor's Choice **Agate House.** A fairly flat 1-mi trip takes you to an eight-room pueblo sit-
★ ting high on a knoll. *Moderate.* ⊠ *Trailhead: 26 miles south of Painted Desert Visitor Center.*

Blue Mesa. Although it's only 1 mile long and significantly steeper than the rest, this trail at the park's midway point is one of the most popular and worth the effort. *Moderate.* ⊠ *Trailhead: 14 miles south of Painted Desert Visitor Center.*

Painted Desert Rim. The 1-mile trail is at its best in early morning or late afternoon, when the sun accentuates the brilliant red, blue, purple, and other hues of the desert and petrified forest landscape. *Moderate.* ⊠ *Trail runs between Tawa Point and Kachina Point, 1 mile north of Painted Desert Visitor Center; drive to either point from Visitor Center.*

DIFFICULT **Kachina Point.** This is the trailhead for wilderness hiking. A 1-mile trail leads to the Wilderness Area, but from there you're on your own; with no developed trails, hiking here is cross-country style. Expect to see strange formations, beautifully colored landscapes, and maybe, just maybe, a pronghorn antelope. *Difficult.* ⊠ *Trailhead: on the northwest side of the Painted Desert Inn National Historic Landmark.*

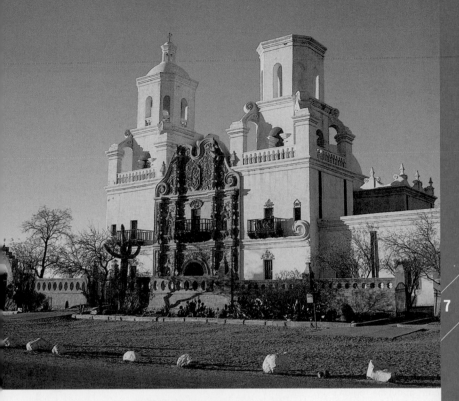

TUCSON

WELCOME TO TUCSON

TOP REASONS TO GO

★ **Get close to the cacti:** Unique to this region, the saguaro is the quintessential symbol of the Southwest. See them at Sabino Canyon and Saguaro National Park.

★ **Enjoy Mexican food:** Tucson boasts that it's the "Mexican Food Capital," and you won't be disappointed at any of the authentic restaurants.

★ **Explore the Arizona–Sonora Desert Museum:** Anyone who thinks that museums are boring hasn't been here, where you can learn about the region's animals, plants, and geology up close in a gorgeous, mostly outdoor setting.

★ **Tour Mission San Xavier del Bac:** The "White Dove of the Desert" is the oldest building in Tucson. Ornate carvings and frescoes inside add to the mystical quality of this active parish on the Tohono O'odham Reservation.

★ **Stroll the U of A campus:** Stop in at one of the five museums, then walk University Boulevard and 4th Avenue for a taste of Tucson's hipper element.

1 Downtown. Three historic districts here—Barrio Historico, El Presidio, and Armory Park—encompass the Downtown area.

2 The University of Arizona. The 353-acre campus, classified as an arboretum, has several top-rated museums. At the west entrance, University Boulevard is lined with boutiques, cafés, and bookstores.

3 Central and Eastside. This mostly residential area is home to Tucson's zoo, its largest indoor shopping mall (Park Place), and its best municipal golf course (Randolph Park).

GETTING ORIENTED

The metropolitan Tucson area covers more than 500 square miles in a valley ringed by mountains—the Santa Catalinas to the north, the Santa Ritas to the south, the Rincons to the east, and the Tucson Mountains to the west. Saguaro National Park bookends Tucson, with one section on the far east side and the other out west near the Arizona–Sonora Desert Museum. The central portion of the city has most of the shops, restaurants, and businesses, but not many tourist sights. Downtown's historic district and the neighboring university area are much smaller and easily navigated on foot. Up north in the Catalina Foothills, you'll find first-class resorts, restaurants, and hiking trails, most with spectacular views of the entire valley.

4 Catalina Foothills. North of River Road the land becomes hilly and streets wind up to beautiful homes and resorts. At the east end, Sabino Canyon is a must for hikers.

5 Northwest. Suburban sprawl at its finest, this part of town just keeps growing. A dude ranch and a few riding stables are holdouts from a quieter era.

6 Westside. The untamed Tucson Mountain region embraces miles of saguaro forests, the Arizona–Sonora Desert Museum, and Mission San Xavier del Bac on the Tohono O'odham Reservation.

TUCSON FOOD: NORTH OF THE BORDER

While Tucson ensures that authentic south-of-the-border culinary and cultural influences aren't lost in translation, it also cooks up plenty of cross-border sway. The growing University metropolis boasts eats from around the world and mixes these tastes with more local flavors.

Above: Peppers are the star ingredient in many Southwestern dishes. Top right: Tamales use corn flour and corn husks. Lower right: Chocolate, chiles, and spices make a savory mole sauce.

Emerging from an era of meat and potatoes and carne and frijoles—all of which it still does exceptionally well—Tucson has become a foodie tour de force. You can indulge in authentic chicken mole (rich sauce including chiles and chocolate) and *carne seca* (dried beef); fill up on some local/world fusion food; or get good and greasy with a Sonoran hot dog.

Start with some classic Mexican dishes such as tamales (filled masa dough wrapped in a corn husk) or enchiladas (corn tortillas filled with meat or cheese). But today even Mexican-American foods are evolving into a new generation of creations. Do you prefer the chimichangas (deep-fried burritos) that purportedly originated at El Charro Café or the mango-filled ones at Mi Nidito for dessert? Taste and decide for yourself.

FOODIE FESTIVALS

4th Avenue Street Fair. Hit Tucson's 4th Avenue Street Fair, usually held in May and December, where you can munch on every kind of festival food imaginable. ☎ 520/624–5004 ⊕ www.fourthavenue.org.

Tucson Culinary Festival. In October visit Casino del Sol for the Tucson Culinary Festival. Sample foods, wines, and killer margaritas by local indie chefs. ☎ 520/343–9985 ⊕ www.tucsonoriginals.com.

SAY CHEESE

Many identify Mexican food by bright, glistening layers of cheddar that render the entrée below it unrecognizable. Not that there's anything wrong with that, but true Mexico-style meals are untouched by orange cheese. Authentic dishes are served with much smaller rations of white cheese, usually *queso blanco* or *panela*—mild cheeses that become soft and creamy when heated, but don't melt—and *cotija*, a Mexican-style Parmesan. These cheeses now appear on non-Hispanic menus, too.

PICK A PEPPER

Another key to authentic Mexican food is its heat source: fresh peppers. These heat-tolerant plants were once a south-of-the-border specialty; increased demand has led to their being raised in the southern United States, where they've had a growing impact on regional cuisine. There are endless varieties of the spicy fruit, but here are some more commonly seen on local menus.

Green and Red: Often roasted and peeled for stews and broths, sauces, rubs, marinades, confectionery, chili, and chiles rellenos. Green chiles are unripe, with mild to medium-high heat. Red chiles are ripe, with maximum heat.

Jalapeño: These flavorful green peppers can range from mild to hot and are served pickled, canned, deep-fried

for "poppers," or as a garnish for everything from salads to nachos.

Chipotle: When select jalapeños mature from green to a deep red, they're prime for the wood-smoking process that creates chipotle (chee-*pote*-lay) peppers. Their distinct flavor is popular in sauces, marinades, and salsas.

Habañero: This thumb-shape pepper is one of the hottest. A little goes a long way in cooking. It's most often found in chili recipes and hot sauces.

Poblano: This green pepper, aka *pasilla,* is usually mild, but can sometimes pack a punch. Dried, it's an ancho chili. The poblano is used for moles (mo-lays).

SONORAN DOG DAYS

El Guero Canelo. Talk about fusion. Take the American tradition of ballpark franks, give it a Mexican spin, and you'll have a Sonoran hot dog, created by and sold in El Guero Canelo restaurants and their strategically placed taco stands. The dogs are made with *bolillos* (oval-shape baguettes), wrapped in bacon and topped with pinto beans, grilled peppers and onions, tomatoes, mayo, mustard, and jalapeño sauce. There are two other locations, one in Central and one on the Eastside, but the original eatery in South Tucson has the most colorful vibe. ✉ *5201 S. 12th Ave., South* ☎ *520/295–9005* ⊕ *www. elguerocanelo.com.*

7

TUCSON AND SOUTHERN ARIZONA SHOPPING

Despite the waves of modernity that continue to wash over it, southern Arizona always emerges with reverence for its cultural influences and attention to detail, making it one of the best places to shop in the Southwest—even if you're just browsing.

Above: Papier-mâché skulls celebrate *El Día de los Muertos* (The Day of the Dead). Right: Ceramics are popular crafts in Tucson and nearby Tubac.

With its proximity to Mexico, its numerous artisan and Indian communities, a prominent wine region, and a storied past, this booming area is bursting with rare culinary and curio items, home and garden decor, fine art, folklore, and clothing. Tucson has a wealth of wares, but a great way to find some firsthand bargains and have some fun is to go straight to the source—like Amado, Tubac, and Bisbee for resident fine art and serious souvenir shopping; Tombstone, where Old West kitsch and curios are alive and well; and Sonoita, Elgin, and Willcox for some of the state's award-winning wines. The shopping list goes on, but your bucks can stop right here. There are many southern Arizona specialties to leave room for in your suitcase, or for which to bring an extra bag altogether.

EVENTS TO SHOP

Tubac Festival of the Arts. This rural artisan extravaganza in February brings artists from around the country to exhibit their eclectic, fine, and tourist-oriented art. ☎ *520/398-2704* ⊕ *www.tubacaz. com/festival.*

Tucson Gem and Mineral Show. Shop like a rock star in February at this two-week gem and mineral show—the world's largest. ☎ *520/322–5773* ⊕ *www.tgms.org.*

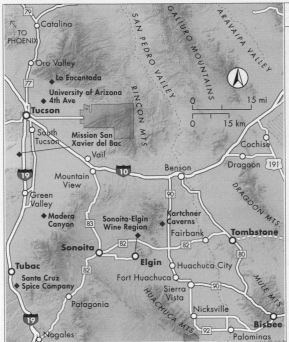

TOP SHOPS

Native and Mexican influence: Given the influences on the area, "ethnic" art is always in, especially pottery, baskets, rugs, furniture, and Mexican crafts including signature folk art honoring *El Día de los Muertos* (The Day of the Dead), depicting skeletons of the dearly departed. Check out **Del Sol** (✉ *435 N. 4th Ave. Central* ☎ *520/628–8765*) and **Picante** (✉ *2932 E. Broadway, Central* ☎ *520/320–5699*) in Tucson or visit **San Xavier Plaza** at Mission San Xavier del Bac on the Tohono O'odham Indian Reservation.

Consumables: For flavorful finds, wines from regional vineyards such as **Callaghan Vineyards** and **Keeling Schaefer Vineyards** are a winning gift, as are local seasonings from **Santa Cruz Chili & Spice Co.**, near Tubac. Weekend farmers' markets are a great source for locally produced honey and prickly pear jellies.

Fashionable Finds: Not so much into local flare? Make your way to outdoor mall **La Encantada,** where you'll find upscale chains and designer brands, as well as a selection of restaurants.

⇨ *Shops without addresses are listed in Chapter 7 or Chapter 8 of this guide.*

QUICK BITES

Delectables. In the University and 4th Avenue area, Delectables is a convenient eatery to pop into. There's a solid selection of fresh gourmet salads, soups, sandwiches, and desserts. ✉ *533 N. 4th Ave., University* ☎ *520/884–9289* ⊕ *www. delectables.com.*

Maynards. If you're in the Downtown district, stop at Maynards in the beautifully restored historic train depot. There's a restaurant, bar, and casual market/eatery on-site. An abundant farmers' market sets up on the patio Saturdays from 9–1. ✉ *400 N. Toole Ave., Downtown* ☎ *520/545–0577* ⊕ *www. maynardsmarket.com.*

Vivace. Tucson's St. Philip's Plaza is at the base of the Catalina Foothills, in the north-central part of town, and features upscale shops, great atmosphere, and acclaimed eats, including Vivace, which serves fresh pastas and salads, and its new sister restaurant, Scordato's Pizzeria. It also has one of the loveliest dining patios in town. Top-notch farmers' markets take place in the plaza on weekend mornings. ✉ *4310 N. Campbell Ave., Foothills* ☎ *520/795–7221* ⊕ *www. vivacetucson.com* ⊗ *Closed Sun.*

Updated by
Mara Levin

The Old Pueblo, as Tucson is affectionately known, is built upon a deep Native American, Spanish, Mexican, and Old West foundation. Arizona's second-largest city is both a bustling center of business and development, with its fair share of ubiquitous strip malls and tract-homes, as well as a relaxed university and resort town.

Metropolitan Tucson has more than 850,000 residents, including thousands of snowbirds, who flee colder climes to enjoy the sun that shines on the city more than 340 days out of 365.

The city has a tri-cultural (Hispanic, Anglo, Native American) population, and offers visitors the chance to see how these cultures interact and to sample their flavorful cuisine.

In terms of outdoor activities, the city is particularly popular among golfers, and there are several hiking trails surrounding the city in the Santa Catalina Mountains and Saguaro National Park. If the weather is too hot to stay outdoors comfortably, consider a cooler alternative like a museum, such as the Arizona State Museum or the Center for Creative Photography.

The city has a relaxed vibe, largely due to the population of students attending Arizona State University. While high-tech industries have moved into the area, the economy still relies heavily on the university and tourism—although, come summer, you'd never guess; when the snowbirds and students depart, Tucson can be a sleepy place.

TUCSON PLANNER

WHEN TO GO

Summer lodging rates (late May to September) are hugely discounted, even at many of the resorts, but there's a good reason: summer in Tucson is hot! Swimming and indoor activities like visiting museums (and spa treatments) are doable; but only the hardiest hikers and golfers stay out past noon in summer.

Tucson averages only 12 inches of rain a year. Winter temperatures hover around 65°F during the day and 38°F at night. Summers are unquestionably hot—July averages 104°F during the day and 75°F at night—but, as Tucsonans are fond of saying, "It's a dry heat."

The International Gem and Mineral Show descends on Tucson the first two weeks in February; book your hotel in advance or you'll be hard-pressed to find a room.

FESTIVALS AND EVENTS

FEBRUARY **Tucson Gem and Mineral Show.** This huge two-week trade show in February, with multiple venues in and around downtown, is the largest of its kind in the world. Most vendors sell to the public as well as wholesale. The Tucson Convention & Visitors Bureau website (http://www.visit-tucson.org/events/gem-show/) has a lot of information about the event. ☎ 520/322–5773 ⊕ www.tgms.org.

La Fiesta de los Vaqueros. America's largest outdoor midwinter rodeo is at the Tucson Rodeo Grounds the third weekend in February. ☎ 520/294–8896 ⊕ www.tucsonrodeo.com.

JULY **Saguaro Harvest.** The majestic saguaro's fruit is harvested at Colossal Cave Mountain Park around late June. ☎ 520/647–7121 ⊕ www.colossalcave.com.

PLANNING YOUR TIME

Even if you have only one day, you can experience both the wild and developed parts of Tucson. You can visit the Arizona–Sonora Desert Museum in the morning and combine it with a stop at Mission San Xavier del Bac or Old Tucson Studios. On the way back to town, stop in Downtown's Barrio Historico and El Presidio neighborhoods to meander through the adobe-lined streets, then have dinner at one of the outstanding Mexican restaurants in Downtown or South Tucson.

Another option is spending a half day in Saguaro National Park. ■TIP→ Set out for a desert visit in the early morning when it's cooler and the liveliest time for wildlife. If you're based in the Foothills, you can choose Sabino Canyon instead; the saguaros are almost as plentiful and the vistas are equally rewarding. Nature in the morning can be combined with an afternoon in the university area: visit any of the five campus museums, then stroll University Boulevard and 4th Avenue for ethnic eats and vintage boutiques.

If you have another day for exploring and like to shop, head south towards the Mexican border. If you haven't seen Mission San Xavier yet, it's directly en route to Tubac, an artists' colony with historic sights as well as galleries. You can then head back toward Tucson, stopping at the Titan Missile Museum or at one of the casinos.

GETTING HERE AND AROUND

You can fly to Tucson International Airport (TUS), which is 8½ miles south of Downtown, off the Valencia exit of Interstate 10, but cheaper, nonstop flights into Phoenix—a two-hour drive away on Interstate 10—are often easier to find. Once in town, a car is essential to get to the outlying tourist sights.

AIR TRAVEL

Air Contacts Tucson International Airport (TUS) ☎ 520/573–8100 ⊕ www.flytucsonairport.com.

GROUND TRANSPOR- TATION

Many hotels have a courtesy airport shuttle; inquire when making reservations. The Arizona Stagecoach shuttle will carry you between the airport and all parts of Tucson and Green Valley for $9 to $41, depending on the location.

Ground Transportation Contact Arizona Stagecoach ☎ 520/889–1000 ⊕ www.azstagecoach.com.

BUS TRAVEL

Within the city limits, public transportation, which is geared primarily to commuters, is available through Sun Tran, Tucson's bus system.

Bus Contact Sun Tran ☎ 520/792–9222 ⊕ www.suntran.com.

CAR TRAVEL

You'll need a car to get around Tucson and the surrounding area, and it makes sense to rent at the airport; all the major car-rental agencies are represented. To save a little on cost, Carefree Rent-a-Car, a local company, rents reliable used cars at good rates.

Driving time from the airport to the center of town varies, but it's usually less than a half hour; add 15 minutes to any destination during rush hours (7:30 am–9 am and 4:30 pm–6 pm). Parking isn't a problem in most parts of town, except near the university, where there are several pay lots.

Car Rental Contact Carefree Rent-a-Car ✉ 6941 E. 22nd St., Eastside ☎ 520/790–2655.

TAXI TRAVEL

Taxi rates vary widely since they're unregulated, but the taxi companies listed here charge $2 per mile plus an initial pickup fee ($2.50 from the airport, $2 from elsewhere in town). It's always wise to inquire about the cost before getting into a cab. It should be about $20 from the airport to central Tucson. AAA Sedan transports travelers in a little more comfort (in Lincoln town cars or SUVs) for a little more money (the flat rate into central Tucson is $35). Yellow Cab dispatchers and drivers speak English and Spanish.

Taxi Contacts AAA Sedan ☎ 520/573–8152. **VIP Taxi** ☎ 520/798–1111 ⊕ www.taxiwithus.com. **Yellow Cab** ☎ 520/624–6611, 520/300–0000 ⊕ www. aaayellowaz.com.

TRAIN TRAVEL

Amtrak serves the city with westbound trains (to Los Angeles, CA) and eastbound trains daily.

NATIVE CULTURES

Mexican-Americans make up about 30% of Tucson's population, and play a major role in all aspects of daily life. The city's south-of-the-border soul is visible in its tile-roof architecture, mariachi festivals, and abundance of Mexican restaurants. Native Americans have a strong presence as well, especially the Tohono O'odham and the Pascua Yaqui. Mission San Xavier del Bac, a thriving reservation parish, is a good spot to experience religious festivals and to sample fry bread, a favorite Indian snack.

Amtrak ✉ *400 E. Toole Ave., Downtown* ☎ *800/872-7245, 800/872-7245* ⊕ *www.amtrak.com.*

VISITOR INFORMATION

Metropolitan Tucson Convention and Visitors Bureau. The visitor center in La Placita Village is open 9–5 weekdays and 9–4 weekends. ✉ *100 S. Church Ave., Suite 7199, Downtown* ☎ *520/624-1817, 800/638-8350* ⊕ *www.visittucson.org.*

EXPLORING

Central Tucson—which has most of the shops, restaurants, and businesses—is roughly bounded by Craycroft Road to the east, Oracle Road to the west, River Road to the north, and 22nd Street to the south. The older Downtown section, east of Interstate 10 off the Broadway-Congress exit, is smaller and easy to navigate on foot. Downtown streets don't run on any sort of grid, however, and many are one-way, so it's best to get a good, detailed map. The city's Westside area is the vast region west of Interstates 10 and 19, which includes the western section of Saguaro National Park and the San Xavier Indian Reservation.

DOWNTOWN TUCSON

The area bordered by Franklin Street on the north, Cushing Street on the south, Church Avenue on the east, and Main Avenue on the west contains more than two centuries of Tucson's history, dating from the original walled fortress, El Presidio de Tucson, built by the Spanish in 1776, when Arizona was still part of New Spain. A good deal of the city's history was destroyed in the 1960s, when large sections of Downtown's barrio were bulldozed to make way for the Tucson Convention Center, high-rises, and parking lots.

However, within the area's three small historic districts it's still possible to explore Tucson's cultural and architectural past. Adobe—brick made of mud and straw, cured in the hot sun—was used widely as a building material in early Tucson because it provides natural insulation from the heat and cold and because it's durable in Tucson's dry climate. When these buildings are properly made and maintained, they can last for centuries. Driving around Downtown Tucson, you'll see adobe houses painted in vibrant hues such as bright pink and canary yellow.

Revitalization is in full swing Downtown, especially along Congress Street, where multiple restaurants and bars are now thriving, and a new streetcar line—scheduled for completion in early 2014—will shuttle riders between Downtown and the 4th Avenue/university areas.

GETTING HERE AND AROUND

Downtown only approaches bustling on weekdays at lunchtime and 5–6 pm for the evening rush hour. It's pretty easy to find metered street parking (free after 6 pm); otherwise, there is ample parking in several parking garages all within a few blocks of Congress Street.

7

"A" Mountain
(Sentinel Peak) . **1**

Children's
Museum
Tucson **5**

El Tiradito
(The Castaway) . **3**

Pima County
Courthouse **7**

Santa Cruz
River Park **2**

St. Augustine
Cathedral **4**

Tucson Museum
of Art and Historic
Block **6**

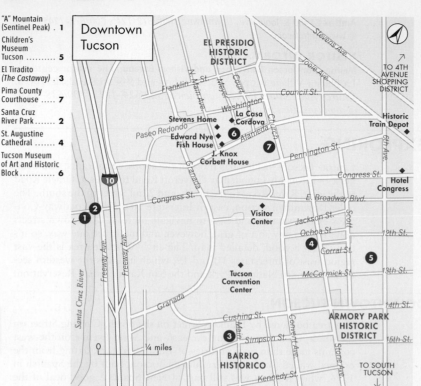

TOP ATTRACTIONS

"A" Mountain. The original name of this mountain, Sentinel Peak, west of Downtown, came from its function as a lookout point for the Spanish, though the Pima village and cultivated fields that once lay at the base of the peak are long gone. In 1915 fans of the University of Arizona football team whitewashed a large "A" on its side to celebrate a victory, and the tradition has been kept up ever since—the permanent "A" is now red, white, and blue. During the day the peak's a great place to get an overview of the town's layout; at night the city lights below form a dazzling carpet, but the teenage hangout–make-out scene may make some uncomfortable. ⊠ *Congress St. on Sentinel Peak Rd., Downtown.*

FAMILY **Children's Museum Tucson.** Youngsters are encouraged to touch and explore the science, language, and history exhibits here. They can examine a patient in the Medical Center and shop for healthy food in the Wellness Town Grocery Store. Investigation Station has air-pressure tubes where balls and scarves whiz around, and there's an Enchanted Forest for all ages to climb, build, and burn off steam. ⊠ *200 S. 6th Ave., Downtown* ☎ *520/792–9985* ⊕ *www.childrensmuseumtucson. org* ⊠ *$8* ⊗ *Tues.–Fri. 9–5, weekends 10–5.*

Downtown Historic Districts. North of the Convention Center and the government buildings that dominate Downtown, **El Presidio Historic**

District is an architectural thumbnail of the city's former self. The north–south streets Court, Meyer, and Main are sprinkled with traditional Mexican adobe houses sitting cheek by jowl with territorial-style houses with wide attics and porches. Paseo Redondo, once called Snob Hollow, is the wide road along which wealthy merchants built their homes.

The area most closely resembling 19th-century Tucson is the **Barrio Historico,** also known as Barrio Viejo. The narrow streets of this neighborhood, including Convent Avenue, have a good sampling of thick-walled adobe houses. The colorfully painted houses are close to the street, hiding the yards and gardens within.

To the east of the Barrio Historico, across Stone Avenue, is the **Armory Park** neighborhood, mostly constructed by and for the railroad workers who settled here after the 1880s. The brick or wood territorial-style homes here were the Victorian era's adaptation to the desert climate. ⊠ *Downtown.*

El Tiradito (*The Castaway*). No one seems to know the details of the story behind this little shrine, but everyone agrees a tragic love triangle was involved. A bronze plaque indicates only that it's dedicated to a sinner who is buried here on unconsecrated ground. The candles that line the cactus-shrouded spot attest to its continuing importance in local Catholic lore. People light candles and leave *milagros* (miracles; little icons used in prayers for healing) for loved ones. A modern-day miracle: the shrine's inclusion on the National Register of Historic Places helped prevent a freeway from plowing through this section of the Barrio Historico. ⊠ *Main Ave., south of Cushing St., Downtown.*

Pima County Courthouse. This pink Spanish colonial–style building with a mosaic-tile dome is among Tucson's most beautiful historic structures. Still in use, it was built in 1927 on the site of the original single-story adobe court of 1869; a portion of the old presidio wall can be seen in the south wing of the courthouse's second floor. At the side of the building, the county assessor's office has a diorama depicting the area's early days. ⊠ *115 N. Church Ave., between Alameda and Pennington Sts., Downtown* ⊕ *www.sc.pima.gov* ✉ *Free* ☉ *Weekdays 8–4:30, Sat. 8–noon.*

Tucson Museum of Art and Historic Block. The five historic buildings on this block are listed in the National Register of Historic Places. You can enter La Casa Cordova, the Stevens Home, the J. Knox Corbett House, and the Edward Nye Fish House, but the Romero House, believed to incorporate a section of the presidio wall, is not open to the public.

In the center of the museum complex, connecting the modern buildings to the surrounding historic houses, is the Plaza of the Pioneers, honoring Tucson's early citizens. The museum building, the only modern structure in the complex, houses a permanent collection of modern, contemporary, and Asian art and hosts traveling shows.

Permanent and changing exhibitions of Western art fill the **Edward Nye Fish House,** an 1868 adobe that belonged to an early merchant, entrepreneur, and politician, and his wife. The building is notable for its 15-foot beamed ceilings and saguaro cactus–rib supports.

There are free docent tours of the museum, and you can pick up a self-guided tour map of El Presidio district. **La Casa Cordova,** one of the oldest buildings in Tucson, is also one of the best local examples of a Sonoran row house. This simple but elegant design is a Spanish style adapted to adobe construction. The oldest section of La Casa Cordova, constructed around 1848, has been restored to its original appearance, and is the Mexican Heritage Museum. El Nacimiento, a permanent installation of nativity scenes and depictions of Mexican family life, is on display here from November through March.

The **J. Knox Corbett House** was built in 1906–07 and occupied by members of the Corbett family until 1963. The original occupants were J. Knox Corbett, a successful businessman, postmaster, and mayor of Tucson, and his wife, Elizabeth Hughes Corbett, an accomplished musician and daughter of Tucson pioneer Sam Hughes. Tucson's Hi Corbett field (now the baseball field for the U of A Wildcats) is named for their grandnephew, Hiram. The two-story, Mission Revival–style residence has been furnished with Arts and Crafts pieces: Stickley, Roycroft, Tiffany, and Morris are among the more famous manufacturers represented.

The **Stevens Home** was where the wealthy politician and cattle rancher Hiram Stevens and his Mexican wife, Petra Santa Cruz, entertained many of Tucson's leaders during the 1800s. A drought brought the Stevens's cattle ranching to a halt in 1893, and Stevens killed himself in despair after unsuccessfully attempting to shoot his wife (the bullet was deflected by the comb she wore in her hair). The 1865 house was restored in 1980, and now houses the Tucson Museum of Art's permanent collections of pre-Columbian, Spanish-colonial, and Latin American folk art. Admission to the museum and all four homes is free on the first Sunday of every month. ■TIP➔ There's free parking in a lot behind the museum at Washington and Meyer streets. ✉ *140 N. Main Ave., Downtown* ☎ *520/624–2333* ⊕ *www.tucsonmuseumofart. org* ✉ *$10* ⊙ *Wed., Fri. and Sat. 10–5; Thurs. 10–8; Sun. noon–5. Free guided tours Oct.–Apr., Wed.–Sun. at 11* ⊙ *Closed Mon. and Tues.*

QUICK BITES

Cafe A La C'Art. On the patio of the Stevens Home, part of the Tucson Museum of Art and Historic Block, this cafe serves breakfast frittatas, burritos, and pancakes as well as delightful salads, soups, and sandwiches weekdays from 7 to 3 (weekends 8 to 3), and delectable dinners Thurs.-Sat. from 5 to 9. ✉ *150 N. Main Ave., Downtown* ☎ *520/628–8533* ⊕ *www. cafealacarttucson.com.*

WORTH NOTING

Santa Cruz River & River Park. When Europeans arrived in what is now Arizona, the Santa Cruz River had wide banks suitable for irrigation; over time its banks have been narrowed and contained and are now lined by River Park. These days it's a dry wash, or arroyo, most of the year, but sudden summer thunderstorms and rainwater from upper elevations can turn it into a raging river in a matter of hours. It's a favorite spot for walkers, joggers, and bicyclists. The park has a bike path, restrooms, drinking fountains, and sculptures created by local artists. ⊠ *W. Congress St. at Bonita Ave., Downtown* ⊕ *www.pima. gov/nrpr/parks.*

St. Augustine Cathedral. Although the imposing white-and-beige, late-19th-century, Spanish-style building was modeled after the Cathedral of Queretaro in Mexico, a number of its details reflect the desert setting: above the entryway, next to a bronze statue of St. Augustine, are carvings of local desert scenes with saguaro cacti, yucca, and prickly pears—look closely and you'll find the horned toad. Compared with the magnificent facade, the modernized interior is a bit disappointing. ■ **TIP→ For a distinctly Southwestern experience, attend the maria-chi mass celebrated Sunday at 8 am.** ⊠ *192 S. Stone Ave., Downtown* ☏ *520/623–6351* ⊕ *www.augustinecathedral.org/* ⊠ *Free* ⊙ *Daily 7–6.*

THE UNIVERSITY OF ARIZONA

The U of A (as opposed to rival ASU, in Tempe) is a major economic influence in Tucson, with a student population of more than 34,000. The land for the university was "donated" by a couple of gamblers and a saloon owner in 1891—their benevolence reputedly inspired by a bad hand of cards—and $25,000 of territorial (Arizona was still a territory back then) money was used to build Old Main, the original building, and hire six faculty members. Money ran out before Old Main's roof was placed, but a few enlightened citizens pitched in funds to finish it. Most of the city's populace was less than enthusiastic about the institution: they were disgruntled when the 13th Territorial Legislature granted the University of Arizona to Tucson and awarded Phoenix what was considered the real prize—an insane asylum and a prison.

The university's flora is impressive—it represents a collection of plants from arid and semiarid regions around the world. An extremely rare mutated, or "crested," saguaro grows at the northeast corner of the Old Main building. The long, grassy mall in the heart of campus—itself once a vast cactus garden—sits atop a huge underground student activity center, and makes for a pleasant stroll on a balmy evening.

GETTING HERE AND AROUND
If you drive, leave your car in a university garage or lot; those on 2nd Street at Mountain Avenue, on Speedway Boulevard at Park Avenue, on Tyndall Avenue south of University Boulevard, and on 2nd Street at Euclid Avenue are the most convenient. Parking is free in these garages on weekends and holidays. Both the campus and the shopping/dining district just west along University Boulevard are best explored on foot. The new streetcar route, scheduled to be completed in early 2014, runs west along University Boulevard, down 4th Avenue and into Downtown.

PLANNING YOUR TIME
Call ahead to verify hours for the university's museums, or visit the University of Arizona website (⊕ *www.arizona.edu*) for parking maps and the latest visitor information.

7

U of A Campus Walking Tour

This tour takes in the highlights of the university area: Start at the northwest corner of campus, at Euclid and 2nd streets, at the public parking garage, then walk a half block east on 2nd Street to the **Arizona History Museum** to see how far the Old Pueblo has come in 100 years. A block south on Park Avenue, just inside the main gate of the university, is the **Arizona State Museum**, the place to explore Native American culture. Heading east on University Boulevard and deeper into the campus, you'll pass Old Main and the crested saguaro. As the road curves to the left, University Boulevard turns into the campus mall. The Student Union, which houses a huge food court, and University Bookstore are on your left; the sculpture in front of the complex depicts Arizona–Mexico border struggles. Cross over to the south side of the mall (watch out for Frisbees) and take a peek inside the old gymnasium, then continue east, passing the steps leading down to the underground activity center, and you'll come to the **Flandrau Science Center and Planetarium**. Check telescope-viewing schedules, see a light show, or stock up on science-oriented gifts here.

Walk north on Cherry, then turn left onto 2nd Street, passing several fraternity and sorority houses. Turn right on Olive Road to find the **Center for Creative Photography**, home to most of photographer Ansel Adams's negatives and a slew of other exhibits in this medium. Across from the center is the **University of Arizona Museum of Art**. From here it's a short walk west on Speedway Boulevard to Park Avenue, where you can go south to 2nd Street and return to the Arizona Historical Society's Museum and the parking lot.

For more college culture, continue down Park to University Boulevard and turn right. This area is the hub of off-campus activity, with restaurants, cafés, and trendy boutiques. You can walk or take the new streetcar along University to **4th Avenue**, Tucson's last bastion of bohemia, for shopping and people-watching.

If you drive, leave your car in a university garage; those on 2nd Street at Mountain Avenue, on Speedway Boulevard at Park Avenue, on Tyndall Avenue south of University Boulevard, and on 2nd Street at Euclid Avenue are the most convenient. Parking is free in these garages on weekends and holidays.

TOP ATTRACTIONS

4th Avenue. Students and counterculturists favor this 0.5-mi strip of 4th Avenue, where vintage-clothing stores rub shoulders with ethnic eateries from Guatemalan to Greek. After dark, 4th Avenue bars pulse with live and recorded music. ⊠ *University* ☎ *520/624–5004* ⊕ *www. fourthavenue.org/*.

FAMILY **Arizona History Museum.** The museum houses the headquarters of the state Historical Society and has exhibits exploring the history of southern Arizona, the Southwest United States, and northern Mexico, starting with the Hohokam Indians and Spanish explorers. The harrowing "Life on the Edge: A History of Medicine in Arizona" exhibit promotes

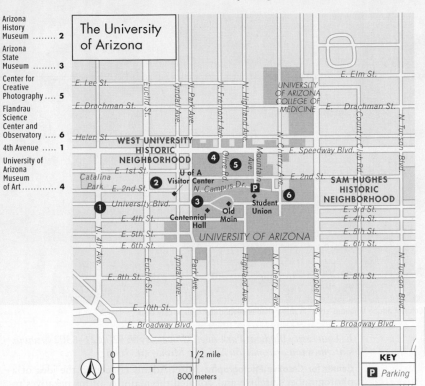

Arizona History Museum **2**

Arizona State Museum **3**

Center for Creative Photography **5**

Flandrau Science Center and Observatory **6**

4th Avenue **1**

University of Arizona Museum of Art **4**

The University of Arizona

E. Elm St.

E. Lee St.

E. Drachman St.

UNIVERSITY OF ARIZONA COLLEGE OF MEDICINE

E. Drachman St.

Helen St.

WEST UNIVERSITY HISTORIC NEIGHBORHOOD

E. Speedway Blvd.

E. 1st St.

Catalina Park

E. 2nd St.

U of A Visitor Center

N. Campus Dr.

E. 2nd St.

SAM HUGHES HISTORIC NEIGHBORHOOD

University Blvd.

E. 4th St.

Centennial Hall

Old Main

Student Union

E. 3rd St.

E. 4th St.

E. 5th St.

UNIVERSITY OF ARIZONA

E. 5th St.

E. 6th St.

E. 6th St.

E. 8th St.

E. 8th St.

E. 10th St.

E. Broadway Blvd.

E. Broadway Blvd.

0   1/2 mile
0   800 meters

KEY

P *Parking*

a new appreciation of modern drugstores in present-day Tucson. Children enjoy the exhibit on copper mining (with an atmospheric replica of a mine shaft and camp) and the stagecoaches in the transportation area.

Flanking the entrance to the museum are statues of two men: Father Kino, the Jesuit who established San Xavier del Bac and a string of other missions, and John Greenaway, indelibly linked to Phelps Dodge, the copper-mining company that helped Arizona earn statehood in 1912.

The library has an extensive collection of historic Arizona photographs and sells inexpensive reprints. Park in the garage at the corner of 2nd and Euclid streets and get a free parking pass in the museum. ⊠ *949 E. 2nd St., University* ☎ *520/628–5774* ⊕ *www.arizonahistoricalsociety. org/museums* ☞ *$5* ⊘ *Mon.–Sat. 10–4; library Mon.–Fri. 9–4.*

Arizona State Museum. Inside the main gate of the university is Arizona's oldest museum, dating from territorial days (1893) and recognized as one of the world's most important resources for the study of Southwestern cultures. Exhibits include the largest collections of Southwest Indian pottery and basketry, as well as "Paths of Life: American Indians of the Southwest"—a permanent exhibit that explores the cultural traditions, origins, and contemporary lives of 10 native tribes of Arizona and Sonora, Mexico. Admission is free for children under 18. ⊠ *1013*

Colorful adobe buildings come in many shades beyond the natural clay color.

E. University Blvd., at Park Ave., University ☎ *520/621–6302* ⊕ *www. statemuseum.arizona.edu* ✉ *$5* ⊘ *Mon.–Sat. 10–5.*

Center for Creative Photography. Ansel Adams conceived the idea of a photographer's archive and donated the majority of his negatives to this museum. In addition to its superb collection of his work, the center has works by other major photographers, including Paul Strand, W. Eugene Smith, Edward Weston, and Louise Dahl-Wolfe. Changing exhibits in the main gallery display selected pieces from the collection. On the first Friday of every month, a themed display of photos from the archives is set up, unframed, in the print study room for up-close viewing and discussion with docents. ✉ *1030 N. Olive Rd., north of 2nd St., University* ☎ *520/621–7968* ⊕ *www.creativephotography.org* ✉ *Free* ⊘ *Weekdays 9–5, weekends 1–4.*

FAMILY **Flandrau Science Center and Planetarium.** Attractions include a 16-inch public telescope for evening stargazing, hands-on science exhibits, planetarium shows, and a Mineral Museum, which displays more than 2,000 rocks and gems, some quite rare. ✉ *1601 E. University Blvd., at Cherry Ave., University* ☎ *520/621–4515, 520/621–7827 recorded message* ⊕ *www.flandrau.org* ✉ *$7 for museum, observatory free* ⊘ *Museum Mon.–Wed. 10–3, Thurs. and Fri. 10–3 and 6–9, Sat. 10–9, Sun. 1–4; Planetarium and laser shows Thurs.–Sun. (call for schedule); Observatory Wed.–Sat. 7 pm–10 pm (weather permitting).*

QUICK
BITES

Just outside the west campus gate, University Boulevard is lined with student-oriented eateries.

Gentle Ben's Brewing Company. Beer lovers should head to Gentle Ben's, a friendly, laid-back burger-and-brew pub that also makes a scrumptious veggie burger. The deck upstairs offers a good view of the sunset. ✉ *865 E. University Blvd., University* ☎ *520/624–4177* ⊕ *www.gentlebens.com.*

Kababeque. From curry to kebab, the tasty and plentiful dishes at Kababeque satisfy for a quick bite Indian-style. ✉ *845 E. University Blvd., University* ☎ *520/388–4500* ⊕ *www.tucsonindianrestaurant.com.*

Sinbad's. Nestled in the verdant Geronimo Plaza, Sinbad's serves falafel and other Middle Eastern fare, and has a great patio. ✉ *810 E. University Blvd., University* ☎ *520/623–4010* ⊗ *No lunch Sun.*

WORTH NOTING
University of Arizona Museum of Art. This small museum houses a collection of over 6,000 artworks, mainly European and American paintings from the Renaissance through modern day, including works by Georgia O'Keeffe and Jackson Pollock. A highlight is the Kress Collection's *retablo* from Ciudad Rodrigo: 26 panels of an altarpiece made in the 1490s by Fernando Gallego. ✉ *Fine Arts Complex, 1031 N Olive Rd., north of 2nd St., University* ☎ *520/621–7567* ⊕ *www.artmuseum.arizona.edu* 🎟 *$5* ⊗ *Tues.–Fri. 9–5, weekends noon–4.*

CENTRAL TUCSON AND EASTSIDE

Tucson expanded north and east from the university during the 1950s and '60s, and currently continues to spread southeast. The sights worth seeing in this mostly residential area include the Tucson Botanical Gardens, the small Reid Park Zoo, and the Fort Lowell Park and Museum. Colossal Cave Mountain Park and Pima Air and Space Museum are on the southeast outskirts. Saguaro National Park East is on the far east side of town.

PLANNING YOUR TIME
If it's warm, visit outdoor attractions such as the zoo or Tucson Botanical Gardens in the morning; note that Colossal Cave stays at a constant, cool temperature, so it's a good option on a hot day.

CENTRAL TUCSON
FAMILY **Fort Lowell Park and Museum.** Fertile soil and proximity to the Rillito River once enticed the Hohokam to construct a village on this site. Centuries later, a fort (in operation from 1873 to 1891) was built here to protect the fledgling city of Tucson against the Apaches. The former commanding officer's quarters at this quirky fort museum has artifacts from military life in territorial days. The park has a playground, ball fields, tennis courts, and a duck pond. Admission to the museum is two-for-one on the first Saturday of every month. ✉ *2900 N. Craycroft Rd., Central* ☎ *520/885–3832* ⊕ *www.arizonahistoricalsociety.org* 🎟 *Museum $3* ⊗ *Fri. and Sat. 10–4.*

FAMILY **Reid Park Zoo.** This small but well-designed zoo won't tax the children's—or your—patience. There are plenty of shady places to sit, a wonderful gift shop, and a snack bar to rev you up when your energy

Colossal Cave
Mountain Park .. **5**

Fort Lowell
Park and
Museum **3**

Pima Air
and Space
Museum **4**

Reid Park
Zoo **2**

Tucson Botanical
Gardens **1**

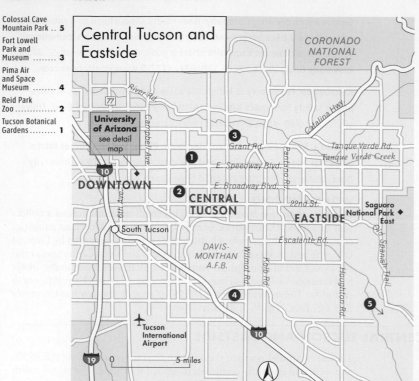

Central Tucson and Eastside

flags. You can feed carrots to the zoo's friendly giraffes each morning at about 9:30 ($2). The new African elephants habitat and the South American section with rain forest exhibits and exotic birds are also popular. If you're visiting in summer, go early in the day when the animals are active. The park surrounding the zoo has a number of imaginative playground structures and a lake where you can feed ducks and rent paddleboats. ⊠ *Reid Park, 1100 S. Randolph Way, off 22nd St., Central* ☏ *520/791–4022* ⊕ *www.tucsonzoo.org* ⊠ *$9* ◷ *Sept.–May 9–4; June–Aug. 8–3.*

Tucson Botanical Gardens. The 5 acres are home to a variety of experiences: a tropical greenhouse; a sensory garden, where you can touch and smell the plants and listen to the abundant birdlife; historical gardens that display the Mediterranean landscaping the property's original owners planted in the 1930s; a garden designed to attract birds; and a cactus garden. Other gardens showcase wildflowers, Australian plants, and Native American crops and herbs. From October through April, interact with butterflies from all over the world in their own greenhouse. A delightful café is open for breakfast and lunch daily October–early May. All paths are wheelchair accessible. ⊠ *2150 N. Alvernon Way, Central* ☏ *520/326–9686* ⊕ *www.tucsonbotanical.org* ⊠ *$13 Oct.– Apr.; $8 May–Sept.* ◷ *Daily 8:30–4:30.*

EASTSIDE

FAMILY **Colossal Cave Mountain Park.** This limestone grotto 20 mi east of Tucson is the largest dry cavern in the world. Guides discuss the fascinating crystal formations and relate the many romantic tales surrounding the cave, including the legend that an enormous sum of money stolen in a stagecoach robbery is hidden here.

Forty-five-minute cave tours begin every 30 minutes and require a 0.5-mi walk and climbing 363 steps. The park includes a ranch area with trail rides ($30 per hour), a gemstone-sluicing area, a small museum, a desert tortoise habitat, nature trails, a butterfly garden, a snack bar, and a gift shop. Parking is $5 per vehicle. Take Broadway Boulevard or 22nd Street east to Old Spanish Trail. ⊠ *16721 E. Old Spanish Trail, Eastside* ☎ *520/647–7275* ⊕ *www.colossalcave.com* ⊠ *Cave tour $13* ⊙ *Oct.–mid-Mar., daily 9–5; mid-Mar.–Sept., daily 8–5.*

Pima Air and Space Museum. This huge facility ranks among the largest private collections of aircraft in the world. More than 300 airplanes are on display in hangars and outside, including a presidential plane used by both John F. Kennedy and Lyndon B. Johnson; a full-scale replica of the Wright brothers' 1903 Wright Flyer; the SR-71 reconnaissance jet; and a mock-up of the X-15, the world's fastest aircraft. World War II planes are particularly well represented.

Meander on your own (even leashed pets are allowed) or take a free walking tour led by volunteer docents. The open-air tram tour (an additional $6 fee) narrates all outside aircraft. Hour-long van tours of Aerospace Maintenance and Regeneration Group (AMARG)—affectionately called "The Boneyard"—at nearby Davis-Monthan Air Force Base provide an eerie glimpse of hundreds of mothballed aircraft lined up in rows on a vast tract of desert. This $7 AMARG tour, available only on weekdays on a first-come, first-served basis, is a photographer's delight. An on-site restaurant, The Flight Grill, is open daily from 9:30 to 4:30. ⊠ *6000 E. Valencia Rd., I–10, Exit 267, Eastside* ☎ *520/574–0462* ⊕ *www.pimaair.org* ⊠ *$15.50* ⊙ *Daily 9–5, last admission at 4.*

CATALINA FOOTHILLS

Considered by some to be the "Beverly Hills of Tucson," the Catalina Foothills area is home to posh resorts and upscale shopping. Because the neighborhood backs on the beautiful Santa Catalina Mountains, it also has an abundance of hiking trails.

PLANNING YOUR TIME

It may be hard to choose from the shopping, hiking, golf, and spa options along the Skyline Drive/Sunrise Drive corridor, but you can plan to spend at least a few hours strolling or hiking in Sabino Canyon. Shopping and dining at La Encantada or the smaller complexes across the road can easily fill the other half of a day. If you want to venture farther into the mountains, head northeast up to Mount Lemmon: it's time-consuming (a one-hour drive each way), but the higher elevation and cooler temperatures make it an excellent destination in summer.

Tucson History: City in the Foothills

Native Americans have lived along the waterways in this valley for thousands of years. During the 1500s Spanish explorers arrived to find Pima Indians growing crops in the area. Father Eusebio Francisco Kino, a Jesuit missionary whose influence is still strongly felt throughout the region, first visited the area in 1687, and returned a few years later to build missions.

NATIVE AMERICANS AND THE PRESIDIO

The name "Tucson" came from the Native American word *stjukshon* (pronounced *stook*-shahn), meaning "spring at the foot of a black mountain." The springs at the foot of Sentinel Peak, made of black volcanic rock, are now dry. The name was pronounced *tuk*-son by the Spanish explorers who built a wall around the city in 1776 to keep Native Americans from reclaiming it. At the time, this *presidio* (fortified city), called San Augustín del Tucson, was the northernmost Spanish settlement in the area, and present-day Main Avenue is a quiet reminder of the former Camino Real ("royal road") that

stretched from this tiny walled fort all the way to Mexico City.

CHANGING ALLEGIANCES

Four flags have flown over Tucson— Spanish, Mexican, Confederate, and, finally, the Stars and Stripes. Tucson's allegiance changed in 1820 when Mexico declared independence from Spain, and again in 1853 when the Gadsden purchase made it part of the United States, though Arizona didn't become a state until 1912. In the 1850s the Butterfield stage line was extended to Tucson, bringing adventurers, a few settlers, and more than a handful of outlaws. The arrival of the railroad in 1880 marked another spurt of growth, as did the opening of the University of Arizona in 1891.

MODERN TIMES

Tucson's 20th-century growth occurred after World War I, when veterans with damaged lungs sought the dry air and healing power of the sun, and again during World War II with the opening of Davis-Monthan Air Force Base and the rise of local aeronautical industries. It was also around this time that air-conditioning made the desert climate hospitable year-round.

DeGrazia Gallery in the Sun. Arizonan artist Ted DeGrazia, who depicted Southwest Native American and Mexican life in a manner some find kitschy and others adore, built this sprawling, spacious, single-story museum with the assistance of Native American friends, using only natural material from the surrounding desert.

You can visit DeGrazia's workshop, former home, tranquil chapel, and grave. Although the original works are not for sale, the museum's gift shop has a wide selection of prints, ceramics, and books by and about the colorful artist. ⊠ *6300 N. Swan Rd., Foothills* ☎ *520/299–9191* ⊕ *www.degrazia.org* ⊠ *Free* ☉ *Daily 10–4.*

Mount Lemmon. Part of the Santa Catalina range, Mount Lemmon— named for Sara Lemmon, the first woman to reach the peak of this mountain, in 1881—is the southernmost ski slope in the continental United States, but you don't have to be a skier to enjoy the area: in

De Grazia's
Gallery
in the Sun **2**

Mount
Lemmon **3**

Sabino
Canyon **1**

Catalina
Foothills

summer, it's a popular place for picnicking, and there are 150 miles of marked and well-maintained trails for hiking. The mountain's 9,157-foot elevation brings relief from summer heat.

Mount Lemmon Highway twists its way for 28 miles up the mountainside. Every 1,000-foot climb in elevation is equivalent, in terms of climate, to traveling 300 miles north: you'll move from typical Sonoran Desert plants in the Foothills to vegetation similar to that found in southern Canada at the top. Rock formations along the way look as though they were carefully balanced against each other by sculptors from another planet.

Even if you don't make it to the top of the mountain, you'll find stunning views of Tucson at Windy Point, about halfway up. Look for a road on your left between the Windy Point and San Pedro lookouts; it leads to Rose Canyon lake, a lovely reservoir.

Just before you reach the ski area, you'll pass through the tiny alpine-style village of **Summerhaven**, which has some casual restaurants, gift shops, and pleasant lodges.

■**TIP**➜ There are no gas stations on Mount Lemmon Highway, so gas up before you leave town and check the road conditions in winter. To reach the highway, take Tanque Verde Road to Catalina Highway, which becomes Mount Lemmon Highway as you head north.

✉ *Mount Lemmon Hwy., North-east* ☎ *520/576–1400 recorded snow report, 520/547–7510 winter road conditions* 🎫 *$5 per vehicle* 🕐 *Daily, depending on snow in winter.*

Coronado National Forest. At milepost 18 of your ascent, on the left-hand side of the road, is the Palisades Ranger Station of Coro-

nado National Forest. Rangers have information on the mountain's campgrounds, hiking trails, and picnic spots. ☎ *520/749–8700* ⊕ *www. fs.fed.us/r3/coronado* 🕐 *Daily 8–4:30.*

Mt. Lemmon Ski Valley. Mount Lemmon Highway ends at Mount Lemmon Ski Valley. Skiing and snowboarding depend on natural conditions—there's no artificial snow, so call ahead. There are 21 runs, ranging from beginner to advanced. Lift tickets cost $40 for an all-day pass and $32 for a half-day pass starting at 12:30 pm. Equipment rentals and instruction are available.

Off-season you can take a ride on the chairlift ($9), which whisks you to the top of the slope—some 9,100 feet above sea level. Many ride the lift, then hike on one of several trails that crisscross the summit. There are some concessions right at the ski lift; the Iron Door Restaurant, across the road, serves sandwiches, soups, and homemade pies alongside gorgeous views. ✉ *10300 Ski Run Rd., Mount Lemmon* ☎ *520/576–1321* ⊕ *www.skithelemmon.com* 🕐 *Closed Tues.–Wed.*

Mt. Lemmon Sky Center. At the University of Arizona's research observatory on Mount Lemmon, visitors can plumb the night sky on the highest mountain in the area using the largest public-viewing telescope in the Southwest. A five-hour stargazing program is offered nightly (weather-permitting), and includes astronomy lessons, telescope viewing, and a light dinner. The cost ($60 for adults; $30 for kids under 18) is discounted Monday to Wednesday. ✉ *Ski Run Rd., Mt. Lemmon* ☎ *520/626–8122* ⊕ *www.skycenter.arizona.edu.*

Fodor's Choice **Sabino Canyon.** Year-round, but especially in summer, locals flock to
★ Coronado National Forest to hike, picnic, and enjoy the waterfalls, streams, swimming holes, saguaros, and shade trees. No cars are allowed, but a narrated tram ride (about 45 minutes round-trip) takes you up a WPA-built road to the top of the canyon; you can hop off and on at any of the nine stops or hike any of the numerous trails.

There's also a shorter tram ride (or you can walk) to adjacent Bear Canyon, where a rigorous but rewarding hike leads to the popular Seven Falls (it'll take about 1½–2 hours each way from the drop-off point, so carry plenty of water). If you're in Tucson near a full moon between April and November, take the special night tram and watch the desert come alive with nocturnal critters. ✉ *Sabino Canyon Rd. at Sunrise Dr., Foothills* ☎ *520/749–2861 recorded tram information, 520/749–8700 visitor center* ⊕ *www.fs.fed.us/r3/coronado* 🎫 *$5 per vehicle, tram $3–$8* 🕐 *Visitor center: Daily 8–4:30; call for tram schedules.*

NORTHWEST TUCSON AND WESTSIDE

Once a vast, open space dotted with horse ranches, Northwest Tucson is now a rapidly growing residential area encompassing the townships of Oro Valley and Marana. Families and retirees are moving here in droves, and the traffic congestion proves the point, but you'll also find first-rate golf resorts and restaurants here, as well as the oases of Tohono Chul Park and Catalina State Park, which calm the senses.

The Westside is far less developed, and beautiful vistas of saguaro-studded hills are around every bend. Saguaro National Park West, the Desert Museum, Old Tucson Studios, and the San Xavier mission are all in this section of town. If you're interested in the flora and fauna of the Sonoran Desert—as well as some of its appearances in the cinema—heed the same advice given the pioneers: go west.

PLANNING YOUR TIME

A good idea is to start the morning at Saguaro National Park and then head over to the Arizona–Sonora Desert Museum, where you can lunch at Ironwood Terrace or the more upscale Ocotillo Café. How long you spend at Saguaro National Park depends on whether you choose a short walk to see petroglyphs at Signal Hill on the Loop Drive (an hour should suffice) or hike a longer mountain trail, but leave yourself at least two hours for your visit at the Desert Museum. The hottest part of an afternoon can be spent ducking in and out of attractions at Old Tucson Studios or enjoying the indoor sanctuary of San Xavier mission, although the mission is also a good stop if you're heading out of town to Tubac or Tumacácori.

TOP ATTRACTIONS

FAMILY
Fodor's Choice
★

Arizona–Sonora Desert Museum. The name "museum" is a bit misleading, since this delightful site is actually a zoo, aquarium, and botanical garden featuring the animals, plants and, yes, even fish of the Sonoran Desert. Hummingbirds, coatis, rattlesnakes, scorpions, bighorn sheep, bobcats, and Mexican wolves all busy themselves in ingeniously designed habitats.

An Earth Sciences Center has an artificial limestone cave to climb through and an excellent mineral display. The coyote and javelina (wild, piglike mammals with oddly oversize heads) exhibits have "invisible" fencing that separates humans from animals, and at the Raptor Free Flight show (October–April daily at 10 and 2), you can see the powerful birds soar and dive, untethered, inches above your head.

The restaurants are above average, and the gift shop, which carries books, jewelry, and crafts, is outstanding. ■TIP➜ June through August, the museum stays open until 10 pm every Saturday, which provides a great opportunity to see nocturnal critters. ⊠ 2021 N. Kinney Rd., Westside ☎ 520/883–2702 ⊕ www.desertmuseum.org ☏ $14.50 ⊗ Mar.–May, daily 7:30–5; June–Sept., daily 7–5; Oct.–Feb., daily 8:30–5.

Fodor's Choice
★

Mission San Xavier del Bac. The oldest Catholic church in the United States still serving the community for which it was built, San Xavier was founded in 1692 by Father Eusebio Francisco Kino, who established

Arizona–
Sonora
Desert
Museum 1

Mission
San Xavier
del Bac 4

Old Tucson
Studios 2

Tohono Chul
Park 3

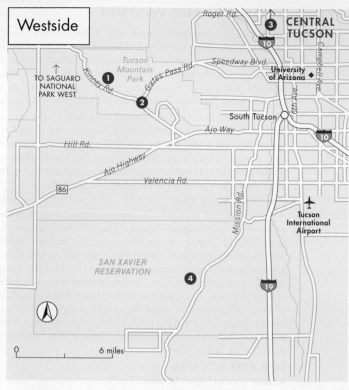

22 missions in northern Mexico and southern Arizona. The current structure was made out of native materials by Franciscan missionaries between 1777 and 1797, and is owned by the Tohono O'odham tribe.

The beauty of the mission, with elements of Spanish, baroque, and Moorish architectural styles, is highlighted by the stark landscape against which it is set, inspiring an early-20th-century poet to dub it the White Dove of the Desert.

Inside, there's a wealth of painted statues, carvings, and frescoes. Paul Schwartzbaum, who helped restore Michelangelo's masterwork in Rome, supervised Tohono O'odham artisans in the restoration of the mission's artwork, completed in 1997; Schwartzbaum has called the mission the Sistine Chapel of the United States. Mass is celebrated at 8:30 am Tuesday through Friday in the church, Saturday afternoon at 5:30, and three times on Sunday morning. Call ahead for information about special celebrations.

Across the parking lot from the mission, San Xavier Plaza has a number of crafts shops selling the handiwork of the Tohono O'odham tribe, including jewelry, pottery, friendship bowls, and woven baskets with man-in-the-maze designs. ✉ *1950 W. San Xavier Rd., 9 mi southwest of Tucson on I–19, Westside* ☎ *520/294–2624* ⊕ *www.sanxaviermission. org* 🎟 *Free* ☉ *Church daily 7–5, museum and gift shop daily 8–5.*

QUICK
BITES

Wa:k Snack Shop. For wonderful Indian fry bread—large, round pieces of dough taken fresh from the hot oil and served with sweet or savory toppings like honey, powdered sugar, beans, meats, or green chiles—stop in the Wa:k Snack Shop at the back of San Xavier Plaza. You can also have breakfast or a lunch of Mexican food here, and if you're lucky, local dancers will be performing for one of the many tour groups that stop here. ⊠ *San Xavier Plaza, 1950 W. San Xavier Rd., 9 miles southwest of Tucson on I-19, Westside.*

Tohono Chul Park. A 48-acre desert garden retreat designed to promote the conservation of arid regions, Tohono Chul—"desert corner" in the language of the Tohono O'odham—uses demonstration gardens, a greenhouse, and a geology wall to explain this unique desert area. Nature trails, a small art gallery, gift shops (including a great selection of desert plants), and a bistro can all be found at this peaceful spot. You can visit the restaurant and gift shops without paying admission. ⊠ *7366 N. Paseo del Norte, Northwest* ☎ *520/742–6455* ⊕ *www.tohonochulpark.org* ⊠ *$8* ⊗ *Park and restaurant daily 8–5.*

WORTH NOTING

OFF THE
BEATEN
PATH

Biosphere 2. In the town of Oracle, about 30 minutes northwest of Tucson, this unique, self-contained cluster of ecosystems opened in 1991 as a facility to test nature technology and human interaction with it. Now managed by the University of Arizona, the biomes include tropical rain forest, savanna, desert, thorn scrub, marsh, and ocean areas. The newest biome, the Landscape Evolutionary Observatory, tracks rainfall in simulated desert environments to study the effects of climate change on water sources and plant life in this region.

Guided walking tours, which last about an hour, take you inside the biomes, and a brief film gives an overview of Biosphere projects, from the original "human missions"—where scientists literally ate, slept, and breathed their work in a closed system—to current research. A snack bar overlooks the Santa Catalina Mountains. ⊠ *32540 S. Biosphere Rd., AZ 77, Milepost 96.5, Northwest, Oracle* ☎ *520/838–6200* ⊕ *www.b2science.org* ⊠ *$20* ⊗ *Daily 9–4.*

FAMILY **Old Tucson.** This film studio–theme park, originally built for the 1940 motion picture *Arizona*, has been used to shoot countless movies, such as *Rio Bravo* (1959) and *The Quick and the Dead* (1994), and the TV shows *Gunsmoke, Bonanza,* and *Highway to Heaven.* Actors in Western garb perform and roam the streets talking to visitors.

Youngsters enjoy the simulated gunfights, rides, stunt shows, and petting farm, while adults might appreciate the screenings of old Westerns, studio tour, and the little-bit-bawdy Grand Palace Hotel's Dance Hall Revue. There are plenty of places to eat and to buy souvenirs. Horseback riding is available for an additional charge. ⊠ *Tucson Mountain Park, 201 S. Kinney Rd., Westside* ☎ *520/883–0100* ⊕ *www.oldtucson.com* ⊠ *$16.95* ⊗ *Jan.–April daily 10–5; May and Oct.–Dec., Fri.–Sun. 10-5* ⊗ *Closed June–Sept.*

7

WHERE TO EAT

Tucson boldly proclaims itself to be the "Mexican Food Capital of the United States" and most of the Mexican food in town is Sonoran-style. It's the birthplace of the chimichanga (Spanish for "whatchamacallit"), a flour tortilla filled with meat or cheese, rolled, and deep-fried.

This means prolific use of cheese, mild peppers, corn tortillas, pinto beans, and beef or chicken. The best Mexican restaurants are concentrated in South Tucson and Downtown, although some favorites have additional locations around town. If Mexican's not your thing, there are plenty of other options: you won't have any trouble finding excellent sushi, Thai, Italian, and Ethiopian food at reasonable prices.

For sampling local flavors, there are several Southwestern restaurants in town. Up in the Foothills, upscale Southwestern cuisine flourishes at such restaurants as the Grill at Hacienda del Sol Resort. A recent trend in Tucson dining is combining hip restaurants with chic shopping locations. Choose from sushi, steak, Italian, or Mexican at La Encantada in the Foothills. Casas Adobes Plaza, in the Northwest, is home to upscale shops alongside Wildflower Grill, Bluefin Seafood Bistro, and trendy, thin-crust pizza at Sauce—and the gelato shop here is handy for dessert. At St. Philip's Plaza, in the lower Foothills, art galleries and boutiques surround Vivace, which has lovely patio dining.

Cheaper but no less tasty fare as varied as Indian, Guatemalan, and Middle Eastern can be enjoyed on the west side of U of A's campus, along University Boulevard and 4th Avenue—a great area for people-watching and barhopping as well as quelling hunger pangs.

On Friday and Saturday nights and during the Gem Show (first two weeks of February), reservations are usually a good idea at upscale and popular restaurants. Dress ranges from casual to casual dressy here—jackets for men aren't required at any restaurant, even at resorts. Although the city's selection of restaurants is impressive, Tucson doesn't have much in the way of late-night dining; many restaurants in town are shuttered by 9 pm.

Prices in the reviews are the average cost of a main course at dinner or, if dinner isn't served, at lunch. Use the coordinate (⊕ B2) at the end of each listing to locate a site on the corresponding map.

DOWNTOWN TUCSON

$$ MEXICAN Fodor's Choice ★

🍴 **Café Poca Cosa.** At what is arguably Tucson's most creative Mexican restaurant, the chef prepares recipes inspired by different regions of her native country. The menu, which changes daily, might include chicken mole or pork *pibil* (made with a tangy Yucatecan barbecue seasoning). Servings are plentiful, and each table gets a stack of warm corn tortillas and a bowl of beans to share. Order the daily Plato Poca Cosa, and the chef will select one beef, one chicken, and one vegetarian entrée for you to sample. The bold-color walls of the contemporary interior are hung with Latin American art. [$] *Average main: $16* ✉ *110 East Pennington St., Downtown* ☎ *520/622–6400* 🌐 *www.cafepocacosatucson.com* ✍ *Reservations essential* 🕒 *Closed Sun. and Mon.* ⊕ *B5.*

BEST BETS FOR TUCSON DINING

Fodor's offers a listing of quality dining experiences at every price range, from the city's best cheap eateries to its most upscale restaurants. Here, we've compiled our top picks by price and experience. The best properties—in other words, those that provide a remarkable experience in their price range—are designated in the listings with the Fodor's Choice logo.

Fodor's Choice ★

Beyond Bread, $, p. 380

Café Poca Cosa, $$, p. 374

Maynards, $$$, p. 376

Best by Price

$

Beyond Bread, p. 380

El Minuto Café, p. 376

Sauce, p. 384

Tucson Tamale Company, p. 380

Zemam's, p. 381

Zinburger, p. 383

$$

Bangkok Cafe, p. 377

Café Poca Cosa, p. 374

Downtown Kitchen & Cocktails, p. 376

Feast, p. 380

$$$-$$$$

Acacia, p. 382

The Grill at Hacienda del Sol, p. 382

JaxKitchen, p. 384

Maynards, p. 376

Best by Cuisine

AMERICAN

Feast, $$, p. 380

JaxKitchen, $$$, p. 384

Kingfisher Bar and Grill, $$, p. 380

Wildflower Grill, $$, p. 384

ITALIAN

North, $$, p. 383

Tavolino, $$, p. 383

Vivace, $$$, p. 383

Zona 78, $$, p. 381

MEXICAN

Café Poca Cosa, $$, p. 374

El Charro, $$, p. 376

El Minuto Café, $, p. 376

Micha's, $, p. 385

Mi Nidito, $, p. 385

SOUTHWESTERN

Acacia, $$$, p. 382

The Grill at Hacienda del Sol, $$$$, p. 382

Best by Experience

BEST BREAKFAST

Arizona Inn Restaurant, $$$$, p. 377

The B Line, $, p. 377

Cup Café, $$, p. 376

Tohono Chul Garden Bistro, $$, p. 384

BEST PATIO DINING

Maynards, $$$, p. 376

Tohono Chul Garden Bistro, $$, p. 384

Vivace, $$$, p. 383

MOST KID-FRIENDLY

Beyond Bread, $, p. 380

Pinnacle Peak Steakhouse, $$, p. 382

Sauce, $, p. 384

GOOD FOR GROUPS

Bluefin Seafood Bistro, $$$, p. 383

Feast, $$, p. 380

North, $$, p. 383

Tavolino, $$, p. 383

HOT SPOTS

Café Poca Cosa, $$, p. 374

Cup Café, $$, p. 376

Zinburger, $, p. 383

LATE-NIGHT DINING

Cup Café, $$, p. 376

Kingfisher Bar and Grill, $$, p. 380

Zinburger, $, p. 383

SPECIAL OCCASION

Acacia, $$$, p. 382

The Grill at Hacienda del Sol, $$$$, p. 382

Maynards, $$$, p. 376

7

$$ AMERICAN

🍴 **Cup Café.** This charming spot off the lobby of Hotel Congress is at the epicenter of Tucson's hippest Downtown scene, but it's also a down-home, friendly place. Try the eggs, potatoes, chorizo, and cheese for breakfast or an ahi tuna salad for lunch. The "Heartbreaker" appetizer—Brie melted over artichoke hearts and apple slices on a baguette—complements such entrées as chicken cordon bleu, house-smoke beef brisket or potato-wrapped salmon. It's open late—until 10 pm weeknights and midnight on weekends—and becomes crowded in the evening with patrons from Club Congress, the hotel's nightclub. [$] *Average main: $13* ✉ *Hotel Congress, 311 E. Congress St., Downtown* ☎ *520/798–1618* 🌐 *www.hotelcongress.com* ✥ *B5.*

$$ MODERN AMERICAN

🍴 **Downtown Kitchen & Cocktails.** Ever-evolving maverick and master chef Janos Wilder has returned to the Downtown dining scene, delighting city planners striving to energize this district. The menu draws inspiration from warm-weather regions around the world. Dishes like calamari with mango, roasted peanuts, and green chile vinaigrette, and honey-soy-ginger duck breast fuse beautifully with Janos's French technique and Southwestern flavors. The interior, decorated in soft blues and greens and exposed brick walls, affords relaxation and quiet conversation. Janos's emphasis on locally grown, organic foods informs the seasonally changing menu, but you can always get his signature J Dawg, a Sonoran hot dog with black beans, bacon, and smoked poblano chile crema, along with other lighter fare at the bar, which stays open until midnight Thursday to Saturday. [$] *Average main: $20* ✉ *135 S. 6th Ave., Downtown* ☎ *520/623–7700* 🌐 *www.downtownkitchen.com* 🕒 *No lunch weekends* ✥ *B5.*

$$ MEXICAN

🍴 **El Charro Café.** Started by Monica Flin in 1922, the oldest Mexican restaurant in town still serves splendid versions of the Mexican-American staples Flin claims to have originated, most notably *chimichangas* and cheese crisps. The tortilla soup and *carne seca* chimichanga, made with beef that is air-dried on the premises—on the roof, actually—are delicious. Located in an old stone house in El Presidio Historic District, the colorful restaurant and bar exude festive—if slightly touristy—vibes. [$] *Average main: $12* ✉ *311 N. Court Ave., Downtown* ☎ *520/622–1922* 🌐 *www.elcharrocafe.com* ✥ *B5.*

$ MEXICAN

🍴 **El Minuto Café.** Popular with local families and the business crowd at lunch, this bustling restaurant is in Tucson's Barrio Historico neighborhood and stays open until 11 pm Friday and Saturday and 10 pm the rest of the week. For more than 50 years El Minuto has served *topopo* salads (a crispy tortilla shell heaped with beans, guacamole, and many other ingredients), huge burritos, and green-corn tamales (in season) made just right. The spicy *menudo* (tripe soup) is reputed to be a great hangover remedy. [$] *Average main: $9* ✉ *354 S. Main Ave., Downtown* ☎ *520/882–4145* 🌐 *www.elminutocafe.com* ✥ *B5.*

$$$ FRENCH
Fodor's Choice ★

🍴 **Maynards.** An anchor in the downtown district, this French-inspired bistro, bar, and gourmet take-out market takes up part of Tucson's historic train depot. Clever thematic touches—a dining room fashioned long and narrow like a train car, with wheel-like divider walls and lamps made from rail spikes—and the attentive yet relaxed service evoke the romance of a largely bygone era. Choose a table by the window and watch the trains go by. Or if you prefer, sit outside on the vast patio overlooking the tracks. Menu choices range from starters like fresh oysters and steak tartare to bouillabaisse, coq au vin, and burgers served with *pommes frites*. The market sells house-made sandwiches and snacks to take out (or dine in at the large community table), as well as locally made products like wines, tamales, and soaps. [$] *Average main: $25* ✉ *400 N. Toole Ave., Downtown* ☎ *520/545–0577* 🌐 *www.maynardsmarket.com* ✣ *B5.*

UNIVERSITY OF ARIZONA

$$$$ EUROPEAN 🍴 **Arizona Inn Restaurant.** At the Arizona Inn, one of Tucson's oldest and most elegant restaurants, dine on the patio overlooking the lush grounds or enjoy the view from the dining room, which has Southwestern details from the 1930s. The culinary range is broad, from roasted duck in a tart cherry demi-glace to a vegetarian tomato and mushroom cannelloni. Locals mostly come for weekday power breakfasts, business or special occasion lunches, and Sunday brunch. [$] *Average main: $34* ✉ *Arizona Inn, 2200 E. Elm St., University* ☎ *520/325–1541* 🌐 *www.arizonainn.com* ✣ *C4.*

$$ GREEK 🍴 **Athens on 4th Avenue.** The tranquil dining room in this Greek spot off 4th Avenue is furnished with lace curtains, white stucco walls, and potted plants. Enjoy classics like *kotopoulo stin pita* (grilled chicken breast with a yogurt-cucumber sauce on fresh pita), moussaka, or the *pastitsio* (a casserole made with pasta, meat, and béchamel). The house favorite is braised lamb shoulder in a light tomato sauce over pasta or potatoes—call to reserve your order of the lamb ahead of time. [$] *Average main: $18* ✉ *500 N. 4th Ave., at 6th St., University* ☎ *520/624–6886* 🌐 *www.athenson4th.com* 🕒 *Closed Sun. No lunch* ✣ *B5.*

$ AMERICAN 🍴 **The B Line.** In the heart of 4th Avenue's amalgam of antique clothing stores, pubs, and natural-food grocers, this casual café in a converted 1920s bungalow attracts a mix of students, professors, downtown professionals, and artists with its simple but refined meals and desserts. Homemade biscuit sandwiches and excellent coffee start the day; the lunch–dinner menu features soups, salads, pastas, burritos, and 13 brews on tap. People-watching as a secondary pleasure doesn't get any better than sitting against the wraparound window looking out on 4th Avenue. [$] *Average main: $9* ✉ *621 N. 4th Ave., University* ☎ *520/882–7575* 🌐 *www.blinerestaurant.com* ✣ *B4.*

CENTRAL TUCSON

$$ THAI 🍴 **Bangkok Cafe.** This is not only the best Thai food in town, it is top-notch for Thai-food fans. The bright, spacious café offers favorite Thai dishes, along with exceptionally pleasant service and reasonable prices; the Thoong Tong appetizer of fried veggie-filled pouches is blissfully good. The spice-heat level of any dish can be adjusted at your request, from 1 through 5 (just keep in mind that a 5 might cause steam to blow out the top of your head). There are plenty of options for vegetarians, and tofu is available to add to any dish. Try to avoid the dinner rush (6:30–8:30) on weekends, or you might wait a while to

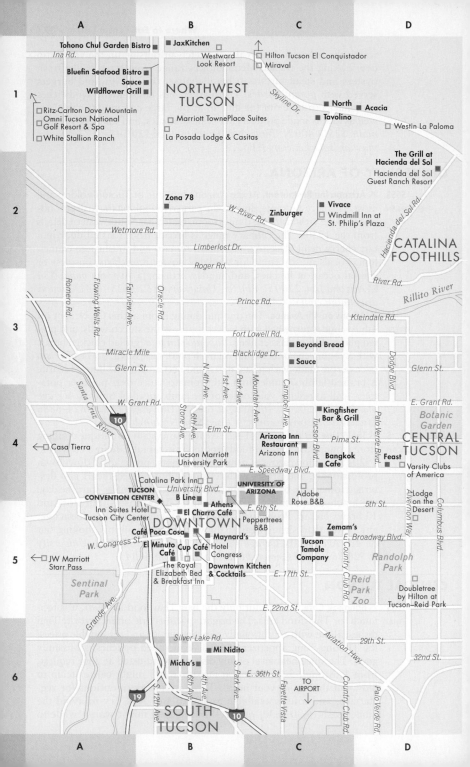

A   **B**   **C**   **D**

Tohono Chul Garden Bistro ■   ■ JaxKitchen   □
Ina Rd.   □ Hilton Tucson El Conquistador
   Westward   □ Miraval
   Look Resort

Bluefin Seafood Bistro ■
Sauce ■   **NORTHWEST**
Wildflower Grill ■   **TUCSON**   Skyline Dr.

1   ■ North   ■ Acacia
□ Ritz-Carlton Dove Mountain   ■ Tavolino
□ Omni Tucson National   □ Marriott TownePlace Suites   □ Westin La Paloma
Golf Resort & Spa
□ White Stallion Ranch   La Posada Lodge & Casitas

   The Grill at
   Hacienda del Sol
   Hacienda del Sol
Zona 78 ■   Guest Ranch Resort

2   ■ Vivace
   Zinburger ■   □ Windmill Inn at
   W. River Rd.   St. Philip's Plaza   **CATALINA**
   FOOTHILLS
Wetmore Rd.

Limberlost Dr.   River Rd.

Roger Rd.   Rillito River

Romero Rd.   Prince Rd.
Flowing Wells Rd.   Kleindale Rd.

3   Fort Lowell Rd.
   Fairview Ave.   Oracle Rd.   ■ Beyond Bread   Dodge Blvd.   Glenn St.
Miracle Mile   Blacklidge Dr.   ■ Sauce
Glenn St.
   E. Grant Rd.
   Botanic
W. Grant Rd.   ■ Kingfisher   Garden
   Bar & Grill
Santa Cruz River   Stone Ave.   N. 4th Ave.   1st Ave.   Park Ave.   Mountain Ave.   Campbell Ave.   Tucson Blvd.   Pima St.   **CENTRAL**
4   Elm St.   Arizona Inn   Palo Verde Blvd.   **TUCSON**
← Casa Tierra   Restaurant   ■ Feast   Columbus Blvd.
   Tucson Marriott   Arizona Inn   ■ Bangkok   ■ Varsity Clubs
   University Park   Café   of America
   E. Speedway Blvd.
   Catalina Park Inn   **UNIVERSITY OF**   □ Lodge
TUCSON   University Blvd.   **ARIZONA**   on the
CONVENTION CENTER ◆   B Line ■   □ Adobe   5th St.   Desert
Inn Suites Hotel   ■ Athens   E. 6th St.   Rose B&B
Tucson City Center   ■ El Charro Café   □ Peppertrees   ■ Zemam's   E. Broadway Blvd.
   DOWNTOWN   B&B   Tucson   Randolph
Café Poca Cosa ■   Maynard's ■   Tamale   Park
5   El Minuto   Cup Café ■   Hotel   Company   Reid
← JW Marriott   Café ■   Congress   E. 17th St.   Park   Doubletree
Starr Pass   The Royal   Downtown Kitchen   Zoo   by Hilton at
   Elizabeth Bed   & Cocktails   Tucson–Reid Park
Sentinal   & Breakfast Inn
Park   E. 22nd St.

Grande Ave.   Silver Lake Rd.   29th St.
   ■ Mi Nidito   32nd St.
6   Micha's ■   E. 36th St.
   TO
   AIRPORT
   ↓
SOUTH
TUCSON

A   **B**   **C**   **D**

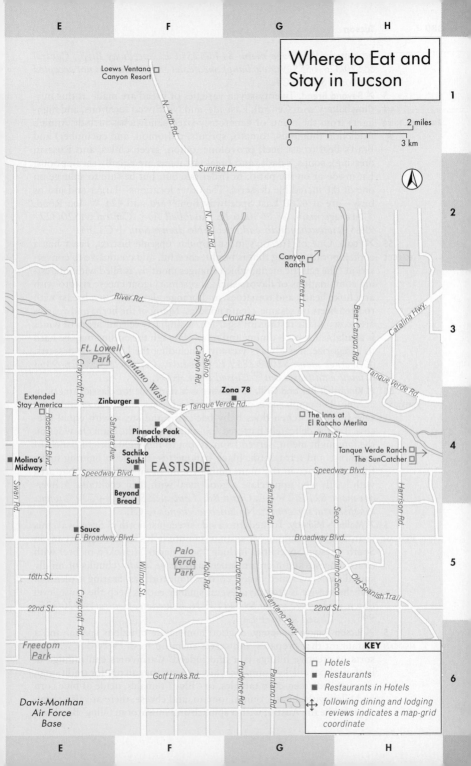

Where to Eat and Stay in Tucson

0   2 miles

0   3 km

Loews Ventana Canyon Resort ☐

N. Kolb Rd.

Sunrise Dr.

N. Kolb Rd.

Canyon Ranch ☐ ↗

Larrea Ln.

Bear Canyon Rd.

Catalina Hwy.

River Rd.

Cloud Rd.

Tanque Verde Rd.

Ft. Lowell Park

Pantano Wash

Sabino Canyon Rd.

Craycroft Rd.

Rosemont Blvd.

Extended Stay America ☐

Zinburger ■

Sahuara Ave.

Pinnacle Peak Steakhouse ■

Sachiko Sushi ■

Molina's Midway ■

E. Speedway Blvd.

EASTSIDE

Beyond Bread ■

Swan Rd.

■ Sauce

E. Broadway Blvd.

16th St.

Wilmot St.

22nd St.

Craycroft Rd.

Freedom Park

Zona 78 ■

E. Tanque Verde Rd.

The Inns at El Rancho Merlita ☐

Pima St.

Tanque Verde Ranch ☐

The SunCatcher ☐

Speedway Blvd.

Harrison Rd.

Pantano Rd.

Palo Verde Park

Kolb Rd.

Prudence Rd.

Pantano Pkwy.

Broadway Blvd.

Seco

Camino Seco

Old Spanish Trail

22nd St.

Golf Links Rd.

Prudence Rd.

Pantano Rd.

Davis-Monthan Air Force Base

KEY

☐ Hotels

■ Restaurants

■ Restaurants in Hotels

↔ following dining and lodging reviews indicates a map-grid coordinate

be seated. [$] *Average main: $14* ✉ *2511 E. Speedway Blvd., Central* ☎ *520/323–6555* 🌐 *www.bangkokcafe.net* ✍ *Reservations not accepted* 🕒 *Closed Sun.* ✥ *C4.*

$ CAFÉ Fodor's Choice ★ 🍴 **Beyond Bread.** Twenty-seven varieties of bread are made at this bustling bakery with Central, Eastside, and Northwest locations, and highlights from the menu of generously-sized sandwiches include Annie's Addiction (hummus, tomato, sprouts, red onion, and cucumber) and Brad's Beef (roast beef, provolone, onion, green chiles, and Russian dressing); soups, salads, and breakfast items are equally scrumptious. Eat inside or on the patio, or order takeout, but be sure to splurge on one of the incredible desserts. The other locations—larger and just as busy—are at 6260 East Speedway Boulevard and 421 W. Ina Road. [$] *Average main: $8* ✉ *3026 N. Campbell Ave., Central* ☎ *520/322–9965* 🌐 *www.beyondbread.com* 🕒 *No dinner Sun.* ✥ *C3, F4.*

$$ ECLECTIC 🍴 **Feast.** One of Tucson's most popular upscale bistros, Feast has a contemporary setting that is bright, cheerful, and conducive to conversation. The eclectic menu, which changes monthly, is filled with interesting combinations of flavors such as rosemary-goat cheese risotto with artichoke hearts and tomatoes, and orange-glazed chicken breast with roasted beets on sesame-cream noodles. Many of the herbs and veggies are grown in the restaurant's garden. A similarly eclectic array of wines is available for both dining and retail. Though the cuisine may be hard to categorize, it is always yummy—including the homemade desserts. [$] *Average main: $20* ✉ *3719 E. Speedway, Central* ☎ *520/326–9363* 🌐 *www.eatatfeast.com* 🕒 *Closed Mon.* ✥ *D4.*

$$ AMERICAN 🍴 **Kingfisher Bar and Grill.** Kingfisher is a standout for classic American cuisine. The emphasis is on fresh seafood, especially oysters and mussels, but the kitchen does baby back ribs and steak with equal success. Try the delicately battered fish-and-chips or the clam chowder on the late-night menu, served from 10 pm to midnight. Bright panels of turquoise and terra-cotta, black banquettes, and neon lighting make for a chic space in the main dining room, or sit in the cozy bar area with locals who appreciate a good meal with their cocktails. [$] *Average main: $21* ✉ *2564 E. Grant Rd., Central* ☎ *520/323–7739* 🌐 *www.kingfishertucson.com* 🕒 *No lunch weekends* ✥ *C4.*

$ MEXICAN 🍴 **Molina's Midway.** Tucked into a side street just north of Speedway, this charming, unassuming Mexican restaurant holds its own against any in South Tucson. Specialties include "Sinchiladas" (chicken or beef with chiles, cheese, and a cream sauce) and *carne asada* (chunks of mildly spiced steak) wrapped in soft corn or flour tortillas. Seating is plentiful and the service is friendly; several smaller rooms keep the noise level down. [$] *Average main: $9* ✉ *1138 N. Belvedere, Central* ☎ *520/325–9957* 🕒 *Closed Mon.* ✥ *E4.*

$ MEXICAN 🍴 **Tucson Tamale Company.** A good homemade tamale is special and a restaurant that prepares and serves them up fresh every day with all sorts of creative fillings is a find indeed. Carnivores can indulge in beef, pork, or chicken tamales while vegetarians can opt for traditional, cheese-filled green-corn tamales, or "Blue" tamales, made of blue corn and filled with squash, onion, tomato, and cheese; there are also vegan choices like the Austin, with a spinach and mushroom filling. Breakfast

Work up your appetite hiking through the desert before enjoying some of the best Mexican food north of the border.

tamales and eggs are served on weekend mornings. Salad, rice, and black beans are side options; most items are gluten-free and made without animal fat. Eat here in the no-frills dining area, or take your tamales to go. [$] *Average main: $8* ✉ *2545 E. Broadway Blvd., Central* ☎ *520/305–4760* 🌐 *www.tucsontamalecompany.com* ✥ *C5.*

$ ETHIOPIAN 🍴 **Zemam's.** It can be hard to get a table in this small, friendly eatery with a loyal following. The sampler plate of any three items allows you to try dishes like *yesimir wat* (a spicy lentil dish) and *lega tibs* (a milder beef dish with a tomato sauce). Most of the food has a stew-like consistency, so don't come if you feel the need to crunch. Everything is served on a communal platter with *injera,* a spongy bread, and eaten with the hands. Alcohol is bring-your-own. [$] *Average main: $12* ✉ *2731 E. Broadway Blvd., Central* ☎ *520/323–9928* 🌐 *www.zemams.com* ✍ *Reservations not accepted* 🕒 *Closed Mon.* ✥ *C5.*

$$ ITALIAN 🍴 **Zona 78.** Fresh food takes on a whole new meaning at this contemporary bistro emphasizing inventive pizzas, pastas, and salads. The casual interior's focal point is a huge stone oven, where the pies are fired with toppings like Australian blue cheese, kalamata olives, sausage, and even chicken with peanut sauce. Whole-wheat crust is an option, and there are also baked salmon and chicken entrées. The house-made mozzarella is delectable, either on top of a pizza or in a salad with organic tomatoes. The newer eastside location at 7301 East Tanque Verde Road has the same low-key, neighborhood feel. [$] *Average main: $15* ✉ *78 W. River Rd., Central* ☎ *520/888–7878* 🌐 *www.zona78.com* ✥ *B2, G4.*

EASTSIDE

$$ STEAKHOUSE FAMILY 🍴 **Pinnacle Peak Steakhouse.** Anybody caught eating newfangled foods like fish tacos here would probably be hanged from the rafters—along with the ties snipped from city slickers who overdressed. This cowboy steakhouse serves basic, not stellar, fare: mesquite-broiled steak, ribs, chicken, and grilled fish with salad and pinto beans. The restaurant is part of the somewhat kitschy, family-friendly Trail Dust Town, a re-creation of a turn-of-the-20th-century town, complete with a working antique carousel, a narrow-gauge train, and Western stunt shows staged outside nightly at 7 and 8. Expect a long wait on weekends. [$] *Average main: $16* ✉ *6541 E. Tanque Verde Rd., Eastside* ☎ *520/296–0911* 🌐 *www.traildusttown.com* ✍ *Reservations not accepted* ⏲ *No lunch* ✣ *F4.*

$ JAPANESE 🍴 **Sachiko Sushi.** Don't let the bland interior or the strip-mall setting dissuade you; many locals consider this the best Japanese restaurant in Tucson. Inside, you'll find perfectly prepared sushi and sashimi, generous combinations of tempura and teriyaki, and friendly service. The owner's wife is Korean, so you'll also find quite a few Korean classics, like beef and pork *bulgogi* (barbecued with vegetables) and tofu kimchi, on the menu. Try a bowl of udon noodles, served in broth with assorted meat, seafood, or vegetables; it's a satisfying meal in itself. [$] *Average main: $12* ✉ *1101 North Wilmot Rd., Eastside* ☎ *520/886–7000* 🌐 *www.sachikosushitucson.com* ⏲ *No lunch Sun.* ✣ *F4.*

CATALINA FOOTHILLS

$$$ SOUTHWESTERN 🍴 **Acacia.** One of Tucson's premier chefs, Albert Hall, relocated his fine-dining restaurant to high in the Catalina Foothills, so now patrons can enjoy stunning city views from both the restaurant and the expansive, more casual bar. Roasted plum tomato and basil soup, a recipe from Hall's mom, is a favorite starter. Creative dishes like wild salmon with a pecan honey-mustard glaze and wood-roasted quail filled with pancetta, mozzarella, roasted tomatoes, and Oaxacan risotto are among the many tempting, organically grown (or raised) entrées. Vegetarians have choices here, too, including a sweet corn and green chile custard with roasted vegetables, fettuccini and wild mushrooms, and an Asian noodle salad. [$] *Average main: $24* ✉ *3001 E. Skyline Drive, Gallery Row, Foothills* ☎ *520/232–0101* 🌐 *www.acaciatucson.com* ✣ *D1.*

$$$$ SOUTHWESTERN 🍴 **The Grill at Hacienda del Sol.** Tucked into the Foothills and surrounded by spectacular flowers and cactus gardens, this special-occasion restaurant, a favorite among locals hosting out-of-town visitors, provides an alternative to the chili-laden dishes of most Southwestern nouvelle cuisine. Wild-mushroom bisque, grilled buffalo in dark choclate mole, and pan-seared sea bass are among the menu choices at this luxurious guest ranch resort. Lower-priced tapas such as tequila-steamed mussels and carne asada tacos can be enjoyed on the more casual outdoor patio, accompanied by live flamenco guitar music on weekends. The lavish Sunday brunch buffet is worth a splurge. [$] *Average main: $38* ✉ *Hacienda del Sol Guest Ranch Resort, 5501 N. Hacienda Del Sol Rd., Foothills* ☎ *800/728–6514* 🌐 *www.haciendadelsol.com* ✣ *D3.*

$$ ITALIAN 🍴 **North.** This trendy eatery in upscale La Encantada Shopping Center melds an urban-loft look with rustic Italian touches, including bright red chairs and metal tables. North draws crowds who come for the excellent thin-crust pizzas, pasta, fish, and steak, all prepared in the open kitchen. Alfresco dining on the wraparound patio affords views of the city and quieter conversation; on most evenings the expansive bar area inside buzzes with Tucson's young professionals. [$] *Average main: $18* ✉ *La Encantada Shopping Center, 2995 E. Skyline Dr., Foothills* ☎ *520/299–1600* 🌐 *www.foxrc.com* ✣ *C1.*

$$ ITALIAN 🍴 **Tavolino.** Italian classics like lasagna del forno, ravioli del zucca, and osso buco have never tasted better than at Chef Mossimo's Tavolino, tucked into a small complex of art galleries across from La Encantada Mall. All the pastas are house-made, and even the bread—a pizza dough recipe—is scrumptious. Wood-fired pizzas and the slow-roasted pork loin are deservedly popular. The mostly Italian wine list includes some excellent selections from Pietro Rinaldi (Mossimo's brother's vineyards), just to keep it all in the family. [$] *Average main: $19* ✉ *2890 E. Skyline Dr., Foothills* ☎ *520/531–1913* 🌐 *www.tavolinoristorante.com* ⏲ *Closed Sun.* ✣ *C1.*

$$$ ITALIAN 🍴 **Vivace.** A nouvelle Italian bistro in the lovely St. Philip's Plaza, Vivace has long been a favorite with Tucsonans. Wild mushrooms and goat cheese in puff pastry is hard to resist as a starter. The fettuccini with grilled salmon is a nice, lighter alternative to such entrées as a rich osso buco. For dessert, the molten chocolate cake with spumoni is worth the 20 minutes it takes to create. Patio seating overlooking the pretty, flower-filled courtyard is especially inviting on warm evenings. [$] *Average main: $26* ✉ *4310 N. Campbell Ave., St. Philip's Plaza, Foothills* ☎ *520/795–7221* 🌐 *www.vivacetucson.com* ⏲ *Closed Sun.* ✣ *C2.*

$ AMERICAN 🍴 **Zinburger.** Have a glass of wine or a cocktail with your gourmet burger and fries at this high-energy, somewhat noisy, and unquestionably hip burger joint. Open until 11 pm on Friday and Saturday (late by Tucson standards), Zinburger delivers tempting burgers—try the Kobe beef with cheddar and wild mushrooms—and decadent milk shakes made of exotic combinations like dates and honey or melted chocolate with praline flakes. A few creative salads, including one with ahi tuna, round out the menu. The restaurant also has a second location on the northeast side of town. [$] *Average main: $10* ✉ *1865 E. River Rd., Foothills* ☎ *520/299–7799* 🌐 *www.foxrc.com* ✣ *C2.*

NORTHWEST TUCSON

$$$ SEAFOOD 🍴 **Bluefin Seafood Bistro.** What's a nice little fish restaurant doing in the middle of the desert? Consistently turning out fresh, well-prepared seafood like cashew-crusted mahimahi, Scottish salmon, and a mixed grill of lobster, shrimp, and scallops in a classy setting. Tucked into the Casas Adobes Plaza, the two-story bistro has three comfortable seating areas: in the brick-walled bar (where "mussel madness" is a daily happy-hour lure), upstairs in the mellow dining room, or outside on the patio. The late-night menu, which includes New England and Manhattan clam chowder, is served until 10 pm on Friday and Saturday, providing a less expensive, lighter option in this part of town. [$] *Average main: $22*

⊠ *Casas Adobes Plaza, 7053 N. Oracle Rd., Northwest* ☎ *520/531–8500* ⊕ *www.bluefintucson.com* ✢ *B1.*

$$$ ✕ **JaxKitchen.** With just the right blend of culinary inventiveness, upbeat
MODERN energy, and value, Jax serves up modern comfort food in a cozy, sophis-
AMERICAN ticated setting more reminiscent of Chicago or Boston than the Sonoran
Desert. Their unique versions of "street tacos" (made with duck confit
and corn with chile cream) and tomato soup with grilled Brie and Gru-
yère cheeses are heavenly, and the daily fish entrée is served with Meyer
lemon–infused risotto. The dining room is cleverly divided by a half
wall, so conversation still feels intimate even when the place is bustling.
Save room for the red velvet cake or milk and cookies like your mother
never served—a plate of assorted warm cookies surrounding a cup of
bourbon-spiked milk to dip them in. You'll want to make a reservation
here, even on weeknights. $ *Average main: $21* ⊠ *7286 N. Oracle Rd.,
Northwest* ☎ *520/219–1235* ⊕ *www.jaxkitchen.com* ⊘ *Closed Mon.
No lunch Sun.–Tues.* ✢ *B1.*

$ ✕ **Sauce.** Modern Italian fuses with fast food here at North Restau-
ITALIAN rant's casual little sister in Casas Adobes Plaza. Delicious thin-crust
pizzas, chopped salads, pastas, and panini are ordered at the counter
in this lively, family-friendly spot decorated in a contemporary twist
on the colors of Italy's flag—green, white, and tomato-red. The food
is fast, fresh, and affordable, without sacrificing sophisticated taste.
Two additional locations, on East Broadway in Eastside and North
Campbell in Central, are identical in both decor and menu. $ *Aver-
age main: $9* ⊠ *Casas Adobes Plaza, 7117 N. Oracle Rd., Northwest*
☎ *520/297–8575* ⊕ *www.foxrc.com* ✢ *B1, E5.*

$$ ✕ **Tohono Chul Garden Bistro.** The food at Tohono Chul Garden Bistro is
SOUTHWESTERN excellent, but what many come for is the location inside a wildlife sanc-
tuary, surrounded by flowering desert gardens. The Southwestern interior has Mexican tile, light wood, and a cobblestone courtyard. Dine on
the back patio to watch hummingbirds and butterflies. House favorites
include prickly pear and pistachio chicken on croissant, vegan quiche (a
tofu-and-garbanzo custard with veggies), burgers, and assorted salads.
Open daily 8–5, the bistro also serves breakfast, afternoon high tea,
and a popular weekend brunch. $ *Average main: $13* ⊠ *Tohono Chul
Park, 7366 N. Paseo del Norte, Northwest* ☎ *520/742–6455* ⊕ *www.
tohonochulpark.org* ⊘ *No dinner* ✢ *B1.*

$$ ✕ **Wildflower Grill.** A glass wall separates the bar from the dining area,
AMERICAN where an open kitchen, high ceiling with painted flowers, and blue-
green banquettes complete the light and airy effect. Wildflower Grill is
well known for its creative American fare and stunning presentation,
and the menu has compelling choices like a salmon and seafood bouil-
labaise; bow-tie pasta with grilled chicken, tomatoes, spinach, and pine
nuts; and red wine-braised short ribs. The decadently huge desserts are
equally top-notch. Request a banquette or seating on the patio in the
evening if you want quiet conversation, as the room can be noisy. $ *Av-
erage main: $20* ⊠ *Casa Adobes Plaza, 7037 N Oracle Rd., Northwest*
☎ *520/219–4230* ⊕ *www.foxrc.com* ✢ *B1.*

SOUTH TUCSON

$
MEXICAN
✕ **Micha's.** Family-owned for 37 years, this local institution in the heart of South Tucson is a nondescript Mexican diner serving some of the best Sonoran classics this side of the border. House specialties include *machaca* (shredded beef) enchiladas and *chimichangas*, and *cocido*, a hearty vegetable-beef soup. Homemade chorizo spices up breakfast, which is served daily. $ *Average main: $10* ✉ *2908 S. 4th Ave., South* ☎ *520/623–5307* ⊕ *www.michascatering.com* ☉ *No dinner Mon.* ✛ *B6.*

$
MEXICAN
✕ **Mi Nidito.** A perennial favorite among locals (the wait is worth it), Mi Nidito—"my little nest"—has also hosted its share of visiting celebrities. Following President Clinton's lunch here, the rather hefty Presidential Plate (bean tostada, taco with barbecued meat, chiles rellenos, chicken enchilada, and beef tamale with rice and beans) was added to the menu. Top that off with the mango *chimichangas* for dessert, and you're talkin' executive privilege. $ *Average main: $10* ✉ *1813 S. 4th Ave., South* ☎ *520/622–5081* ⊕ *www.minidito.net* ☉ *Closed Mon. and Tues.* ✛ *B6.*

WHERE TO STAY

When it comes to places to spend the night, the options in Tucson run the gamut: there are luxurious desert resorts, bed-and-breakfasts ranging from bedrooms in modest homes to private cottages nestled on wildlife preserves, and small to medium-size hotels and motels.

If you like being able to walk to sights, shops, and restaurants, plan on staying in the Downtown or University neighborhoods. You won't find a hotter scene than Downtown's Hotel Congress, with nightly music pulsing at Club Congress or the Rialto Theatre across the street. For a quieter but equally convenient base, opt for one of the charming B&Bs near the U of A campus.

The posh resorts, primarily situated in the Catalina Foothills and Northwest areas, although farther away from town, have many activities on-site, as well as some of Tucson's top-rated restaurants, golf courses, and spas, and can arrange transportation to shopping and sights. Tucson's JW Marriott Starr Pass is the only one southwest of town; seemingly isolated, it's actually closer to Downtown and the Westside sights.

For a unique experience, you can check into one of several Southwestern-style dude ranches—among them a former cattle ranch from the 1800s—on the outskirts of town (unless otherwise indicated, price categories for guest ranches include all meals and most activities).

If you're seeking accommodations that can change your life, book a stay at one of Tucson's world-class health spas, Canyon Ranch or Miraval. Both provide pampering, serenity, and guidance for attaining an improved sense of well-being.

Summer rates (late May through September) are up to 60% lower than those in winter. Note that unless you book months in advance, you'll be hard-pressed to find a Tucson hotel room at any price the week before and during the huge gem and mineral show, which is held the first two

BEST BETS FOR TUCSON LODGING

Fodor's offers a selective listing of quality lodging experiences at every price range, from the city's best budget motel to its most sophisticated luxury hotel. Here, we've compiled our top recommendations by price and experience. The very best properties—in other words, those that provide a particularly remarkable experience in their price range—are designated in the listings with the Fodor's Choice logo.

Fodor'sChoice ★

Arizona Inn, $$$, p. 387

Canyon Ranch, $$$$, p. 390

Casa Tierra, $$, p. 393

Hacienda del Sol Guest Ranch Resort, $$, p. 390

Hotel Congress, $, p. 387

Loews Ventana Canyon Resort, $$$, p. 390

White Stallion Ranch, $$$$, p. 392

Best by Price

$

Catalina Park Inn Bed & Breakfast, p. 388

Hotel Congress, p. 387

Inn Suites Hotel Tucson City Center, p. 387

La Posada Lodge and Casitas, p. 392

$$

Adobe Rose Bed and Breakfast, p. 387

Casa Tierra, p. 393

Hacienda del Sol Guest Ranch Resort, p. 390

Inns at El Rancho Merlita, p. 390

Lodge on the Desert, p. 388

Peppertrees Bed & Breakfast, p. 388

$$$–$$$$

Arizona Inn, p. 387

JW Marriott Starr Pass, p. 393

Loews Ventana Canyon Resort, p. 390

Westin La Paloma, p. 391

Westward Look Resort, p. 392

White Stallion Ranch, p. 392

The Ritz-Carlton Dove Mountain, p. 392

Best By Experience

BEST B&BS

Casa Tierra, $$, p. 393

Catalina Park Inn Bed & Breakfast, $, p. 388

Peppertrees Bed & Breakfast, $$, p. 388

Royal Elizabeth Bed and Breakfast Inn, $$, p. 387

BEST RESORTS

JW Marriott Starr Pass, $$$, p. 393

Loews Ventana Canyon Resort, $$$, p. 390

The Ritz-Carlton Dove Mountain, $$$$, p. 392

Westin La Paloma, $$$, p. 391

BEST SPAS

Canyon Ranch, $$$$, p. 390

JW Marriott Starr Pass, $$$, p. 393

Miraval, $$$$, p. 392

The Ritz-Carlton Dove Mountain, $$$$, p. 392

Westin La Paloma, $$$, p. 391

GREAT VIEWS

Casa Tierra, $$, p. 393

JW Marriott Starr Pass, $$$, p. 393

Loews Ventana Canyon Resort, $$$, p. 392

Tanque Verde Ranch, $$$, p. 390

Westward Look Resort, $$$, p. 392

MOST KID-FRIENDLY

Hilton Tucson El Conquistador, $$, p. 391

Tanque Verde Ranch, $$$, p. 390

Westin La Paloma, $$$, p. 391

White Stallion Ranch, $$$$, p. 392

MOST ROMANTIC

Arizona Inn, $$$, p. 387

Hacienda del Sol Guest Ranch Resort, $$, p. 390

JW Marriott Starr Pass, $$$, p. 393

The Ritz-Carlton Dove Mountain, $$$$, p. 392

weeks in February. Also, resorts typically charge an additional daily fee for "use of facilities," such as pools, tennis courts, and exercise classes and equipment, so be sure to ask what's included when you book a room.

Prices in the reviews are the lowest cost of a standard double room in high season. For expanded hotel reviews, visit Fodors.com. Use the coordinate (✢ B2) at the end of each listing to locate a site on the corresponding map.

DOWNTOWN TUCSON

$ **▦ Hotel Congress.** This hotel built in 1919 has been artfully restored to
HOTEL its original Western version of art deco; it's now the center of Tucson's
Fodor'sChoice hippest scene and a great place to stay for younger or more adventurous
★ visitors. **Pros:** prime location; good restaurant; funky and fun. **Cons:** no elevator to guest rooms; no TVs in rooms; noise from nightclub. Ⓢ *Rooms from: $125* ✉ *311 E. Congress St., Downtown* ☎ *520/622–8848, 800/722–8848* ⊕ *www.hotelcongress.com* ⤳ *40 rooms* ⦿ *No meals* ✢ *B5.*

$ **▦ Inn Suites Hotel Tucson City Center.** Just north of the Presidio district
HOTEL of Downtown, this circa 1980 hotel is next to Interstate 10 but quiet nevertheless. **Pros:** free breakfast and cocktails; affordable. **Cons:** little character; long walk to Downtown attractions (but there is a free shuttle service). Ⓢ *Rooms from: $75* ✉ *475 N. Granada Ave., Downtown* ☎ *520/622–3000, 877/446–6589* ⊕ *www.innsuites.com* ⤳ *265 rooms, 35 suites* ⦿ *Breakfast* ✢ *B5.*

$$ **▦ The Royal Elizabeth Bed and Breakfast Inn.** Fans of Victoriana will adore
B&B/INN this B&B in the Armory Park historic district. **Pros:** large and well-appointed rooms; beautiful common areas; a sense of privacy as well as B&B camaraderie. **Cons:** pricey for Downtown; neighbors aren't very lively (next door to a funeral home). Ⓢ *Rooms from: $209* ✉ *204 S. Scott Ave., Downtown* ☎ *520/670–9022* ⊕ *www.royalelizabeth.com* ⤳ *6 rooms* ⦿ *Breakfast* ✢ *B5.*

UNIVERSITY OF ARIZONA

$$ **▦ Adobe Rose Bed and Breakfast.** The comfortable rooms in this 1933
B&B/INN adobe home just east of the University vary in size and amenities. **Pros:** sumptuous breakfasts that can be prepared gluten-free; homelike yet private. **Cons:** some rooms are small; about a mile walk to University Boulevard and 4th Avenue sights. Ⓢ *Rooms from: $160* ✉ *940 N. Olsen Ave., University* ☎ *520/318–4644, 800/328–4122* ⊕ *www.aroseinn.com* ⤳ *6 rooms* ⦿ *Breakfast* ✢ *C4.*

$$$ **▦ Arizona Inn.** Although near the University and many sights, the beauti-
HOTEL fully landscaped lawns and gardens of this 1930 inn seem far from the
Fodor'sChoice hustle and bustle. **Pros:** unique historical property; emphasis on service.
★ **Cons:** rooms may not be modern enough for some; close to University Medical Center but long walk (1.5 miles) from the main campus. Ⓢ *Rooms from: $329* ✉ *2200 E. Elm St., University* ☎ *520/325–1541, 800/933–1093* ⊕ *www.arizonainn.com* ⤳ *72 rooms, 20 suites, 3 casitas* ⦿ *No meals* ✢ *C4.*

$ B&B/INN 🏨 **Catalina Park Inn Bed & Breakfast.** Classical music plays softly in the living room of this beautifully restored 1927 neoclassical house. **Pros:** rooms are large and quiet with up-to-date technology (DVDs, flat-screen TVs, and iPod docks); comfortable beds; charming hosts. **Cons:** West University location is not quite as bucolic as east of campus; closed late summer. [$] *Rooms from: $139* ✉ *309 E. 1st St., University* ☎ *520/792–4541, 800/792–4885* 🌐 *www.catalinaparkinn.com* 🛏 *6 rooms* 🕒 *Closed July and Aug.* 🍴 *Breakfast* ✣ *B4.*

$$ B&B/INN 🏨 **Peppertrees Bed & Breakfast.** This restored 1905 Victorian, just west of the U of A campus, has both rooms and self-contained apartment units. **Pros:** comfortably furnished and meticulously clean; very convenient. **Cons:** often booked far in advance. [$] *Rooms from: $155* ✉ *724 E. University Blvd., University* ☎ *520/622–7167* 🌐 *www.peppertreesinn.com* 🛏 *2 rooms, 1 suite, 2 guesthouses* 🍴 *Breakfast* ✣ *B4.*

$$ HOTEL 🏨 **Tucson Marriott University Park.** With the University of Arizona less than a block from the front door, this clean, contemporary hotel is an ideal place to stay when visiting the campus. **Pros:** excellent location; clean. **Cons:** generic rooms; uninspired restaurant. [$] *Rooms from: $190* ✉ *880 E. 2nd St., University* ☎ *520/792–4100, 888/236–2427* 🌐 *www.marriott.com* 🛏 *234 rooms, 16 suites* 🍴 *No meals* ✣ *B4.*

CENTRAL TUCSON

$ HOTEL 🏨 **Doubletree by Hilton at Tucson-Reid Park.** A sprawling, 1970s-era hotel and conference center, the Doubletree sits directly across the street from Randolph Park, Tucson's best municipal golf course, and Reid Park, which houses the city zoo, a lake with paddleboats, and numerous play areas. **Pros:** attractive gardens; close to recreation and restaurants. **Cons:** large, older property; smallish rooms. [$] *Rooms from: $149* ✉ *445 S. Alvernon Way, Central* ☎ *520/881–4200, 800/222–8733* 🌐 *doubletree3.hilton.com* 🛏 *295 rooms* 🍴 *No meals* ✣ *D5.*

$ HOTEL 🏨 **Extended Stay America.** If you're seeking convenience and value (and don't mind a certain blandness), this modern chain property will suffice. **Pros:** central location; cheap. **Cons:** no pool; some road noise in front rooms. [$] *Rooms from: $65* ✉ *5050 E. Grant Rd., Central* ☎ *520/795–9510, 800/804–3724* 🌐 *www.extendedstayamerica.com* 🛏 *120 rooms* 🍴 *Breakfast* ✣ *E4.*

$$ HOTEL 🏨 **Lodge on the Desert.** A charming hacienda-style hotel originally built in the 1930s has gotten a long-awaited face-lift and now offers modern comfort in an old-world setting. **Pros:** quiet, garden setting; central location. **Cons:** no views to speak of; no gym or spa (though in-room massages and gym passes are available, for a fee). [$] *Rooms from: $169* ✉ *306 N. Alvernon Way, Central* ☎ *520/320–2000, 877/498–6776* 🌐 *www.lodgeonthedesert.com* 🛏 *83 rooms, 20 suites* 🍴 *No meals* ✣ *D5.*

$ HOTEL 🏨 **Varsity Clubs of America.** This sports-themed time-share facility also doubles as a hotel, so it may have some or all of its one- and two-bedroom suites available for rental at any given time. **Pros:** apartment style; common areas include a billiards room, cozy library with fireplace, and a putting green. **Cons:** little curb appeal; bland decor in suites; availability varies by season. [$] *Rooms from: $169* ✉ *3855 E. Speedway Blvd.,*

Fodor's Choice ★

Hacienda del Sol Canyon Ranch

Loews Ventana Canyon Resort White Stallion Ranch

Hotel Congress Arizona Inn

Central ☎ *520/318–3777, 888/594–2287* ⊕ *www.diamondresorts.com* ⤴ *60 suites* ⦿ *No meals* ✛ *D4.*

EASTSIDE

$$　⊞ **The Inns at El Rancho Merlita.** Few bed-and-breakfasts offer the historic
B&B/INN　charm, elegance, and pampering that this mid-century Southwestern
estate, the former retreat of cosmetics mogul Merle Norman, delivers.
Pros: historic, charming home and grounds; excellent breakfast. **Cons:**
a little far from town for some. Ⓢ *Rooms from: $175* ⊠ *1924 N. Corte
El Rancho Merlita, Eastside* ☎ *520/495–0071, 888/218–8418* ⊕ *www.
ranchomerlita.com* ⤴ *8 rooms* ⦿ *Breakfast* ✛ *G4.*

$$　⊞ **The SunCatcher.** The three rooms in this B&B are decorated in honor
B&B/INN　of three groups who settled the Old West: Cowboys, Native Americans,
and Spaniards. **Pros:** quiet escape from civilization; all rooms have
separate entrances; scrumptious European breakfasts. **Cons:** on the far
east side of town. Ⓢ *Rooms from: $160* ⊠ *105 N. Avenida Javelina,
Eastside* ☎ *520/885–0883, 877/775–8355* ⊕ *www.suncatchertucson.
com* ⤴ *3 rooms* ⦿ *Breakfast* ✛ *H4.*

$$$　⊞ **Tanque Verde Ranch.** The most upscale of Tucson's guest ranches and
RESORT　one of the oldest in the country, the Tanque Verde sits on 640 beau-
ALL-INCLUSIVE　tiful acres in the Rincon Mountains next to Saguaro National Park
FAMILY　East. **Pros:** authentic Western experience; loads of all-inclusive activi-
ties; great riding. **Cons:** expensive; at the eastern edge of town; all-
inclusive package excludes alcohol. Ⓢ *Rooms from: $350* ⊠ *14301 E.
Speedway Blvd., Eastside* ☎ *520/296–6275, 800/234–3833* ⊕ *www.
tanqueverderanch.com* ⤴ *49 rooms, 25 suites* ⦿ *All-inclusive* ✛ *H4.*

CATALINA FOOTHILLS

$$$$　⊞ **Canyon Ranch.** This award-winning resort draws an international
RESORT　crowd of well-to-do health seekers to its superb spa facilities on 70
ALL-INCLUSIVE　acres in the desert Foothills. **Pros:** a stay here can be a life-changing
Fodor'sChoice　experience; gorgeous setting. **Cons:** very pricey; not family-friendly.
★　Ⓢ *Rooms from: $425* ⊠ *8600 E. Rockcliff Rd., Foothills* ☎ *520/749–
9000, 800/742–9000* ⊕ *www.canyonranch.com* ⤴ *240 rooms* ⦿ *All-
inclusive* ✛ *G2.*

$$　⊞ **Hacienda del Sol Guest Ranch Resort.** This 32-acre hideaway in the
RESORT　Santa Catalina Foothills is a charming and more intimate alternative to
Fodor'sChoice　the larger resorts. **Pros:** outstanding restaurant and bar; buildings and
★　landscaping are stunningly beautiful. **Cons:** not enough resort amenities
for some (no golf or spa, just a few massage rooms). Ⓢ *Rooms from:
$209* ⊠ *5501 N. Hacienda Del Sol Rd., Foothills* ☎ *520/299–1501,
800/728–6514* ⊕ *www.haciendadelsol.com* ⤴ *22 rooms, 8 suites* ⦿ *No
meals* ✛ *D2.*

$$$　⊞ **Loews Ventana Canyon Resort.** This is one of the most luxurious and
RESORT　prettiest of the big resorts, with dramatic stone architecture and an
FAMILY　80-foot waterfall cascading down the mountains. **Pros:** this place has
Fodor'sChoice　everything: great golf, full spa, hiking, and even a kids' playground.
★　**Cons:** some rooms overlook the parking lot. Ⓢ *Rooms from: $329*
⊠ *7000 N. Resort Dr., Foothills* ☎ *520/299–2020, 800/234–5117*

Downtown Tucson is close to the Tucson Mountains, which fill with blooms in springtime.

🌐 *www.loewshotels.com/Ventana-Canyon-Resort* ⇨ *384 rooms, 14 suites* 🍴 *No meals* ✥ *F1.*

$$$ RESORT FAMILY 🏨 **Westin La Paloma.** Popular with business travelers and families, this sprawling resort has grand views of the Santa Catalina Mountains above and the city below. **Pros:** top-notch golf, tennis, and spa. **Cons:** so big it can feel crowded at pool areas and mazelike going to and from guest rooms. [$] *Rooms from: $239* ✉ *3800 E. Sunrise Dr., Foothills* ☎ *520/742–6000, 800/937–8461* 🌐 *www.westinlapalomaresort.com* ⇨ *455 rooms, 32 suites* 🍴 *No meals* ✥ *D1.*

$$ HOTEL 🏨 **Windmill Inn & Suites at St. Philip's Plaza.** This all-suites hotel is in a chic shopping plaza filled with boutiques, galleries, good restaurants, and a weekend farmers' market. **Pros:** so many shops and restaurants to walk to, so little time; bicycles are available for treks along the adjacent Rillito River Path. **Cons:** sure, it's a suite, but both rooms are small. [$] *Rooms from: $150* ✉ *4250 N. Campbell Ave., Foothills* ☎ *520/577–0007, 800/547–4747* 🌐 *www.windmillinns.com* ⇨ *122 suites* 🍴 *Breakfast* ✥ *C2.*

NORTHWEST TUCSON

$$ RESORT FAMILY 🏨 **Hilton Tucson El Conquistador.** A huge copper mural of cowboys and cacti, and a wide view of the Santa Catalina Mountains grace the lobby of this golf and tennis resort. **Pros:** great variety of on-site activities; low-key. **Cons:** huge place; location is farther northwest than most resorts, adding on driving time to restaurants and in-town sights. [$] *Rooms from: $209* ✉ *10000 N. Oracle Rd., Northwest* ☎ *520/544–*

5000, 800/325–7832 ⊕ *www.hiltonelconquistador.com* ↪ *328 rooms, 57 suites, 43 casitas* ¶Óǀ *No meals* ✛ *C1.*

$
HOTEL

▦ **La Posada Lodge and Casitas.** This 1960s motor lodge has been reborn as a Santa Fe–style boutique hotel with a Latin theme. **Pros:** good location; good value; attractive grounds. **Cons:** service is inconsistent; rooms are not large. Ⓢ *Rooms from: $99* ⊠ *5900 N. Oracle Rd., Northwest* ☎ *520/887–4800, 800/810–2808* ⊕ *www.laposadalodge.com* ↪ *72 rooms* ¶Óǀ *Breakfast* ✛ *B1.*

$
HOTEL

▦ **Marriott TownePlace Suites.** With full kitchens in all of its studio, one-bedroom, and two-bedroom suites, this property is suitable for short or extended stays. **Pros:** convenient location; well-equipped units. **Cons:** no restaurant; kind of sterile-looking. Ⓢ *Rooms from: $129* ⊠ *405 W. Rudasill Rd., Northwest* ☎ *520/292–9697* ⊕ *www.marriott.com/towneplace* ↪ *76 suites* ¶Óǀ *Breakfast* ✛ *B1.*

$$$$
RESORT

▦ **Miraval.** Giving Canyon Ranch a run for its money, this New Age health spa 30 miles north of Tucson has a secluded desert setting and beautiful Southwestern rooms. **Pros:** very high-end getaway in the middle of nowhere; tranquil. **Cons:** very posh attitude makes some uncomfortable; expensive. Ⓢ *Rooms from: $525* ⊠ *5000 E. Via Estancia Miraval, Catalina* ☎ *520/825–4000, 800/232–3969* ⊕ *www.miravalresorts.com* ↪ *102 rooms* ¶Óǀ *All meals* ✛ *C1.*

$$
RESORT

▦ **Omni Tucson National Golf Resort & Spa.** Perfect for couples with differing ideas on how to spend a vacation, Omni Tucson National is both a premier golf resort and a full-service European-style spa, where you can be coiffed, waxed, and wrapped to your heart's content. **Pros:** outstanding golf; friendly, relaxed environment. **Cons:** tucked away in Northwest Tucson; too sedate for some. Ⓢ *Rooms from: $199* ⊠ *2727 W. Club Dr., Northwest* ☎ *520/297–2271, 800/843–6664* ⊕ *www.omnihotels.com* ↪ *143 rooms, 24 suites* ¶Óǀ *No meals* ✛ *A1.*

$$$
RESORT

▦ **The Ritz-Carlton, Dove Mountain.** The most elegant and exclusive of Tucson's golf and tennis resorts is the ever-posh Ritz-Carlton, set in the rolling hills of Marana, about 20 miles northwest of central Tucson. **Pros:** great golf; top-notch service. **Cons:** somewhat isolated location in the far Northwest. Ⓢ *Rooms from: $299* ⊠ *15000 N. Secret Springs Dr., Marana* ☎ *520/572–3000, 800/241–3333* ⊕ *www.ritzcarlton.com/dovemountain* ↪ *250 rooms* ¶Óǀ *No meals* ✛ *A1.*

$$$
RESORT

▦ **Westward Look Resort.** Originally the 1912 homestead of William and Mary Watson, this laid-back lodging with gorgeous city views and desert gardens has Southwestern character and all the amenities you expect at a major resort. **Pros:** horseback riding; excellent spa; pleasant nature trails; you can actually park near your room. **Cons:** no golf (privileges at private club 4 mi away); pool areas are rather plain. Ⓢ *Rooms from: $249* ⊠ *245 E. Ina Rd., Northwest* ☎ *520/297–1151, 800/722–2500* ⊕ *www.westwardlook.com* ↪ *244 rooms* ¶Óǀ *No meals* ✛ *B1.*

$$$$
RESORT
ALL-INCLUSIVE
Fodor's Choice
★

▦ **White Stallion Ranch.** A 3,000-acre working cattle ranch run by the hospitable True family since 1965, this place is the real deal. **Pros:** solid dude-ranch experience; very charming hosts; satisfying for families as well as singles or couple; airport shuttle. **Cons:** no TV in rooms; alcohol not included in the rate—you must pay extra, or bring your own. Ⓢ *Rooms from: $350* ⊠ *9251 W. Twin Peaks Rd., Northwest*

☎ *520/297–0252, 888/977–2624* 🌐 *www.wsranch.com* 🛏 *24 rooms, 17 suites* 🍴 *All-inclusive* ⊕ *A1.*

WESTSIDE

$$ B&B/INN Fodor's Choice ★ 🏨 **Casa Tierra.** For a real desert experience, head to this B&B on 5 acres near the Desert Museum and Saguaro National Park West. **Pros:** peaceful; great Southwest character. **Cons:** far from town (30-minute drive); two-night minimum stay; closed in summer. [$] *Rooms from: $165* ✉ *11155 W. Calle Pima, Westside* ☎ *520/578–3058, 866/254–0006* 🌐 *www.casatierratucson.com* 🛏 *3 rooms, 1 suite* 🕒 *Closed mid-June–mid-Aug.* 🍴 *Breakfast* ⊕ *A4.*

$$$ RESORT 🏨 **JW Marriott Starr Pass.** Set amid saguaro forests and mesquite groves in the Tucson Mountains (yet only 15 minutes from Downtown), this is the city's largest resort. **Pros:** posh and beautiful; excellent spa; great walking-hiking paths. **Cons:** expensive; parking structure is quite far from lobby areas and guest rooms. [$] *Rooms from: $319* ✉ *3800 W. Starr Pass Blvd., Westside* ☎ *520/792–3500* 🌐 *www.jwmarriottstarrpass.com* 🛏 *538 rooms, 37 suites* 🍴 *No meals* ⊕ *A5.*

NIGHTLIFE AND THE ARTS

NIGHTLIFE

The majority of Tucson's bars and clubs, many with live music or a DJ, are clustered along Congress Street Downtown and on 4th Avenue. In addition, most of the major resorts have late spots for drinks or dancing. The Westward Look Resort's Lookout Bar, with its expansive view and classic rock band on Friday and Saturday nights, is popular for dancing. The bars at Westin La Paloma, Hacienda del Sol, and Loews Ventana have live acoustic music on weekends.

DOWNTOWN

BARS AND CLUBS

Club Congress. The city's main venue for cutting-edge bands and singer-songwriters, Club Congress has a mixed-bag crowd of alternative rockers, international travelers, and college kids. There is live indie rock and folk/roots during the week, while Friday and Saturday nights bring more rock and dance parties. ✉ *Hotel Congress, 311 E. Congress St., Downtown* ☎ *520/622–8848* 🌐 *www.hotelcongress.com.*

La Cocina. Hear some of the best local talent play folk-rock, blues, and jazz Wednesday to Saturday nights at this restaurant and bar in the courtyard of Old Town Artisans. Sit under the stars and order from the late-night menu until 2 am. ✉ *Old Town Artisans, 201 N. Court Ave., Downtown* ☎ *520/622–0351* 🌐 *www.lacocinatucson.com* 🕒 *Closed Sun. and Mon. nights.*

UNIVERSITY
BARS AND CLUBS

GAY AND
LESBIAN

IBT's (It's 'Bout Time). Tucson's most popular gay men's bar, IBT's (It's 'Bout Time) has rock and disco DJ music and drag shows Wednesday and Saturday nights. Expect long lines on weekends. ☒ *616 N. 4th Ave., University* ☎ *520/882–3053* ⊕ *www.ibtstucson.com.*

ROCK

Plush. Alternative-rock bands like Camp Courageous and Greyhound Soul are hosted at the intimate Plush, as well as local performers with a loyal following. ☒ *340 E. 6th St., at 4th Ave., University* ☎ *520/798–1298* ⊕ *www.plushtucson.com.*

CENTRAL AND EASTSIDE
BARS AND CLUBS

BLUES AND
JAZZ

Boondocks. The unofficial home of the Blues Heritage Foundation, Boondocks hosts local and touring jazz and classic rock singer-songwriters. ☒ *3306 N. 1st Ave., Central* ☎ *520/690–0991* ⊕ *www. boondockslounge.com.*

Old Pueblo Grille. This restaurant and bar has live jazz on Sunday nights. ☒ *60 N. Alvernon Way, Central* ☎ *520/326–6000* ⊕ *www. oldpueblogrille.com.*

COUNTRY AND
WESTERN

The Maverick Live Country Club. An excellent house band gets the crowd two-stepping Tuesday through Saturday nights. ☒ *6622 E. Tanque Verde Rd., Eastside* ☎ *520/298–0430* ⊕ *www.tucsonmaverick.com.*

ROCK

El Parador. This spot has a DJ on Friday night and a live salsa band Saturday night, with dance lessons at 10 pm. ☒ *2744 E. Broadway, Central* ☎ *520/881–2744* ⊕ *www.elparadortucson.com.*

The Shelter. You can go totally retro at the Shelter, a former bomb shelter decked out in plastic 1960s kitsch, lava lamps, and JFK memorabilia, which plays Elvis videos and music by the likes of Burt Bacharach and Martin Denny. ☒ *4155 E. Grant Rd., Central* ☎ *520/326–1345* ⊕ *www. thesheltercocktaillounge.com.*

SOUTH AND SOUTHEAST
BARS AND CLUBS

Nimbus Brewing Company. This is the place for acoustic blues, folk, and bluegrass, not to mention good, cheap food and microbrew beer. ☒ *3850 E. 44th St., Southeast* ☎ *520/745–9175* ⊕ *www.nimbusbeer.com.*

CASINOS

Two Native American tribes operate casinos on their Tucson-area reservations west of the airport. They're quite unlike their distant and much grander cousins in Las Vegas and Atlantic City. Don't expect much glamour, ersatz or otherwise: these casinos are more like glorified video arcades, though you can lose money much faster. You'll be greeted by a wall of cigarette smoke (the reservation is exempt from antismoking laws) and the wail of slot machines, video poker, blackjack, roulette, and craps machines. The only "live" gaming is keno, bingo, blackjack, and certain types of poker. No one under age 21 is permitted.

Casino del Sol. A few miles west of the Casino of the Sun is their newer, larger facility, Casino del Sol, with live poker and blackjack, bingo, and slots. An del Sol, a first-rate Asian-fusion restaurant; the excellent PY

Steakhouse; and several casual eateries provide multiple dining options. A 215-room hotel and conference center opened in 2012, followed by a golf course in 2013. An adjacent 4,600-seat outdoor amphitheater books entertainers like Counting Crows and James Taylor. ☒ *5655 W. Valencia Rd., Westside* ☎ *520/838–6506, 855/765–7829* ⊕ *www. casinodelsol.com.*

Casino of the Sun. The Pascua Yaqui tribe's original gaming venture has slot and video-gambling machines only, and one casual restaurant. ☒ *7406 S. Camino de Oeste, off W. Valencia Rd. about 5 miles west of I-19, Southwest* ☎ *520/838–6506, 855/765-7829* ⊕ *www.casinodelsol. com.*

Desert Diamond Casinos. The Tohono O'odham tribe operates the Desert Diamond Casinos, which has an indoor concert venue, a hotel and conference center, and plenty of one-armed bandits and video poker in addition to live keno, bingo, and Stud High, Texas Hold'em, Omaha, and Stud Lo poker. ☒ *7350 S. Old Nogales Hwy., 1 mile south of Valencia, just west of the airport, South* ☎ *520/294–7777, 866/332–9467* ⊕ *www.desertdiamondcasino.com.*

THE ARTS

For a city of its size, Tucson is abuzz with cultural activity. It's one of only 14 cities in the United States with a symphony as well as opera, theater, and ballet companies. Wintertime, when Tucson's population swells with vacationers, is the high season, but the arts are alive and well year-round. The low cost of Tucson's cultural events comes as a pleasant surprise to those accustomed to paying East or West Coast prices: symphony tickets are as little as $20 for some performances, and touring Broadway musicals can often be seen for $35. Parking is plentiful and frequently free.

The free *Tucson Weekly* (⊕ *www.tucsonweekly.com*) and the "Caliente" section of the *Arizona Daily Star* (⊕ *www.azstarnet.com*) both hit the stands on Thursday, and have listings of what's going on in town.

MAJOR VENUES

Centennial Hall. Dance, music, and other performances take place at the University of Arizona's Centennial Hall. ☒ *1020 E. University Blvd., University* ☎ *520/621–3341* ⊕ *www.uapresents.org.*

Fox Tucson Theatre. A refurbished old movie palace, the art deco Fox Theatre hosts film festivals and mostly folk-rock concerts. ☒ *17 W. Congress St., Downtown* ☎ *520/547–3040* ⊕ *www.foxtucsontheatre.org.*

Rialto Theatre. One of Tucson's hottest venues, the Rialto Theatre, once a silent-movie theater, now reverberates with the sounds of hard rock, jazz, folk, and world-music concerts. You can experience great musicians up close for reasonable ticket prices. ☒ *318 E. Congress St., Downtown* ☎ *520/740–1000* ⊕ *www.rialtotheatre.com.*

Tucson Convention Center. Much of the city's cultural activity, including opera, touring Broadway shows, and Tucson Symphony concerts, takes place at the Tucson Convention Center. The Music Hall and the

Leo Rich Theater are part of this complex. ⊠ *260 S. Church Ave., Downtown* ☎ *520/791–4101* ⊕ *www.tucsonaz.gov/tcc.*

Ticketmaster. Each season brings visiting opera, theater, and dance companies to Tucson. Tickets to many events can be purchased through Ticketmaster, which has outlets at most Fry's Marketplace stores around town. ☎ *800/745–3000* ⊕ *www.ticketmaster.com.*

MUSIC

Arizona Friends of Chamber Music. A Wednesday-night chamber-music series is hosted by the Arizona Friends of Chamber Music at the Leo Rich Theater in the Tucson Convention Center from October through April. They also have a music festival the first week of March. ☎ *520/577–3769* ⊕ *www.arizonachambermusic.org.*

Arizona Opera Company. This company is based in Tucson and puts on five major productions each year at the Tucson Convention Center's Music Hall. ☎ *520/293–4336* ⊕ *www.azopera.com.*

Arizona Symphonic Winds. The Arizona Symphonic Winds performs a series of free indoor concerts during winter, and has a spring–summer concert schedule outdoors at Udall Park in Northeast Tucson. Performances in the park are usually at 7 pm, but you need to arrive at least an hour early for a good spot on the grass. ⊕ *www.azsymwinds.org.*

Tucson Jazz Society. Tucson's small but vibrant jazz scene encompasses everything from afternoon jam sessions in the park to Sunday jazz brunches at resorts in the Foothills. Call the Tucson Jazz Society for information. ☎ *520/903–1265* ⊕ *www.tucsonjazz.org.*

Tucson Pops Orchestra. In May, June, and September the Tucson Pops Orchestra gives free concerts on Sunday evenings at the DeMeester Outdoor Performance Center in Reid Park. Arrive about an hour before the music starts (usually at 7 pm) to stake your claim on a viewing spot. ☎ *520/722–5853* ⊕ *www.tucsonpops.org.*

Tucson Symphony Orchestra. Part of Tuscon's cultural scene since 1929, this orchestra performs at the Tucson Convention Center and at sites in the Foothills and the Northwest from October through May. ⊠ *443 S. Stone Ave., Downtown* ☎ *520/882–8585 box office* ⊕ *www. tucsonsymphony.org.*

POETRY

Tucson Poetry Festival. The first weekend in April brings the Tucson Poetry Festival and its four days of readings and related events, including workshops, panel discussions, and a poetry slam. Such internationally acclaimed poets as Jorie Graham and Sherman Alexie have participated. ⊕ *www.tucsonpoetryfestival.org.*

THEATER

Arizona Repertory Theatre. Performances occur throughout the academic year on campus at this University of Arizona theater. ⊠ *1025 N. Olive St., University* ☎ *520/621–7008* ⊕ *www.tftv.arizona.edu.*

Arizona Theatre Company. Arizona's state theater performs classical pieces, contemporary drama, and musical comedy at the historic Temple of Music and Art from September through May. It's worth coming just to see the beautifully restored historic Spanish colonial–Moorish-style theater; dinner at the adjoining Temple Café is a tasty prelude. ⊠ *Temple of Music and Art, 330 S. Scott Ave., Downtown* ☎ *520/622–2823 box office, 520/884–8210 company office* ⊕ *www.arizonatheatre.org.*

Borderlands Theater. This company presents new plays about Southwest border issues—often multicultural and bilingual—at venues throughout Tucson, usually from October through April. ⊠ *40 W. Broadway, Downtown* ☎ *520/882–7406* ⊕ *www.borderlandstheater.org.*

FAMILY **Gaslight Theatre.** Children of all ages love the clever, original melodramas at the Gaslight Theatre, where hissing at the villain and cheering the hero are part of the audience's duty. ⊠ *7010 E. Broadway, Eastside* ☎ *520/886–9428* ⊕ *www.thegaslighttheatre.com.*

Invisible Theatre. Contemporary plays and musicals are presented here. ⊠ *1400 N. 1st Ave., Central* ☎ *520/882–9721* ⊕ *www.invisibletheatre. com.*

SHOPPING

Much of Tucson's retail activity is focused around malls, but shops with more character and some unique wares can be found in the city's open plazas: Old Town Artisans (Meyer Avenue and Washington Street), St. Philip's Plaza (River Road and Campbell Avenue), Casas Adobes Plaza (Oracle and Ina roads), and La Encantada (Skyline Drive and Campbell Avenue).

The 4th Avenue neighborhood near the University of Arizona—especially between 2nd and 9th streets—is fertile ground for unusual items in the artsy boutiques, galleries, and secondhand-clothing stores. For in-town deals, the outlet stores at the Foothills Mall in Northwest Tucson score high marks.

If you're seeking work by regional artists, there are excellent galleries Downtown and in the Catalina Foothills; or you might want to drive down to Tubac, a community 45 miles south of Tucson (⇨ *see Side Trips Near Tucson).*

San Xavier Plaza, across from San Xavier mission and also part of the Tohono O'odham Reservation, is a good place to find vendors and stores selling the work of this and other area tribes.

DOWNTOWN
MALLS AND SHOPPING CENTERS
Old Town Artisans Complex. Across from the Tucson Museum of Art, the Old Town Artisans complex has a large selection of Southwestern wares, including Native American jewelry, baskets, Mexican handicrafts, pottery, and textiles, as well as La Cocina Restaurant and bar. ⊠ *201 N. Court Ave., Downtown* ☎ *520/623–6024* ⊕ *www. oldtownartisans.com.*

GALLERIES
Etherton Gallery. This gallery specializes in vintage, classic, and contemporary photography but also represents artists in other mediums. ⊠ *135 S. 6th Ave., Downtown* ☎ *520/624–7370* ⊕ *www.ethertongallery.com.*

Local ceramics and other arts and crafts are popular in Tucson and the nearby town of Tubac.

Obsidian Gallery. This gallery sells exquisite glass, ceramic, and jewelry pieces. ⊠ *Historic Depot, 410 N. Toole Ave., #130, Downtown* ☎ *520/577–3598* ⊕ *www.obsidian-gallery.com.*

Philabaum Glass Gallery and Studio. Magnificent handblown glass vases, artwork, table settings, and jewelry are made and sold at this gallery. ⊠ *711 S. Sixth Ave., Downtown* ☎ *520/884–7404* ⊕ *www. philabaumglass.com* ⊘ *Closed Sun.-Mon.*

UNIVERSITY OF ARIZONA
ARTS AND CRAFTS
Del Sol. This shop specializes in Mexican folk art, jewelry, and Southwest-style clothing. ⊠ *435 N. 4th Ave., University* ☎ *520/628–8765* ⊕ *www.delsolstores.com.*

Native Seeds/SEARCH. Dedicated to preserving native crops and traditional farming methods, Native Seeds/SEARCH sells 350 kinds of seeds as well as Native American foods, baking mixes, and crafts. ⊠ *3061 N. Campbell Ave., University* ☎ *520/622–5561* ⊕ *www.nativeseeds.org.*

BOOKS
Antigone Books. This lovely independent bookstore on 4th Avenue specializes in books by and about women and also sells creative feminist cards, gifts, and T-shirts. ⊠ *411 N. 4th Ave., University* ☎ *520/792–3715* ⊕ *www.antigonebooks.com.*

Book Stop. This is a wonderful browsing place for used, rare, and out-of-print books. ⊠ *214 N. 4th Ave., University* ☎ *520/326–6661* ⊕ *www. bookstoptucson.com.*

CENTRAL
MALLS AND SHOPPING CENTERS

Broadway Village. Tucson's first shopping center, Broadway Village was built in 1939. Although small by today's standards, this outdoor complex and neighboring strip of shops houses several noteworthy stores: Zocalo for colonial Mexican furniture and art, Yikes! for fabulous off-the-wall toys, and Picante for a wonderful assortment of Mexican/Latin American clothing and crafts. ⊠ *2926 E. Broadway Blvd., at Country Club Rd., Central* ⊕ *www.broadwayvillagetucson.com.*

The Lost Barrio Tucson. Located in an old warehouse district, The Lost Barrio is a cluster of 10 shops with Southwestern and ethnic art, furniture, and funky gifts (both antique and modern). ⊠ *Park Ave. and 12th St., south of Broadway, Central* ⊕ *www.lostbarriotucson.com.*

BOOKS

Bookmans Entertainment Exchange. A Tucson institution, Bookmans carries an enormous and eclectic selection of used and new books, movies, music, magazines, games, and musical instruments in three spacious locations. ⊠ *1930 E. Grant Rd., Central* ☎ *520/325-5767* ⊕ *www. bookmans.com.*

CLOTHING

Arizona Hatters. For that Stetson you've always wanted, Arizona Hatters is your best bet. ⊠ *2790 N. Campbell Ave., Central* ☎ *520/292-1320* ⊕ *www.arizonahatters.com.*

EASTSIDE
MALLS AND SHOPPING CENTERS

Park Place. This busy enclosed mall has an extensive food court, a 20-screen cineplex, and more than 120 stores, including Macy's and Dillard's department stores. ⊠ *5870 E. Broadway Blvd., Eastside* ☎ *520/747-7575* ⊕ *www.parkplacemall.com.*

ARTS AND CRAFTS

B&B Cactus Farm. You'll pass this cactus farm en route to Saguaro National Park East. There's a huge selection of cacti and succulents, and they'll ship anywhere in the country. ⊠ *11550 E. Speedway Blvd., Eastside* ☎ *520/721-4687* ⊕ *www.bandbcactus.com* ☯ *Closed Sun.–Mon.*

JEWELRY

Abbott Taylor Jewelers. Abbott Taylor creates custom designs in diamonds and other precious stones. ⊠ *6383 E. Grant Rd., Eastside* ☎ *520/745-5080* ⊕ *www.atdiamonds.com.*

CATALINA FOOTHILLS
MALLS AND SHOPPING CENTERS

La Encantada. The newest outdoor mall in the area, La Encantada has close to 50 stores (and five restaurants) decidedly aimed at affluent consumers. North, a nouvelle Italian bistro, and Ra Sushi are the standout eateries. Trendy tenants include Crate & Barrel, Pottery Barn, Coach, Apple, and Tiffany & Co., plus AJs, a gourmet grocery that also serves casual meals. ⊠ *Skyline Dr. and Campbell Ave., Foothills* ☎ *520/615-2561* ⊕ *www.laencantadashoppingcenter.com.*

St. Philip's Plaza. More than a dozen chic boutiques and galleries are arranged around Spanish-style outdoor courtyards at St. Philip's Plaza. The restaurant Vivace is located here, and an excellent farmers' market is held on Saturday and Sunday mornings. ⊠ *4280 N. Campbell Ave., at River Rd., Foothills* ⊕ *www.stphilipsplaza.com.*

Tucson Mall. This indoor mall has Dillard's, Macy's, H & M, and more than 200 specialty shops. For tasteful Southwestern-style T-shirts, belts, jewelry, and prickly pear candies, check out the shops on "Arizona Avenue," a section on the first floor that's devoted to regional items. The popular Cheesecake Factory is also here, on the mall's perimeter. ⊠ *4500 N. Oracle Rd., at Wetmore Rd., Central* ☏ *520/293–7330* ⊕ *www.tucsonmall.com.*

ARTS AND CRAFTS

Bahti Indian Arts. This shop is owned and run by Mark Bahti, whose father, Tom, literally wrote the book on Native American art, including an early definitive work on kachinas. The store sells high-quality jewelry, pottery, rugs, art, and more. ⊠ *St. Philip's Plaza, 4330 N. Campbell Ave., Foothills* ☏ *520/577–0290* ⊕ *www.bahti.com.*

Grey Dog Trading Company. There's an ample selection of jewelry, kachinas, weaving, pottery, and Zuni fetishes at this store. ⊠ *St. Philip's Plaza, 4320 North Campbell Ave., Suite 130, Foothills* ☏ *520/881–6888* ⊕ *www.greydogtrading.com.*

GALLERIES

Gallery Row at El Cortijo. Galleries that collectively represent regional and national artists working in all mediums, including Native American, Western, and contemporary painting, crafts, and jewelry make up this complex. ⊠ *3001 E. Skyline Dr., at Campbell Ave., Foothills.*

Madaras Gallery. Bright watercolor prints of cacti and animals by the popular local artist Diana Madaras can be found at this gallery, at El Cortijo. ⊠ *El Cortijo, 3001 E. Skyline Dr., #101, Foothills* ☏ *520/615–3001* ⊕ *www.madaras.com.*

JEWELRY

Beth Friedman. For unsurpassed designs in silver and semiprecious stones, visit Beth Friedman's. The store also carries an eclectic selection of ladies' apparel, fine art, and home furnishings. ⊠ *Joesler Village, 1865 E. River Rd., Suite 121, Foothills* ☏ *520/577–6858* ⊕ *www.bethfriedman.com.*

NORTHWEST AND WESTSIDE

MALLS AND SHOPPING CENTERS

Casas Adobes Plaza. This outdoor, Mediterranean-style shopping center originally served the ranchers and orange-grove owners in this once remote part of town, now the city's fastest-growing area. There's a Whole Foods grocery store, the superb Wildflower and Bluefin restaurants, a gelato shop, upscale pizzas at Sauce, Starbucks, and diverse boutiques and gift shops. ⊠ *7001-7153 North Oracle Rd., Northwest* ⊕ *www.casasadobesplaza.com.*

Foothills Mall. This mall has a Barnes & Noble Superstore, a Saks Fifth Avenue outlet store, and many other outlets including Old Navy, Nike, and Adidas. A 16-screen cineplex (including Tucson's only IMAX theater) and the brewpub Thunder Canyon Brewery round out the place. ⊠ *7401 N. La Cholla Blvd., at Ina Rd., Northwest* ☎ *520/219–0650* ⊕ *www.shopfoothillsmall.com.*

ARTS AND CRAFTS

Antigua de Mexico. This place sells well-made furniture and crafts that you are not likely to find elsewhere in town. ⊠ *3235 W. Orange Grove Rd., Northwest* ☎ *520/742–7114* ⊕ *www.antiguademexico.us.*

Tucson's Map and Flag Center. For topographical maps of just about anywhere, including specialty guides to Arizona, visit Tucson's Map and Flag Center. ⊠ *3239 N. 1st Ave., Central* ☎ *520/887–4234* ⊕ *www. mapsmithus.com.*

SOUTH TUCSON

CLOTHING

Stewart Custom Boots. This company has been making handmade leather boots since the 1940s. It is open Mon.–Thurs., and Fri.–Sat. by appointment only. ⊠ *30 W. 28th St., at S. Sixth Ave., South* ☎ *520/622–2706* ⊕ *www.stewartbootcompany.com.*

SPAS

From day spas to top-rated destination spas to a multitude of posh resorts, the array of wellness treatments in Tucson is wide. Many Tucson spas feature treatments that incorporate Native American traditions and desert plants. Most of the resorts and destination spas—including Canyon Ranch (⇨ *see Where to Stay*)—lie in the Foothills or Northwest, while popular day spas are located around town.

Gadabout. Pampering from head to toe is what awaits at this popular day spa with five locations around town. Hair stylists and "nail therapists" are friendly and skilled; massages, facials, waxing, and makeup lessons are also on the menu, at lower prices than you'll pay at a resort. Each 50-minute facial includes a soothing neck, shoulder, hand, and foot moisturizing massage. If you want your friends back home to envy your Arizona tan, even if you don't have hours to spend soaking up rays, try the "Sun Glow" massage, an exfoliating scrub and UV-free tanning application all in one. ⊠ *3207 E. Speedway, Central* ☎ *520/325– 0000* ⊕ *www.gadabout.com* ☞ *$65 50-minute massage. Hair salon. Services: facials, massage, scrubs, waxing and tinting, nail treatment.*

Hashani Spa at JW Marriott Starr Pass. The tri-level modern Hashani Spa, built on a hillside just east of the JW Marriott, connects to the main resort via a walkway above a wildlife area, but it feels a world away. The top level houses the salon and a shop selling activewear and high-end skin and beauty products. Sleek, Asian-inspired indoor/outdoor lounge areas, a gym, and a dance/yoga studio occupy the middle level; the lower floor is for heavenly treatments like the hot desert stone massage and the signature creosote body wrap. After your spa service, lie out or lunch poolside; then make your own aromatherapy sachet to take home. ⊠ *3800 W. Starr Pass Blvd., Southwest* ☎ *520/791–6117* ⊕ *www. hashanispa.com* ☞ *$125 50-minute massage. Hair salon, hot tub, pool,*

7

steam room. *Gym with: cardio machines, free weights, weight-training equipment. Services: aromatherapy, body wraps, facials, massage, nail treatment, scrubs, waxing and tinting. Classes and programs: dance classes, fitness analysis, guided hikes, nutritional counseling, personal training, tone and cardio, yoga.*

Lakeside Spa at Loews Ventana Canyon Resort. The Lakeside Spa seems quiet and unassuming, but their array of treatments and fitness opportunities is abundant. Take in the sweeping desert views along the trail on the daily 7-mile guided power walk or from the serene pool area during an aqua fitness class. Fortify your skin for the dry climate by choosing a signature spa treatment like the Sedona Sacred Ritual, which begins with an Arizona red-clay wrap, adds a face and scalp massage, and finishes with an ultra-hydrating body massage using jojoba lotion. On your way back to reality, indulge in a sundress, yoga pants, or locally made lotions from the well-stocked spa shop. ⊠ *7000 N. Resort Dr., Foothills* ☎ *520/299–2020, 800/234–5117* ⊕ *www.loewshotels. com/en/Ventana-Canyon-Resort/spa* ☞ *$115 50-minute massage, $185 80-minute Sacred Sedona Ritual. Hair salon, outdoor hot tub, pool, saunas, steam rooms. Gym with: cardio machines, free weights, weight-training equipment. Services: aromatherapy, body wraps, facials, massage, nail treatments, scrubs, waxing and tinting. Classes and programs: aerobics, aqua fitness, guided power walks, personal training, Pilates, yoga.*

The Red Door Spa at Westin La Paloma. Glamour and body bliss combine at this Elizabeth Arden spa connected to the Westin La Paloma Resort. Renowned for their state-of-the-art skin and makeup products—including the aptly named anti-aging line, Prevage for Face—the Red Door also delivers first-rate Swedish and hot-stone massages, which can be experienced in an outdoor cabana. Check yourself in for an Ultimate Arden facial or the 110-minute "Stress Melter Ritual" (exfoliating scrub, custom body wrap, and signature massage); either way, you'll leave feeling and looking *mah*-velous. ⊠ *3666 E. Sunrise Dr., Foothills* ☎ *520/742–7866* ⊕ *www.westinlapalomaresort.com/red-door-spa* ☞ *$135 50-minute massage or facial, $250 110-minute Stress Melter Ritual. Hair salon, outdoor hot tub, saunas, steam rooms. Services: aromatherapy, body wraps, facials, makeup application, massage, nail treatment, scrubs, waxing and tinting.*

The Ritz-Carlton Spa, Dove Mountain. Are you an earth element who needs a little more fire in your life? Perhaps your wood, water, and metal are out of balance. "Embracing Your Elements," the signature service at the 17,000-square-foot Dove Mountain Spa, will help you realign all five elements in a rejuvenating 90-minute massage, skin brush, aromatherapy, and face/scalp treatment based upon your birthdate. Before and after, relax indoors in the men's, ladies', or co-ed lounge areas, or by the secluded infinity pool with a tanning "island" in the center. As you might expect from Ritz-Carlton, spas don't come much more luxurious than this. ⊠ *15000 N. Secret Springs Dr., Marana* ☎ *520/572–3030, 800/542–8680* ⊕ *www.ritzcarlton.com/dovemountain* ☞ *$150 50-minute massage, $210 80-minute massage, $245 90-minute "Embracing Your Elements" treatment. Hair salon, outdoor hot tub, pool, sauna.*

Gym with cardio machines, free weights, weight-training equipment. Services: aromatherapy, body wraps, facials, massage, nail treatment, scrubs, Vichy shower, waxing. Classes and programs: Pilates, yoga, Zumba.

SPORTS AND THE OUTDOORS

Fall, winter, and spring in Tucson are mild with little rainfall, making the Tucson area wonderful for outdoor sports. The city has miles of bike paths (shared by joggers and walkers), plenty of open spaces with memorable desert views, and some of the best golf courses in the country. Hikers enjoy the desert trails in Saguaro National Park, Sabino Canyon, and Catalina State Park—all within 20 minutes of central Tucson. In summer there are cooler treks in nearby mountain ranges—Mount Lemmon to the north and Madera Canyon to the south. Equestrians can find scenic trails at one of the many area stables or dude ranches.

ADVENTURE TOURS

Baja's Frontier Tours. This operator explores the natural and cultural history of Tucson and the greater Southwest by van and motorcoach. Expert naturalists accompany the tours. ☎ 520/887–2340 ⊕ *www. bajasfrontiertours.com.*

Southwest Trekking. Top-notch guided mountain biking, hiking, and camping outings are arranged by this outfitter. ☎ 520/296–9661 ⊕ *www.swtrekking.com.*

BALLOONING

Balloon America. Passengers can soar above Sabino Canyon and the Santa Catalinas in a hot-air balloon. Tours depart from the east side of Tucson October through May. ☎ 520/299–7744 ⊕ *www.balloonrideusa.com.*

Fleur de Tucson Balloon Tours. Operating out of the Northwest from October through April, this company arranges flights over the Tucson Mountains and Saguaro National Park West. ✉ *4635 N. Caida Pl.* ☎ 520/403–8547 ⊕ *www.fleurdetucson.net.*

BICYCLING

Tucson is one of America's top bicycling cities and has well-maintained bikeways, routes, lanes, and paths all over the city. Scenic-loop roads in both sections of Saguaro National Park are rewarding rides for all levels of cyclists, though the West district's road is unpaved.

GABA (*Greater Arizona Bicycling Association*). Most bike stores in Tucson carry the monthly newsletter of the Tucson chapter of GABA, which lists rated group rides, local bike rentals, and more. ⊕ *www. bikegaba.org.*

Pima Association of Governments. You can pick up a map of Tucson-area bike routes here. ✉ *177 N. Church Ave., Suite 405, Downtown* ☎ 520/792–1093 ⊕ *www.pagnet.org.*

EQUIPMENT AND RENTALS

Cycle Tucson. This company rents road, mountain, and hybrid bikes, and delivers them to your door. ✉ *7049 E. Tanque Verde Rd, Suite 126, Foothills* ☎ 520/245–6011 ⊕ *www.cycletucson.com.*

Don't let the name fool you—the Arizona–Sonora Desert Museum is also a zoo and botanical garden.

Fair Wheel Bikes. Mountain bikes and road bikes can be rented by the day or week here. They also organize group rides of varying difficulty. ⊠ *1110 E. 6th St., University* ☎ *520/884–9018.*

BIRD-WATCHING

The naturalist and illustrator Roger Tory Peterson (1908–96) considered Tucson one of the country's top birding spots, and avid "life listers"—birders who keep a list of all the birds they've sighted and identified—soon see why. In the early morning and early evening Sabino Canyon is alive with cactus and canyon wrens, hawks, and quail. Spring and summer, when species of migrants come in from Mexico, are great hummingbird seasons. In the nearby Santa Rita Mountains and Madera Canyon you can see elegant trogons nesting in early spring. The area also supports species usually found only in higher elevations.

Tucson Audubon Society and Nature Shop. You can get the latest birding word on the local Audubon Society's 24-hour line; sightings of rare or interesting birds in the area are recorded regularly. The society's shop organizes free local outings for birders and carries field guides, bird feeders, binoculars, and natural-history books. ⊠ *300 E. University Blvd., Suite 120, University* ☎ *520/629–0510* ⊕ *www.tucsonaudubon.org.*

Wild Bird Store. This shop is an excellent resource for bird-watching information, feeders, books, and trail guides. ⊠ *3160 E. Fort Lowell Rd., Central* ☎ *520/322–9466* ⊕ *www.wildbirdsonline.com.*

TOURS

Several companies operate birding tours in the Tucson area.

Borderland Tours. Bird-watching tours throughout the state and internationally are led by this company, whose owner, Richard Taylor, has written several photo field guides, including *Birds of Southeastern Arizona.* ⊠ *2550 W. Calle Padilla, Northwest* ☎ *520/882–7650* ⊕ *www. borderland-tours.com.*

Wings. A Tucson-based company, Wings leads ornithological expeditions worldwide and locally. ⊠ *1643 N. Alvernon Way, 109, Central* ☎ *520/320–9868, 866/547–9868* ⊕ *www.wingsbirds.com.*

GOLF

Tee off after 1 pm at many of Tucson's courses, and you can shave off nearly half the greens fee. The city's public courses also have lower fees Monday through Thursday. All Tucson area courses dramatically reduce greens fees in summer.

RESOURCES

Golf Stop Inc. This shop, owned and run by two LPGA pros, can fit you with pro shop brands and custom clubs, repair your old irons, or give you lessons. ⊠ *6155 E. Broadway, Eastside* ☎ *520/790–0941* ⊕ *www. golfstopinc.biz.*

Tucson Parks and Recreation Department. To reserve a tee time at one of the city's municipal courses, call the Tucson Parks and Recreation Department or reserve online up to six days in advance. ☎ *520/791–4653 general golf information, 520/791–4336 automated tee-time reservations* ⊕ *www.tucsoncitygolf.com.*

MUNICIPAL COURSES

One of Tucson's best-kept secrets is that the city's five low-priced municipal courses are maintained to standards usually found only at the best country clubs. All five have pro shops, driving ranges and putting greens, snack bars, and rental clubs.

Dell Urich Golf Course. Adjacent to Randolph and formerly known as Randolph South, Dell Urich is a pretty 18-hole in-town course with tall trees and dramatic elevation changes. ⊠ *600 S. Alvernon Way, Central* ☎ *520/791–4161* ⊕ *www.tucsoncitygolf.com/dell-urich-golf-course.html* ⚑ *18 holes. 6633 yds. Par 70. Greens Fee: $54* ⌖ *Facilities: Driving range, putting green, golf carts, rental clubs, pro shop, golf academy/lessons, snack bar.*

El Rio Golf Course. This is a par-70 course with 18 holes of tight fairways, small greens, and two lakes on fairly flat terrain west of downtown. You'll have nice views of the nearby Tucson Mountains. ⊠ *1400 W. Speedway Blvd., Westside* ☎ *520/791–4229* ⊕ *www.tucsoncitygolf. com/el-rio-golf-course.html* ⚑ *18 holes. 6936 yds. Par 70. Greens Fee: $43.* ⌖ *Facilities: Driving range, putting green, golf carts, pull carts, rental clubs, pro shop, lessons, snack bar.*

Fred Enke Golf Course. This hilly, semi-arid (less grass and more native vegetation) 18-hole course is in the southeastern part of town. ⊠ *8251 E. Irvington, Eastside* ☎ *520/791–2539* ⊕ *www.tucsoncitygolf.com/ fred-enke-golf-course.html* ⚑ *18 holes. 6567 yds. Par 72. Greens Fee: $43.* ⌖ *Facilities: Driving range, putting green, golf carts, rental clubs, pro shop, lessons, snack bar.*

7

Fodor's Choice

★

Randolph Park Golf Course–North Course. This long, scenic 18-hole course has hosted the LPGA Tour for many years and is the flagship of Tucson's municipal courses. ✉ *600 S. Alvernon Way, Central* ☎ *520/791–4161* ⊕ *www.tucsoncitygolf.com/randolph-north-golf-course.html* ⅃ *18 holes. 6863 yds. Par 72. Greens Fee: $54.* ☞ *Facilities: Driving range, putting green, golf carts, pull carts, rental clubs, pro shop, golf academy/lessons, snack bar.*

Silverbell Golf Course. With spacious fairways and ample greens, this course has an 18-hole layout along the Santa Cruz River northwest of town. Greens fee includes a cart; walkers can play 9 holes for $25. ✉ *3600 N. Silverbell Rd., Northwest* ☎ *520/791–5235* ⊕ *www.tucsoncitygolf.com/silverbell-golf-course.html* ⅃ *18 holes. 6936 yds. Par 70. Greens Fee: $42.* ☞ *Facilities: Driving range, putting green, golf carts, pull carts, rental clubs, pro shop, golf academy/lessons, snack bar.*

PUBLIC COURSES

Arizona National Golf Club. This is a gorgeous 18-hole, Robert Trent Jones, Jr.–designed course at the base of the Rincon Mountains on the eastern edge of town. ✉ *9777 E. Sabino Greens Dr., Eastside* ☎ *520/749–3636* ⊕ *www.arizonanationalgolfclub.com* ⅃ *18 holes. 6776 yds. Par 71. Greens Fee: $60.* ☞ *Facilities: Driving range, putting green, golf carts, rental clubs, pro shop, golf academy/lessons, restaurant, bar, snack bar.*

Dorado Golf Course. With an 18-hole, par-62 executive course, Dorado Golf Course is good for those who want to play just a few short rounds. There's a putting green but no driving range or lessons. ✉ *6601 E. Speedway Blvd., Eastside* ☎ *520/885–6751* ⅃ *18 holes. 3751 yds. Par 62. Greens Fee: $35.* ☞ *Facilities: Putting green, golf carts, pull carts, rental clubs, pro shop, snack bar.*

Esplendor Resort & Country Club. South of Tucson, this reasonably priced Robert Trent Jones Sr.–designed course, with an on-site restaurant and country club facilities, is one of Arizona's lesser-known gems. At a higher elevation, it's also cooler than Tucson, making for a great golf getaway in the summer. ✉ *1069 Camino Carampi, Rio Rico* ☎ *800/288–4746, 520/281–8567* ⊕ *www.esplendor-resort.com* ⅃ *18 holes. 6135 yds. Par 72. Greens Fee: $48.* ☞ *Facilities: Driving range, putting green, golf carts, pull carts, rental clubs, pro shop, golf academy/lessons, restaurant, bar, snack bar.*

San Ignacio Golf Club. Designed by Arthur Hills, San Ignacio is a challenging 18-hole desert course in Green Valley. ✉ *4201 S. Camino del Sol, Green Valley* ☎ *520/648–3469* ⊕ *www.sanignaciogolf.com* ⅃ *18 holes. 5865 yds. Par 71. Greens Fee: $58.* ☞ *Facilities: Driving range, putting green, golf carts, rental clubs, pro shop, golf academy/lessons, restaurant, bar.*

Tubac Golf Resort. A par-71 course 45 minutes south of Tucson, Tubac Golf Resort will look familiar to you if you've seen the movie *Tin Cup.* The rolling hills and pastoral land surrounding these 27 holes are a change from desert golf environs. A pro shop, an excellent restaurant, and a cantina are on-site at this resort. ✉ *1 Ave. De Otero Rd., Tubac* ☎ *520/398–2211* ⊕ *www.tubacgolfresort.com* ⅃ *27 holes. 6375 yds. Par 71. Greens Fee: $99.* ☞ *Facilities: Driving range, putting green,* *golf carts, rental clubs, pro shop, golf academy/lessons, restaurant, bar, snack bar.*

RESORT COURSES

Avid golfers check into one of Tucson's many tony resorts and head straight for the links. The resort courses listed here are open to the public, but resort guests pay slightly lower greens fees. All have complete country-club facilities. Those who don't mind getting up early to beat the heat will find some excellent golf packages at these places in summer.

Hilton Tucson El Conquistador. This resort has 45 holes of golf tucked into the Santa Catalina Foothills. The three courses—one par-72, one par-71, and one 9-hole, par 35—have panoramic views of the city. ⊠ *10555 N. La Canada Dr., Northwest* ☎ *520/544–1800* ⊕ *www. hiltonelconquistador.com* ⚑ *Cañada course: 18 holes. 6713 yds. Par 72. El Conquistador course: 18 holes. 6801 yds. Par 71. Pusch Ridge Course: 9 holes. 2788 yds. Par 35. Greens Fee: $89.* ☞ *Facilities: Driving range, putting green, golf carts, rental clubs, pro shop, golf academy/ lessons, restaurant, bar, snack bar.*

Fodor'sChoice ★ **Lodge at Ventana Canyon.** There are two beautiful 18-hole Tom Fazio–designed courses here. Their signature hole, No. 3 on the mountain course, is a favorite of golf photographers for its panoramic views and majestic saguaros. Guests staying up the road at Loews Ventana Canyon Resort have privileges here. ⊠ *6200 N. Clubhouse Lane, Foothills* ☎ *520/577–1400, 800/828–5701* ⊕ *www.thelodgeatventanacanyon. com* ⚑ *36 holes. Canyon Course: 6819, Mountain Course: 6898 yds. Par 72. Greens Fee: $159.* ☞ *Facilities: Driving range, putting green, golf carts, rental clubs, pro shop, golf academy/lessons, restaurant, bar, snack bar.*

Omni Tucson National Golf Resort. Cohost of an annual PGA winter open, this resort offers 36 holes: the Catalina Course, designed by Robert Van Hagge and Bruce Devlin, a traditional par-73 course with eight lakes and gorgeous, long par 4s; and the Sonoran Course, a par-70 desert course. ⊠ *2727 W. Club Dr., Northwest* ☎ *520/297–2271* ⊕ *www. tucsonnational.com* ⚑ *Catalina Course: 18 holes. 6610 yds. Par 7. Sonoran Course: 18 holes. 6065 yds. Par 70. Greens Fee: $190.* ☞ *Facilities: Driving range, putting green, golf carts, rental clubs, pro shop, golf academy/lessons, restaurant, bar, snack bar.*

Starr Pass Golf Resort. With 27 magnificent holes in the Tucson Mountains, Starr Pass was developed as a Tournament Player's Course. Managed by Arnold Palmer, it's become a favorite of visiting pros; playing its No. 15 signature hole has been likened to threading a moving needle. Guests at the JW Marriott Starr Pass Resort have privileges (and pay lower green fees) here. ⊠ *3645 W. Starr Pass Blvd., Westside* ☎ *520/670–0406* ⊕ *www.jwmarriottstarrpass.com* ⚑ *27 holes. 6731 yds. Par 71. Greens Fee: $215.* ☞ *Facilities: Driving range, putting green, golf carts, rental clubs, pro shop, golf academy/lessons, restaurant, bar, snack bar.*

7

HIKING

For hiking inside Tucson's city limits, you can test your skills climbing trails up "A" Mountain (Sentinel Peak), but there are also hundreds of other trails in the immediate Tucson area. The Santa Catalina Mountains, Sabino Canyon, and Saguaro National Park East and West beckon hikers with waterfalls, birds, critters, and huge saguaro cacti. ⇨ *For hiking trails in Saguaro, see Saguaro National Park in this chapter.*

FAMILY

Fodor's Choice

★

Bear Canyon Trail. Also known as Seven Falls Trail, this route in Sabino Canyon is a three- to four-hour, 7.8-mile round-trip that is moderately easy and fun, crossing the stream several times on the way up the canyon.

Be sure to bring plenty of water. Kids enjoy the boulder-hopping, and all are rewarded with pools and waterfalls as well as views at the top. The trailhead can be reached from the parking area by either taking a five-minute Bear Canyon Tram ride or walking the 1.8-mi tram route. *Easy.* ☒ *Sabino Canyon Rd. at Sunrise Dr., Foothills* ☎ *520/749–2861* ⊕ *www.fs.usda.gov/coronado.*

Catalina State Park. This park is crisscrossed by hiking trails. One of them, the moderately easy, two-hour, 5.5-mi round-trip **Romero Canyon Trail**, leads to Romero Pools, a series of natural *tinajas,* or stone "jars," filled with water much of the year. The trailhead is on the park's entrance road, past the restrooms on the right side. *Moderate.* ☒ *11570 N. Oracle Rd., Northwest* ☎ *520/628–5798* ⊕ *www.pr.state.az.us/parks/cata/index.html.*

RESOURCES

Sierra Club. The Club's local chapter, The Rincon Group, welcomes out-of-towners on weekend hikes, ranging in level of difficulty. ☒ *738 N. 5th Ave., University* ☎ *520/620–6401* ⊕ *www.arizona.sierraclub.org/rincon.*

Summit Hut. For hiking on your own, this store has an excellent collection of hiking reference materials, supplies, and a friendly staff who will help you plan your trip. Packs, tents, bags, and climbing shoes can be rented and purchased here. The other store branch is located on the Westside at 605 East Wetmore Road. ☒ *5045 E. Speedway Blvd., Eastside* ☎ *520/325–1554* ⊕ *www.summithut.com.*

HORSEBACK RIDING

Bandit Outfitters. This outfitter leads riders on one-hour, two-hour, sunset, and cowboy cookout rides near Saguaro National Park East and through Colossal Cave Park. ☒ *16600 Colossal Cave Rd., Eastside* ☎ *520/647–3450* ⊕ *www.banditoutfitters.com.*

Cocoraque Ranch. Wranglers lead riders through their working cattle ranch and along trails into Saguaro National Park West. Cattle drives can also be arranged. ☒ *6255 N. Diamond Hills Lane, Westside* ☎ *520/682–8594* ⊕ *www.cocoraque.com.*

Pantano Riding Stables. This is a reliable operator of one- and two-hour rides on the far east side of town. ☒ *4450 S. Houghton Rd., Eastside* ☎ *520/298–8980* ⊕ *www.horsingaroundarizona.com.*

Pusch Ridge Stables. Adjacent to Catalina State Park, Pusch Ridge Stables takes riders along the beautiful western side of the Santa Catalina Mountains, and can serve up a cowboy-style breakfast, lunch, or dinner on the trail; one- and two-hour rides are also available. ✉ *13700 N. Oracle Rd., Northwest* ☎ *520/825-1664* ⊕ *www.puschridgestables.com.*

RODEO

FAMILY **Tucson Rodeo.** In late February, Tucson hosts **Fiesta de Los Vaqueros,** the largest annual winter rodeo in the United States, a nine-day extravaganza with more than 600 events and a crowd of more than 44,000 spectators a day at the Tucson Rodeo Grounds.

The rodeo kicks off with a 2-mile parade of Western and fancy-dress Mexican *charros*, wagons, stagecoaches, and horse-drawn floats; it's touted as the largest nonmotorized parade in the world. Local schoolkids especially love the celebration—they get a two-day holiday from school. Daily seats at the rodeo vary from $12 to $25. ✉ *4823 S. 6th Ave., South* ☎ *520/741-2233* ⊕ *www.tucsonrodeo.com.*

> **WORD OF MOUTH**
>
> "In the American West, temperature is more a function of elevation rather than how far north or south you are. This is why you can be enjoying a swimming pool in Tucson but then drive to the top of Mt Lemmon for snow (in February) and alpine conditions. This is also why Tucson will be cooler than Phoenix even though it is farther south." —peterboy

---

SAGUARO NATIONAL PARK

Saguaro National Park West: 14 miles west of central Tucson; Saguaro National Park East: 12 miles east of central Tucson.

Saguaro National Park's two distinct sections flank the city of Tucson. Perhaps the most familiar emblem of the Southwest, the towering saguaros, are found only in the Sonoran Desert. Saguaro National Park preserves some of the densest stands of these massive cacti.

Known for their height (often 50 feet) and arms reaching out in weird configurations, these slow-growing giants can take 15 years to grow a foot high and up to 75 years to grow their first arm. The cacti can live up to 200 years and weigh up to 2 tons. In late spring (usually May), the succulent's top is covered with tiny white blooms—the Arizona state flower. The cacti are protected by state and federal laws, so don't disturb them.

ORIENTATION

Saguaro West. Also called the Tucson Mountain District, this is the park's smaller, more-visited section. Here you'll find a Native American video about saguaros at the visitor center, hiking trails, an ancient Hohokam petroglyph site at Signal Hill, and a scenic drive through the park's densest desert growth. This section is near the Arizona–Sonora Desert Museum in Tucson's Westside, and many opt for combining these sights.

Saguaro East. Also called the Rincon Mountain District, this area encompasses 57,930 acres of designated wilderness area, an easily accessible scenic loop drive, several easy and intermediate trails through the cactus forest, and opportunities for adventure and backcountry camping at six rustic campgrounds.

WHEN TO GO

Saguaro never gets crowded; however, most people visit in milder weather, October through April. December through February can be cool, and are likely to see gentle rain showers. The spring days from March through May are bright and sunny with wildflowers in bloom. Because of high temperatures, from June through September it's best to visit the park in the early morning or late afternoon. The intense summer heat puts off most hikers, at least at lower elevations, but lodging prices are much cheaper—rates at top resorts in Tucson drop by as much as 70%. Cooler temperatures return in October and November, providing perfect weather for hiking and camping throughout the park.

PLANNING YOUR TIME
SAGUARO IN ONE DAY

Before setting off, choose which section of the park to visit and pack a lunch (there's no food service in either park district). Also bring plenty of water—you're likely to get dehydrated in the dry climate—or purchase a reusable bottle at the visitor center (there are water stations in both districts of the park).

In the western section, start out by watching the 15-minute video at the **Red Hills Visitor Center,** then stroll along the 0.5-mile-long **Desert Discovery Trail.**

Drive north along Kinney Road, then turn right onto the graded dirt **Bajada Loop Drive.** Before long you'll soon see a turnoff for the **Hugh Norris Trail** on your right. If you're game for a steep 45-minute hike uphill, this trail leads to a perfect spot for a picnic. Hike back down and drive along the Bajada Loop Drive until you reach the turnoff for **Signal Hill.** From here it's a short walk to the **Hohokam petroglyphs.**

Alternatively, in the eastern section, pick up a free map of the hiking trails at the **Saguaro East Visitor Center.** Drive south along the paved **Cactus Forest Drive** to the Javelina picnic area, where you'll see signs for the **Freeman Homestead Trail,** an easy 1-mile loop that winds through a stand of mesquite as interpretive signs describe early inhabitants in the Tucson basin. If you're up for more difficult hiking, you might want to tackle part of the **Tanque Verde Ridge Trail,** which affords excellent views of saguaro-studded hillsides.

Along the northern loop of Cactus Forest Drive is **Cactus Forest Trail,** which branches off into several fairly level paths. You can easily spend the rest of the afternoon strolling among the saguaros.

GETTING HERE AND AROUND

Both districts are about a half-hour drive from central Tucson. To reach Rincon Mountain District (east section) from Interstate 10, take Exit 275, then go north on Houghton Road for 10 miles. Turn right on Escalante and left onto Old Spanish Trail, and the park will be on the

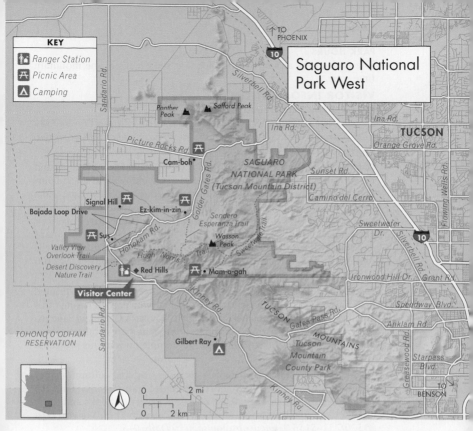

Saguaro National Park West

↑ TO
PHOENIX

10

TUCSON

Ina Rd.

Orange Grove Rd.

Silverbell Rd.

Panther
Peak

▲ Safford Peak

Picture Rocks Rd.

Cam-boh

Ina Rd.

SAGUARO
NATIONAL PARK
(Tucson Mountain District)

Sunset Rd.

Golden Gates Rd.

Signal Hill

Ez-kim-in-zin

Bajada Loop Drive

Sendero
Esperanza Trail

Wasson
▲ Peak

Camino del Cerro

Sweetwater Trail

Sweetwater
Dr.

10

Silverbell Rd.

Grant Rd.

Flowing Wells Rd.

Sus

Hohokam Rd.

Valley View
Overlook Trail

Hugh Norris Trail

Desert Discovery
Nature Trail

Red Hills

Mam-a-gah

Ironwood Hill Dr.

Visitor Center

Speedway Blvd.

TOHONO O'ODHAM
RESERVATION

Sandario Rd.

KinneyRd.

Gilbert Ray

Gates Pass Rd.

TUCSON

MOUNTAINS

Tucson
Mountain
County Park

Anklam Rd.

Greasewood Rd.

Starpass
Blvd.

Kinney Rd.

TO
BENSON

0 ——— 2 mi

0 ——— 2 km

right side. If you're coming from town, go east on Speedway Boulevard to Houghton Road. Turn right on Houghton and left onto Old Spanish Trail.

To reach the Tucson Mountain District (west section) from Interstate 10, take Exit 242 or Exit 257, then go west on Speedway Boulevard (the name will change to Gates Pass Road), follow it to Kinney Road, and turn right.

As there's no public transportation to or within Saguaro, a car is a necessity. In the western section, Bajada Loop Drive takes you through the park and to various trailheads; Cactus Forest Drive does the same for the eastern section.

PARK ESSENTIALS

PARK FEES AND PERMITS

Admission to Saguaro is $10 per vehicle and $5 for individuals on foot or bicycle; it's good for seven days from purchase at both park districts. Annual passes cost $25. For camping at one of the primitive campsites in the east district (the closest campsite is 6 miles from the trailhead), obtain a required backcountry permit for $6 nightly from the Saguaro East Visitor Center up to two months in advance.

PARK HOURS

The park opens at sunrise and closes at sunset. It's in the mountain time zone.

VISITOR INFORMATION

PARK CONTACT INFORMATION

Saguaro National Park ✉ *3693 S. Old Spanish Trail, Tucson* ☎ *520/733– 5158 Saguaro West, 520/733–5153 Saguaro East* ⊕ *www.nps.gov/sagu.*

VISITOR CENTERS

Red Hills Visitor Center. Take in gorgeous views of nearby mountains and the surrounding desert from the center's large windows and shaded outdoor terrace. A spacious gallery is filled with educational exhibits, and a lifelike display simulates the flora and fauna of the region. A 15-minute slide show, "Voices of the Desert," provides a poetic, Native American perspective of the saguaro. Park rangers and volunteers provide maps and suggest hikes to suit your interests. The well-stocked gift shop sells reusable water bottles that you can fill at water stations outside. ✉ *2700 N. Kinney Rd., Saguaro West* ☎ *520/733–5158* ⊗ *Daily 9–5.*

Saguaro East Visitor Center. Stop here to pick up free maps and printed materials on various aspects of the park, including maps of hiking trails and backcountry camping permits (Red Hills Visitor Center, in Saguaro West, does not offer permits). Exhibits at the center are comprehensive, and a relief map of the park lays out the complexities of this protected landscape.

Two 20-minute slide shows explain the botanical and cultural history of the region, and there is a short self-guided nature walk along the paved Cactus Garden Trail. A small, select variety of books and other gift items are sold here, too. ✉ *3693 S. Old Spanish Trail, Saguaro East* ☎ *520/733–5153* ⊕ *www.nps.gov/sagu* ⊗ *Daily 9–5.*

EXPLORING

SCENIC DRIVES

Unless you're ready to lace up your hiking boots for a long desert hike, the best way to see Saguaro National Park is from the comfort of your car.

Bajada Loop Drive. This 6-mile drive winds through thick stands of saguaros and past two picnic areas and trailheads to a few short hikes, including one to a petroglyph site. Although the road is unpaved and moderately bumpy, it's a worthwhile trade-off for access to some of the park's densest desert growth. It's one way between Hugh Norris Trail and Golden Gate Road, so if you want to make the complete circuit, travel counterclockwise. The road is susceptible to flash floods during the monsoon season (July and August), so check road conditions at the visitor center before proceeding. This bumpy route is also popular among bicyclists. ✉ *Saguaro West.*

Cactus Forest Drive. This paved 8-mile drive provides a great overview of all Saguaro East has to offer. The one-way road, which circles clockwise, has several turnouts with roadside displays that make it easy to pull over and admire the scenery; you can also stop at two picnic areas

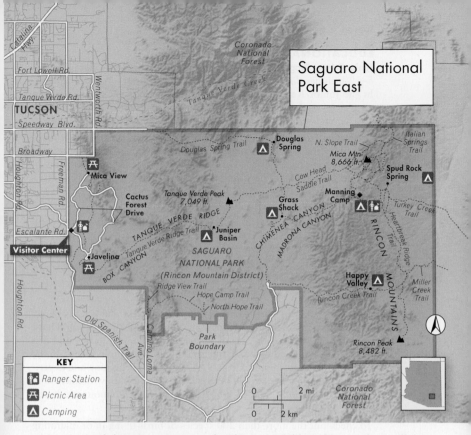

Saguaro National Park East

Coronado National Forest

Tanque Verde Creek

TUCSON

Catalina Hwy.
Fort Lowell Rd.
Tanque Verde Rd.
Speedway Blvd.
Broadway
Houghton Rd.
Freeman Rd.
Wentworth Rd.

Douglas Spring Trail
Douglas Spring
N. Slope Trail
Mica Mtn 8,666 ft.
Italian Springs Trail
Spud Rock Spring
Mica View
Cactus Forest Drive
Tanque Verde Peak 7,049 ft.
Cow Head Saddle Trail
Grass Shack
Manning Camp
Turkey Creek Trail
Escalante Rd.
Visitor Center
TANQUE VERDE RIDGE
Tanque Verde Ridge Trail
Juniper Basin
CHIMENEA CANYON
MADRONA CANYON
RINCON MOUNTAINS
Heartbreak Ridge Trail
Javelina
BOX CANYON
SAGUARO NATIONAL PARK
(Rincon Mountain District)
Ridge View Trail
Hope Camp Trail
North Hope Trail
Happy Valley
Miller Creek Trail
Rincon Creek Trail
Houghton Rd.
Old Spanish Trail
Camino Loma Alta
Park Boundary
Rincon Peak 8,482 ft.
Coronado National Forest

0   2 mi
0   2 km

KEY
🧍 *Ranger Station*
🏕 *Picnic Area*
🔺 *Camping*

and three easy nature trails. This is a good bicycling route as well, but watch out for snakes and javelinas traversing the roads. This road is open from 7 am to sunset daily. ⊠ *Saguaro East.*

HISTORIC SITES

Manning Camp. The summer home of Levi Manning, onetime Tucson mayor, was a popular gathering spot for the city's elite in the early 1900s. The cabin can be reached only on foot or horseback via one of several challenging high-country trails: Douglas Spring Trail to Cow Head Saddle Trail (12 mi), Turkey Creek Trail (7.5 mi), or Tanque Verde Ridge Trail (15.4 mi). The cabin itself is not open for viewing. ⊠ *Douglas Spring Trail (6 miles) to Cow Head Saddle Trail (6 miles), Saguaro East.*

SCENIC STOPS

FAMILY **Signal Hill.** The most impressive petroglyphs, and the only ones with explanatory signs, are on the Bajada Loop Drive in Saguaro West. An easy five-minute stroll from the signposted parking area takes you to one of the largest concentrations of rock carvings in the Southwest. You'll have a close-up view of the designs left by the Hohokam people between AD 900 and 1200, including large spirals some believe are astronomical markers. ⊠ *Bajada Loop Dr., 4.5 miles north of visitor center, Saguaro West.*

EDUCATIONAL OFFERINGS

Junior Ranger Program. Usually offered during June, a day camp for kids 5–12 includes daily hikes and workshops on pottery and petroglyphs. In the **Junior Ranger Discovery program,** young visitors can pick up an activity pack any time of the year and complete it within an hour or two. ⊠ *Saguaro East and Red Hills Visitor Centers* ☎ *520/733–5153.*

Orientation Programs. Daily programs at both park districts introduce visitors to the desert. You might find presentations on bats, birds, or desert blooms, naturalist-led hikes (including moonlight hikes), and, in summer only, films. Check online or call for the current week's activities. ⊠ *Saguaro East and Red Hills Visitor Centers* ☎ *520/733–5153* 🖅 *Free* ☉ *Daily.*

Ranger Talks. These are a great way to hear about wildlife, geology, and archaeology. ⊠ *Saguaro East and Red Hills Visitor Centers* ☎ *520/733–5153* 🖅 *Free* ☉ *Nov.–Apr.*

SPORTS AND THE OUTDOORS

BICYCLING

Scenic drives in the park—Bajada Loop in the west and Cactus Forest Drive in the east—are also popular among cyclists, though you'll have to share the roads with cars. Bajada Loop Drive is a gravel and dirt road, so it's quite bumpy and only suitable for mountain bikers. In the east section, Cactus Forest Drive is great for both beginning and experienced mountain bikers who don't mind sharing the path with hikers and the occasional horse; Hope Camp Trail is also open to mountain bikes.

BIRD-WATCHING

To check out the more than 200 species of birds living in or migrating through the park, begin by focusing your binoculars on the limbs of the saguaros, where many birds make their home. In general, early morning and early evening are the best times for sightings. In winter and spring, volunteer-led birding hikes begin at the visitor centers.

The finest areas to flock to in Saguaro East (the Rincon Mountain District) are the Desert Ecology Trail, where you may find rufous-winged sparrows, verdins, and Cooper's hawks along the washes, and the Javelina picnic area, where you'll most likely spot canyon wrens and black-chinned sparrows. At Saguaro West (the Tucson Mountain District), sit down on one of the visitor center benches and look for ash-throated flycatchers, Say's phoebes, curve-billed thrashers, and Gila woodpeckers. During the cooler months, keep a lookout for wintering neotropical migrants such as hummingbirds, swallows, orioles, and warblers.

HIKING

The park has more than 100 miles of trails. The shorter hikes, such as the Desert Discovery and Desert Ecology trails, are perfect for those looking to learn about the desert ecosystem without expending too much energy.

■**TIP→** Rattlesnakes are commonly seen on trails; so are coyotes, javelinas, roadrunners, Gambel's quail, and desert spiny lizards. Hikers should keep their distance from all wildlife.

EASY

Cactus Garden Trail. This 100-yard paved trail in front of the Saguaro East Visitor Center is wheelchair accessible, and has resting benches and interpretive signs about common desert plants. *Easy.* ⊠ *Trailhead: next to Saguaro East Visitor Center, Saguaro East.*

FAMILY **Desert Discovery Trail.** Learn about plants and animals native to the region on this paved path in Saguaro West. The 0.5-mile loop is wheelchair accessible, and has resting benches and ramadas (wooden shelters that supply shade for your table). *Easy.* ⊠ *Trailhead: 1 mi north of Red Hills Visitor Center, Saguaro West* ☎ *520/733–5158.*

FAMILY **Desert Ecology Trail.** Exhibits on this 0.25-mile loop near the Mica View picnic area explain how local plants and animals subsist on limited water. ⊠ *Trailhead: 2 mi north of Saguaro East Visitor Center.*

Freeman Homestead Trail. Learn a bit about the history of homesteading in the region on this 1-mile loop. Look for owls living in the cliffs above as you make your way through the lowland vegetation. *Easy.* ⊠ *Trailhead: Javelina picnic area, 2 mi south of Saguaro East Visitor Center.*

Signal Hill Trail. This 0.25-mile trail in Saguaro West is an easy, rewarding ascent to ancient petroglyphs carved a millennium ago by the Hohokam people. *Easy.* ⊠ *Trailhead: 4.5 mi north of Red Hills Visitor Center on Bajada Loop Dr., Saguaro West.*

MODERATE

Cactus Forest Trail. This 2.5-mile one-way loop drive in the east district is open to pedestrians, bicyclists, and equestrians. It is a moderately easy walk along a dirt path that passes historic lime kilns and a wide variety of Sonoran Desert vegetation. While walking this trail, keep in mind that it is one of the only off-road trails for bicyclists. *Moderate.* ⊠ *Trailhead: 2 mi south of Saguaro East Visitor Center, off Cactus Forest Dr., Saguaro East.*

Douglas Spring Trail. This challenging 6-mile trail leads almost due east into the Rincon Mountains. After a half mile through a dense concentration of saguaros you reach the open desert. About 3 miles in is Bridal Wreath Falls, worth a slight detour in spring when melting snow creates a larger cascade. Blackened tree trunks at the Douglas Spring Campground are one of the few traces of a huge fire that swept through the area in 1989. *Moderate.* ⊠ *Trailhead: eastern end of Speedway Blvd., Saguaro East.*

Fodor'sChoice
★ **Hope Camp Trail.** Well worth the 7-mile round-trip trek, this Rincon Valley Area route rewards hikers with gorgeous views of the Tanque Verde Ridge and Rincon Peak. The trail is also open to mountain bicyclists. *Moderate.* ⊠ *Trailhead: from Camino Loma Alta trailhead to Hope Camp, Saguaro East.*

Sendero Esperanza Trail. Follow a sandy mine road for the first section of this 6-mile trail in Saguaro West, then ascend via a series of switchbacks to the top of a ridge and cross the Hugh Norris Trail. Descending on the other side, you'll meet up with the King Canyon Trail. The Esperanza ("Hope") Trail is often rocky and sometimes steep, but rewards include ruins of the Gould Mine, dating back to 1907. *Moderate.* ⊠ *Trailhead:*

Saguaro National Park Flora and Fauna

The saguaro may be the centerpiece of Saguaro National Park, but more than 1,200 plant species, including 50 types of cactus, thrive in the park. Among the most common cacti here are the prickly pear, barrel cactus, and teddy bear cholla—so named because it appears cuddly, but rangers advise packing a comb to pull its barbed hooks from unwary fingers.

For many of the desert fauna, the saguaro functions as a high-rise hotel. Each spring the Gila woodpecker and gilded flicker create holes in the cactus and then nest there. When they give up their temporary digs, elf owls, cactus wrens, sparrow hawks, and other birds move in, as do dangerous Africanized honeybees.

You may not encounter any of the park's six species of rattlesnake or the Gila monster, a venomous lizard, but avoid sticking your hands or feet under rocks or into crevices. Look where you're walking; if you do get bitten, get to a clinic or hospital as soon as possible. Not all snakes pass on venom; 50% of the time the bite is "dry" (nonpoisonous).

Wildlife, from bobcats to jackrabbits, is most active in early morning and at dusk. In spring and summer, lizards and snakes are out and about but tend to keep a low profile during the midday heat.

1.5 mi east of the intersection of Bajada Loop Dr. and Golden Gate Rd., Saguaro West.

Sweetwater Trail. Though technically within Saguaro West, this trail is on the eastern edge of the district, and affords access to Wasson Peak from the eastern side of the Tucson Mountains. After gradually climbing 3.4 miles it ends at King Canyon Trail (which would then take you on a fairly steep 1.2 mile climb to Wasson Peak). Long and meandering, this little-used trail allows more privacy to enjoy the natural surroundings than some of the more frequently used trails. *Moderate.* ⊠ *Trailhead: western end of El Camino del Cerro Rd., Saguaro West.*

Valley View Overlook Trail. On clear days you can spot the distinctive slope of Picacho Peak from this 1.5-mile trail in Saguaro West. Even on an overcast day you'll be treated to splendid vistas of Avra Valley. *Moderate.* ⊠ *Trailhead: 3 mi north of Red Hills Visitor Center on Bajada Loop Dr., Saguaro West.*

DIFFICULT

Fodor's Choice ★ **Hugh Norris Trail.** This 10-mile trail through the Tucson Mountains is one of the most impressive in the Southwest. It's full of switchbacks, and some sections are moderately steep, but at the top of 4,687-foot Wasson Peak you'll enjoy views of the saguaro forest spread across the *bajada* (the gently rolling hills at the base of taller mountains). *Difficult.* ⊠ *Trailhead: 2.5 mi north of Red Hills Visitor Center on Bajada Loop Dr., Saguaro West.*

King Canyon Trail. This 3.5-mile trail is the shortest, but steepest, route to the top of Wasson Peak in Saguaro West. It meets the Hugh Norris Trail less than half a mile from the summit. The trail, which begins across

Saguaro cacti are easy to anthropomorphize because of their giant "arms."

from the Arizona–Sonora Desert Museum, is named after the Copper King Mine. It leads past many scars from the search for mineral wealth. Look for petroglyphs in this area. *Difficult.* ⊠ *Trailhead: 2 mi south of Red Hills Visitor Center, Saguaro West.*

Tanque Verde Ridge Trail. Be rewarded with spectacular scenery on this 15.4-mile trail through desert scrub, oak, alligator juniper, and piñon pine at the 6,000-foot peak, where views of the surrounding mountain ranges from both sides of the ridge delight. *Difficult.* ⊠ *Trailhead: Javelina picnic area, 2 mi south of Saguaro East Visitor Center.*

SHOPPING

The visitor centers in both districts sell books, gifts, film, and single-use cameras, as well as a few necessities such as sunscreen, bug repellent, and reusable water bottles. For other items, you'll have to drive a few miles back towards town.

SIDE TRIPS NEAR TUCSON

Interstate 19 heads south from Tucson through Tubac to Nogales at the border of Mexico, carrying with it history buffs, bird-watchers, hikers, art enthusiasts, duffers, and shoppers. The road roughly follows the Camino Real (King's Road), which the conquistadors and missionaries traveled from Mexico up to what was once the northernmost portion of New Spain.

Side Trips
Near Tucson

THE ASARCO MINERAL DISCOVERY CENTER

15 miles south of Tucson off Interstate 19.

GETTING HERE AND AROUND

From Interstate 19 south take Exit 80. Turn right (west) onto Pima Mine Road and the entrance will be almost immediately on your left.

EXPLORING

ASARCO Mineral Discovery Center. This center (American Smelting and Refining Co. is abbreviated) is designed to elucidate the importance of mining to everyday life. Exhibits include a walk-through model of an ore crusher, video stations that explain refining processes, and a film on extraction of minerals from the earth. The big draw, though, is the yawning open pit of the Mission Mine, some 2 miles long and 1.75 miles wide because so much earth has to be torn up to extract the 1% that is copper. It's impressive, but doesn't bolster the case the center tries to make about how environmentally conscious mining has become. Tours of the pit take about one hour; the last one starts at 3:30. In summer, tours are only on Saturday. ⊠ *1421 W. Pima Mine Rd.* ☎ *520/625–8233* ⊕ *www.mineraldiscovery.com* 🖃 *$8* 🕐 *Tues.–Sat. 9–5.*

TITAN MISSILE MUSEUM

25 miles south of Tucson.

GETTING HERE AND AROUND

From Interstate 19, take Exit 69, Duval Mine Road, approximately 1 mile west to the museum.

EXPLORING

Titan Missile Museum. Now a National Historic Landmark, the Titan Missile Museum makes for a sobering visit. During the cold war Tucson was ringed by 18 of the 54 Titan II missiles maintained in the United States. After the SALT II treaty with the Soviet Union was signed in 1979, this was the only missile-launch site left intact.

> **WORD OF MOUTH**
>
> "Titan Missile [Museum] on Duval Mine Road in Green Valley is often highly praised for being a worthwhile stop. It is especially good if you like (or remember) history from the '60s."   —CollegeMom

Guided tours, running every hour on the hour (and more frequently when there are enough visitors and volunteer docents), last about an hour and take you down 55 steps into the command post, where a ground crew of four lived and waited. Among the sights is the 103-foot, 165-ton, two-stage liquid-fuel rocket. Now empty, it originally held a nuclear warhead with 214 times the explosive power of the bomb that destroyed Hiroshima. ⊠ *1580 W. Duval Mine Rd., I–19, Exit 69, Green Valley* ☎ *520/625–7736* ⊕ *www.titanmissilemuseum. org* ⊠ *$9.50* ⊙ *Daily 9–5; last tour departs at 4.*

MADERA CANYON

61½ miles southeast of Tucson.

GETTING HERE AND AROUND

From Interstate 19, take Exit 63 (Continental Road) east for about a mile, then turn right (southeast) on White House Canyon Road for 12½ miles (it turns into Madera Canyon Road).

EXPLORING

Madera Canyon. This is where the Coronado National Forest meets the Santa Rita Mountains—among them Mount Wrightson, the highest peak in southern Arizona, at 9,453 feet. With approximately 200 miles of scenic trails, the recreation area is a favorite destination for hikers. Higher elevations and thick pine cover make it especially popular with Tucsonans looking to escape the summer heat.

Trails vary from a steep trek up Mount Baldy to a paved, wheelchair-accessible path. Birders flock here year-round; about 400 avian species have been spotted in the area. The small, volunteer-run visitor center is open only on weekends. ⊠ *Madera Canyon Rd., Madera Canyon* ☎ *520/281–2296 Nogales Ranger District office* ⊕ *www.fs.usda.gov/ coronado* ⊠ *$5* ⊙ *Daily.*

TUBAC

45 miles south of Tucson at Exit 40 off Interstate 19.

Established in 1726, Tubac is the site of the first European settlement in Arizona. A year after the Pima Indian uprising in 1751, a military garrison was established here to protect Spanish settlers, missionaries, and peaceful Native American converts of the nearby Tumacácori Mission. It was from here that Juan Bautista de Anza led 240 colonists across the desert—the expedition resulted in the founding of San Francisco in 1776. In 1860 Tubac was the largest town in Arizona. Today, the quiet little town is a popular art colony. More than 80 shops sell such crafts as carved wooden furniture, hand-thrown pottery, delicately painted tiles, and silkscreen fabrics (many shops are closed Monday). You can also find Mexican pottery and trinkets without having to cross the border. The annual **Tubac Festival of the Arts** has been held in February for more than 50 years.

GETTING HERE AND AROUND

When you exit Interstate 19 at Tubac Road, signs will point you east into Tubac village. There's plenty of free parking, and you can pick up a free map of the village at any of the shops.

ESSENTIALS

Visitor Information Tubac Chamber of Commerce ☎ *520/398-2704* ⊕ *www. tubacaz.com.*

EXPLORING

Tubac Presidio Park and Museum. There's an archaeological display of portions of the original 1752 fort at this museum, run by volunteers of the Tubac Historical Society. In addition to the visitor center and the adjoining museum, which has detailed exhibits on the history of the early colony, the park includes Tubac's well-preserved 1885 schoolhouse. ✉ *1 Burruel St.* ☎ *520/398-2252* ⊕ *www.tubacpresidiopark. com* ⌧ *$5* ⊘ *Daily 9–5.*

WHERE TO EAT AND STAY

For expanded hotel reviews, visit Fodors.com.

$$
MEXICAN
Fodor's Choice
★

✕ **Elvira's.** This colorful and deservedly popular restaurant, a fixture in Nogales, Mexico since 1927, moved across the border and now serves delicious Sonoran classics in Tubac village. Try one of the five Chicken moles (a sauce using chocolate as its base), ranging from sweet to nutty to spicy, and you'll know why Chef Ruben has such a devoted following. Chiles rellenos, enchiladas, and heartier steak and fish selections don't disappoint either. Save room for the divine flan dessert, a creamier version of traditional Mexican custard with caramel sauce. Live music on Friday and Saturday nights adds festivity to this gem of an eatery in a quiet little town. ⓢ *Average main: $18* ✉ *2221 E. Frontage Rd.* ☎ *520/398-9421* ⊕ *www.elvirasrestaurant.com* ⊘ *Closed Mon.; no dinner Sun.*

$
AMERICAN

✕ **Tubac Deli & Coffee Co.** Smack in the middle of Tubac village, this is a very convenient and friendly place to "set awhile" with the locals. From breakfast pastries and quiche to generous sandwiches, salads, and soups, this pleasant little eatery is open daily from 6:30 am until

5 pm. $ *Average main: $8* ✉ *6 Plaza Rd.* ☎ *520/398–3330* ⊕ *www. tubacdeli.com.*

$

B&B/INN

⊡ **Amado Territory Inn.** Although this quiet, friendly B&B is directly off the highway frontage road, it feels worlds away. **Pros:** good breakfast; pleasant garden areas for strolling. **Cons:** only the common room has a TV; not walking distance to Tubac village. $ *Rooms from: $129* ✉ *3001 E. Frontage Rd., off Exit 48 of I–19, Amado* ⊕ *www.amadoterritoryinn. com* ⥵ *9 rooms, 1 3-bedroom house* ⍥ *Breakfast.*

$

B&B/INN

⊡ **Tubac Country Inn.** Down the lane from the shops and eateries of Tubac village is this charming two-story inn. **Pros:** rooms are spacious, comfortably furnished, and have separate entrances; in Tubac village. **Cons:** no B&B camaraderie here—it feels more like you're staying in someone's guest cottage. $ *Rooms from: $130* ✉ *13 Burruel St.* ☎ *520/398– 3178* ⊕ *www.tubaccountryinn.com* ⥵ *5 rooms* ⍥ *Breakfast.*

SPORTS AND THE OUTDOORS
HIKING
Juan Bautista de Anza National Historic Trail. You can tread the same road as the conquistadors: the first 4.5 miles of the Juan Bautista de Anza National Historic Trail from Tumacácori to Tubac were dedicated in 1992. You'll have to cross the Santa Cruz River—which is usually low— three times to complete the hike, and the path is rather sandy, but it's a pleasant journey along the tree-shaded banks of the river. *Moderate.* ☎ *415/623–2344* ⊕ *www.nps.gov/juba.*

TUMACÁCORI NATIONAL HISTORIC PARK

3 miles south of Tubac.

GETTING HERE AND AROUND
Take Exit 29 off Interstate 19 and follow signs half a mile to the park (from Tucson, go under the highway to East Frontage Road and turn left).

EXPLORING
Tumacácori National Historic Park. The site where Tumacácori National Historic Park now stands was visited by missionary Father Eusebio Francisco Kino in 1691, but the Jesuits didn't build a church here until 1751. You can still see some remnants of this simple structure, but the main attraction is the mission of San José de Tumacácori, built by the Franciscans around 1799–1803. A combination of circumstances— Apache attacks, a bad winter, and Mexico's withdrawal of funds and priests—caused the remaining inhabitants to flee in 1848. Persistent rumors of wealth left behind by both the Franciscans and the Jesuits led treasure seekers to pillage the site; it still bears those scars. The site was finally protected in 1908, when it became a national monument.

Information about the mission and the Anza trail is available at the visitor center, and guided tours are available daily October through March. A small museum displays some of the mission's artifacts, and sometimes fresh tortillas are made on a wood-fire stove in the courtyard. In addition to a Christmas Eve celebration, costumed historical high masses are held at Tumacácori in spring and fall. An annual fiesta the first weekend of December has arts and crafts and food booths. ✉ *1891 E. Frontage Rd., I–19, Exit 29, Tumacácori* ☎ *520/398–2341* 🌐 *www.nps.gov/tuma* 🎟 *$3* 🕒 *Daily 9–5.*

EN ROUTE **Santa Cruz Chili & Spice Co.** Across the street from the Tumacácori National Historic Park, the Santa Cruz Spice Factory packs and sells 240 varieties of herbs and spices, including the owner's home-grown chili powders and pastes, if you want to take a taste of the Southwest home. A little museum, tasting area, and store are open Monday through Saturday. ✉ *1868 E. Frontage Rd., Tumacácori* ☎ *520/398–2591* 🌐 *www.santacruzchili.com.*

WHERE TO STAY

For expanded hotel reviews, visit Fodors.com.

$ RESORT 🏨 **Esplendor Resort at Rio Rico.** This secluded hotel and conference center has a historic, rather than hokey, Western feel, with vistas of open prairie and an elongated bar reminiscent of a Tombstone saloon. **Pros:** great golf and tennis; a sense of leaving the world behind; 15-minute drive to Mexico. **Cons:** somewhat isolated; golf and tennis are across the highway (shuttle bus provided). [$] *Rooms from: $99* ✉ *1069 Camino Caralampi, off I–19 at Rio Rico Rd., Rio Rico* ☎ *520/281–1901, 800/288–4746* 🌐 *www.esplendor-resort.com* 🛏 *179 rooms* 🍴 *No meals.*

SOUTHERN ARIZONA

WELCOME TO SOUTHERN ARIZONA

TOP REASONS TO GO

★ **Tour Kartchner Caverns:** The underground world of a living "wet" cave system is a rare and wonderful sensory experience. You'll see a multicolor limestone kingdom and probably feel "cave kiss" droplets grace your head; just *don't touch anything.*

★ **Hike in the Chiricahuas:** Stunning "upside-down" rock formations, flourishing wildlife, and relatively easy trails make for great hiking in this unspoiled region. The 3.4-mile Echo Canyon Loop Trail is a winner.

★ **Explore Bisbee:** Board the Queen Mine Train and venture into the life of a copper miner at the turn of the last century. Afterward, check out the narrow, hilly town's Victorian houses and thriving shops.

★ **Stargaze at Kitt Peak:** Clear skies and dry air provide ideal conditions for stargazing; the evening observation program, with top-notch telescopes and enthusiastic guides, is an excellent introduction to astronomy.

1 Southeast Arizona. Old West history, colorful limestone caverns, bizarre hoodoo formations, sweeping "Sky Islands," Arizona's wine country, rolling grasslands, a world-renowned birding paradise, and rustic ranch retreats create a perfect mix of historical adventure and outdoor recreation.

GETTING ORIENTED

Southern Arizona ranges from the searing deserts surrounding Organ Pipe Cactus National Monument and the town of Yuma in the southwest to the soaring "Sky Islands"—steep hills that rise from the desert floor into the clouds—and rolling grasslands in the southeast. Towns are few and far between in the southwestern corner of the state, where the desert and dry climate rule. In stark contrast, the varied terrain in the southeastern region ranges from pine-forested mountains and cool canyons to desert grasslands and winding river valleys. A complex network of highways links the many communities situated in this part of the state, where the next town or attraction is just over the hill, making the decision on which way you want to go next the hardest part of traveling.

8

2 Southwest Arizona. The historical Yuma Territorial Prison, a world-class observatory, national wildlife refuges, Colorado River recreation, and Organ Pipe Cactus National Monument keep visitors busy in this remote desert region.

EXPERIENCE THE WILD WEST

Arizona's identity was forged like horseshoes by cattle, copper, and the men who chased both. The "Old West" stretches as long as a cowboy's yarn and as broad as a 19th-century cattle drive. Follow the echoes of gunslingers like Wyatt Earp, or drink in majestic landscapes popularized on the silver screen.

Above: You can still ride a stagecoach in Tombstone. Top right: Western watchers will find Canyon de Chelly familiar. Lower right: Tours go deep into the Cooper Queen Mine.

In 1862, when Arizona became a U.S. territory, it began to fill immediately with fortune-seekers. In towns like Bisbee (copper) and Tombstone (silver), the discovery of a single ore begot legendary boom-and-bust mining cycles. Precious metal brought miners, then speculators, real wealth, and services including saloons and brothels. Just as quickly, the ore ran out, and envy, shoot-outs, and desolation followed. With the arrival of railroads in 1880, Arizona's stock grew from a few thousand to a million plus in less than 20 years—but ranchers were also shortsighted and the "boom" subsided just as fast. Still, cowboy life is one of the most enduring icons of Americana.

TOURISM BONANZA

Movies like *Gunfight at the O.K. Corral* started a renaissance in many ghost towns, and the modern "boom" is tourism. Main Street's drinking and gambling establishments have given way to B&Bs (try **School House Inn Bed & Breakfast** in Bisbee), historic bars (visit **Crystal Palace** in Tombstone), and boutiques (**55 Main Gallery** in Bisbee).

SOUTHERN ARIZONA WILD WEST ROAD TRIP

Start your Old West explorations in Tucson with a half day at the **Old Tucson Studios** and a stop at **Mission San Xavier del Bac**. Kids will love the simulated gunfights, rides, and stunt shows at the studios where *Gunsmoke* and *Bonanza* were filmed. Mom and Dad can channel the West in a more contemplative way inside the 18th-century mission where the bad guys no doubt went for sanctuary or forgiveness.

Southeast Arizona may be the most dense and interesting corner in which to explore various aspects of the Old West. The Apache tribe, led by Cochise and later Geronimo, held out for decades against U.S. troops and settlers amid the 12 ranges of the Coronado National Forest, before surrendering in 1886. Imagine warrior-tribes in the canyons and rock formations of the **Chiricahua National Monument**, where spotting jaguar, rare deer, and flora are treasures in their own right.

Also in the southeast, Tombstone and Bisbee were centers of mining (silver and copper, respectively) and the wealth, larger-than-life characters, and movie depictions that came with them. **Tombstone** is more touristy, but the historic Allen Street buildings and the re-creation of the gunfight at the O.K. Corral are so steeped in Old West history (Wyatt Earp and Doc Holliday walked away but three of the notorious Clanton gang weren't so lucky) that it's worth a visit. More authentic experiences await in **Bisbee**. Don a light jacket when you take the 75-minute underground tour of the **Copper Queen Mine**, or if you're prone to claustrophobia, stick to the **Bisbee Mining and Historical Museum**, which served as the company's offices.

ELSEWHERE IN ARIZONA

In north-central Arizona, **Jerome** and **Prescott** are two other boom-towns worth a half-day's exploration. Jerome was once known as the Billion Dollar Copper Camp, but its 15,000-person population dwindled to 50 before rebounding to today's 500 or so. Stop for a hearty burger in the **Haunted Hamburger/Jerome Palace,** where the resident ghost purportedly hangs out upstairs. Thirty miles away, Prescott is home to the world's oldest rodeo during July's **Frontier Days** and has regular live music at the historic bars on **Whiskey Row**.

Thanks to Hollywood, the wide-open vistas of the West are some of the most recurring images of a bygone era. Fortunately for you, **Monument Valley** and **Canyon de Chelly** in northeast Arizona remain virtually unchanged from the way that cowboys and Native Americans experienced them in the 19th century.

8

Updated by
Mara Levin

Southern Arizona can do little to escape its cliché-ridden image as a landscape of cow skulls, tumbleweed, dried-up riverbeds, and mother lodes—but it doesn't need to. Abandoned mining towns and sleepy Western hamlets dot a lonely landscape of rugged rock formations, deep pine forests, dense mountain ranges, and scrubby grasslands.

South of Sierra Vista, just above the Mexican border, a stone marker commemorates the spot where the first Europeans set foot in what is now the United States. In 1540, 80 years before the pilgrims landed at Plymouth Rock, Spanish conquistador Don Francisco Vásquez de Coronado led one of Spain's largest expeditions from Mexico along the fertile San Pedro River valley, where the little towns of Benson and St. David are found today. They'd come north to seek the legendary Seven Cities of Cibola, where Native American pueblos were rumored to have doors of polished turquoise and streets of solid gold. The wealth of the region, however, lay in its rich veins of copper and silver, not tapped until more than 300 years after the Spanish marched on in disappointment. Once word of this cache spread, these parts of the West quickly became much wilder: fortune seekers who rushed to the region came face-to-face with the Chiricahua Apaches, led by Cochise and Geronimo, while Indian warriors battled encroaching settlers and the U.S. Cavalry sent to protect them.

Although the search for mineral booty in southeastern Arizona is more notorious, the western side of the state wasn't untouched by the rage to plunder. Interest in going for the gold in California gave rise to the town of Yuma: the Colorado River had to be crossed to get to the West Coast, and Fort Yuma was established in part to protect the Anglo ferry business at a good fording point from Indian competitors. The Yuma Tribe lost that battle, but another group of Native Americans, the Tohono O'odham, fared better in this part of the state. Known for a long time as the Papago—or "bean eaters"—they were deeded a large portion of their ancestral homeland by the U.S. Bureau of Indian Affairs.

SOUTHERN ARIZONA PLANNER

WHEN TO GO

As you might expect, the desert areas are popular in winter, and the cooler mountain areas are more heavily visited in summer. If you're seeking outdoor adventure, spring and fall are the best times to visit this part of the state. The region is in full bloom by late March and early April, and spring and fall are the peaks of birding season.

FESTIVALS AND EVENTS

JANUARY **Wings Over Willcox.** This birding extravaganza the third week in January is highlighted by the morning flights of thousands of wintering sandhill cranes lifting off from the Willcox Playa. ☎ 520/384–2272 ⊕ *www.wingsoverwillcox.com.*

FEBRUARY **Cochise Cowboy Poetry and Music Gathering.** In Sierra Vista, this festival in early February showcases Western culture, history, and folklore. ☎ 520/417–6960 ⊕ *www.cowboypoets.com.*

OCTOBER **The Rex Allen Days.** A rodeo and Western music and dance fill the first weekend in October, in Willcox. ☎ 520/384–2272 ⊕ *www.rexallendays.org.*

Helldorado Days. The third weekend of October, history comes alive in Tombstone with gunfights in the streets, a parade, and an 1880s fashion show. ☎ 888/457–3929 ⊕ *www.tombstonechamber.com.*

PLANNING YOUR TIME

The diverse geography of the region and the driving distances between sights require that you strategize when planning your trip. With Tucson as a starting point, the rolling hills and grasslands of Sonoita and Patagonia are little more than an hour away, as are the underground marvels in Kartchner Caverns (to the southeast) and the starry skies above Kitt Peak Observatory (to the southwest). You can explore the Old West of Tombstone, Bisbee, and the surrounding ghost towns in one day, or more leisurely in two. If you're heading to the cactus-studded hillsides at Organ Pipe Cactus National Monument, leave yourself at least a full day to explore the monument and the nearby town of Ajo. A trek through the stunning Chiricahua rock formations calls for an overnight stay, since the area is a 2½-hour drive southeast of Tucson.

GETTING HERE AND AROUND

Tucson is the major starting point for exploring both the southwest region and the southeast corner of the state. Yuma's remote location on the California–Arizona border makes it a destination in itself, and while it can be reached on a lengthy three-hour drive from Tucson or Phoenix, it's most easily accessed through Yuma International Airport.

CAR TRAVEL

The best way to explore southeastern Arizona is on a leisurely road trip. The intricate network of highways in the San Pedro Valley provides looping access to the many scenic vistas and Old West communities, which makes the drive an integral part of the adventure. In stark contrast, a drive through the southwestern portion of the state is filled with long stretches of desert broken infrequently with tiny towns and intermittent gas stations. If you're heading west, pack a lunch, a few games, and plenty of music for entertainment along the way.

A car is essential in southern Arizona. The best plan is to fly into Tucson, which is the hub of the area, or Phoenix, which has the most flights. You can rent a car from several national companies at Yuma International Airport.

TRAIN TRAVEL

Amtrak trains run three times a week from Tucson to Benson and Yuma.

RESTAURANTS

In southern Arizona cowboy fare is more common than haute cuisine. There are exceptions, though, especially in the wine-growing area of Sonoita and in the trendy town of Bisbee, both popular for weekend outings from Tucson. And, as one would expect, Mexican food dominates menus.

Prices in the reviews are the average cost of a main course at dinner or, if dinner is not served, at lunch.

HOTELS

There are plenty of chain hotels found throughout the southern region of Arizona, especially along the interstate highways, but why settle for boring basics in this beautiful and historic corner of the state? For the best experience, seek out an old-fashioned room in a historic hotel, a rustic casita at a working cattle ranch, or a spacious suite in a homey bed-and-breakfast. There are a few scattered dude ranches in the sweeping grasslands to the south. It's usually not hard to find a room any time of the year, but keep in mind that prices tend to go up in high season (winter and spring) and down in low season (summer through early fall).

Prices in the reviews are the lowest cost of a standard double room in high season. For expanded reviews, facilities, and current deals, visit Fodors.com.

SOUTHEAST ARIZONA

From the rugged mountain forests to the desert grasslands of Sierra Vista, the southeast corner of Arizona is one of the state's most scenic regions. Much of this area is part of Cochise County, named in 1881 in honor of the chief of the Chiricahua Apache. Cochise waged war against troops and settlers for 11 years, and was respected by Indians and non-Indians alike for his integrity and leadership. Today Cochise County is dotted with small towns, many of them smaller—and tamer—than they were in their heyday. Cochise County encompasses 6, and part of the seventh, of the 12 mountain ranges that compose the 1.7-million-acre Coronado National Forest.

In the valleys between southeastern Arizona's jagged mountain ranges you'll discover the 19th-century charm of Bisbee—Queen of the Copper Camps. You can explore the eerie hoodoos and spires of Chiricahua National Monument and walk in the footsteps of the legendary Apaches, who valiantly stood against the U.S. Army until Geronimo's final surrender in 1886. This is also where you can travel through the grassy plains surrounding Sonoita and Elgin—the heart of Arizona's wine country.

A trip to this historically and ecologically important corner of the state will also take you to Fort Huachuca, the oldest continuously operating military installation in the Southwest; to southeastern Arizona's "Sky Islands," the lush microclimates in the Huachuca and Chiricahua mountains where jaguars roam and migratory tropical birds flit through the canopy; and to historic mining and military towns, the tenacious survivors of the Old West—including Bisbee, Sierra Vista, and Tombstone.

> **WORD OF MOUTH**
>
> "Tombstone is touristy, but I'm an Old West fan and loved it. I'd allow one full day there and... tour the Bird Cage and the courthouse."   —Beatle

TOMBSTONE

70 miles southeast of Tucson, 24 miles south of Benson via AZ 80, 28 miles northeast of Sierra Vista via AZ 90.

When prospector Ed Schieffelin headed out in 1877 to seek his fortune along the arid washes of San Pedro Valley, a patrolling soldier warned that all he'd find was his tombstone. Against all odds, his luck held out: he evaded bands of hostile Apaches, braved the harsh desert terrain, and eventually stumbled across a ledge of silver ore. The town of Tombstone was named after the soldier's offhand comment.

The rich silver lodes from the area's mines attracted a wide mix of fortune seekers ranging from prospectors to prostitutes and gamblers to gunmen. But as the riches continued to pour in, wealthy citizens began importing the best entertainment and culture that silver could purchase. Even though saloons and gambling halls made up two out of every three businesses on Allen Street, the town also claimed the Cochise County seat, a cultural center, and fancy French restaurants. By the early 1880s the notorious boomtown was touted as the most cultivated city west of the Mississippi.

In 1881 a shoot-out between the Earp brothers and the Clanton gang ended with three of the "cowboys" (Billy Clanton and Tom and Frank McLaury) dead and two of the Earps (Virgil and Morgan) and Doc Holliday wounded. The infamous "gunfight at the O.K. Corral" and the ensuing feud between the Earp brothers and the Clanton gang firmly cemented Tombstone's place in the Wild West—even though the actual course of events is still debated by historians.

All in all, Tombstone's heyday lasted only a decade, but the colorful characters attached to the town's history live on—immortalized on the silver screen in such famous flicks as *Gunfight at the O.K. Corral, Tombstone,* and *Wyatt Earp.* The town's tourist industry parallels Hollywood hype. As a result, the main drag on Allen Street looks and feels like a movie set (even though most of the buildings are original), complete with gunning desperados, satin-bedecked saloon girls, and

8

leather-clad cowboys. Today, the "Town Too Tough to Die" attracts a kitschy mix of rough-and-tumble bikers, European tourists, and pulp-fiction thrill seekers looking to walk the boardwalks of Tombstone's infamous past.

GETTING HERE AND AROUND

Start your tour of this tiny town and pick up a free map at the visitor center. As you drive into Tombstone on U.S. 80, historic Allen Street parallels the highway one block west. The visitor center sits in the middle, on the corner of Allen and 4th Street. Park along any side street or at one of the free lots on 6th Street. There's a self-guided walking tour, but the best way to get the lay of the land is to take the 15-minute **stagecoach ride** ($10, $5 for kids) around downtown. Drivers, dressed in cowboy attire, relate a condensed version of Tombstone's notorious past. You'll also pass the Tombstone Courthouse and travel down Toughnut Street, once called Rotten Row—because of the lawyers who lived there.

ESSENTIALS

Visitor Information Tombstone Visitor Center ⊠ 104 S. 4th St., at Allen St. ☎ 520/457-3929 ⊕ www.tombstonechamber.com ⊙ Mon.–Thurs. 9–4; Fri.–Sun. 9–5.

CLOSE UP

The Legend of Wyatt Earp and the O.K. Corral

Popularized in dime novels and on the silver screen, the legend of Wyatt Earp follows the American tradition of the tall tale. This larger-than-life hero of the Wild West is cloaked with romance and derring-do. Stripped of the glamour, though, Earp emerges as a man with a checkered past who switched from fugitive to lawman several times during his long life.

Born in 1848, Wyatt Berry Stapp Earp earned renown as the assistant city marshal of Dodge City. Wyatt and his brothers James, Virgil, and Morgan moved to Tombstone in 1879, and it was here that they, along with Wyatt's friend Doc Holliday, made their mark in history. Wyatt ran a gambling concession at the Oriental Saloon, and Virgil became Tombstone's city marshal. When trouble began to brew with the Clanton gang, Virgil recruited Wyatt and Morgan as deputy policemen. The escalating animosity

between the "cowboys" and the Earps peaked on October 26, 1881, at the O.K. Corral—a 30-second gunfight that left three of the Clanton gang dead and Morgan and Virgil wounded. Doc Holliday was grazed, but Wyatt walked away from the fight uninjured. And then the real trouble for the Earps began.

In December, Virgil was shot and crippled by unknown assailants, and on March 18, 1882, Morgan was shot to death in a pool hall. In retribution, Wyatt went on a bloody vendetta. After the smoke had settled, the remaining "cowboys" were dead and Wyatt had left Tombstone for good. He made the rounds of mining camps in the West and up into Alaska, then settled in California. He died on January 13, 1929. His legend lives on in movies such as *Tombstone* and *Wyatt Earp*.

8

EXPLORING
TOP ATTRACTIONS

FAMILY **O.K. Corral and Tombstone Historama.** Vincent Price narrates the dramatic version of the town's fascinating past in the Historama—a 26-minute multimedia presentation that provides a solid overview. At the adjoining, authentic **O.K. Corral,** a recorded voice-over details the town's famous shoot-out, while life-size figures of the gunfight's participants stand poised to shoot. A reenactment of the gunfight at the O.K. Corral is held daily at 2 pm in an outdoor theater next door ($4). Photographer C.S. Fly, whose studio was next door to the corral, didn't record this bit of history, but Geronimo and his pursuers were among the historic figures he did capture with his camera. Many of his fascinating Old West images and his equipment may be viewed at the **Fly Exhibition Gallery & Studio.** ⊠ *326 Allen St., between 3rd and 4th Sts.* ☎ *520/457–3456* ⊕ *www.ok-corral.com* ✉ *Historama, O.K. Corral, and Fly Exhibition Gallery & Studio $6; gunfight reenactment $4* ⊙ *Daily 9–5; Historama shows every half hr 9:30–4:30.*

Tombstone Epitaph Museum. You can see the original printing presses for the town's newspaper and watch a video about the production process at the Tombstone Epitaph Museum. The newspaper was founded in 1880 by John P. Clum, a colorful character in his own right, and is still publishing today. You can purchase one of the newspaper's special editions—*The Life and Times of Wyatt Earp*, *The Life and Times of Doc Holliday*, or *Tombstone's Pioneering Prostitutes.* ✉ *9 S. 5th St.* ☎ *520/457–2211* ⊕ *www.ok-corral.com* ✏ *Free* ☉ *Daily 9:30–5.*

WORTH NOTING

The Bird Cage Theater. A Tombstone institution, known as the wildest, wickedest night spot between Basin Street and the Barbary Coast, the Bird Cage Theater is a former music hall where Enrico Caruso, Sarah Bernhardt, and Lillian Russell—among others—performed. It was also the site of the longest continuous poker game recorded: the game started when the Bird Cage opened in 1881 and lasted eight years, five months, and three days. Some of the better-known players included Diamond Jim Brady, Adolphus Busch (of brewery fame), and William Randolph Hearst's father. The cards were dealt round the clock; players had to give a 20-minute notice when they were planning to vacate their seats, because there was always a waiting list of at least 10 people ready to shell out $1,000 (the equivalent of about $30,000 today) to get in. In all, some $10 million changed hands.

When the mines closed in 1889, the Bird Cage was abandoned but the building has remained in the hands of the same family, who threw nothing out. You can walk on the stage visited by some of the top traveling performers of the time, see the faro table once touched by the legendary gambler Doc Holliday, and pass by the hearse that carried Tombstone's deceased to Boot Hill. The basement, which served as an upscale bordello and gambling hall, still has all the original furnishings and fixtures intact, and you can see the personal belongings left behind by the ladies of the night when the mines closed and they, and their clients, headed for California. ✉ *535 E. Allen St., at 6th St.* ☎ *520/457–3421* ⊕ *www. tombstonebirdcage.com* ✏ *$10* ☉ *Daily 9–6.*

Boot Hill Graveyard. This graveyard, where the victims of the O.K. Corral shoot-out are buried, is on the northwest corner of town, facing U.S. 80. Chinese names in one section of the "bone orchard" bear testament to the laundry and restaurant workers who came from San Francisco during the height of Tombstone's mining fever. One of the more amusing epitaphs at the cemetery, however, is engraved on the headstone of Wells Fargo agent Lester Moore; it poetically lists the cause of his untimely demise: "Here lies Lester Moore, four slugs from a .44, no les, no more." If you're put off by the commercialism of the place—you enter through a gift shop that sells novelty items in the shape of tombstones—remember that Tombstone itself is the result of crass acquisition. ✉ *U.S. 80* ☎ *520/457–3300* ✏ *Free* ☉ *Daily 8–Dusk.*

Rose Tree Inn Museum. Originally a boardinghouse for the Vizina Mining Company and later a popular hotel, the Rose Tree Inn Museum has 1880s period rooms. Covering more than 8,600 square feet, the Lady Banksia rose tree, planted by a homesick bride in 1885, is reported to be the largest of its kind in the world. The best time to see the tree is from April to May, when its tiny white roses bloom. Romantics can purchase a healthy clipping from the tree to plant in their own yards. The museum might not look like much from the outside, but the collectibles

SOUTHERN ARIZONA BIRD-WATCHING

Southern Arizona is one of the best areas for bird-watching in the United States; nearly 500 species have been spotted here. To the east, birders flock to the Patagonia–Sonoita Creek and Ramsey Canyon preserves, the San Pedro Riparian National Conservation Area, the ponds and dry lakebeds south of Willcox, and the Portal–Cave Creek area in the Chiricahua Mountains near the New Mexico border. To the west, the Buenos Aires and Imperial national wildlife refuges are among the many places famed for their abundance of avian visitors. All in all, more than a quarter of the birds found in North America nest in the rich habitats provided by the secluded canyons and diverse microclimates of southern Arizona's "Sky Islands." Some of the most coveted avian species spotted in this birder's paradise include painted redstarts, elegant trogons, violet-crowned hummingbirds, north-ern goshawk, and sulphur-bellied flycatchers.

Ramsey Canyon, near Sierra Vista, holds the birding claim to fame as the "Hummingbird Capital of the United States." The proliferation of the colorful, winged wonders (14 species in all) is the focus of the Southwest Wings Birding and Nature Festival, held in August. Get up close and personal with these tiny birds at feeder stations in Miller's Canyon or by participating in guided walks and activities during Fiesta de las Aves in early May. For more information on birding sites and educational programs in the area, contact the **Southeastern Arizona Birding Observatory** (☎ *520/432–1388* ⊕ *www.sabo.org*); or pick up an Arizona birding trail guide for $3 at the **Tucson Audubon Nature Shop** (✉ *300 E. University Blvd., #120, Tucson* ☎ *520/629–0510* ⊕ *www. tucsonaudubon.org*) or at the visitor center in Bisbee.

and tree make this one of the best places to visit in town. ✉ *118 S. 4th St., at Toughnut St.* ☎ *520/457–3326* ⚄ *$5* ⊘ *Daily 9–5.*

Tombstone Courthouse State Park. For an introduction to the town's—and the area's—past, visit the Tombstone Courthouse State Historic Park. This redbrick 1882 county courthouse offers exhibits on the area's mining and ranching history and pioneer lifestyles; you can also see the restored 1904 courtroom and district attorney's office. The two-story building housed the Cochise County jail, a courtroom, and public offices until the county seat was moved to Bisbee in 1929. The stately building became the cornerstone of Tombstone's historic-preservation efforts in the 1950s, and was Arizona's first operational state park. Today you can relax with an outdoor lunch at the park's tree-shaded picnic tables. ✉ *219 E. Toughnut St., at 3rd St.* ☎ *520/457–3311* ⊕ *www.azstateparks.com/Parks/TOCO* ⚄ *$5* ⊘ *Daily 9–5.*

Tombstone Western Heritage Museum. Aficionados of the Old West have most likely seen the photograph of Billy Clanton in his coffin, which was taken after his demise at the infamous gunfight at the O.K. Corral. But Steve Elliott, owner of the Tombstone Western Heritage Museum, offers another glimpse of this cowboy—one with his eyes wide open. The 5-inch-by-7-inch black-and-white photograph, taken by C.S. Fly

A visit to Tombstone isn't complete without witnessing the re-created gunfight at the O.K. Corral.

in the 1880s, shows the Clantons, the McLaury brothers, and Billy Claiborne all saddled up and ready to ride. According to Elliott, it is the only known photograph of Billy Clanton taken while he was still among the living. Other relics of the Old West at the museum include 1880s dentist's tools, clay poker chips, historic photographs, vintage firearms, and a stagecoach strongbox. ⊠ *517 Fremont St., at 6th St.* ☎ *520/457–3933* ⊕ *www.thetombstonemuseum.com* ⊠ *$7.50* ⊙ *Mon.–Sat. 10–5, Sun. 1–5.*

WHERE TO EAT AND STAY
For expanded hotel reviews, visit Fodors.com.

$
AMERICAN
FAMILY
✕ **Longhorn Restaurant.** You won't find anything fancy at this noisy eatery across the street from Big Nose Kate's Saloon, but you will find generous helpings of basic American and Mexican food at decent prices. The menu covers everything from breakfast to dinner with such entrées as omelets, burgers, steaks, tacos, and enchiladas. The food is a little bland, but the rustic environment and easy accessibility keep this long-time establishment in the running. Ⓢ *Average main: $11* ⊠ *501 E. Allen St.* ☎ *520/457–3405* ⊕ *www.bignosekates.info/longhorn.html.*

$
HOTEL
🏨 **Holiday Inn Express.** Nestled into a hill just outside town, this newer two-story property offsets basic rooms with spectacular views of the mountains and desert valley. **Pros:** clean; modern; pool and hot tub. **Cons:** longer walk (or three-minute drive) into town; no elevator (request a ground-floor room if you don't want to climb stairs). Ⓢ *Rooms from: $119* ⊠ *580 W. Randolph Way* ☎ *520/457–9507* ⊕ *www.hitombstone.com* ⇗ *60 rooms* ❙⦿❙ *Breakfast.*

$ B&B/INN 🏨 **Marie's Engaging Bed & Breakfast.** Filled with Western kitsch, curios, and family portraits, Marie's has the feel of a stay at Grandma's house without the obligation. **Pros:** friendly hosts; convenient location. **Cons:** two rooms in the main house share a bathroom. [$] *Rooms from: $103* ✉ *101 N. 4th St* ☎ *520/457–3831, 877/457–3831* 🌐 *www.mariesbandb.com* 🛏 *3 rooms, 1 with bath* 🍴 *Breakfast.*

NIGHTLIFE

Big Nose Kate's Saloon. This popular pub was once part of the original Grand Hotel, built in 1881. Saloon girls encourage visitors to get into the 1880s spirit by dressing up in red-feather boas and dusters. Occasionally an acoustic concert livens things up even more. ✉ *417 E. Allen St., between 4th and 5th Sts.* ☎ *520/457–3107* 🌐 *www.bignosekates.com.*

Crystal Palace Saloon. If you're looking to wet your whistle, stop by the Crystal Palace, where a beautiful mirrored mahogany bar, wrought-iron chandeliers, and tinwork ceilings date back to Tombstone's heyday. Locals come here on weekends to dance to live country-and-western music. ✉ *436 E. Allen St., at 5th St.* ☎ *520/457–3611* 🌐 *www.crystalpalacesaloon.com.*

SHOPPING

Several souvenir shops and old-time photo emporiums await in the kitschy collection of stores lining Allen Street.

Silver Hills Trading Co. This store offers everything from Native American jewelry to Southwestern and Old West souvenirs, including replica guns and Tombstone sheriff badges. ✉ *504 E. Allen St.* ☎ *520/457–3335* 🌐 *www.silverhillstrading.com.*

T. Miller's Tombstone Mercantile. Get into the spirit of the Old West by purchasing high-quality, 1880s-style clothing and jewelry, as well as Western art and antique furniture, at T. Miller's Tombstone Mercantile. Refuel for more shopping or shoot-outs with a root beer float from the on-site ice cream and sandwich shop. ✉ *530 E. Allen St.* ☎ *520/457–2405* 🌐 *www.tombstonemercantileco.com.*

Tombstone Old West Books. Well-stocked Tombstone Old West Books has a wide selection of books about Cochise County and the Old West. ✉ *401 E. Allen St.* ☎ *520/457–2252* 🌐 *www.tombstoneoldwestbooks.com* 🕓 *Closed Sun.*

8

BISBEE

Fodor's Choice ★

24 miles southeast of Tombstone on AZ 80.

Like Tombstone, Bisbee was a mining boomtown, but its wealth was in copper, not silver, and its success continued much longer. The gnarled Mule Mountains aren't as impressive as some of the other mountain ranges in southern Arizona, but their rocky canyons concealed one of the richest mineral sites in the world.

Jack Dunn, a scout with Company C from Fort Huachuca chasing hostile Apaches in the area, first discovered an outcropping of rich ore here in 1877. By 1900 more than 20,000 people lived in the crowded canyons around the Bisbee mines. Phelps Dodge purchased all the major mines by the Great Depression, and mining continued until 1975, when the mines were closed for good. In less than 100 years of mining, the area surrounding Bisbee yielded more than $6.1 billion of mineral wealth.

> ## WORD OF MOUTH
>
> "Certainly take the Copper Queen Mine tour; it's great. Exploring Bisbee on your own is also fun. Be sure to visit the old county building/jail." —bigtyke

Once known as the Queen of the Copper Camps, Bisbee is no longer one of the biggest cities between New Orleans and San Francisco. It was rediscovered in the early 1980s by burned-out city dwellers and revived as a kind of Woodstock West. The population is a mix of retired miners and their families, aging hippie jewelry makers, and enterprising restaurateurs and boutique owners from all over the country.

GETTING HERE AND AROUND
If you want to head straight into town from U.S. 80, get off at the Brewery Gulch interchange. You can cross under the highway, taking Main, Commerce, or Brewery Gulch streets, all of which intersect at the large public parking lot. Next door, the visitor center is a good place to start your visit of this historic mining town. It offers up-to-date information on attractions, dining, lodging, tours, and special events.

TOURS
Lavender Jeep Tours. Tom Mosier, a native of Bisbee, gives the Lavender Jeep Tours for $25 to $49. He regales locals and visitors with tales of the town and tours of the surrounding region, including ghost towns. ⊠ 10 Copper Queen Plaza ☎ 520/432–5369 ⊕ www.lavenderjeeptours.com.

Fodor's Choice
★ **Southeastern Arizona Bird Observatory.** This nonprofit organization offers guided birding tours, educational programs, and detailed information about birding in the region. Tours range from morning walks and evening "owl prowls" to one-week hummingbird trips. During the Fiesta de las Aves, the first week in May, you can participate in multiple birding activities each day; sign up to observe a hummingbird banding session, where you can assist researchers. ☎ 520/432–1388 ⊕ www.sabo.org.

ESSENTIALS
Visitor Information Bisbee Visitors Center ⊠ 478 N. Dart Rd. ☎ 520/432–3554, 866/224-7233 ⊕ www.discoverbisbee.com ⊙ Mon.–Fri. 10–5, Sat.–Sun. 10–4.

EXPLORING
TOP ATTRACTIONS
Bisbee Mining and Historical Museum. This museum is housed in a redbrick structure built in 1897 to serve as the Copper Queen Consolidated Mining Offices. The rooms today are filled with colorful exhibits, photographs, and artifacts that offer a glimpse into the everyday life of Bisbee's early mining community. The exhibit "Bisbee: Urban Outpost on the Frontier" paints a fascinating portrait of how this "Shady Lady" of a mining town transformed into a true mini–urban center. Upstairs, the "Digging In" exhibit shows you everything you ever wanted to know about copper mining, including what it felt and sounded like in

a mining car. This was the first rural museum in the United States to become a member of the Smithsonian Institution Affiliations Program, and it tells a story you can take with you as you wander through Bisbee's funky streets. ✉ *5 Copper Queen Plaza* ☎ *520/432–7071* ⊕ *www. bisbeemuseum.org* ✑ *$7.50* ☉ *Daily 10–4.*

FAMILY **Copper Queen Mine Underground Tour.** For a lesson in mining history, take the Copper Queen Mine Underground Tour. The mine is less than 0.5 mile to the east of the Lavender Pit, across AZ 80 from downtown at the Brewery Gulch interchange. Tours are led by Bisbee's retired copper miners, who are wont to embellish their spiel with tales from their mining days. The 75-minute tours (you can't enter the mine at any other time) go into the shaft via a small open train, like those the miners rode when the mine was active. Before you climb aboard, you're outfitted in miner's garb—a yellow slicker and a hard hat with a light that runs off a battery pack. You may want to wear a sweater or light coat under your slicker, because temperatures inside are cool. You'll travel thousands of feet into the mine, up a grade of 30 feet (not down, as many visitors expect). Reservations are suggested. ✉ *478 N. Dart Rd.* ☎ *520/432–2071, 866/432–2071* ⊕ *www.queenminetour.com* ✑ *Mine tour $13* ☉ *Tours daily at 9, 10:30, noon, 2, and 3:30.*

Main Street. Bisbee's Main Street is alive and retailing. This hilly commercial thoroughfare is lined with appealing art galleries, antiques stores, crafts shops, boutiques, and restaurants—many in well-preserved turn-of-the-20th-century brick buildings.

WORTH NOTING

Brewery Gulch. A short street running north–south, Brewery Gulch is adjacent to the Copper Queen Hotel. In the old days the brewery housed here allowed the dregs of the beer that was being brewed to flow down the street and into the gutter. Nowadays, this narrow road is home to Bisbee's nightlife.

Copper Queen Hotel. Built a century ago and still in operation, the Copper Queen Hotel is behind the Mining and Historical Museum. It has housed the famous as well as the infamous: General John "Black Jack" Pershing, John Wayne, Theodore Roosevelt, and mining executives from all over the world made this their home away from home. Though the restaurant fare is basic, the outdoor bar area is a great spot for enjoying a margarita and people-watching. The hotel also hosts three resident ghosts. Take a minute to look through the journal at the front desk where guests have described their haunted encounters. ✉ *11 Howell Ave.* ☎ *520/432–2216* ⊕ *www.copperqueen.com.*

Lavender Pit Mine. About 0.25 mile after AZ 80 intersects with AZ 92, you can pull off the highway into a gravel parking lot, where a short, typewritten history of the Lavender Pit Mine is attached to the hurricane fence (Bisbee isn't big on formal exhibits). The hole left by the copper miners is huge, with piles of lavender-hue "tailings," or waste, creating mountains around it. Arizona's largest pit mine yielded some 94 million tons of copper ore before mining activity came to a halt. ✉ *AZ 80.*

WHERE TO EAT

$$ ✕ **Bisbee's Table.** You might not expect diversity at a place with a reputa-
AMERICAN tion for having the best burger in town, but this restaurant delivers with
salads, sandwiches, fajitas, pasta, salmon, steaks, and ribs. The dining
room, built to resemble an old train depot, fills up fast on weekends.
Its location directly across the street from the Mining Museum makes
for a convenient meal. $ *Average main: $16* ⊠ *2 Copper Queen Plaza*
☎ *520/432–6788* ⊕ *www.thebisbeegrille.blogspot.com.*

$$ ✕ **Café Roka.** This is the deserved darling of the hip Bisbee crowd. The
ITALIAN constantly changing northern Italian–style evening menu is not exten-
Fodor's Choice sive, but whatever you order—gulf shrimp tossed with lobster ravioli,
★ roasted quail, New Zealand rack of lamb—will be wonderful. Por-
tions are generous, and all entrées come with soup, salad, and sorbet.
Exposed-brick walls and soft lighting form the backdrop for original
artwork, and the 1875 bar harks back to Bisbee's glory days. Reservations are strongly advised. $ *Average main: $20* ⊠ *35 Main St.*
☎ *520/432–5153* ⊕ *www.caferoka.com* ☉ *Closed Sun.–Tues. No lunch.*

WHERE TO STAY

For expanded hotel reviews, visit Fodors.com.

$ ⊡ **Canyon Rose Suites.** Steps from the heart of downtown, this all-suites
HOTEL inn includes seven pretty and spacious units of varying size, all with
hardwood floors, 10-foot ceilings, and fully equipped kitchens. **Pros:**
quiet, yet just off Main Street; well-equipped, attractive suites; easy
parking behind building. **Cons:** no breakfast or common area; no elevator (guest rooms are on second floor). $ *Rooms from: $99* ⊠ *27 Sub-
way St.* ☎ *520/432–5098, 866/296–7673* ⊕ *www.canyonrose.com* ⇥ *7
suites* ⦿ *No meals.*

$ ⊡ **Letson Loft Hotel.** This beautifully restored boutique hotel is perched
B&B/INN above the galleries and shops of Main Street and well appointed
with upscale comforts. **Pros:** luxurious amenities; comfy, pillow-top
mattresses. **Cons:** some noise from Main Street below; no elevator
(all guest rooms are upstairs). $ *Rooms from: $115* ⊠ *26 Main St.*
☎ *520/432–3210, 877/432–3210* ⊕ *www.letsonlofthotel.com* ⇥ *8
rooms* ⦿ *Breakfast.*

$ ⊡ **School House Inn.** You might flash back to your classroom days at this
B&B/INN B&B, a schoolhouse built in 1918 at the height of Bisbee's mining days.
Fodor's Choice **Pros:** well-preserved property; exceedingly friendly hosts; hearty veg-
★ etarian breakfast. **Cons:** a mile walk or short drive into town. $ *Rooms
from: $89* ⊠ *818 Tombstone Canyon Rd.* ☎ *520/432–2996, 800/537–
4333* ⊕ *www.schoolhouseinnbb.com* ⇥ *6 rooms, 3 suites* ⦿ *Breakfast.*

$ ⊡ **Shady Dell Vintage Trailer Court.** For a blast to the past, stay in one of
RENTAL the funky vintage aluminum trailers at this trailer park south of town,
Fodor's Choice where accommodations range from a 1952 10-foot homemade unit to
★ a 1951 33-foot Royal Mansion. **Pros:** unique (how many vintage trailer-
park hotels with a hip vibe are out there?); fun; cheap. **Cons:** walking
to the public restrooms in the middle of the night. $ *Rooms from: $87*
⊠ *1 Old Douglas Rd.* ☎ *520/432–3567* ⊕ *www.theshadydell.com* ⇥ *10
trailers* ⦿ *No meals.*

NIGHTLIFE

Once known for shady ladies and saloons, Brewery Gulch retains a few shadows of its rowdy past.

St. Elmo Bar. Established in 1902, St. Elmo Bar is decorated with an assortment of the past and present—a 1922 official map of Cochise County hangs next to a neon beer sign. Locals and tourists hang out here from lunchtime on. The jukebox plays during the week, but on weekends Buzz and the Soul Senders rock the house with rhythm and blues. ⊠ *36 Brewery Ave.* ☎ *520/432–5578.*

SHOPPING

55 Main Gallery. Artist studios, galleries, and boutiques in historic buildings line Main Street, which runs though Tombstone Canyon. 55 Main Gallery is just one of many art galleries selling contemporary work along the main drag. ⊠ *55 Main St.* ☎ *520/432–4694* ⊕ *www.55maingallery.com.*

Belleza Gallery. This unusual gallery is owned and operated by Bisbee's Women's Transition Project, which aids homeless women and their children. Belleza features the artwork of local and national artists, as well as Adirondack chairs and birdhouses made by women receiving assistance from the program. The gallery's 50% commission goes directly into funding the Transition Project. ⊠ *27 Main St.* ☎ *520/432–5877* ⊕ *www.bellezagallery.org.*

Killer Bee Guy. A trip to Bisbee wouldn't be complete without a stop at the Killer Bee Guy. Beekeeper Reed Booth has appeared on cable TV; you can sample his honey butters and mustards and pick up some killer honey recipes. ⊠ *20 Main St.* ☎ *877/227–9338* ⊕ *www.killerbeeguy.com.*

Old Bisbee Roasters. In Peddlers Alley, grab a free cup of freshly brewed espresso from Old Bisbee Roasters, whose shop is just down the road. ⊠ *7 Naco Rd.* ☎ *866/432–5063* ⊕ *www.oldbisbeeroasters.com.*

Optimo Custom Panama Hatworks. Nationally renowned Optimo Custom Panama Hatworks is popular for its custom, handwoven Panama hats. It also sells works of beaver, cashmere, hare, and rabbit felt. ⊠ *47 Main St.* ☎ *520/432–4544, 888/346–3428* ⊕ *www.optimohatworks.com.*

SONOITA

55 miles west of Bisbee on AZ 90 to AZ 82; 34 miles southeast of Tucson on Interstate 10 to AZ 83; 57 miles west of Tombstone on AZ 82.

The grasslands surrounding modern-day Sonoita captured the attention of early Spanish explorers, including Father Eusebio Francisco Kino, who mapped and claimed the area in 1701. The Tuscan-like beauty of the rolling, often green hills framed by jutting mountain ranges has been noticed by Hollywood filmmakers. As you drive along AZ 83 and AZ 82 you might recognize the scenery from movies filmed here, including *Oklahoma* and *Tin Cup.*

Today this region is known for its family-run vineyards and wineries, as well as for its ranching history. Sonoita's "town," at the junction of AZ 83 and AZ 82 (known by locals as "the crossroads"), consists of a few restaurants and shops, an inn and a gas station, but it's the nearby wineries that draw the crowds. There are often weekend events at the

8

ARIZONA WINERIES: A GRAPE ESCAPE

The soil and climate in the Santa Cruz Valley southeast of Tucson are ideal for growing grapes, even if "Arizona wine country" may sound odd. Wine grapes first took root in the region 400 years ago, when the Spanish missionaries planted the first vines of "mission" grapes for the production of sacramental wine. But it wasn't until the 1970s that the first commercial vinifera grapes were planted here as part of an agricultural experiment. The hardier vines, such as Syrahs, Grenaches, and Malvasias, seem to tolerate the summer heat and retain good acidity.

Connoisseurs have debated the merits of the wines produced in this area since 1974, but if you want to decide for yourself, tour some of the region's wineries. **Callaghan**

Vineyards, Canelo Hills Winery, Rancho Rossa Vineyards, Hops & Vines, Dos Cabezas Wineworks, Village of Elgin Winery, Sonoita Vineyards, Kief-Joshua Vineyards, Lightning Ridge Cellars, and Wilhelm Family Vineyards all have something to tantalize the taste buds. You can purchase a wine glass at the first tasting room you choose, then take it with you to any of the other wineries for a reduced tasting fee.

Farther east, vineyards are springing up around Willcox, and elsewhere in the state, vineyards south of Sedona along lower Oak Creek are garnering attention as well. ⇨ See the listings in this chapter and Chapter 4, North-Central Arizona, for contact info.

wineries, including live jazz concerts and the Blessing of the Vines in spring and the Harvest Festival in fall. Summer is also a good time to visit, when you can escape the heat of Tucson, sample some of Arizona's vintages, and chat with local vintners.

GETTING HERE AND AROUND
To explore the wineries of southern Arizona, head south on AZ 83 from Sonoita and then east on Elgin Road. Most of the growers are in and around the tiny village of Elgin, 9 miles southeast of Sonoita. The best times to visit the vineyards are Friday through Sunday, when most are open for tastings (though a few are open daily). To plot your course through Arizona's wine country, check out the Sonoita/Elgin Wine Trail map from Arizona Wine Growers Association.

ESSENTIALS
Winery Information Arizona Wine Growers Association (⊕ www. arizonawine.org).

WINERIES
AZ Hops & Vines. With interesting varietals (try Zinnerpeace, a smooth and light Zinfandel), a hip vibe, and bottomless bowls of Cheetos to accompany tastings, AZ Hops & Vines splashed onto the Sonoita wine-tour scene in 2012. Open Friday through Sunday, 10–6, this spunky winery atop a pretty hillside boasts outdoor seating and a petting zoo. ✉ 3450 Hwy. 82 ☎ 520/955–4249 ⊕ www.azhopsandvines.com.

Fodor's Choice ★ **Callaghan Vineyards.** This vineyard, open Friday through Sunday 11–3, produces some of the best wine in Arizona. Its Buena Suerte ("good luck" in Spanish) Cuvée is a favorite, and its 1996 fumé blanc is considered one of the top wines in the United States. ✉ *336 Elgin Rd., Elgin* ☏ *520/455–5322* ⊕ *www. callaghanvineyards.com.*

Canelo Hills Vineyard & Winery. Open Friday through Sunday 11–4, Canelo Hills Winery specializes in full-bodied red wines and chardonnays. The grapes for their award-winning wines are all Arizona-grown and their wine is produced on-site. ✉ *342 Elgin Rd., Elgin* ☏ *520/455–5499* ⊕ *www. canelohillswinery.com.*

Dos Cabezas WineWorks. Award-winning reds and whites (some have been served at The White House) can be sampled Thursday through Sunday 10:30–4:30 at Dos Cabezas Wineworks, near the intersection of Highways 82 and 83. You can taste all their wines and keep the glass for $15. ✉ *3248 Hwy. 82* ☏ *520/455–5141* ⊕ *www.doscabezaswinery.com.*

Kief-Joshua Vineyards. Winemaker Kief Manning uses the traditional methods of open fermentation and barrel aging he learned in Australia. The winery is open daily 11–5. If you're here on a Sunday, Manning and his chef dish up omelets with locally grown veggies to complement the wines produced from organically grown grapes. ✉ *370 Elgin Rd., Elgin* ☏ *520/455–5582* ⊕ *www.kj-vineyards.com.*

Lightning Ridge Cellars. You might think you're in Italy when you visit Lightning Ridge Cellars, housed in a Tuscan-style building perched on a pretty hillside and open Friday through Sunday 11–4. The wide porch with Adirondack chairs and a bocce ball court invite you to linger awhile after sampling Italian varietals like their Sangiovese and Primitivo wines. ✉ *2368 Hwy. 83, Elgin* ☏ *520/678–8220* ⊕ *www. lightningridgecellars.com.*

Rancho Rossa Vineyards. Known for its dry and fruity varietals, Rancho Rossa Vineyards offers tastings Friday through Sunday 10:30–3:30. All of the fruit used to make the wines is estate-grown–something to brag about in these parts. Philanthropists as well as oenologists, they donate a portion of wine sales to local and national charities. ✉ *32 Cattle Ranch La., Elgin* ☏ *520/455–0700* ⊕ *www.ranchorossa.com.*

Sonoita Vineyards. This vineyard, known for its high-quality reds, offers tours and tastings daily 10–4. Originally planted in the early 1970s as an experiment by Dr. Gordon Dutt, former agriculture professor at the University of Arizona, this was the first commercial vineyard in Arizona. ✉ *290 Elgin-Canelo Rd., Elgin* ☏ *520/455–5893* ⊕ *www. sonoitavineyards.com.*

Village of Elgin Winery. Stop for tastings daily 10–4 at Village of Elgin Winery, one of the largest producers of wines in the state and the home to Tombstone Red, which the winemaker claims is "great with scorpion,

8

tarantula, and rattlesnake meat." ✉ *471 Elgin Rd., Elgin* ☎ *520/455–9309* 🌐 *www.elginwines.com.*

Wilhelm Family Vineyards. You can tour as well as taste at Wilhelm Family Vineyards, open Friday through Sunday 11–5, which produces seven red varietals, including a homegrown Syrah and tempranillo. ✉ *21 Mountain Ranch Dr., Elgin* ☎ *520/455–9291* 🌐 *www.wilhelmfamilyvineyards.com.*

WHERE TO EAT AND STAY

For expanded hotel reviews, visit Fodors.com.

$$ AMERICAN 🍴 **Steak Out Restaurant & Saloon.** A frontier-style design and a weathered-wood exterior help to create the mood at this Western restaurant and bar known for its tasty margaritas and live country music played on weekend evenings. Built and owned by the family that operates the Sonoita Inn next door, the restaurant serves cowboy fare: mesquite-grilled steaks, ribs, chicken, and fish. [$] *Average main: $20* ✉ *3235 AZ 83* ☎ *520/455–5205* 🌐 *www.azsteakout.com* ⏲ *No lunch weekdays.*

$ B&B/INN 🏨 **Sonoita Inn.** The owner of this small hotel also owned the Triple Crown–winning racehorse Secretariat, and the inn, built to resemble a huge barn, celebrates the horse's career with photos, racing programs, and press clippings. **Pros:** cheery equestrian decor; walk to restaurants. **Cons:** some road noise. [$] *Rooms from: $109* ✉ *3243 AZ 82* ☎ *520/455–5935, 800/696–1006* 🌐 *www.sonoitainn.com* 🔑 *18 rooms* 🍽 *Breakfast.*

$ B&B/INN 🏨 **The Walker Ranch.** If you've ever fantasized about living on a horse ranch, this B&B will be an easy place to settle into and a hard place to leave. **Pros:** attractive rooms and suites; tranquil setting. **Cons:** if you want breakfast, it costs extra. [$] *Rooms from: $120* ✉ *99 Curly Horse Rd.* ☎ *520/455–4631* 🌐 *www.thewalkerranch.com* 🔑 *8 rooms* 🍽 *No meals.*

SPORTS AND THE OUTDOORS

HORSEBACK RIDING

Arizona Horseback Experience. If you want to see the region from atop a trusty steed, Arizona Horseback Experience saddles 'em up for 3-hour, all-day, or overnight rides. You can opt for more or less challenging terrain—climbing mountains or loping along in lower elevations—within the Coronado National Forest. On the wine-tasting ride, they'll lead you to a vineyard (but they can't make you drink); you'll even get a souvenir glass and bottle of wine. ✉ *16 Coyote Ct.* ☎ *520/455–5696* 🌐 *www.horsebackexperience.com.*

PATAGONIA

12 miles southwest of Sonoita via AZ 82, 18 miles northeast of Nogales via AZ 82.

Served by a spur of the Atchison, Topeka, and Santa Fe Railroad, Patagonia was a shipping center for cattle and ore. The town declined after the railroad departed in 1962, and the old depot is now the town hall. Today, with the migration of artists and health-conscious urban refugees here in recent years, art galleries, natural food stores, and yoga/

Pilates studios coexist with real Western saloons in this tiny, tree-lined village in the Patagonia Mountains. The surrounding region is a prime birding destination, with more than 275 species of birds found around Sonoita Creek.

GETTING HERE AND AROUND

As you approach Patagonia on AZ 82 from either direction, the galleries and restaurants are either along the highway (called Naugle Avenue through town) or one block south on McKeown Avenue. There's plenty of street parking.

VISITOR INFORMATION

Patagonia Visitor Center/Patagon Bike Rental. The Patagonia Visitor Center shares cozy quarters with Patagon Bike Rental in this storefront on Patagonia's small main drag. Pick up free maps and information, and rent a mountain, road, or comfort bike to explore the region. Many of the old mining roads attract cyclists looking for a little challenge and great vistas. ⊠ *305 McKeown Ave.* ☎ *520/604–0258, 888/794–0060* ⊕ *www.patagoniaaz.com.*

EXPLORING

Nature Conservancy Patagonia–Sonoita Creek Preserve. At the Nature Conservancy Patagonia–Sonoita Creek Preserve, 1,350 acres of cottonwood-willow riparian habitat are protected along the Patagonia–Sonoita Creek watershed. More than 275 bird species have been sighted here, along with white-tailed deer, javelina, coatimundi (raccoonlike animals native to the region), desert tortoise, and snakes. There's a self-guided nature trail; guided walks are occasionally offered (call to inquire). Three concrete structures near an elevated berm of the Railroad Trail serve as reminders of the land's former use as a truck farm. To reach the preserve from Patagonia, make a right on 4th Avenue; at the stop sign, turn left onto Blue Haven Road. This paved road soon becomes dirt, and leads to the preserve in about 1.25 miles. The admission fee is good for seven days. ⊠ *Blue Haven Rd.* ☎ *520/394–2400* ⊕ *www.nature.org/patagonia* 🎫 *$5* ☉ *Apr.–Sept., Wed.–Sun. 6:30–4; Oct.–Mar., Wed.–Sun. 7:30–4.*

FAMILY **Patagonia Lake State Park.** Five miles south of town, Patagonia Lake State Park is the spot for water sports, birding, picnicking, and camping. Formed by the damming of Sonoita Creek, the 265-acre reservoir lures anglers with its largemouth bass, crappie, bluegill, and catfish; it's stocked with rainbow trout in the wintertime. You can rent rowboats, paddleboats, canoes, and fishing gear at the marina. Most swimmers head for Boulder Beach. The adjoining Sonoita Creek State Natural Area is home to giant cottonwoods, willows, sycamores, and mesquites; nesting black hawks; and endangered species. From mid-October to mid-April, rangers offer guided birding and discovery tours by pontoon boat ($5) on Saturday and Sunday at 9, 10:15, and 11:30 am (call to sign up); free guided bird walks are on Monday and Friday at 9 am. ⊠ *400 Lake Patagonia Rd.* ☎ *520/287–6965* ⊕ *www.azstateparks.com/ patagonia* 🎫 *$10 per vehicle weekdays; $15 weekends* ☉ *Park daily (gates closed 10 pm–4 am); visitor center mid-Oct.–mid-Apr., Wed.– Sun. 8–4:30.*

Bird-watchers flock to Ramsey Canyon Preserve for rare ecosystems where deserts meet mountains.

WHERE TO EAT

$ CAFÉ 🍴 **Gathering Grounds.** This colorful café and espresso bar, which also doubles as an art gallery featuring local artists, serves healthful breakfasts and imaginative soups, salads, and sandwiches through the late afternoon. Beverage choices include organic fair-trade coffees; ice cream, cakes, and cookies draw the local younger set. [$] *Average main: $7* ✉ *319 McKeown Ave.* ☎ *520/394–2009* 🕒 *No dinner.*

$ PIZZA 🍴 **Velvet Elvis Pizza Company.** There aren't too many places where you can enjoy a pizza heaped with organic veggies, a crisp salad of organic greens tossed with homemade dressing, freshly pressed juice (try the beet-, apple-, and lime-juice concoction), organic wine, and microbrewed or imported beer while surrounded by images of Elvis *and* the Virgin Mary. Owner Cecilia San Miguel uses a 1930s dough recipe for the restaurant's delightful whole wheat crust; daily specials such as Carne Adobada, tender roasted pork in a red chili sauce, and curried vegetable stew entice those who may seek a lower-carb alternative. [$] *Average main: $12* ✉ *292 Naugle Ave.* ☎ *520/394–2102* 🌐 *www.velvetelvispizza.com* 🕒 *Closed Mon.–Wed.*

$ AMERICAN 🍴 **Wagon Wheel Saloon.** The restaurant at the Wagon Wheel, serving basic ribs, steaks, and burgers, is a more recent development, but the cowboy bar, with its neon beer signs and mounted moose head, has been around since the early 1950s. This is where every Stetson-wearing ranch hand in the area comes to listen to the country jukebox and down a longneck, maybe accompanied by some jalapeño poppers. [$] *Average main: $9* ✉ *400 W. Naugle Ave.* ☎ *520/394–2433.*

WHERE TO STAY

For expanded hotel reviews, visit Fodors.com.

$$$$
RESORT
ALL-INCLUSIVE
FAMILY

Circle Z Ranch. Rimmed by giant sycamore, ash, and cottonwood trees and surrounded by the Patagonia–Sonoita Creek Preserve, this seasonal guest ranch served as a setting in the movie *Red River* and in several episodes of *Gunsmoke*. **Pros:** excellent dude ranch experience in a lush, rather than desert, setting; laid-back and friendly staff and guests. **Cons:** all-inclusive is pricey. $ *Rooms from: $400* ⊠ *AZ 82, 4 miles southwest of town* ☎ *520/394–2525, 888/854–2525* ⊕ *www.circlez.com* ⤳ *24 rooms* ☉ *Closed mid-May–Oct.* ⦿ *All-inclusive.*

$
B&B/INN

Duquesne House Bed & Breakfast/Gallery. Built as a miners' board-inghouse at the turn of the 20th century, this adobe home has rooms painted in pastel Southwest colors, lovingly and whimsically detailed by a local artist, and decorated with hand-stitched quilts and Mexican folk art. **Pros:** quiet location only a couple of blocks from town; cheerful, contemporary interior. **Cons:** few amenities. $ *Rooms from: $125* ⊠ *357 Duquesne Ave.* ☎ *520/394–2732* ⊕ *www.theduquesnehouse.com* ⤳ *4 suites* ⊟ *No credit cards* ⦿ *Breakfast.*

SHOPPING

Patagonia is quickly turning into a shopping destination in its own right. Unlike the trendy shops in nearby Tubac, the stores here have reasonable prices in addition to small-town charm.

Creative Spirit Artists Gallery. This gallery features a thoughtful selection of jewelry, paintings, photography, quilts, and pottery by more than 60 local artists. ⊠ *317 McKeown Ave.* ☎ *520/394–2100* ⊕ *www.azcreativespirit.com.*

Global Arts Gallery. Everything from local art and antiques to Native American jewelry, Middle Eastern rugs, and exotic musical instruments is showcased at Global Arts. ⊠ *315 McKeown Ave.* ☎ *520/394–0077* ⊕ *www.globalartsgallery.com.*

Fodor's Choice
★

High Spirits Flutes. You can peruse and purchase Odell Borg Native American flutes at their factory store. Not only beautiful, the flutes' five-note pentatonic scale makes them easy to learn to play. ⊠ *714 Red Rock Ave., off Harshaw Rd.* ☎ *800/394–1523* ⊕ *www.highspirits.com.*

Mesquite Grove Gallery. Regina Medley, a talented local painter, weaver, and jewelry maker, markets her lovely wares at Mesquite Grove Gallery, along with other regional artists' work. ⊠ *371 McKeown Ave.* ☎ *520/400–7230* ⊕ *www.reginamedley.com.*

SIERRA VISTA

42 miles east of Patagonia, 70 miles southeast of Tucson, 30 miles southeast of Sonoita, via AZ 82 to AZ 90.

A characterless military town on the outskirts of Fort Huachuca, Sierra Vista is nonetheless a good base from which to explore the more scenic areas that surround it—and at 4,620 feet above sea level the whole area has a year-round temperate climate. There are quite a few fast-food and chain restaurants for your basic dining needs, and more than 1,100 rooms in area hotels, motels, and B&Bs offer shelter for the night.

8

Fort Huachuca, headquarters of the army's Global Information Systems Command, is the last of the great Western forts still in operation. It dates back to 1877, when the Buffalo Soldiers (yes, Bob Marley fans—*those* Buffalo Soldiers), the first all-black regiment in the U.S. forces, came to aid settlers battling invaders from Mexico, Indian tribes reluctant to give up their homelands, and assorted American desperadoes on the lam from the law back East.

GETTING HERE AND AROUND

The most direct route to Sierra Vista from Interstate 10 is a straight shot south on AZ 90 (about 30 miles). If you're not going to Fort Huachuca, take a left on the Route 90 bypass to reach the shopping centers, most of the chain motels, and the intersection of AZ 92, which takes you to Ramsey Canyon and Coronado National Memorial. If you're going to the fort, stay on AZ 90 and the fort will be on your right. From here, Fry Boulevard will lead you through town to the AZ 92.

EXPLORING

FAMILY **Coronado National Memorial.** Those driving to Coronado National Memorial, dedicated to Francisco Vásquez de Coronado, will see many of the same stunning vistas of Arizona and Mexico the conquistador saw when he trod this route in 1540 seeking the mythical Seven Cities of Cibola. Hikers come here for both the excellent views and the opportunity to walk the 1-mile Yaqui Trail, the southernmost leg of the 800-mile Arizona Trail, that ends at the Mexico border. It's a little more than 3 miles via car or hike up a dirt road from the visitor center to Montezuma Pass Overlook, and another 0.5 mile on foot to the top of the nearly 7,000-foot Coronado Peak, where the views are best. Miller Peak Trail is a difficult but rewarding 12-mile round-trip to the highest point in the Huachuca Mountains (Miller Peak is 9,466 feet). Kids ages 5 to 12 can participate in the memorial's Junior Ranger program, explore Coronado Cave, and dress up in replica Spanish armor. The turnoff for the monument is 16 miles south of Sierra Vista on AZ 92; the visitor center is 5 miles farther. ⊠ *4101 E. Montezuma Canyon Rd., Hereford* ☎ *520/366–5515* ⊕ *www.nps.gov/coro* 🆓 *Free* ☉ *Visitor center daily 8–4.*

Fort Huachuca Museum. Three miles from the fort's main gate are the Fort Huachuca museums. The late-19th-century bachelor officers' quarters and the annex across the street provide a record of military life on the frontier. More often than not, you'll be sharing space with new cadets learning about the history of this far-flung outpost. Motion sensors activate odd little sound bites in the multimedia experience. Another half block south, the **U.S. Army Intelligence Museum** focuses on American intelligence operations from the Apache Scouts through Desert Storm. Code machines, codebooks, decoding devices, and other intelligence-gathering equipment are on display. Enter the main gate of Fort Huachuca on AZ 90, west of Sierra Vista. You need a driver's license or other photo identification to get on base. ⊠ *Grierson Ave. and Boyd St., off AZ 90, west of Sierra Vista, Fort Huachuca* ☎ *520/533–3638* ⊕ *www.huachucamuseum.com* 🆓 *Free* ☉ *Mon.–Sat. 9–4* ☉ *Closed Sun.*

Fodor's Choice **Ramsey Canyon Preserve.** Managed by the Nature Conservancy, Ramsey Canyon Preserve marks the convergence of two mountain and desert systems: this spot is the northernmost limit of the Sierra Madre and the southernmost limit of the Rockies, and it's at the edge of the Chihuahuan and Sonoran deserts. Visitors to this world-famous bird-watching hot spot train their binoculars skyward hoping to catch a glimpse of some of the preserve's most notable inhabitants. Painted redstarts nest, and 14 magnificent species of hummingbirds congregate here from spring through autumn—the jewels of this pristine habitat. Even for nonbirders, the beauty of the canyon makes this a destination in its own right. The rare stream-fed, sycamore-maple riparian corridor provides a lush contrast to the desert highlands at the base of the mountains. Guided hikes begin at 9 am Monday, Thursday, and Saturday from March through October. Stop at the visitor center for maps and books on the area's natural history, flora, and fauna. To get here, take AZ 92 south from Sierra Vista for 6 miles, turn right on Ramsey Canyon Road, and then go 4 miles to the preserve entrance. Admission is good for seven days. ✉ *27 Ramsey Canyon Rd., Hereford* ☎ *520/378–2785* ⊕ *www.nature.org* ✉ *$5* ⊗ *Daily 8–5.*

> **WORD OF MOUTH**
>
> "Ramsey Canyon is a nature preserve administered by the Nature Conservancy and is loaded with wildlife…especially hummingbirds…you're gonna love it there!!"   —peterboy

OFF THE BEATEN PATH   **San Pedro Riparian National Conservation Area.** The San Pedro River, partially rerouted underground by an 1887 earthquake, may not look like much, but it sustains an impressive array of flora and fauna. To maintain this fragile creek-side ecosystem, 56,000 acres along the river were designated a protected riparian area in 1988. More than 350 species of birds come here, as well as 82 mammal species and 45 reptiles and amphibians. Forty thousand years ago this was the domain of woolly mammoths and mastodons: many of the huge skeletons in Washington's Smithsonian Institute and New York's Museum of Natural History came from the massive fossil pits in the area. As evidenced by a number of small, unexcavated ruins, the migratory Indian tribes who passed through thousands of years later also found this valley hospitable, in part because of its many useful plants. Information, guided tours, books, and gifts are available from the volunteer staff at San Pedro House, a visitor center operated by Friends of the San Pedro River (⊕ *www.sanpedroriver.org*). ✉ *San Pedro House, 9800 AZ 90* ☎ *520/508–4445, 520/439–6400 Sierra Vista BLM Office* ⊕ *www. az.blm.gov* ✉ *Free* ⊗ *Visitor center daily 9:30–4:30, conservation area daily sunrise–sunset.*

WHERE TO EAT AND STAY
For expanded hotel reviews, visit Fodors.com.

$$ **✕ The Mesquite Tree.** Ask a local for the best restaurant in town, and
STEAKHOUSE   you'll probably be directed to a chain restaurant near the shopping mall (folks tend to be literal in these parts); but if you're willing to drive a few miles south toward Ramsey Canyon, most agree that The Mesquite Tree towers above them all. This unassuming steak house turns

8

out fish and chicken classics, like Trout Piccata and Chicken Florentine, just as consistently as their tasty rib eyes and T-bones. Generous entrées include a salad and choice of potato, rice, or veggies. [$] *Average main: $20* ✉ *6398 S. AZ 92, Hereford* ☎ *520/378–2758* 🌐 *www.mesquitetreesierravista.com* ⏲ *Closed Mon. No lunch.*

$$ B&B/INN Fodor's Choice ★ 🏨 **Casa de San Pedro.** Bird-watchers are drawn to this contemporary hacienda-style B&B abutting the San Pedro Riparian National Conservation Area. **Pros:** gracious hosts; tranquil setting; midway between Bisbee and Sierra Vista. **Cons:** some may feel too isolated. [$] *Rooms from: $169* ✉ *8933 S. Yell Lane, Hereford* ☎ *520/366–1300, 888/257–2050* 🌐 *www.bedandbirds.com* 🛏 *10 rooms* 🍴 *Breakfast.*

$$ B&B/INN 🏨 **Ramsey Canyon Inn Bed & Breakfast.** The Ramsey Canyon Preserve is an internationally renowned bird haven, and the nearby Ramsey Canyon Inn is a bird-watcher's delight. **Pros:** perfect base for birding and hiking; comfortable rooms. **Cons:** a little dull for nonbirders. [$] *Rooms from: $150* ✉ *29 Ramsey Canyon Rd., Hereford* ☎ *520/378–3010* 🌐 *www.ramseycanyoninn.com* 🛏 *6 rooms, 2 suites* 🍴 *Breakfast.*

$ HOTEL 🏨 **Windemere Hotel & Conference Center.** This updated hotel complex, across from the area's shopping mall, is on AZ 92 in what used to be the eastern outskirts of Sierra Vista but is now a rapidly growing commercial corridor. **Pros:** pleasant common areas and pool complex; free hot breakfast and evening cocktails. **Cons:** generic feel compared to other lodging options. [$] *Rooms from: $88* ✉ *2047 S. AZ 92* ☎ *520/459–5900, 800/825–4656* 🌐 *www.windemerehotel.com* 🛏 *149 rooms, 3 suites* 🍴 *Breakfast.*

CHIRICAHUA NATIONAL MONUMENT

65 miles northeast of Sierra Vista on AZ 90 to Interstate 10 to AZ 186; 58 miles northeast of Douglas on U.S. 191 to AZ 181; 36 miles southeast of Willcox.

GETTING HERE AND AROUND

Though more remote than other sights in southeastern Arizona, Chiricahua National Monument is well worth the two-hour drive from Tucson. You'll be rewarded with unique, stunning scenery and unspoiled wilderness for birding and hiking. The nearest gas stations are in Willcox or Sunizona, so be sure to fill your tank first.

EXPLORING

FAMILY Fodor's Choice ★ **Chiricahua National Monument.** Vast fields of desert grass are suddenly transformed into a landscape of forest, mountains, and striking rock formations as you enter the 12,000-acre Chiricahua National Monument. The Chiricahua Apache—who lived in the mountains for centuries and, led by Cochise and Geronimo, tried for 25 years to prevent white pioneers from settling here—dubbed it the Land of the Standing-Up Rocks. Enormous outcroppings of volcanic rock have been worn by erosion and fractured by uplift into strange pinnacles and spires. Because of the particular balance of sunshine and rain in the area, in April and May visitors will see brown, yellow, and red leaves coexisting with new green foliage. Summer in Chiricahua National Monument is exceptionally wet: from July through September there are

CLOSE UP

Geronimo: No Bullet Shall Pass

The fearless Apache war shaman Geronimo, known among his people as "one who yawns," fought to the very last in the Apache Wars. His surrender to General Nelson Miles on September 5, 1886, marked the end of the Indian Wars in the West. Geronimo's fleetness in evading the massed troops of the U.S. Army and his legendary immunity to bullets made him the darling of sensationalistic journalists, and he was the most famous outlaw in America.

When the combined forces of the U.S. Army and Mexican troops failed to rout the powerful shaman from his territory straddling Arizona and Mexico, General Miles sent his officer Lieutenant Gatewood and relatives of Geronimo's renegade band of warriors to persuade Geronimo to parley with Miles near the mouth of Skeleton Canyon, at the edge of the Peloncillo Mountains. After several days of talks, Geronimo and his warriors agreed to the presented treaty and surrendered their arms.

Geronimo related the scene years later: "We stood between his troopers and my warriors. We placed a large stone on the blanket before us. Our treaty was made by this stone, as it was to last until the stone should crumble to dust; so we made the treaty, and bound each other with an oath." However, the political promises quickly unraveled, and the most feared of Apache medicine men spent the next 23 years in exile as a prisoner of war. He died on February 17, 1909, never having returned to his beloved homeland, and was buried in the Apache cemetery in Fort Sill, Oklahoma.

In 1934 a stone monument was built on State Route 80 in Apache, Arizona, as a reminder of Geronimo's surrender in 1886. The 16-foot-tall monument lies 10 miles northwest of the actual surrender site in Skeleton Canyon, where an unobtrusive sign and a pile of rocks mark the place where the last stone was cast.

8

thunderstorms nearly every afternoon. Few other areas in the United States have such varied plant, bird, and animal life. Deer, coatimundi, peccaries, and lizards live among the aspen, ponderosa pine, Douglas fir, oak, and cypress trees—to name just a few.

Chiricahua National Monument is an excellent area for bird-watchers, and hikers have more than 17 miles of scenic trails. The admission fee is good for seven days. Hiking trail maps are available at the visitor center. The most popular and rewarding hike is the moderately easy **Echo Canyon Loop Trail**. This 3.4-mile path winds through cavelike grottos, brilliant rock formations, and a wooded canyon. Birds and other wildlife are abundant here. ✉ *AZ 181, 36 miles southeast of Willcox* ☎ *520/824–3560* ⊕ *www.nps.gov/chir* ✉ *$5* ☉ *Visitor center daily 8–4:30.*

Keeling Schaefer Vineyards. The picturesque Keeling Schaefer Vineyards, 12 miles south of Chiricahua National Monument, is garnering attention from wine mavens especially for its fruity Grenaches and Three Sisters Syrah. Vines from the Napa Valley region of California were planted on this beautiful property set among sycamores and rolling hills. Tours and tastings here are available by appointment only; their tasting room in downtown Willcox is open Thursday through Sunday, 11–5. ✉ *10277 E. Rock Creek Lane, Pearce* ☎ *520/824–2500* 🌐 *www.keelingschaefervineyards.com.*

WHERE TO STAY

Lodging is a bit of a challenge in this remote area. For those preferring to sleep indoors, the closest accommodations are about a half-hour drive, either north to one of several modern chain hotels in Willcox or to a B&B or guest ranch south of the monument. Within the monument there are 22 first-come, first-served campsites at Bonita Canyon Campground ($12). Some of the most beautiful and untouched camping areas in Arizona are nearby, in the Chiricahua Mountains. Backcountry campsites at Sunny Flat ($10) in the Cave Creek area, part of the Coronado National Forest (☎ *520/364–3468* 🌐 *www.fs.usda.gov/coronado*), have toilets and water.

For expanded hotel reviews, visit Fodors.com.

$ B&B/INN 🏨 **Dreamcatcher Bed and Breakfast.** All four rooms of this U-shape hacienda have large walk-in showers, ceiling fans, and private entrances that open onto a flower-filled courtyard. **Pros:** excellent value; tranquil; convenient to Chiricahuas. **Cons:** isolated location. [$] *Rooms from: $90* ✉ *13097 S. Hwy. 181, Pearce* ☎ *520/824–3127* 🌐 *www.dreamcatcherbnb.com* 🛏 *3 rooms, 1 suite* 💳 *No credit cards* 🍴 *Breakfast.*

$ HOTEL 🏨 **Portal Peak Lodge.** This barracks-style structure on the eastern side of Chiricahua National Monument near the New Mexico border is notable less for its rooms (clean and pleasant but nondescript) than for its winged visitors: the elegant trogon, 14 types of hummingbird, and 10 species of owl are among the 330 varieties of birds that flock to nearby Cave Creek canyon. **Pros:** inexpensive; decks outside each room; on-site restaurant and store. **Cons:** very isolated setting. [$] *Rooms from: $85* ✉ *1215 Main St., Portal* ☎ *520/558–2223* 🌐 *www.portalpeaklodge.com* 🛏 *16 rooms* 🍴 *No meals.*

$$$ B&B/INN 🏨 **Sunglow Guest Ranch.** Named after the ghost town of Sunglow, this lodge consists of eleven casitas—some with connecting rooms to be configured for families—decked out in Southwestern style with fireplaces. **Pros:** very isolated (a great escape); many on-site activities (even massages). **Cons:** very isolated (it's a 30-minute drive to hike in the Chiricahuas). [$] *Rooms from: $299* ✉ *14066 S. Sunglow Rd., Pearce* ☎ *520/824–3334, 866/786–4569* 🌐 *www.sunglowranch.com* 🛏 *11 casitas* 🍴 *Some meals.*

FORT BOWIE NATIONAL HISTORICAL SITE

8 miles northwest of Chiricahua National Monument.

GETTING HERE AND AROUND

From Chiricahua National Monument, take AZ 186 west (about a 30-minute drive); 5 miles north of the junction with AZ 181, signs direct you to an unpaved road leading to the fort. Upon entering the site, you'll drive down a winding gravel road to the parking area, where

Remote Chiricahua National Monument is filled with dramatic "upside-down" or "standing-up" volcanic rock formations.

a moderately challenging walking trail leads 1½ miles to the visitor center and ruins.

EXPLORING

Fort Bowie National Historical Site. It's a bit of an outing to get to the site of Arizona's last battle between Native Americans and U.S. troops in the Dos Cabezas (Two-Headed) Mountains, but history buffs will find it an interesting hike with the added benefit of high-desert scenic beauty. Once a focal point for military operations—the fort was built here because Apache Pass was an important travel route for Native Americans and wagon trains—it now serves as a reminder of the brutal clashes between the two cultures. The fort itself is virtually in ruins, but there's a small ranger-staffed visitor center with historical displays, restrooms, and books for sale.

Points of interest along the 1.5-mile trail leading to the visitor center and ruins, indicated by historic markers, include the remnants of an Apache wickiup (hut), the fort cemetery, Apache Springs (their water source), and the **Butterfield stage stop,** a crucial link in the journey from east to west in the mid-19th century that happened to be in the heart of Chiricahua Apache land. Chief Cochise and the stagecoach operators ignored one another until sometime in 1861, when hostilities broke out between U.S. Cavalry troops and the Apache. After an ambush by the chief's warriors at Apache Pass in 1862, U.S. troops decided a fort was needed in the area, and Fort Bowie was built within weeks. There were skirmishes for the next 10 years, followed by a peaceful decade. Renewed fighting broke out in 1881. Geronimo, the new leader of the Indian warriors, finally surrendered in 1886 and was detained here.

The trail is moderately easy, with little elevation gain but rocky in some areas. ⊠ *3327 S. Old Fort Bowie Rd., Apache Pass Rd., 26 miles southeast of Willcox, Bowie* ☎ *520/847–2500* ⊕ *www.nps.gov/fobo* 🎫 *Free* ⊙ *Daily 8–4:30.*

WILLCOX

26 miles northwest of Fort Bowie National Historical Site on AZ 186.

The small town of Willcox, in the heart of Arizona ranching country, began in the late 1870s as a railroad construction camp called Maley. When the Southern Pacific Railroad line arrived in 1880, the town was renamed in honor of the highly regarded Fort Bowie commander, General Orlando B. Willcox. Once a major shipping center for cattle ranchers and mining companies, the town has preserved its rustic charm; the downtown area looks like an Old West movie set. An elevation of 4,167 feet means moderate summers and chilly winters, ideal for growing apples, and apple pie fans from as far away as Phoenix make pilgrimages to sample the harvest. The climate also seems favorable for growing grapes, and Willcox has sprouted a few vineyards and tasting rooms in the last couple of years.

GETTING HERE AND AROUND

The small, historic downtown area of Willcox is just a few blocks north of Interstate 10 from Exit 340. Take Rex Allen Drive, turn right on Haskell Avenue, then left on Maley Street and left onto Railroad Avenue for an authentic glimpse of southern Arizona circa 1912, including mercantile stores, banks, and the railroad depot. Museums, wine-tasting rooms, and a few restaurants are also here.

ESSENTIALS

Visitor Information Willcox Chamber of Commerce & Agriculture ⊠ *1500 N. Circle I Rd.* ☎ *520/384–2272, 800/200–2272* ⊕ *www.willcoxchamber.com.* **Willcox Wineries** ⊕ *www.willcoxwines.com.*

EXPLORING

TOP ATTRACTIONS

Apple Annie's Orchards. Pick your own apples just outside town at Apple Annie's Orchards from August to October. Peaches are ready July through September; veggies ripen mid-summer through fall. Or stop at their in-town country store, next to the Willcox Chamber of Commerce, for delicious homemade pies, fudge, and fruit butters. ⊠ *2081 W. Hardy Rd.* ☎ *520/384–2084* ⊕ *www.appleannies.com.*

Chiricahua Regional Museum and Research Center. Learn about the fierce Chiricahua Apaches and the fearless leaders Cochise and Geronimo at this research center, located in downtown Willcox. Other interesting tidbits about the area can be found in displays featuring the U.S. Cavalry, a nice collection of rocks and minerals, and relics of the famed Butterfield Overland Stage Route. One oddity the museum points out is that the memoirs of Civil War general Orlando Willcox, for whom the town was named, don't even mention a visit to Arizona. ⊠ *127 E. Maley St.* ☎ *520/384–3971* 🎫 *$2* ⊙ *Mon.–Sat. 10–4.*

Muleshoe Ranch Cooperative Management Area. Outside Willcox is the headquarters for the Muleshoe Ranch Cooperative Management Area, nearly 50,000 acres of riparian desert land in the foothills of the Galiuro Mountains that are jointly owned and managed by the Nature Conservancy, the U.S. Forest Service, and the U.S. Bureau of Land Management. It's a 30-mile drive on a dirt road to the ranch—it takes about an hour—but the scenery, wildlife, and hiking are worth the bumps.

The varied terrain of mesquite bosks, desert grasslands, and rocky canyons is home to a diverse array of wildlife, including desert tortoise, javelina, mule deer, hognose skunk, Montezuma quail, and great horned owl. You might also catch a glimpse of roaming bands of coatimundi—unusual looking omnivores resembling land-bound monkeys. Backcountry mountain-biking trips can be arranged by the ranch, and overnight accommodations are available. Hiking is self-guided, and Nature Conservancy staff can suggest trails to suit your interests.

To reach the ranch, take Exit 340 off Interstate 10 and head south on Rex Allen Drive. Turn right on Bisbee Avenue, continue to Airport Road, turn right again, and after 15 miles take the right fork at a junction just past a group of mailboxes and continue to the end of the road. ⊠ *6502 N. Muleshoe Ranch Rd.* ☎ *520/212–4295* ⊕ *www.nature.org* ⊙ *June–Aug., weekends 9–4; Sept.–May, Thurs.–Mon. 9–4.*

FAMILY **Rex Allen Arizona Cowboy Museum.** The Rex Allen Arizona Cowboy Museum, in Willcox's historic district, is a tribute to Willcox's most famous native son, cowboy singer Rex Allen. He starred in several rather average cowboy movies during the 1940s and '50s for Republic Pictures, but he's probably most famous as the friendly voice that narrated Walt Disney nature films of the 1960s. Check out the glittery suits the star wore on tour—they'd do Liberace proud. A special family rate is $5. ⊠ *150 N. Railroad Ave.* ☎ *520/384–4583* ⊕ *www.rexallenmuseum. org* ⊡ *$2* ⊙ *Mon.–Sat. 10–4* ⊙ *Sun. by appointment only.*

WORTH NOTING

Willcox Commercial Store. Established in 1881, the Willcox Commercial Store, near the Rex Allen Cowboy Museum, is the oldest retail establishment in Arizona. Locals like to say that Geronimo used to shop here. Today it's a clothing and general store, with a large selection of Western wear. ⊠ *180 N. Railroad Ave.* ☎ *520/384–2448.*

Willcox Playa. If you visit in winter, you can see some of the more than 10,000 sandhill cranes that roost at the Willcox Playa, a 37,000-acre area resembling a dry lake bed 10 miles south of Willcox. They migrate in late fall and head north to nesting sites in February, and bird-watchers migrate to Willcox the third week in January for the annual Wings over Willcox bird-watching event held in their honor. ⊠ *Kansas Settlement Rd., 3 miles south of AZ 186, Cochise.*

WHERE TO EAT AND STAY
For expanded hotel reviews, visit Fodors.com.

$ ✕ **Salsa Fiesta Mexican Restaurant.** You can't miss the bright neon lights of
MEXICAN this little restaurant, just south of Interstate 10 at Exit 340 in Willcox. The interior is cheerful and clean, with tables, chairs, and walls painted in a spicy medley of hot pink, purple, turquoise, green, and orange. The

8

menu consists of Mexican standards, and the salsa bar runs the gamut from mild to superhot. There is a modest selection of domestic and Mexican beers, and takeout is available. $ *Average main: $8* ✉ *1201 W. Rex Allen Dr.* ☎ *520/384–4233* ⏲ *Closed Tues.*

$$ RENTAL 🏨 **Muleshoe Ranch.** This turn-of-the-20th-century ranch, run by the Arizona chapter of the Nature Conservancy, has five comfortable casitas with kitchens and modern plumbing, set in the pristine grassland foothills of the Galiuro Mountains. **Pros:** good hiking, birding and stargazing in unspoiled setting; hot springs. **Cons:** no services nearby—closest town is Willcox (30 miles away). $ *Rooms from: $180* ✉ *6502 N. Muleshoe Rd.* ☎ *520/212–4295* 🌐 *www.nature.org* 🛏 *5 units* ⏲ *Closed June–Aug.* 🍴 *No meals.*

TEXAS CANYON

Fodor's Choice ★ *16 miles southwest of Willcox off Interstate 10.*

A dramatic change of scenery along Interstate 10 will signal that you're entering Texas Canyon. The rock formations here are exceptional—huge boulders appear to be delicately balanced against each other.

GETTING HERE AND AROUND

Get off Interstate 10 at Exit 318, and then turn right onto Dragoon Road. The Amerind Foundation is a mile down on the left, and Triangle T Guest Ranch, with lodging and a restaurant, is next door.

EXPLORING

The Amerind Foundation. Texas Canyon is the home of the Amerind Foundation (a contraction of "American" and "Indian"), founded by amateur archaeologist William Fulton in 1937 to foster understanding about Native American cultures. The research facility and museum are housed in a Spanish colonial–style structure designed by noted Tucson architect H.M. Starkweather. The museum's rotating displays of archaeological materials, crafts, and photographs give an overview of Native American cultures of the Southwest and Mexico.

The adjacent Fulton–Hayden Memorial Art Gallery displays an assortment of art collected by William Fulton. Permanent exhibits include the work of Tohono O'odham women potters, an exquisite collection of Hopi kachina dolls, prized paintings by acclaimed Hopi artists, Pueblo pottery ranging from prehistoric pieces to modern ceramics, and archaeological exhibits on the Indian cultures of the prehistoric Southwest. The museum's gift shop has a superlative selection of Native American art, crafts, and jewelry. ✉ *2100 N. Amerind Rd., 1 mile southeast of I–10, Exit 318, Dragoon* ☎ *520/586–3666* 🌐 *www.amerind.org* 🎟 *$8* ⏲ *Tues.–Sun. 10–4.*

WHERE TO STAY

For expanded hotel reviews, visit Fodors.com.

$$ B&B/INN 🏨 **Cochise Stronghold Bed & Breakfast.** Nestled in the Dragoon Mountains and bordered on three sides by national forest land, Cochise Stronghold Bed & Breakfast beckons nature lovers and anyone seeking solitude in a beautiful setting. **Pros:** great breakfast; peace and quiet. **Cons:** remote

location. $ *Rooms from: $179* ✉ *Pearce* ☎ *520/826–4141* ⊕ *www. cochisestrongholdbb.com* ⇗ *3 units* ⧌ *Breakfast.*

$$
B&B/INN

⌂ **Triangle T Guest Ranch.** Enjoy the romance of the Old West at this historic ranch situated on 160 acres of prime real estate in Texas Canyon. **Pros:** horseback riding (extra fee) and hiking trails; good base for exploring the region. **Cons:** expensive for this area; isolated. $ *Rooms from: $159* ✉ *4190 Dragoon Rd., at Exit 318 off I–10, Dragoon* ☎ *520/586–7533* ⊕ *www.triangletguestranch.com* ⇗ *11 casitas* ⧌ *Breakfast.*

BENSON

12 miles west of Texas Canyon, 50 miles southeast of Tucson via Interstate 10.

Back in its historic heyday as a Butterfield stagecoach station, and later as the hub of the Southern Pacific Railroad, Benson was just a place to stop on the way to somewhere else. Not much has changed, except that a few more visitors come through for a meal or to fill their gas tanks, following the 1974 discovery of a pristine cave beneath the Whetstone Mountains west of Benson, culminating 25 years later with the opening of Kartchner Caverns State Park, one of the most remarkable living cave systems in the world.

GETTING HERE AND AROUND

Amtrak runs trains from Tucson to the Benson depot three times a week. The Benson Visitor Center is inside the train depot on 4th Street, the main drag through this sleepy town. Benson Taxi offers transport services in the Benson area, as well as to Tombstone, Bisbee, and Kartchner Caverns, which lies a few miles west.

ESSENTIALS

Transportation Contacts Benson Taxi ☎ *520/586–1294.* **Benson train station** ✉ *4th St. at San Pedro Ave.*

EXPLORING

The San Pedro Valley Arts and Historical Museum. Though the city is undergoing some modern development, you can see the story of Benson's past at this free museum open Tuesday through Saturday (but closed in August). Exhibits include a re-creation of an old-fashioned grocery store, a horse-drawn schoolbus, quilts, and railroad paraphernalia. ✉ *180 S. San Pedro Ave., at E. 5th St.* ☎ *520/586–3070* ⊕ *www. bensonmuseum.com* ▣ *Free* ☉ *Tues.–Fri. 10–4, Sat. 10–2* ☉ *Closed Aug.*

Singing Wind Bookshop. As you pass Benson on Interstate 10, watch for Ocotillo Avenue, Exit 304. Take a left and drive about 2.25 miles, where a mailbox with a backward "SW" signals that you've come to the turnoff for Singing Wind Bookshop. Make a right at the mailbox onto Singing Wind Road and drive 0.5 mile to the shop. You might meet Winifred Bundy, who also runs the ranch. She knows just about every regional author around, so this unique bookshop-on-a-ranch has signed copies of books on almost any Southwestern topic. This chatty bibliophile also frequently shares her love of the area with visitors, throwing

8

in choice tidbits about obscure sights and her literary friends' favorite haunts. She doesn't take credit cards, though. ✉ *700 W. Singing Wind Rd.* ☎ *520/586–2425* ⏲ *Daily 9–5.*

WHERE TO EAT AND STAY

For expanded hotel reviews, visit Fodors.com.

$ AMERICAN 🍴 **Reb's Café.** For a more traditional take on Southwestern food—none of that newfangled nouvelle stuff—this unpretentious diner is of the cowboy variety. It serves Mexican food and a little Italian, but it really prides itself on steaks and hamburgers, and a darned good breakfast (served all day). [$] *Average main: $7* ✉ *1020 W. 4th St.* ☎ *520/586–3856.*

$ HOTEL 🏨 **Comfort Inn Benson.** The closest lodging to Kartchner Caverns State Park, this modern motel sits just off Interstate 10 at the "Kartchner Corridor," a few miles west of Benson. **Pros:** clean; friendly; convenient location. **Cons:** just off the highway; not particularly serene or scenic. [$] *Rooms from: $89* ✉ *630 S. Village Loop* ☎ *520/586–8800* 🌐 *www.choicehotels.com* 🛏 *62 rooms* 🍽 *Breakfast.*

KARTCHNER CAVERNS STATE PARK

9 miles south of Benson on AZ 90.

GETTING HERE AND AROUND

Amateur cavers discovered Kartchner Caverns in 1974. From Exit 302 off Interstate 10, take AZ 90 for 9 miles.

EXPLORING

FAMILY Fodor's Choice ★ **Kartchner Caverns.** The publicity that surrounded the official opening of Kartchner Caverns in November 1999 was in marked contrast to the secrecy that shrouded their discovery 25 years earlier and concealed their existence for 14 years. The two young spelunkers, Gary Tenen and Randy Tufts, who stumbled into what is now considered one of the most spectacular cave systems anywhere, played a fundamental role in its protection and eventual development. Great precautions have been taken to protect the wet-cave system—which comprises 13,000 feet of passages and two chambers as long as football fields—from damage by light and dryness.

The Discovery Center introduces visitors to the cave and its formations, and hour-long guided tours take small groups into the upper cave. Spectacular formations include the longest soda straw stalactite in the United States at 21 feet and 2 inches. The Big Room is viewed on a separate tour: it holds the world's most extensive formation of brushite moonmilk, the first reported occurrence of turnip shields, and the first noted occurrence of birdsnest needle formations. Other funky and fabulous formations include brilliant red flowstone, rippling multihued stalactites, delicate white helictites, translucent orange bacon, and expansive mud flats. It's also the nursery roost for female cave myotis bats from April through September, during which time the lower cave is closed in an effort to foster the cave's unique ecosystem. Kartchner Caverns is a wet, "live" cave, meaning that water still rises up from the surface to increase the multicolor calcium carbonate formations already visible.

DID YOU KNOW?

Abandoned mining gear, like this ore loading chute, is all that remains of some of southern Arizona's former boomtowns. Copper, silver, and gold have all attracted miners at different times.

The total cavern size is 2.4 miles long, but the explored areas cover only 1,600 feet by 1,100 feet. The average relative humidity inside is 99%, so visitors are often graced with "cave kisses," water droplets from above. Because the climate outside the caves is so dry, it is estimated that if air got inside, it could deplete the moisture in only a few days, halting the growth of

the speleothems that decorate its walls. To prevent this, there are 22 environmental monitoring stations that measure air and soil temperature, relative humidity, evaporation rates, air trace gases, and airflow inside the caverns. ■TIP➔ Tour reservations are required, and should be made well in advance. If you're here and didn't make a reservation, you may be in luck: sometimes same-day reservations are available (call or arrive early for these). Hiking trails, picnic areas, and campsites ($25 with hook-ups) are available on the park's 550 acres; and the Bat Cave Café, open daily, serves pizza, hot dogs, salads, and sandwiches. ⊠ *AZ 90, 9 miles south of Exit 302 off I–10* ☎ *520/586–4100 information, 520/586–2283 tour reservations* ⊕ *www.azstateparks. com* ☒ *Rotunda/Throne Room tour or Big Room tour $22.95; Park admission $6 per vehicle up to 4 people, $2 each additional person (fees waived for cave tour ticket holders)* ☉ *Daily 7:30–6; cave tours, by reservation, daily 8–4.*

SOUTHWEST ARIZONA

The turbulent history of the West is writ large in this now-sleepy part of Arizona. It's home to the Tohono O'odham Indian Reservation (the largest in the country after the Navajo Nation's) and towns such as Ajo, created—and almost undone—by the copper-mining industry, and Nogales, along the U.S.–Mexico border. Yuma, abutting the California border, was a major crossing point of the Colorado River as far back as the time of the conquistadors.

These days people mostly travel *through* Sells, Ajo, and Yuma en route to the closest beaches. During the school year, especially on warm weekends and semester breaks, the 130-mile route from Tucson to Ajo is busy with traffic headed southwest to Puerto Penasco (Rocky Point), Mexico, the closest access to the sea for Arizonans. All summer long, Interstate 8 takes heat-weary Tucsonans and Phoenicians to San Diego, California, and Yuma is the midpoint.

Natural attractions are a lure in this starkly scenic region: Organ Pipe Cactus National Monument provides trails for desert hikers and birders, and Buenos Aires and Imperial wildlife refuges—homes to many unusual species—are important destinations for birders and other nature-watchers. Much of the time, however, your only companions will be the low-lying scrub and cactus, and the mesquite, ironwood, and palo verde trees.

BUENOS AIRES NATIONAL WILDLIFE REFUGE

66 miles southwest of Tucson.

GETTING HERE AND AROUND

From Tucson, take AZ 86 west 22 miles to AZ 286; go south 40 miles to Milepost 8, and it's another 3 miles east to the preserve headquarters.

EXPLORING

Buenos Aires National Wildlife Refuge. Remote Buenos Aires National Wildlife Refuge, in the Altar Valley and encircled by seven mountain ranges, is the only place in the United States where the Sonoran–savanna grasslands that once spread over the entire region can still be seen. The fragile ecosystem was almost completely destroyed by overgrazing, and a program to restore native grasses is currently in progress. In 1985 the U.S. Fish and Wildlife Service purchased the Buenos Aires Ranch—now headquarters for the 115,000-acre preserve—to establish a reintroduction program for the endangered masked bobwhite quail.

Bird-watchers consider Buenos Aires unique because it's the only place in the United States where they can see a "grand slam" (four species) of quail: Montezuma quail, Gambel's quail, scaled quail, and masked bobwhite. If it rains, the 100-acre Aguirre Lake, 1.5 miles north of the headquarters, attracts wading birds, shorebirds, and waterfowl—in all,

BORDER TOWN SAFETY: NOGALES, MEXICO

Nogales used to draw tourists and locals, who would park on the American side and walk across the border. Though shopping bargains and cheap bars are enticing, safety issues have changed in recent years.

⚠ **Drug-related violence in Mexico—especially near the U.S. border—has increased to the point that the U.S. government strongly discourages travel in and around Mexico border towns. Check 🌐 www.state.gov/travel for updates and details.**

If you must cross, bring your passport, remain alert, and stay in the central area on Avenida Obregón, which begins a few blocks west of the border entrance and runs north–south.

more than 320 avian species have been spotted there. They share the turf with deer, coati, badgers, bobcats, and mountain lions. Touring options include a 10-mile auto tour through the area; nature trails; a 3.8-mile guided hike in Brown Canyon (offered 2nd and 4th Saturdays–call to sign up); a boardwalk through the marshes at Arivaca Cienega; and guided bird walks, also at Arivaca Cienega, on Saturdays at 8 am November through April. ✉ *AZ 286, at milepost 7.5, Sasabe* ☎ *520/823–4251* 🌐 *www.fws.gov/refuges* 🎟 *Free* 🕒 *Visitor center daily 7:30–4 Sept.–May and weekdays 7:30–4 June–Aug.; closed weekends June-Aug. Refuge open 24 hrs.*

WHERE TO STAY

For expanded hotel reviews, visit Fodors.com.

$$$$ B&B/INN 🏨 **Rancho de la Osa.** This tranquil ranch, set on 250 eucalyptus-shaded acres near the Mexican border and Buenos Aires preserve, was built in 1889, and two adobe structures were added in the 1920s to accommodate guests. **Pros:** good riding; good food and extensive wine list; pretty setting. **Cons:** pricey; somewhat isolated for those interested in touring the region. [$] *Rooms from: $480* ✉ *AZ 286, Sasabe* ☎ *520/823–4257, 800/872–6240* 🌐 *www.ranchodelaosa.com* 🛏 *19 rooms* 🍴 *All meals.*

KITT PEAK NATIONAL OBSERVATORY

70 miles northwest of Buenos Aires National Wildlife Refuge on AZ 286 to AZ 86; 56 miles southwest of Tucson.

GETTING HERE AND AROUND

To reach Kitt Peak from Tucson, take Interstate 10 to Interstate 19 south, and then AZ 86. After 44 miles on AZ 86, turn left at the AZ 386 junction and follow the winding mountain road 12 miles up to the observatory. In inclement weather, contact the highway department to confirm that the road is open. To get to Sells (for the nearest food and gas), from the base of the mountain, it's 20 miles west on AZ 86.

EXPLORING

Kitt Peak National Observatory. Funded by the National Science Foundation and managed by a group of more than 20 universities, Kitt Peak National Observatory is part of the Tohono O'odham Reservation. After much discussion back in the late 1950s, tribal leaders agreed to share a small section of their 4,400 square miles with the observatory's telescopes. Among these is the McMath-Pierce, the world's largest solar telescope, which uses piped-in liquid coolant. From the visitors' gallery you can see into the telescope's light-path tunnel, which goes down hundreds of feet into the mountain. Kitt Peak scientists use these high-power telescopes to conduct vital solar research and observe distant galaxies.

The visitor center has exhibits on astronomy, information about the telescopes, and hour-long guided tours ($9.75 per person) that depart daily at 10, 11:30, and 1:30. Complimentary brochures enable you to take self-guided tours of the grounds, and there's a picnic area about 1.5 miles below the observatory. The observatory sells snacks and drinks, but there are no restaurants or gas stations within 20 miles of Kitt Peak. The observatory offers a nightly observing program ($49 per person); reservations are necessary. ⌧ *AZ 386, Pan Tak* ☎ *520/318–8726* ⊕ *www.noao.edu* ⌧ *Free* ☉ *Visitor center daily 9–4.*

SELLS

32 miles southwest of Kitt Peak via AZ 386 to AZ 86.

The Tohono O'odham Reservation, the second largest in the United States, covers 4,400 square miles between Tucson and Ajo, stretching south to the Mexican border and north almost to the city of Casa Grande. To the south of Kitt Peak, the 7,730-foot Baboquivari Peak is considered sacred by the Tohono O'odham as the home of their deity, I'itoi ("elder brother"). Less than halfway between Tucson and Ajo, Sells—the tribal capital of the Tohono O'odham—is a good place to stop for gas or a soft drink. Much of the time there's little to see or do in Sells, but in winter an annual rodeo and fair attract thousands of Native American visitors.

GETTING HERE AND AROUND

If you're traveling east or west along AZ 86, take the exit for the Sells Hospital to explore this tiny town, which consists of a few stores, offices, and a school (about a half-mile from the highway). The Papago Cafe sits at the highway exit. To get into town, drive south past the hospital, and go over the bridge.

WHERE TO EAT

$ × **Basha's Deli & Bakery.** At the Sells Shopping Center, the good-size
SOUTHWESTERN market Basha's Deli & Bakery can supply all the makings for a picnic. ⓢ *Average main: $7* ⌧ *Topawa Rd., at AZ 86* ☎ *520/383–2546.*

$ × **Papago Cafe.** For traditional Indian and Mexican food like fry bread,
SOUTHWESTERN tacos, and chili, try the Papago Cafe, open weekdays breakfast through dinner, and Saturdays for breakfast and lunch only. ⓢ *Average main: $9* ⌧ *AZ 86, near Chevron Station* ☎ *520/383–3510* ☉ *Closed Sun.*

AJO

90 miles northwest of Sells on AZ 86.

"Ajo" (pronounced *ah*-ho) is Spanish for garlic, and some say the town got its name from the wild garlic that grows in the area. Others claim

8

the word is a bastardization of the Indian word *au-auho,* referring to red paint derived from a local pigment.

For many years Ajo, like Bisbee, was a thriving Phelps Dodge Company town. Copper mining had been attempted in the area in the late 19th century, but it wasn't until the 1911 arrival of the Calumet & Arizona Mining Company that the region began to be developed profitably. Calumet and Phelps Dodge merged in 1935, and the huge pit mine produced millions of tons of copper until it closed in 1985. Nowadays Ajo is pretty sleepy; the town's population of 4,000 has a median age of 51, and most visitors are on their way to or from Rocky Point, Mexico. At the center of town is a sparkling white Spanish-style plaza. The shops and restaurants that line the plaza's covered arcade today are rather modest. Unlike Bisbee, Ajo hasn't yet drawn an artistic crowd—or the upscale boutiques and eateries that tend to follow. Chain stores and fast-food haven't made a beeline here either—you'll find only one Dairy Queen and a Pizza Hut in this remote desert hamlet.

GETTING HERE AND AROUND

As you drive into Ajo on AZ 85, you'll see the small historical plaza, with a few shops, a pharmacy, and a library, immediately on your right. After jogging west for several blocks and changing its name three times, the highway turns north again, becomes 2nd Avenue, and takes you out of town, past the Cabeza Prieta Wildlife Refuge and north to Gila Bend.

EXPLORING

Cabeza Prieta National Wildlife Refuge. The 860,000-acre Cabeza Prieta National Wildlife Refuge, about 10 minutes from Ajo, was established in 1939 as a preserve for endangered bighorn sheep and other Sonoran Desert wildlife. A free permit, essentially a "hold-harmless" agreement, is required to enter, and only those with four-wheel-drive, high-clearance vehicles, or all-terrain vehicles—needed to traverse the rugged terrain—can obtain one from the refuge's visitor center. ✉ *1611 N. 2nd Ave.* ☎ *520/387–6483* 🌐 *www.fws.gov/refuges* 🎟 *Free* 🕘 *Visitor center weekdays 8–4, refuge daily dawn–dusk.*

WHERE TO EAT AND STAY

For expanded hotel reviews, visit Fodors.com.

$ SOUTHWESTERN 🍴 **100 Estrella.** It can be hard to decide which burger to order from the dozen or so on the menu here. In the mood for the popular bacon and avocado burger, the "bleu cheese," or the free range bison burger? If you're brave enough for something spicier, try "Summer in Ajo"—a beef patty with jalapeño, green chile, onions, and pepperjack cheese. Herbivores can find veggie burgers, organic veggie pizzas, and salads with tepary beans, a Native American legume loaded with protein, fiber, and flavor. The bar at this colorful eatery offers 10 beers on draft and a good selection of bottled brews. [$] *Average main: $9* ✉ *100 Estrella Ave.* ☎ *520/387–3110* 🕘 *Closed Sun.*

$ B&B/INN 🏨 **The Guest House Inn.** Built in 1925 to accommodate visiting Phelps Dodge VIPs, this lodging is a favorite for birders: guests can head out early to nearby Organ Pipe National Monument or just sit on the patio and watch the quail, cactus wrens, and other warblers that fly in to visit. **Pros:** pleasant hosts; well-preserved home. **Cons:** may be a little sedate

Kitt Peak National Observatory is open to visitors during the day, but it's easy to enjoy the night sky here.

for some. [$] *Rooms from: $89* ✉ *700 Guest House Rd.* ☎ *520/387–6133* 🌐 *www.guesthouseinn.biz* 🛏 *4 rooms* 🍴 *Breakfast.*

ORGAN PIPE CACTUS NATIONAL MONUMENT

32 miles southwest of Ajo on AZ 86 to AZ 85.

GETTING HERE

From Ajo, drive to Why and take AZ 85 south for 22 miles to reach the visitor center.

SAFETY AND PRECAUTIONS

Be aware that Organ Pipe has become an illegal border crossing hot spot. Migrant workers and drug traffickers cross from Mexico under the cover of darkness. At this writing, much of Puerto Blanco Drive is closed indefinitely to the public. A two-way road that only travels 5 of the 53 miles on Puerto Blanco Drive is open, but the rest of the road remains closed due to continuing concerns over its proximity to the U.S.–Mexico border. Even so, park officials emphasize that tourists only occasionally have been the victims of isolated property crimes—primarily theft of personal items from parked cars. Visitors are advised by rangers to keep valuables locked and out of plain view and not to initiate contact with groups of strangers whom they may encounter on hiking trails.

EXPLORING

Organ Pipe Cactus National Monument. The largest habitat north of the border for organ-pipe cacti, Organ Pipe Cactus National Monument is near Cabeza Prieta National Wildlife Refuge but is much more accessible to visitors. These multiarmed cousins of the saguaro are fairly common in Mexico but rare in the United States. Because they tend to grow on the warmer, usually south-facing, slopes, you won't be able to see many of them unless you take either the 21-mile scenic loop **Ajo Mountain Drive** (a one-way, winding dirt road) or **Puerto Blanco Drive,** which is a two-way, 53-mile dirt road, of which only the first 5 miles are currently open to the public.

A campground at the monument has 208 RV (no hookups) and tent sites ($12). Facilities include a dump station with potable water, showers, flush toilets, grills, and picnic tables. Ranger-led tours and talks are offered January through March. ✉ *10 Organ Pipe Dr., Ajo* ☎ *520/387–6849* ⊕ *www.nps.gov/orpi* ✉ *$8 per vehicle* ☉ *Visitor center daily 8:30–4:30.*

YUMA

232 miles northwest of Organ Pipe Cactus National Monument, 170 miles northwest of Ajo.

Today many people think of Yuma as a convenient stop between Phoenix or Tucson and San Diego—and this was equally true in the relatively recent past. It's difficult to imagine the lower Colorado River, now dammed and bridged, as either a barrier or a means of transportation, but until the early part of the 20th century this section of the great waterway was a force to contend with. Records show that since at least 1540 the Spanish were using Yuma (then the site of a Quechan Indian village) as a ford across a relatively shallow stretch of the Colorado.

Three centuries later, the advent of the shallow-draft steamboat made the settlement a point of entry for fortune seekers heading through the Gulf of California to mining sites in eastern Arizona. Fort Yuma was established in 1850 to guard against Indian attacks, and by 1873 the town was a county seat, a U.S. port of entry, and an army depot.

The steamboat shipping business, undermined by the completion of the Southern Pacific Railroad line in 1877, was finished off by the building of Laguna Dam in 1909. During World War II Yuma Proving Ground was used to train bomber pilots, and General Patton readied some of his desert war forces for battle at classified areas near the city. Many who served here during the war returned to Yuma to retire, and the city's economy now relies largely on tourism. The population swells during the winter months with retirees from cold climates who park their homes on wheels at one of the many RV communities. One fact may explain this: according to National Weather Service statistics, Yuma is the sunniest city in the United States.

GETTING HERE AND AROUND

AZ 8 runs through Yuma, which is approximately halfway between Casa Grande and the California coast. Most of the interesting historic sights are at the north end of town. Stop in at the Yuma Convention and Visitors Bureau, on the grounds of Quartermaster Depot State Park, and pick up a walking-tour guide to the historic downtown area. The town's largest shopping center, Yuma Palms, sits just to the east side of U.S. 8 (at the 16th Street exit). More than a half dozen modern hotels—the most convenient choices for lodging—are a stone's throw from here.

Yuma is accessible by two commercial airlines: US Airways has direct flights to Yuma from Phoenix and United Express flies nonstop from Los Angeles to Yuma.

Yuma City Cab has the best taxi service in Yuma.

Amtrak trains run three times a week from Tucson west to Yuma.

ESSENTIALS

Transportation Contacts Yuma City Cab ☎ 928/782–4444. **Yuma train station** ✉ 281 Gila St. **Yuma International Airport (YUM)** ☎ 928/726–5882 ⊕ www.yumainternationalairport.com.

Visitor Information Yuma Convention and Visitors Bureau ✉ 201 N. 4th Ave., at Quartermaster Depot Park ☎ 928/783–0071, 800/293–0071 ⊕ www. visityuma.com ⊘ Daily 9–5.

EXPLORING

Quartermaster Depot State Historic Park. On the other side of the river from Fort Yuma, the Civil War–period quartermaster depot resupplied army posts to the north and east and served as a distribution point for steamboat freight headed overland to Arizona forts. The 1853 home of riverboat captain G.A. Johnson is the depot's earliest building and the centerpiece of Quartermaster Depot State Historic Park. The residence also served as a weather bureau and home for customs agents, among other functions, and the guided tour through the house provides a complete history. Also on display are antique surreys and more "modern" modes of transportation like a 1931 Model A Ford pickup. You can visit a re-creation of the Commanding Officer's Quarters, complete with period furnishings. The Yuma Visitors Bureau is also here. ✉ 201 N. 4th Ave., between 1st St. and I-8 ☎ 928/783–0071 ⊕ www.azstateparks. com ☞ $4 ⊘ Daily 9–4:30. Closed Mon. June–Sept.

Sanguinetti House Museum. This adobe-style museum, run by the Arizona Historical Society, was built around 1870 by merchant E.F. Sanguinetti; it exhibits artifacts from Yuma's territorial days and details the military presence in the area. If you're dining at the Garden Café this makes for an interesting stop, but it's not worth a visit on its own, especially if you plan on visiting the more popular Quartermaster Depot State Historic Park. ✉ 240 S. Madison Ave. ☎ 928/782–1841 ⊕ www. arizonahistoricalsociety.org ☞ $3 ⊘ Tues.–Sat. 10–4.

Yuma River Tours. You can take a boat ride up the Colorado with Yuma River Tours. Canoe, kayak, cruise on a stern-wheeler, or book 12- to 45-person jet-boat excursions through Smokey Knowlton, who has been exploring the area for more than 35 years. ✉ 1920 Arizona Ave. ☎ 928/783–4400 ⊕ www.yumarivertours.com.

FAMILY **Yuma Territorial Prison State Historic Park.** The most notorious tourist sight in town, Yuma Territorial Prison, now an Arizona state historic park, was built for the most part by the convicts who were incarcerated here from 1876 until 1909, when the prison outgrew its location. The hilly site on the Colorado River, chosen for security purposes, precluded further expansion.

Visitors gazing today at the tiny cells that held six inmates each, often in 115°F heat, are likely to be appalled, but the prison—dubbed the

8

Crested saguaros at Organ Pipe National Monument are found alongside the monument's namesake cacti and other succulent plants.

Country Club of the Colorado by locals—was considered a model of enlightenment by turn-of-the-20th-century standards: in an era when beatings were common, the only punishments meted out here were solitary confinement and assignment to a dark cell. The complex housed a hospital as well as Yuma's only public library, where the 25¢ that visitors paid for a prison tour financed the acquisition of new books.

The 3,069 prisoners who served time at what was then the territory's only prison included men and women from 21 different countries. They came from all social classes and were sent up for everything from armed robbery and murder to polygamy. R.L. McDonald, incarcerated for forgery, had been the superintendent of the Phoenix public school system. Chosen as the prison bookkeeper, he absconded with $130 of the inmates' money when he was released.

The mess hall opened as a museum in 1940, and the entire prison complex was designated a state historic park in 1961. ⊠ *1 Prison Hill Rd., near Exit 1 off Interstate 8* ☎ *928/783–4771* ⊕ *www.yumaprison.org* ⌨ *$6* ⊙ *Daily 9–5* ⊙ *Closed Tues. and Wed. June–Sept.*

WHERE TO EAT

$ ✕ **The Garden Café.** Before or after a visit to the Sanguinetti House
CAFÉ Museum, this adjoining café is a good place to stop for breakfast or lunch. The charming dining spot features lush gardens and aviaries on the outdoor patio, historical photos on the walls, and a menu of homemade salads, soups, and sandwiches. Favorites include the quiche, served with homemade fruit bread, and the tortilla soup. Breakfasts are top-notch, too. One of the best times to visit is Sunday brunch—complete with carne asada, tortillas, potatoes, scrambled eggs, a layered

ham-and-egg strata, breakfast meats, fruit, and dessert. $ *Average main: $10* ✉ *250 S. Madison Ave.* ☎ *928/783–1491* ⚅ *Reservations not accepted* ⊘ *Closed Mon. No dinner. Closed June–Sept.*

$ ✗ **La Fonda.** A Yuma institution, La Fonda opened as a tortilla factory in
MEXICAN 1940, then added a colorful restaurant onto the original building in 1982; locals have been enjoying the carne asada, pollo asado, and chile rellenos here ever since. Only canola oil is used (not lard), and all the sauces and marinades are made fresh, as are the corn tortillas, which many say are the best in town. Save room for the homemade desserts—the flan and fried ice cream are fabulous. Open for breakfast (served all day), lunch, and early dinner, La Fonda closes at 8 so the employees can go home to their families. $ *Average main: $9* ✉ *1095 S. 3rd Ave.* ☎ *928/783–6902* ⊕ *www.lafondarestaurantandtortillafactory.com* ⊘ *Closed Sun.*

$ ✗ **Lutes Casino.** Packed with locals at lunchtime, this large, funky res-
SOUTHWESTERN taurant and bar claims to be the oldest pool hall and domino parlor in Arizona. It's a great place for a burger and a brew. The "Especial" combines a cheeseburger and a hot dog and adds a generous dollop of Lutes's "special sauce." $ *Average main: $5* ✉ *221 S. Main St.* ☎ *928/782–2192* ⊕ *www.lutescasino.com.*

$$$ ✗ **River City Grill.** This hip downtown restaurant is a favorite dining spot
AMERICAN for locals and visitors. It gets a bit loud on weekend nights, but the camaraderie of diners is well worth it. Owners Nan and Tony Bain dish out a medley of flavors drawing on Mediterranean, Pacific Rim, Indian, and Caribbean influences. For starters you can sample everything from Vietnamese spring rolls to curried mussels. Entrées include delicacies like grilled wild salmon, rack of lamb, and such vegetarian dishes as ricotta-and-spinach ravioli. $ *Average main: $22* ✉ *600 W. 3rd St.* ☎ *928/782–7988* ⊕ *www.rivercitygrillyuma.com* ⊘ *No lunch weekends.*

WHERE TO STAY

For expanded hotel reviews, visit Fodors.com.

$ **Best Western Coronado Motor Hotel.** This Spanish tile–roofed motor
HOTEL hotel was built in 1938 and has been well cared for. **Pros:** convenient to AZ 8, and a short walk from the historic downtown area; retro property; full breakfast at restaurant. **Cons:** some highway noise in rooms. $ *Rooms from: $99* ✉ *233 S. 4th Ave.* ☎ *928/783–4453, 800/528–1234* ⊕ *www.bestwestern.com* ⇄ *86 rooms* ⦿| *Breakfast.*

$ **Clarion Suites Yuma.** One wing of this sprawling hotel surrounds a
HOTEL well-manicured courtyard with a fountain; another faces the pool and Cabana Club, where the complimentary breakfast and happy-hour drinks are served. **Pros:** spacious suites; quiet. **Cons:** no restaurant. $ *Rooms from: $89* ✉ *2600 S. 4th Ave.* ☎ *928/726–4830* ⊕ *www.clarionyuma.com* ⇄ *164 suites* ⦿| *Breakfast.*

$ **Hilton Garden Inn Yuma-Pivot Point.** One of the newer hotels in town,
HOTEL the Hilton Garden Inn Yuma caters to families and business travelers equally, with well-equipped rooms, a pleasant pool area, and convenience to historic sights, the river park, and the highway. **Pros:** comfortable rooms; pool, hot tub, and gym; easy walk to historic Old Town area. **Cons:** generic property. $ *Rooms from: $109* ✉ *310 N. Madison Ave.* ☎ *928/783–1500* ⊕ *www.yumapivotpoint.hgi.com* ⇄ *150 rooms* ⦿| *No meals.*

8

SHOPPING

Art studios, antiques shops, and specialty boutiques have taken advantage of downtown Yuma's face-lift.

Bard Date Company. The retail outlet of the Bard Date Company is a great place to sample and purchase all grades of the high-fiber, fat-free fruit grown in this region, including delicious date shakes. ✉ *245 S. Main St.* ☎ *928/341–9966* ⊕ *www.barddate.com* ⊘ *Closed Sun.*

Colorado River Pottery. This shop features handcrafted bowls, vases, and dishes. ✉ *67 W. 2nd St.* ☎ *928/343–0413* ⊕ *www.coloradoriverpottery. com.*

Prickly Pear. This store is packed with an assortment of gourmet coffees and teas, turquoise jewelry, hand-carved furniture, and wall art. ✉ *324 S. Main St.* ☎ *928/343–0390* ⊘ *Closed Sun.–Mon.*

IMPERIAL NATIONAL WILDLIFE REFUGE

30 miles north of Yuma on U.S. 95.

GETTING HERE AND AROUND

From Yuma, take U.S. 95 north and follow the signs to the refuge. It's about a 40-minute drive, and between January and March look for army paratroopers taking practice jumps as you pass the Yuma Proving Ground.

EXPLORING

FAMILY **Imperial National Wildlife Refuge.** A guided tour is the best way to visit this 25,765-acre wildlife refuge, created by backwaters formed when the Imperial Dam was built. Something of an anomaly, the refuge is home both to species indigenous to marshy rivers and to creatures that inhabit the adjacent Sonoran Desert—desert tortoises, coyotes, bobcats, and bighorn sheep. Mostly, though, this is a major bird habitat. Thousands of waterfowl and shorebirds live here year-round, and migrating flocks of swallows pass through in spring and fall. During those seasons, expect to see everything from pelicans and cormorants to Canada geese, snowy egrets, and some rarer species.

Canoes can be rented at Martinez Lake Marina, 3.5 miles southeast of the refuge headquarters. It's best to visit from mid-October through May, when it's cooler and the ever-present mosquitoes are least active. Kids especially enjoy the 1.3-mile Painted Desert Nature Trail, which winds through the different levels of the Sonoran Desert. From an observation tower at the visitor center you can see the river, as well as the fields where migrating birds like to feed. You can sign up for guided walks (including evening walks when the moon is full) from November through March (call ahead). ✉ *Martinez Lake Rd., Martinez Lake* ☎ *928/783–3371* ⊕ *www.fws.gov/refuges* 🖾 *Free* ⊘ *Visitor center Apr.– Oct., weekdays 7:30–4; Nov.–Mar., weekdays 7:30–4, weekends 9–4.*

NORTHWEST ARIZONA AND SOUTHEAST NEVADA

WELCOME TO NORTHWEST ARIZONA AND SOUTHEAST NEVADA

TOP REASONS TO GO

★ **Get wet:** Boating, fishing, and water adventure top the list of favorite activities on the cool Colorado River and the adjoining lakes of Havasu, Mohave, and Mead.

★ **Experience a slice of England:** Pass under on a boat or stroll over London Bridge in Lake Havasu City.

★ **Drive the open road:** Take a road trip on legendary Route 66 and cruise the longest remaining stretch of the Mother Road from Seligman to Kingman.

★ **Take a walk on the wild side:** For Vegas-style gambling and glitz spend some quality play time in the twin riverside cities of Laughlin, Nevada, and Bullhead City, Arizona.

★ **Hike Hualapai:** Take a break from the desert and climb the cool climes of Hualapai Mountain Park—the highest point in western Arizona.

Laughlin, Nevada's casinos are just over the Colorado River.

1 Northwest Arizona. Take a drive down memory lane on the longest remaining stretch of historic Route 66—roll down the windows and watch the sweeping desert views pass you by. Along the way, check out the funky little ghost towns of Oatman and Chloride and make a splash in the cool blue waterways of Lakes Mohave, Mead, and Havasu.

2 Southeast Nevada. Laughlin attracts laid-back gamblers and elite entertainers looking for all of the glitz and glamour of Las Vegas without the high prices and large crowds. Take a quick jaunt into Nevada for a look at the monumental Hoover Dam and a hand or two of black-jack in a riverside casino.

Rt. 66 is a classic American route for road trips.

HISTORIC
US
66

GETTING ORIENTED

In the far northwestern corner of Arizona, the fast-growing communities of Lake Havasu and Laughlin/Bullhead City are good bases for outdoor recreation and gaming, respectively. Kingman, the Mohave County seat and a historic shipping center, is an ideal launch pad for exploring historic and quirky Route 66. The Colorado River flows out of the Grand Canyon to the north and then sweeps directly south, serving as the western border of the state of Arizona and supplying the lifeblood to the otherwise desolate desert region. Created from dams on the mighty Colorado River, Lakes Mead, Mohave, and Havasu provide a common link in the tristate area by offering some of the best water recreation around.

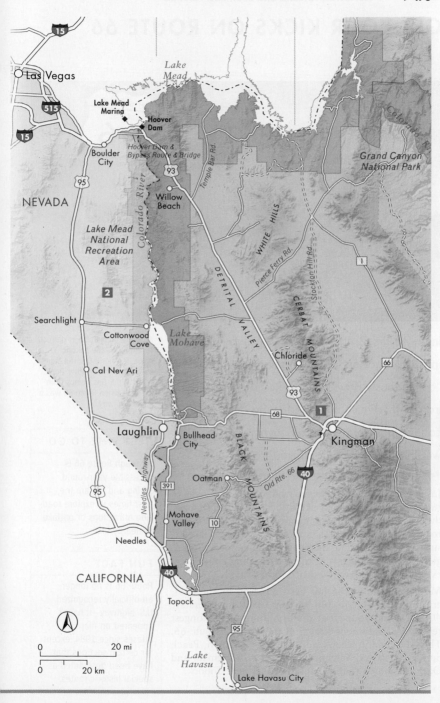

GET YOUR KICKS ON ROUTE 66

In 1938 the 2,400 miles of roadway connecting Chicago and Los Angeles was declared "continuously paved." U.S. Route 66 had been transformed from a ragged string of local lanes connecting isolated small towns into an "all-weather" highway that eased travel.

Above: A convertible is perfect for exploring the historic route. Top right: Colorful signs abound on the "Mother Road." Lower right: Gas pumps from the time when Route 66 was a major highway.

Just as the road crews changed what had been a string of rutty dirt roads into a paved roadbed, Route 66 changed the social landscape as communities adapted to the new road. The needs of travelers were met by new concepts, such as the gas station, the diner, and the motel. Nostalgic remnants from this retro road-tripping culture still exist along this stretch of the "Mother Road."

Most of old Route 66 has been replaced by the modern interstate system, but at Exit 139 from Interstate 40 you'll find yourself at the beginning of the longest remaining continuous stretch of the original Route 66. This 160-mile journey leads through Seligman, Peach Springs, Truxton, Valentine, Hackberry, Kingman, and Oatman, and on to the Colorado River near Topock.

BEST TIME TO GO

Although Route 66 is accessible year-round, spring and fall are the best times to explore roadside attractions or partake of nearby hikes.

FUN FACT

Route 66 is no longer an officially recognized U.S. highway—it hasn't appeared on maps or atlases since 1984, except for certain sections that have been designated as special historic routes.

BEST WAYS TO EXPLORE

SHOP FOR RETRO COLLECTIBLES IN OATMAN

The Leather Shop of Oatman. You can get in the spirit of the Old West with the leather jackets, Western gun holsters, and moccasins offered at this shop. ⊠ *162 Main St., Oatman* ☎ *928/768–3833* ⊕ *www.theleathershopofoatman.com.*

Main Street Emporium. This emporium offers a wide array of handcrafted items including Western-themed wall art, hand-woven blankets, and cholla cactus candles. ⊠ *150 Main St., Oatman* ☎ *928/788–3298* ⊕ *www.main-st-emporium.com.*

Ore House. Browse through a nice selection of Indian jewelry, colorful gems, pottery, textiles, and Southwestern art at the Ore House. ⊠ *194 Main St., Oatman* ☎ *928/768–3839.*

SIGN HERE

One of the joys of exploring Route 66 is admiring the vintage signage along the way.

Delgadillo's Snow Cap Drive-in. In Seligman, you can stop here for a "small soda" and to view the old Coca-Cola and Burma Shave signs. In fact, the whole town is rife with old signs and cars. ⊠ *301 W Chino Ave., Seligman* ☎ *928/422–3291.*

Hackberry General Store. At this store, which is both a shop and museum dedicated to Mother Road memorabilia, you can pose for pictures with vintage cars, kitschy signs, ancient gas pumps, and highway memorabilia while sipping sarsaparilla from a bottle of Route 66 Beer. ⊠ *11255 E. AZ 66, Hackberry* ☎ *928/769–2605* ⊕ *hackberrygeneralstore.com.*

Wigwam Motel. In eastern Arizona, the parking lot of the Wigwam Motel—where the rooms are inside 30-foot-tall wood-and-concrete tepees—you'll see a vast collection of classic cars, from a '59 Chevy Impala to a '51 Studebaker Land Cruiser. ⊠ *811 W. Hopi Dr., Holbrook* ☎ *928/241–8413* ⊕ *www.sleepinawigwam.com.*

QUICK BITES

Oatman Hotel. This allegedly haunted landmark on Oatman's historic main drag has very basic rooms. Claims that Carole Lombard and Clark Gable honeymooned here have been largely debunked, but this quirky establishment contains a fun little restaurant that's renowned for its juicy buffalo burgers and addictively filling "burro ears"—house-made potato chips served with tangy salsa. The rambling dining room has an astounding number of dollar bills plastered on its walls. ⊠ *181 Main St., Oatman* ☎ *928/768–4408.*

West Side Lilo's. An unassuming roadhouse along Route 66 in Seligman, West Side Lilo's is a must for exceptionally well-prepared, hearty short-order cooking. The prodigious breakfast burritos, green-chile stew, hefty cheese-burgers, and famously massive cinnamon buns are a hit with regulars and tourists. One "slice" of the famous carrot cake is equal to three or four slices at most restaurants. ⊠ *415 W. AZ 66, Seligman* ☎ *928/422–5456.*

9

Updated
by Andrew
Collins and
Michael
Weatherford

Northwestern Arizona and southeastern Nevada comprise a unique blend of deserts, mountains, and 1,000 miles of shoreline. Despite the superficial aridity of much of the landscape, the region bubbles with an abundance of springs and artesian wells. Without these water sources seeping from the rocks and sand, this wide-open region would never have developed into the major crossroads it is today.

The defining feature of the region is the Colorado River. Since the late Pleistocene epoch when Paleo-Indians first set foot in the river that was once described as "too thick to drink and too thin to plow," the Colorado has been a blessing and a barrier. Prehistoric traders from the Pacific Coast crossed the river at Willow Beach on their way to trade shells for pelts with the Hopi Indians and other Pueblo tribes farther east. When gold was discovered in California in 1848, entrepreneurs built ferries up and down the river to accommodate the miners drawn to the area by what Cortez called "a disease of the heart for which the only cure is gold." Prosperity followed, particularly for Kingman.

Every spring the snowmelt of the Rocky Mountain watershed of the Colorado River rushed through high basaltic canyons like water through a garden hose and washed away crops and livestock. Harnessing such a powerful river required no ordinary dam. In 1935, notched into the steep and narrow confines of Black Canyon on the border separating Arizona and Nevada, 726-foot high Hoover Dam took control of the Colorado River and turned its power into electricity and its floodwaters into the largest man-made reservoir in the United States: Lake Mead. In 2010, the similarly dramatic Hoover Dam Bypass (also known as the Mike O'Callaghan–Pat Tillman Memorial Bridge) opened just south of the dam, vastly reducing the time it takes for automobiles to cross over the Colorado River.

Today, thousands of vehicles travel through northwestern Arizona and southeastern Nevada every day. For many who view the area through the glass of their air-conditioned vehicles, the landscape is a daunting vision of distant mountains shimmering in the heat. But for those who pull over and step into the clean open air, the area offers an enchanting blend of past and present, earth and sky, river and wind.

NORTHWEST ARIZONA AND SOUTHEAST NEVADA PLANNER

WHEN TO GO

Unlike many destinations, the communities in northwestern Arizona don't have distinct high and low seasons. The arid climate and clear winter skies attract "snowbirds," retirees flocking south to escape the harsh northern climes. On the flip side, the hot, sunny summer months attract sports enthusiasts looking to cavort in the cool, blue waterways—despite searing temperatures that occasionally top 110°F.

Lake Havasu City plays host to hordes of college revelers during spring break in March and Kingman fills up fast during the annual Route 66 Fun Run drive in May. Things simmer down a bit during the rest of spring as well as the fall months. Overall, expect fairly busy weekends during the summer months and sold-out rooms during sporting events and fishing tournaments.

Hualapai Mountain Park is the one part of northwestern Arizona that is high-altitude enough to get occasionally heavy snow in winter.

FESTIVALS AND EVENTS

LATE APRIL– EARLY MAY
Route 66 Fun Run. This three-day event in early May is a 40-mile drive along the longest remaining section of the "Mother Road." ☎ 928/753–5001 ⊕ www.azrt66.com.

SEPTEMBER
Andy Devine Days. The festival honors the film and television actor with a parade and an impressive rodeo. ☎ 928/753–6106 ⊕ www.kingmanrodeoaz.com.

OCTOBER
London Bridge Days. Lake Havasu City heats up with a weeklong Renaissance festival, a parade, and British-themed contests. ☎ 928/453–8686 ⊕ www.golakehavasu.com.

PLANNING YOUR TIME

Kingman is an ideal base for exploring Lake Mead National Recreation Area, the ghost towns of Oatman and Chloride, and the forested Hualapai Mountain Park. You'll need at least a day to enjoy water sports on Lake Mead, whereas an hour or two is enough to explore the funky little ghost towns. Visitors to Lake Havasu should spend a night or two to get a real sense of this recreation hub, although you can get a quick taste by making a day trip from Kingman or Bullhead City. Water activities dominate the scene here, but in a shorter visit you can check out London Bridge, go on a birding expedition at Havasu National Wildlife Refuge, or a foray into the quaint if touristy shops in English Village. Fans of gambling can just hop across the Colorado River to Laughlin and spend hours or days reveling in the glitz and glitter—there's also a large casino on the Arizona side in Parker, an hour south of Lake Havasu City.

9

■TIP➜ Remember that Arizona, in the mountain time zone, doesn't observe daylight saving time, but the neighboring states of Nevada and California, both in the Pacific time zone, do. When scheduling interstate travel, double-check all times to avoid confusion and missed connections.

GETTING HERE AND AROUND

AIR TRAVEL

Kingman (IGM) has very limited air service. Laughlin-Bullhead City (IFP) is presently served only by charters, but has been lobbying for scheduled commercial service—stay tuned. Most visitors arriving by plane reach this part of the state after first flying into Las Vegas (two hours from Laughlin) or Phoenix (four hours from Kingman or Lake Havasu City) and renting a car.

CAR TRAVEL

Most visitors drive to this corner of the state—after all, Kingman is on the longest remaining stretch of Route 66. At first glance, the country-side can seem a bit stark and remote, but there are many surprises in this part of the world, including the strange-looking Joshua tree, the defining plant of the Mojave Desert. Historic Route 66 crosses east–west and curves north of Interstate 40, which provides the fastest path across the region. U.S. 93 is the main route for north–south travel. All of these roads are in excellent condition. On Interstate 40 high winds occasionally raise enough blowing dust to restrict visibility. In winter, ice may be present on Interstate 40 east of Kingman, as well as on sections of Route 66. Most of the county roads are improved dirt roads, but washboard sections bounce you around a bit, so take your time and drive no faster than prudence dictates. Beware that many maps and GPS devices show what appear to be viable dirt roads that may actually be unmaintained or even abandoned—stick with established routes if you're ever unsure. ■TIP➜ Fuel up while you're in this part of Arizona—all grades of gasoline can be as much as 50¢ to 75¢ per gallon less in Kingman and Bullhead City than across the border in Nevada and California.

TRAIN TRAVEL

Kingman is the only city in this region served by Amtrak; the *Southwest Chief* train stops in Kingman on its daily run between Los Angeles and Chicago (via Albuquerque).

RESTAURANTS

Dining in this remote corner of the state is quite casual, though also affordable. You're more likely to find a 1950s-inspired diner, a taqueria, or a family-owned café than a sophisticated, high-end eatery. For the most part you'll find home-cooked American and Southwestern favorites. The few higher-end dining options are in Lake Havasu and across the Colorado River in Laughlin's casinos, where steak houses are particularly prolific. *Prices in the reviews are the average cost of a main course at dinner or, if dinner isn't served, at lunch.*

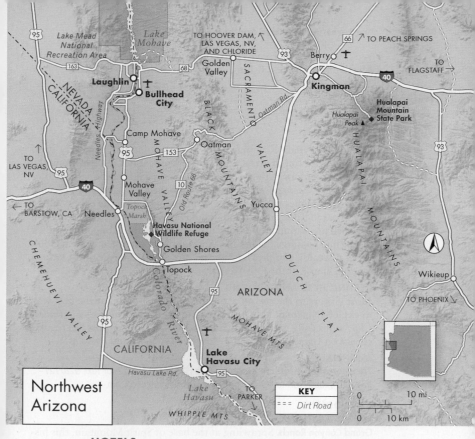

Northwest Arizona

HOTELS

Mid-priced chain accommodations abound in Kingman and Lake
Havasu, and to a lesser extent Bullhead City—though the casino resorts
across the river in Laughlin are among the best values in the region.
Lake Havasu City has a few somewhat upscale resorts, as does Laughlin, with its several glittery but reasonably priced gaming properties.
Staying in a houseboat on Lake Havasu or Lake Mead puts a decidedly
different twist on water recreation. These floating rooms with a view
can be maneuvered into countless coves and inlets, allowing for peaceful solitude rarely found on the busy beaches and popular waterways.
*Prices in the reviews are the lowest cost of a standard double room in
high season. For expanded reviews, facilities, and current deals, visit
Fodors.com.*

NORTHWEST ARIZONA

Towns like Kingman hark back to the glory days of the old Route 66,
and the ghost towns of Chloride and Oatman bear testament to the
mining madness that once reigned in the region. Water-sports fans, or
those who just want to laze on a houseboat, enjoy Lake Havasu, where

you'll find the misplaced English icon, the London Bridge, and Lake Mead, one of the best fishing spots in the state.

KINGMAN

200 miles northwest of Phoenix, 149 miles west of Flagstaff via Interstate 40.

The highway past Kingman may seem desolate, and the city itself doesn't have a ton of attractions, but the mountains that surround the area offer outdoor activities in abundance, especially along the Colorado River. Water sports play a big part in the area's recreation because about 1,000 miles of freshwater shoreline lie within the county along the Colorado River and around Lakes Havasu, Mohave, and Mead—all of which are within a one-hour drive of this major stopping point for fishing and boating aficionados. And for those interested in the region's mineral wealth, the nearby "ghost" towns of Chloride and Oatman offer a glimpse of the Old West.

GETTING HERE AND AROUND

Most visitors to the region arrive by car, which is by far the best way to explore Kingman and area sites. Additionally, Amtrak's *Southwest Chief* stops daily in Kingman, and the town's small airport has regular service on Great Lakes Airlines from Los Angeles and Prescott.

ESSENTIALS

Transportation Contacts Kingman Cab ☎ *928/753–1222 for taxi, 928/727–1311 for shuttle van to other cities* ⊕ *www.kingmancabco.com.*

EXPLORING

TOP ATTRACTIONS

Grand Canyon Ranch. Sprawling at the base of Spirit Mountain, this historic 106,000-acre working cattle ranch takes guests on an adventure to the Old West. Corriente cattle still roam the hills and their cowboy caretakers guide horseback tours and horse-drawn wagon rides through the rugged countryside. Tap Duncan (a member of the Hole-in-the-Wall Gang) lived here, and Andy Devine supposedly spent some time working here. The ranch now offers rustic cabins, home-cooked meals, horseback riding, wagon rides, and a helicopter tour of Grand Canyon West. Take U.S. 93 north from Kingman 40 miles and turn right onto Pierce Ferry Road. Follow the paved road for 29 miles, then turn right onto the unpaved Diamond Bar Ranch Road. The Grand Canyon West Ranch is 5.5 miles farther on the right side of the road. Located just 14 miles southwest of Grand Canyon West, the ranch is a popular stopping-off point for day-trippers seeking spectacular canyon views in this remote region. Call ahead to arrange your visit. A variety of packages are available, with or without meal plans, depending on which activities you're interested in. ⊠ *3750 E. Diamond Bar Ranch Rd., Meadview* ☎ *702/736–8787, 800/359–8727* ⊕ *www.grandcanyonranch.com* ⊜ *Reservations essential.*

Fodor's Choice
★

Hualapai Mountain Park. You haven't truly hiked in northwestern Arizona until you've hiked in Hualapai Mountain Park. A 15-mile drive from town up Hualapai Mountain Road leads to the park's more than 2,300 wooded acres, with 10 miles of developed and undeveloped hiking trails, picnic areas, ATV trails, rustic cabins ($70 to $125 per night), and RV (full hookups) and tent areas. Along the park's trail system you'll find a striking variety of plant life such as prickly pear cactus and Arizona walnut. Abundant species of birds and mammals such as the piñon jay and the Abert squirrel live here, and pristine stands of unmarred aspen mark the higher elevations. Any of the trails can be hiked in about three hours. The **Hayden Peak Trail** is a branch of a 16-mile trail system, which links with many other trails at a high elevation. The popular **Aspen Peak Trail** is shorter, 2 miles one way. Trail maps are available at the park office. Keep in mind the terrain in the park ranges from 5,000 to 8,500 feet above sea level, and snow—sometimes heavy—is common in winter. ⊠ *6250 Hualapai Mountain Rd.* ☎ *928/681–5700, 877/757–0915 for cabin reservations* ⊕ *www.mcparks.com* ⊠ *$5.*

OFF THE BEATEN PATH

Chloride. The ghost town of Chloride, Arizona's oldest silver-mining camp, takes its name from a type of silver ore mined here. During its heyday, from 1900 to 1920, some 60 mines operated in the area: silver, gold, lead, zinc, molybdenum, and even turquoise were mined here. Around 370 folks live in Chloride today; there's a restaurant, saloon, convenience store, motel, and two RV parks. Sights include the old jail, Chloride Baptist Church, and the Jim Fritz Museum.

Western artist Roy Purcell painted the large murals on the rocks on the east edge of town—10 feet high and almost 30 feet across, they depict a goddess figure, intertwined snakes, and Eastern and Native American symbols. To reach the murals, follow signs from the east end of Highway 125 along the unpaved road—it's a slow, twisting drive best attempted with four-wheel drive. Outdoors enthusiasts can take advantage of the miles of hiking trails and explore the mineral-rich hills with excellent rockhounding opportunities.

Mock gunfights in the streets mark high noon on the first and third Saturdays each month (except December, when no gunfights are staged). In early October the entire town turns out for Old Miner's Day—the biggest event of the year featuring a parade, bazaar, bake sale, and family-friendly contests (St. Patrick's Day is also a big to-do here).

The marked turnoff on Highway 125 for Chloride is about 12 mi north of Kingman on U.S. 93. For more information, contact the **Chloride Chamber of Commerce** (⊠ *4940 Tennessee Ave., Chloride* ☎ *928/565–9419* ⊕ *www.chloridearizona.com*). ⚠ **Give wide berth to abandoned mine entrances and shafts, which are often unstable and can cave in without warning.** Experts believe there are more than 200,000 abandoned mines in Arizona, many in the rich mineral regions such as the one surrounding Chloride. ⊕ *www.chlorideaz.com.*

WORTH NOTING

Bonelli House. History buffs should check out the 1915 Bonelli House, an excellent example of Anglo-territorial architecture, featuring a facade of light-gray quarried stone and whitewashed wood accents, a very popular style in the early 1900s. It is one of more than 60 buildings in the Kingman business district listed on the National Register of Historic

9

Northwest Arizona is full of interesting pit stops off Historic Route 66.

Places and contains period pieces including a large wall clock that was once the only clock in Kingman. ✉ *430 E. Spring St.* ☎ *928/753–3175* 🌐 *www.mohavemuseum.org/bonel.html* ✉ *$4 includes admission to Historic Route 66 Museum and the Mohave Museum of History and Arts* ☉ *Weekdays 11–3 and by appt.*

Kingman Railroad Museum. Developed in 2012 by Kingman's active legion of railroad aficionados, the Whistler Stop Railroad Club, this museum is set inside the town's vintage 1907 Santa Fe Railroad depot and contains vintage model train layouts from the 1940s through the 1960s, plus additional memorabilia chronicling the region's rail history. ✉ *400 E. Andy Devine Ave.* ☎ *928/718–1440* 🌐 *www.whistlestoprailroadclub. org* ✉ *$2* ☉ *Tues.–Sun. 9–5.*

Mohave Museum of History and Arts. This museum includes an Andy Devine Room with memorabilia from Devine's Hollywood years and, incongruously, a portrait collection of every president and first lady. There's an exceptional library collection of research materials related to the region. There's also an exhibit of carved Kingman turquoise, displays on Native American art and artifacts, and a diorama depicting the mid-19th-century expedition of Lt. Edward Beale, who led his camel-cavalry unit to the area in search of a wagon road along the 35th parallel. You can follow the White Cliffs Trail from downtown to see the deep ruts cut into the desert floor by the wagons that came to Kingman after Beale's time. ✉ *400 W. Beale St.* ☎ *928/753–3195* 🌐 *www. mohavemuseum.org* ✉ *$4 includes admission to Historic Route 66 Museum and the Bonelli House* ☉ *Weekdays 9–5, Sat. 1–5.*

FAMILY **Powerhouse.** The Powerhouse building is a great first stop for visitors. The **Kingman Visitor Center** (☎ 928/753–6106, 866/427–7866 ⊕ *www.kingmantourism.org*), in a converted 1907 electrical plant, has the usual brochures to acquaint you with local attractions. Pick up a walking tour map, which highlights 27 historic sights, including Locomotive Park—home to the 1928 steam locomotive Engine No. 3759.

Inside the visitor center, the **Powerhouse Route 66 Museum** (☎ 928/753–9889 ☜ *$4 includes admission to the Bonelli House and the Mohave Museum of History and Arts*) provides a nostalgic look at the evolution of the famous route that started as a footpath followed by prehistoric Indians and evolved into a length of pavement

> ### ANDY DEVINE
>
> Kingman's most famous citizen is Andy Devine (1905–77). The raspy-voiced Western character actor appeared in more than 400 films, most notably as the comic cowboy sidekick "Cookie" to Roy Rogers in 10 films. He also played "the Cheerful Soldier" in *The Red Badge of Courage* and was in several John Wayne flicks, including *The Man Who Shot Liberty Valance, Stagecoach,* and *Island in the Sky.* On the last weekend of September each year, Kingman celebrates its favorite son with the Andy Devine Days Rodeo (⊕ *www.kingmanrodeoaz.com*), parade, and community fair.

that reached from Chicago, Illinois, to Santa Monica, California. **Memory Lane,** also inside the Powerhouse, is a store crammed with kitschy souvenirs.

The first weekend of May each year, the Historic Route 66 Association of Arizona holds the three-day Route 66 Fun Run, a 40-mile drive that attracts classic car buffs. Admission to the Historic Route 66 Museum also includes a visit to the nearby Mohave Museum of History and Arts and the Bonelli House. ✉ *The Powerhouse, 120 W. Rte. 66* ☎ *866/427–7866, 928/753–6106* ⊕ *www.kingmantourism.org* ☉ *Daily 9–5.*

EN ROUTE   Traveling north from Kingman, keep an eye out for the strange-looking namesakes of the **Joshua Tree Forest** (*Yucca brevifolia*). This native of the dry Mojave Desert isn't a tree, but actually a member of the lily family. Standing as tall as 40 feet, the alien-looking plant can be recognized by its gangly limbs ending in dense clumps of dark green, bayonet-shape leaves. Mormon emigrants traveling through the area in the mid-19th century named the towering plants after the biblical figure Joshua. From February through March, Joshua trees bloom in clusters of creamy white blossoms. The trees don't branch until after they bloom, and, because they rely on perfect conditions to flower, they don't bloom every year—you're most likely to see blossoms following a rainy December or January.

WHERE TO EAT AND STAY

For expanded hotel reviews, visit Fodors.com.

$ ✗ **El Palacio.** Set in a century-old building in the heart of Kingman's
MEXICAN   historic downtown, this regional chain is a reliable choice for well-prepared Mexican favorites and Southwest specialties—and what many believe are the best chiles rellenos in the area. Other notable options

include *machaca con huevos* (scrambled eggs with shredded beef and vegetables), carne asada tacos, *sopa del mar* (seafood stew with cilantro and lemon), and chicken mole poblano. A comprehensive drink menu includes a selection of Mexican beers, guava and banana margaritas, and fruity sangria. ⓢ *Average main: $11* ✉ *401 E. Andy Devine Ave.* ☎ *928/718–0018* ⊕ *www.elpalacioofchandler.com.*

$

AMERICAN
FAMILY

✕ **Mr. D'z Route 66 Diner.** This popular spot serves up road food with a '50s flair for breakfast, lunch, and dinner. (Even Oprah and Gayle King stopped here on their cross-country adventure several years ago.) The jukebox spins favorites, and tributes to Elvis and Marilyn Monroe adorn the walls in this old-fashioned diner decked out in bright turquoise and hot pink. Expect low prices and large servings of your favorite burgers, milk shakes, and more substantial fare (chicken-fried steak, baby-back ribs) at dinner, plus handcrafted root beer made on the premises. ⓢ *Average main: $10* ✉ *105 E. Andy Devine Ave.* ☎ *928/718–0066* ⊕ *www.mrdzrt66diner.com.*

$

BARBECUE

✕ **Redneck's Southern Pit BBQ.** Drop by this unassuming storefront eatery in Kingman's historic downtown for tender, perfectly seasoned and smoked barbecue. Pulled pork sandwiches, Cajun-style andouille sausage platters, and sides of mac-and-cheese, baked beans, and chunky potato salad are favorites among the lunch crowd. At dinner, dig into hefty platters of juicy ribs or smoked bone-in chicken breasts. There's also an ice cream shop on premises—all the easier to enjoy that homemade peach cobbler a la mode. ⓢ *Average main: $10* ✉ *420 E. Beale St.* ☎ *928/757–8227* ⊕ *www.redneckssouthernpitbbq.com* ⊘ *Closed Sun.–Mon.*

$

HOTEL

🛏 **Best Western Plus–King's Inn & Suites.** Conveniently located at the intersection of Interstate 40 and U.S. 93, this hotel has clean, spacious rooms and is a good base for visiting Hualapai Mountain Park, Laughlin, and the ghost towns of Chloride and Oatman. **Pros:** several restaurants are within walking distance; nicely kept rooms; hot breakfast included. **Cons:** traffic can be heard from the highway. ⓢ *Rooms from: $89* ✉ *2930 E. Andy Devine Ave.* ☎ *928/753–6101, 800/750–6101* ⊕ *www.bestwesternarizona.com* ⤳ *101 rooms* ⎮◉⎮ *Breakfast.*

NIGHTLIFE

Fodor's Choice
★

Cellar Door Wine Bar. With more than 20 wines by the glass (priced with a very reasonable mark-up) plus a noteworthy selection of imported and craft beers, this wine bar provides a sophisticated but low-key after-dark option in historic downtown Kingman. There's live music many evenings, and you can accompany your wine-sipping with a few well-prepared small plates, from cheese platters to bruschetta topped with tomatoes and mozzarella. There is also a retail wine shop here. Cellar Door is open till 10 pm weekdays, and midnight on Friday and Saturday; it's closed Sunday–Tuesday. ✉ *414 E. Beale St.* ☎ *928/753–3885* ⊕ *www.the-cellar-door.com.*

EN
ROUTE

Oatman. A worthwhile if hokey stop between Kingman and Bullhead City, the ghost town of Oatman lies along old Route 66. It's a straight shot across the Mojave Desert valley for a while, but then the road narrows and winds precipitously for about 15 miles through the Black Mountains. Oatman's main street is right out of the Old West; scenes from a number of films, including *How the West Was Won,* were shot here. It still has a remote, old-time feel: many of the natives carry side-arms, and they're not acting. You can wander into one of the three saloons or visit the shabbily endearing **Oatman Hotel**. Several times a day, resident actors entertain visitors with mock gunfights on the main drag.

Several curio shops and eclectic boutiques line the length of Main Street. The burros that often come in from nearby hills and meander down the street, however, are the town's real draw. A couple of stores sell carrots to folks who want to feed these "wild" beasts, which at last count numbered about a dozen and which leave plenty of evidence of their visits in the form of "road apples"—so watch your step. For information about the town and its attractions, contact the **Oatman Chamber of Commerce** (☎ *928/768–6222* ⊕ *www.oatmangoldroad.org*). ⊠ *Oatman.*

LAKE HAVASU CITY

60 miles southwest of Kingman on Interstate 40 to AZ 95.

If there's an Arizona Riviera, this is it. Lake Havasu has more than 45 miles of lake shoreline—it's actually a dammed section of the Colorado River—and the area gets less than 4 inches of rain annually, which means it's almost always sunny. Spring, winter, and fall are the best times to visit; in summer, temperatures often exceed 100°F. You can rent everything from water skis to Jet Skis, small fishing boats to large houseboats. The lake area has about a dozen RV parks and camp-grounds, more than 120 boat-in campsites, and hundreds of hotel and motel rooms. There are golf and tennis facilities, as well as fishing guides who'll help you find, and catch, the big ones. This city of about 53,000 has grown rapidly over the past couple of decades, and downtown has become steadily more upscale—at least compared with the rest of northwestern Arizona.

Learn about the purchase and reconstruction of London Bridge at the exhibit showcased at the Lake Havasu City Visitor Center, which is also a great place to pick up other information on area attractions.

GETTING HERE AND AROUND

You can explore downtown and the lakefront easily on foot, but most visitors arrive by car—the city lies about 25 miles south of Interstate 40 via AZ 95, and about 100 miles north of Interstate 10 via AZ 95. In town, call Amore Shuttle & Sedan Service for local taxi service. River City Shuttle offers service from Lake Havasu to several Laughlin casinos as well as to McCarran Airport in Las Vegas.

ESSENTIALS

Transportation Contacts Amore Shuttle & Sedan Service ☎ *928/854–7744* ⊕ *www.amoreshuttlelhc.com.* **Aloha Airport Express** ☎ *928/854–5253, 888/948–3427* ⊕ *www.azaloha.com.*

Visitor Information Lake Havasu City Visitor Center ⊠ *422 English Village* ☎ *928/855–5655, 800/242–8278* ⊕ *www.golakehavasu.com.*

EXPLORING

Bill Williams River National Wildlife Refuge. This 6,055-acre desert oasis contains the largest surviving cottonwood-willow woodland in the region. The refuge is a favorite byway of neotropical migratory birds such as the flashy vermilion flycatcher and the brilliant summer tanager. ⊠ *60911 AZ 95, between mileposts 160 and 161, 23 miles south of Lake Havasu City, Parker* ☎ *928/667–4144* ⊕ *www.fws.gov/southwest/ refuges/arizona/billwill.html.*

Fodor's Choice
★ **Havasu National Wildlife Refuge.** Situated between Needles and Lake Havasu City, this spectacular 37,515-acre refuge is home to wintering Canada geese and other waterfowl, such as the snowy egret and the great blue heron. More than 315 species have been observed resting and nesting here. ⊠ *Off Oatman-Topock Hwy., exit 1 off Interstate 40 at CA/AZ border, then follow signs to refuge entrance, Topock* ☎ *760/326–3853* ⊕ *www.fws.gov/refuge/Havasu.*

Lake Havasu Museum of History. This museum takes an in-depth look at the history of the region with exhibits on the Chemehuevi Indians, London Bridge, Parker Dam, the mining industry, and historic steamboat operation. ⊠ *320 London Bridge Rd.* ☎ *928/854–4938* ⊕ *www. havasumuseum.com* ⊠ *$4* ⊙ *Tues.–Sat. 1–4.*

Fodor's Choice
★ **London Bridge.** Remember the old nursery rhyme "London Bridge Is Falling Down"? Well, it was. In 1968, after about 150 years of constant use, the 294-foot-long landmark was sinking into the Thames. When Lake Havasu City founder Robert McCullough heard about this predicament, he set about buying London Bridge, having it disassembled, shipped more than 5,000 miles to northwestern Arizona, and rebuilt, stone by stone. The bridge was reconstructed on mounds of sand and took three years to complete. When it was finished, a mile-long channel was dredged under the bridge and water was diverted from Lake Havasu through the Bridgewater Channel. Today, the entire city is centered on this unusual attraction. At the east base of the bridge, a colorful re-creation of an **English Village** houses a few curio shops and restaurants and offers good views of the channel of cool blue water flowing under London Bridge. On the west side, you'll find a handful of more urbane restaurants as well as the hip **Heat Hotel.** ⊠ *1550 London Bridge Rd.*

OFF THE BEATEN PATH

'Ahakhav Tribal Preserve. The 1,253-acre preserve, which includes a 3.5-acre park and 250 acres of aquatic habitat, is on the Colorado Indian Tribes Reservation and is a top spot in the area for bird-watching and hiking. Some 350 species of migratory and native birds live around the region or visit on their annual migrations. The best bird-watching is along the shoreline of the backwater area branching off the Colorado River. The 3-mile hiking trail has exercise stations along the way, and a trail extension will lead you to the tribal historical museum and gift shop. From AZ 95 in Parker, which is at the southern end of Lake Havasu, head west on Mohave Road for about 2 miles. When you reach the "Parker Indian Rodeo Association" sign, continue 0.5 miles farther and turn left at the "Tribal Preserve" sign at Rodeo Road. ⊠ *Rodeo*

Rd., off of Mohave Rd. and AZ 95, Parker ☎928/669–2664 ⊕ *www. parkeraz.org/Ahakhav.html* ⊗ *Daily dawn–dusk.*

WHERE TO EAT

$$$
AMERICAN

✗ **Cha-Bones.** Fiber-optic lighting, mod hanging lamps, and water sculptures create a contemporary vibe at this hip, elegant restaurant a short drive north of London Bridge. Superbly prepared steaks and seafood are the key draw, from 24-ounce porterhouse cuts to cioppino in a saffron-tomato broth, but also consider the barbecue ribs and linguine with chicken and poblano chiles. There's also an extensive tapas list, including yam fries with honey-key-lime sauce and seared ahi, and a great selection of wine and cocktails. $ *Average main: $22* ✉ *112 London Bridge Rd.* ☎928/854–5554 ⊕ *www.chabones.com.*

$
MEXICAN

✗ **Chico's Tacos.** This always-hopping taqueria in the nondescript Basha's Shopping Center serves reliably good Mexican food. It's not fancy, but this clean and comfortable short-order joint turns out tasty tacos, enchiladas, flautas, burritos, and fajitas served with chicken, grilled fish, carne asada, and other meat and veggie options. Six different salsas at the salsa bar add a bit of spice to the mix. $ *Average main: $6* ✉ *1641 N. McCulloch Blvd.* ☎928/680–7010.

$$
MODERN
AMERICAN
Fodor's Choice
★

✗ **College Street Brewhouse.** Although it's in a somewhat industrial area a short drive north of downtown, this lively, high-ceilinged restaurant and microbrewery with an enormous patio enjoys nice views of the lake. The craft beers, especially the crisp but balanced IPA and refreshing unfiltered American wheat, are reason alone to stop by, but chef Theary So also turns out consistently tasty, artfully presented comfort food that pairs well with the brews. Worthy starters include lump crab–stuffed fried avocados and green chile mac-and-cheese. Entrées include hefty sandwiches (note the first-rate pastrami burger topped with cabbage chow-chow and Swiss cheese), pizzas, and several Cajun-influenced dishes, with scallop-and-shrimp jambalaya topping the list. $ *Average main: $14* ✉ *1940 College Dr.* ☎928/854–2739 ⊕ *www. collegestreetbrewhouseandpub.com.*

$$
AMERICAN

✗ **Juicy's River Café.** This downtown locals' favorite is cozy and very popular—it fills up fast, especially for breakfast and on Sunday mornings. The chicken-fried steak with biscuits and eggs is legendary. The varied menu of lunch and dinner standards includes burgers with barbecue sauce, cheddar, and smoked bacon; meat loaf; pot roast Stroganoff; and homemade soups and desserts. Great service is paired with reasonable prices. $ *Average main: $16* ✉ *25 N. Acoma Blvd.* ☎928/855–8429, 877/584–2970 ⊕ *www.juicysrivercafe.com* ⊗ *No dinner Sun. mid-Sept– May. No dinner Sat.–Thurs. June–mid-Sept.*

$
ITALIAN

✗ **La Vita Dolce.** This informal, bustling, family-run restaurant with indoor and outdoor seating serves tasty, straightforward Italian fare, from classic pastas and grills—spaghetti and meatballs, portobello-mushroom ravioli, veal piccata—and a small but creative selection of thin-crust pizzas. The Maui Waui with capicola ham, sweet pineapple, and marinara sauce is a local favorite. Appetizers are half off and beer and wine are discounted during the daily happy hour (3–6 pm). $ *Average main: $13* ✉ *231 Swanson Ave.* ☎928/208–4138 ⊕ *www. lavitadolcehavasu.com.*

9

$$$

AMERICAN

✗ **Shugrue's.** The Shugrue's in Sedona came first, but this branch lives up to the original's excellent reputation. More relaxed than the Sedona oupost, this attractive space set on a bluff overlooking London Bridge has one of the best wine lists in town plus consistently well-prepared steaks, seafood, and other traditional American and international dishes. Highlights include flat bread with Havarti cheese, portabella mushrooms, and olive-tomato tapenade for a starter and baked Dijon–garlic–crusted halibut with sea scallops and tomato concasse as a main course. Be sure to request a table with a bridge view. Ⓢ *Average main: $22* ⊠ *1425 McCulloch Blvd.* ☎ *928/453–1400* ⊕ *www.shugrues.com.*

WHERE TO STAY

For expanded hotel reviews, visit Fodors.com.

$

RESORT

⛉ **Havasu Springs Resort.** On a low peninsula reaching into Lake Havasu, this moderately priced resort 15 miles north of Parker comprises four motel buildings, each with different attributes and many with expansive views of the water or desert. **Pros:** comprehensive dining and recreation; affordable; nice lakeside beachfront. **Cons:** the most economical rooms have dated furnishings; RV traffic; 30-minute drive from Lake Havasu City. Ⓢ *Rooms from: $72* ⊠ *2581 AZ 95, Parker* ☎ *928/667–3361* ⊕ *www.havasusprings.com* ⌁ *38 rooms, 4 suites, 3 apartments* ⦿ *No meals.*

$$

HOTEL

Fodor's Choice

★

⛉ **Heat Hotel.** The hip rooms at this sleek, angular-looking boutique hotel on the west side of London Bridge capture the see-and-be-seen playfulness of Vegas, making it a hit with well-heeled, stylish visitors. **Pros:** stylish and posh decor; steps from London Bridge and many restaurants; swanky bar and cabana area. **Cons:** might be a bit too trendy and modern for some tastes; bar and pool area can be a scene on weekends and during spring break. Ⓢ *Rooms from: $189* ⊠ *1420 McCulloch Blvd.* ☎ *928/854–2833, 888/898–4328* ⊕ *www.heathotel.com* ⌁ *17 rooms, 8 suites* ⦿ *No meals.*

$

RESORT

FAMILY

⛉ **The Nautical Beachfront Resort.** This expansive waterfront resort on a scenic stretch of Thompson Bay is a favorite choice of families and sports enthusiasts. **Pros:** lots of recreation amenities on-site; set on a beautiful and relatively quiet section of lakefront; spacious rooms. **Cons:** $20 daily resort fee; 20-minute walk to restaurants and shops at London Bridge. Ⓢ *Rooms from: $149* ⊠ *1000 McCulloch Blvd. N* ☎ *928/855–2141, 800/892–2141* ⊕ *www.nauticalinn.com* ⌁ *138 suites* ⦿ *No meals.*

NIGHTLIFE

Clubbing and barhopping are increasingly popular pastimes among visitors to Lake Havasu. Most of the top venues in town are located in hotels and restaurants, including Heat Hotel, College Street Brewhouse, and Cha-Bones among them. ⇨ *See Where to Eat and Where to Stay in Lake Havasu City for reviews.*

BlueWater Resort & Casino. A big nightlife draw around Lake Havasu is BlueWater Casino, 40 miles south in the town of Parker. The gaming area comprises 475 slot machines, plus blackjack, poker, and bingo, and it adjoins a full-service resort with a concert hall, bars, a movie theater, restaurants, a 164-slip marina, and a 200-room hotel. ⊠ *11300*

Resort Dr., Parker ☏ *928/669–7777, 888/243–3360* ⊕ *www.bluewaterfun.com.*

Fodor's Choice **Desert Bar.** Set down a remote mining road in the Buckskin Mountains roughly midway between Lake Havasu City and Parker, the quirky Desert Bar, aka the Nellie E. Saloon, is one of the region's most fabled curiosities. It's only open on weekends and occasional holidays (from noon until sunset), from Labor Day through Memorial Day. This cash-only, solar-powered entertainment compound is a work in progress, comprising indoor and outdoor bars, a stage with live music throughout the day, a horseshoe pit, a covered footbridge, and a nondenominational church that's the occasional site of weddings. ✉ *Cienega Springs Rd., off AZ 95, 5 miles south of Lake Havasu City (follow signs), Parker* ⊕ *www.thedesertbar.com.*

> **LODGING ALTERNATIVE: HOUSEBOATS**
>
> What houseboats lack in speed and maneuverability they make up for in comfort and shade. **Lake Havasu Houseboats** has some of the most luxurious boats on the lake and the crew makes certain that boaters get the best instruction and tips for their travel into cool blue waters. Boats sleep 10 or more and have sundecks, waterslides, kitchens, and plenty of other amenities. Expect to pay $850 to $2,500 per night during the summer high season—the longer you rent, the less costly it is per day. ✉ *1000 McCulloch Blvd., Lake Havasu City* ☏ *800/843-9218* ⊕ *www.lakehavasuhouseboating.com*

SPORTS AND THE OUTDOORS
BOAT TOURS

There's no white water on the Colorado River below Hoover Dam. Instead, the river and its lakes offer many opportunities to explore the gorges and marshes that line the shores. If you prefer to do it yourself, look into the canoe and kayak rentals available on Lakes Mead, Mohave, and Havasu. Raft adventures will take you through the Topock Gorge near Lake Havasu, or you can take a trip upriver from Willow Beach 12 miles to the base of Hoover Dam. Along the way, chances are good you'll see bighorn sheep moving along the steep basaltic cliffs, and depending on the season, you can view hundreds of different types of migrating birds.

Blue Water Jet Boat Tours. From September through May, Blue Water Jet Boat Tours takes guests on a 2½-hour narrated trip up the Colorado River to Topock Gorge in the climate-controlled *Starship*. Other tours run to Bill Williams Wildlife Refuge (3 hours) and around the lake's famed lighthouses (1½ hours). Prices range from $24 to $38 per person, depending on the tour. ✉ *501 English Village* ☏ *928/855-7171, 888/855-7171* ⊕ *www.coloradoriverjetboattours.com* ۞ Closed June–Aug.

FAMILY **Desert River Outfitters.** Kayakers can choose between Davis Dam to Rotary Park half-day ($35 per person) paddling trips along the Colorado River Heritage Trail and all-day trips from Topock Gorge ($50 per person) to the upper reaches of Lake Havasu. The full-day trips are for intermediate kayakers and are available only from mid-October to mid-April; the others are suitable for beginners and can be undertaken year-round. Some excursions are offered in the evening, by moonlight. ⊠ *1034 AZ 95, Bullhead City* ☎ *888/529–2533* ⊕ *www. desertriveroutfitters.com.*

Jerkwater Canoe Co. Jerkwater offers three different one-day paddling trips, including exploratory excursions in Topock Gorge and Black Canyon—rates are from $41 to $78 per person, depending on the trip. Multiday trips along several scenic stretches of the Colorado River are also available. ⊠ *13003 Powell Lake Rd., Topock* ☎ *928/768–7753, 800/421–7803* ⊕ *www.jerkwatercanoe.com.*

Western Arizona Canoe & Kayak Outfitter (WACKO). This outfitter gets the outdoor adventure going with paddling trips of Topock Gorge, Lake Havasu, and Bill Williams Wildlife Refuge. Excurions cost $40 to $48 per person. ☎ *928/855–6414, 888/881–5038* ⊕ *www.azwacko.com.*

GOLF

The Courses at London Bridge Golf Club. You can play on two beautifully laid-out 18-hole courses at this golf club set along the shore of Lake Havasu, with stunning views of the mountains. The Nassau course runs a bit shorter than Olde London, but both are similarly challenging, with tight fairways and demanding, relatively small greens on the former and ample bunkers and water hazards on the latter. ⊠ *2400 Clubhouse Dr.* ☎ *928/855–2719* ⊕ *www.londonbridgegc.com* ⅄. *Nassau Course: 18 holes. 6,140 yds. Par 72. Olde London Course: 18 holes. 6,466 yds. Par 71. Greens Fee: $65* ⌦ *Facilities: driving range, putting green, golf carts, pull carts, rental clubs, pro shop, lessons, restaurant, bar, snack bar.*

WATER SPORTS

When construction of Parker Dam was completed in 1938, the reservoir it created to supply water to Southern California and Arizona became Lake Havasu. The lake is a 45-mile-long playground for water sports of all kinds. Whether it's waterskiing, jet skiing, stand-up paddling, powerboating, houseboating, swimming, fishing, or you name it, if water is required, it's happening on Lake Havasu.

With a boat, you have more options: you can find a quiet, secluded cove or beach to swim or fish. If you have a need for speed, you can plane up and down the lake with or without a skier in tow.

Cattail Cove State Park. On the eastern shore of the lake 15 miles south of Lake Havasu City is 2,000-acre Cattail Cove State Park, a popular spot for fishing and boating (you can rent boats at the marina). There are 61 first-come, first-served campsites ($15–$26) with access to electricity and water, and public restrooms with showers. ⊠ *AZ 95, 15 miles south of Lake Havasu* ☎ *928/855–1223* ⊕ *www.pr.state.az.us/parks/ CACO/index.html* 🖃 *$10 per vehicle on weekdays, $15 on weekends* ☾ *Sunrise–10 pm.*

Lake Havasu State Park. Near the London Bridge, Lake Havasu State Park has an interpretive nature garden and a level 1.75-mile trail that's perfect for watching the sunset. With three boat ramps, extensive docking, electrical hookups, and about 45 first-come, first-served campsites

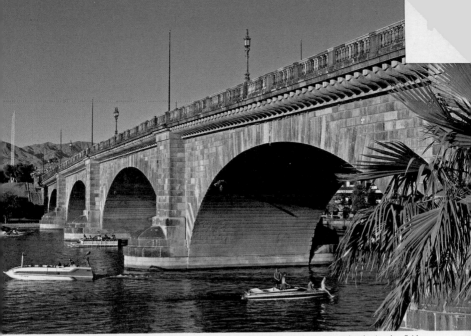
On Lake Havasu, boaters combine recreation with a bit of English history as they pass under the London Bridge.

($30–$35 daily, including day-use fee), it's an extremely popular spot in summer. ✉ *699 London Bridge Rd.* ☎ *928/855–2784* ⊕ *www.pr.state. az.us/parks/LAHA/index.html* ✉ *$10 per vehicle on weekdays, $15 on weekends* ☉ *Sunrise–10 pm.*

9

EQUIPMENT AND RENTALS If you don't have the equipment or the vessel necessary to enjoy your water sport, you can rent one from a number of reputable merchants.

Arizona Water Sports. You can rent Jet Skis, jet boats, ski boats, and pontoon boats here, as well as a variety of other water toys, from wakeboards to inner tubes. The company also has branches down at Parker Dam and at Blue Water Resort & Casino, in Parker. ✉ *655 Kiowa Ave.* ☎ *928/453–5558, 800/393–5558* ⊕ *www.arizonawatersports.com.*

AZ Built Sports. In addition to renting motorboats, outrigger canoes, and kayaks—not to mention a wide variety of bikes—AZ Built Sports offers stand-up paddleboards, which have become an extremely popular way to play and exercise on the lake. ✉ *191 Swanson Ave.* ☎ *928/505–8669* ⊕ *www.azbuiltsports.com.*

Sand Point Marina and RV Park. You can rent everything from Jet Skis to pontoon boats, by the day or by the week, at this park, which has a 104-slip marina, convenience store, and café. ✉ *7952 S. Sandpoint Rd.* ☎ *928/855–0549* ⊕ *www.sandpointresort.com.*

SOUTHEAST NEVADA

Laughlin, Nevada, and Bullhead City, Arizona, are separated by a unique state line: the Colorado River. It's an interesting juxtaposition of cities, with the casino lights of Laughlin sparkling across the river from Bullhead City. Sixty miles upstream, just southeast of Las Vegas, Boulder City is prim, languid, and full of historic neighborhoods, small businesses, parks, greenbelts—and not a single casino. Over the hill from town, enormous Hoover Dam blocks the Colorado River as it enters Black Canyon. Backed up behind the dam is incongruous, deep-blue Lake Mead, the focal point of water-based recreation for southern Nevada and northwestern Arizona and the major water supplier to seven Southwest states. The lake is ringed by miles of rugged desert country. Less than half a mile downstream from the Hoover Dam and Lake Mead, another engineering marvel, a bridge spanning the river canyon and linking northwestern Arizona to southeastern Nevada, opened in fall 2010. It's dramatically reduced traffic across Hoover Dam.

BULLHEAD CITY, ARIZONA, AND LAUGHLIN, NEVADA

35 miles west of Kingman via U.S. 93 to AZ 68.

Laughlin, Nevada, is separated from Arizona by the Colorado River. Its founder, Don Laughlin, bought an eight-room motel here in 1964 and basically built the town from scratch. By the early 1980s Laughlin's Riverside Hotel-Casino was drawing gamblers and river rats from northwestern Arizona, southeastern California, and even southern Nevada, and his success attracted other casino operators. Today Laughlin is the state's third major resort area, attracting more than 3 million visitors annually. The city fills up, especially in winter, with both retired travelers who spend at least part of winter in Arizona and a younger resort-loving crowd. The big picture windows overlooking the Colorado River lend a bright, airy, and open feeling unique to Laughlin casinos. Take a stroll along the river walk, then make the return trip by water taxi ($4 one-way, $20 all day). Boating, using Jet Skis, fishing, and plain old wading are other options for enjoying the water.

TIMING

The state of Nevada is in the Pacific time zone, while Arizona is in the mountain time zone. Arizona doesn't observe daylight saving time, however. As a result, in summer Nevada and Arizona observe the same hours.

GETTING HERE AND AROUND

To get to Laughlin from Kingman by car, follow U.S. 93 north for 3 miles, and then head west on AZ 68 for about 30 miles.

Mills Tours, River City Shuttle, and Tri State Shuttle offer regular service from McCarran International Airport to Laughlin/Bullhead City. Reservations for all shuttle services are required.

Lucky Cab & Limo Company of Nevada services Laughlin and Bullhead City. For another approach in getting from casino to casino in Laughlin, hop aboard a water taxi with River Passage. Fares can be purchased at the casino dock ticket booths.

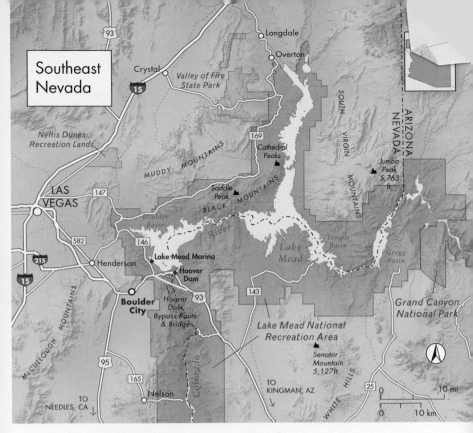

Southeast Nevada

ESSENTIALS

Airport Laughlin/Bullhead International Airport. The airport is for charter flights only, though various carriers have been working to obtain scheduled passenger service. ☎ *928/754–2134.*

Bus Contacts Mills Tours ☎ *877/454–3734.* **Tri State Shuttle** ✉ *1528 Alta Vista Rd., Bullhead City, Arizona* ☎ *800/801–8687* ⊕ *www.tristateairportshuttle. com.*

Rental Cars Avis-Airport ☎ *928/754–4686* ⊕ *www.avis.com.* **Enterprise-Airport** ☎ *928/754–2700* ⊕ *www.enterprise.com.* **Hertz-Airport** ☎ *928/754–4111* ⊕ *www.hertz.com.*

Taxis Lucky Cab & Limo Company of Nevada ☎ *702/298–2299.* **River Passage.** The river taxis that ferry people from hotel to hotel along the Mojave River are a fun way to casino-hop. It's $4 per trip or $20 for a day pass. ☎ *928/754–4391.*

Train Contacts Amtrak. Amtrak does not provide direct service to Laughlin, but its Southwest Chief makes a daily stop in Kingman, Arizona. Connections are made by bus, with daily Greyhound service from Kingman to Laughlin. ☎ *800/872–7245* ⊕ *www.amtrak.com.*

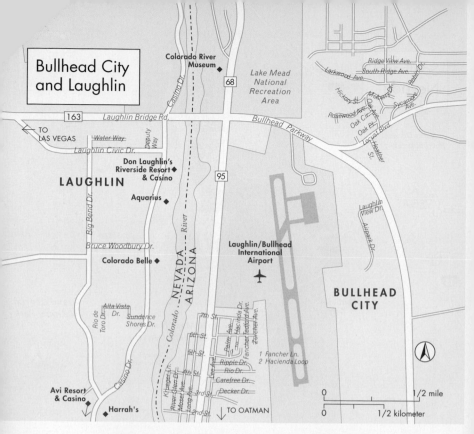

Bullhead City and Laughlin

Visitor Information Laughlin Chamber of Commerce ✉ *1585 S. Casino Dr.* ☎ *702/298-2214, 800/227-5245* ⊕ *www.laughlinchamber.org.*

EXPLORING

FAMILY **Colorado River Museum.** Across the Laughlin Bridge, ¼ mi to the north on the Arizona side of the river, the Colorado River Museum displays the rich past of the tristate region where Nevada, Arizona, and California converge. The museum is a bit ramshackle, but earnest volunteers guide you through the haphazard array of artifacts from the Mojave Indian tribe and the gold rush era in nearby Oatman. There's a model of Fort Mohave, rock and fossil specimens, and the first telephone switchboard used in Bullhead City. ✉ *2201 Hwy. 68, Bullhead City, Arizona* ☎ *928/754-3399* ✉ *$2; children under 12 free* ⊘ *Sept.–June, Tues.–Sat. 10–4.*

Searchlight Historic Museum. Searchlight was once the biggest boomtown in southern Nevada, and some of its rich mining and railroad history is now compressed into a one-room museum, in a building shared with a library and community center. There is recorded narration, a recreated assayer's office, and an exhibit devoted to Clara Bow, the silent screen star who lived near Searchlight after marrying screen cowboy Rex Bell. ✉ *200 Michael Wendell Way, Searchlight* ✤ *On the way to Laughlin from Las Vegas on U.S. 95, turn off at Cottonwood Cove Road, drive* *almost a mile to the end of town and turn left on Michael Wendell Way* ☎ *702/297–1682* 🌐 *www.searchlighthistoricmuseum.org* 🎟 *Free* 🕘 *Weekdays 9–5, Sat. 9–1.*

OFF THE BEATEN PATH

Christmas Tree Pass Road. Christmas Tree Pass Road is a dirt road that provides a gorgeous drive through the Lake Mead National Recreation Area to an extensive petroglyph site in Grapevine Canyon. This side route runs 16 mi through a desert landscape sacred to several historical and modern native tribes. The pass cuts through the rough-cut Newberry Range near legendary Spirit Mountain, with several turnouts (but no designated hiking trails) before the Grapevine Canyon trail. It's the kind of drive you imagined when you bought your grocery-getter SUV, but one that also should make sedan drivers extremely wary. Sedans can take a shorter, easier route to the Grapevine Canyon trail by instead approaching from the Laughlin side (U.S. 163), which reduces the dirt-and-gravel drive to two of its easier miles. The Grapevine trail has a parking lot with latrines (no running water) and a quarter-mile walk to the springs, which served as the central gathering point for Yuman- and Numic-speaking tribes, whose messages are etched on the canyon boulders. It's a more pleasant walk in the winter, when more water is usually channeling through the canyon. The trail around the springs also offers a chance to see desert wildflowers and blooming cacti in spring and early summer. The drive reconnects with U.S. 163 15 mi northwest of Laughlin. ✉ *U.S. 95, 14 mi south of Searchlight, Searchlight.*

WHERE TO EAT

$ SEAFOOD 🍴 **Joe's Crab Shack.** With a fun beachfront atmosphere and relaxing river views on the largest outdoor-dining patio in Laughlin, this popular restaurant features fish-and-chips, seafood platters, po'boy sandwiches, crab-stuffed shrimp, steam pots, crab nachos or heaping mounds of crab in a bucket. [$] *Average main: $14* ✉ *Golden Nugget, 2300 S. Casino Dr.* ☎ *702/298–7143* 🌐 *www.joescrabshack.com.*

$$ AMERICAN 🍴 **Pints Brewery and Sports Bar.** Laughlin's only microbrewery pumps out 700 barrels of beer each year. Sample the six choices of handcrafted ales and stout, all of which pair nicely with the wood-fired specialty pizzas, gourmet hamburgers, and mesquite-grilled steaks. The pub is open daily and around the clock for breakfast, lunch and dinner. [$] *Average main: $15* ✉ *Colorado Belle, 2100 S. Casino Dr.* ☎ *702/298–4000, 866/352–3553* 🌐 *www.coloradobelle.com.*

$$$$ STEAKHOUSE 🍴 **The Range Steakhouse.** This counterpart to the Harrah's Las Vegas steak house of the same name is Laughlin's most prestigious dining room. Some menu items change seasonally to augment standards such as seafood pasta, ahi tuna, lamb chops, and a surf-and-turf platter. Riverfront views and an extensive wine list add to the elegant experience. [$] *Average main: $35* ✉ *Harrah's, 2900 S. Casino Dr.* ☎ *702/298–6832* 🌐 *www.harrahslaughlin.com* 🕘 *No lunch.*

$$$ STEAKHOUSE 🍴 **Saltgrass Steakhouse.** This casual eatery serves up Texas-size portions of such favorites as certified Angus steaks, herb-crusted prime rib, and barbecue baby back ribs. Other menu items include salads, sandwiches, hamburgers, chicken, and seafood. It's open for dinner daily and all day Sunday. [$] *Average main: $22* ✉ *Golden Nugget, 2300 S. Casino Dr.* ☎ *702/298–7153* 🌐 *www.saltgrass.com* 🕘 *No lunch Mon.–Sat.*

WHERE TO STAY

At each resort you visit, visit guest services for a player's card. These casino programs quickly rack up points for cash and discounts.

For expanded hotel reviews, visit Fodors.com.

$$ RESORT **Aquarius.** The old Flamingo Laughlin got a new name with a makeover and resort-wide renovations. **Pros:** business center; a 3,000-seat outdoor amphitheater hosts big-name entertainers; spacious buffet with Colorado River views. **Cons:** Cafe opens out to casino noise and smoke; high hallway traffic; Wi-Fi only free in Starbucks (It's $12 for 24 hours if you want it in your room). *Rooms from: $65 ✉ 1900 S. Casino Dr. ☎ 702/298–5111, 800/352–6464 🌐 www.aquariuscasinoresort.com ⇨ 1,907 rooms, 82 suites 🍴 No meals.*

$$ RESORT FAMILY **Avi Resort & Casino.** The only tribally owned casino in Nevada is run by the Fort Mojave tribe (said fort once occupied the land) and has more of a relaxed, resort vibe than hotels on the Casino Drive strip. **Pros:** Sunday champagne brunch; 8-plex movie theater; KidQuest children's center; free Wi-Fi in all rooms (a Laughlin rarity). **Cons:** location is 10 mi south of the main drag (though some consider that a "pro"); room refrigerators available on first-come, first-served basis (fee $10). *Rooms from: $65 ✉ 10000 Aha Macav Pkwy. ☎ 702/535–5555, 800/284–2946 🌐 www.avicasino.com ⇨ 455 rooms, 29 spa suites 🍴 No meals.*

$$ RESORT **Colorado Belle.** A Nevada anomaly—a riverboat casino that's actually on a river—this 608-foot replica of a Mississippi paddle wheeler has nautical-theme rooms with views of the Colorado River and special events on its outdoor plaza. **Pros:** makes good use of its outdoor space; microbrewery; decent family-friendly restaurants. **Cons:** some of the riverfront rooms have noisier motel-style exterior entry; fee for in-room Wi-Fi ($5.99 per hour or $9.99 for 24 hours); room service is continental breakfast only. *Rooms from: $65 ✉ 2100 S. Casino Dr. 🌐 www.coloradobelle.com ⇨ 1,119 rooms, 49 suites.*

$ RESORT FAMILY **Don Laughlin's Riverside Resort Hotel and Casino.** Town founder Don Laughlin still runs this northernmost joint himself. **Pros:** charter flights to the resort from all over the country; family destination features an oudoor concert venue and indoor showroom; arcade, bowling center, six-plex movie theater, and supervised playtime at Don's Kid Kastle. **Cons:** casino has low-ceiling, 1970s atmosphere; incidental fees for Wi-Fi ($8.99 for 24 hours) some in-room refrigerators; rambling layout; serious devotion to cigarettes on the "smoking" side of the casino. *Rooms from: $45 ✉ 1650 S. Casino Dr. ☎ 702/298–2535, 800/227–3849 🌐 www.riversideresort.com ⇨ 1,400 rooms 🍴 No meals.*

$$ RESORT **Edgewater Hotel Casino.** This 26-story hotel has a large casino with more than 1,000 machines. **Pros:** central location on the river walk; complimentary wheelchairs when available; beauty salon. **Cons:** incidental fees for Wi-Fi ($9.95 for 24 hours) and for refrigerators ($10); design doesn't fully exploit riverfront location (no views from buffet or steak house); swimming pool fills up fast. *Rooms from: $60 ✉ 2020 S. Casino Dr. ☎ 702/298–2453, 800/677–4837 🌐 www.edgewater-casino.com ⇨ 1,356 rooms 🍴 No meals.*

$$ ⛏ **Golden Nugget Laughlin.** Although its casino is smaller than most of its
RESORT local contemporaries, this resort is home to two of the best restaurants
in town and the first choice of Sunday brunches. **Pros:** local nightlife
scene at The Nightclub; attached parking garage; Sunday champagne
brunch at Harlow's. **Cons:** limited room availability; the only no-smok-
ing area is a detached area in the slot section of the casino. $ *Rooms
from: $65* ✉ *2300 S. Casino Dr.* ☎ *702/298–7111, 800/950–7700*
⊕ *www.goldennugget.com* ➷ *300 rooms* ✺ *No meals.*

$ ⛏ **Harrah's.** This is the classiest joint in Laughlin: it comes with a pri-
RESORT vate sand beach and two casinos (one is no-smoking). **Pros:** separate
family and adult towers and pools; smoking and no-smoking casinos;
air-charter flights from all over the United States directly to resort for
player card members. **Cons:** pools fill up fast; long lines for guest ser-
vices; incidental fees for Wi-Fi ($10.95 for 24 hours). $ *Rooms from:
$50* ✉ *2900 S. Casino Dr.* ☎ *702/298–4600, 800/427–7247* ⊕ *www.
harrahslaughlin.com* ➷ *1,505 rooms* ✺ *No meals.*

$ ⛏ **Pioneer Hotel and Gambling Hall.** Although other casinos stress the new,
RESORT the Pioneer retains its laid-back Western theme and decor from the craps
table right inside the front door to the kitschy Western trimmings of
Sassy Sue's saloon, an enclosed bar with picture-window river views.
You can spot this small (by high-rise standards) casino from the river
walkway by looking for the neon mascot, River Rick—he's Vegas Vic's
brother. **Pros:** 40 designated pet rooms; Colorado River view rooms
available. **Cons:** Wi-Fi service available; refrigerators upon request pri-
oritized for medical needs; no elevator in deluxe and river-view build-
ings; many rooms still original motel units with outdoor entry. $ *Rooms
from: $50* ✉ *2200 S. Casino Dr.* ☎ *702/298–2442, 800/634–3469*
⊕ *www.pioneerlaughlin.com* ➷ *416 rooms* ✺ *No meals.*

$ ⛏ **The River Palms.** This 25-story tower offers terrific views from most
RESORT rooms, but the two-level casino has an odd design with much space
devoted to a gaping second-floor "cut-out" that allows you to peer
below but involves much circling around and taking escalators between
levels. **Pros:** no old motel units, so every room has some high-rise view.
Cons: small sports book; limited restaurant choice for a property of
its size; transitional feel to the casino layout; Wi-Fi is $11.99 per day;
no free refrigerators unless for medical reasons ($10 rental). $ *Rooms
from: $50* ✉ *2700 S. Casino Dr.* ☎ *702/298–2242, 800/835–7903*
⊕ *www.river-palms.com* ➷ *1,000 rooms* ✺ *No meals.*

$ ⛏ **Tropicana Laughlin.** The only large casino not on the river's side of
RESORT Casino Drive competes with 1,495 renovated, value-priced rooms. **Pros:**
rooms have an airy, contemporary feel with plantation shutters and
quality beds; in-room Wi-Fi. **Cons:** must cross Casino Drive to see the
river and access most casinos; mediocre restaurants. $ *Rooms from:
$39* ✉ *2121 S. Casino Dr.* ☎ *702/298–4200, 800/243–6846* ⊕ *www.
tropicanax.com* ➷ *1,495 rooms* ✺ *No meals.*

9

BOULDER CITY

78 miles north of Laughlin on NV 163 and U.S. 95; 76 miles northwest of Kingman on U.S. 93.

In the early 1930s Boulder City was built by the federal government to house 5,000 construction workers on the Hoover Dam project. A strict moral code was enforced to ensure timely completion of the dam, and to this day, the model city is the only community in Nevada in which gambling is illegal. (Note that the two casinos at either end of Boulder City are just outside the city limits.) After the dam was completed, the town shrank but was kept alive by the management and maintenance crews of the dam and Lake Mead. Today it's a vibrant little Southwestern town.

GETTING HERE AND AROUND

It takes about 75 minutes via U.S. 93 to get from Kingman to Boulder City.

ESSENTIALS

Boulder City Chamber of Commerce ⊠ *465 Nevada Way* ☎ *702/293–2034* ⊕ *www.bouldercitychamber.com* ⊙ *Weekdays 9–5.*

EXPLORING

Boulder Dam Hotel. Be sure to stop at the Dutch Colonial style Boulder Dam Hotel, built in 1933. On the National Register of Historic Places, the 20-room bed-and-breakfast once was a favorite getaway for notables, including the man who became Pope Pius XII and actors Will Rogers, Bette Davis, and Shirley Temple. ⊠ *1305 Arizona St.* ⊕ *www.boulderdamhotel.com.*

Boulder City/Hoover Dam Museum. The Boulder City/Hoover Dam Museum in the rear of the hotel gives you a quick, compact history of the city and dam-building process. If you're going to the dam and paying for the tour and exhibits there, you probably don't need this one as well; but if you don't plan to pop for the dam tour, this one covers the basics. ☎ *702/294–1988* ⊕ *www.bcmha.org* 💲*$2* ⊙ *Mon.–Sat. 10–5.*

HOOVER DAM

7 miles east of Boulder City via U.S. 93; 67 miles northwest of Kingman via U.S. 93.

GETTING HERE AND AROUND

Hoover Dam is about a 75-minute drive from Kingman via U.S. 93; it's about 15 minutes from Boulder City.

EXPLORING

FAMILY
Fodor's Choice
★

Hoover Dam. In 1928 Congress authorized $175 million for construction of a dam on the Colorado River to control destructive floods, provide a steady water supply to seven Colorado River Basin states, and generate electricity. Considered one of the seven wonders of the industrial world, the art deco Hoover Dam is 726 feet high (the equivalent of a 70-story building) and 660 feet thick (more than the length of two football fields) at the base. Construction required 4.4 million cubic yards of concrete—enough to build a two-lane highway from San Francisco to New York. Originally referred to as Boulder Dam, the structure was later officially named Hoover Dam in recognition of President Herbert Hoover's role in the project. Look for artist Oskar Hansen's plaza sculptures, which include the 30-foot-tall *Winged Figures of the Republic* (the statues and terazzo floor patterns were copied at the new Smith Center for the Performing Arts in Downtown Las Vegas).

The tour itself is a tradition that dates back to 1937, and you can still see the old box office on top of the dam. But now the ticketed tours originate in the modern visitor center, with two choices of tour. The cheaper, most popular one is the **Powerplant Tour**, which starts every 15 minutes or so. It's a half-hour, guided tour that includes a short film and then a 537-foot elevator ride to two points of interest: a less-than-overwhelming view of a diversion tunnel, and the more impressive eight-story room housing still-functional power generators. Self-paced exhibits follow the guided portion, with good interactive museum exhibits and a great indoor/outdoor patio view of the dam from the river side. The more extensive **Hoover Dam Tour** includes everything on the Powerplant Tour but limits the group size to 20 and spends more time inside the dam, including a peek through the air vents. Tours run from 9 to 5 in the winter and 9 to 6 in the summer. Visitors for both tours submit to security screening comparable to an airport. January and February are the slowest months, and mornings generally are less busy. The top of the dam is open to pedestrians and vehicles, but you have to remain in your vehicle after sundown. The new bypass bridge is the way to and from Arizona. Those willing to pass a security checkpoint (with inspections at the discretion of officers) can still drive over the dam for sightseeing, but cannot continue into Arizona; you have to turn around and come back after the road dead-ends at a scenic lookout (with a snack bar and store) on the Arizona side. ■TIP➔ The dam's High Scaler Café is fine for a cold drink or an ice-cream cone, and the outdoor café tables even have misters. But you can skip the $9 burger by having lunch in Boulder City instead. ⊠ *U.S. 93, east of Boulder City* ☎ *702/494–2517, 866/730–9097* ⊕ *www.usbr. gov/lc/hooverdam* ⊠ *Powerplant Tour $11, expanded Hoover Dam Tour $30, visitor center only $8; garage parking $7 (free parking on Arizona-side surface lots)* ۞ *Daily 9–5* ☞ *Security, road, and Hoover Dam crossing information: 888/248–1259.*

SPORTS AND THE OUTDOORS

RAFTING Black Canyon, just below Hoover Dam, is the place for river running near Las Vegas. You can launch a raft here on the Colorado River year-round. On the Arizona side, the 11-mile run to Willow Beach, with its vertical canyon walls, bighorn sheep on the slopes, and feeder streams and waterfalls coming off the bluffs, is reminiscent of rafting the Grand Canyon. The water flows at roughly 5 mph, but some rapids, eddies, and whirlpools can cause difficulties, as can headwinds, especially for inexperienced rafters.

If you want to go paddling in Black Canyon on your own, you need to make mandatory arrangements with one of the registered outfitters. They provide permits ($12) and the National Park Service entrance fee ($5) as well as launch and retrieval services. You can get a list of outfitters at ☎ 702/494–2204, or go to the paddle-craft and rafting-tours

section on the Bureau of Land Management's website (⊕ *www.usbr.gov/lc/hooverdam*).

Black Canyon/Willow Beach River Adventures. If you're interested in seeing the canyon on large motor-assisted rafts, Black Canyon/Willow Beach River Adventures is a group excursion launching most mornings from the Hacienda Casino and Hotel. You only get wet if you want to, and a picnic lunch on the river bank is included. The trip is $88 for adults, or $33 for a half-hour "post card" tour. ⊠ *Depart from Hacienda Casino and Hotel, U.S. 93, Boulder City* ☎ *800/455–3490* ⊕ *www.blackcanyonadventures.com.*

WORD OF MOUTH

"While it is not hallowed ground in the sense of Gettysburg or Independence Hall, Hoover Dam is a stirring reminder to me of what we have accomplished as a people in an even more difficult time. I recommend it highly, and will visit again." —MRand

LAKE MEAD

About 4 miles from Hoover Dam on U.S. 93, 67 miles northwest of Kingman.

GETTING HERE AND AROUND

From Hoover Dam, travel west on U.S. 93 to its intersection with Lakeshore Drive to reach Alan Bible Visitors Center.

EXPLORING

Lake Mead. Lake Mead, which is actually the Colorado River backed up behind Hoover Dam, is the nation's largest man-made reservoir: it covers 225 square miles, is 110 miles long, and has an irregular shoreline that extends for 550 miles. You can get information about the lake's history, ecology, recreational opportunities, and the accommodations available along its shore at the Alan Bible Visitors Center. People come to Lake Mead primarily for boating, but a few areas or shoreline are cultivated for swimming: **Boulder Beach** is the closest to Las Vegas, only a mile or so from the visitor center.

Angling and house boating are favorite pastimes; marinas strung along the Nevada shore rent houseboats, personal watercraft, and ski boats. At least 1 million fish are harvested from the lake every year including the popular striped and largemouth bass. It's stocked with rainbow trout on a weekly basis from late October through March. You can fish here 24 hours a day, year-round (except for posted closings). You must have a fishing license from either Nevada or Arizona (details are on the National Park Service website), and if you plan to catch and keep trout, a separate trout stamp is required. Willow Beach is a favorite for anglers looking to catch rainbow trout; Cathedral Cove and Katherine are good for bass fishing. Divers can explore the murk beneath, including the remains of a B-29 Superfortress, which crashed into the Overton Arm of the lake in 1948. Other activities abound, including waterskiing, sailboarding, canoeing, kayaking, and snorkeling. ⊠ *601 Nevada Way, Boulder City* ☎ *702/293–8990* ⊕ *www.nps.gov/lame* ☑ *$10 per vehicle, good for 7 days; lake-use fees $16 1st vessel, good for 7 days. Annual pass is $30 per vehicle or per vessel.*

SPORTS AND THE OUTDOORS

FAMILY **Echo Bay Resort and Marina.** Echo Bay Resort and Marina, on the Overton Arm of the north side of the lake, has boat rentals, RV facilities, a gift shop, and snack bar. It used to have a restaurant and hotel rooms but those are closed indefinitely. However, it has "flotels"—houseboat rentals that stay moored at the marina but do not go out on the lake. ✉ *600 Echo Bay Rd, Overton* ☎ *702/394–4000* ⊕ *www.echobay lakemead.com.*

Lake Mead Marina. Lake Mead Marina, at Hemenway Harbor near Hoover Dam, has a general store, rentals, and a floating restaurant. It's the closest marina to the public beach, Boulder Beach. If you haven't been to Lake Mead in a few years, the marina was moved in 2008 due to dropping water levels but has stayed put since. Boat rentals and personal watercraft are available through the **Las Vegas Boat Harbor** (702/293–1191 or 877/765–3745). ✉ *490 Horsepower Cove Rd., Boulder City* ☎ *702/293–3484* ⊕ *www.boatinglakemead.com.*

Lake Mead Cruises. At Lake Mead Cruises you can board the 300-passenger *Desert Princess,* an authentic Mississippi-style paddle wheeler that plies a portion of the lake; brunch and dinner cruises are available seasonally. Ninety-minute sightseeing cruises occur year-round. ✉ *Hemenway Boat Harbor near Boulder Beach* ☎ *702/293–6180* ⊕ *www.lakemeadcruises.com* 🍽 *Prices start at $25. Advance tickets available online.*

SCUBA
DIVING AND
SNORKELING
The creation of Lake Mead flooded a huge expanse of land, and, as a result, sights of the deep abound for scuba divers. Wishing Well Cove has steep canyon drop-offs, caves, and clear water. Castle Cliffs and Virgin Basin both have expansive views of white gypsum reefs and submerged sandstone formations. In summer Lake Mead is like a bathtub, reaching 85°F on the surface and staying at about 80°F down to 50 feet below the surface. Divers can actually wear bathing suits rather than wet suits to do some of the shallower dives. But visibility—which averages 30 feet to 35 feet overall—is much better in the winter months before the late-spring surface-algae bloom obscures some of the deeper attractions from snorkelers. Be aware that Lake Mead's level has dropped because of low snowfall in the Rockies. This has had some effect on diving conditions; the once sunken ghost town of St. Thomas, for example, is now only partially submerged.

Outfitters American Cactus Divers ✉ *3985 East Sunset Rd., Suite B, Las Vegas* ☎ *702/433–3483* ⊕ *www.americancactusdivers.com.* **Desert Divers Supply** ✉ *5720 E. Charleston Blvd., West Side, Las Vegas* ☎ *702/438–1000* ⊕ *www. nsra.info/desertdivers/divers.php.*

TRAVEL SMART
ARIZONA

GETTING HERE AND AROUND

Most visitors to Arizona arrive either by car via one of the main east–west interstates, Interstate 40 or Interstate 10/8, or by air into the state's major airport in Phoenix. (Smaller but still significant numbers fly into Tucson.) Most visitors who fly in rent cars; public transportation is limited and limiting, and this vast state is ideally suited for car touring. The state's highways are well maintained, have minimal congestion outside of Phoenix, and have high speed limits (up to 75 mph on interstates); so traveling even significant distances by car isn't a great challenge, and the scenery throughout most of the state is stunning.

▌ AIR TRAVEL

Despite its high passenger volume, lines at the check-in counters and security checkpoints at Phoenix Sky Harbor are usually brisk and efficient, although during busy periods (spring break, holiday weekends, and so on) you should anticipate longer waits and arrive at the airport 30 to 60 minutes earlier than you would otherwise. Because Phoenix is the hub for Southwest and US Airways, it has direct flights to most major U.S. cities and a number of international destinations elsewhere in North America (Calgary, Cancún, Edmonton, Guadalajara, Mexico City, Puerto Vallarta, San José [Costa Rica], Toronto, and Vancouver among them), as well as nonstop service to London on British Airways. As of this writing, US Airways was in merger talks with American Airlines; the completion of this deal would vastly expand this network and likely increase the number of destinations with direct service from Phoenix. Sample flying times from major cities are: one hour from Los Angeles, three hours from Chicago, and five hours from New York City. Keep in mind that several destinations have only seasonal nonstop service

from Phoenix (usually from mid-autumn through mid-spring).

AIRPORTS

Major gateways to Arizona include Phoenix Sky Harbor International (PHX), about 3 miles southeast of Phoenix city center, and Tucson International Airport (TUS), about 8½ miles south of the central business area.

Phoenix Sky Harbor International Airport is one of the busiest airports in the world for takeoffs and landings but rarely suffers from congestion or lengthy lines. Its spacious, modern terminals are easily navigable, with plenty of dining options as well as free Wi-Fi. Sky Harbor's three passenger terminals are connected by interterminal buses that run regularly throughout the day.

Tucson International Airport has one terminal that has a smattering of restaurants and free Wi-Fi. Although it services far fewer passengers per day than Sky Harbor, it does offer nonstop flights to a number of major metropolitan areas around the western half of the country (Atlanta is the only eastern city with direct service).

Airport Info Phoenix Sky Harbor International ☏ *602/273–3300* ⊕ *www.phxskyharbor. com.* **Tucson International Airport** ☏ *520/573–8100* ⊕ *www.flytucsonairport.com.*

FLIGHTS

Phoenix is a hub for Southwest Airlines and US Airways. These carriers offer direct flights in and out of Phoenix to most of the country's larger metro areas; Southwest also has direct flights from Tucson to Albuquerque, Chicago, Denver, Las Vegas, Los Angeles, and San Diego, and US Airways has numerous daily connections between Tucson and Phoenix. The nation's other major airlines also fly into Phoenix and have a few flights into Tucson as well.

Among the smaller carriers, Alaska Airlines has direct service from Phoenix to

Portland and Seattle, and from Tucson to Seattle. Frontier connects Phoenix with Denver. Hawaiian Airlines flies from Phoenix to Honolulu. JetBlue has service from Phoenix to Boston and New York. Sun Country Airlines has seasonal service from Phoenix to Minneapolis. Canada's WestJet connects Phoenix with Calgary, Edmonton, Kelowna, Regina, Saskatoon, Vancouver, Victoria, and Winnipeg.

Within Arizona, US Airways Express flies from Phoenix to Flagstaff and Yuma. Great Lakes Aviation flies to Kingman from Los Angeles and Prescott; to Page from Denver, Farmington (NM), Las Vegas, Phoenix, and Prescott; to Prescott from Kingman, Los Angeles, Moab (UT), and Page; and to Show Low from Phoenix and Farmington. Scenic Airlines flies from Las Vegas to the Grand Canyon.

Airline Contacts Alaska Airlines ☎ *800/252-7522* ⊕ *www.alaskaair.com.* **American Airlines** ☎ *800/433-7300* ⊕ *www. aa.com.* **Delta Airlines** ☎ *800/221-1212* ⊕ *www.delta.com.* **jetBlue** ☎ *800/538-2583* ⊕ *www.jetblue.com.* **Southwest Airlines** ☎ *800/435-9792* ⊕ *www.southwest.com.* **United Airlines** ☎ *800/864-8331* ⊕ *www. united.com.* **US Airways** ☎ *800/428-4322* ⊕ *www.usairways.com.*

Smaller Airlines Frontier Airlines ☎ *800/432-1359* ⊕ *www.flyfrontier.com.* **Great Lakes Airlines** ☎ *800/554-5111* ⊕ *www.greatlakesav.com.* **Hawaiian Airlines** ☎ *800/367-5320* ⊕ *www.hawaiianair. com.* **Scenic Airlines** ☎ *866/235-9422* ⊕ *www.scenic.com.* **Sun Country Airlines** ☎ *800/359-6786* ⊕ *www.suncountry.com.* **WestJet** ☎ *888/937-8538* ⊕ *www.westjet. com.*

▌ CAR TRAVEL

A car is a necessity in Arizona, as even bigger cities are challenging to get around in using public transportation. Distances are considerable, but you can make excellent time on long stretches of interstate and other four-lane highways with speed limits of up to 75 mph (even rural two-lane highways often have speed limits of 65 mph). In cities, freeway limits are between 55 mph and 65 mph. If you venture off major thoroughfares, slow down. Many rural roadways have no shoulders; on many twisting and turning mountain roads speed limits dip to 25 mph, and police officers often patrol heavily near entrances to small town centers, where speed limits drop precipitously. For the most part, the scenery you'll take in while driving makes road-tripping worth the time and effort.

At some point you'll probably pass through one or more of the state's 22 Native American reservations. Roads and other areas within reservation boundaries are under the jurisdiction of reservation police and governed by separate rules and regulations. Observe all signs, and respect Native Americans' privacy. Be careful not to hit any animals, which often wander onto the roads; the fines can be very high.

Note that in Phoenix certain lanes on interstates are restricted to carpools and multi-occupant vehicles. Seat belts are required at all times. Tickets can be given for failing to comply. Driving with a blood-alcohol level higher than 0.08 will result in arrest and seizure of your driver's license. Fines are severe. Radar detectors are legal in Arizona, as is driving while talking on handheld phones (although texting while driving is illegal in Phoenix and Tucson, and other municipalities are considering a similar ban).

Always strap children under age five into approved child-safety seats. In Arizona children must wear seat belts regardless of where they're seated. In Arizona you may turn right at a red light after stopping if there's no oncoming traffic.

Information Arizona Department of Public Safety ☎ *602/223-2000* ⊕ *www.azdps.gov.* **Arizona Department of Transportation** ☎ *511 Arizona road information from within the state, 888/411-7623 Arizona road information from outside the state* ⊕ *www.az511.com.*

GASOLINE

Gas stations, many of them open 24 hours, are widely available in larger towns and cities and along interstates. However, you'll encounter some mighty lonely and long stretches of highway in certain remote sections of Arizona; in these areas it's not uncommon to travel 50 or 60 miles between service stations. It's prudent to play it safe when exploring the far-flung corners of the state and keep your tank at least half full. Gas prices in Arizona are slightly higher than the national average but generally lower than in neighboring Nevada and California.

PARKING

Parking is plentiful and either free or very inexpensive in most Arizona towns, even Phoenix and Tucson. During very busy times, however, such as holidays, parking in smaller popular places like Sedona, Flagstaff, Scottsdale, and Bisbee can prove a little challenging.

ROAD CONDITIONS

The highways in Arizona are well maintained, but there are some natural conditions to keep in mind.

Desert heat. Vehicles and passengers should be well equipped for searing summer heat in the low desert. If you're planning to drive through the desert, make sure you're well stocked with radiator coolant, and carry plenty of water, a good spare tire, a jack, a cell phone, and emergency supplies. If you get stranded, stay with your vehicle and wait for help to arrive.

Dust storms. Dust storms are common on the highways and interstates that traverse the open desert (Interstate 10 statewide, and Interstate 8 between Casa Grande and Yuma). These usually occur from May to mid-September, causing extremely low visibility. They also occur occasionally in northeastern Arizona around the Navajo and Hopi regions. If you're on the highway, pull as far off the road as possible, turn on your headlights to stay visible, and wait for the storm to subside.

Flash floods. Warnings about flash floods shouldn't be taken lightly. Sudden downpours send torrents of water racing into low-lying areas so dry that they're unable to absorb such a huge quantity of water quickly. The result can be powerful walls of water suddenly descending upon these low-lying areas, devastating anything in their paths. If you see rain clouds or thunderstorms coming, stay away from dry riverbeds (also called arroyos or washes). If you find yourself in one, get out quickly. If you're with a car in a long gully, leave your car and climb out of the gully. You simply won't be able to outdrive a speeding wave. The idea is to get to higher ground immediately when it rains. Major highways are mostly flood-proof, but some smaller roads dip through washes; most roads that traverse these low-lying areas will have flood warning signs, which should be seriously heeded during rainstorms. Washes filled with water shouldn't be crossed unless you can see the bottom. By all means, don't camp in these areas at any time, interesting as they may seem.

Fragile desert life. The dry and easily desecrated desert floor takes centuries to overcome human damage. Consequently, it's illegal for four-wheel-drive and all-terrain vehicles and motorcycles to travel off established roadways.

Winter snow and ice. First-timers to Arizona sometimes doubt the intensity and prevalence of icy and snowy winter weather in the state's higher elevations: the Interstate 40 corridor, Grand Canyon region, north-central and northeastern Arizona, as well as some high-elevation communities in eastern Arizona. It's not uncommon for Phoenix to enjoy dry weather and temperatures in the 50s and 60s, while Flagstaff—just 140 miles north—is getting heavy snow and high winds. The North Rim of the Grand Canyon is closed from around the end of October through mid-May due to snow. Always check on weather conditions before planning trips to northern and eastern Arizona from late fall through mid-spring.

ROADSIDE EMERGENCIES

In the event of a roadside emergency, call 911. Depending on the location, either the state police or the county sheriff's department will respond. Call the city or village police department if you encounter trouble within the limits of a municipality. Native American reservations have tribal police headquarters, and rangers assist travelers within U.S. Forest Service boundaries.

Information Automobile Association (AAA). ☎ 800/222-4357 ⊕ www.aaa.com.

CAR RENTAL

Car-rental rates in Phoenix typically begin around $25 a day or $125 a week for an economy car with air-conditioning, automatic transmission, and unlimited mileage—rates vary according to supply and demand, tending to be lower in summer and higher in winter. This doesn't include taxes and fees on car rentals, which can range from about 15% to 50%, depending on pickup location. The base tax rate at Sky Harbor Airport is about 30%. When you add the daily fees (which are about $6 or more a day), taxes and fees can add up to almost half the cost of the car rental. Taxes outside the airport are typically around 25% or less.

Check the Internet or local papers for discounts and deals. Local rental agencies also frequently offer lower rates.

Most agencies in Arizona won't rent to you if you're under the age of 21, and several major agencies won't rent to anyone under 25.

In Arizona the car-rental agency's insurance is primary; therefore, the company must pay for damage to third parties up to a preset legal limit, beyond which your own liability insurance kicks in.

Major Rental Agencies Alamo ☎ 855/533-1196 ⊕ www.alamo.com. **Avis** ☎ 800/633-3469 ⊕ www.avis.com. **Budget** ☎ 800/218-7992 ⊕ www.budget.com. **Hertz** ☎ 800/654-3131 ⊕ www.hertz.com. **National Car Rental** ☎ 877/222-9058 ⊕ www.nationalcar.com.

▌ TRAIN TRAVEL

Amtrak's *Southwest Chief* operates daily between Los Angeles and Chicago, stopping in Needles, California (near the Arizona border), Kingman, Williams Junction (from which bus transfers are available to the scenic Grand Canyon Railway), Flagstaff, Winslow, and Gallup, New Mexico (near the Arizona border). The *Sunset Limited* travels three times each week between Los Angeles and New Orleans, with stops at Yuma, Maricopa (about 25 miles south of Phoenix), Tucson, and Benson. There's a connecting bus (a three-hour trip) between Flagstaff and Phoenix.

Train Info Amtrak ☎ 800/872-7245 ⊕ www.amtrak.com.

ESSENTIALS

∎ ACCOMMODATIONS

Arizona's hotels and motels run the gamut from world-class resorts to budget chains and from historic inns, bed-and-breakfasts, and mountain lodges to dude ranches, campgrounds, houseboat rentals, and RV parks. Make reservations well in advance for the high season—winter in the desert and summer in the high country. A few areas, such as Sedona and the Grand Canyon's South Rim, stay relatively busy year-round, so book as soon as you can. Tremendous bargains can be found off-season, especially in the Phoenix and Tucson areas in summer, when even the most exclusive establishments may cut their rates by half or more.

Phoenix and Tucson have the most variety of accommodations in the state, with Flagstaff offering the largest number in the northern part of the state. Lodgings in Sedona and in some of the smaller, more exclusive desert communities can be pricey, but there are inexpensive chains in or near just about every resort-oriented destination. That said, even the budget chains in these areas can have rates in at least the upper double-digits.

The Grand Canyon area is relatively pricey, but camping, cabins, and dorm-style resorts on or near the national park grounds offer lower rates. ∎TIP➔ If you plan to stay at the Grand Canyon, make lodging reservations as far as a year in advance—especially if you're looking to visit in summer. You might have a more relaxing visit, and find better prices, in one of the gateway cities: Tusayan, Williams, and Flagstaff to the south, and Jacob Lake, Fredonia, and Kanab, Utah, to the north. Of all of these, Flagstaff has the best variety of lodging options in all price ranges.

After booking, get confirmation in writing and have a copy handy when you check in. Be sure you understand the hotel's cancellation policy. Some places allow you to cancel without any kind of penalty—even if you prepaid to secure a discounted rate—if you cancel at least 24 hours in advance. Others require you to cancel a week in advance or penalize you the cost of one night. Small inns and B&Bs are most likely to require you to cancel far in advance. Most hotels allow children under a certain age to stay in their parents' room at no extra charge, but others charge for them as extra adults; find out the cutoff age for discounts.

Our local writers vet every hotel to recommend the best overnights in each price category, from budget to expensive. Unless otherwise specified, you can expect private bath, phone, and TV in your room. *For expanded reviews, facilities, and current deals, visit Fodors.com. Prices in the reviews are the lowest cost of a standard double room in high season.*

BED-AND-BREAKFASTS

Arizona is one of the better destinations in the country when it comes to B&Bs. You'll find luxurious Spanish colonial–style compounds and restored Victorian inns in the more upscale destinations, such as Tucson, Sedona, Flagstaff, and Prescott, as well as less fancy lodges virtually everywhere. Check with the Arizona Association of Bed and Breakfast Inns for details on its many members throughout the state. The Arizona Trails Travel Service also has an extensive list of B&Bs and other lodgings, and can also help with vacation packages, guided tours, and golf vacations. BedandBreakfast.com has booking services and emails deals and promotions to its subscribers. Mi Casa Su Casa offers properties in a range of styles, from adobe haciendas in areas like Sedona and Tucson to pine cabins in the White Mountains.

Reservation Services Arizona Association of Bed and Breakfast Inns ⊕ *www.arizona-bed-breakfast.com.* **Arizona Trails**

Travel Services ☎ *480/837–4284, 888/799–4284* ⊕ *www.arizonatrails.com.* **Bedan-dBreakfast.com** ☎ *512/322–2710* ⊕ *www.bedandbreakfast.com.* **Bed & Breakfast Inns Online** ☎ *800/215–7365* ⊕ *www.bbonline.com.* **BnB Finder.com** ☎ *888/469–6663* ⊕ *www.bnbfinder.com.* **Mi Casa Su Casa** ☎ *480/990–0682, 800/456–0682* ⊕ *www.azres.com.*

DUDE–GUEST RANCHES

Guest ranches afford visitors a close encounter with down-home cooking, activities, and culture. Most of the properties are situated around Tucson and Wickenburg, northwest of Phoenix. Some are resort-style compounds where guests are pampered, whereas smaller, family-run ranches expect *everyone* to join in the chores. Horseback riding and other outdoor recreational activities are emphasized. Many dude ranches are closed in summer. The Arizona Dude Ranch Association provides names and addresses of member ranches and their facilities and policies.

Information Arizona Dude Ranch Association ☎ *520/823–4277* ⊕ *www.azdra.com.*

∎ COMMUNICATIONS

INTERNET

As in all major U.S. cities, high-speed Internet and Wi-Fi connections are ubiquitous at hotels throughout the state, even in remote areas (sometimes at high-end resorts or business hotels, especially in big cities, there's a fee of $5 to $15 per day, though free Wi-Fi is increasingly becoming the norm). There are also typically free connections at cafés (including Starbucks), restaurants, and other businesses. In a few extremely remote areas you'll find fewer ways to get online, but usually a local café or motel has Wi-Fi.

∎ EATING OUT

Two distinct cultures—Native American and Sonoran—have had the greatest influence on native Arizona cuisine.

Chiles, beans, corn, tortillas, and squash are common ingredients for those restaurants that specialize in regional cuisine (cactus is just as tasty but less common). Mom-and-pop taquerias are abundant, especially in the southern part of the state. In Phoenix, Tucson, Sedona, Flagstaff, and increasingly Bisbee, Prescott, Lake Havasu City, and a growing number of smaller communities, you'll find hip, intriguing restaurants specializing in contemporary American and Southwestern cuisine—often with an emphasis on local produce and meats—as well as some excellent purveyors of Asian cuisine, with Thai, Chinese, and Japanese leading the way. *Prices in the reviews are the average cost of a main course at dinner or, if dinner is not served, at lunch.*

RESERVATIONS AND DRESS

Regardless of where you are, it's a good idea to make a reservation if you can. In some places (some top restaurants in Scottsdale and Tucson, for example) it's expected. We only mention them specifically when reservations are essential (there's no other way you'll ever get a table) or when they're not accepted. For popular restaurants, book as far ahead as you can (often 30 days), and reconfirm as soon as you arrive. (Large parties should always call ahead to check the reservations policy.) We mention dress only when men are required to wear a jacket or a jacket and tie.

Online reservation services, such as OpenTable, make it easy to book a table before you even leave home.

Contacts OpenTable ⊕ *www.opentable.com.*

WINES, BEER, AND SPIRITS

Although Arizona isn't typically associated with viticulture, the region southeast of Tucson, stretching to the Mexico border, has several microclimates ideal for wine growing. The iron- and calcium-rich soil is similar to that of the Burgundy region in France, and, combined with the temperate weather and lower-key atmosphere, has enticed several independent and family-run wineries to open in the past few decades in the Elgin, Sonoita, and Nogales areas, with a somewhat more nascent but increasingly respected crop of them having developed north of Phoenix, around Sedona and Verde Valley. Microbreweries are another fast-growing presence in Arizona, with a number of good ones in Phoenix, Tucson, Sedona, and Flagstaff, and other notables in Lake Havasu City, Prescott, Bisbee, and a few other towns.

In Arizona you must be 21 to buy any alcohol. Bars and liquor stores are open daily, including Sunday, but must stop selling alcohol at 2 am. Smoking is prohibited in bars and restaurants that serve food. You'll find beer, wine, and alcohol at most supermarkets. Possession and consumption of alcoholic beverages is illegal on Native American reservations.

Contact Arizona Craft Brewers Guild ⊕ *www.azbrewguild.com.* **Arizona Wine Growers Association** ☎ *623/236–2338* ⊕ *www.arizonawine.org.*

▌HEALTH

ANIMAL BITES

Wherever you're walking in desert areas, particularly between April and October, keep a lookout for rattlesnakes. You're likely not to have any problems if you maintain distance from snakes that you see—they can strike only half of their length, so a 6-foot clearance should allow you to remain unharmed, especially if you don't provoke them. If you're bitten by a rattler, don't panic. Get to a hospital within two to three hours of the bite. Try to keep the area that has been bitten below heart level, and stay calm, as increased heart rate can spread venom more quickly. Keep in mind that 30% to 40% of bites are dry bites, where the snake uses no venom (still, get thee to a hospital). Avoid night hikes without rangers, when snakes are on the prowl and less visible.

Scorpions and Gila monsters are less of a concern, since they strike only when provoked. To avoid scorpion encounters, look before touching: never place your hands where you can't see, such as under rocks and in holes. Likewise, if you move a rock to sit down, make sure that scorpions haven't been exposed. Campers should shake out shoes in the morning, since scorpions like warm, moist places. If you're bitten, see a ranger about symptoms that may develop. Chances are good that you won't need to go to a hospital. Children are a different case, however: scorpion stings can be fatal for them. Always try to keep an eye on what they may be getting their hands into to avoid the scorpion's sting. Gila monsters are relatively rare and bites are even rarer, but bear in mind that the reptiles are most active between April and June. Should a member of your party be bitten, it's most important to release the Gila monster's jaws as soon as possible to minimize the amount of venom released. This can usually be achieved with a stick, an open flame, or immersion of the animal in water.

DEHYDRATION

This underestimated danger can be very serious, especially considering that one of the first major symptoms is the inability to swallow. It may be the easiest hazard to avoid, however; simply drink every 10–15 minutes, up to a gallon of water per day when outside in summer, and keep well hydrated other times of year, too, as even cool winter days can be very dry.

HYPOTHERMIA

Temperatures in Arizona can vary widely from day to night—as much as 40°F. Be sure to bring enough warm clothing for hiking and camping, along with wet-weather gear. It's always a good idea to pack an extra set of clothes in a large, waterproof plastic bag that would stay dry in any situation. Exposure to the degree that body temperature dips below 95°F produces the following symptoms: chills, tiredness, then uncontrollable shivering and irrational behavior, with the victim not always recognizing that he or she is cold. If someone in your party is suffering from any of these symptoms, wrap him or her in blankets and/or a warm sleeping bag immediately and try to keep him or her awake. The fastest way to raise body temperature is through skin-to-skin contact in a sleeping bag. Drinking warm liquids also helps.

SUN EXPOSURE

Wear a hat and sunglasses and put on sunblock to protect against the burning Arizona sun. And watch out for heatstroke. Symptoms include headache, dizziness, and fatigue, which can turn into convulsions and unconsciousness and can lead to death. If someone in your party develops any of these conditions, have one person seek emergency help while others move the victim into the shade and wrap him or her in wet clothing (is a stream nearby?) to cool down.

▮ HOURS OF OPERATION

Most museums in Arizona's larger cities are open daily. A few are closed Monday, and hours may vary between May and September (off-season in the major tourist centers of Phoenix and Tucson). Call ahead when planning a visit to lesser-known museums or attractions, whose hours may vary considerably. Major attractions are open daily.

Most retail stores are open 10 am–6 pm, although stores in malls tend to stay open until 9 pm. Those in less-populated areas are likely to have shorter hours and may be closed Sunday. Shopping centers are often open Sunday noon–5 or later.

▮ MONEY

ITEM	AVERAGE COST
Cup of Coffee	$2.50
Glass of Wine	$6
Glass of Beer	$4
Sandwich	$6
1-Mile Taxi Ride in Phoenix	$7
Museum Admission	$10

Prices throughout this guide are given for adults. Substantially reduced fees are almost always available for children, students, and senior citizens.

▮ PACKING

Pack casual clothing and resort wear for a trip to Arizona. Stay cool in cotton fabrics and light colors. T-shirts, polo shirts, sundresses, and lightweight shorts, trousers, skirts, and blouses are useful year-round in all but the higher-elevation parts of the state, where cooler temperatures mandate warmer garb. Bring sun hats, swimsuits, sandals, and sunscreen—essential warm-weather items. Bring a sweater and a warm jacket in winter, necessary from November through April in the high country—anywhere around Flagstaff and in the White Mountains. And don't forget jeans and sneakers or sturdy walking shoes year-round.

SHIPPING SPORTING EQUIPMENT

If you're driving here, lugging your gear isn't much of a hassle. But travelers arriving by plane may find hauling bags of clubs, mountain bikes, and skis a bit daunting. Sports Express specializes in shipping gear. The service isn't cheap, but it's highly reliable and convenient.

Contact Sports Express ☎ *800/357-4174* ⊕ *www.sportsexpress.com.*

SAFETY

Arizona's track record in terms of crime is not unlike that of other U.S. states, if a little higher than average in Phoenix and Tucson. In these big cities you should take the same precautions you would anywhere—be aware of what's going on around you, stick to well-lighted and populous areas, and quickly move away from any situation or people that might be threatening.

■**TIP→** Check the U.S. government travel advisory before you plan a trip to the Mexico border towns. Visitors should take extra precautions.

Contacts Transportation Security Administration (*TSA*). ⊕ *www.tsa.gov.* **U.S. Department of State** ⊕ *travel.state.gov.*

TAXES

Arizona state sales tax (called a transaction privilege tax), which applies to all purchases except food in grocery stores, is 6.6%. Individual counties and municipalities then add their own sales taxes, which add another few percentage points. Sales taxes don't apply on Indian reservations.

TIME

Arizona is in the mountain time zone, but neighboring California and Nevada are in the Pacific time zone. Arizona doesn't use daylight saving time, though, and as a result, from spring through fall Arizona observes the same hours as Nevada and California and is an hour behind Utah and New Mexico. ■**TIP→** The Navajo Nation does observe daylight saving time, so it's always the same time on Navajo territory as in mountain time zone areas outside Arizona. Timeanddate.com can help you figure out the correct time anywhere.

Information Timeanddate.com ⊕ *www. timeanddate.com/worldclock.*

TIPPING

The customary tip for taxi drivers is 15%–20%, with a minimum of $2. Bellhops are usually given $1–$2 per bag. Hotel maids should be tipped $2 per day of your stay. A doorman who hails a cab can be tipped $1–$2. You should also tip your hotel concierge for services rendered; the size of the tip depends on the difficulty of your request, as well as the quality of the concierge's work. For an ordinary dinner reservation or tour arrangements, $3–$5 should do; if the concierge scores seats at a popular restaurant or show or performs unusual services (getting your laptop repaired, finding a good pet-sitter, etc.), $10 or more is appropriate.

Waiters should be tipped 15%–20%, though at higher-end restaurants a solid 20% is more the norm. Many restaurants add a gratuity to the bill for parties of six or more. Ask what the percentage is if the menu or bill doesn't state it. Tip $1 per drink you order at the bar, though if at an upscale establishment, those $15 martinis warrant a $2 tip.

TOURS

ARCHAEOLOGY

The Archaeological Conservancy offers a number of tours covering significant sites around the country, including a couple of trips that often involve sites in Arizona. Based in southwestern Colorado, Crow Canyon Archaeological Center has a few different trips that touch on portions of Arizona. These vary year to year, but have included hiking in Carrizo Mountain Country, Hopi kachina and silver-jewelry workshops, backcountry archaeology in Canyon de Chelly, and archaeology along the Colorado River. Utah's Southwest EdVentures, part of the Four Corners School of Outdoor Education, can work with you to customize your own trip through

Arizona's Hopi and Navajo regions, and they also offer a number of scheduled group trips that touch on mostly northeastern Arizona.

Contacts Archaeological Conservancy ☎ *505/266–1540* ⊕ *www. americanarchaeology.org.* **Crow Canyon Archaeological Center** ☎ *970/565–8975, 800/422–8975* ⊕ *www.crowcanyon.org.* **Southwest Ed-Ventures** ☎ *435/587–2156, 800/525–4456* ⊕ *www.fourcornersschool.org.*

BICYCLING

A number of companies offer extensive bike tours that cover parts of the Southwest. Backroads organizes a six-day biking and hiking trip through Utah and northern Arizona national parks. Scottsdale-based AOA Adventures offers a variety of bike trips throughout the state. For a six-day bike excursion through Tucson's Saguaro National Park and down through Tombstone and Bisbee, book the Cactus Classic Tour through Bicycle Adventures.

■**TIP**➔ Most airlines accommodate bikes as luggage, provided they're dismantled and boxed.

Contacts AOA Adventures ☎ *480/945–2881, 866/455–1601* ⊕ *www.aoa-adventures.com.* **Backroads** ☎ *510/527–1555, 800/462–2848* ⊕ *www.backroads.com.* **Bicycle Adventures** ☎ *800/443–6060* ⊕ *www.bicycleadventures. com.*

GOLF

Golfpac organizes golf vacations all over the world, Phoenix, Scottsdale, and Tucson being among its most popular destinations.

Contact Golfpac ☎ *888/848–8941* ⊕ *www. golfpactravel.com.*

HIKING

Scottsdale-based AOA Adventures offers multiday hiking and biking tours through some of the state's most dramatic scenery, from the Grand Canyon to Havasupai. Timberline Adventure has hiking tours in the Grand Canyon as well as in Chiricahua National Monument and the Sonoran Desert near Tucson.

Contact AOA Adventures ☎ *480/945–2881, 866/455–1601* ⊕ *www.aoa-adventures.com.* **Timberline Adventures** ☎ *303/368–4418, 800/417–2453* ⊕ *www.timbertours.com.*

NATIVE AMERICAN HISTORY

You can explore a number of parts of the state important to indigenous peoples—Sedona, the Grand Canyon, Hopi Country, Antelope Canyon, Canyon de Chelly—on walking, float-trip, and jeep tours offered by Native American Journeys.

Contact Native American Journeys ☎ *928/284–4735* ⊕ *www. nativeamericanjourneys.com.*

NATURAL HISTORY

Victor Emanuel Nature Tours is another excellent tour operator, offering four different tours throughout the year that emphasize bird-watching throughout the state. Off the Beaten Path has a variety of tours in northern Arizona and elsewhere in the Southwest. Tours by Arizona-based Naturalist Journeys emphasize birding and geology, and venture into southeastern Arizona as well as the Grand Canyon region.

Contacts Naturalist Journeys ☎ *520/558–1146, 866/900–1146* ⊕ *www. naturalistjourneys.com.* **Off the Beaten Path** ☎ *406/586–1311, 800/445–2995* ⊕ *www. offthebeatenpath.com.* **Victor Emanuel Nature Tours** ☎ *512/328–5221, 800/328–8368* ⊕ *www.ventbird.com.*

RIVER-RAFTING

Rafting on the Colorado River through the Grand Canyon is a once-in-a-lifetime experience for many who try it. Numerous reliable companies offer rafting tours through the canyon, including Action Whitewater Adventures, OARS, Western River Expeditions, and Wilderness River Adventures.

Contacts Action Whitewater Adventures ☎ *801/375–4111, 800/453–1482* ⊕ *www. riverguide.com.* **OARS** ☎ *209/736–4677, 800/346–6277* ⊕ *www.oars.com.* **Western River Expeditions** ☎ *801/942–6669,*

866/904–1160 ⊕ www.westernriver.com. Wilderness River Adventures ☎ 800/992-8022 ⊕ www.riveradventures.com.

■ VISITOR INFORMATION

For local tourism information, see specific chapters and towns. Many of Arizona's Native American reservations have websites and helpful information. Some require permits for visiting certain areas.

Visitor Information Arizona Office of Tourism ☎ 602/364–3700, 866/275–5816 ⊕ www.arizonaguide.com.

Native American Contacts Arizona Commission of Indian Affairs ☎ 602/542–4426 ⊕ www.indianaffairs.state.az.us. **Gila River Indian Community** ☎ 520/562–9715 ⊕ www.gilariver.org. **Hopi Tribe** ☎ 928/283–4500 ⊕ www.hopiartstrail.com. **Discover Navajo** ☎ 928/871–6436 ⊕ www.discovernavajo.com. **Salt River Pima-Maricopa Indian Community** ☎ 480/362–7740 ⊕ www.srpmic-nsn.gov. **Tohono O'odham Nation** ☎ 520/383–0211 ⊕ www.tonation-nsn.gov. **White Mountain Apache Nation** ☎ 928/369–2036 ⊕ www.wmat.nsn.us.

ONLINE RESOURCES

Information of particular interest to outdoorsy types can be found on the website for Arizona State Parks. The site for the National Park Service has links to many of Arizona's parks. The Great Outdoor Recreation Page (GORP) is another font of information for hikers, skiers, and the like.

There's a handful of excellent general-interest sites related to travel in Arizona. A very good bet is the *Arizona Republic*–sponsored ⊕ *azcentral.com*, which provides news, reviews, and travel information on the entire state, with a particular emphasis on Phoenix. Alternative newsweeklies are another helpful resource, among them the Phoenix *New Times*. For the southern part of the state, look for *Tucson Weekly*. In Flagstaff and north-central Arizona, check out Flagstaff Live.

Contacts Arizona State Parks ☎ 602/542–4174, 800/285–3703 ⊕ www.azstateparks.com. **AzCentral.com** ⊕ www.azcentral.com. **Flagstaff Live!** ⊕ www.flaglive.com. **Great Outdoor Recreation Page (GORP)** ⊕ www.gorp.com. **National Park Service** ⊕ www.nps.gov. **Phoenix New Times** ⊕ www.phoenixnewtimes.com. **Tucson Weekly** ⊕ www.tucsonweekly.com.

INDEX

A

"A" Mountain (Sentinel Peak), 358
Abyss, The, 153
Accommodations, 508–509
Adventure tours, 175, 403
Agate Bridge, 340, 344
Agate House, 342, 346
'Ahakhav Tribal Preserve, 486–487
Air tours, 142, 158–159, 300–301
Air travel, 504–505
Airports, 12, 504
  Grand Canyon, 146, 147
  North-Central Arizona, 205, 223, 251
  Northeast Arizona, 297
  Northwest Arizona and Southeast Nevada, 492, 493
  Phoenix, Scottsdale, and Tempe, 54
  Southern Arizona, 478
  Tucson, 355–356
Ajo, 463–465
Ajo Mountain Drive, 466
AJ's Fine Foods (shop), 51
Alpine, 335–336
Amangiri ☒, 307–308
Amerind Foundation, 456
Andy Devine Days, 477
Antelope Canyon, 33, 301, 304–305
Antiques and collectibles, shopping for, 110
Apache Cultural Museum, 319
Apache-Sitgreaves National Forest, 37
Apache Trail, 133–134, 136–140
Apache Cultural Center, 319
Apple Annie's Orchards, 454
Arboretum, 35, 134, 136
Archaeology tours, 512–513
Arcosanti, 132
Arizona Doll and Toy Museum, 57
Arizona Grand Resort ☒, 21
Arizona History Museum, 362–363
Arizona Inn ☒, 387
Arizona Museum of Natural History, 69
Arizona Opera Company, 105
Arizona Science Center, 21, 56

Arizona Sealife Aquarium, 69
Arizona Snowbowl, 206
Arizona-Sonora Desert Museum, 19, 35, 348, 371
Arizona State Museum, 363–364
Arizona State University, 69
Armory Park, 359
Art galleries and museums.
  ⇨ See Museums and Art galleries
Art Walk, 50
Artlink Phoenix First Fridays, 56
Arts and crafts, shopping for, 51, 108, 109, 110–111, 166, 214, 231, 258, 270, 273, 277, 279, 281, 282, 285, 287, 295, 299–300, 397–398, 399, 400, 401
ASARCO Mineral Discovery Center, 418
Aspen Peak Trail, 481
ASU Karsten Golf Course
ASU Memorial Union, 69

B

Babbitt Brothers Building, 206, 208
Bacavi, 283
Backpacking, 240
Bajada Loop Drive, 410, 412
Ballooning
  North-Central Arizona, 239
  Phoenix, Scottsdale, and Tempe, 117–118
  Tucson, 403
Barrio Historico, 359
Bars and lounges
  gay and lesbian, 100, 101, 102, 394
  Phoenix, Scottsdale, and Tempe, 99–103
  Tucson, 393–395
Baseball, 117
Basin and Range Province, 30
Bear Canyon Trail, 408
Bear Wallow Wilderness Area, 337
Bed and breakfasts, 508–509
Bell Rock, 225
Benson, 457–458
Besh-Ba-Gowah Archaeological Park, 138
Betatakin, 296

Beyond Bread ✕, 380
Bicycling
  Eastern Arizona, 323–324, 336
  Grand Canyon, 142, 159, 170, 179
  North-Central Arizona, 215, 217, 241
  Phoenix, Scottsdale, and Tempe, 118
  tours, 513
  Tucson, 403–404, 414
Bill Williams River National Wildlife Refuge, 486
Binkley's Restaurant ✕, 129
Biosphere 2 Center, 373
Bird Cage Theater, 434
Bird-watching, 33
  Eastern Arizona, 337
  Grand Canyon, 178
  North-Central Arizona, 244
  Northwest Arizona, 486
  Southern Arizona, 435, 438, 449, 451, 461–462, 470
  Tucson, 404–405, 414
Bisbee, 424, 427, 437–441
Bisbee Mining and Historical Museum, 427, 438–439
Bitter Springs, 297
Black Mesa, 288
Blair's Dinnebito Trading Post, 299–300
Blazin' M Ranch, 229
Blue Mesa Trail, 340, 346
Blue Range Primitive Area, 335
Blue Vista, 331
Blues, Jazz, and Rock, 100, 394
Boat tours, 309–310, 467, 489–490
Boating, 18, 258, 305, 308–310, 489–490, 499, 501, 502
Bola ties, 51
Bonelli House, 481–482
Books, 111, 398, 399, 514
Boot Hill Graveyard, 434
Boulder Beach, 502
Boulder City, NV, 498
Boulder City Chamber of Commerce, 498
Boulder City/Hoover Dam Museum, 498
Boulder Dam Hotel, 498
Boulders Resort and Golden Door Spa, The ☒, 129
Bourbon Steak ✕, 82–83

Boyce Thompson Arboretum, 35, 134, 136
Brewery Gulch (Bisbee), 439
Bright Angel Point, 168
Bright Angel Trail, 18, 160
Buenos Aires National Wildlife Refuge, 461–462
Bullhead City, 492–497
Bus travel
Grand Canyon, 146, 147
North-Central Arizona, 204, 223
Northwest Arizona and Southeast Nevada, 492, 493
Phoenix, Scottsdale, and Tempe, 54
Tucson, 356
Business hours, 511
Butterfield stage stop, 453–454
Butterfly Lodge Museum, 328

C

Cabeza Prieta National Wildlife Refuge, 35, 464
Cacti, 348
Cactus Forest Drive, 410, 412–413
Café Poca Cosa ✕, 24, 374
Café Roka ✕, 440
Callaghan Vineyards, 24, 442–443
Camelback Market, 48
Camelback Mountain and Echo Canyon Recreation Area, 18, 122
Cameron Trading Post, 19, 24, 287–288
Camping, 21
Eastern Arizona, 318, 345
Grand Canyon, 142, 196
North-Central Arizona, 250
Northeast Arizona, 277, 310
Northwest Arizona and Southeast Nevada, 485, 490–491
Southern Arizona, 466
Canoeing, 18, 470, 490
Canyon de Chelly, 21, 33, 258, 270–273, 276
Canyon Ranch ⬚, 390
Canyon X, 33
Canyons, 32–33
Cape Royal, 168
Car rentals, 507
Car travel, 12, 505–507
Eastern Arizona, 312, 315–316
Grand Canyon, 146, 147
North-Central Arizona, 205, 223, 224, 242, 246, 250

Northeast Arizona, 266, 268, 294, 295, 297, 306, 307
Northwest Arizona and Southeast Nevada, 472, 478
Phoenix, Scottsdale, and Tempe, 54
Southern Arizona, 429–430
Tucson, 356
Carefree, 127, 129–131
Carefree-Cave Creek Chamber of Commerce, 127
Carl Hayden Visitor Center, 306
Casa de San Pedro ⬚, 450
Casa Grande Ruins National Monument, 19, 133
Casa Malpais Archaeological Park, 332
Casa Tierra ⬚, 393
Casinos, 101, 102, 103, 394–395, 472, 488–489
Catalina Foothills, 348, 367–370, 382–383, 390–391, 399–400
Catalina State Park, 408
Cathedral Rock, 225–226
Cathedral Rock Trail, 226
Cave Creek, 127, 129–131
Cave Creek Museum, 127
Caverns
North-Central Arizona, 209
Northeast Arizona, 283
Southern Arizona, 21, 424, 458, 460
Tucson, 367
Cellar Door Wine Bar, 484
Center for Creative Photography, 364
Central Highlands, 30
Changing Hands Bookstore, 111
Chapel of the Holy Cross, 226
Chelsea's Kitchen ✕, 75
Children, activities for, 21.
⇨ See also specific regions
Children's Museum of Phoenix, 56
Children's Museum Tucson, 358
Chiricahua National Monument, 37, 427, 450–452
Chiricahua Regional Museum and Research Center, 19, 454
Chloride, 481
Christmas Tree Pass Road, 495
Churches
North-Central Arizona, 226
Tucson, 361, 371–372

Chuska Mountains, 271–272
Claypool, 136
Cliff pueblos
Betatakin, 296
Canyon de Chelly, 272
Casa Malpais Archaeological Park, 332
Keet Seel, 296
Montezuma Castle National Monument, 19, 21, 242–243
Tonto National Monument, 138–139
Tuzigoot National Monument, 19, 244–245
Walnut Canyon National Monument, 18, 219–220
Climate, 12, 13
Clothing, shopping for, 236, 399, 401
Coal Canyon, 283
Coconino National Forest, 200, 214–215
Coffeehouses, 100
College Street Brewhouse ✕, 487
Colleges and universities
Tempe, 69
Tucson, 348, 361–365, 377, 387–388, 394, 398
Colorado Plateau, 30
Colorado River, 182–189
Colorado River Discovery (waterborne tours), 300–301
Colorado River Museum, 19, 494
Colossal Cave Mountain Park, 367
Comedy clubs, 100, 102, 103
Communications, 509
Copper Queen Hotel, 439
Copper Queen Mine Underground Tour, 427, 439
Coronado National Forest, 370
Coronado National Memorial, 448
Coronado Trail, 312, 330–331
Cosanti Originals, 51, 109
Country & Western clubs, 102, 394
Courthouse Butte, 229
Crack-in-Rock Ruin, 222
Credit cards, 7
Crystal Forest, 341, 344
Cuisine, 24, 48–49, 350–351
Cultural Center, 319

D

Dance
Phoenix, 105
Dance clubs, *102, 103*
De Grazia's Gallery in the Sun, *368*
Dead Horse Ranch State Park, *244*
Deer Valley Rock Art Center, *125*
Desert Bar, *489*
Desert Botanical Garden, *15, 19, 35, 57, 61*
Desert Caballeros Western Museum, *131*
Desert Discovery Trail, *410, 415*
Desert Rose Inn and Cabins ⌨ , *294*
Desert View and Watchtower, *153*
Desert View Drive, *151*
Desert View Information Center, *149*
Deserts, *34–35*
Devine, Andy, *483*
Dining, *7, 509–510.* ⇨ *See also* Restaurants
Eastern Arizona, 316, 320, 322, 325–326, 328, 333, 345
Grand Canyon, 148, 181, 190–193
North-Central Arizona, 204, 210–211, 229–232, 245, 247–248, 252–253
Northeast Arizona, 266, 269, 272, 279, 281, 285–286, 289, 291, 294, 298, 304–305, 307
Northwest Arizona and Southeast Nevada, 478, 483–484, 487–488, 495
Phoenix, Scottsdale, and Tempe, 42, 48–49, 69–86, 129, 132, 138
Southern Arizona, 430, 436, 440, 444, 446, 449–450, 455–456, 458, 463, 464–465, 468–469
Tucson, 348, 350–351, 374–385, 420–421
Dinosaur Tracks, *285*
Doney Mountain, *222*
Dude-guest ranches, *21, 509*

E

Earp, Wyatt, *433*
Eastern Arizona, *10, 311–346*
camping, 318, 345
children, attractions for, 321, 327, 346
dining, 316, 320, 322, 325–326, 328, 333, 345
guided tours, 332, 335
itineraries, 315, 340–341
lodging, 316, 321, 322–323, 326, 327, 328–329, 334, 335–336, 337
nightlife and the arts, 329, 334
Petrified Forest, 312, 340–346
Round Valley and Coronado Trail, 312, 330–338
prices, 316
shopping, 334
sports and the outdoors, 312, 316, 321–322, 323–324, 326–327, 329–330, 334–335, 336, 337–338, 345–346
timing the visit, 315, 320, 322, 325, 327, 328, 330, 335, 337, 340
transportation, 312, 315–316, 320, 322, 325, 327, 328, 330, 332, 335, 337, 341
visitor information, 341
White Mountains, 312, 316–330
Echo Cliffs, *178, 297*
Edward Nye Fish House, *359–360*
El Presidio Historic District (Tucson), *358–359*
El Tiradito, *359*
El Tovar Dining Room ✕ , *190*
El Tovar Hotel ⌨ , *193*
Elephant Feet, *287*
Elote Café ✕ , *230*
Elvira's ✕ , *420*
Encanto Park, *62*
Enchantment Resort ⌨ , *233–234*
Explore Navajo Interactive Museum, *285*

F

FEZ ✕ , *79*
5th Avenue (Scottsdale), *64*
FireSky Resort & Spa ⌨ , *94*
First Mesa, *280*
Fish Creek Canyon, *140*
Fishing
Eastern Arizona, 316, 321, 324, 329, 334, 336
Grand Canyon, 142, 179
North-Central Arizona, 229
Northeast Arizona, 310
Northwest Arizona, 480, 501
Southern Arizona, 445
Flagstaff, *200, 205–215, 217–218*
Flandrau Science Center and Observatory, *364*
Flora and fauna, *38–39, 169, 344, 416*
Fly Exhibition Gallery, *433*
Food, shopping for, *51, 108, 109*
Fort Apache Historical Park, *319*
Fort Apache Indian Reservation, *319*
Fort Bowie National Historical Site, *452–454*
Fort Huachuca Museums, *448*
Fort Lowell Park and Museum, *365*
Fort Verde State Historic Park, *244*
Four Corners Monument, *293*
Four Seasons Scottsdale at Troon North ⌨ , *95*
Four-wheeling, *118–119.* ⇨ *See also* Jeep tours
4th Avenue (Tucson), *362*
Fredonia, *177*
Frontier Town, *127*
Fulton-Hayden Memorial Art Gallery, *456*

G

Gay and lesbian bars, *100, 101, 102, 394*
Geology, *40, 208–209, 228*
Geronimo, *451*
Ghost towns
Northwest Arizona, 481
Phoenix, Scottsdale, and Tempe, 134
Giant Logs, *341*
Giant Logs Interpretive Loop Trail, *344*
Gilbert Ortega Jewelry and Gallery, *51*
Glen Canyon Dam and Lake Powell, *259*
Glen Canyon National Recreation Area, *258, 306*
Globe, *136, 138*
Gobbler Trail, *337*
Gold Canyon Golf Resort, *119*
Goldfield Ghost Town, *134*
Golf, *20*
Eastern Arizona, 315, 321–322, 324, 326, 336

North-Central Arizona, 239
Northeast Arizona, 301
Northwest Arizona and Southeast Nevada, 490
Phoenix, Scottsdale, and Tempe, 42, 46–47, 119–121, 131
tours, 513
Tucson, 405–407
Goosenecks Region, UT, 293–295
Goulding's Lodge ⌸ , 295
Goulding's Trading Post, 295
Governor Hunt's Tomb, 62–63
Grand Canyon Lodge ⌸ , 166, 168, 195
Grand Canyon Lodge Dining Room ✕ , 191
Grand Canyon National Park, 10, 14, 141–198
bicycling, 142, 159, 170, 179
camping, 142, 196
cell phones, 148
children, attractions for, 21, 158, 170, 172, 178, 181
crowds, 157
dining, 148, 181, 190–193
educational offerings, 158, 170
fees, 147
festivals and seasonal events, 145
fishing, 142, 179
flora & fauna, 169
free attractions, 165
guided tours, 149, 158–159, 162, 164–165, 172, 173–174, 175, 188
hiking, 20, 142, 160–162, 170, 172
horseback riding, 179–180
itineraries, 145–146
jeep tours, 162, 164
lodging, 148–149, 193–198
mule rides, 142, 164–165, 172
nearby attractions, 177–181
North Rim and environs, 142, 147, 150, 166–170, 172, 191, 195
park hours, 148
permits, 147
picnic spots, 190
prices, 148, 149
rafting, 142, 180–181, 186–187, 188
shopping, 165–166
skiing, 165, 181
South Rim & environs, 142, 146–147, 149–153, 155–162, 164–166, 181, 190, 193–195

sports and the outdoors, 142, 158–162, 164–165, 170, 172, 175, 179–181
timing the visit, 144
transportation, 146–147, 173, 175–176
visitor information, 149–150, 176, 177–178
West Rim & Havasu Canyon, 142–143, 172–177, 197–198
Grand Canyon Railway, 147
Grand Canyon Skywalk, 174–175
Grand Canyon Ranch, 480
Grand Canyon Visitor Center, 150
Grand Canyon West, 173–175
Greasewood Flat (country & western club), 102
Green's Peak, 332
Greer, 327–330

H

Hacienda del Sol Guest Ranch Resort ⌸ , 390
Hall of Flame, 61
Hannagan Meadow, 337–338
Hano, 280
Hassayampa River Preserve, 131–132
Havasu Canyon, 33, 175–177
Havasu Falls, 18, 176
Havasu National Wildlife Refuge, 486
Havasupi Tribe, 175–176, 184
Hayden Peak Trail, 481
Health concerns, 510–511
Heard Museum, 15, 19, 21, 42, 61
Heard Museum North Scottsdale, 65–66
Heard Museum Shop, 108
Heartline Café ✕ , 230–231
Heat Hotel ⌸ , 488
Helicopter tours, 142, 158–159
Heritage Inn Bed & Breakfast ⌸ , 326
Heritage Square, 57
Hermit Road (Grand Canyon), 151
Hermits Rest, 155
Hieroglyphic Point, 317
High Spirits Flutes (shop), 447
Highway 67, 166
Hiking, 18, 20, 35, 37
Eastern Arizona, 316, 323–324, 326–327, 330, 336, 337–338, 345–346

Grand Canyon, 20, 142, 160–162
North-Central Arizona, 204, 214–215, 240, 245, 256
Northeast Arizona, 273, 276, 296, 301, 310
Northwest Arizona and Southeast Nevada, 472
Phoenix, Scottsdale, and Tempe, 121–123, 134
Southern Arizona, 424
tours, 513
Tucson, 408, 414–417, 421
Historama, 433
Historic Downtown District (Flagstaff), 206, 208
Hohokam petroglyphs, 410, 413
Holbrook, 346
Hole-in-the-Rock, 62
Homolovi Ruins State Park, 218
Hoover Dam, 498–499, 501
Hoover Dam Tour, 499
Hope Camp Trail, 415
Hopi Arts Trail and Tours, 282\
Hopi Cultural Center, 281
Hopi Cultural Center Restaurant ✕ , 24, 281
Hopi Mesas, 258, 278–283
Hopi Point, 153, 155
Horseback riding, 33
Grand Canyon, 179–180
North-Central Arizona, 240, 256
Northeast Arizona, 276
Phoenix, Scottsdale, and Tempe, 123, 131
Southern Arizona, 444
Tucson, 408–409
Hot-air ballooning. ➪ See Ballooning
Hot Air Expeditions, 117–118
Hotel Congress ⌸ , 387
Hotel Monte Vista, 206
Hotel Palomar Phoenix ⌸ , 87
Hotels, 7, 508. ➪ See also Lodging
prices, 7, 87, 149, 205, 267, 316, 385, 387, 430, 479
Hotevilla, 283
House of Tricks ✕ , 86
Houseboating, 18, 308–309, 489, 501
Houses, historic
Eastern Arizona, 325
Grand Canyon, 151
North-Central Arizona, 206, 208

Northwest Arizona and Southeast Nevada, 481–482
Phoenix, Scottsdale, and Tempe, 57
Southern Arizona, 467
Tucson, 359–360
Hualapai Mountain Park, 37, 480–481
Hualapai Tribe, 174
Hubbell Trading Post National Historic Site, 276–278
Hubbell Trading Post Store, 19, 258
Hugh Norris Trail, 410, 416
Hyatt Regency Scottsdale Resort and Spa at Gainey Ranch 🖭, 95

I

Imperial National Wildlife Refuge, 470
Inscription Rock, 278–279
Internet, 509
Island Trail, 220
Itineraries, 25–27

J

J. Knox Corbett House, 360
J & G Steakhouse ✕, 75–76
Jacob Lake, 177, 197
Jade Bar, 100
Jasper Forest, 340, 344
Jeep tours, 20
Grand Canyon, 162, 164
North-Central Arizona, 224, 240–241
Northeast Arizona, 276
Phoenix, Scottsdale, and Tempe, 118–119
Southern Arizona, 438
Jerome, 200, 246–250
Jerome State Historic Park, 246–247
Jewelry, shopping for, 236, 399, 400
John Wesley Powell Memorial Museum, 297–298
Joshua Tree Forest, 483
Juan Bautista de Anza National Historic Trail, 421
Junior Ranger Program for Families, 21, 158, 170, 414
JW Marriott Desert Ridge Resort & Spa ✕, 21, 93

K

Kactus Jack (shop), 51
Kai ✕, 24, 85–86

Kartchner Caverns State Park, 21, 424, 458, 460
Kayaking, 18, 490
Kayenta, 288–290
Keams Canyon Trading Post, 19, 278–279
Keeling Schaeffer Vineyards, 24, 451–452
Keet Seel, 296
Kingman, 480–485
Kingman Railroad Museum, 482
Kinishba Ruins, 319
Kitt Peak National Observatory, 424, 462–463
Kolb Studio, 151
Kykotsmovi, 282

L

La Grande Orange ✕, 76
La Posada Hotel 🖭, 220
Lake Havasu City, 485–491
Lake Havasu Museum of History, 486
Lake Havasu State Park, 490–491
Lake Mead, 501–502
Lake Powell, 304, 306
Laughlin, NV, 492–497
Lava Flow Trail, 221
Lava River Cave, 209
Lavender Jeep Tours, 438
Lavender Pit Mine, 439
Lees Ferry, 177
Lenox Crater, 221
Lipan Point, 155
Little House Museum, 332, 407
Lodge at Ventana Canyon (golf course), 407
Lodging, 7, 21, 508–509. ⇨ See also Camping; Hotels
Eastern Arizona, 316, 321, 322–323, 326, 327, 328–329, 334, 335–336, 337
Grand Canyon, 148–149, 193–198
North-Central Arizona, 204–205, 211–212, 220, 232–234, 248–249
Northeast Arizona, 267, 269, 273, 281, 286–287, 289, 293, 294–295, 298–299, 307–309
Northwest Arizona and Southeast Nevada, 479, 484, 488, 496–497
Phoenix, Scottsdale, and Tempe, 86–99, 129, 132, 138

Southern Arizona, 430, 436–437, 440, 444, 447, 450, 452, 456–457, 458, 462, 469
Tucson, 385–393, 421, 422
Loews Ventana Canyon Resort 🖭, 390–391
London Bridge, 472, 486
London Bridge Days, 477
Lookout Studio, 151
Los Dos Molinos ✕, 24
Lost Dutchman Mine, 137
Lowell Observatory, 21, 208

M

Madera Canyon, 33, 419
Main Street (Bisbee), 439
Main Street Arts District (Scottsdale), 64
Manning Camp, 413
Marble Canyon, 177, 178–179
Margaritas, 16
Maricopa Point, 155
Marshall Way Arts District (Scottsdale), 64
Massacre Cave Overlook, 271
Mather Point, 156
Matt's Big Breakfast ✕, 74
Maynards ✕, 376–377
Meteor Crater, 21, 219
Mexican Hat, UT, 294
Miami, 136
Microbreweries, 102, 103
Mii Amo Spa, 237
Mine Museum, 247
Mining operations
Grand Canyon, 155
North-Central Arizona, 246–247
Northeast Arizona, 283, 288
Northwest Arizona and Southeast Nevada, 481
Phoenix, Scottsdale, and Tempe, 134, 137
Southern Arizona, 438–439
Tucson, 418
Mishongnovi, 281
Mission, The ✕, 24
Mission San Xavier del Bac, 348, 371–372
Mittens, 290
Moenkopi Legacy Inn & Suites 🖭, 286
Mogollon Rim, 319
Mohave Museum of History and Arts, 482–483
Mohave Point, 156
Money matters, 511
Montezuma Castle National Monument, 19, 21, 242–243

Montezuma Well, *242–243*
Monument Valley, *15, 21, 258–259, 288–296*
Monument Valley Navajo Tribal Park, *290–292, 293*
Monument Valley Visitor Center, *290–291*
Monuments, national. ⇨ *See* National monuments
Mooney Falls, *176*
Moran Point, *156*
Motels. ⇨ *See* Lodging
Mount Humphreys, *18*
Mount Lemmon, *368–370*
Mount Lemmon Ski Valley, *370*
Mount Lemmon Sky Center, *370*
Mountain biking, *37, 215, 217, 241*
Mountains, *36–37*
Mule rides, *33, 164–165, 172*
Muleshoe Ranch Cooperative Management Area, *455*
Mummy Cave Overlook, *271*
Museum of Northern Arizona. *19, 208–209*
Museums and art galleries
Eastern Arizona, *319, 325, 328, 332, 333, 341*
Grand Canyon, *153, 178*
North-Central Arizona, *208–209, 218, 219, 247, 251–252*
Northeast Arizona, *268, 285, 297–298*
Northwest Arizona and Southeast Nevada, *482, 483, 486, 494–495, 498*
Phoenix, Scottsdale, and Tempe, *19, 21, 35, 42, 56, 57, 61–62, 63, 65–67, 69, 125, 127, 131, 134*
Southern Arizona, *433–436, 438–439, 448, 454, 455, 457, 467, 468*
Tucson, *19, 358, 359–360, 362–364, 365, 367, 368, 371, 419, 420*
Music, classical
Grand Canyon, *145*
North-Central Arizona, *235, 255*
Phoenix, *105*
Tucson, *396*
Music, popular
North-Central Arizona, *235, 249, 254–255*
Phoenix, Scottsdale, and Tempe, *100, 102*

Southern Arizona, *437*
Tucson, *394*
Musical Instrument Museum (MIM), *61*
Mystery Castle, *61*

N

National Geographic Visitor Center Grand Canyon, *178*
National monuments
Grand Canyon, *178*
North-Central Arizona, *18, 21, 33, 37, 219–220, 221–222, 242–243, 244–245*
Northeast Arizona, *293, 295–296, 307*
Phoenix, Scottsdale, and Tempe, *19, 133, 138–139*
Southern Arizona, *450–451, 465–466*
National parks. ⇨ *See* Parks, national
Native American
crafts, *51, 108, 110, 166, 236, 258, 270, 273, 277, 279, 281, 282, 285, 287, 295, 299–300, 363, 400, 482*
culture, *13, 19, 20, 174, 260–261, 262, 263, 272, 281, 288, 318, 319, 356, 368, 421–422, 451, 456, 482*
history tours, *513*
petroglyph sites, *125, 219, 222, 317, 326–327, 338, 342, 344, 410, 413*
reservation life and rules, *260, 261, 263*
Native American sites
Eastern Arizona, *312, 317, 318, 319, 326–327, 332, 335, 338, 342, 344–345, 346*
Grand Canyon, *151, 153, 157–158, 174–175*
North-Central Arizona, *200, 218, 219–220, 221–222*
Northeast Arizona, *258, 260–261, 268, 271, 278–283, 288, 290–291, 295–296*
Northwest Arizona and Southeast Nevada, *482–483, 486–487*
Phoenix, Scottsdale, and Tempe, *62, 63, 125, 133, 138*
Southern Arizona, *428, 448, 450, 453–454, 456*
Tucson, *410, 413, 421–422*
Natural history tours, *513*

Nature Conservancy Patagonia-Sonoita Creek Preserve, *445*
Navajo Arts and Crafts Enterprises, *270, 287*
Navajo Bridge, *179*
Navajo Code Talkers Memorial Museum, *285*
Navajo Cultural Center of Kayenta, *288*
Navajo Interactive Museum, *285*
Navajo Nation Council Chambers, *268*
Navajo Nation East, *258, 267–273, 276–278*
Navajo Nation Fair, *268*
Navajo Nation Museum, *268*
Navajo Nation West, *258, 283–288*
Navajo National Monument, *295–296*
Navajo National Zoological & Botanical Park, *268*
Navajo Point, *156*
Nevada. ⇨ *See* Northwest Arizona and Southeast Nevada
Newspaper Rock, *340, 342, 344*
Noca ✕, *76*
Nogales, Mexico, *462*
North-Central Arizona, *10, 199–256*
camping, *250*
children, attractions for, *208–209, 219, 226, 228, 229, 251*
dining, *204, 210–211, 229–232, 245, 247–248, 252–253*
festivals and seasonal events, *203, 213*
Flagstaff, *200, 205–215, 217–218*
Flagstaff side trips, *218–222*
guided tours, *205, 210, 222, 223, 239, 240–241*
itineraries, *203–204, 224, 246, 251*
lodging, *204–205, 21–212, 220, 232–234, 248–249, 253–254*
nightlife and arts, *212–213, 234–235, 249, 254*
prices, *204, 205, 224*
Sedona and Oak Creek Canyon, *200, 222–241*
shopping, *214, 235–236, 249–250, 255*
spas, *237–238*

sports and the outdoors, 204,
214–215, 217–218, 229,
238–241, 245, 256
timing the visit, 203
transportation, 204, 205, 206,
218, 221, 223–224, 242,
246, 250–251
Verde Valley, Jerome, and
Prescott, 200, 242–256
visitor information, 206, 224,
246, 251
North Rim Drive (Canyon de
Chelly), 271
North Rim Visitor Center, 150
Northeast Arizona, 10,
257–310
camping, 277, 310
children, attractions for, 268,
285, 288
dining, 266, 269, 272, 279,
281, 285–286, 289, 291,
294, 298, 304–305, 307
festivals and seasonal events,
265
Glen Canyon Dam and Lake
Powell, 296–301, 304–310
guided tours, 258, 266, 273,
276, 282, 283, 293, 300–
301, 304, 309–310
Hopi Mesas, 258, 278–283
itineraries, 265, 270
lodging, 267, 269, 273, 281,
286–287, 289, 293, 294–295,
288–289, 307–309
Monument Valley, 15, 21,
258–259, 288–296
Navajo Nation East, 258,
267–273, 276–278
Navajo Nation West, 258,
283–288
prices, 266, 267
reservation rules, 260, 261,
263
shopping, 270, 273, 277–278,
279, 281–282, 285, 287–288,
295, 299–300, 309
sports and the outdoors,
258, 273, 276, 293, 296,
300–301, 305, 309–310
timing the visit, 265
transportation, 265–266, 268,
270, 276–277, 279, 280,
282, 285, 288, 291, 295,
297, 301, 306, 307
visitor information, 267, 271,
278, 281, 290–291, 297
**Northern Arizona University
Observatory,** 209

**Northwest Arizona and South-
east Nevada,** 10, 471–502
camping, 485
children, attractions for, 483,
489–490, 494, 502
dining, 478, 483–484, 487–
488, 495
festivals and seasonal events,
477
ghost towns, 481
guided tours, 499, 501
itineraries, 477–478
lodging, 479, 484, 488, 489,
496–497
nightlife, 484, 488–489
Northwest Arizona, 479–491
prices, 478, 479
shopping, 475, 485
Southeast Nevada, 492–502
sports and the outdoors, 472,
489–491, 499, 501, 502
timing the visit, 477
transportation, 472, 478, 480,
485, 492, 493, 501
visitor information, 483, 485,
494, 498

O

O.K. Corral (Tombstone), 433
O.K. Corral & Stable, 123
Oak Creek Canyon, 21, 33,
228
Oak Creek Vineyards, 226
Oatman, 484–485
**Oatman Chamber of Com-
merce,** 485
Oatman Hotel, 485
Old Oraibi, 282–283
Old Town Scottsdale, 64, 110
Old Tucson Studios, 373
O'Leary Peak, 221
**Organ Pipe Cactus National
Monument,** 35, 465–466
Outdoor activities. ⇨ *See*
Sports and the outdoors

P

Packing, 13, 511–512
Page, 297–301
Page Springs Cellars, 24
Painted Desert, 14, 142, 178,
285
**Painted Desert Inn National
Historic Site,** 340, 341, 344
Painted Desert Scenic Drive,
342
Painted Desert Visitor Center,
340, 341
Pane Bianco ✕ , 79

Papago Park, 62–63
Parks, national
Grand Canyon National Park,
10, 14, 141–198
Glen Canyon National Recre-
ation Area, 258, 306
Petrified Forest National Park,
14, 35, 312, 340–346
Saguaro National Park, 35,
409–417
Tumacácori National Historic
Park, 421–422
Parks, state
North-Central Arizona, 21,
209–210, 218, 226, 228,
229, 244, 246–247
Northwest Arizona, 490–491
Southern Arizona, 445, 458,
460, 467–468
Tucson, 408
Patagonia, 444–447
Patagonia Lake State Park,
445
**Patagonia-Sonoita Creek Pre-
serve,** 445
Pepe's Taco Villa ✕ , 79
Peralta Trail, 134
Petrified Forest National Park,
14, 35, 312, 340–346
Petroglyphs, 125, 219, 222,
317, 326–327, 338, 342,
344, 410, 413
**Phippen Museum of Western
Art,** 251
Phoenician, The ⓣ , 92
Phoenician Golf Club, 121
**Phoenix, Scottsdale and
Tempe,** 10, 41–140
Apache Trail, 133–134,
136–140
Camelback Corridor, 108
children, attractions for, 56, 57,
61–63, 69, 92, 93, 94, 95,
98, 106, 107, 122, 123, 125,
127, 131, 138
climate, 52–53
dining, 42, 48–49, 69–86, 129,
132, 138
downtown Phoenix, 55–57, 70,
74, 87, 89, 99–100, 103–104
festivals and seasonal events,
53, 56, 64, 69
Glendale, 109–110
greater Phoenix, 57, 61–63,
75–77, 89, 92–94, 100–101,
103–104, 108–110
guided tours, 55, 65, 123, 136,
139
history, 59

itineraries, 53–55
Litchfield Park, 94
lodging, 86–99, 129, 132, 138
nightlife and the arts, 99–107, 130, 132
north central Phoenix, 77–81, 92–93, 108–109
Paradise Valley, 81, 93–94, 109
prices, 70, 87
Scottsdale, 10, 52–55, 64–67, 82–85, 94–95, 98, 101–102, 104–105, 110–111
shopping, 50–51, 107–111, 130
side trips near Phoenix, 124–140
south Phoenix, 81–82, 94, 109–110
spas, 44–45, 92, 93, 94, 95, 98, 112–116, 129, 130
sports and the outdoors, 46–47, 116–124, 131, 134
Tempe, 10, 52–55, 67–69, 85–86, 98–99, 102–103, 105, 111
transportation, 54–56, 64, 68, 125, 127, 131, 132, 133, 134, 136, 138, 139, 140
visitor information, 55, 127, 131, 138
Phoenix Art Museum, 21, 61–62
Phoenix Symphony Orchestra, 105
Phoenix Zoo, 63
Photography, 35
Pima Air and Space Museum, 367
Pima County Courthouse, 359
Pima Point, 156
Pinetop-Lakeside, 322–324
Pioneer Living History Village, 125
Pioneer Museum, 209
Plane travel. ⇨ See Air travel
Planes of Fame Air Museum, 178
Planetariums and observatories
Grand Canyon, 153
North-Central Arizona, 208, 209
Southern Arizona, 462–463
Tucson, 364, 370
Point Imperial, 168
Point Sublime, 168
Pointe Hilton Squaw Peak Resort ⚄, 93
Powell Memorial, 153
Powerhouse, 483

Powerhouse Route 66 Museum, 483
Powerplant Tour, 499
Prescott, 200, 250–256
Prescott National Forest, 200, 250
Prices
dining, 7, 70, 148, 204, 266, 316, 374, 430, 478
lodging, 7, 87, 149, 205, 267, 316, 385, 387, 430, 479
Pueblo Grande Museum and Cultural Park, 62
Puerco Pueblo, 340, 344
Puerto Blanco Drive, 466

Q

Quartermaster Depot State Historic Park, 467
Queen Mine Train, 424

R

Rafting, 18, 20, 33, 123, 142, 180–181, 186–187, 188, 499–500, 513–514
Railroads
Grand Canyon, 147
North-Central Arizona, 243–244
Rainbow Bridge National Monument, 307
Rainbow Forest Museum, 341
Rainbow Room ✕, 307
Rainbow Trout Farm, 229
Ramsey Canyon Preserve, 33, 449
Rancho de los Caballeros ⚄, 132
Rancho Pinot ✕, 82
Randolph Park Golf Course, 406
Ranger programs, 21, 158, 170, 239, 414
Rawhide Western Town and Steakhouse at the Wild Horse Pass, 107
Red Hills Visitor Center, 410, 412
Red Raven Restaurant ✕, 192
Red Rock geology, 228
Red Rock State Park, 229
Reid Park Zoo, 365–366
Renée Cushman Art Collection Museum, 333
Reno Trail, 337
Reservations and dress, 509–510

Restaurants, 5, 509–510. ⇨ See also Dining
prices, 7, 70, 148, 204, 266, 316, 374, 430, 478
Rex Allen Arizona Cowboy Museum, 455
Rim Trail, 160, 220
Riordan State Historic Park, 209–210
Road trips, 16
Rock Art Ranch, 219
Rock climbing, 37, 217
Rodeos, 17, 409
Roosevelt Point, 169
Rose Peak, 331
Rose Spring Trail, 337
Rose Tree Inn Museum, 434–435
Rosson House Museum, 57
Round Valley, 312, 330–338
Route 66, 474–475
Route 66 Fun Run, 477
Royal Palms Resort & Spa ⚄, 92

S

Sabino Canyon, 348, 370
Safety, 462, 465, 512
Saguaro East, 410
Saguaro East Visitor Center, 410, 412
Saguaro National Park, 35, 348, 409–417
Saguaro West, 409
Sailplaning-soaring, 124
St. Augustine Cathedral, 361
St. Peter's Dome, 332
Salsa, 16
Salt River Canyon, 317–319
San Carlos Apache Indian Reservation, 319
San Francisco Peaks, 37
San Francisco Volcanic Field, 220–222
San Pedro Riparian National Conservation Area, 449
San Pedro Valley Arts and Historical Society Museum, 457
Sanctuary on Camelback Mountain ⚄, 93–94
Sanctuary Spa at Sanctuary Camelback Mountain, 114
Sanguinetti House Museum, 467
Santa Catalina Mountains, 37
Santa Cruz Chili & Spice Co., 422
Santa Cruz River & River Park, 360–361

Santa Fe Depot, *206*
School House Inn Bed & Breakfast ⊡ , *440*
Scottsdale, *10, 14–15, 41, 43, 50–55, 64–67, 82–85, 94–95, 98, 101–102, 104–105, 110–111.* ⇨ *See also* Phoenix, Scottsdale, and Tempe
Scottsdale ArtWalk, *64*
Scottsdale Arts Festival, *50*
Scottsdale Center for the Performing Arts, *66–67*
Scottsdale Culinary Festival, *48*
Scottsdale Fashion Square, *50*
Scottsdale Historical Museum, *67*
Scottsdale Museum of Contemporary Art, *67*
Scuba diving and snorkeling, *502*
Searchlight Historic Museum, *494–495*
Second Mesa, *280–282*
Sedona, *14, 200, 222–241*
Sedona Golf Resort, *239*
Sedona Vortex Tour, *223*
Sells, *463*
Shady Dell Vintage Trailer Court ⊡ , *440*
Sharlot Hall Museum, *251*
Shemer Arts Center, *63*
Shopping
   Eastern Arizona, 334
   Grand Canyon, 165–166
   North-Central Arizona, 214, 235–236, 249–250, 255
   Northeast Arizona, 270, 273, 277–278, 279, 281–282, 285, 287–288, 295, 299–300, 309
   Northwest Arizona and Southeast Nevada, 475, 485
   Phoenix, Scottsdale and Tempe, 42, 50–51, 107–111
   Southern Arizona, 437, 441, 447, 470
   Tucson, 352–353, 397–401, 417
Show Low, *319–322*
Shungopavi, *280*
Sichomovi, *280*
Sierra Vista, *447–448*
Signal Hill, *410, 413*
Sinagua people, *219, 221–222*
Singing Wind Bookshop, *457–458*
Skiing
   Eastern Arizona, 316, 324, 327, 330, 331, 336
   Grand Canyon, 142, 165, 181

North-Central Arizona, 217–218
Tucson, 370
Skywalk (Grand Canyon), *174–175*
Slide Rock State Park, *21, 226, 228*
Slot canyons, 307
Smoki Museum, *251–252*
Snoopy Rock, *21, 228*
Snowboarding, *217–218, 324*
Snowflake-Taylor, *324–327*
Sonoita, *441–444*
Sonoita Vineyards, *443*
South Mountain Park, *63*
Southeast Nevada. ⇨ *See* Northeast Arizona and Southeast Nevada
Southeastern Arizona Bird Observatory, *435, 438*
Southern Arizona, *10, 423–470*
   camping, 466
   children, attractions for, 433, 439, 445, 448, 450–457, 455, 470
   dining, 430, 436, 440, 444, 446, 449–450, 455–456, 458, 463, 464–465, 468–469
   festivals and seasonal events, 429
   guided tours, 438, 439, 467, 470
   itineraries, 427, 429
   lodging, 430, 436–437, 440, 444, 447, 450, 452, 456–457, 458, 462, 469
   nightlife, 437, 441
   prices, 430
   safety, 462, 465
   shopping, 437, 441, 447, 470
   southeast Arizona, 424, 430–460
   southwest Arizona, 425, 460–470
   sports and the outdoors, 424, 435, 444
   timing the visit, 429
   transportation, 429–430, 432, 438, 442, 445, 448, 450, 452–453, 454, 456, 457, 458, 462, 463, 464, 465, 466–467, 470
   visitor information, 432, 438, 442, 445, 454, 467
   wineries, 442–444, 451–452
Spa at Sedona Rouge, The, *238*
Spa Avania at the Hyatt Regency Scottsdale at Gainey Ranch, *115*

Spas, *20, 42, 44–45, 92, 93, 94, 95, 112–116, 129, 237–238, 401–403*
Spider Rock Overlook, *271*
Sports and the outdoors. ⇨ *See* specific regions; specific sports
Sports outfitters, *116–117, 236, 335*
Springerville-Eagar, *331–335*
Springerville-Eagar Regional Chamber of Commerce, *332*
Springerville Volcanic Field, *332*
Stagecoach rides, *432*
Stargazing, *17, 22–23, 424*
State parks. ⇨ *See* Parks, state
Steamboat Rock, *278*
Stevens Home, *360*
Stinson Museum, *325*
Summerhaven, *369*
Sun Devil Stadium, *69*
Sunrise Park Resort, *327*
Sunset Crater Volcano National Monument, *37, 221*
Superior, *136*
Superstition Mountain Museum, *134*
Superstition Mountains, *133–134*
Superstition Wilderness, *37*
Surgeon's House ⊡ , *249*
Symbols, *7*

T

T. Cook's at the Royal Palms ✕ , *76*
Taliesin West, *64–65, 66*
Taxes, *512*
Taxis
   Grand Canyon, 146
   North-Central Arizona, 206
   Northwest Arizona and Southeast Nevada, 492, 493
   Phoenix, Scottsdale, and Tempe, 54–55
   Southern Arizona, 467
   Tucson, 356
Taylor Museum, *325*
Telephones, *148*
Tempe, *10, 41–43, 52–55, 67–69, 85–86, 98–99, 102–103, 105, 111.* ⇨ *See also* Phoenix, Scottsdale, and Tempe
Tempe Festival of the Arts, *69*
Tempe Town Lake, *69*
Tennis, *124*
Tepees, The, *340, 345*

Texas Canyon, *456–457*
Theater
North-Central Arizona, 213
Phoenix, Scottsdale, and
Tempe, 106–107
Tucson, 396–397
Theodore Roosevelt Lake Reservoir & Dam, *139*
Third Mesa, *282–283*
Time zones, *512*
Timing the visit, *12*
Tinderbox Kitchen ✕, *211*
Tipping, *512*
Titan Missile Museum, *419*
Tohono Chul Park, *373*
Tombstone, *427, 431–437*
Tombstone Courthouse State Historic Park, *435*
Tombstone Epitaph Museum, *433–434*
Tombstone Visitor Center, *432*
Tombstone Western Heritage Museum, *435–436*
Tonto National Monument, *138–139*
Tortilla Flat, *140*
Totem Pole, *290*
Totsonii Ranch, *276*
Tours and packages, *512–514*
Tovrea Castle, *62*
Trailview Overlook, *156*
Train travel, *511* ⇨ *See also* Railroads
Grand Canyon, 147
North-Central Arizona, 205, 243–244
Northwest Arizona and Southeast Nevada, 478, 493
Phoenix, Scottsdale, and Tempe, 54
Southern Arizona, 430
Tucson, 356–357
Transportation, *12, 504–507*
Travel times, *12*
Trolley travel, *224*
Troon North* (golf course), *120*
Tuba City, *283, 285–287*
Tuba City Trading Post, *285*
Tubac, *420–421*
Tubac Presidio State Historic Park and Museum, *420*
Tubing, *124*
Tucson, *10, 347–422*
Catalina Foothills, 348, 367–370, 382–383, 390–391, 399
central and East Tucson, 348, 365–367, 377, 380–381, 388, 390, 394, 399–400

children, attractions for, 358, 362–363, 364, 365–366, 367, 371, 373, 397, 409, 413, 415
climate, 354–355
dining, 348, 350–351, 374–385, 420–421
downtown, 348, 357–361, 374, 376–377, 387, 393, 397–398
eastside, 348, 367, 382, 390, 399
educational offerings, 414
fees, 411
festivals and seasonal events, 355, 396
flora & fauna, 416
guided tours, 360, 362, 373, 404–405
history, 368
itineraries, 355
lodging, 385–393, 421, 422
nightlife and the arts, 393–397
northwest Tucson and the Westside, 348, 371–373, 383–384, 391–393, 400–401
permits, 411
prices, 374, 385, 387
Saguaro National Park, 409–417
shopping, 352–353, 397–401, 417
side trips, 417–422
south Tucson, 385, 394–395
spas, 401–403
sports and the outdoors, 370, 403–409, 414–417, 421
timing the visit, 354–355, 410
transportation, 355–357, 361, 410–411, 418, 419, 420, 421
University of Arizona, 348, 361–365, 377, 387–388, 394, 398
visitor information, 357, 412, 420
Tucson Botanical Gardens, *366*
Tucson Gem and Mineral Show, *352, 355*
Tucson Museum of Art and Historic Block, *359–360*
Tumacácori National Historic Park, *421–422*
Tusayan, *177, 191–192, 195*
Tusayan Ruin and Museum, *153*
Tuzigoot National Monument, *19, 244–245*
Twin Knolls, *332*
Twin Rocks Cafe ✕, *294*

U

U.S. Army Intelligence Museum, *448*
U.S. 89, *178*
U.S. 89A, *178–179*
University of Arizona, *348, 361–365, 377, 387–388, 394, 398*
University of Arizona Museum of Art, *365*
Utah, *293–295*

V

Vail Building, *208*
Valley of the Sun. ⇨ *See* Phoenix, Scottsdale, and Tempe
Verde Canyon Railroad, *243–244*
Verde Valley, *200, 242–250*
Vermilion Cliffs National Monument, *178*
View Hotel, The 🏠, *293*
View Restaurant ✕, *291*
Vintage clothing and furniture, shopping for, *109*
Visitor information, *514.* ⇨ *See also* specific regions
Vista Encantada, *169*
Volcanic remains, *221, 332*
Vortex tour, *223*

W

Wahweap, *306–310*
Walhalla Overlook, *169*
Walking tours, *35, 224, 276, 362*
Walnut Canyon National Monument, *18, 219–220*
Walpi, *280*
Waltz, Jacob "The Dutchman", *134, 137*
Water sports, *18, 490–491, 502*
Waterfalls, *176*
Weather, *12, 13*
Weaver's Needle, *134*
Web sites, *514*
Westin Kierland Resort & Spa 🏠, *21, 95*
Whiskey Row* (Prescott), *252*
White House Ruin, *271*
White House Ruin Trail, *271*
White Mesa Natural Bridge, *288*
White Mountains, *37, 312, 316–330*

White Stallion Ranch ⊡, 392–393
Wickenburg, 131–132
Wild West Shows, 107, 426–427
Wilde Meyer Galleries, 51, 110–111
Wildlife refuges
North-Central Arizona, 244
Northwest Arizona and Southeast Nevada, 486
Phoenix, Scottsdale, and Tempe, 131–132
Southern Arizona, 35, 445, 449, 455, 461–462, 464, 470
Willcox, 454–456

Willcox Commercial Store, 455
Willcox Playa, 455
Williams, 177, 192–193, 197
Willow Stream Spa at Fairmont Scottsdale Princess, 115–116
Window Rock, 267–270
Window Rock Navajo Tribal Park & Veteran's Memorial, 268
Wine shops, 108, 109
Wineries, 24, 245, 442–444, 451–452
Winslow, 220
Wupatki National Monument, 221–222

Y

Yaki Point, 156–157
Yavapai Geology Museum, 150
Yavapai Point, 157–158
Yuma, 466–470
Yuma River Tours, 467
Yuma Territorial Prison State Historic Park, 467–468

Z

Zoos
Northeast Arizona, 268
Phoenix, 63
Tucson, 365–366

PHOTO CREDITS

Front cover (Organ Pipe Cactus National Monument): Ed Callaert. 1, Kerrick James. 2-3 Kerrick Jones. 5, Christophe Testi/Shutterstock. Chapter 1: Experience Arizona: 8-9, gary718/ Shutterstock. 10, Wilde Meyer Gallery. 11 (left and right), Metropolitan Tucson Convention & Visitors Bureau. 14 (top left), National Park Service. 14(bottom left), Mike Norton/Shutterstock. 14 (right) and 15 (left and top center), Kerrick James. 15 (top right), Katrina Brown/Shutterstock. 15 (bottom right), Daniel Gratton/Shutterstock. 16, Kerrick James. 17 and 18, Metropolitan Tucson Convention & Visitors Bureau. 19 (left), luchschen/Shutterstock. 19 (right), Paul Markow/Rancho de los Caballeros. 20, Royal Palms Resort and Spa. 22, Jeffrey Kramer, Fodors.com member. 24, Royal Palms Resort and Spa. 28-29, Adventurephoto/age fotostock. 30, julius fekete/Shutterstock. 32 (top), Jim West/age fotostock. 32 (bottom), Peter Mukherjee/iStockphoto. 33, NPS. 34 (top), iShootPhotos, LLC/iStockphoto. 34 (bottom), Kenneth Bosma/Flickr. 35, James Metcalf/iStockphoto. 36 (top), Tom Grundy/Shutterstock. 36 (bottom), Anton Foltin/Shutterstock. 37, Anton Foltin/Shutterstock. 38 (left), Frank Leung/iStockphoto. 38 (top center), IPK Photography/Shutterstock. 38 (bottom center), Dominic Sherony/wikipedia. org. 38 (top right), gary yim/Shutterstock. 38 (bottom right), Steve Byland/Shutterstock. 39 (top left), Mike Norton/Shutterstock. 39 (bottom left), EuToch/Shutterstock. 39 (top center), Nina B/Shutterstock. 39 (bottom center), robert van beets/iStockphoto. 39 (right), Walter Siegmund/wikipedia.org. 40 (left), Ashok Rodrigues/iStockphoto. 40 (top right), Daryl Faust/Shutterstock. 40 (bottom right), Eric Foltz/iStockphoto. Chapter 2: Phoenix, Scottsdale and Tempe: 41, Kerrick James. 42, John C. Russell/ Four Seasons Hotels & Resorts. 43, Barbara Kraft/Four Seasons Hotels & Resorts. 44, Royal Palms Resort and Spa. 45 (top), Sanctuary on Camelback Mountain, Scottsdale. 45 (bottom), InterContinental Hotels Group. 46, Starwood Hotels & Resorts.47 (top), David Peeters/iStockphoto. 47 (bottom), The Boulders Resort & Golden Door Spa. 48 and 49 (top), Nicky HedayatZedeh. 49 (bottom), John Pozniak/wikipedia.org. 50, Damian Davies / age fotostock. 51, Wilde Meyer Gallery. 52, Paul Markow/ Rancho de los Caballeros. 58 and 67, Kerrick James. 78, 80, Royal Palms Resort and Spa. 96 (top left), Mark Boisclair Photography, Inc. 96 (top right), VFM/FireSky Resort & Spa. 96 (center left), Reddie Henderson. 96 (center right), John Ellis. 96 (bottom left), Sanctuary on Camelback Mountain, Scottsdale. 96 (bottom right), Hilton Worldwide. 97 (top left), The Phoenician. 97 (top right), The Westin Kierland Resort & Spa. 97 (bottom left), JW Marriott Desert Ridge Resort. 97 (bottom right), Barbara Kraft/Four Seasons Hotels & Resorts. 104, Kerrick James. 106, Stuart Pearce/age fotostock. 112, Wilde Meyer Gallery. 122, JW Marriott Desert Ridge Resort. 128 (top), The Boulders Resort & Golden Door Spa. 128 (bottom), Mark Boisclair Photography. 135 and 139, Kerrick James. Chapter 3: Grand Canyon National Park: 141 and 143 (top and bottom), National Park Service. 144, Nickolay Stanev/Shutterstock. 154, poutnik/Shutterstock. 158, National Park Service. 171, Kerrick James. 180, Mark Lellouch/National Park Service. 182–83, Christophe Testi/Shutterstock. 184, Anton Foltin/Shutterstock. 185, Geir Olav Lyngfjell/Shutterstock. 186 (top and bottom) and 187 (top), Kerrick James. 187 (bottom), NPS. 188, Mark Lellouch/NPS. 189, Kerrick James. 194, Kerrick James. Chapter 4: North-Central Arizona: 199, Kerrick James. 200, Tom Grundy/Shutterstock. 201 (top), sochigirl/Shutterstock. 201 (bottom), Tom Grundy/Shutterstock. 202, David M. Schrader/Shutterstock. 213, Zack Frank/Shutterstock. 216, Kerrick James. 227 and 230, Kerrick James. 233, Lindy Drew. 247, Kerrick James. 248, LouLouPhotos/Shutterstock. Chapter 5: Northeast Arizona: 257, Kerrick James. 258 (left), Sourav and Joyeeta Chowdhury/Shutterstock. 258 (right), Katrina Brown/Shutterstock. 259 (top and bottom), Aramark Parks & Destinations. 260, Sylvain Grandadam/age fotostock. 261 (top), Library of Congress Prints and Photographs Division. 261 (bottom), SuperStock/age fotostock. 262, Frank Staub/ age fotostock. 263, Wolfgang Staudt/Wikimedia Commons. 264, Robcsee/Shutterstock. 274-75, 284, 292, 299, 302-303, and 305, Kerrick James.308, CAN BALCIOGLU/Shutterstock. Chapter 6: Eastern Arizona: 311, Kerrick James. 312, George Burba/Shutterstock. 313 (top), Mike Norton/ Shutterstock. 313 (bottom), Zack Frank/Shutterstock. 314, Jeffrey M. Frank/Shutterstock. 320, Raymond Forbes/ age fotostock. 329, 333, 339, and 342, Kerrick James. 345, Sebastien Burel/Shutterstock. Chapter 7: Tucson: 347, 348, and 349 (top and bottom), Metropolitan Tucson Convention & Visitors Bureau. 350, Floris Slooff/Shutterstock. 351 (top), Miguel Malo/iStockphoto. 351 (bottom), stu_spivack/Flickr. 352, Jose Gil/Shutterstock. 354, Metropolitan Tucson Convention & Visitors Bureau. 364, Kerrick James. 381, Metropolitan Tucson Convention & Visitors Bureau. 389 (top left), Hacienda del Sol Guest Ranch Resort. 389 (top right), Canyon Resort 7 Hotel. 389 (center left), Loews Ventana Canyon. 389 (center right), White Stallion Ranch. 389 (bottom left), Hotel Congress, Tucson AZ by Mike. 389 (bottom right), Arizona Inn.391, 398, and 417, Metropolitan Tucson Convention & Visitors Bureau. 404, Phil Coleman. Chapter 8: Southern Arizona: 423, Kerrick James. 424 (top), Kevin Cole/wikipedia.org. 424 (bottom), Mark Godfrey/The Nature Conservancy. 425 (top and bottom). Metropolitan Tucson Convention & Visitors Bureau. 426, Walter Bibikow/age fotostock. 427 (top), Nickolay Stanev/

NOTES

NOTES

NOTES